Topic relevant selected content from the highest rated entries, typeset, printed and shipped.

Combine the advantages of up-to-date and in-depth knowledge with the convenience of printed books.

A portion of the proceeds of each book will be donated to the Wikimedia Foundation to support their mission: to empower and engage people around the world to collect and develop educational content under a free license or in the public domain, and to disseminate it effectively and globally.

The content within this book was generated collaboratively by volunteers. Please be advised that nothing found here has necessarily been reviewed by people with the expertise required to provide you with complete, accurate or reliable information. Some information in this book maybe misleading or simply wrong. The publisher does not guarantee the validity of the information found here. If you need specific advice (for example, medical, legal, financial, or risk management) please seek a professional who is licensed or knowledgeable in that area.

References

Article Licenses

Contents

Articles

The trio reunited in 1956. They signed a new recording contract with Capitol Records (for whom Patty had become a featured soloist) and released a dozen singles through 1959, some rock-and-roll flavored and not very well received, and three hi-fi albums, including a vibrant LP of songs from the dancing 1920s with Billy May's orchestra. In 1962, they signed with Dot Records and recorded a series of stereo albums until 1964, both re-recordings of earlier hits, as well as new material, including "I Left My Heart In San Francisco", "Still", "The End of the World", "Puff the Magic Dragon", "Sailor", "Satin Doll", the theme from *Come September*, and the theme from *A Man and a Woman*. They toured extensively during the 1960s, favoring top nightclubs in Las Vegas, Nevada, California, and London, England.

Eldest sister LaVerne died of cancer in 1967 after a year-long bout with the illness,[15] during which she was replaced by singer Joyce DeYoung. LaVerne had founded the original group, and often acted as the peacemaker among the three during the sisters' lives, more often siding with her parents, to whom the girls were extremely devoted, than with either of her sisters. Their last appearance together as a trio was on The Dean Martin Show on September 27, 1966.

After LaVerne died, Maxene and Patty continued to perform as a duo until 1968, when Maxene announced she would become the Dean of Women at Tahoe Paradise College,[16] teaching acting, drama and speech at a Lake Tahoe college and worked with troubled teens, and Patty was once again eager to be a soloist.[17]

Comeback

Patty and Maxine's careers experienced a resurgence when Bette Midler recorded her own version of their song "Boogie Woogie Bugle Boy" in 1973. The next year, the pair debuted on Broadway in the Sherman Brothers' nostalgic World War II musical: *Over Here!* which premiered at the Shubert Theatre to rave reviews. This was a follow-up to Patty's success in "Victory Canteen", a 1971 California revue. *Over Here!* starred Maxene and Patty (with Janie Sell filling in for LaVerne and winning a Tony Award for her performance) and was written with both sisters in mind for the leads. It launched the careers of many now notable theater, film, and television icons including John Travolta, Marilu Henner, Treat Williams and Ann Reinking. It was the last major hurrah for the sisters and was cut short due to a lawsuit initiated by Patty's husband against the show's producers, squashing an extensively scheduled road tour.[18]

Patty immediately distanced herself from Maxene, who claimed until her death that she was not aware of Patty's motives regarding the separation. She appealed to Patty for a reunion, personally if not professionally, both in public and in private, but to no avail. Maxene suffered a serious heart attack while performing in Illinois in 1982 and underwent quadruple bypass surgery, from which she successfully recovered. Patty visited her sister while she was hospitalized. Now sometimes appearing as "Patti" (but still signing autographs as "Patty") she re-emerged in the late 1970s as a regular panelist on *The Gong Show*. Maxene had a successful comeback as a cabaret soloist in 1979 and toured worldwide for the next 15 years, recording a solo album in 1985 entitled "Maxene: An Andrews Sister" for Bainbridge Records. Patty started her own solo act in 1981, but did not receive the critical acclaim her sister had for her performances, even though it was Patty who was considered to be the "star" of the group for years. The critics' major complaint was that Patty's show concentrated too much on Andrews Sisters material, which did not allow Patty's own talents as a very expressive and bluesy vocalist to shine through.

The two sisters did reunite, albeit briefly, on October 1, 1987, when they received a star on Hollywood's Walk of Fame, even singing a few bars of "Beer Barrel Polka" for the *Entertainment Tonight* cameras. An earthquake shook the area that very morning and the ceremony was nearly cancelled, which caused Patty to joke, "Some people said that earthquake this morning was LaVerne because she couldn't be here, but really it was just Maxene and me on the telephone." Besides this, and a few brief private encounters, they remained somewhat estranged for the last few years.

Shortly after her Off-Broadway debut in New York City in a show called *Swingtime Canteen*, Maxene suffered another heart attack and died at Cape Cod Hospital on October 21, 1995, making Patty the last surviving Andrews

Sister. Not long before she died, Maxene told music historian William Ruhlmann, "I have nothing to regret. We got on the carousel and we each got the ring and I was satisfied with that. There's nothing I would do to change things if I could...Yes, I would. I wish I had the ability and the power to bridge the gap between my relationship with my sister, Patty."[19] Upon hearing the news of her sister's death, Patty became very distraught. As her husband Wally went to her, he fell on a flight of stairs and broke both wrists. Patty did not attend her sister's memorial services in New York, nor in California. Said Bob Hope of Maxene's passing, "She was more than part of The Andrews Sisters, much more than a singer. She was a warm and wonderful lady who shared her talent and wisdom with others."[19]

Retirement and deaths

Instrumental to the sisters' success over the years were their parents, Olga and Peter; their orchestra leader and musical arranger, Vic Schoen (1916–2000); music publishing giant Lou Levy, who died only days after Maxene, and was their manager from 1937–51 and was also Maxene's husband from 1941–49;[20] and Jack and David Kapp, who founded Decca Records. Maxene was the mother of two adopted children, Peter and Aleda Ann.

LaVerne married Lou Rogers,[15] a trumpet player in Vic Schoen's band, in 1948, and remained with him until her death (he died in 1995, five days after Maxene's death and five days before Levy's).[21] Patty Andrews married agent Marty Melcher in 1947 and left him in 1949, when he pursued a romantic relationship with Doris Day. She then married Walter Weschler, the trio's pianist, in 1951. Patty Andrews died of natural causes at her home in Northridge, California on January 30, 2013, just 17 days before her 95th birthday. Walter Wechsler, her husband of 60 years, died on August 28, 2010, at the age of 88. [7] Patty and Walter were parents to foster daughter Pam Dubois.[14] The sisters were interred in the Forest Lawn Memorial Park Cemetery in Glendale, California, close to their parents.[22]

Legacy

Until the advent of the Supremes, the sisters were the most imitated of all female singing groups and influenced many artists, including Mel Tormé, Les Paul and Mary Ford, The Four Freshmen, The McGuire Sisters, The Manhattan Dolls, The Lennon Sisters, The Pointer Sisters, The Manhattan Transfer, The Puppini Sisters, Barry Manilow, and Bette Midler. Even Elvis Presley was a fan. Most of the Andrews Sisters' music has been restored and released in compact disc form, yet over 300 of their original Decca recordings, a good portion of which was hit material, has yet to be released by MCA/Decca in over 50 years. Many of these Decca recordings have been used in such television shows and Hollywood movies as *Homefront*, *ER*, *The Brink's Job*, *National Lampoon's Christmas Vacation*, *Swing Shift*, *Raggedy Man*, *Summer of '42*, *Slaughterhouse-Five*, *Maria's Lovers*, *Harlem Nights*, *In Dreams*, *Murder in the First*, *L.A. Confidential*, American Horror Story, *Just Shoot Me*, Gilmore Girls, *Mama's Family*, *War and Remembrance*, *Jakob the Liar*, *Lolita*, *The Polar Express*, *The Chronicles of Narnia*, *Molly: An American Girl on the Home Front*, *Memoirs of a Geisha*, and *Bon Voyage, Charlie Brown (and Don't Come Back!!)*. Comical references to the trio in television sitcoms can be found as early as *I Love Lucy* and as recently as *Everybody Loves Raymond*. In 2007, their version of "Bei Mir Bist Du Schön" was included in the game *BioShock*, a first-person shooter that takes place in an alternate history 1960, and later in 2008, their song "Civilization" (with Danny Kaye) was included in the Atomic Age-inspired video game *Fallout 3*. The 2010 video game *Mafia II* features numerous Andrews Sisters songs, with 'Boogie Woogie Bugle Boy', 'Strip Polka' and 'Rum And Coca-Cola'. The 2011 video game *L.A. Noire* features the song Pistol Packin' Mama, where the sisters perform a duet with Bing Crosby.

Christina Aguilera used the Andrews Sisters' "Boogie Woogie Bugle Boy" to inspire her song "Candyman" (released as a single in 2007) from her hit album *Back to Basics*. The song was co-written by Linda Perry. The London based trio the Puppini Sisters uses their style harmonies on several Andrews Sisters and other hits of the 1940s and 1950s as well as later rock and disco hits. The trio has said their name is a tribute to The Andrews Sisters. The Manhattan Dolls, a New York City-based touring group, performs both the popular tunes sung by the Andrews Sisters and some of the more obscure tunes such as "Well Alright" and "South American Way" as well.

In 2008 and 2009, the BBC produced *The Andrews Sisters: Queens of the Music Machines*, a one-hour documentary on the history of the Andrews Sisters from their upbringing to the present. The American premier of the show was June 21, 2009, in their birthplace of Mound, Minnesota. In 2008, Mound dedicated "The Andrews Sisters Trail". The sisters spent summers in Mound[2] with their uncles Pete and Ed Solie, who had a grocery store there. Maxene Andrews always said that the summers in Mound created a major sense of "normalcy" and "a wonderful childhood" in a life that otherwise centered on the sisters' careers. The Westonka Historical Society has a large collection of Andrews Sisters memorabilia.

Musical innovators

When the sisters burst upon the music scene in the late 1930s, they shook a very solid musical foundation: producing a slick harmonic blend by singing at the top of their lungs while trying - successfully - to emulate the blare of three harmonizing trumpets,[23] with a full big band racing behind them. Some bandleaders of the day, such as Artie Shaw and his musicians, resented them for taking the focus away from the band and emphasizing the vocals instead. They were in as high demand as the big bandleaders themselves, many of whom did not want to share the spotlight and play back-up to a girl trio.

Nevertheless, they found instant appeal with teenagers and young adults who were engrossed in the swing and jazz idioms, especially when they performed with nearly all of the major big bands, including those led by Glenn Miller, Benny Goodman, Buddy Rich, Tommy Dorsey, Jimmy Dorsey, Gene Krupa, Joe Venuti, Freddie Slack, Eddie Heywood, Bob Crosby (Bing's brother), Desi Arnaz, Guy Lombardo, Les Brown, Bunny Berigan, Xavier Cugat, Paul Whiteman, Ted Lewis, Nelson Riddle and mood-master Gordon Jenkins, whose orchestra and chorus accompanied them on such successful soft and melancholy renditions as "I Can Dream, Can't I?" (which shot to number one on *Billboard* and remained in the Top 10 for 25 weeks), "I Wanna Be Loved", "There Will Never Be Another You", and the inspirational "The Three Bells" (the first recorded English version of the French composition), along with several solo recordings with Patty, including a cover version of Nat King Cole's "Too Young", "It Never Entered My Mind", "If You Go", and "That's How A Love Song Is Born".

"Boogie Woogie Bugle Boy" can be considered an early recording of rhythm and blues or jump blues.

Many styles

While the sisters specialized in swing, boogie-woogie, and novelty hits with their trademark lightning-quick vocal syncopations, they also produced major hits in jazz, ballads, folk, country-western, seasonal, and religious titles, being the first Decca artists to record an album of gospel standards in 1950. Their versatility allowed them to pair with many different artists in the recording studios, producing Top 10 hits with the likes of Bing Crosby (the only recording artist of the 1940s to sell more records than The Andrews Sisters), Danny Kaye, Dick Haymes, Carmen Miranda, Al Jolson, Ray McKinley, Burl Ives, Ernest Tubb, Red Foley, Dan Dailey, Alfred Apaka, and Les Paul. In personal appearances, on radio and on television, they sang with everyone from Rudy Vallee, Judy Garland and Nat "King" Cole to Jimmie Rodgers, Andy Williams, and The Supremes. Some obvious 1930's song styles can be heard with early contemporary harmonizers of their day with the Boswell Sisters, and the Three X Sisters.

Films

Maxene, Patty, and LaVerne appeared in 17 Hollywood films. Their first picture, *Argentine Nights*, paired them with another enthusiastic trio, the Ritz Brothers.[24] Universal Pictures, always budget-conscious, refused to hire a choreographer, so the Ritzes taught the sisters some eccentric steps. Thus, in *Argentine Nights* and the sisters' next film, *Buck Privates*, the Andrews Sisters dance like the Ritz Brothers.

Buck Privates, with Abbott and Costello, featured the Andrews Sisters' best-known song, "Boogie Woogie Bugle Boy". This Don Raye-Hughie Prince composition was nominated for Best Song at the 1941 Academy Awards ceremony.

Universal hired the sisters for two more Abbott and Costello comedies, and then promoted them to full-fledged stardom in B musicals. *What's Cookin', Private Buckaroo*, and *Give Out, Sisters* (the latter portraying the sisters as old women) were among the team's popular full-length films.

The Andrews Sisters have a specialty number in the all-star revue *Hollywood Canteen* (1944). They can be seen singing "You Don't Have to Know the Language" with Bing Crosby in Paramount's *Road to Rio* with Bob Hope, that year's highest-grossing movie. Their singing voices are heard in two full-length Walt Disney features ("Make Mine Music"[25] which featured Johnny Fedora and Alice Blue Bonnet, and "Melody Time", which introduced *Little Toot*, both of which are available on DVD today).

Stage and radio shows

The Andrews Sisters were the most sought-after entertainment property in theater shows worldwide during the 1940s and early 1950s, always topping previous house averages. The trio headlined at the London Palladium in 1948 and 1951 to sold-out crowds. They hosted their own radio shows for ABC and CBS from 1944–1951, singing specially-written commercial jingles for such products as Wrigley's chewing gum, Dole pineapples, Nash motor cars, Kelvinator home appliances, Campbell's soups, and Franco-American food products.

Setting records

They recorded 47 songs with crooner Bing Crosby, 23 of which charted on *Billboard*, thus making the team one of the most successful pairings of acts in a recording studio in show business history. Their million-sellers with Crosby included "Pistol Packin' Mama", "Don't Fence Me In", "South America, Take It Away", and "Jingle Bells", among other yuletide favorites.

The sisters' popularity was such that after the war they discovered some of their records had actually been smuggled into Germany after the labels had been changed to read "Hitler's Marching Songs". Their recording of *Bei Mir Bist Du Schön* became a favorite of the Nazis, until it was discovered that the song's composers were of Jewish descent. Still, it did not stop concentration camp inmates from secretly singing it, this is most likely since the song was originally a Yiddish song "Bei Mir Bistu Shein", and had been popularized within the Jewish community before it was recorded as a more successful "cover" version by the Andrews sisters.

Along with Bing Crosby, separately and jointly, The Andrews Sisters were among the performers who incorporated ethnic music styles into America's Hit Parade, popularizing or enhancing the popularity of songs with melodies originating in Brazil, Czechoslovakia, France, Ireland, Israel, Italy, Mexico, Russia, Spain, Sweden and Trinidad, many of which their manager chose for them.

The Andrews Sisters became the most popular female vocal group of the first half of the 20th century.[26]

- between 75-100 million records sold from a little over 600 recorded tunes
- 113 charted Billboard hits, 46 reaching Top 10 status (more than Elvis Presley or The Beatles)
- 17 Hollywood films (more than any other singing group in motion picture history)[27]
- record-breaking theater and cabaret runs all across America and Europe;

- countless appearances on radio shows from 1935 to 1960 (including their own)
- guest spots on every major television show of the 1950s and 1960s, including those hosted by Ed Sullivan, Milton Berle, Perry Como, Frank Sinatra, Dean Martin, Sammy Davis, Jr., Johnny Carson, Joey Bishop, Art Linkletter and Jimmy Dean.

Early comparative female close harmony trios were the Boswell Sisters, the Pickens Sisters, and the Three X Sisters.

Repertoire

Hit records

Year	Single	Chart positions		
		US	US R&B	US Country
1938	"Bei Mir Bist Du Schön"	1	-	-
	"Nice Work If You Can Get It"	12	-	-
	"Joseph, Joseph"	18	-	-
	"Ti-Pi-Tin"	12	-	-
	"Shortenin' Bread"	16	-	-
	"Says My Heart"	10	-	-
	"Tu-li-Tulip Time"	9	-	-
	"Sha-Sha"	17	-	-
	"Lullaby To a Jitterbug"	10	-	-
1939	"Pross-Tchai (Goodbye)"	15	-	-
	"Hold Tight, Hold Tight"	2	-	-
	"You Don't Know How Much You Can Suffer"	14	-	-
	"Beer Barrel Polka (Roll Out the Barrel)"	4	-	-
	"Well All Right (Tonight's the Night)"	5	-	-
	"Ciribiribin (They're So In Love)"(with Bing Crosby)	13	-	-
	"Yodelin' Jive"(with Bing Crosby)	4	-	-
	"Chico's Love Song"	11	-	-
1940	"Say Si Si (Para Vigo Me Voy)"	4	-	-
	"The Woodpecker Song"	6	-	-
	"Down By the O-Hi-O"	21	-	-
	"Rhumboogie"	11	-	-
	"Ferryboat Serenade"	1	-	-
	"Hit the Road"	27	-	-
	"Beat Me Daddy, Eight to the Bar"	2	-	-

1941	"Scrub Me, Mama, With a Boogie Beat"	10	-	-
	"Boogie Woogie Bugle Boy"	6	-	-
	"I Yi, Yi, Yi, Yi (I Like You Very Much)"	11	-	-
	"(I'll Be With You) In Apple Blossom Time"	5	-	-
	"Aurora"	10	-	-
	"Sonny Boy"	22	-	-
	"The Nickel Serenade"	22	-	-
	"Sleepy Serenade"	22	-	-
	"I Wish I Had a Dime (For Every Time I Missed You)"	20	-	-
	"Jealous"	12	-	-
1942	"The Shrine of St. Cecilia"	3	-	-
	"I'll Pray For You"	22	-	-
	"Three Little Sisters"	8	-	-
	"Don't Sit Under the Apple Tree"	16	-	-
	"Pennsylvania Polka"	17	-	-
	"That's the Moon, My Son"	18	-	-
	"Mister Five By Five"	14	-	-
	"Strip Polka"	6	-	-
	"Here Comes the Navy"	17	-	-
1943	"East of the Rockies"	18	-	-
	"Pistol Packin' Mama"(with Bing Crosby)	2	3	1
	"Victory Polka"(with Bing Crosby)	5	-	-
	"Jingle Bells"(with Bing Crosby)	19	-	-
	"Shoo-Shoo Baby"	1	-	-
1944	"Down In the Valley"	20	-	-
	"Straighten Up and Fly Right"	8	-	-
	"Tico Tico"	24	-	-
	"Sing a Tropical Song"	24	-	-
	"Is You Is Or Is You Ain't My Baby"(with Bing Crosby)	2	-	-
	"A Hot Time In the Town of Berlin"(with Bing Crosby)	1	-	-
	"Don't Fence Me In"(with Bing Crosby)	1	9	-
1945	"Rum and Coca Cola"	1	3	-
	"Accentuate the Positive"(with Bing Crosby)	2	-	-
	"The Three Caballeros"(with Bing Crosby)	8	-	-
	"One Meat Ball"	15	-	-
	"Corns For My Country"	21	-	-
	"Along the Navajo Trail"(with Bing Crosby)	2	-	-
	"The Blond Sailor"	8	-	-

1946	"Money Is the Root of All Evil"	9	-	-
	"Patience and Fortitude"	12	-	-
	"Coax Me a Little Bit"	24	-	-
	"South America, Take It Away"(with Bing Crosby)	2	-	-
	"Get Your Kicks On Route 66"(with Bing Crosby)	14	-	-
	"I Don't Know Why"	17	-	-
	"House of Blue Lights"	15	-	-
	"Rumors Are Flying"(with Les Paul)	4	-	-
	"Winter Wonderland"(with Guy Lombardo)	22	-	-
	"Christmas Island"(with Guy Lombardo)	7	-	-
1947	"Tallahassee"(with Bing Crosby)	10	-	-
	"There's No Business Like Show Business"(with Bing Crosby and Dick Haymes)	25	-	-
	"On the Avenue"	21	-	-
	"Near You"	2	-	-
	"The Lady From 29 Palms"	7	-	-
	"The Freedom Train"(with Bing Crosby)	21	-	-
	"Civilization (Bongo, Bongo, Bongo)"(with Danny Kaye)	3	-	-
	"Jingle Bells"(with Bing Crosby)(re-entry)	21	-	-
	"Santa Claus Is Comin' To Town"(with Bing Crosby)	22	-	-
	"Christmas Island"(with Guy Lombardo)(re-entry)	20	-	-
	"Your Red Wagon"	24	-	-
	"How Lucky You Are"	22	-	-
1948	"You Don't Have To Know the Language"(with Bing Crosby)	21	-	-
	"Teresa"(with Dick Haymes)	21	-	-
	"Toolie Oolie Doolie (The Yodel Polka)"	3	-	-
	"I Hate To Lose You"	14	-	-
	"Heartbreaker"	21	-	-
	"Sabre Dance"	20	-	-
	"Woody Woodpecker"(with Danny Kaye)	18	-	-
	"Blue Tail Fly"(with Burl Ives)	24	-	-
	"Underneath the Arches"	5	-	-
	"You Call Everybody Darling"	8	-	-
	"Cuanto La Gusta"(with Carmen Miranda)	12	-	-
	"160 Acres"(with Bing Crosby)	23	-	-
	"Bella Bella Marie"	23	-	-

1949	"Christmas Island"(with Guy Lombardo)(re-entry)	26	-	-
	"The Pussy Cat Song (Nyow! Nyot! Nyow!)"(Patty Andrews w/Bob Crosby)	12	-	-
	"More Beer!"	30	-	-
	"I'm Bitin' My Fingernails and Thinking of You"(with Ernest Tubb)	30	-	2
	"Don't Rob Another Man's Castle"(with Ernest Tubb)	-	-	6
	"I Can Dream, Can't I?"	1	-	-
	"The Wedding of Lili Marlene"	20	-	-
	"She Wore a Yellow Ribbon"(with Russ Morgan)	22	-	-
	"Charley, My Boy"(with Russ Morgan)	15	-	-
1950	"Merry Christmas Polka"(with Guy Lombardo)	18	-	-
	"Have I Told You Lately That I Love You"(with Bing Crosby)	24	-	-
	"Quicksilver"(with Bing Crosby)	6	-	-
	"The Wedding Samba"(with Carmen Miranda)	23	-	-
	"I Wanna Be Loved"	1	-	-
	"Can't We Talk It Over"	22	-	-
	"A Bushel and a Peck"	22	-	-
1951	"A Penny a Kiss, a Penny a Hug"	17	-	-
	"Sparrow in the Tree Top"(with Bing Crosby)	8	-	-
	"Too Young"(Patty Andrews)	19	-	-
1955	"Suddenly There's a Valley"(Patty Andrews)	69	-	-

Other songs

Highest chart positions on Billboard; with Vic Schoen and his orchestra, unless otherwise noted:

- "Joseph! Joseph!" (1938) (#18)
- "Ti-Pi-Tin" (1938) (#12)
- "Shortenin' Bread" (1938) (#16)
- "Says My Heart" (1938) (#10)
- "Tu-Li-Tulip Time" (with Jimmy Dorsey and his orchestra) (1938) (#9)
- "Sha-Sha" (with Jimmy Dorsey and his orchestra)(1938) (#17)
- "Lullaby to a Jitterbug" (1938) (#10)
- "Pross Tchai (Goodbye-Goodbye)" (1939) (#15)
- "You Don't Know How Much You Can Suffer" (1939) (#14)
- "Ciribiribin (They're So in Love)" (with Bing Crosby & Joe Venuti and his orchestra) (1939) (#13)
- "Chico's Love Song" (1939) (#11)
- "The Woodpecker Song" (1940) (#6)
- "Down By the O-HI-O" (1940) (#21)
- "Rhumboogie" (1940) (#11)
- "Hit the Road" (1940) (#27)
- "Scrub Me Mama with a Boogie Beat" (1940) (#10)
- "I Yi, Yi, Yi, Yi (I Like You Very Much)" (1941) (#11)
- "Aurora" (1941) (#10)
- "Sonny Boy" (1941) (#22)

- "The Nickel Serenade" (1941) (#22)
- "Sleepy Serenade" (1941) (#22)
- "I Wish I Had a Dime (For Ev'rytime I Missed You)" (1941) (#20)
- "Jealous" (1941) (#12)
- "I'll Pray For You" (1942) (#22)
- "Three Little Sisters" (1942) (#8)
- "Pennsylvania Polka" (1942) (#17)
- "That's the Moon, My Son" (1942) (#18)
- "Mister Five By Five" (1942) (#14)
- "Strip Polka" (1942) (#6)
- "Here Comes the Navy" (1942) (#17)
- "East of the Rockies" (1943) (#18)
- "Down in the Valley (Hear that Train Blow)" (1944) (#20)
- "Straighten Up and Fly Right" (1944) (#8)
- "Sing a Tropical Song" (1944) (#24)
- "Tico-Tico no Fubá" (1944) (#24)
- "Corns for My Country" (1945) (#21)
- "The Three Caballeros" (with Bing Crosby) (1945) (#8)
- "One Meat Ball" (1945) (#15)
- "The Blond Sailor" (1945) (#8)
- "Money Is the Root of All Evil (Take it Away, Take it Away, Take it Away)" (with Guy Lombardo and his Royal Canadians) (1946) (#9)
- "Patience and Fortitude" (1946) (#12)
- "Coax Me a Little Bit" (1946) (#24)
- "Get Your Kicks on Route 66" (with Bing Crosby) (1946) (#14)
- "I Don't Know Why (I Just Do)" (1946) (#17)
- "The House of Blue Lights" (with Eddie Heywood and his orchestra) (1946) (#15)
- "Winter Wonderland" (with Guy Lombardo and his Royal Canadians) (1946) (#22)
- "Christmas Island" (with Guy Lombardo and his Royal Canadians) (1946: #7; 1947: #20; 1949: #26)
- "Tallahassee" (with Bing Crosby) (1947) (#10)
- "There's No Business Like Show Business" (with Bing Crosby and Dick Haymes) (1947) (#25)
- "On the Avenue" (with Carmen Cavallaro at the piano) (1947) (#21)
- "The Lady from 29 Palms" (1947) (#7)
- "The Freedom Train" (1947) (#21)
- "Your Red Wagon" (1947) (#24)
- "How Lucky You Are" (1947) (#22)
- "You Don't Have to Know the Language" (with Bing Crosby) (1948) (#21)
- "Teresa" (with Dick Haymes) (1948) (#21)
- "Heartbreaker" (with The Harmonica Gentlemen) (1948) (#21)
- "(Everytime They Play the) Sabre Dance" (with The Harmonica Gentlemen) (1948) (#20)
- "I Hate to Lose You" (1948) (#14)
- "The Woody Woodpecker Song" (with Danny Kaye and The Harmonica Gentlemen) (1948) (#18)
- "The Blue Tail Fly (Jimmy Crack Corn)" (with Burl Ives, vocal and guitar accompaniment) (1948) (#24)
- "You Call Everybody Darling" (recorded in London with Billy Ternant and his orchestra) (1948) (#8)
- "Cuanto La Gusta" (with Carmen Miranda) (1948) (#12)
- "A Hundred and Sixty Acres" (with Bing Crosby) (1948) (#23)
- "Bella Bella Marie" (1948) (#23)

- "More Beer!" (1949) (#30)
- "I'm Biting My Fingernails and Thinking of You" (with Ernest Tubb and The Texas Troubadors directed by Vic Schoen) (1949) (#30)
- "The Wedding of Lili Marlene" (with Gordon Jenkins and his orchestra and chorus) (1949) (#20)
- "The Pussy Cat Song (Nyow! Nyot Nyow!)" (Patty Andrews and Bob Crosby) (1949) (#12)
- "She Wore a Yellow Ribbon" (with Russ Morgan and his orchestra) (1949) (#22)
- "Charley, My Boy" (with Russ Morgan and his orchestra) (1949) (#15)
- "Merry Christmas Polka" (with Guy Lombardo and his Royal Canadians) (1950) (#18)
- "Have I Told You Lately that I Love You?" (with Bing Crosby) (1950) (#24)
- "Quicksilver" (with Bing Crosby) (1950) (#6)
- "The Wedding Samba" (with Carmen Miranda) (1950) (#23)
- "Can't We Talk it Over?" (with Gordon Jenkins and his orchestra and chorus) (1950) (#22)
- "A Bushel and a Peck" (1950) (#22)
- "A Penny a Kiss-A Penny a Hug" (1950) (#17)
- "Sparrow in the Treetop" (with Bing Crosby) (1951) (#8)
- "Too Young" (Patty Andrews with Victor Young and his orchestra) (1951) (#19)
- "Torero" Capitol F 3965 (recorded on March 31, 1958)

Film and theatre

(partial list)

Filmography

- *Argentine Nights* (Universal Pictures, 1940)[28]
- *Buck Privates* (Universal Pictures, 1941)
- *In the Navy* (Universal Pictures, 1941)[28]
- *Hold That Ghost* (Universal Pictures, 1941)
- *Private Buckaroo* (Universal Pictures, 1942)[28]
- *Give Out, Sisters* (Universal Pictures, 1942)
- *How's About It* (Universal Pictures, 1943)
- *Always a Bridesmaid* (Universal Pictures, 1943)
- *Swingtime Johnny* (Universal Pictures, 1943)
- *Moonlight and Cactus* (Universal Pictures, 1944)
- *Follow the Boys* (Universal Pictures, 1944)
- *Hollywood Canteen* (Warner Brothers, 1944)
- *Her Lucky Night* (Universal Pictures, 1945)
- *Make Mine Music* (Walt Disney Studios, 1946)
- *Road to Rio* (Paramount Pictures, 1947)[28]
- *Melody Time* (Walt Disney Studios, 1948)[28]
- *Brother, Can You Spare a Dime?* (1975)

Soundtracks

- *What's Cookin'?* (Universal Pictures, 1942)[28]
- *Breach* (background music) (2007)
- *Land of the Lost* (2009)

Broadway

- *Over Here!* (1974; Shubert Theater, New York City, 9 months)

Dance

- *Company B* (1991; Choreographed by Paul Taylor, Performed by Paul Taylor Dance Company, American Ballet Theatre, and Miami City Ballet)

As Muppets

They were parodied on "Sesame Street" as the Androoze Sisters, named Mayeeme (Audrey Smith), Pattiz (Maeretha Stewart), and Lavoorrnee (Kevin Clash).

References

[1] http://www.cmgww.com/music/andrews

[2] http://www.foxnews.com/entertainment/2013/01/30/last-surviving-andrews-sisters-member-patty-andrews-dies-at-4/?test=latestnews

[3] boogie-woogie (http://www.collinsdictionary.com/dictionary/english/boogie-woogie). CollinsDictionary.com. Collins English Dictionary - Complete & Unabridged 11th Edition. Retrieved November 26, 2012.

[4] The American Heritage Dictionary of the English Language, Fourth Edition copyright ©2000 by Houghton Mifflin Company, Updated in 2009 CITED IN "Boogie-Woogie" (http://www.thefreedictionary.com/boogie-woogie), *FreeDictionary.com*.

[5] "Vocal Group Hall of Fame - The Andrews Sisters" (http://www.vocalgroup.org/inductees/andrews_sisters.htm). . Retrieved January 31, 2013.

[6] (http://uk.real.com/music/artist/The_Andrews_Sisters/). UK Real.com article on The Andrews Sisters.

[7] http://www.startribune.com/entertainment/189120371.html

[8] SHOLOM SECUNDA The Story of Bei Mir Bist du Schön (http://www.dvrbs.com/swing/SholomSecunda-BeiMirBistDuSchoen.htm)

[9] Jill Serjeant (January 30, 2013). "Last of 1940s hitmakers Andrews Sisters dies in California" (http://www.reuters.com/article/2013/01/30/us-pattyandrews-idUSBRE90T1HW20130130). "Reuters". . Retrieved February 3, 2013.

[10] Andrews, Maxene and Bill Gilbert. *Over Here, Over There: The Andrews Sisters and the USO Stars in World War II*. New York: Kensington Publishing Corp, 1993.

[11] Adam Bernstein (January 30, 2013). "Patty Andrews, the last surviving member of the Andrews Sisters, dies at 94" (http://articles.washingtonpost.com/2013-01-30/local/36647222_1_boswell-sisters-sister-act-andrews-sisters). "Washington Post". . Retrieved February 3, 2013.

[12] Bob Beverage, Ron Peluso. "Christmas of Swing" (http://www.historytheatre.com/files/play-guide_christmas-of-swing_2012.pdf). "HistoryTheater.com". p. 4. . Retrieved February 3, 2013.

[13] Los Angeles Times article (http://proquest.umi.com/pqdweb?did=435022642&sid=5&Fmt=10&clientId=48776&RQT=309&VName=HNP) (PDF) December 22, 1954.

[14] Natalie Finn (January 30, 2013). "Patty Andrews Dies, Singer Was Last Surviving Member of the Andrews Sisters" (http://www.eonline.com/news/383541/patty-andrews-dies-singer-was-last-surviving-member-of-the-andrews-sisters). "E Online.com". . Retrieved February 3, 2013.

[15] Los Angeles Times article (http://proquest.umi.com/pqdweb?did=521603392&sid=6&Fmt=10&clientId=48776&RQT=309&VName=HNP) (PDF) May 9, 1967.

[16] St Petersburg Times August 10, 1968 (http://news.google.com/newspapers?id=cqJQAAAAIBAJ&sjid=u1wDAAAAIBAJ&pg=5642,6029172&dq=andrews+sisters&hl=en)

[17] St. Petersburg Times (http://news.google.com/newspapers?id=hR0MAAAAIBAJ&sjid=u1wDAAAAIBAJ&dq=andrews sisters&pg=5682,6029193) August 10, 1968.

[18] http://news.google.com/newspapers?id=cD9SAAAAIBAJ&sjid=hHkDAAAAIBAJ&pg=4875,1202172&dq=andrews+sisters&hl=en St. Petersburg Times - December 27, 1974.

[19] Sforza, John (2004). *Swing It!: The Andrews Sisters Story* (http://books.google.com/books?id=IPoMEFJgOwUC&pg=PA171). United States of America: University Press of Kentucky. p. 171. ISBN 9780813190990. .

[20] Los Angeles Times article (http://proquest.umi.com/pqdweb?did=408941231&sid=1&Fmt=10&clientId=48776&RQT=309& VName=HNP) PDF February 4, 1940.

[21] http://books.google.com/books?id=9mE2-RxDyZsC&pg=PA409

[22] "The Andrews Sisiters - Bio" (http://www.imdb.com/name/nm1679536/bio). "IMDb". . Retrieved Fevruary 3, 2013.

[23] "Patty Andrews, last surviving member of Andrews sisters, remembered for rallying troops" (http://www.washingtonpost.com/ entertainment/music/patty-andrews-last-surviving-member-of-singing-andrews-sisters-dead-at-94/2013/01/30/ 2da038ec-6b45-11e2-9a0b-db931670f35d_story.html). The Associated Press. The Washington Post. January 31, 2013. . Retrieved February 1, 2013.

[24] Los Angeles Times article (http://proquest.umi.com/pqdweb?did=409280301&sid=1&Fmt=10&clientId=48776&RQT=309& VName=HNP) PDF May 15, 1940.

[25] Los Angeles Times article (http://proquest.umi.com/pqdweb?did=415221731&sid=3&Fmt=10&clientId=48776&RQT=309& VName=HNP) (PDF) Hedda Hopper. June 30, 1946.

[26] Schoifet, Mark (January 30, 2013). "Patty Andrews, Last Survivor of Wartime Sister Trio, Dies at 94" (http://www.businessweek.com/ news/2013-01-30/patty-andrews-last-survivor-of-wartime-sister-trio-dies-at-94). *Bloomberg* (BusinessWeek). . Retrieved January 31, 2013.

[27] "Biography for The Andrews Sisters" (http://www.imdb.com/name/nm1679536/bio). IMDb.com. . Retrieved January 31, 2013.

[28] "The Andres Sisters" (http://www.imdb.com/name/nm1679536/). IMDb. . Retrieved February 3, 2013.

- Nimmo, H. Arlo. *The Andrews Sisters.* Jefferson: McFarland & Co, Inc., 2004.
- Sforza, John. *Swing It! The Andrews Sisters Story.* Lexington: The University Press of Kentucky, 2000.

External links

- Andrews Sisters Official website (http://www.cmgww.com/music/andrews/)
- Andrews Sisters on BigBands.net (http://www.bigbands.net/andrewsbio.htm)
- Vocal Group Hall of Fame page on the Andrews Sisters (http://www.vocalgroup.org/inductees/ andrews_sisters.htm)
- Maxene Andrews (http://www.findagrave.com/cgi-bin/fg.cgi?page=gr&GRid=3052) at *Find a Grave*
- Laverne Andrews (http://www.findagrave.com/cgi-bin/fg.cgi?page=gr&GRid=2092) at *Find a Grave*
- Patty Andrews (http://www.findagrave.com/cgi-bin/fg.cgi?page=gr&GRid=104311861) at *Find a Grave*

(I'll Be With You) In Apple Blossom Time

"(I'll Be With You) In Apple Blossom Time"	
Written by	Albert Von Tilzer
Lyrics by	Neville Fleeson
Published	1920
Recorded by	Artie Shaw, Harry James, The Andrews Sisters, Vera Lynn, Nat King Cole, Jo Stafford, Anne Shelton, Chet Atkins, Louis Prima, Tab Hunter, Rosemary June, Ray Conniff, The Bachelors, Wayne Newton, Barry Manilow

"(I'll Be With You) In Apple Blossom Time" is a popular song written by Albert Von Tilzer and lyricist Neville Fleeson, and copyrighted in 1920.

The song has been recorded by numerous artists including Artie Shaw (1937), Harry James, The Andrews Sisters (US no. 5, 1941), Vera Lynn, Nat King Cole, Jo Stafford (1946), Anne Shelton, Chet Atkins, Louis Prima, Tab Hunter (US no. 31, 1959), Rosemary June (UK no. 14, 1959), Ray Conniff, The Bachelors, Wayne Newton (US no. 52, 1965),Barry Manilow,Emmy Rossum.<Allmusic.com [1]</ref>

References

[1] http://www.allmusic.com/search/track/I%27ll+Be+With+You+in+Apple+Blossom+Time/order:default-asc

A Bushel and a Peck

"A Bushel and a Peck" is a popular song written by Frank Loesser and published in 1950. The song was introduced in the Broadway musical *Guys and Dolls*, which opened at the 46th Street Theater on November 24, 1950. It was performed on stage by Vivian Blaine, who later reprised her role as Miss Adelaide in the 1955 film version of the play. "A Bushel and a Peck," however, was not included in the film.

A recording by Perry Como and Betty Hutton (made on September 12, 1950 and released by RCA Victor Records as catalog number 47-3930) first reached the Billboard magazine charts on October 27, 1950 and lasted 18 weeks on the chart, peaking at #6.[1]

Another contemporary recording that had some popularity was by Margaret Whiting and Jimmy Wakely (recorded on September 13, 1950 and released by Capitol Records as catalog number 1234). The record first reached the Billboard magazine charts on October 20, 1950 and lasted 13 weeks on the chart, peaking at #13.[1]

Doris Day's recording (made on September 13, 1950 and released by Columbia Records as 78rpm catalog number 39008 and 45rpm catalog number 6-838) made the chart on January 5, 1951 at #30 for one week.[1] Many other recording artists also did versions of the song.

On Cash Box magazine's Best-Selling Record charts, where all versions of the song are combined, the song reached #5 on December 2, 1950.

The song gained so much popularity before the musical actually began that it was moved from its original spot opening the second act into the first act.

The number, in context of the show, can be performed either as "Miss Adelaide and her Chick Chick Chickedies," where the girls are dressed in yellow feathers, or as "Miss Adelaide and the Hot Box Farmerettes," where skimpy plantation outfits are worn (often jean cutoffs and checkered racing shirts or short gingham sundresses).

Recorded versions

- The Andrews Sisters (1953)
- Vivian Blaine (1953)
- Perry Como and Betty Hutton (1950)
- Doris Day (1950)
- Johnny Desmond (1953)
- Connie Haines (1950)
- Margaret Whiting and Jimmy Wakely (1950)
- Sharon, Lois & Bram From the LP In The Schoolyard
- VeggieTales Junior's Bedtime Songs (2002)
- Dan Zanes & Friends Rocket Ship Beach (1990)
- Faith Prince Guys and Dolls 1992 Broadway Revival Cast Recording

References

[1] Whitburn, Joel (1973). *Top Pop Records 1940-1955*. Record Research.

Beat Me Daddy, Eight to the Bar

"Beat Me Daddy, Eight to the Bar"	
Sheet music for "Beat Me Daddy, Eight to the Bar"	
Single by Will Bradley and His Orchestra featuring Ray McKinley	
B-side	"Beat Me Daddy, Eight to the Bar Pt. 2"
Released	1940
Format	10" 78 rpm record
Recorded	May 21, 1940
Genre	Boogie woogie
Length	2:39
Label	Columbia (Cat. no. 35530)
Writer(s)	Don Raye, Hughie Prince, Eleanore Sheehy

"Beat Me Daddy, Eight to the Bar" is a song written in 1940 by Don Raye, with credit given to Ray McKinley. It follows the American boogie-woogie tradition of syncopated piano music. The song was first recorded in 1940 by the Will Bradley orchestra, with Freddie Slack on piano. The recording placed in *Billboard*'s "Leading Music Box Records of 1941" at number ten.[1]

The title adopts 1940s hipster slang coined by Raye's friend, Ray McKinley, a drummer and lead singer in the Jimmy Dorsey band in the 1930s. McKinley kicked off certain uptempo songs by asking pianist Freddie Slack — nicknamed "Daddy" — to give him a boogie beat, or "eight to the bar". For that reason Raye gave partial songwriting credit to McKinley. (The song was formally published under McKinley's wife's name, Eleanore Sheehy, because McKinley was under a songwriting contract with another publisher.) The nickname "Daddy Slack" was also used in the 1941 recording by "Pig Foot Pete" with Don Raye singing in Slack's band.

Other versions

- Versions of this song have been hits for the Andrews Sisters. Their later hit, "Boogie Woogie Bugle Boy", which praises a fictional trumpet player, resembles this hit. Both songs were written by Don Raye and Hughie Prince.
- Glenn Miller and His Orchestra in 1940 on RCA Victor Bluebird.
- Woody Herman in 1940 on Decca.
- Commander Cody and his Lost Planet Airmen on their album *Lost in the Ozone*.
- Ella Fitzgerald recorded this song with arrangements by Russell Garcia on her 1959 Verve release *Get Happy!*.
- Referred to in a Sesame Street song "Boogie-Woogie Piggies [2]".

References

[1] "Leading Music Box Records of 1941". *Billboard* (Nielsen Business Media, Inc.) **54** (5): 66. January 31, 1941. ISSN 0006-2510.
[2] http://muppet.wikia.com/wiki/The_Boogie-Woogie_Piggies

Beer Barrel Polka

"*Škoda lásky*" ("Beer Barrel Polka") Roll Out the Barrel

Memorial plaque of the author with the song's name in Czech, German and English

Beer Barrel Polka, also known as **Roll Out the Barrel**, is a song which became popular worldwide during World War II. The music was composed by the Czech musician Jaromír Vejvoda in 1927.[1] Eduard Ingriš wrote the first arrangement of the piece, after Vejvoda came upon the melody and sought Ingriš's help in refining it. At that time, it was played without lyrics as *Modřanská polka* ("Polka of Modřany"). Its first text was written later (in 1934) by Václav Zeman – with the title **Škoda lásky**[2] ("Wasted Love").

The polka became famous around the world. In June 1939, "Beer Barrel Polka", as recorded by Will Glahé, was #1 on the Hit Parade. This version was distributed by Shapiro Bernstein. Glahé's earlier 1934 recording sold many copies in its German version *Rosamunde* (it is possible the reason for the rapid spread was due to the occupation of Czechoslovakia by Nazi Germany, and subsequent emigration of thousands of Czechs to other parts of the world, bringing this catchy tune with them). The authors of the English lyrics were Lew Brown and Wladimir Timm. Meanwhile, the song was recorded and played by many others such as Andrews Sisters in 1939, Glenn Miller Orchestra, Benny Goodman, and Billie Holiday. Bobby Vinton also had his version of the song, which peaked at #33 in 1975.

During World War II, versions in many other languages were created and the song was popular among soldiers, regardless of their alliances. It was claimed many times that the song was written in the country where it had just become a hit. Its actual composer was not widely known until after the war.

Popular culture

- The song became a signature song of well-known entertainer Liberace.
- Since the 1970s, it (usually the Frankie Yankovic version) has been played during the seventh inning stretch at Milwaukee Brewers baseball games, as well as becoming one of the state of Wisconsin's unofficial state songs as it is also played at numerous University of Wisconsin sporting events, as well as Green Bay Packers home games, and Milwaukee Panthers basketball games, including after every home win.
- The Australian Rugby League Football Club, Cronulla-Sutherland Sharks has a club song known as 'Sharks Forever' which is sung to the tune of Beer Barrel Polka.
- Brave Combo and Jimmy Sturr & His Orchestra made their own compositions of "Beer Barrel Polka".
- Arthur Miller's play *Death of a Salesman* features a recording of a young girl whistling this song.
- Chico Marx of the Marx Brothers playes a variation of this song in the movie *At the Circus* and *A Night in Casablanca*.

- The Wiggles sang this song on their album and video *Sailing Around the World*.
- In the Disney movie *The North Avenue Irregulars*, a scene features a tape recorder playing The Andrews Sisters' version of the song while Patsy Kelly, Barbara Harris, and Virginia Capers sing along with it.
- Bobby Vinton recorded "Beer Barrel Polka" in 1975.
- In an episode of Mr. Bean: The Animated Series, the Queen of England sings a portion of the song with a piano accompaniment.
- In an episode of The Critic, a trained bear plays the song for Jay Sherman, the critic, trying to stay a part of his show.
- An instrumental version is featured in the 1941 film "Meet John Doe".

Names in other languages

- Basque: *Gora ta gora beti*
- Chinese: 啤酒桶波尔卡/啤酒桶波爾卡
- Croatian: *Rozamunda*
- Czech: *Škoda lásky*
- Danish: *Hvor er min Kone*
- Dutch: *Rats, kuch en bonen*
- Finnish: *Tonttujen joulupolkka*
- French: *Frida oum Papa*
- German: *Rosamunde*

- Hungarian: *Sej-haj Rozi*
- Italian: *Rosamunda*
- Japanese: *Biya daru polka*
- Norwegian: *Hvor er min kone*
- Polish: *Banda* or *My młodzi, my młodzi, nam bimber nie zaszkodzi.../Szkoda miłości*
- Portuguese (Brazil): *Barril de chope*
- Russian: *Розамунда*
- Spanish: *Polka del Barril*, *Polca de la Cerveza* or *Barrilito de Cerveza*
- Swedish: *Ut i naturen*

External links

- Midi: [3], [4], [5]

Notes

[1] Greene, Victor. *A Passion for Polka: Old-Time Ethnic Music in America*. University of California Press, 1992, p. 131.
[2] Greene 1992, p. 131.
[3] http://ingeb.org/Lieder/rosamund.mid
[4] http://ingeb.org/Lieder/rosamun2.mid
[5] http://ingeb.org/Lieder/rosamun3.mid

Bei Mir Bistu Shein

"Bei Mir Bis Du Shein"	
Song by Andrews Sisters	
Genre	Swing
Language	English
Writer	Sammy Cahn and Saul Chaplin
Composer	Sholom Secunda
Producer	Harms, Inc.

"**Bei Mir Bistu Shein**" (Yiddish: ביי מיר ביסטו שיין, "To Me You're Beautiful") is a popular Yiddish song composed by Jacob Jacobs (lyricist) and Sholom Secunda (composer) for a 1932 Yiddish comedy musical, *I Would If I Could* (in Yiddish, *Men Ken Lebn Nor Men Lost Nisht*, "You could live, but they won't let you"), which closed after one season. The score for the song transcribed the Yiddish title as "**Bay mir bistu sheyn**".[1] The original Yiddish version of the song (in C minor) is a dialogue between two lovers who share lines of the song.

The fame

The song became famous with English lyrics but retaining the Yiddish title, "Bei Mir Bistu Shein." It also appeared with a Germanized title "Bei Mir Bist Du Schön."

In 1937 Sammy Cahn heard a performance of the song, sung in Yiddish by African-American performers Johnnie and George at the Apollo Theater in Harlem. Grossinger's Catskill Resort Hotel proprietor Jenny Grossinger claimed to have taught the song to Johnnie and George while they were performing at the resort.[2] On seeing the response, Cahn got his employer to buy the rights so he (together with Saul Chaplin) could rewrite the song with English language lyrics and rhythms more typical of swing music. Secunda sold the publishing rights to the song for a mere US$30 which later he split with Jacobs. Cahn then convinced the still unknown Andrews Sisters to perform the song (recorded November 24, 1937). It became their first major hit, earning them a gold record, the first ever to a female vocal group. The song is performed by Renata Flores in the 1980 film *The Last Metro* and by Janis Siegel in the 1993 film *Swing Kids*. It was also a worldwide hit.

Original poster of the show, in Yiddish. New York, 1938

Over time, the song grossed some $3 million, with Secunda and Jacobs missing significant royalties. In 1961 the copyright on the song expired, and the ownership reverted to Secunda and Jacobs, who signed a contract with Harms, Inc., securing proper royalties.[3]

Other versions

There have been several songs with the tune in the Soviet Union. In particular, in 1943, a Russian-language song for the music was produced with satirical anti-Nazi lyrics titled *"Baron von der Pshik"* ("Барон фон дер Пшик") by Anatoli Fidrovsky, music arrangement by Orest Kandat.[4] Initially it was recorded by the jazz orchestra (director Nikolay Minkh) of the Baltic Fleet Theatre;[5] later it was included into the repertoire of Leonid Utyosov's jazz orchestra.[4]

In Nazi Germany it was also a hit until its Jewish origins were discovered, at which point it was promptly banned.[6]

In the late Soviet period, a similar version came out under the name "In the Cape Town Port", lyrics to which was written by another Jewish national and a native of Leningrad, Pavel Gandelman. That Soviet song was performed by a Russian singers Larisa Dolina and Arkady Severny.

There is a Swedish version called "Bär ner mig till sjön", which means "Carry me down to the lake".

Shasta (soft drink) Beverage Company adapted the song for a 1976 T.V. advertisement for Shasta Root Beer ("its root beer Mr. Shane ...").

In November 2011, Ilhama Gasimova released her single *Bei Mir Bist Du Sheen* featuring DJ OGB, a modern version of Yiddish song.[7]

Recorded versions

In addition to the original (or modified/translated) lyrics, a number of songs are known which borrowed only the popular tune of *Bei Mir...*, with completely unrelated text.

0-9

- 8 to the Bar

A

- Acker Bilk
- Adrian Rollini & His Novelty Trio & Quintet
- Al Bowlly
- The Andrews Sisters
- Arthur Murray Orchestra

B

- The Barry Sisters
- Belle Baker
- Benny Goodman
- Billy Cotton & His Band
- Bob Wilber
- Booker Ervin
- Budapest Klezmer Band, a traditional style Yiddish version switching to English for the last 40 seconds.[8]
- Buddy Clark

L

- Larisa Dolina (as *V Keiptaunskom portu* - In Cape Town port)[9]
- Lee Press-on and the Nails
- The Leningrad Dixieland Jazz Band
- The Lennon Sisters. Released on a single by Dot Records as catalog number 45-16423 in 1963[10]
- Leroy Jones
- Lionel Hampton and His Orchestra
- Listen Up!
- Los Albertos
- Louis Prima & Keely Smith. Released on the EP *Louis & Keely* by Dot Records as catalog number DEP-1093 in 1960[11]

M

- Martha Tilton
- Max Raabe & das Palast Orchester
- Mieczysław Fogg & Henryk Wars Orchestra (1938)
- Moreno

N

- Natasza Urbańska
- New Orleans Jazz Vipers
- Nina Hagen

C

- Charlie and his Orchestra
- The Clark Sisters
- Cora Green (in the 1938 race film *Swing!*)
- The Crew-Cuts

D

- Dan Barrett
- Dick Hyman
- Dennis Bell (Ballabio)
- Dukes of Dixieland

E

- Ella Fitzgerald
- Eydie Gormé & Steve Lawrence. Released on the LP *Eydie and Steve Sing the Golden Hits* by ABC-Paramount Records as catalog number ABC 311 in 1960[12]

F

- The Flying Neutrinos
- Frida Boccara (as "Pour Lui Je Suis Belle")

G

- Garland Wilson
- Gevolt (on album AlefBase, 2011)[16]
- Giora Feidman
- Glenn Miller
- Gołda Tencer
- Gordon Jenkins
- Gordon Webster
- Greta Keller
- Guy Lombardo

H

- Bettina Hermlin and Andrej Hermlin with his *Swing Dance Orchestra*

I

- Ilhama Gasimova with DJ OGB, a 2009 pop recording based on the Andrews Sisters' English version at higher speed and without the introductory section.[17]

J

- Jack Teagarden
- The Jackson Five (on the Carol Burnett Show, January 25, 1975)
- Janis Siegel
- Judy Garland
- June Christy. Recorded on June 20, 1952. Released on a 78rpm record by Capitol Records as catalog number 2199[18]

K

- Tatiana Kabanova (as *S Odesskogo Kichmana*)[22]
- Klezmer Conservatory Band
- Psoy Korolenko

P

- The Puppini Sisters. Released on the CD *Betcha Bottom Dollar* by Universal Music as catalog number 06 0251 70622 7 6 in 2006[13]

Q

- Quadro Nuevo

R

- Ramsey Lewis and His Gentlemen of Swing. Released on the LP *Ramsey Lewis and His Gentlemen of Swing* by Argo Records as catalog number LP 611 in 1958[14]
- Ray Anthony
- The Red Elvises with the title "My Darling Lorraine"
- Regina Carter. Released on the 2006 album "I'll Be Seeing You: A Sentimental Journey"
- Robin McKelle. Released on the CD *Introducing Robin McKelle* by Cheap Lullaby Records as catalog number 37 6010 60712 4 96 in 2006[15]
- Ronn Metcalfe

S

- Sammy Cahn
- Severny, Arkasha (*V Keiptaunskom portu* 1972)
- Shelly Manne
- Slim Gaillard
- A parody of this song, "The Bear Missed the Train", was written by the Smith Street Society Jazz Band in 1964 and became a favorite on Jean Shepherd's radio narratives.[19]
- it:Sorelle Marinetti
- Swing Kids

T

- Teddy Wilson
- Teresa Brewer. Released on a single by Amsterdam Records as catalog number 85029 in 1973[20]
- Terry Gibbs
- Tom Cunningham
- Karsten Troyke

U

- Utyosov, Leonid (*Baron Fod Der Pshik*[4] and *S Odesskogo Kichmana*[21])

V

- Vagabond Opera
- The Village Stompers

W

- Waldeck
- Willie "The Lion" Smith

Z

- Zarah Leander with Einar Groth's orchestra. Swedish lyrics: Tage Tall. Recorded on April 21, 1938. Released on a 78 rpm record by Odeon as catalog number D 2978, SA 255 956[23]

Notes

[1] *Funny it doesn't sound Jewish* (http://books.google.com/books?id=-jQzZfNYKWsC&pg=PA57&dq="bay+mir+is+do"&hl=en&
     ei=WOdiTYCHCoassAO4kdDSCA&sa=X&oi=book_result&ct=result&resnum=2&sqi=2&ved=0CDAQ6AEwAQ#v=onepage&q&
     f=false)

[2] Whitfield, S. J. (2001). *In Search of American Jewish Culture*. UPNE. pp. 1–2. ISBN 978-1-58465-171-0.

[3] Sholom Secunda - The Story of Bei Mir Bist Du Schoen (http://www.dvrbs.com/swing/SholomSecunda-BeiMirBistDuSchoen.htm), from
     the Milken Archive of Jewish American Music

[4] Search results for "Kandat" (http://www.russian-records.com/search.php?search_keywords=Kandat) at russian-records.com

[5] (Russian) (http://samuraev.narod.ru/music/schans/s006.htm)

[6] http://www.milkenarchive.org/works/view/583#/works/program_notes/583

[7] "Bei Mir Bistu Shein" with Ilhama Gasimova, featuring DJ OGB (http://www.youtube.com/watch_popup?v=r4B90Knx57w)

[8] Budapest Klezmer Version (http://www.youtube.com/watch?v=ZUVEq6NC7mM)

[9] V Keiptaunskom portu (Odessa motif), words by Pavel Gandelman, youtube (http://www.youtube.com/watch?v=kXT835cyhng)
     (Russian)

[10] Dot Records (http://www.soulfulkindamusic.net/dot.htm)

[11] Dot Album Discography, Part 1 (http://www.bsnpubs.com/dot/dota.html)

[12] Second Hand Songs - Medium: Eydie Steve Sing the Golden Hits - Eydie Gormé and Steve Lawrence (http://www.secondhandsongs.com/
     medium/64335)

[13] Second Hand Songs - Medium: Betcha Bottom Dollar - The Puppini Sisters (2006) (http://www.secondhandsongs.com/medium/21386)

[14] Second Hand Songs - Medium: Ramsey Lewis and His Gentlemen of Swing - Ramsey Lewis and His Gentlemen of Swing (http://www.
     secondhandsongs.com/medium/16649)

[15] Second Hand Songs - Medium: Introducing Robin McKelle - Robin McKelle (2006) (http://www.secondhandsongs.com/medium/29738)

[16] "Gevolt - AlefBase - Bay Mir Bistu Sheyn" (http://soundcloud.com/gevolt/gevolt-alefbase-11-bay-mir). . (Metal Version)

[17] "Bei Mir Bistu Shein" with Ilhama Gasimova, featuring DJ OGB (http://www.youtube.com/watch_popup?v=r4B90Knx57w)

[18] Capitol Records in the 2000 - 2499 series (http://www.78discography.com/Capitol2000.htm)

[19] Eugene B. Bergmann, *Excelsior, You Fathead!: The Art and Enigma of Jean Shepherd*, 2005, ISBN 1-55783-600-0, p. 203

[20] Teresa Brewer (http://www.rocky-52.net/chanteursb/brewer_t.htm)

[21] (Russian war video) (http://www.youtube.com/watch?v=4wrxW9VVU9o)

[22] S Odesskogo Kichmana (Odessa motif) youtube (http://www.youtube.com/watch?v=VbLXPfhhL_E&feature=related) **(Russian)**

[23] Zarah Leander (http://medlem.spray.se/filmoch78or/zarlea.htm)

External links

- Bay Mir Bist Du Sheyn (http://yi.wikisource.org/wiki/×□×□×□Ö·_×□×□×¨_×□×□×¡×□×□_×©×□×□×□) Original
  lyrics in Yiddish at Wikisource

- Page on the song at Yiddish Radio Project (http://www.yiddishradioproject.org/exhibits/ymis/ymis.
  php3?pg=2) site

- Bei Mir Bist Du Schoen - Sholem Secunda, Jacob Jacobs, Sammy Cahn and Saul Chaplin (Lyrics and Chords)
  (http://www.guntheranderson.com/v/data/beimirbi.htm)

- History of Bei Mir Bistu Shein featuring archival film clips (https://www.youtube.com/
  watch?v=04WH5ewE2RM) on YouTube **(Russian)**

- The Andrews Sisters sing Bei Mir Bistu Shein with new English lyrics (1937) (https://www.youtube.com/
  watch?v=4Vvo3MaFcxw) on YouTube

- Lyricist's granddaughter tells "The Real Story of Bei Mir Bistu Shein" (https://www.youtube.com/
  watch?v=4Vvo3MaFcxw) on YouTube

- Full lyrics of this song (http://www.metrolyrics.com/bei-mir-bist-du-schoen-lyrics-andrews-sisters.html) at
  MetroLyrics

Bette Midler

Bette Midler	
 Midler backstage at the Grammy Awards, February 1990	
Background information	
Birth name	Bette Midler
Also known as	The Divine Miss M
Born	December 1, 1945
Origin	Honolulu, Hawaii, U.S. Territory
Genres	Vocal, pop, adult contemporary, comedy
Occupations	Singer-songwriter, actress, comedian, author, producer, activist
Instruments	Vocals-mezzo soprano, ukulele
Years active	1965–present
Labels	Atlantic (1972–1997) Warner Bros. (1998–2001) Columbia (2002–present)
Associated acts	Barry Manilow
Website	bettemidler.com [1]

Bette Midler (born December 1, 1945), also known by her informal stage name, **The Divine Miss M**, is an American singer-songwriter, actress, comedian, producer and entrepreneur. In a career spanning almost half a century, Midler has been nominated for two Academy Awards, and won three Grammy Awards, four Golden Globes, three Emmy Awards, and a special Tony Award. She has sold over 30 million albums worldwide.[2]

Born in Honolulu, Hawaii, Midler began her professional career in several Off-Off-Broadway plays prior to her engagements in *Fiddler on the Roof* and *Salvation* on Broadway in the late 1960s. She came to prominence in 1970 when she began singing in the Continental Baths, a local gay bathhouse, where she managed to build up a core following. Since then, she has released 13 studio albums as a solo artist. Throughout her career, many of her songs became hits on the record charts, including "The Rose" and "Wind Beneath My Wings" as well as her renditions of "Do You Wanna Dance?", "Boogie Woogie Bugle Boy" and "From a Distance". In 2008, she signed a contract with Caesars Palace in Las Vegas to perform a series of shows titled *Bette Midler: The Showgirl Must Go On*, which ended in January 2010.

Midler made her motion picture debut in 1979 with *The Rose* which earned her a Golden Globe and a nomination for the Academy Award for Best Actress of 1980. In the following years she starred in a string of hit films that includes *Down and Out in Beverly Hills*, *Outrageous Fortune*, *Beaches*, *The First Wives Club*, and *The Stepford Wives* as well as *For the Boys* and *Gypsy*, the latter two for which she won two further Golden Globe Awards in 1992 and 1994.

Early life and family

Midler was born in Honolulu, Hawaii. Her parents moved from Paterson, New Jersey to Honolulu before she was born, and hers was one of the few Jewish families in a mostly Asian neighborhood.[3] Her mother, Ruth (née Schindel), was a seamstress and housewife, and her father, Fred Midler, worked at a Navy base in Hawaii as a painter, and was also a housepainter.[4][5] She was named after actress Bette Davis, though Davis pronounced her first name in two syllables, and Midler uses one, /ˈbɛt/.[6] She was raised in Aiea and attended Radford High School, in Honolulu.[7] She was voted "Most Talkative" in the 1961 school Hoss Election, and in her Senior Year (Class of 1963), "Most Dramatic".[8] Midler majored in drama at the University of Hawaii, but left after three semesters.[9] She earned money in the 1966 film *Hawaii* as an extra,[6] playing an uncredited seasick passenger named Miss David Buff.

Midler married artist Martin von Haselberg on December 16, 1984, about six weeks after their first meeting. Their daughter, Sophie Frederica Alohilani Von Haselberg, was born on November 14, 1986.[10]

Career

Theater work

Midler relocated to New York City in the summer of 1965, using the money from her work in the film *Hawaii*. She landed her first professional onstage role in Tom Eyen's Off-Off-Broadway plays in 1965, *Miss Nefertiti Regrets* and *Cinderella Revisited,* a children's play by day and an adult show by night.[11] From 1966 to 1969, she played the role of Tzeitel in *Fiddler on the Roof* on Broadway.[6] After *Fiddler*, she joined the original cast of *Salvation* in 1969.[12]

She began singing in the Continental Baths, a gay bathhouse in the city, in the summer of 1970.[6] During this time, she became close to her piano accompanist, Barry Manilow, who produced her first album in 1972, *The Divine Miss M*.[11] It was during her time at the Continental Baths that she built up a core following. In the late 1990s, during the release of her album *Bathhouse Betty*, Midler commented on her time performing there, "Despite the way things turned out [with the AIDS crisis], I'm still proud of those days. I feel like I was at the forefront of the gay liberation movement, and I hope I did my part to help it move forward. So, I kind of wear the label of 'Bathhouse Betty' with pride".[13]

Midler starred in the first professional production of The Who's rock opera *Tommy* in 1971, with director Richard Pearlman and the Seattle Opera.[14] It was during the run of *Tommy* that Midler first appeared on *The Tonight Show*.

1972–80: *The Divine Miss M* and success

Midler released her debut album, *The Divine Miss M*, on Atlantic Records, in December 1972. It reached Billboard's Top 10 and became a million-selling Platinum-certified album,[15] earning Midler the 1973 Grammy Award for Best New Artist.[16] It featured three hit singles, with "Do You Wanna Dance?", "Friends", and "Boogie Woogie Bugle Boy", which became Midler's first No. 1 Adult Contemporary hit. "Bugle Boy" became a very successful rock cover of the classic swing tune originally introduced and popularized in 1941 by the famous Andrews Sisters, of whom Midler has repeatedly referenced as her idols and inspiration, as far back as her first appearances on *The Tonight Show Starring Johnny Carson*. Midler told Carson in an interview that she always wanted to move like the sisters, and Patty Andrews once remembered, "When I first heard the introduction on the radio, I thought it was our old record. When Bette opened at the Amphitheater in Los Angeles, Maxene and I went backstage to see her. Her first words were, 'What else did you record?'"[17] During another one of Midler's concerts, Maxene went on stage and presented her with an honorary bugle. Bette recorded other Andrews Sisters hits, including "In the Mood" and "Lullaby of Broadway."[17]

Her self-titled follow-up album was released at the end of 1973. It reached Billboard's Top 10 and eventually sold close to a million copies in the United States alone.[18] Midler returned to recording with the 1976 and 1977 albums, *Songs for the New Depression* and *Broken Blossom*. In 1974, she received a Special Tony Award for her contribution to Broadway,[19] with *Clams on the Half Shell Revue* playing at the Minskoff Theater. From 1975–1978, she also provided the voice of Woody the Spoon on the PBS educational series *Vegetable Soup*. In 1977, Midler's first television special, *Ol' Red Hair is Back*, premiered, featuring guest stars Dustin Hoffman and Emmett Kelly. It went on to win the *Emmy Award*[20] for Outstanding Special — Comedy-Variety or Music.[21]

Midler at the premiere of *The Rose*, 1979

Midler made her first motion picture in 1979, starring in the 1960s-era rock and roll tragedy *The Rose*, as a drug-addicted rock star modeled after Janis Joplin.[6] That year, she also released her fifth studio album, *Thighs and Whispers*. Midler's first foray into disco was a commercial and critical failure and went on to be her all-time lowest charting album, peaking at No. 65 on the *Billboard* album chart.[22] Soon afterward, she began a world concert tour, with one of her shows in Pasadena being filmed and released as the concert film *Divine Madness* (1980).

Her performance in *The Rose* earned her an Academy Award nomination for Best Actress, a role for which she won the Golden Globe for Best Actress (Comedy or Musical).[6] The film's acclaimed soundtrack album sold over two million copies in the United States alone, earning a Double Platinum certification.[15] The single version of the song held the No. 1 position on Billboard's Adult Contemporary chart for five consecutive weeks and reached No. 3 on Billboard's Hot 100. It earned Midler her first Gold single[15] and won the Grammy award for Best Pop Vocal Performance, Female.[16]

1981–1989: *Wind Beneath My Wings*, *Beaches* and chart comeback

Midler worked on the troubled comedy project *Jinxed!* in 1981. However, during production, there was friction with co-star Ken Wahl and the film's director, Don Siegel. Released in 1982, the film was a major flop. Midler did not appear in any other films until 1986. During those four years, she concentrated on her music career and in 1983, released the album *No Frills*, produced by Chuck Plotkin, who was best known for his work with Bob Dylan and Bruce Springsteen. The album included three single releases: the ballad "All I Need To Know", a cover of Detroit native Marshall Crenshaw's "You're My Favorite Waste of Time" – which Midler fell in love with after flipping his 45 of "Someday Someway" – and Midler's take on the Rolling Stones cover "Beast of Burden". The rock and New Wave album became Midler's third lowest charting album in the U.S.

Midler performed on USA for Africa's 1985 fund-raising single "We Are the World", and participated at the Live Aid event at JFK Stadium in Philadelphia.[23] Also in 1985, she signed a multi-picture deal with the Walt Disney Studios. She was subsequently cast by director Paul Mazursky in *Down and Out in Beverly Hills*, beginning a successful comedic acting career.[6] She followed that role with *Ruthless People* (1986), *Outrageous Fortune* (1987), and *Big Business* (1988).[6] Later in 1988, Midler lent her voice to the animated character Georgette, a snobbish poodle, in Disney's *Oliver & Company*, and had a hit with the tearjerker *Beaches*, co-starring Barbara Hershey.[6] The accompanying soundtrack remains Midler's all-time biggest selling disc, reaching No. 2 on *Billboard*'s album chart and with U.S. sales of four million copies. It featured her biggest hit, "Wind Beneath My Wings", which went to No. 1 on *Billboard*'s Hot 100, achieved Platinum status,[15] and won Midler her third Grammy Award — for

Record of the Year – at the 1990 telecast.[16]

1990s

Midler in Los Angeles, 1990.

Midler's 1990 cover of the Julie Gold song "From a Distance", the first offering from her seventh studio album *Some People's Lives* (1990), topped the *Billboard* Adult Contemporary charts and achieved platinum status in the US. The same year, she starred along with Trini Alvarado as the title character in John Erman's drama film *Stella*. The third feature film adaptation of the 1920 novel *Stella Dallas* by Olive Higgins Prouty, Midler portrayed a vulgar single mother living in Watertown, New York, who, determined to give her daughter all the opportunities she never had, ultimately makes a selfless sacrifice to ensure her happiness. The movie scored mediocre reviews.[24][25] while Midler received her first Razzie Award nomination for Worst Actress.[26]

She co-starred with Woody Allen in the 1991 film *Scenes from a Mall*, again for Paul Mazursky. In the film, Allen's character reveals to his author wife Deborah, played by Midler, after years of a happy marriage, that he has had an affair, resulting in her request for divorce. The movie performed poorly,[27] and received a mixed reception by critics.[28][29][30] Midler faired somewhat better with her other 1991 project *For the Boys*, on which she reteamed with *The Rose* director Mark Rydell. A historical musical drama, it tells the story of 1940s actress and singer Dixie Leonard, played by Mider, who teams up with Eddie Sparks, a famous performer to entertain American troops. While the film received a mixed reception from critics, Midler earned rave review for her portrayal. The following year she was awarded her second Golden Globe and received her second Academy Award nomination for Best Actress.[26]

Midler turned down the lead role in the musical comedy *Sister Act* in 1992, which instead went to Whoopi Goldberg.[31] Midler won an Emmy Award in 1992 for her performance on the penultimate episode of *The Tonight Show Starring Johnny Carson* in May 1992, during which she sang an emotion-laden "One for My Baby (and One More for the Road)" to Johnny Carson. That night, Midler began singing "Here's That Rainy Day", Carson's favorite song; Carson joined in a few lyrics later.[32] In 1993, she starred with Sarah Jessica Parker and Kathy Najimy in the Walt Disney comedy fantasy film, *Hocus Pocus*, as Winifred Sanderson, the head witch of the Sanderson Sisters.[6][33] Released to initially mixed reviews, through various outlets such as strong DVD sales and annual record-breaking showings on 13 Nights of Halloween, the film has achieved cult status over the years.[34][34][35][36] Her television work includes an Emmy-nominated version of the stage musical *Gypsy* and a guest appearance as herself in Fran Drescher's *The Nanny*.

She appeared on *Seinfeld* in the 1995 episode "The Understudy", which was the season finale of that show's sixth season in 1995. Her 1997 HBO special *Diva Las Vegas* earned her a third Emmy Award, for Outstanding Performance in a Variety or Music Program.[21] Midler's other 1990s films include *The First Wives Club* (1996).[6] In 1997, Midler, along with her co-stars from *The First Wives Club*, Goldie Hawn, and Diane Keaton, was a recipient of the Women in Film Crystal Award, which honors "outstanding women who, through their endurance and the excellence of their work, have helped to expand the role of women within the entertainment industry".[37]

2000–05

Midler starred in her own sitcom in 2000, *Bette*, which featured Midler playing herself, a divine celebrity who is adored by her fans. Airing on CBS, initial ratings were high, marking the best sitcom debut for the network in more than five years, but viewers percentage soon declined, resulting into the show's cancellation in early 2001.[38] Midler openly griped about the show's demanding shooting schedule, while the show itself was also reportedly rocked by backstage turmoil, involving the replacement of co-star Kevin Dunn whose departure was attributed to his behind-the scenes bickering with Midler by the media.[38] Critically praised however, Midler was awarded a People's Choice Award for her performance in the show and received a Golden Globe Award nomination the following year.[26] Also in 2000, Midler made an uncredited cameo appearance in Nancy Meyers' fantasy rom–com *What Women Want*, starring Mel Gibson and Helen Hunt.[39] In the film, she portrayed a therapist who realizes that central character Nick, played by Gibson, is able to understand women's thoughts.[39] Released to genereally mixed reviews, it became the then-most successful film ever directed by a woman, taking in $183 million in the United States, and grossing upward of $370 million worldwide.[40][41]

The same year Midler starred in *Isn't She Great* and *Drowning Mona*. In Andrew Bergman's *Isn't She Great*, a highly fictionalized account of the life and career of author Jacqueline Susann, she played alongside Nathan Lane and Stockard Channing, portraying Susann with her early struggles as an aspiring actress relentlessly hungry for fame, her relationship with press agent Irving Mansfield, her success as the author of *Valley of the Dolls*, and her battle with and subsequent death from breast cancer. The dramedy garnered largely negative reviews by critics, who dismissed it as "bland material [that] produces entirely forgettable comic performances."[42] For her performance in the film, Midler received her second Golden Raspberry Award nomination for Worst Actress at the 21st ceremony.[26] In Nick Gomez's dark comedy *Drowning Mona*, Midler appeared along with Danny DeVito and Jamie Lee Curtis, playing title character Mona Dearly, a spiteful, loud-mouthed, cruel and highly unpopular woman, whose mysterious death is investigated. Another critical fiasco, reviewers noted that the film "drowns itself in humor that never rises above sitcom level."[43]

Bette or Bust, a book chronicling Midler's Divine Miss Millennium Tour, was released in 2001. After nearly three decades of erratic record sales, Midler was dropped from the Warner Music Group in 2001. Following a reported long-standing feud with Barry Manilow, the two joined forces after many years in 2003 to record *Bette Midler Sings the Rosemary Clooney Songbook*. Now signed to Columbia Records, the album was an instant success, being certified gold by RIAA. One of the *Clooney Songbook* selections, "This Ole House", became Midler's first Christian radio single shipped by Rick Hendrix and his positive music movement. The album was nominated for a Grammy the following year.[44]

Throughout 2003 and 2004, Midler toured the United States in her new show, *Kiss My Brass*, to sell-out audiences. Also in 2004, she appeared in a supporting role in Frank Oz' science fiction satire *The Stepford Wives*, a remake of the 1975 film of the same name also based on the Ira Levin novel. Also starring Nicole Kidman, Matthew Broderick, Christopher Walken and Glenn Close, Midler played Bobbie Markowitz, a writer and recovering alcoholic. The project underwent numerous production problems that occurred throughout its shooting schedule, with reports of problems on-set between director Oz and the actors being rampant in the press. Oz later blamed Midler — who was amid recording her next album and rehearsing for her tour — for being under a lot of stress by other projects and making "the mistake of bringing her stress on the set".[45] While the original book and film had tremendous cultural impact, the remake was marked by poor reviews by many critics, and a financial loss of approximately $40 million at the box office.[46][47]

An Australian tour in early 2005, *Kiss My Brass Down Under*, was equally successful. Midler joined forces again with Manilow for another tribute album, *Bette Midler Sings the Peggy Lee Songbook*. Released in October 2005, the album sold 55,000 copies the first week of release, returned Midler to the top ten of US *Billboard* 200,[48] and was nominated for a Grammy Award.[49]

2006–present

Midler released a new Christmas album entitled *Cool Yule* in 2006, which featured a duet of Christmastime pop standards "Winter Wonderland"/"Let It Snow" with Johnny Mathis. Well-received, the album received a Grammy Award nomination for Best Traditional Pop Vocal Album in 2007.[50] The same year, Midler returned to the big screen, appearing in *Then She Found Me*, Helen Hunt's feature film directorial debut. Also starring Hunt along with Matthew Broderick and Colin Firth, the comedy-drama film tells the story of a 39-year-old Brooklyn elementary school teacher, who after years is contacted by the flamboyant host of a local talk show, played by Midler, who introduces herself as her biological mother. Critical response to the film was mixed; whereas some critics praised the film for having strong performances, others felt the film was bogged down by a weak script and technical issues.

Midler debuted her Vegas show entitled *Bette Midler: The Showgirl Must Go On* at The Colosseum at Caesars Palace on February 20, 2008. It comprised The Staggering Harlettes, 20 female dancers called The Caesar Salad Girls and a 13-piece band. The show played its final performance on January 31, 2010, after a two-year run,[51] and was nominated for a Primetime Emmy Award for Outstanding Variety, Music, or Comedy Special in 2011.[52] Also in 2008, another compilation album by Midler, *Jackpot: The Best Bette*, was released. It reached number 66 on the US *Billboard* 200 chart, and number six in the United Kingdom, where it was certified platinum for sales of over 300,000 copies.[53] Her only film appearance that year, Milder has a small role in Diane English's comedy film *The Women*, starring Meg Ryan, Annette Bening and Eva Mendes among others. An updated version of the George Cukor-directed 1939 film of the same name based on a 1936 play by Clare Boothe Luce. Upon its release, the

Midler at the 2010 HRC Annual Dinner.

film was widely panned by critics who found it was "a toothless remake of the 1939 classic, lacking the charm, wit and compelling protagonists of the original."

She appeared on the Bravo TV show *My Life on the D-List* with Kathy Griffin in June 2009. December of the same year, she appeared in the *Royal Variety Performance*, an annual British charity event attended by Queen Elizabeth II. Midler performed "In My Life" and "Wind Beneath My Wings" as the closing act.[54] In 2010, Midler voiced the character Kitty Galore in the animated film *Cats & Dogs: The Revenge of Kitty Galore*. The film was a success, grossing $112 million worldwide.[55] In November 2010, Midler released *Memories of You*, another compilation of lesser known tracks from her catalog. Midler is one of the producers of the Broadway production of the musical *Priscilla Queen of the Desert* which opened in February 2011.[56] In June 2012, she received the Sammy Cahn Lifetime Achievement Award at the Songwriters Hall of Fame in New York in recognition of her having "captivated the world" with her "stylish presentation and unmistakable voice".[57]

Midler co-starred alongside Billy Crystal in the family movie *Parental Guidance*, released in 2012.

Charity work

Midler founded the New York Restoration Project (NYRP) in 1995, a non-profit organization with the goal of revitalizing neglected neighborhood parks in economically disadvantaged neighborhoods of New York City.[6] These include Highbridge Park, Fort Washington Park, and Fort Tryon Park in upper Manhattan and Roberto Clemente State Park and *Bridge Park* in the Bronx.[58]

When the city planned in 1991 to auction 114 community gardens for commercial development, Midler led a coalition of greening organizations to save them. NYRP took ownership of 60 of the most neglected plots. Today, Midler and her organization work with local volunteers and community groups to ensure that these gardens are kept safe, clean and vibrant. In 2003, Midler opened Swindler Cove Park, a new 5-acre (20,000 m^2) public park on the Harlem River shore featuring specially designed educational facilities and the Peter Jay Sharp Boathouse, the first community rowing facility to be built on the Harlem River in more than 100 years. The organization offers free in-school and after-school environmental education programming to students from high-poverty Title I schools.[58]

Discography

Studio albums

• 1972: *The Divine Miss M*	• 1995: *Bette of Roses*
• 1973: *Bette Midler*	• 1998: *Bathhouse Betty*
• 1976: *Songs for the New Depression*	• 2000: *Bette*
• 1977: *Broken Blossom*	• 2003: *Sings the Rosemary Clooney Songbook*
• 1979: *Thighs and Whispers*	• 2005: *Sings the Peggy Lee Songbook*
• 1983: *No Frills*	• 2006: *Cool Yule*
• 1990: *Some People's Lives*	

Tours

• 1970–72: *Continental Baths Tour*	• 1982–83: *De Tour*
• 1972: *Cross Country Tour*	• 1993: *Experience the Divine*
• 1973: *The Divine Miss M Tour*	• 1994: *Experience the Divine Again!*
• 1975: *Clams on the Half Shell Revue*	• 1997: *Diva Las Vegas*
• 1975–76: *The Depression Tour*	• 1999: *Bathhouse Betty Club Tour*
• 1977–78: *An Intimate Evening with Bette*	• 1999–2000: *The Divine Miss Millennium Tour*
• 1978: *The Rose Live in Concert*	• 2003–04: *Kiss My Brass*
• 1978: *World Tour*	• 2005: *Kiss My Brass Down Under*
• 1979–80: *Bette! Divine Madness*	• 2008–10: *The Showgirl Must Go On*
• 1980: *Divine Madness: Pasadena*	

Filmography

Film

Year	Title	Role	Notes
1966	*Hawaii*	Passenger	uncredited
1968	*The Detective (1968 film)*	Girl at Party	uncredited
1969	*Goodbye, Columbus*	Wedding Guest	uncredited, cut scene
1972	*Scarecrow in a Garden of Cucumbers*	unknown	voice
1974	*The Thorn*	Virgin Mary	Also known as *The Divine Mr. J*; blocked distribution of film
1979	*The Rose*	Mary Rose Foster	Golden Globe Award for Best Actress – Motion Picture Musical or Comedy Golden Globe Award New Star of the Year – Actress Nominated — Academy Award for Best Actress Nominated — BAFTA Award for Best Actress in a Leading Role
1980	*Divine Madness!*	Herself/ Divine Miss M.	concert film Nominated — Golden Globe Award for Best Actress – Motion Picture Musical or Comedy
1982	*Jinxed!*	Bonita Friml	

1986	*Down and Out in Beverly Hills*	Barbara Whiteman	Nominated — Golden Globe Award for Best Actress — Motion Picture Musical or Comedy
1986	*Ruthless People*	Barbara Stone	American Comedy Award for Funniest Actress in a Motion Picture
1987	*Outrageous Fortune*	Sandy Brozinsky	American Comedy Award for Funniest Actress in a Motion Picture Nominated — Golden Globe Award for Best Actress — Motion Picture Musical or Comedy
1988	*Big Business*	Sadie Shelton/Sadie Ratliff	American Comedy Award for Funniest Actress in a Motion Picture
1988	*Oliver & Company*	Georgette	voice
1988	*Beaches*	C. C. Bloom	
1989	*The Lottery*		Short film
1990	*Stella*	Stella Claire	
1991	*For the Boys*	Dixie Leonard	Golden Globe Award for Best Actress — Motion Picture Musical or Comedy Nominated — Academy Award for Best Actress
1991	*Scenes from a Mall*	Deborah Fifer	
1993	*Gypsy*	Mama Rose	Television film Golden Globe Award for Best Actress in a Miniseries or Television Film Nominated — Primetime Emmy Award for Outstanding Lead Actress — Miniseries or a Movie
1993	*Hocus Pocus*	Winifred 'Winnie' Sanderson	Nominated — Saturn Award for Best Actress
1995	*Get Shorty*	Doris Saphron	uncredited American Comedy Award for Funniest Supporting Actress in a Motion Picture
1996	*The First Wives Club*	Brenda Cushman	National Board of Review Award for Best Cast Nominated — Satellite Award for Best Actress - Motion Picture Musical or Comedy
1997	*That Old Feeling*	Lilly Leonard	
1999	*Get Bruce*	Herself	
1999	*Fantasia 2000*	Herself / Hostess	(segment "Piano Concerto No. 2, Allegro, Opus 102")
2000	*What Women Want*	Dr. J.M. Perkins	uncredited
2000	*Isn't She Great*	Jacqueline Susann	
2000	*Drowning Mona*	Mona Dearly	
2004	*The Stepford Wives*	Bobbie Markowitz	
2007	*Then She Found Me*	Bernice Graves	
2008	*The Women*	Leah Miller	
2010	*Cats & Dogs: The Revenge of Kitty Galore*	Kitty Galore	
2012	*Parental Guidance*	Diane Decker	

Television

Year	Title	Role	Notes
1976	*Vegetable Soup*	Woody the Spoon	Voice role
1976	*The Bette Midler Show*	Herself	Television special
1977	*Ol' Red Hair is Back*	Herself	Television special Primetime Emmy Award for Outstanding Comedy-Variety or Music Special Nominated — Primetime Emmy Award for Outstanding Writing for a Variety, Music or Comedy Program
1984	*Art Or Bust*	Herself/ Divine Miss M.	Television special
1984	*Video Music Awards*	Herself/ co-host	Awards Show
1990	*Earth Day Special*	Mother Nature	
1992	*The Tonight Show Starring Johnny Carson*	Herself	Primetime Emmy Award for Individual Performance in a Variety or Music Program
1993	*The Simpsons*	Herself	"Krusty Gets Kancelled"
1995	*Seinfeld*	Herself	"The Understudy"
1997	*Diva Las Vegas*	Herself/ Divine Miss M.	Television special Primetime Emmy Award for Individual Performance in a Variety or Music Program Nominated — Primetime Emmy Award for Outstanding Comedy-Variety or Music Special
1997	*The Nanny*	Herself	"You Bette Your Life"
1998	*Murphy Brown*	Caprice Feldman	"Never Can Say Goodbye"
1999	*Jackie's Back*	Herself	
2000–01	*Bette*	Bette	18 episodes TV Guide Award – Actress of the Year in a New Series Nominated — Golden Globe Award for Best Actress – Television Series Musical or Comedy
2008	*Strictly Come Dancing*	Herself	Performed *Wind Beneath My Wings*
2009	*Loose Women*	Herself	Guest Host
2009	*Dancing on Ice*	Herself	Performed
2009	*Strictly Come Dancing*	Herself	Performed *The Rose*
2009	*The One Show*	Herself	Guest
2009	*The Royal Variety Performance*	Herself	Performed
2009	*The Marriage Ref*	Herself	Guest
2009	*Kathy Griffin: My Life on the D-List*	Herself	Guest / toured Las Vegas nightlife w/Kathy
2010	*The Showgirl Must Go On*	Herself	HBO TV Special (December 31)
2010	*Paul O'Grady's Christmas*	Herself	Guest

Stage shows

Year	Title	Role	Notes
1967	*Fiddler on the Roof*	Tzeitel	Musical
1970	*Salvation*	Betty Lou	Off-Broadway musical
1973	*Bette Midler*	Herself	Concerts
1975	*Bette Midler's Clams on the Half Shell Revue*	Herself	Revue
1979	*Bette! Divine Madness*	Herself	Concerts
2011	*Priscilla, Queen of the Desert*		Musical; Producer

Grammy Awards

Year	Award	Performance	Result
1974	Best New Artist	—	Won
	Album of the Year	*The Divine Miss M*	Nominated
	Best Female Pop Vocal Performance	"Boogie Woogie Bugle Boy"	Nominated
1981	Best Female Pop Vocal Performance	"The Rose"	Won
	Record of the Year		Nominated
1990	Record of the Year	"Wind Beneath My Wings"	Won
	Best Female Pop Vocal Performance		Nominated
1991	Best Female Pop Vocal Performance	"From a Distance"	Nominated
	Record of the Year		Nominated
2004	Best Traditional Pop Vocal Album	*Bette Midler Sings the Rosemary Clooney Songbook*	Nominated
2007	Best Traditional Pop Vocal Album	*Bette Midler Sings the Peggy Lee Songbook*	Nominated
2008	Best Traditional Pop Vocal Album	*Cool Yule*	Nominated

- The year given is the year of the ceremony.
- In 1981 the album *In Harmony: A Sesame Street Record* won the Grammy for Best Recording for Children, Midler was one of the various artists featured. This Grammy was awarded to the producers, David Levine and Lucy Simon.
- "Wind Beneath My Wings" also won the Grammy for Song of the Year. This Grammy was awarded to the songwriters, Larry Henley and Jeff Silbar.
- "From a Distance", recorded by Midler in 1990, won that year's Grammy for Song of the Year. This Grammy was awarded to the songwriter, Julie Gold.

Bibliography

- *Bette Midler: A View From a Broad* (Simon & Schuster, 1980).
- *The Saga of Baby Divine* (Crown Publishers, 1983).

References

[1] http://bettemidler.com/

[2] Sinead Garvan (November 26, 2010). "Bette Midler: I wouldn't make it now" (http://www.bbc.co.uk/news/entertainment-arts-11842187). BBC News. . Retrieved 2011-07-25.

[3] "The Religious Affiliation of Singer, Actress, Comedian Bette Midler" (http://www.adherents.com/people/pm/Bette_Midler.html). Adherents.com. October 8, 2005. . Retrieved 2011-07-25.

[4] "Bette Midler, Biography (1945–)" (http://www.filmreference.com/film/58/Bette-Midler.html). FilmReference.com. . Retrieved 2011-07-28.

[5] "Bette Midler: The Divine Miss Bubbe" (http://www.jewishjournal.com/the_ticket/item/bette_midler_the_divine_miss_bubbe). Jewish Journal. 2012-12-12. . Retrieved 2012-12-18.

[6] Stated on *Inside the Actors Studio*, 2004

[7] The Class of 1963! We're Radgrads! (http://www.radgrad63.org/rg_senior2.html)

[8] High School Hoss Elections (http://www.radgrad63.org/rg_classnewsp.html)

[9] "Bette Midler: 62 and Heading for Vegas!". *The Oprah Winfrey Show*. January 28, 2008. Harpo Productions, Inc.

[10] "Bette Midler" (http://jwa.org/encyclopedia/article/midler-bette). Jewish Women's Archive. . Retrieved 2011-07-25.

[11] Richard Corliss (March 17, 2004). "That Old Feeling: Best Bette Yet" (http://www.time.com/time/columnist/corliss/article/0,9565,601990,00.html). *Time*. . Retrieved 2011-07-25.

[12] "Bette Midler" (http://broadwayworld.com/people/Bette_Midler/). BroadwayWorld.com. . Retrieved 2011-07-28.

[13] "Bette Midler" (http://delveintothedivine.com/bio/bettebathhouse.html). *Houston Voice* (DelveIntoTheDevine.com). October 23, 1998. . Retrieved 2011-07-28.

[14] Melinda Bargreen (July 22, 2005). "Glynn Ross, 90, turned Seattle into opera destination" (http://seattletimes.nwsource.com/html/entertainment/2002394625_ross22.html). *The Seattle Times* (Seattletimes.com). . Retrieved 2011-07-25.

[15] "Gold & Platinum Searchable database-Bette Midler" (http://www.riaa.com/goldandplatinumdata.php?content_selector=gold-platinum-searchable-database). Recording Industry Association of America. . Retrieved 2011-07-28.

[16] "Past Winners Search-Midler" (http://www.grammy.com/nominees/search?artist=midler&title=&year=All&genre=All). Grammy.com. . Retrieved 2011-07-28.

[17] Sforza, John: "Swing It! The Andrews Sisters Story;" University Press of Kentucky, 2000; 289 pages.

[18] Joel Whitburn (May 1, 2002). *Top Adult Contemporary 1961–2001*. Menomonee Falls, WI: Record Research, Inc. 3rd edition. p. 170. ISBN 978-0-89820-149-9.

[19] "Search Past Winners-1974" (http://www.tonyawards.com/p/tonys_search?start=15&year=1974&award=All&lname=&fname=&show=). TonyAwards.com. . Retrieved August 23, 2010.

[20] "Bette Midler" (http://www.emmys.com/celebrities/bette-midler). Emmys.com. . Retrieved 2012-12-18.

[21] "Awards for Bette Midler" (http://www.imdb.com/name/nm0000541/awards). imdb. . Retrieved 2011-07-25.

[22] "Thighs and Wispers" (http://www.betteontheboards.com/boards/album-09.htm). betteontheboards.com. . Retrieved 2011-07-25.

[23] "'We Are The World' Tune Brings Out The Best of America's 46 Stars" (http://books.google.com/books?id=CbMDAAAAMBAJ&pg=PA16&dq=jackson+"we+are+the+world"&lr=&as_drrb_is=q&as_minm_is=0&as_miny_is=&as_maxm_is=0&as_maxy_is=&num=100&as_brr=3&ei=E4EmSvWKIZj2MPnR0ZUL#v=onepage&q=jackson "we are the world"&f=false). *Jet* (Google Books): p. 16. February 18, 1985. . Retrieved 2011-07-28.

[24] "MOVIE REVIEWS : Melodrama: Was this 'Stella,' a loony Midler remake, really necessary?" (http://movies.nytimes.com/movie/review?res=9C0CEED6123FF931A35751C0A966958260). Los Angeles Times. . Retrieved 2012-06-10.

[25] "Stella" (http://rogerebert.suntimes.com/apps/pbcs.dll/article?AID=/19900202/REVIEWS/2020305). Chicago Sun Times. . Retrieved 2012-06-10.

[26] "Awards for Bette Midler" (http://www.imdb.com/name/nm0000541/awards). *IMDb*. imdb.com. . Retrieved 2010-02-18.

[27] "THREE-DAY WEEKEND BOX OFFICE : A Replay of the Top Fhree" (http://articles.latimes.com/1991-02-26/entertainment/ca-1833_1_weekend-box-office). Los Angeles Times. . Retrieved 2012-06-10.

[28] "Review/Film; A Marriage On and Off The Rocks" (http://movies.nytimes.com/movie/review?res=9D0CE0DB163EF931A15751C0A967958260). The New York Times. . Retrieved 2012-06-10.

[29] "Scenes from a Mall" (http://rogerebert.suntimes.com/apps/pbcs.dll/article?AID=/19910222/REVIEWS/102220302/1023). Chicago Sun Times. . Retrieved 2012-06-10.

[30] "MOVIE REVIEW : Down and Out in Beverly Center : A Slice of L.A.--Without the Bite" (http://articles.latimes.com/1991-02-22/entertainment/ca-1467_1_movie-beverly-center). Los Angeles Times. . Retrieved 2012-06-10.

[31] Lynn Hirschburg (October 8, 2000). "Meta-Midler" (http://www.nytimes.com/2000/10/08/magazine/meta-midler.html?scp=4&sq=johnny carson midler&st=nyt&pagewanted=1). *New York Times*: p. 14. . Retrieved 2011-07-25.

[32] Bill Saporito (March 31, 2003). "Great Performances to Savor" (http://www.time.com/time/magazine/article/0,9171,1004565-1,00. html). *Time*. . Retrieved 2011-07-25.

[33] "Hocus Pocus (1993)" (http://www.imdb.com/title/tt0107120/). IMDb. . Retrieved 2011-07-25.

[34] "Five Reasons Why 'Hocus Pocus' is One of the Greatest Cult Classic Films" (http://www.ibtimes.com/articles/235708/20111021/ hocus-pocus-abc-family.htm). International Business Times. . Retrieved 2011-11-03.

[35] "ABC Family's "13 Nights of Halloween 2011" Scares Up Record Crowd" (http://tvbythenumbers.zap2it.com/2011/11/01/ abc-familyâ\lls-13-nights-of-halloween-2011-scares-up-record-crowd/109316/). TV By the Numbers. . Retrieved 2011-11-03.

[36] "HOCUS POCUS - Where are they now?" (http://www.celebuzz.com/2011-10-31/ cast-of-cult-halloween-hit-hocus-pocus-where-are-they-now-photos/). Oh No They Didn't. . Retrieved 2011-11-03.

[37] "Past Recipients" (http://wif.org/past-recipients). wif.org. . Retrieved May 9, 2011.

[38] "CBS Reportedly Cancels 'Bette'" (http://abcnews.go.com/Entertainment/story?id=108743&page=1). *ABC News*. ABC News. March 6, 2001. . Retrieved 2010-02-18.

[39] McCarthy, Todd (December 10, 2000). "*What Women Want* review" (http://www.variety.com/review/VE1117796916?refcatid=31). *Variety*. . Retrieved 2012-10-01.

[40] Griffin, Nancy (December 14, 2003). "Diane Keaton Meets Both Her Matches" (http://www.nytimes.com/2003/12/14/movies/ film-diane-keaton-meets-both-her-matches.html). *The New York Times*. . Retrieved 2010-02-02.

[41] Kaufman, Amy (January 1, 2010). "No Complications For Meyers" (http://www.boston.com/ae/movies/articles/2010/01/01/ nothing_complicated_about_director_meyerss_attention_to_detail/). *Los Angeles Times*. . Retrieved 2010-02-18.

[42] "Isn't She Great (2000)" (http://www.rottentomatoes.com/m/isnt_she_great/). *RottenTomatoes*. RottenTomatoes.com. . Retrieved 2012-10-01.

[43] "Drowning Mona (2000)" (http://www.rottentomatoes.com/m/drowning_mona/). *RottenTomatoes*. RottenTomatoes.com. . Retrieved 2012-10-01.

[44] "Complete list of 46th annual Grammy winners and nominees" (http://www.chicagotribune.com/sns-grammys-nominees,0,3626237. story). *Chicago Tribune*. Associated Press. . Retrieved February 11, 2012.

[45] "Nicole Kidman-Frank Oz's Tense Remake" (http://www.contactmusic.com/news-article/frank-oz.s-tense-remake). contactmusic.com. February 10, 2003. .

[46] "The Stepford Wives (2004)" (http://boxofficemojo.com/movies/?id=stepfordwives.htm). Boxofficemojo.com. . Retrieved 2010-09-20.

[47] "Stepford Wives 2004 budget details" (http://www.the-numbers.com/movies/2004/STEPF.php). The Numbers. . Retrieved 2010-09-20.

[48] "Sings the Peggy Lee Songbook-Bette Midler" (http://www.billboard.com/#/album/bette-midler/sings-the-peggy-lee-songbook/ 736948). *Billboard*. . Retrieved 2011-07-28.

[49] "49th Annual Grammy Awards Winners List" (http://web.archive.org/web/20070305201811/http://www.grammy.com/ GRAMMY_Awards/49th_Show/list.aspx). National Academy of Recording Arts and Sciences. Archived from the original (http://www2. grammy.com/GRAMMY_Awards/49th_Show/list.aspx) on March 5, 2007. . Retrieved February 11, 2012.

[50] "Bette Midler's Array of Awards" (http://www.bootlegbetty.com/awardsandnominations.htm). Bootleg Betty. . Retrieved 2011-07-25.

[51] John Katsilometes (November 5, 2009). "Bette Midler's residency at Caesars Palace to end Jan. 31" (http://www.lasvegassun.com/blogs/ kats-report/2009/nov/05/midlers-residency-caesars-palace-end-jan-31/). *Las Vegas Sun* (lasvegassun.com). . Retrieved 2011-07-25.

[52] "Bette Midler: The Showgirl Must Go On" (http://www.emmys.com/shows/bette-midler-showgirl-must-go). Emmys.com. . Retrieved 2012-12-18.

[53] "Bette Midler – Jackpot: The Best Bette" (http://acharts.us/album/38034). charts.us. . Retrieved 2011-07-25

[54] Robin Duke (December 8, 2009). "The Royal Variety Performance" (http://www.thestage.co.uk/reviews/review.php/26531/ the-royal-variety-performance). *The Stage*. . Retrieved 2011-07-25.

[55] "Cats & Dogs: The Revenge of Kitty Galore (2010)" (http://boxofficemojo.com/movies/?id=catsanddogs2.htm). Box Office Mojo. 2010-10-21. . Retrieved 2012-12-18.

[56] Andrew Gans (February 28, 2011). "Priscilla Queen of the Desert Kicks Up Its Heels on Broadway Starting Feb. 28" (http://www.playbill. com/events/event_detail/21056-Priscilla-Queen-of-the-Desert-at-Palace-Theatre). *Playbill*. . Retrieved 2011-07-28.

[57] "BBC News - Bette Midler to receive Songwriter Hall Of Fame award" (http://www.bbc.co.uk/news/entertainment-arts-17302078). Bbc.co.uk. 2012-03-08. . Retrieved 2012-12-18.

[58] "About NYRP" (http://www.nyrp.org/About/our_mission_and_strategic_plan_). New York Restoration Project. . Retrieved 2011-07-25.

Further reading

- *A View From A Broad* 1981
- *The Saga of Baby Divine* (Crown Publishers, 1984), ISBN 978-0-517-55040-3
- *Bette: An Intimate Biography of Bette Midler* by George Mair (Birch Lane Press, 1995), ISBN 1-55972-272-X

External links

- Official Website (http://bettemidler.com/)
- Bette Midler (http://www.imdb.com/name/nm541/) at the Internet Movie Database
- Bette Midler (http://www.ibdb.com/person.asp?ID=4524) at the Internet Broadway Database
- Bette Midler (http://www.lortel.org/LLA_archive/index.cfm?search_by=people&first=Bette&last=Midler& middle=) at the Internet Off-Broadway Database
- Bette Midler (http://www.tvguide.com/celebrities/bette-midler/141779) at TVGuide.com

Bing Crosby

Bing Crosby	
 Crosby on June 15, 1942	
Background information	
Birth name	Harry Lillis Crosby
Born	May 3, 1903[1] Tacoma, Washington, US
Died	October 14, 1977 (aged 74) La Moraleja, Alcobendas, Madrid, Spain
Genres	Traditional pop, jazz, vocal[2]
Occupations	Singer, actor
Instruments	Vocals
Years active	1926–1977
Labels	Brunswick, Decca, Reprise, RCA Victor, Verve, United Artists
Associated acts	Bob Hope, Dixie Lee, Peggy Lee, Dean Martin, Frank Sinatra, Fred Astaire, The Rhythm Boys, Rosemary Clooney, David Bowie, Louis Armstrong
Website	[bingcrosby.com bingcrosby.com]

Harry Lillis "Bing" Crosby (May 3, 1903 – October 14, 1977)[3] was an American singer and actor. Crosby's trademark bass-baritone voice made him one of the best-selling recording artists of the 20th century, with over half a billion records in circulation.[4]

A multimedia star, from 1934 to 1954 Bing Crosby was a leader in record sales, radio ratings and motion picture grosses.[5] His early career coincided with technical recording innovations; this allowed him to develop a laid-back, intimate singing style that influenced many of the popular male singers who followed him, including Perry Como,[6] Frank Sinatra, and Dean Martin. *Yank* magazine recognized Crosby as the person who had done the most for American G.I. morale during World War II and, during his peak years, around 1948, polls declared him the "most admired man alive," ahead of Jackie Robinson and Pope Pius XII.[7][8] Also in 1948, the *Music Digest* estimated that Crosby recordings filled more than half of the 80,000 weekly hours allocated to recorded radio music.[8]

Crosby exerted an important influence on the development of the postwar recording industry. He worked for NBC at the time and wanted to record his shows; however, most broadcast networks did not allow recording. This was primarily because the quality of recording at the time was not as good as live broadcast sound quality. While in Europe performing during the war, Crosby had witnessed tape recording, on which The Crosby Research Foundation would come to have many patents. The company also developed equipment and recording techniques such as the Laugh Track which are still in use today.[9] In 1947, he invested $50,000 in the Ampex company, which built North America's first commercial reel-to-reel tape recorder. He left NBC to work for ABC because NBC was not interested in recording at the time. This proved beneficial because ABC accepted him and his new ideas.[9] Crosby then became the first performer to pre-record his radio shows and master his commercial recordings onto magnetic tape. He gave one of the first Ampex Model 200 recorders to his friend, musician Les Paul, which led directly to Paul's invention of multitrack recording. Along with Frank Sinatra, Crosby was one of the principal backers behind the famous United Western Recorders recording studio complex in Los Angeles.[10]

During the "Golden Age of Radio," performers often had to recreate their live shows a second time for the west coast time zone. Through the medium of recording, Crosby constructed his radio programs with the same directorial tools and craftsmanship (editing, retaking, rehearsal, time shifting) being used in motion picture production. This became the industry standard.

Crosby won an Academy Award for Best Actor for his role as Father Chuck O'Malley in the 1944 motion picture *Going My Way*, and was nominated for his reprise of the role in *The Bells of St. Mary's* the next year, becoming the first of four actors to be nominated twice for playing the same character. In 1963, Crosby received the first Grammy Global Achievement Award.[11] Crosby is one of the 22 people to have three stars on the Hollywood Walk of Fame (a star for Motion Pictures, Radio, and Audio Recording).

In 1983, six years after Crosby's death, son Gary Crosby published his autobiography, *Going My Own Way*, which revealed the effect of his alcoholism and difficult childhood as a result of his mother's alcoholism and his father's alleged emotional and physical abuse. Some, especially his brother Phillip, claimed the abuse did not take place and that Gary's tellings were instead exaggerated accounts of corporal punishment.[12] Despite the opposing viewpoints, the book damaged for some Bing Crosby's image as an ideal, low-keyed father.

Early life

Crosby was born in Tacoma, Washington, on May 3, 1903,[1] in a house his father built at 1112 North J Street.[13] In 1906, Crosby's family moved to Spokane, Washington.[14] In 1913, Crosby's father built a house at 508 E. Sharp Ave.[15] The house now sits on the campus of Bing's alma mater Gonzaga University[16] and formerly housed the Alumni Association.

He was the fourth of seven children: brothers Larry (1895–1975), Everett (1896–1966), Ted (1900–1973), and Bob (1913–1993); and two sisters, Catherine (1904–1974) and Mary Rose (1906–1990). His parents were Harry Lincoln Crosby (1870–1950), a bookkeeper, and Catherine Helen (known as Kate) (née Harrigan; 1873–1964). Crosby's mother was a second generation Irish-American.[17] His father was of English descent; some of his ancestors had emigrated to what would become the U.S. in the 17th century, and included *Mayflower* passenger William Brewster (c. 1567 – April 10, 1644).[18]

In 1910, six-year-old Harry Crosby was forever renamed. The Sunday edition of the *Spokesman-Review* published a feature called "The Bingville Bugle".[19][20] Written by humorist Newton Newkirk, *The Bingville Bugle* was a parody of a hillbilly newsletter filled with gossipy tidbits, minstrel quips, creative spelling, and mock ads. A neighbor, 15-year-old Valentine Hobart, shared Crosby's enthusiasm for "The Bugle" and noting Crosby's laugh, took a liking to him and called him "Bingo from Bingville". Eventually the last vowel was dropped and the nickname stuck.[21]

In 1917, Crosby took a summer job as property boy at Spokane's "Auditorium," where he witnessed some of the finest acts of the day, including Al Jolson, who held Crosby spellbound with his ad libbing and spoofs of Hawaiian songs. Crosby later described Jolson's delivery as "electric".[22]

Popular success

Music

In 1923, Bing Crosby was invited to join a new band composed of high school students much younger than himself. Al Rinker, Miles Rinker, James Heaton, Claire Pritchard and Robert Pritchard, along with drummer Bing Crosby, formed the Musicaladers, who performed at dances both for high school students and club-goers. The group disbanded after two years.[23]

By 1925, Crosby had formed a vocal duo with partner Al Rinker, brother of singer Mildred Bailey. Mildred introduced Al and Bing to Paul Whiteman, who was at that time America's most famous bandleader. Hired for $150 a week, they made their debut on December 6, 1926 at the Tivoli Theatre (Chicago). Their first recording was "I've Got The Girl," with Don Clark's Orchestra, but the Columbia-issued record did them no vocal favors, as it was inadvertently recorded at a speed slower than it should have been, which increased the singers' pitch when played at 78 rpm. Throughout his career, Bing Crosby often credited Mildred Bailey for getting him his first important job in the entertainment business.

Even as the Crosby and Rinker duo was increasing in popularity, Whiteman added a third member to the group. The threesome, now including pianist and aspiring songwriter Harry Barris, were dubbed "The Rhythm Boys". They joined the Whiteman touring act, performing and recording with musicians Bix Beiderbecke, Jack Teagarden, Tommy Dorsey, Jimmy Dorsey, and Eddie Lang and Hoagy Carmichael, and appeared together in a Whiteman movie.

Crosby soon became the star attraction of the Rhythm Boys, and in 1928 he had his first number one hit with the Whiteman orchestra, a jazz-influenced rendition of "Ol' Man River". However, Crosby's reported taste for alcohol and his growing dissatisfaction with Whiteman led to his quitting the Rhythm Boys to join the Gus Arnheim Orchestra. During his time with Arnheim, the other two Rhythm Boys were increasingly pushed to the background as the emphasis was on Crosby. Harry Barris wrote several of Crosby's subsequent hits including "At Your Command," "I Surrender Dear", and "Wrap Your Troubles In Dreams". But the members of the band had a falling out and split, setting the stage for Crosby's solo career.[24]

On September 2, 1931, Crosby made his solo radio debut.[25] Before the end of the year, he signed with both Brunswick Records and CBS Radio. Doing a weekly 15-minute radio broadcast, Crosby quickly became a huge hit.[24] His songs "Out of Nowhere", "Just One More Chance", "At Your Command" and "I Found a Million Dollar Baby (in a Five and Ten Cent Store)" were all among the best selling songs of 1931.[24]

As the 1930s unfolded, Crosby became the leading singer in America. Ten of the top 50 songs for 1931 featured Crosby, either solo or with others. A so-called "Battle of the Baritones" with singing star Russ Columbo proved short-lived, replaced with the slogan "Bing Was King." Crosby played the lead in a series of sound era musical comedy short films for Mack Sennett, signed witgh Paramount and starred in his first full-length feature, 1932's *The Big Broadcast*, the first of 55 films in which he received top billing. He would appear in 79 pictures, and signed a long-term deal with Jack Kapp's new record company Decca in late 1934,

Around this time, Crosby co-starred on radio with The Carl Fenton Orchestra on a popular CBS radio show. By 1936, he'd replaced his former boss, Paul Whiteman, as the host of NBC's *Kraft Music Hall*, the weekly radio program where he remained for the next ten years. "Where the Blue of the Night (Meets the Gold of the Day)", which showcased one of his then-trademark whistling interludes, became his theme song and signature tune.

Crosby's much-imitated style helped take popular singing beyond the kind of "belting" associated with boisterous performers like Al Jolson, who had been obliged to reach the back seats in New York theatres without the aid of the microphone. As Henry Pleasants noted in *The Great American Popular Singers*, something new had entered

American music, a style that might be called "singing in American" with conversational ease. This new sound led to the popular epithet "crooner".

Crosby in *Road to Singapore* (1940)

Crosby made numerous live appearances before American troops fighting in the European Theater. He also learned how to pronounce German from written scripts and would read propaganda broadcasts intended for the German forces. The nickname "Der Bingle" was common among Crosby's German listeners and came to be used by his English-speaking fans. In a poll of U.S. troops at the close of World War II, Crosby topped the list as the person who had done the most for G.I. morale, ahead of President Franklin Delano Roosevelt, General Dwight Eisenhower, and Bob Hope.

"White Christmas"

The biggest hit song of Crosby's career was his recording of Irving Berlin's "White Christmas", which he first introduced on a Christmas Day radio broadcast in 1941 (of which no extant copy is known), and soon thereafter in his 1942 movie *Holiday Inn*. Crosby's recording hit the charts on October 3, 1942, and rose to No. 1 on October 31, where it stayed for 11 weeks. A holiday perennial, the song was repeatedly re-released by Decca, charting another 16 times. It topped the charts again in 1945, and for a third time in January 1947. The song remains the best-selling single of all time.[24] According to Guinness World Records, Crosby's recording of "White Christmas" has "sold over 100 million copies around the world, with at least 50 million sales as

From *White Christmas* trailer (1954)

singles."[26] Crosby's recording was so popular that he was obliged to re-record it in 1947 using the same musicians and backup singers; the original 1942 master had become damaged due to its frequent use in pressing additional singles. Though the two versions are very similar, it is the 1947 recording which is most familiar today. Crosby was dismissive of his role in the song's success, saying later that "a jackdaw with a cleft palate could have sung it successfully."

Motion pictures

See Bing Crosby filmography

Bob Hope, Bing Crosby, and Dorothy Lamour in *Road to Bali* (1952)

With 1,077,900,000 movie tickets sold, Crosby is by that measure the third most popular actor of all time, behind Clark Gable and John Wayne.[27] The Quigley Publishing Company's *International Motion Picture Almanac* lists Crosby in a tie for second on the "All Time Number One Stars List" with Clint Eastwood, Tom Hanks, and Burt Reynolds.[28] Crosby's most popular film, *White Christmas*, grossed $30 million in 1954 ($260 million in current value).[27] Crosby won an Academy Award for Best Actor for *Going My Way* in 1944, and was nominated for the 1945 sequel, *The Bells of Saint Mary's*. He received critical acclaim for his performance as an alcoholic entertainer in *The Country Girl*, and received his third Academy Award nomination.

Crosby starred with Bob Hope in seven *Road to* musical comedies between 1940 and 1962, cementing the two entertainers as an on-and-off duo, despite never officially declaring themselves a "team" in the sense that Laurel and Hardy or Dean Martin and Jerry Lewis were teams. The series consists of *Road to Singapore* (1940), *Road to Zanzibar* (1941), *Road to Morocco* (1942), *Road to Utopia* (1946), *Road to Rio* (1947), *Road to Bali* (1952), and *The Road to Hong Kong* (1962), and Crosby and Hope were planning another entry called *The Road to the Fountain of Youth* in 1977, which was dropped upon Crosby's death. Appearing solo, Crosby and Hope frequently made note of the other during their various appearances, typically in a comically insulting fashion, and they appeared together countless times on stage, radio, and television over the decades as well as cameos in several additional films.

Crosby with Bob Hope in *Road to Bali* (1952)

By the late 1950s, Crosby's singing career had evolved into that of an avuncular elder statesman, and his albums *Bing Sings Whilst Bregman Swings* and *Bing With A Beat* sold reasonably well,[24] even in the rock 'n roll era. In 1960, Crosby starred in *High Time*, a collegiate comedy with Fabian and Tuesday Weld that foretold the emerging gap between older Crosby fans and a new generation of films and music.[24]

Warner Bros. cartoons occasionally caricatured Crosby, alternately as an animal and as himself. His recognizable appearance popped up in *I've Got to Sing a Torch Song*, *Hollywood Steps Out* and *What's Up, Doc?*, while bird versions appeared in *The Woods Are Full of Cuckoos*, *Swooner Crooner* and *Curtain Razor*. *Bingo Crosbyana* had an insect version of him.

Television

The Fireside Theater (1950) was Crosby's first television production. The series of 26-minute shows was filmed at Hal Roach Studios rather than performed live on the air. The "telefilms" were syndicated to individual television stations.

Crosby was a frequent guest on the musical variety shows of the 1950s and 1960s. He was especially closely associated with ABC's variety show *The Hollywood Palace*. He was the show's first and most frequent guest host, and appeared annually on its Christmas edition with his wife Kathryn and his younger children. In the early 1970s he made two famous late appearances on the *Flip Wilson Show*, singing duets with the comedian. Crosby's last TV appearance was a Christmas special filmed in London in September 1977 and aired just weeks after his death. It was on this special that Crosby recorded a duet of "The Little Drummer Boy" and "Peace on Earth" with the flamboyant rock star David Bowie. It was rush-released as a single 45-rpm record, and

Crosby and his family in a skit for his 1974 Christmas special.

has since become a staple of holiday radio, and the final popular hit of Crosby's career. At the end of the century, *TV Guide* listed the Crosby-Bowie duet as one of the 25 most memorable musical moments of 20th-century television.

Bing Crosby Productions, affiliated with Desilu Studios and later CBS Television Studios, produced a number of television series, including Crosby's own unsuccessful ABC sitcom *The Bing Crosby Show* in the 1964–1965 season (with co-stars Beverly Garland and Frank McHugh). The company produced two ABC medical dramas, *Ben Casey* (1961–1966) and *Breaking Point* (1963–1964), the popular *Hogan's Heroes* (1965–1971) military comedy on CBS, as well as the lesser-known show *Slattery's People* (1964–1965). Another show that Crosby Productions produced was the game show *Beat the Odds*.

Singing style and vocal characteristics

Crosby was one of the first singers to exploit the intimacy of the microphone, rather than using the deep, loud "vaudeville style" associated with Al Jolson and others. Crosby's love and appreciation of jazz music helped bring the genre to a wider mainstream audience. Within the framework of the novelty singing style of The Rhythm Boys, Crosby bent notes and added off-tune phrasing, an approach that was firmly rooted in jazz. He had already been introduced to Louis Armstrong and Bessie Smith prior to his first appearance on record. Crosby and Armstrong would remain professionally friendly for decades, notably in the 1956 film *High Society*, where they sang the duet "Now You Has Jazz."

During the early portion of his solo career (about 1931–1934), Crosby's emotional, often pleading style of crooning was popular. But Jack Kapp (manager of Brunswick and later Decca) talked Crosby into dropping many of his jazzier mannerisms, in favor of a straight-ahead clear vocal style.

Crosby's last portrait taken backstage at the Palladium theater under a 40 watt bulb in 1977, the year of his death.

Crosby also elaborated on a further idea of Al Jolson's: phrasing, or the art of making a song's lyric ring true. His success in doing so was influential. "I used to tell Sinatra over and over," said Tommy Dorsey, "there's only one singer you ought to listen to and his name is Crosby. All that matters to him is the words, and that's the only thing that ought to for you, too."

Vocal critic Henry Pleasants wrote:

[While] the octave B flat to B flat in Bing's voice at that time [1930s] is, to my ears, one of the loveliest I have heard in forty-five years of listening to baritones, both classical and popular, it dropped conspicuously in later years. From the mid-1950s, Bing was more comfortable in a bass range while maintaining a baritone quality, with the best octave being G to G, or even F to F. In a recording he made of 'Dardanella' with Louis Armstrong in 1960, he attacks lightly and easily on a low E flat. This is lower than most opera basses care to venture, and they tend to sound as if they were in the cellar when they get there.[29]

Career statistics

Crosby's was among the most popular and successful musical acts of the 20th century. Although Billboard Magazine operated under different methodologies for the bulk of Crosby's career, his chart numbers remain astonishing: 383 chart singles, including 41 No. 1 hits. Crosby had separate charting singles in every calendar year between 1931 and 1954; the annual re-release of "White Christmas" extended that streak to 1957. He had 24 separate popular singles in 1939 alone. Billboard's statistician Joel Whitburn determined Crosby to be America's most successful recording act of the 1930s, and again in the 1940s.

Crosby with Danny Kaye in *White Christmas* (1954)

For 15 years (1934, 1937, 1940, 1943–1954), Crosby was among the top 10 in box office drawing power, and for five of those years (1944–1948) he was tops in the world.[24] He sang four Academy Award-winning songs – "Sweet Leilani" (1937), "White Christmas" (1942), "Swinging on a Star" (1944), "In the Cool, Cool, Cool of the Evening" (1951) – and won the Academy Award for Best Actor for his role in *Going My Way* (1944).

He collected 23 gold and platinum records, according to the book *Million Selling Records*. The Recording Industry Association of America did not institute its gold record certification program until 1958, by which point Crosby's record sales were barely a blip; prior to that point, gold records are awarded by an artist's own record company. Universal Music, current owner of Crosby's Decca catalog, has never requested RIAA certification for any of his hit singles.

Although often overlooked in many Crosby biographies, Bing charted an impressive 23 Billboard hits from 47 recorded songs with the immensely popular Andrews Sisters, whose Decca record sales were second only to Bing's throughout the 1940s. Patty, Maxene, and LaVerne were his most frequent collaborators on disc from 1939–1952, a partnership which produced four million-selling singles: "Pistol Packin' Mama," "Jingle Bells," "Don't Fence Me In," and "South America, Take it Away." They made one film appearance together in "Road to Rio" singing "You Don't Have to Know the Language," and they sang together countless times on radio shows throughout the 1940s and 1950s (appearing as guests on each other's shows quite often, as well as on many shows for the Armed Forces Radio Service during World War Two and beyond). The quartet's Top-10 Billboard hits from 1943–1945 (including "The Vict'ry Polka," "There'll Be a Hot Time in the Town of Berlin (When the Yanks Go Marching In)," and "Is You Is or Is You Ain't (Ma' Baby?)") helped provide the musical soundtrack for America's greatest generation during the dark war years.[30]

In 1962, Crosby was given the Grammy Lifetime Achievement Award. He has been inducted into the halls of fame for both radio and popular music. In 2007 Crosby was inducted into the Hit Parade Hall of Fame, and in 2008 into the Western Music Hall of Fame.[31]

Entrepreneurship

Mass media

Crosby's radio career took a significant turn in 1945, when he clashed with NBC over his insistence that he be allowed to pre-record his radio shows. (The live production of radio shows was also reinforced by the musicians' union and ASCAP, which wanted to ensure continued work for their members.) In *On the Air: The Encyclopedia of Old-Time Radio*, historian John Dunning wrote about German engineers having developed a tape recorder with a near-professional broadcast quality standard:

> [Crosby saw] an enormous advantage in prerecording his radio shows. The scheduling could now be done at the star's convenience. He could do four shows a week, if he chose, and then take a month off. But the networks and sponsors were adamantly opposed. The public wouldn't stand for 'canned' radio, the networks argued. There was something magic for listeners in the fact that what they were hearing was being performed, and heard everywhere, at that precise instant. Some of the best moments in comedy came when a line was blown and the star had to rely on wit to rescue a bad situation. Fred Allen, Jack Benny, Phil Harris, and, yes, Crosby were masters at this, and the networks weren't about to give it up easily.

Crosby's insistence eventually factored into the further development of magnetic tape sound recording and the radio industry's widespread adoption of it.[32][33][34] He used his clout, both professional and financial, to innovate new methods of reproducing audio of his performances. But NBC (and competitor CBS) were also insistent, refusing to air prerecorded radio programs. Crosby walked away from the network and stayed off the air for seven months, creating a legal battle with Kraft, his sponsor, that was settled out of court. Crosby returned to the air for the last 13 weeks of the 1945–1946 season.

The Mutual network, on the other hand, had pre-recorded some of its programs as early as the 1938 run of *The Shadow* with Orson Welles. And the new ABC network, which had been formed out of the sale of the old NBC Blue network in 1943 following a federal anti-trust action, was willing to join Mutual in breaking the tradition. ABC offered Crosby $30,000 per week to produce a recorded show every Wednesday that would be sponsored by Philco. He would also get an additional $40,000 from 400 independent stations for the rights to broadcast the 30-minute show, which was sent to them every Monday on three 16-inch lacquer/aluminum discs that played ten minutes per side at 33⅓ rpm.

Crosby wanted to change to recorded production for several reasons. The legend that has been most often told is that it would give him more time for his golf game. And he did record his first Philco program in August 1947 so he could enter the Jasper National Park Invitational Golf Tournament in September, just when the new radio season was to start. But golf was not the most important reason.

With Perry Como and Arthur Godfrey

Though Crosby did want more time to tend his other business and leisure activities, he also sought better quality through recording, including being able to eliminate mistakes and control the timing of his show performances. Because his own Bing Crosby Enterprises produced the show, he could purchase the latest and best sound equipment and arrange the microphones his way; the logistics of mic placement had long been a hotly debated issue in every recording studio since the beginning of the electrical era. No longer would he have to wear the hated toupee on his head previously required by CBS and NBC for his live audience shows (he preferred a hat). He could also record short promotions for his latest investment, the world's first frozen orange juice, sold under the brand name Minute Maid. This investment allowed Crosby to make more money by finding a loophole whereby the IRS couldn't tax him at a 77% rate.[35]

The transcription method posed problems, however. The acetate surface coating of the aluminum discs was little better than the wax that Edison had used at the turn of the 19th to 20th century, with the same limited dynamic range and frequency response.

But Murdo MacKenzie of Bing Crosby Enterprises had seen a demonstration of the German Magnetophon in June 1947—the same device that Jack Mullin had brought back from Radio Frankfurt, along with 50 reels of tape, at the end of the war. It was one of the magnetic tape recorders that BASF and AEG had built in Germany starting in 1935. The 6.5mm ferric-oxide-coated tape could record 20 minutes per reel of high-quality sound. Alexander M. Poniatoff ordered his Ampex company, which he'd founded in 1944, to manufacture an improved version of the Magnetophone.

Crosby hired Mullin to start recording his *Philco Radio Time* show on his German-made machine in August 1947, using the same 50 reels of I.G. Farben magnetic tape that Mullin had found at a radio station at Bad Nauheim near Frankfurt while working for the U.S. Army Signal Corps. The crucial advantage was editing. As Crosby wrote in his autobiography:

> By using tape, I could do a thirty-five or forty-minute show, then edit it down to the twenty-six or twenty-seven minutes the program ran. In that way, we could take out jokes, gags, or situations that didn't play well and finish with only the prime meat of the show; the solid stuff that played big. We could also take out the songs that didn't sound good. It gave us a chance to first try a recording of the songs in the afternoon without an audience, then another one in front of a studio audience. We'd dub the one that came off best into the final transcription. It gave us a chance to ad lib as much as we wanted, knowing that excess ad libbing could be sliced from the final product. If I made a mistake in singing a song or in the script, I could have some fun with it, then retain any of the fun that sounded amusing.

Mullin's 1976 memoir of these early days of experimental recording agrees with Crosby's account:

> In the evening, Crosby did the whole show before an audience. If he muffed a song then, the audience loved it – thought it was very funny – but we would have to take out the show version and put in one of the rehearsal takes. Sometimes, if Crosby was having fun with a song and not really working at it, we had to make it up out of two or three parts. This ad lib way of working is commonplace in the recording studios today, but it was all new to us.

Crosby invested US$50,000 in Ampex with an eye towards producing more machines. In 1948, the second season of Philco shows was taped with the new Ampex Model 200 tape recorder using the new Scotch 111 tape from the Minnesota Mining and Manufacturing (3M) company. Mullin explained how one new broadcasting technique was invented on the Crosby show with these machines:

> One time Bob Burns, the hillbilly comic, was on the show, and he threw in a few of his folksy farm stories, which of course were not in Bill Morrow's script. Today they wouldn't seem very off-color, but things were different on radio then. They got enormous laughs, which just went on and on. We couldn't use the jokes, but Bill asked us to save the laughs. A couple of weeks later he had a show that wasn't very funny, and he insisted that we put in the salvaged laughs. Thus the laugh-track was born.

Crosby had launched the tape recorder revolution in America. In his 1950 film *Mr. Music*, Bing Crosby is seen singing into one of the new Ampex tape recorders that reproduced his voice better than anything else. Also quick to adopt tape recording was his friend Bob Hope.

Mullin continued to work for Crosby to develop a videotape recorder (VTR). Television production was mostly live television in its early years, but Crosby wanted the same ability to record that he had achieved in radio. 1950's *The Fireside Theater*, sponsored by Procter and Gamble, was his first television production. Mullin had not yet succeeded with video tape, so Crosby filmed the series of 26-minute shows at the Hal Roach Studios, and the "telefilms" were syndicated to individual television stations.

Crosby did not remain a television producer, but continued to finance the development of videotape. Bing Crosby Enterprises (BCE), gave the world's first demonstration of videotape recording in Los Angeles on November 11, 1951. Developed by John T. Mullin and Wayne R. Johnson since 1950, the device aired what were described as "blurred and indistinct" images, using a modified Ampex 200 tape recorder and standard quarter-inch (6.3 mm) audio tape moving at 360 inches (9.1 m) per second.[36]

TV stations

A Bing Crosby-led group purchased KCOP-TV station in 1954.[37] NAFI Corporation and Bing Crosby purchase together the television station, KPTV, for $4 million on September 1, 1959.[38] In 1960, NAFI purchased KCOP from Crosby's group.[37]

Thoroughbred horse racing

Crosby was a fan of thoroughbred horse racing and bought his first racehorse in 1935. In 1937, he became a founding partner of the Del Mar Thoroughbred Club and a member of its Board of Directors. Operating from the Del Mar Racetrack at Del Mar, California, the group included millionaire businessman Charles S. Howard, who owned a successful racing stable that included Seabiscuit. His son, Lindsay Howard, became one of Crosby's closest friends; Crosby named his son Lindsay after him, and would purchase his 40-room Hillsborough estate from Lindsay in 1965.

Crosby and Lindsay Howard formed Binglin Stable to race and breed thoroughbred horses at a ranch in Moorpark in Ventura County, California. They also established the Binglin stock farm in Argentina, where they raced horses at Hipódromo de Palermo in Palermo, Buenos Aires. A number of Argentine-bred horses were purchased and shipped to race in the United States. On August 12, 1938, the Del Mar Thoroughbred Club hosted a $25,000 winner-take-all match race won by Charles S. Howard's Seabiscuit over Binglin's horse Ligaroti. In 1943, Binglin's horse Don Bingo won the Suburban Handicap at Belmont Park in Elmont, New York.

The Binglin Stable partnership came to an end in 1953 as a result of a liquidation of assets by Crosby, who needed to raise enough funds to pay the hefty federal and state inheritance taxes on his deceased wife's estate.[39] The Bing Crosby Breeders' Cup Handicap at Del Mar Racetrack is named in his honor.

Crosby was also a co-owner of the British colt Meadow Court, with jockey Johnny Longden's friend Max Bell. Meadow Court won the 1965 King George VI and Queen Elizabeth Stakes, and the Irish Derby. In the Irish Derby's winner's circle at the Curragh, Crosby sang "When Irish Eyes Are Smiling."

Though Crosby's stables had some success, he often joked about his horseracing failures as part of his radio appearances. "Crosby's horse finally came in" became a running gag.

Crosby the sportsman

Crosby had an interest in sports. In the 1930s, his friend and former college classmate, Gonzaga head coach Mike Pecarovich appointed Crosby as an assistant football coach.[40] From 1946 until the end of his life, he was part-owner of baseball's Pittsburgh Pirates. Although he was passionate about his team, he was too nervous to watch the deciding Game 7 of the 1960 World Series, choosing to go to Paris with Kathryn and listen to the game on the radio. Crosby had the NBC telecast of the game recorded on kinescope. The game was one of the most famous in baseball history, capped off by Bill Mazeroski's walk-off home run. He apparently viewed the complete film just once, and then stored it in his wine cellar, where it remained undisturbed until it was discovered in December 2009.[41] The restored broadcast was shown on MLB Network in December 2010.

Crosby was also an avid golfer, and in 1978, he and Bob Hope were voted the Bob Jones Award, the highest honor given by the United States Golf Association in recognition of distinguished sportsmanship. He is a member of the World Golf Hall of Fame. In 1937, Bing Crosby hosted the first National Pro-Am Golf Championship, the 'Crosby

Clambake' as it was popularly known, at Rancho Santa Fe Golf Club in Rancho Santa Fe, California, the event's location prior to World War II. Sam Snead won the first tournament, in which the first place check was for $500. After the war, the event resumed play in 1947 on golf courses in Pebble Beach, where it has been played ever since. Now the AT&T Pebble Beach National Pro-Am, it has been a leading event in the world of professional golf.

Crosby first took up golf at 12 as a caddy, dropped it, and started again in 1930 with some fellow cast members in Hollywood during the filming of *The King of Jazz*. Crosby was accomplished at the sport, with a two handicap. He competed in both the British and U.S. Amateur championships, was a five-time club champion at Lakeside Golf Club in Hollywood, and once made a hole-in-one on the 16th at Cypress Point.

Personal life

Crosby was married twice, first to actress/nightclub singer Dixie Lee from 1930 until her death from ovarian cancer in 1952. They had four sons: Gary, twins Dennis and Phillip, and Lindsay. The 1947 film *Smash-Up: The Story of a Woman* is indirectly based on her life. After Dixie's death, Crosby had relationships with model-Goldwyn Girl Pat Sheehan (who married Dennis Crosby in 1958), actresses Inger Stevens and Grace Kelly before marrying the actress Kathryn Grant in 1957. They had three children: Harry (who played Bill in *Friday the 13th*), Mary (best known for portraying Kristin Shepard, the woman who shot J. R. Ewing on TV's *Dallas*), and Nathaniel.

Kathryn converted to Catholicism in order to marry the singer. Crosby was also a registered Republican, and actively campaigned for Wendell Willkie in 1940 against President Roosevelt, arguing that no man should serve more than two terms in the White House. After Willkie lost, Crosby decreed that he would never again make any open political contributions.

Crosby reportedly had an alcohol problem in his youth, and may have been dismissed from Paul Whiteman's orchestra because of it, but he later got a handle on his drinking. *Village Voice* jazz critic and Crosby biographer Gary Giddins says that Louis Armstrong's influence on Crosby "extended to his love of marijuana." Crosby smoked it during his early career when it was still legal, and "surprised interviewers" in the 1960s and 1970s by advocating its decriminalization. According to Giddins, Crosby told his son Gary to stay away from alcohol ("It killed your mother"[42]) and suggested he smoke marijuana instead.[42] Gary said, "There were other times when marijuana was mentioned and he'd get a smile on his face."[42] Gary thought his father's marijuana smoking had influenced his easygoing style in his films.

After Crosby's death, his eldest son, Gary, wrote a highly critical memoir, *Going My Own Way*, depicting his father as cruel, cold, remote, and both physically and psychologically abusive.[43] Dennis also stated that Crosby would abuse Gary the most often.[43]

Gary Crosby wrote:

> We had to keep a close watch on our actions... When one of us left a sneaker or pair of underpants lying around, he had to tie the offending object on a string and wear it around his neck until he went off to bed that night. Dad called it "the Crosby lavalier." At the time the humor of the name escaped me...

> "Satchel Ass" or "Bucket Butt" or "My Fat-assed Kid." That's how he introduced me to his cronies when he dragged me along to the studio or racetrack... By the time I was ten or eleven he had stepped up his campaign by adding lickings to the regimen.

Crosby's sons from his first marriage in 1959. From left: Gary, Lindsay, Phillip and Dennis at center.

Each Tuesday afternoon he weighed me in, and if the scale read more than it should have, he ordered me into his office and had me drop my trousers... I dropped my pants, pulled down my undershorts and bent over. Then he went at it with the belt dotted with metal studs he kept reserved for the occasion. Quite dispassionately, without the least display of emotion or loss of self-control, he whacked away until he drew the first drop of blood, and then he stopped. It normally took between twelve and fifteen strokes. As they came down I counted them off one by one and hoped I would bleed early...

When I saw *Going My Way* I was as moved as they were by the character he played. Father O'Malley handled that gang of young hooligans in his parish with such kindness and wisdom that I thought he was wonderful too. Instead of coming down hard on the kids and withdrawing his affection, he forgave them their misdeeds, took them to the ball game and picture show, taught them how to sing. By the last reel, the sheer persistence of his goodness had transformed even the worst of them into solid citizens. Then the lights came on and the movie was over. All the way back to the house I thought about the difference between the person up there on the screen and the one I knew at home.[44]

It was revealed that Crosby's will had established a blind trust, with none of the sons receiving an inheritance until they reached the age of 65.[45]

However, younger son Phillip vociferously disputed his brother Gary's claims about their father. Around the time Gary made his claim, Phillip stated to the press that "Gary is a whining...crybaby, walking around with a 2-by-4 and just daring people to nudge it off."[46] However, Phillip did not deny that Crosby believed in corporal punishment.[46] In an interview with People, Phillip stated that "we never got an extra whack or a cuff we didn't deserve."[46] During a later interview conducted in 1999 by the Globe, Phillip said:

My dad was not the monster my lying brother said he was; he was strict, but my father never beat us black and blue, and my brother Gary was a vicious, no-good liar for saying so. I have nothing but fond memories of Dad, going to studios with him, family vacations at our cabin in Idaho, boating and fishing with him. To my dying day, I'll hate Gary for dragging Dad's name through the mud. He wrote *Going My Own Way* out of greed. He wanted to make money and knew that humiliating our father and blackening his name was the only way he could do it. He knew it would generate a lot of publicity. That was the only way he could get his ugly, no-talent face on television and in the newspapers. My dad was my hero. I loved him very much. He loved all of us too, including Gary. He was a great father.[12]

Gary Crosby died in 1995 at the age of 62, and 69-year-old Phillip Crosby died in 2004.[47]

Nathaniel Crosby, Crosby's youngest son from his second marriage, was a high-level golfer who won the U.S. Amateur at age 19 in 1981, at the time the youngest-ever winner of that event. Harry Crosby is an investment banker who occasionally makes singing appearances.

Widow Kathryn Crosby dabbled in local theater productions intermittently, and appeared in television tributes to her late husband. Denise Crosby, Dennis Crosby's daughter, is also an actress and is known for her role as Tasha Yar on *Star Trek: The Next Generation*, and for the recurring role of the Romulan Sela (daughter of Tasha Yar) after her withdrawal from the series as a regular cast member. She also appeared in the film adaptation of Stephen King's novel *Pet Sematary*. In 2006, Crosby's niece, Carolyn Schneider, published the laudatory book "Me and Uncle Bing."

Failing health and death

Following his recovery from a life-threatening fungal infection of his right lung in 1974, Crosby emerged from semi-retirement to start a new spate of albums and concerts. In March 1977, after videotaping a concert for CBS to commemorate his 50th anniversary in show business and with Bob Hope looking on, Crosby backed off the stage and fell into an orchestra pit, rupturing a disc in his back and requiring a month in the hospital. His first performance after the accident was his last American concert, on August 16, 1977; when the power went out, he continued singing without amplification. In September, Crosby, his family, and singer Rosemary Clooney began a concert tour of England that included two weeks at the London Palladium. While in England, Crosby recorded his final album, *Seasons*, and his final TV Christmas

Crosby's grave at Holy Cross Cemetery, Culver City, California

special with guest David Bowie (which aired several months after Crosby's death). His last concert was in The Brighton Centre four days before his death, with British entertainer Dame Gracie Fields in attendance. Although it has been reported that Crosby's last photograph was taken with Fields, he was photographed playing golf on the day he died.[48]

At the conclusion of his work in England, Crosby flew alone to Spain to hunt and play golf. Shortly after 6 pm on October 14, Crosby collapsed and died of a massive heart attack on the green after a round of 18 holes of golf near Madrid where he and his Spanish golfing partner had just defeated their opponents. It is widely written that his last words were "That was a great game of golf, fellas."[49] In *Bob Hope's Confessions of a Hooker: My Lifelong Love Affair With Golf*, the comedian recounts hearing that Crosby had been advised by a physician in England to play only nine holes of golf because of his heart condition.

Commemorative Plaque In The Brighton Centre foyer

Legacy

He is a member of the National Association of Broadcasters Hall of Fame in the radio division.[50]

The family launched an official website[51] on October 14, 2007, the 30th anniversary of Crosby's death.

In his autobiography *Don't Shoot, It's Only Me!* (1990), Bob Hope wrote, "Dear old Bing. As we called him, the *Economy-sized Sinatra*. And what a voice. God I miss that voice. I can't even turn on the radio around Christmas time without crying anymore."[52]

Calypso musician Roaring Lion wrote a tribute song in 1939 entitled "Bing Crosby", in which he wrote: "Bing has a way of singing with his very heart and soul / Which captivates the world / His millions of listeners never fail to rejoice / At his golden voice..."[53]

Star on the Hollywood Walk of Fame at 6769 Hollywood Blvd.

Compositions

Crosby wrote or co-wrote lyrics to 17 songs. His composition "At Your Command" was no.1 for three weeks on the U.S. pop singles chart beginning on August 8, 1931. "I Don't Stand a Ghost of a Chance With You" was his most successful composition, recorded by Duke Ellington, Frank Sinatra, Thelonious Monk, Billie Holiday, and Mildred Bailey, among others. Songs co-written by Crosby include:

1. "That's Grandma" (1927), with Harry Barris and James Cavanaugh
2. "From Monday On" (1928), with Harry Barris and recorded with the Paul Whiteman Orchestra featuring Bix Beiderbecke on cornet, no. 14 on US pop singles charts
3. "What Price Lyrics?" (1928), with Harry Barris and Matty Malneck
4. "At Your Command" (1931), with Harry Barris and Harry Tobias, US, no. 1 (3 weeks)
5. "Where the Blue of the Night (Meets the Gold of the Day)" (1931), with Roy Turk and Fred Ahlert, US, no. 4; US, 1940 re-recording, no. 27
6. "I Don't Stand a Ghost of a Chance with You" (1932), with Victor Young and Ned Washington, US, no. 5
7. "My Woman" (1932), with Irving Wallman and Max Wartell
8. "Love Me Tonight" (1932), with Victor Young and Ned Washington, US, no. 4
9. "Waltzing in a Dream" (1932), with Victor Young and Ned Washington, US, no.6
10. "You're Just a Beautiful Melody of Love" (1932), lyrics by Bing Crosby, music by Babe Goldberg
11. "Where Are You, Girl of My Dreams?" (1932), written by Bing Crosby, Irving Bibo, and Paul McVey, featured in the 1932 Universal film *The Cohens and Kellys in Hollywood*
12. "I Would If I Could But I Can't" (1933), with Mitchell Parish and Alan Grey
13. "Where the Turf Meets the Surf" (1941) with Johnny Burke and James V. Monaco.
14. "Tenderfoot" (1953) with Bob Bowen and Perry Botkin, originally issued using the pseudonym of "Bill Brill" for Bing Crosby.
15. "Domenica" (1961)
16. "That's What Life is All About" (1975), with Ken Barnes, Peter Dacre, and Les Reed, US, AC chart, no. 35; UK, no. 41
17. "Sail Away to Norway" (1977)

Grammy Hall of Fame

Bing Crosby was posthumously inducted into the Grammy Hall of Fame, which is a special Grammy award established in 1973 to honor recordings that are at least 25 years old and that have "qualitative or historical significance."

Bing Crosby: Grammy Hall of Fame Awards[54]					
Year Recorded	Title	Genre	Label	Year Inducted	Notes
1942	"White Christmas"	Traditional Pop (single)	Decca	1974	With the Ken Darby Singers
1944	"Swinging on a Star"	Traditional Pop (single)	Decca	2002	
1936	"Pennies from Heaven"	Traditional Pop (single)	Decca	2004	
1944	"Don't Fence Me In"	Traditional Pop (single)	Decca	1998	With the Andrews Sisters

Radio

- The Radio Singers (1931, CBS), sponsored by Warner Brothers, 6 nights a week, 15 minutes.
- *The Cremo Singer* (1931–1932, CBS), 6 nights a week, 15 minutes.
- Unsponsored (1932, CBS), initially 3 nights a week, then twice a week, 15 minutes.
- *Chesterfield's Music that Satisfies* (1933, CBS), broadcast two nights, 15 minutes.
- *Bing Crosby Entertains for Woodbury Soap* (1933–1935, CBS), weekly, 30 minutes.
- *Kraft Music Hall* (1935–1946, NBC), Thursday nights, 60 minutes until January 1943, then 30 minutes.
- Armed Forces Radio (1941–1945; World War II).
- *Philco Radio Time* (1946–1949, ABC), 30 minutes weekly.
- *The Bing Crosby Chesterfield Show* (1949–1952, CBS), 30 minutes weekly.
- *The Minute Maid Show* (1949–1950, CBS), 15 minutes each weekday morning; Bing as disc jockey.
- *The General Electric Show* (1952–1954, CBS), 30 minutes weekly.
- *The Bing Crosby Show* (1954–1956, CBS), 15 minutes, 5 nights a week.
- *A Christmas Sing with Bing* (1955–1962, CBS, VOA and AFRS), 1 hour each year, sponsored by the Insurance Company of North America.
- *The Ford Road Show* (1957–1958, CBS), 5 minutes, 5 days a week.
- *The Bing Crosby – Rosemary Clooney Show (1958–1962, CBS), 20 minutes, 5 mornings a week, with Rosemary Clooney.*

RIAA certification

Album	RIAA[55]
Merry Christmas	Gold
Bing sings	2x platinum
White Christmas	4x platinium

References

[1] Grudens, 2002, p. 236. "Bing was born on May 2, 1903. He always believed he was born on May 2, 1904."

[2] Music Genre: Vocal music (http://www.allmusic.com/explore/genre/d131).*Allmusic. Retrieved October 23, 2008.*

[3] Obituary *Variety*, October 19, 1977.

[4] "Bing Crosby Billboard Biography" (http://www.billboard.com/artist/bing-crosby/3574#/artist/bing-crosby/bio/3574). *Billboard.* . Retrieved October 28, 2009.

[5] Giddins, 2001, p. 8.

[6] Gilliland, John. *Pop Chronicles the 40s: The Lively Story of Pop Music in the 40s.* ISBN 978-1-55935-147-8. OCLC 31611854., cassette 1, side B.

[7] Giddins, 2001, p. 6.

[8] Hoffman, Dr. Frank. "Crooner" (http://www.jeffosretromusic.com/bing.html). . Retrieved December 29, 2006.

[9] Sterling, C. H., & Kittross, J. M. (1990). Stay tuned: A concise history of American broadcasting (2nd ed.). Belmont, CA: Wadsworth.

[10] Cogan, Jim; Clark, William, *Temples of sound : inside the great recording studios* (http://books.google.com/books?id=hO-KQ4o_B2MC&printsec=frontcover), San Francisco : Chronicle Books, 2003. ISBN 0-8118-3594-1

[11] "Lifetime Achievement Award. "Past Recipients"" (http://www.grammy.com/Recording_Academy/Awards/Lifetime_Awards/). Grammy.com. February 8, 2009. . Retrieved February 10, 2010.

[12] Grudens, 2002, p. 59.

[13] Bing Crosby had no birth certificate and his birth date was unconfirmed until his childhood Roman Catholic church released his baptismal record.

[14] Blecha, Peter (August 29, 2005). "the Free Online Encyclopedia of Washington State History" (http://www.historylink.org/index.cfm?DisplayPage=output.cfm&file_id=7445}). HistoryLink.org. . Retrieved January 4, 2011.

[15] Gonzaga History 1980–1989 (September 17, 1986). "Gonzaga History 1980–1989 – Gonzaga University" (http://www.gonzaga.edu/Academics/Libraries/Foley-Library/Departments/Special-Collections/exhibitions/GonzagaHistory1980.asp). Gonzaga.edu. . Retrieved

January 4, 2011.

[16] Bing Crosby and Gonzaga University: 1903 - 1925. "Bing Crosby and Gonzaga University: 1903 - 1925 - Gonzaga University" (http://www.gonzaga.edu/academics/libraries/foley-library/departments/special-collections/Collections/Bing-Crosby-Collection/CrosbyandGonzaga.asp). Gonzaga.edu. . Retrieved 2012-10-15.

[17] Giddins, Gary (2001). *Bing Crosby: A Pocketful of Dreams*.

[18] Giddins, 2001, p. 24.

[19] Newkirk, Newton (March 14, 1909). "The Bingville Bugle" (http://www.spokesmanreview.com/blogs/history/media/bingville.pdf). Spokesman Review. . Retrieved September 25, 2010.

[20] Newkirk, Newton (July 19, 1914). "The Bingville Bugle" (http://leonardodesa.interdinamica.net/comics/lds/bing/bingville.asp). Spokesman Review. . Retrieved September 25, 2010.

[21] Gary Giddins (October 8, 2002). *Bing Crosby: A Pocketful of Dreams − The Early Years, 1903 − 1940, Volume I* (http://books.google.com/books?id=Oa2_zcwucAgC&pg=PA39&lpg=PA39&dq=bing+crosby+bingo+bingville+bugle&source=bl&ots=8DHK9U9Lfl&sig=BLFVQNnhQflUL769bVqYXepaWY8&hl=en&ei=JVqeTI-XM4H68Aa-2cAl&sa=X&oi=book_result&ct=result&resnum=5&ved=0CCcQ6AEwBDgK#v=onepage&q=bing crosby bingo bingville bugle&f=false). Back Bay Books. .

[22] Gilliland, John. *Pop Chronicles the 40s: The Lively Story of Pop Music in the 40s*. ISBN 978-1-55935-147-8. OCLC 31611854., cassette 3, side B.

[23] Giddins, 2001, p. 92-97

[24] Bing Crosby (http://www.allmusic.com/artist/p3094/biography) at Allmusic

[25] "Bing Crosby, Singer" (http://www.radiohof.org/musicvariety/bingcrosby.html). Radio Hall of Fame. . Retrieved September 2, 2010.

[26] *Guinness Book of Records 2007*. Guinness. August 1, 2006. ISBN 978-1-904994-12-1.

[27] "Crosby Movies" (http://www.waynesthisandthat.com/crosbymovies.html). Waynesthisandthat.com. . Retrieved February 10, 2010.

[28] "Top Ten Money Making Stars of the past 79 years" (http://www.quigleypublishing.com/MPalmanac/Top10/Top10_lists.html). Quigley Publishing. . Retrieved August 17, 2011.

[29] Pleasants, H. (1985). The Great American Popular Singers. Simon and Schuster.

[30] Sforza, John: "Swing It! The Andrews Sisters Story;" University Press of Kentucky, 2000; 289 pages.

[31] "Johnny Bond − WMA Hall of Fame" (http://www.westernmusic.com/performers/hof-crosby.html). Westernmusic.com. . Retrieved February 10, 2010.

[32] Hammar, Peter. Jack Mullin: The man and his machines. Journal of the Audio Engineering Society, 37 (6): 490–496, 498, 500, 502, 504, 506, 508, 510, 512; June 1989.

[33] An afternoon with Jack Mullin. NTSC VHS tape, 1989 AES.

[34] *History of Magnetic tape*, section: "Enter Bing Crosby" (http://web.archive.org/web/20040603153341/www.tvhandbook.com/History/History_tape.htm) (WayBack Machine)

[35] "CORPORATIONS: Minute Maid's Man" (http://www.time.com/time/magazine/article/0,9171,799353,00.html). *Time*. October 18, 1948. . Retrieved August 17, 2011.

[36] "Tape Recording Used by Filmless 'Camera'," *New York Times*, November 12, 1951, p. 21. Eric D. Daniel, C. Denis Mee, and Mark H. Clark (eds.), *Magnetic Recording: The First 100 Years*, IEEE Press, 1998, p. 141. ISBN 0-07-041275-8

[37] "KCOP Studio" (http://www.seeing-stars.com/tvstudios/KCOP.shtml). *Seeing Stars: the Television Studios...* . Retrieved March 23, 2011.

[38] Dunevant, Ronald L.. "KPTV Timeline" (http://kptv.home.comcast.net/~kptv/timeline/timeline.htm). *Yesterday's KPTV*. Ronald L. Dunevant. . Retrieved March 23, 2011.

[39] "Time Magazine Article" (http://www.time.com/time/magazine/article/0,9171,822904,00.html). *Time Magazine*. August 3, 1953. . Retrieved January 25, 2007.

[40] Bing Crosby and Gonzaga University: 1925 − 1951 (http://www.gonzaga.edu/Academics/Libraries/Foley-Library/Departments/Special-Collections/Collections/Bing-Crosby-Collection/CrosbyandGonzaga2.asp), Gonzaga University, retrieved June 6, 2011.

[41] Sandomir, Richard (September 23, 2010). "In Bing Crosby's Wine Cellar, Vintage Baseball" (http://www.nytimes.com/2010/09/24/sports/baseball/24crosby.html?_r=1&src=mv). *The New York Times*. . Retrieved September 25, 2010.

[42] Giddins, 2001, p. 181.

[43] Haller, Scot (March 21, 1983). "The Sad Ballad of Bing and His Boys − Child Abuse, Kids & Family Life, Bing Crosby" (http://www.people.com/people/archive/article/0,,20084544,00.html). *People*. . Retrieved January 4, 2011.

[44] Gary Crosby (March 1983). *Going My Own Way* (http://www.nospank.net/crosbyg.htm). Doubleday. ISBN 978-0-385-17055-0. .

[45] Dunn, Ashley (December 13, 1989). "Lindsay Crosby Suicide Laid to End of Inheritance Income" (http://articles.latimes.com/1989-12-13/local/me-242_1_lindsay-crosby). *Los Angeles Times*. . Retrieved August 17, 2011.

[46] "Leah Garchik's Personals" (http://articles.sfgate.com/2004-01-20/bay-area/17409442_1_gary-crosby-bing-crosby-philip-crosby/2). *The San Francisco Chronicle*. January 20, 2004. .

[47] "Philip Crosby, 69, Son of Bing Crosby" (http://query.nytimes.com/gst/fullpage.html?res=9A01E5D61439F933A15752C0A9629C8B63). *New York Times*. January 20, 2004. . Retrieved November 2, 2008.

[48] Thomas, 1977, p. 86-87.

[49] Callahan, Tom (2003-05). "The Bing dynasty: on the 100th anniversary of Crosby's birth, we celebrate the granddaddy of celebrity golf" (http://findarticles.com/p/articles/mi_m0HFI/is_5_54/ai_101967390). Golf Digest. . Retrieved November 2, 2008.

[50] "NAB Hall of Fame" (http://www.nab.org/AM/Template.cfm?Section=Awards7&CONTENTID=11047&TEMPLATE=/CM/ ContentDisplay.cfm). *National Association of Broadcasters.* . Retrieved May 3, 2008.

[51] "The Official Home of Bing Crosby" (http://www.BingCrosby.com). Bingcrosby.com. . Retrieved November 2, 2008.

[52] Hope, Bob (1990). *Don't Shoot, It's Only Me!*. Random House Publishers.

[53] Giddins, 2001, pp. 427–428.

[54] Grammy Hall of Fame Database (http://www.grammy.org/recording-academy/awards/hall-of-fame).

[55] "RIAA certification" (http://web.archive.org/web/20070608063448/http://www.riaa.com/gp/database/default.asp). Archived from the original (http://www.riaa.com/gp/database/default.asp) on June 8, 2007. .

Bibliography

• Giddins, Gary (2001). *Bing Crosby: A Pocketful of Dreams — The Early Years, 1903–1940* (http://books.google. com/books?id=Oa2_zcwucAgC). Little, Brown and Company. ISBN 0-316-88188-0.

• Grudens, Richard (2002). *Bing Crosby — Crooner of the Century* (http://books.google.com/ books?id=Mkz_w-WYiMAC). Celebrity Profiles Publishing Co.. ISBN 1-57579-248-6.

• Macfarlane, Malcolm. *Bing Crosby — Day By Day*. Scarecrow Press, 2001.

• Osterholm, J. Roger. *Bing Crosby: A Bio-Bibliography*. Greenwood Press, 1994.

• Prigozy, R. & Raubicheck, W., ed. *Going My Way: Bing Crosby and American Culture*. The Boydell Press, 2007.

• Thomas, Bob (1977). *The One and Only Bing*. Grosset & Dunlap. ISBN 0-448-14670-3.

Further reading

• Thomas, Nick (2011). *Raised by the Stars: Interviews with 29 Children of Hollywood Actors*. McFarland. ISBN 978-0-7864-6403-6. (Includes an interview with Crosby's son, Harry, and daughter, Mary)

External links

• Official website (http://www.bingcrosby.com)

• Bing Crosby (http://www.imdb.com/name/nm1078/) at the Internet Movie Database

• Bing Crosby (http://tcmdb.com/participant/participant.jsp?participantId=41424) at the TCM Movie Database

• Bing Crosby Collection at Gonzaga University (http://www.gonzaga.edu/Academics/Libraries/Foley-Library/ Departments/Special-Collections/Collections/Bing-Crosby-Collection/default.asp)

• BING magazine (a publication of the ICC) (http://www.bingmagazine.co.uk/)

• Bing Crosby Official 10" (78Rpm) Discography (http://www.discoogle.com/wiki/ Crosby,_Bing_Discography)

• A Bing Crosby Session based discography (http://www.jazzdiscography.com/Artists/Crosby/crosby.html)

• Bing Crosby (http://www.virtual-history.com/movie/person/1815/bing-crosby) at Virtual History

Bob Crosby

George Robert "Bob" Crosby (August 23, 1913 – March 9, 1993) was an American Swing music singer and Dixieland bandleader and vocalist, best known for his group the Bob-Cats.

With Judy Garland in *Presenting Lily Mars*, 1943

Family

The seven Crosby children are: elder boys, Larry (1895–1975), Everett (1896–1966), Ted (1900–1973), Harry, (1903–1977, popularly known as Bing Crosby), two girls, Catherine (1905–1988) and Mary Rose (1907–1990) and Bob. His parents were English-American bookkeeper Harry Lowe Crosby (1871–1950) and Irish-American Catherine Harrigan (1873–1964), (affectionately known as Kate), the daughter of a builder from County Mayo in Ireland.

Career

Singer and bandleader

Bob Crosby began singing in the early 1930s with the Delta Rhythm Boys which included vocalist Ray Hendricks [1] and guitarist Bill Pollard also with Anson Weeks (1931–34) and the Dorsey Brothers (1934–35). He led his first band in 1935, when the former members of Ben Pollack's band elected him as titular leader. He recorded with the Clark Randall Orchestra in 1935, led by Gil Rodin and featuring singer Frank Tennille, whose pseudonym was Clark Randall. Glenn Miller was a member of that orchestra which recorded the Glenn Miller novelty composition "When Icky Morgan Plays the Organ" in 1935.[2] Crosby's "band-within-the-band", the Bob-Cats, was an authentic New Orleans Dixieland style jazz octet featuring soloists drawn from the larger orchestra, many of whom were from New Orleans or were heavily influenced by the music of the Crescent City. In the mid-1930s, with the rise of "swing" music and the popularity of the swing bands ever increasing, the Crosby band managed to authentically combine the fundamental elements of the older jazz style with the then-rising-in-popularity swing style into a sound and big-band style all its own. The resulting music they produced as a big band was a sound and style which few other, if any, big-bands and bandleaders even attempted to emulate. By unapologetically ignoring most of the pop-tunes that were the de facto repertoire of most of the swing bands of the mid- to late- 1930's, and stubbornly sticking to playing many older jazz standards with zeal and in the spirit of their tradition, -all brilliantly translated into a big-band context- the band and especially the Bob-Cats presaged the traditional jazz revival of the 1940s. Most of the band's arrangements were written by bassist Bob Haggart and clarinetist/saxophonist Matty Matlock; other original material also primarily came from band members Joe Sullivan, Bob Zurke, and Eddie Miller in addition to Matlock and Haggart. Crosby's singing voice was remarkably similar to that of his brother Bing, but without its range.

In addition to the above mentioned band members, the Bob Crosby Orchestra and the Bob-Cats also included (at various times) Yank Lawson, Billy Butterfield, Charlie Spivak, Muggsy Spanier, Irving Fazola, Nappy Lamare, Ward Silloway, Warren Smith, Joe Sullivan, Bob Zurke, Jess Stacy, Bob Haggart, Walt Yoder, Jack Sperling and Ray Bauduc and many others who came and went. A much-later press account from 1943 mentions a young trumpeter by the name of Gilbert Portmore who occasionally played with the band.[3]

The orchestra was one of the few bands of its time established as a co-operative corporation of its members, and was managed / presided over by saxophonist Gil Rodin. The band was initially formed out of the ruins of the Ben Pollack Orchestra whose members quit en masse, and needing a vocalist, Crosby was chosen simply for his personality, looks and famous surname. He was made the front man of the band and his name became the band's public identity.[4]

For its theme song, the band chose George Gershwin's song "Summertime", and other hit records in addition to their theme included "South Rampart Street Parade" (its biggest hit), "March of the Bob Cats", "In a Little Gypsy Tea Room", "Whispers in The Dark", "Day In, Day Out", "Down Argentine Way", "You Must Have Been a Beautiful Baby", "Dolores" and "New San Antonio Rose" (last three with Bing Crosby). A novelty bass and drums duet between Haggart and Bauduc, "Big Noise from Winnetka," became a hit in 1938-39.

The enduring popularity of the Bob Cats led by Bob Crosby, whose biography was written by British jazz historian John Chilton, was evident during the frequent reunions in the 1950s and 1960s. Bob Haggart and Yank Lawson organized a band that kept the spirit alive, combining Dixieland and swing with a roster of top soloists. From the late 1960s until the mid-1970s, the group was known as the World's Greatest Jazzband. Since neither leader was happy with that name, they eventually reverted to the Lawson Haggart Jazzband. The Lawson-Haggart group was consistent in keeping the Bob Crosby tradition alive.

Three of his songs ("Way Back Home" (1949), "Happy Times" and "Dear Hearts and Gentle People") were featured in two hit video games, *Fallout 3* and *Fallout: New Vegas*, published by Bethesda Softworks. Most of the popularity of all of these songs were achieved by the use of them in the game trailers, in which they used his lighthearted music to contrast with the combat taking place in the video.

Bob Crosby has two stars on the Hollywood Walk of Fame, for Television and Recording.

Radio

During World War II, Bob Crosby spent 18 months in the Marines, touring with bands in the Pacific. His radio variety series, *The Bob Crosby Show*, aired on NBC and CBS in different runs between the years 1943 to 1950. This was followed by *Club Fifteen* on CBS from 1947 through 1953, minus a brief interlude when he was replaced as host by singer Dick Haymes during parts of 1949 and 1950. During his stint on "Club Fifteen,' he was teamed with the ever-popular Andrews Sisters three nights per week, singing with them and engaging in comedy skits. He first met the trio in 1938 when his orchestra backed their Decca recording of "Begin the Beguine," their popular vocalization of Artie Shaw's big band hit. One can't help when hearing these old "Club Fifteen" broadcasts how eerily similar Bob & The Andrews Sisters sound to the trio's very frequent and hugely successful pairings with brother Bing Crosby on the Decca label. Bob and Patty even scored a hit duet on Decca Records with their duet recording of the novelty "The Pussy Cat Song (Nyow! Nyot Nyow!)" which peaked at No. 12 on Billboard.[5] A half-hour CBS daytime series, *The Bob Crosby Show* followed from 1953–1957. He introduced the Canadian singer Gisele MacKenzie to American audiences and subsequently guest starred in 1957 on her NBC television series, *The Gisele MacKenzie Show*.

On September 14, 1952, Bob replaced Phil Harris as the bandleader on *The Jack Benny Program*, remaining until Benny retired the radio show in 1955 after 23 years. In joining the show, he became the leader of the same group of musicians who had played under Harris. According to Benny writer Milt Josefsberg, the issue was budget. Because radio had strong competition from TV, the program budget had to be reduced, so Bob replaced Phil. Prior to joining Benny on the radio, Crosby, who was based on the East Coast, would often play with Benny during Benny's live New York appearances, and he was seen frequently throughout the 1950s on Benny's television series.

As a performer, Crosby had tremendous charisma and wit combined with a laid back persona. He was able to swap jokes competently with Benny, including humorous references to his brother Bing's wealth and his string of losing racehorses. An exchange during one of the popular Christmas programs ran thus: Crosby muses to Jack that he's bought gifts for everyone but bandmember Frank Remley. When Jack suggests "a cordial, like a bottle of Drambuie," Crosby counters that Drambuie is an after-dinner drink and adds, alluding to Remley's penchant for alcohol, that "Remley never quite makes it to after dinner."

Filmography

- Rhythm on the Roof (1934)
- Collegiate (1936)
- Paramount Headliner: Bob Crosby and His Orchestra (1938)
- Ambercombie Had a Zombie (1941)
- Let's Make Music (1941)
- Merry-Go-Roundup (1941)
- Sis Hopkins (1941)
- Rookies on Parade (1941)
- Reveille With Beverly (1943)
- Presenting Lily Mars (1943)
- Don't Hook Now (1943)
- Thousands Cheer (1943)
- See Here, Private Hargrove (1944)
- Pardon My Rhythm (1944)
- Kansas City Kittie (1944)
- The Singing Sheriff (1944)
- My Gal Loves Music (1944)
- Meet Miss Bobby Sox (1944)
- Pillow to Post (1945, scenes deleted)
- When You're Smiling (1950)
- Two Tickets to Broadway (1951)
- Stars in the Eye (1951)
- The Greatest Show on Earth (1952)
- Road to Bali (1952)
- The Five Pennies (1960)

Television

Bob Crosby guest starred in the television series *The Gisele MacKenzie Show*. He also starred in his own afternoon variety show, The Bob Crosby show, that aired between 1953 and 1957. Bob fronted a TV program in Australia in the 1960s.

Personal life

Crosby married socialite June Kuhn at his home in Spokane on 22 September 1938. They had five children, three boys (Christopher, George and Stephen) and two girls (Cathleen and Junie). Crosby died in 1993 due to complications from cancer.[6]

Notes

[1] http://rayhendricksvocalist.com/

[2] U.S. Library of Congress, Copyright Entries. (http://books.google.com/books?id=pT1jAAAAIAAJ&pg=PA656&lpg=PA656&
dq=WHEN+ICKY+MORGAN+PLAYS+THE+ORGAN+LIBRARY+CONGRESS&source=bl&ots=3drfdV7xyX&
sig=5lQGWjmE1prF0k_NIgRCD5fHCvA&hl=en&sa=X&ei=sauJT9LFONShtwfGk7CzCQ&ved=0CEAQ6AEwAw#v=onepage&q&
f=false)

[3] *Fulton County History* (http://fultonhistory.com/Process small/Newspapers/Fairport NY Monroe County Mail/Fairport NY Monroe
County Mail 1942 - 1943 Grayscale/Fairport NY Monroe County Mail 1942 - 1943 Grayscale - 0633.pdf)

[4] The encyclopedia of big band, lounge, classic jazz and space-age sound (http://www.parabrisas.com/d_crosbybob.php)

[5] Sforza, John: "Swing It! The Andrews Sisters Story;" University Press of Kentucky, 2000; 289 pages

[6] *New York Times* (March 10, 1993): Obituary: Bob Crosby (http://query.nytimes.com/gst/fullpage.
html?res=9F0CEEDD1731F933A25750C0A965958260)

External links

- Big Band Library: Bob Crosby (http://www.bigbandlibrary.com/radioprogramscrosbybob.html)
- Solid!: Bob Crosby (http://www.parabrisas.com/d_crosbybob.php)

Media

- Haendiges Listening Lounge: *The Jo Stafford Show* with vocal by Bob Crosby (http://www.otrsite.com/ra/ra1024.ram)
- Pandora: Bob Crosby (http://www.pandora.com/music/artist/518433b3a73ee2a9)
- Radio Lovers: *The Bob Crosby Show* with Eileen Barton (http://www.radiocrazy.com/shows/B/BigBands/BobCrosbyandEileenBarton1.mp3)
- An episode of *The Bob Crosby Show* from 1954 (http://video.google.com/videoplay?docid=2832495253760127675&ei=rIDLSbH5G5KurgLP4Iz3Bw&q=bob+crosby+show)

Boogie-woogie

Boogie-woogie	
Stylistic origins	Blues
Cultural origins	early 1870s, Piney Woods of Northeast Texas
Typical instruments	Piano
Derivative forms	Rock and roll, Boogie rock
Fusion genres	
Jump blues, Rock and roll, Rockabilly, Swing	

Boogie-woogie is an African American style of piano-based blues that became popular in the late 1930s and early 1940s, but originated much earlier, and was extended from piano, to three pianos at once, guitar, big band, and country and western music, and even gospel. While the blues traditionally depicts a variety of emotions, boogie-woogie is mainly associated with dancing.[1] The lyrics of one of the earliest hits, "Pinetop's Boogie Woogie", consist entirely of instructions to dancers:

> Now, when I tell you to hold yourself, don't you move a peg.

> And when I tell you to get it, I want you to Boogie Woogie!

It is characterized by a regular bass figure, in the left hand. The bass figure is transposed according to the chord changes.

It is not strictly a solo piano style, but is also used to accompany singers and as a solo part in bands and small combos. It is sometimes called *"eight to the bar"*, as much of it is written in common time (4/4) time using eighth notes (quavers) (see time signature). The chord progressions are typically based on **I** - **IV** - **V** - **I** (with many formal variations of it, such as **I/i** - **IV/iv** - **v/I**, as well as chords that lead into these ones.

For the most part, boogie-woogie tunes are twelve-bar blues, although the style has been applied to popular songs such as "Swanee River" and hymns such as "Just a Closer Walk with Thee".

Typical   boogie   woogie   bassline:

History

1870s to 1930s

The origin of the term *boogie-woogie* is unknown, according to *Webster's Third New International Dictionary*. The *Oxford English Dictionary* states that the word is a reduplication of *boogie*, which was used for rent parties as early as 1913.

However, Dr. John Tennison, a San Antonio psychiatrist, pianist, and musicologist has suggested some interesting linguistic precursors.[2] Among them are four African terms, including the Hausa word "Boog" and the Mandingo word "Booga", both of which mean "to beat", as in beating a drum. There is also the West African word "Bogi", which means "to dance",[3] and the Bantu term "Mbuki Mvuki", which means, "Mbuki—to take off in flight" and Mvuki—"to dance wildly, as if to shake off ones clothes".[4] The meanings of all these words are consistent with the percussiveness, dancing, and uninhibited behaviors historically associated with boogie-woogie music. Their African origin is also consistent with the evidence that the music originated among newly emancipated African Americans.

In the sheet music literature prior to 1900, there are at least three examples of the use of the word "Bogie" in titles of music in the archives of the Library of Congress.[5]

In 1901, "Hoogie Boogie" appeared in the title of published sheet music. This is the first known instance where a redoubling of the word "Boogie" occurs in the title of published music. (In 1880, "The Boogie Man" had occurred as the title of published music.)[6] As far as audio recordings are concerned, the first appearance of "Boogie" in the title of a recording appears to be a "blue cylinder" recording made by Edison of the "American Quartet" performing "That Synchopated Boogie Boo" in 1913.[7]

"Boogie" next occurs in the title of Wilbur Sweatman's April 1917 recording of "Boogie Rag". However none of these sheet music or audio recording examples contain the musical elements that would identify them as boogie-woogie.

The 1919 recordings (two takes) of "Weary Blues" by the Louisiana Five contained the same boogie-woogie bass figure as appears in the 1915 "Weary Blues" sheet music by Artie Matthews. Dr. John Tennison has recognized these 1919 recordings as the earliest sound recordings which contain a boogie-woogie bass figure.[6]

Blind Lemon Jefferson used the term "Booga Rooga" to refer to a guitar bass figure that he used in "Match Box Blues".[8] Jefferson may have heard the term from Huddie "Lead Belly" Ledbetter, who played frequently with Jefferson. Lead Belly, who was born in Mooringsport, La. and grew up in Harrison County, Texas in the community of Leigh, said he first heard Boogie Woogie piano in the Caddo Lake Area of northeast Texas in 1899.[9] He said it influenced his guitar-playing. Lead Belly also said he heard boogie-woogie piano in the Fannin Street district of Shreveport, Louisiana. Some of the players he heard were Dave "Black Ivory King" Alexander, or possibly another Dave Alexander known as "Little Dave Alexander" and a piano player called Pine Top (not Pine Top Smith, who was not born until 1904, but possibly Pine Top Williams or Pine Top Hill.)[9][10] Lead Belly was among the first guitar-players to adapt the rolling bass of boogie-woogie piano.

Texas, as the state of origin, became reinforced by Jelly Roll Morton who said he heard the boogie piano style there early in the 20th century; so did Leadbelly and so did Bunk Johnson, according to Rosetta Reitz.[11]

The first time the modern-day spelling of "boogie-woogie" was used in a title of a published audio recording of music appears to be Pine Top Smith's December 1928 recording titled, "Pine Top's Boogie Woogie", a song whose lyrics contain dance instructions to "boogie-woogie".

Earliest attempts to determine a geographical origin for boogie-woogie

The earliest documented inquiries into the geographical origin of boogie-woogie occurred in the late 1930s when oral histories from the oldest living Americans of both African and European descent, revealed a broad consensus that boogie-woogie piano was first played in Texas in the early 1870s. Additional citations place the origins of boogie-woogie in the Piney Woods of northeast Texas. "The first Negroes who played what is called boogie-woogie, or house-rent music, and attracted attention in city slums where other Negroes held jam sessions, were from Texas. And all the Old-time Texans, black or white, are agreed that boogie piano players were first heard in the lumber and turpentine camps, where nobody was at home at all. The style dates from the early 1870s."[12]

"Fast Western" connection to Marshall & Harrison County, Texas

Max Harrison (in the book Jazz edited by Hentoff and McCarthy in 1959) and Mack McCormick (in the liner notes to his Treasury of Field Recordings, VOL. 2) concluded that "Fast Western" was the first term by which boogie-woogie was known.

Also, "In Houston, Dallas, and Galveston — all Negro piano players played that way. This style was often referred to as a 'fast western' or 'fast blues' as differentiated from the 'slow blues' of New Orleans and St. Louis. At these gatherings the ragtime and blues boys could easily tell from what section of the country a man came, even going so far as to name the town, by his interpretation of a piece."[13]

According to Dr. John Tennison, when he interviewed Lee Ree Sullivan in Texarkana in 1986, Sullivan told him that he was familiar with "Fast Western" and "Fast Texas" as terms to refer to boogie-woogie in general, but not to denote the use of any specific bass figure used in boogie-woogie. Sullivan said that "Fast Western" and "Fast Texas" were terms that derived from the "Texas Western" Railroad Company of Harrison County.[14] The company was formed on February 16, 1852, but did not build track from Swanson's Landing at Caddo Lake to Marshall, Texas, until after changing its name to "Southern Pacific" on August 16, 1856.[15] This Texas-based "Southern Pacific" was the first "Southern Pacific" railroad, and was not connected to the more well known "Southern Pacific" originating in San Francisco, California. The Texas-based Southern Pacific Railroad was bought out by the newly-formed Texas and Pacific Railway on March 21, 1872.

Although the "Texas Western" Railroad Company changed its name to "Southern Pacific", Sullivan said the name "Texas Western" stuck among the slaves who constructed the first railway hub in northeast Texas from Swanson's Landing to the city of Marshall[14]

Railroad connection to Marshall & Harrison County, Texas

A key to identifying the geographical area in which boogie-woogie originated is understanding the relationship of boogie-woogie music with the steam railroad, both in the sense of how the music might have been influenced by sounds associated with the arrival of steam locomotives as well as the cultural impact the sudden emergence of the railroad might have had on newly emancipated African Americans.

The railroad did not "arrive" in northeast Texas as an extension of track from existing lines from the north or the east. Rather, the first railroad locomotives and iron rails were brought to northeast Texas via steamboats from New Orleans via the Mississippi and Red Rivers and Caddo Lake to Swanson's Landing, located on the Louisiana/Texas state line. Beginning with the formation of the Texas Western Railroad Company in Marshall, Texas, through the subsequent establishment in 1871 of the Texas and Pacific Railway company, which located its headquarters and shops there, Marshall was the only railroad hub in the Piney Woods of northeast Texas at the time the music developed. The sudden appearance of steam locomotives, and the building of mainline tracks and tap lines to serve logging operations was pivotal to the creation of the music in terms of its sound and rhythm. It was also crucial to the rapid migration of the musical style from the rural barrel house camps to the cities and towns served by the Texas and Pacific Railway Company.

"Although the neighboring states of Arkansas, Louisiana, and Missouri would also produce boogie-woogie players and their boogie-woogie tunes, and despite the fact that Chicago would become known as the center for this music through such pianists as Jimmy Yancey, Albert Ammons, and Meade "Lux" Lewis, Texas was home to an environment that fostered creation of boogie-style: the lumber, cattle, turpentine, and oil industries, all served by an expanding railway system from the northern corner of East Texas to the Gulf Coast and from the Louisiana border to Dallas and West Texas."[16] Alan Lomax, wrote: "Anonymous black musicians, longing to grab a train and ride away from their troubles, incorporated the rhythms of the steam locomotive and the moan of their whistles into the new dance music they were playing in jukes and dance halls. Boogie-woogie forever changed piano playing, as ham-handed black piano players transformed the instrument into a polyrhythmic railroad train."[17]

In the 1986 television broadcast of Britain's *The South Bank Show* about boogie-woogie, music historian Paul Oliver noted: "Now the conductors were used to the logging camp pianists clamoring aboard, telling them a few stories, jumping off the train, getting into another logging camp, and playing again for eight hours, barrel house. In this way the music got around—all through Texas—and eventually, of course, out of Texas. Now when this new form of piano music came from Texas, it moved out towards Louisiana. It was brought by people like George W. Thomas, an early pianist who was already living in New Orleans by about 1910 and writing "New Orleans Hop Scop Blues", which really has some of the characteristics of the music that we came to know as Boogie."[3]

Paul Oliver also wrote that George W. Thomas "composed the theme of the New Orleans Hop Scop Blues – in spite of its title – based on the blues he had heard played by the pianists of East Texas."[18] On February 12, 2007, Paul Oliver confirmed to John Tennison that it was Sippie Wallace who told Oliver that performances by East Texas pianists had formed the basis for George Thomas's "Hop Scop Blues".[19]

George Thomas and his brother Hersal Thomas migrated from Texas to Chicago, and brought boogie-woogie with them. They were an immense influence on other pianists, including Jimmy Yancey, Meade Lux Lewis, Albert Ammons and many others. Many elements that we now know as elements of boogie-woogie are present in Hersal and George Thomas' "The Fives". According to Dr. John Tennison, "although some Boogie Woogie bass figures were present in prior sheet music, the thing that made 'The Fives' so special was the greater amount and variety of Boogie Woogie bass figures that were present in the music as compared to Boogie Woogie bass figures that had been present in previously published sheet music, such as the 1915 "Weary Blues" by Artie Matthews.[20]

"Albert Ammons and Meade 'Lux' Lewis claim that 'The Fives,' [copyrighted in 1921 and published in 1922] the Thomas brothers' musical composition, deserves much credit for the development of modern boogie-woogie. During the 1920s, many pianists featured this number as a 'get off' tune and in the variations played what is now considered boogie-woogie."[21]

Indeed, all modern boogie-woogie bass figures can be found in "The Fives", including swinging, walking broken-octave bass, shuffled (swinging) chord bass (of the sort later used extensively by Ammons, Lewis, and Clarence "Pine Top" Smith), and the ubiquitous "oom-pah" ragtime stride bass.[22]

T&P stops associated with names for boogie-woogie left-hand bass lines

Early generation boogie-woogie players recognized basic boogie-woogie bass lines by geographical locations with which they associated them. Lee Ree Sullivan identified a number of these left hand bass lines for Dr. John Tennison in 1989.[14] From the primitive to the complex, those identifications indicate that the most primitive form of the music was associated with Marshall, Texas – and that the left-hand bass lines grew more complex as the distance from Marshall increased.

The most primitive of these left hand bass lines is the one that was called "the Marshall". It is a simple, four-beats-to-the-bar figure The second-most primitive bass-line, called "the Jefferson", is also four-beats-to-the-bar, but goes down in pitch on the last note in each four-note cycle. It has been suggested that this downturn in pitch reveals a possible New Orleans influence. Jefferson, Texas, about 17 miles north of Marshall, was the westernmost port of a steamboat route that connected to New Orleans via Caddo Lake, the Red River, and the Mississippi

River.[23]

The remaining bass lines rise in complexity with distance from Marshall, Texas as one would expect variations and innovations would occur as the territory in which the music has been introduced expands.

Indications that Marshall & Harrison County Texas is the most likely point of origination of boogie-woogie

In January 2010, Dr. John Tennison summarized his research into the origins of boogie-woogie with the conclusion that Marshall, Texas is "the municipality whose boundaries are most likely to encompass or be closest to the point on the map which is the geographic center of gravity for all instances of Boogie Woogie performance between 1870 and 1880".

Dr. Tennison states: "Given the account of Elliot Paul, and given that Lead Belly witnessed boogie-woogie in 1899 in the Arklatex; and given the North to South migration of the Thomas family; and given the Texas & Pacific headquarters in Marshall in the early 1870s; and given that Harrison County had the largest slave population in the state of Texas; and given the fact that the best-documented and largest-scale turpentine camps in Texas did not occur until after 1900 in Southeast Texas, it is most probable that boogie-woogie spread from Northeast to Southeast Texas, rather than from Southeast to Northeast Texas, or by having developed diffusely with an even density over all of the Piney Woods of East Texas. It would not be surprising if there was as yet undiscovered evidence of the earliest boogie-woogie performances buried (metaphorically or literally) in Northeast Texas."[6]

On May 13, 2010, the Marshall City Commission enacted an official declaration naming Marshall as the "birthplace" of boogie-woogie music, and embarked on a program to encourage additional historical research and to stimulate interest in and appreciation for the early African-American culture in northeast Texas that played a vital role in creating boogie-woogie music.[24]

The City of Marshall, Texas is committed to cooperating with any and all efforts to unearth boogie-woogie history and to honor, celebrate, and re-create the vibrant environment that was catalytic to the creation of the most entertaining, revolutionary, and influential of all American musical forms.

"Birthplace of Boogie Woogie" was registered by the Marshall Convention and Visitors on June 21, 2011 (registration number 3,980,563; Ser. No. 85-064,442, Filed 6-16-2010.)

Development of modern boogie-woogie

A song titled "Tin Roof Blues" was published in 1923 by the Clarence Williams Publishing Company. Compositional credit is given to Richard M. Jones. The Jones composition uses a boogie bass in the introduction with some variation throughout.[25][26] In February 1923 Joseph Samuels' Tampa Blue Jazz Band recorded the George W. Thomas number "The Fives" for Okeh Records, considered the first example of jazz band boogie-woogie.

Jimmy Blythe's recording of "Chicago Stomps" from April 1924 is sometimes called the first complete boogie-woogie piano solo record.

The first boogie-woogie hit was "Pinetop's Boogie Woogie" by Pinetop Smith, recorded in 1928 and first released in 1929. Smith's record was the first boogie-woogie recording to be a commercial hit, and helped establish "boogie-woogie" as the name of the style. It was closely followed by another example of pure boogie-woogie, "Honky Tonk Train Blues" by Meade Lux Lewis, recorded by Paramount Records; (1927), first released in March 1930. The performance emulated a railroad trip, perhaps lending credence to the 'train theory'.

Late 1930s: Carnegie Hall

Boogie-woogie gained further public attention in 1938 and 1939, thanks to the *From Spirituals to Swing* concerts in Carnegie Hall promoted by record producer John Hammond.[1] The concerts featured Big Joe Turner and Pete Johnson performing Turner's tribute to Johnson, "Roll 'Em Pete", as well as Meade Lux Lewis performing "Honky Tonk Train Blues" and Albert Ammons playing "Swanee River Boogie". "Roll 'Em Pete" is now considered to be an early rock and roll song.

These three pianists, with Turner, took up residence in the Café Society night club in New York City where they were popular with the sophisticated set. They often played in combinations of two and even three pianos, creating a richly textured piano performance.

1930s–1940s: Swing

After the Carnegie Hall concerts, it was only natural for swing bands to incorporate the boogie-woogie beat into some of their music. Tommy Dorsey's band had a hit with an updated version of "Pine Top's Boogie Woogie" in 1938, which was the swing era's second best seller, only second to Glenn Miller's "In the Mood". From 1939, the Will Bradley orchestra had a string of boogie hits such as the original versions of "Beat Me Daddy (Eight To The Bar)" and "Down The Road A-Piece", both 1940, and "Scrub Me Mamma With A Boogie Beat", in 1941. The Andrews Sisters sang some boogies, and after the floodgates were open, it was expected that every big band should have one or two boogie numbers in their repertoire, as the dancers were learning to jitterbug and do the Lindy Hop, which required the boogie-woogie beat.

Key figures

Amongst the many pianists who have been exponents of this genre, there are only a few who have had a lasting influence on the music scene. Perhaps the most well known boogie-woogie pianist is Albert Ammons. His "Boogie Woogie Stomp" released in 1936 was a pivotal recording, not just for boogie-woogie but for music. Some of the flattened sevenths in the right hand riffs are similar to licks used by early rock and roll guitarists. Ammons' two main compatriots were Meade 'Lux' Lewis and Pete Johnson. Before these three were playing piano, the two leading pianists were Jimmy Yancey and 'Pine-Top' Smith. Both of these pianists used bass patterns similar to ragtime and stride piano, but the distinctive Boogie-Woogie right hand licks were already in use. Today, Boogie-Woogie is being taken forward by such pianists as Michael Kaeshammer, Rob Rio, Silvan Zingg and particularly Axel Zwingenberger, whose records and performances have a great influence on the contemporary scene.

Derivative forms

In 1939 country artists began playing boogie-woogie when Johnny Barfield recorded "Boogie Woogie". "Cow Cow Boogie" was written for, but not used in, the 1942 movie "Ride 'em Cowboy". This song by Benny Carter, Gene DePaul, and Don Raye successfully combined boogie-woogie and Western, or cowboy music. The lyrics leave no doubt that it was a Western boogie-woogie. It sold over a million records in its original release by Ella Mae Morse and Freddie Slack, and has now been recorded many times.

The trickle of what was initially called hillbilly boogie, or Okie boogie (later to be renamed country boogie), became a flood beginning around late 1945. One notable country boogie from this period was the Delmore Brothers "Freight Train Boogie", considered to be part of the combined evolution of country music and blues towards rockabilly. In 1948 Arthur Smith achieved Top 10 US country chart success with his MGM Records recordings of "Guitar Boogie" and "Banjo Boogie", with the former crossing over to the US pop chart, introducing many people to the potential of the electric guitar.[27] The hillbilly boogie period lasted into the 1950s, the last recordings of this era were made by Tennessee Ernie Ford with Cliffie Stone and his orchestra with the great guitar duo Jimmy Bryant and Speedy West. Bill Haley and the Saddlemen recorded two boogies in 1951.

The boogie beat continued in country music through the end of the 20th century. The Charlie Daniels Band (whose earlier tune "The South's Gonna Do It Again" uses boogie-woogie influences) released "Boogie Woogie Fiddle Country Blues" in 1988,[28] and three years later in 1991 Brooks & Dunn had a huge hit with "Boot Scootin' Boogie".[29]

More representative examples can be found in some of the songs of Western swing pioneer Bob Wills, and subsequent tradition-minded country artists such as Asleep At The Wheel, Merle Haggard, and George Strait.

The popularity of the Carnegie Hall concerts meant work for many of the fellow boogie players and also led to the adaptation of boogie-woogie sounds to many other forms of music. Tommy Dorsey's band had a hit with "T.D.'s Boogie Woogie" as arranged by Sy Oliver and soon there were boogie-woogie songs, recorded and printed, of many different stripes. Most famously, in the big-band genre, the ubiquitous "Boogie Woogie Bugle Boy", which was revamped recently by Christina Aguilera as her 2006 hit, "Candyman".

In the many styles of blues, especially Chicago blues and (more recently) West Coast blues, most pianists were influenced by, and employed, the traditional boogie-woogie styles. Some of the earliest and most influential were Big Maceo Merriweather and, later, Sunnyland Slim. Otis Spann and Pinetop Perkins, two of the best known blues pianists, are heavily boogie-woogie influenced, with the latter taking both his name and signature tune from Pinetop Smith.

The boogie-woogie fad lasted from the late 1930s into the early 1950s,[30] and made a major contribution to the development of jump blues and ultimately to rock and roll, epitomized by Little Richard and Jerry Lee Lewis. Boogie-woogie is still to be heard in clubs and on records throughout Europe and North America. Big Joe Duskin displayed on his 1979 album, *Cincinnati Stomp*, a command of piano blues and boogie-woogie, which he had absorbed at first hand in the 1940s from Albert Ammons and Pete Johnson.[31]

In classical music, the composer Conlon Nancarrow was also deeply influenced by boogie-woogie, as many of his early works for player piano demonstrate. "A Wonderful Time Up There" is a boogie-woogie gospel song. Povel Ramel's first hit in 1944 was *Johanssons boogie-woogie-vals* where he mixed boogie-woogie with waltz. John Lee Hooker took the Boogie-woogie style over to guitar from piano, creating the Boogie song "Boogie Chillen".

Beginning in the 1970s, and continuing to this day, artists such as George Frayne (Commander Cody and His Lost Planet Airmen), keep (mostly) traditional boogie style alive with songs such as "Rock That Boogie", "Too Much Fun", "Beat Me Daddy, Eight to the Bar", and others. In the late 20th and early 21st centuries, Jools Holland has been instrumental in keeping the boogie-woogie tradition alive. Also, multi-instrumentalist Shawn Lee experimented with boogie-woogie in his 2006 soundtrack for the game *Bully*, in the song "Fighting Johnny Vincent".

The Grateful Dead took part in the boogie woogie rhythmic style, they played a dance hall sort of music as they emerged. Over the years there are many examples of them jamming, when they are just playin' Boogie Woogie.

References

[1] Du Noyer, Paul (2003). *The Illustrated Encyclopedia of Music* (1st ed.). Fulham, London: Flame Tree Publishing. p. 165. ISBN 1-904041-96-5.

[2] Boogie Woogie: Development—by John Tennison (A.K.A. Nonjohn)—Updated November 3, 2010 at the Boogie Woogie Foundation http://www.bowofo.org/

[3] *The South Bank Show* (educational television series in Great Britain), episode on Boogie Woogie, 1986, with commentary by Music Historian, Paul Oliver

[4] *They Have a Word for It: A Lighthearted Lexicon of Untranslatable Words and Phrases*, by Howard Rheingold, Published 2000 by Sarabande Books.

[5] page 20, Liner Notes, written by Jean-Christophe Averty, for CD album, *Original Boogie Woogie* by Claude Bolling, 1968, Universal Music S.A.S., France.

[6] Boogie Woogie: Its Origin, Subsequent History, and Continuing Development—by John Tennison (A.K.A. Nonjohn)—Updated November 3, 2010.

[7] Syracuse Digital library at http://digilib.syr.edu/cdm4/item_viewer.php?CISOROOT=/cylinder&CISOPTR=179&CISOBOX=1&REC=1.

[8] *What Do They Want?*, 1990, by Sammy Price (his autobiography.), University of Illinois Press.

[9] *Just Jazz*, edited by Sinclair Traill and The Hon Gerald Lascelles, Chapter 2. "Boogie Woogie" (pages 13–40) written by Ernest Borneman, published 1957 in Great Britain for Peter Davies Ltd by The Windmill Press, Kingswood, Surrey.

[10] "Illuminating The Leadbelly Legend", by Ross Russell, *Down Beat*, August 6, 1970, Vol. 37, No. 15,

[11] Liner Notes by Rosetta Reitz for Album: *Boogie Blues: Women Sing and Play Boogie Woogie*, 1983, Rosetta Records, New York, NY.

[12] Elliot Paul, page 229, Chapter 10, *That Crazy American Music*, published in 1957.

[13] E. Simms Campbell, 1939, pages 112–113, (in Chapter 4 "Blues") in the book, *Jazzmen: The Story of Hot Jazz Told in the Lives of the Men Who Created It*.

[14] Interview with Lee Ree Sullivan, Boogie Woogie pianist, 1986, Texarkana, AR-TX, by John Tennison and Alfred Tennison, Jr.

[15] George C. Werner, "Texas Western Railroad", Handbook of Texas Online, (http://www.tshaonline.org/handbook/online/articles/eqt20), accessed November 06, 2010.

[16] (page 75) *Texan Jazz*, 1996, by Dave Oliphant, University of Texas Press.

[17] Chapter 4, *Lonesome Whistles*, page 170 *The Land Where the Blues Began*, 1993, by Alan Lomax, The New Press, New York, NY.

[18] Page 85, *The Story of the Blues*, 1969, by Paul Oliver, London.

[19] Interview with Paul Oliver by John Tennison, February 12, 2007.

[20] e-mail to Jack and Nancy Canson, November 4, 2010.

[21] "5 Boogie Woogie Piano Solos by All-Star Composers" (a book of sheet music), Copyright 1942, edited by Frank Paparelli, Leeds Music Corporation, RKO Building, Radio City, New York, NY.

[22] History of Boogie Woogie Retrieved April 11, 2008 (http://nonjohn.com/History of Boogie Woogie.htm)

[23] Christopher Long, "Jefferson, TX (Marion County)", Handbook of Texas Online, (http://www.tshaonline.org/handbook/online/articles/hgj02), accessed November 05, 2010.

[24] Lee Hancock, Dallas Morning News, June 18, 2010.

[25] see section on Tin Roof Blues (http://www.gregkoenig.com/basinstreet/articles/blues.htm)

[26] additional information on this song and songs based on it (http://dippermouth.blogspot.com/2007/09/jazzin-babies-blues.html)

[27] Oldies.com (http://www.oldies.com/artist-biography/Arthur-Smith.html)

[28] Lpdiscography.com (http://www.lpdiscography.com/d/Daniels/charlie.htm)

[29] Cmt.com (http://www.cmt.com/artists/az/brooks_and_dunn/25957/album.jhtml)

[30] *Deep Blues* by Robert Palmer 1981 page 130

[31] Russell, Tony (1997). *The Blues: From Robert Johnson to Robert Cray*. Dubai: Carlton Books Limited. p. 108. ISBN 1-85868-255-X.

Further reading

- Silvester, Peter (2009/1988). *The Story of Boogie-Woogie: A Left Hand Like God*. Da Capo Books. ISBN 0-8108-6924-1.

External links

Resources

- From Ammons to Zwingenberger: A brief history of Boogie Woogie (http://www.daniel-paterok.de/en/history-of-boogie)
- The Boogie Woogie Foundation (contains extensive article on the history of Boogie Woogie) (http://www.bowofo.org)

Festivals

- International Boogie Woogie Festival Netherlands (http://www.boogiefestival.nl)
- International Boogie Woogie Festival Switzerland (http://www.boogiefestival.com)
- International Boogie Woogie Festival Dorset UK (http://www.ukboogiewoogiefestival.co.uk)

Boogie Woogie Bugle Boy

"**Boogie Woogie Bugle Boy**" was a major hit for The Andrews Sisters and an iconic World War II tune. This song can be considered an early jump blues recording. The song is ranked #6 on Songs of the Century.

Origins of the song

The song was written by Don Raye and Hughie Prince, and was recorded at Decca's Hollywood studios on January 2, 1941, nearly a year before the United States entered World War II but after the start of a peacetime draft to expand the armed forces in anticipation of American involvement. The flipside was "Bounce Me Brother With a Solid Four". The Andrews Sisters introduced the song in the 1941 Abbott and Costello film *Buck Privates*, which was in production when they made the record. "Boogie Woogie Bugle Boy" was nominated for an Academy Award for Best Song.

It is closely based on an earlier Raye-Prince hit, "Beat Me Daddy, Eight to the Bar," which is about a virtuoso boogie-woogie piano player.

Storyline of the song

According to the lyrics of the song, a renowned Chicago, Illinois street musician is drafted into the U.S. Army during the Peacetime Draft imposed by the Roosevelt Administration. In addition to being famous, the bugler was the "top man at his craft," but the Army had little use for his talents and he was reduced to blowing the wake up call (Reveille) in the morning. This caused the musician to become dejected: "It really brought him down, because he couldn't jam." The Cap (An Army Captain—the Company Commander) took note of the blues man's blues and went out and conscripted more musicians to assemble a band to keep the bugler company. Thereafter, the bugler found his stride, infusing the military marches with his inimitable street flair: "He blows it eight to the bar—in boogie rhythm." Even his morning calls attain some additional flavor: "And now the company jumps when he plays reveille." But, the bugler is not only empowered, he is possibly spoiled, because thereafter, "He can't blow a note if the bass and guitar/Isn't with him."

People who claim to have inspired the song

In an interview broadcast July 3, 2006 on CNN, World War II veteran Bill Arter said he often played in jam sessions with the black unit in Company C, who gave him the nickname Bugle Boy from Company B. Arter was a medic who landed during D-day. There is no evidence that he was the inspiration for the song; however, since it was written before the U.S. entered the war he may have been dubbed the Bugle Boy from Company B in reference to the song, not the other way around.

Articles published in *Stars & Stripes*, as well as Billboard Magazine, and The Cleveland Plain Dealer during WWII credit Clarence Zylman of Muskegon, Michigan, as the original Boogie Woogie Bugler.[1] The lyrics in the song seem to agree with several aspects of Zylman's life. Drafted at age 38, Clarence had been performing for 20 years, beginning with radio station WBBM in Chicago and moving on to several big bands, starting with Paul Specht and Connie Connaughton, and most recently with the Tommy Tucker Orchestra. He brought his playing style to England where he was a bugler for an engineer company, using his trumpet for taps and reveille, eventually being transferred to an army band. Articles in *Billboard* and *The Plain Dealer* (Cleveland, Ohio) support this, including the fact that Clarence was sent to teach other buglers his techniques.

Another claimant to the title (though he seldom mentioned it) would be Harry L. Gish, Jr. (1922–2005). At age 17, after a meteoric rise in the mid 1930s based out of the Ritz Hotel in Paducah, Kentucky, he ventured to New York City where he appeared (studio only) with the Will Bradley "All Star Orchestra" with highly regarded solos on the

Raye-Prince songs "Celery Stalks at Midnight", "Scrub Me Mama With a Boogie Beat", and "The Boogilly Woogilly Piggie". He also performed with the Olsen & Johnson (of *Hellzapoppin'* fame) band, Ray Anthony and was popular in the Plattsburgh, New York (Lake Placid) area before returning to Decca Records in Chicago. He also had a "summer replacement" radio show there for CBS from WBBM radio.

In the 1980s and 1990s he honored many requests to play at services for veterans' funerals, and in 1995, in the character of The Boogie Woogie Bugle Boy (still able to fit in his WWII uniform: he enlisted in the Army Air Corps) he opened the combined service units (American Legion, VFW and others) celebration of the 50th anniversary of the end of WWII in Little Rock, Arkansas, where he opened with "Reveille" and closed the ceremony with "Taps".

Later versions of the song

In 1973, Bette Midler recorded the song. It peaked at number eight on the *Billboard Hot 100* singles chart, and introduced it to a new generation of pop music fans. The track was also a number-one single on the *Billboard* easy listening chart.[2]

In 1987, The Chipettes covered the song for the *Alvin and the Chipmunks* episode "Just One of the Girls."

In 1990, pop/R&B group En Vogue did a shortened version of the song for their album *Born to Sing*, rewording it to sound more urban, i.e. "boogie woogie hip hop boy".

In 2003, Brighton downtempo act Backini remixed a version called *Company B Boy* for their album *Threads*.

In 2006, the Puppini Sisters recorded the song for their album *Betcha Bottom Dollar*.

In 2007, R&B/Gospel group Jerry Lawson and Talk of the Town recorded the song on their album *Jerry Lawson Talk of the Town*.

Katy Perry performing the song alongside Keri Hilson and Jennifer Nettles.

On their 2008 *Live in Concert* DVD, the von Trapp Children sang this song.

In 2010, on *VH1 Divas Salute The Troops* the song performing by Katy Perry, Keri Hilson and Jennifer Nettles.

Homage

- The song inspired the 1941 cartoon *Boogie Woogie Bugle Boy of Company B* produced by Walter Lantz Productions.[3]
- The song is referenced in the animated short Disney musical film, *A Symposium on Popular Songs* in the song, "The Boogie Woogie Bakery Man" written by Robert & Richard Sherman.
- The song was parodied on an early 1980s episode of Chicago-based horror movie show *Son of Svengoolie* as "The Boogie-Woogie Bogeyman of Berwyn".
- In the sitcom Dinosaurs, episode Nuts to War Part 2, Earl, Roy, and Charlene dress up as USO girls and sing the song.
- Christina Aguilera and Linda Perry wrote "Candyman" (released as a single in 2007) from Aguilera's hit album *Back to Basics*, as a tribute to the Andrews Sisters and their "Boogie Woogie Bugle Boy".[4]
- The Miami-based girl group Company B took their name from the song. They recorded their own version of the song in 1989.

- In the *Sesame Street* song "Dance Myself to Sleep", Ernie has Rubber Duckie play the bugle and calls him "The Boogie Woogie Bugle Duck of Sesame Street."
- On an episode of *A Different World*, Whitley, Kim, and Jaleesa dress up in military attire and sing "Boogie Woogie Bugle Boy" to pay homage to their friend Zelmer (played by Blair Underwood), who is about to depart for war in the Persian Gulf.
- On *The Pucca Adventures of Tuck and Brad with their friends from Histeria! and Detention* in the episode "Tuck's Date Night Out" was played went Tuck put on a style the 1940s and the 1950s that aired on February 11, 2005.
- Albert Ammons recorded a boogie-woogie piano elaboration of the Andrews Sisters original, released in February 1944, when the musicians' strike ended.
- The song is featured in the cafe scenes in the movie Molly: An American Girl on the Home Front.
- On the 2005 *Doctor Who* episode *The Doctor Dances*, the Doctor (Christopher Eccleston) dances to an instrumental version of the tune with companion Rose Tyler (Billie Piper).

References

[1] "Boogie Woogie Reveille" (http://books.google.com/books?id=ggwEAAAAMBAJ&pg=PA63&dq=muskegon&lr=& as_pt=MAGAZINES#v=onepage&q=muskegon&f=false). *Billboard* (Billboard) (Vol 55 No. 14). 1943-04-03. . Retrieved 2009-11-04.
[2] Whitburn, Joel (2002). *Top Adult Contemporary: 1961–2001*. Record Research. p. 170.
[3] http://www.imdb.com/title/tt0033424/
[4] Moss, Corey (2007-02-21). "Xtina X Three: Aguilera Has Multiple-Personality Disorder In Clip – Music, Celebrity, Artist News" (http://www.mtv.com/news/articles/1552870/20070220/aguilera_christina.jhtml). MTV. . Retrieved 2012-01-04.

External links

- The Puppini Sisters' official website (http://www.thepuppinisisters.com) (featuring a sample of their version)
- Jerry Lawson's official website (http://jerrylawson.biz/)
- MCA Music v. Earl Wilson (http://ccnmtl.columbia.edu/projects/law/library/cases/case_mcawilson.html) Columbia Law School Arthur W. Diamond Law Library Music Plagiarism Project.
- http://www.thednaoflife.com/40/manners/respect/ american-hero-the-boogie-woogie-bugle-boy-of-company-b-goes-to-heaven-today

Buck Privates

Buck Privates	
Theatrical release poster	
Directed by	Arthur Lubin
Produced by	Alex Gottlieb
Written by	Arthur T. Horman
Starring	Bud Abbott Lou Costello The Andrews Sisters
Music by	Charles Previn
Editing by	Philip Cahn
Distributed by	Universal Pictures
Release date(s)	January 31, 1941 (U.S. release)
Running time	84 min
Country	United States
Language	English
Budget	$245,000 [1]
Box office	$4,000,000 (USA)[1]

Buck Privates is the 1941 comedy/World War II film that turned Bud Abbott and Lou Costello into bona fide movie stars. It was the first service comedy based on the peacetime draft of 1940. The comedy team made two more service comedies before the United States entered the war (*In the Navy* and *Keep 'Em Flying*). A sequel to this movie, *Buck Privates Come Home*, was released in 1947. *Buck Privates* is one of three Abbott and Costello films featuring The Andrews Sisters, who were also under contract to Universal Pictures at the time.

Abbott and Costello performed a radio version of the film on the *Lux Radio Theater* on October 13, 1941.

Plot

Slicker Smith and Herbie Brown (Abbott and Costello) are sidewalk peddlers who hawk neckties out of a suitcase. They are chased by a cop and duck into a movie theater, not realizing that it is now being used as an Army Recruitment Center. Believing that they are signing up for theater prizes, they end up enlisting instead.

Meanwhile, spoiled playboy Randolph Parker (Lee Bowman) and his long-suffering valet, Bob Martin (Alan Curtis), are also enlisting at the old theater. Randolph expects his influential father to pull some strings so he can avoid military service. Bob, on the other hand, takes his military obligations in stride. Tensions between the two men escalate with the introduction of Judy Gray (Jane Frazee), a camp hostess and friend of Bob's upon whom Randolph sets his sights.

At boot camp, Slicker and Herbie are mortified to discover that the policeman who chased them is now their drill sergeant(!). Randolph, meanwhile, learns that his father will not use his influence on his behalf, believing that a year in the Army will do Randolph some good. Life at camp is not so bad, since the Andrews Sisters appear at regular intervals to sing patriotic or sentimental tunes, and Herbie continues to screw up with little consequence.

Randolph decides to skip an army shooting match (that his company eventually loses) to meet with Judy, which causes the rest of his company to resent him. But during a war game exercise, Randolph redeems himself by saving

Bob and coming up with a ruse to win the exercise for his company. He is finally accepted by his unit, and wins Bob's and Judy's admiration in the process. Randolph soon learns that he's been accepted to Officer Training School, but initially refuses thinking that his father's political influence was responsible. However, his commanding officer assures him that his training record (along with recommendations from others in his class) factored in the decision. Randolph later finds out that Bob has also been offered an appointment to OTS, and Judy announces that she will be joining them as a hostess at the OTS training facility.

Production

Buck Privates was filmed from December 13, 1940 through January 11, 1941. It was originally budgeted at $233,000 and meant to shoot over 20 days; in the end it went $12,000 over budget and four days over schedule.[1]

The famous 'drill routine', where Smitty tries to get Herbie and other soldiers to march in formation, was actually a series of shorter takes that were strung together to expand the bit to more than 3 minutes of screen time.[1]

Award nominations

The film received two Academy Award nominations in 1941. Hughie Prince and Don Raye were nominated for an Academy Award for Best Original Song for *Boogie Woogie Bugle Boy* and Charles Previn was nominated for an Academy Award for Original Music Score (Scoring of a Musical Picture).

World War II

Japan used this film as propaganda to demonstrate to its own troops the "incompetence" of the United States Army.[1]

Rerelease

It was re-released in 1948, and again on a double bill with *Keep 'Em Flying* in 1953. It was one of Universal's most successful films ever.

Andrews Sisters

The Andrews Sisters perform four songs during the course of the film: *You're a Lucky Fellow, Mr. Smith, Boogie Woogie Bugle Boy, Bounce Me Brother with a Solid Four*, and *(I'll Be With You When It's) Apple Blossom Time*. Their performance of "Bounce Me Brother with a Solid Four" also features one of the more famous Lindy Hop dance sequences of the swing era. Many dancers from Los Angeles, including Dean Collins, Jewel McGowan, Ray Hirsch, and Patty Lacey, are featured.

The composers of the songs sung by the Andrews Sisters are Don Raye and Hughie Prince, who appear in the film as new recruits alongside Abbott and Costello.

Home media releases

This film has been released three times on DVD. Originally released as single DVD on April 1, 1998, it was released twice as part of two different Abbott and Costello collections. The first time, on *The Best of Abbott and Costello Volume One*, on February 10, 2004, and again on October 28, 2008 as part of *Abbott and Costello: The Complete Universal Pictures Collection*. A Blu-Ray edition was released on April 17, 2012.

References

[1] Bob Furmanek & Ron Palumbo, *Abbott and Costello in Hollywood*, Perigree Books 1991 p 42-48

External links

- *Buck Privates* (http://www.imdb.com/title/tt0033436/) at the Internet Movie Database

Burl Ives

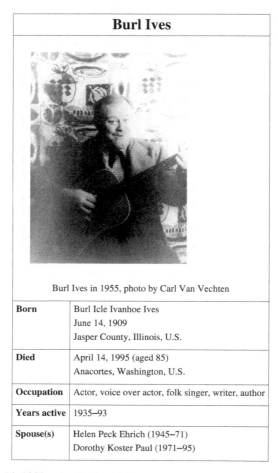

Burl Ives

Burl Ives in 1955, photo by Carl Van Vechten

Born	Burl Icle Ivanhoe Ives June 14, 1909 Jasper County, Illinois, U.S.
Died	April 14, 1995 (aged 85) Anacortes, Washington, U.S.
Occupation	Actor, voice over actor, folk singer, writer, author
Years active	1935–93
Spouse(s)	Helen Peck Ehrich (1945–71) Dorothy Koster Paul (1971–95)

Burl Icle Ivanhoe Ives (June 14, 1909 – April 14, 1995) was an American actor, writer and folk music singer. As an actor, Ives's work included comedies, dramas, and voice work in theater, television, and motion pictures. Music critic John Rockwell said, "Ives's voice ... had the sheen and finesse of opera without its latter-day Puccinian vulgarities and without the pretensions of operatic ritual. It was genteel in expressive impact without being genteel in social conformity. And it moved people."[1]

Life and career

Early life

Ives was born in 1909 near Hunt City, an unincorporated town in Jasper County, Illinois near Newton, Illinois; the son of Levi "Frank" Ives (1880–1947) and Cordelia "Dellie" White (1882–1954). He had six siblings: Audry, Artie, Clarence, Argola, Lillburn, and Norma. His father was at first a farmer and then a contractor for the county and others. One day Ives was singing in the garden with his mother, and his uncle overheard them. He invited his nephew to sing at the old soldiers' reunion in Hunt City. The boy performed a rendition of the folk ballad "Barbara Allen" and impressed both his uncle and the audience.[2]

Ives had a long-standing relationship with the Boy Scouts of America. He was a Lone Scout before that group merged with the Boy Scouts of America in 1924.[3] The collection of his papers at the New York Library for the

Performing Arts includes a photograph of Ives being "inducted" into the Boy Scouts in 1966.[4] Ives received the organization's Silver Buffalo Award, its highest honor.[5] The certificate for the award is hanging on the wall of the Scouting Museum in Valley Forge, Pennsylvania.[6] Ives often performed at the quadrennial Boy Scouts of America jamboree, including the 1981 jamboree at Fort A.P. Hill in Virginia, where he shared the stage with the Oak Ridge Boys.[7] There is a 1977 sound recording of Ives being interviewed by Boy Scouts at the National Jamboree at Moraine State Park, Pennsylvania; on this tape he also sings and talks about Scouting, teaching, etc.[8] Ives is also the narrator of a 28-minute film about the 1977 National Jamboree. In the film, which was produced by the Boy Scouts of America, Ives "shows the many ways in which Scouting provides opportunities for young people to develop character and expand their horizons."[9]

From 1927 to 29, Ives attended Eastern Illinois State Teachers College (now Eastern Illinois University) in Charleston, Illinois, where he played football.[10] During his junior year, he was sitting in English class, listening to a lecture on *Beowulf,* when he suddenly realized he was wasting his time. As he walked out the door, the professor made a snide remark, and Ives slammed the door behind him.[11] Sixty years later, the school named a building after its most famous dropout.[12] Ives was also involved in Freemasonry from 1927 onward.[13]

On July 23, 1929 in Richmond, Indiana, Ives did a trial recording of "Behind the Clouds" for the Starr Piano Company's Gennett label, but the recording was rejected and destroyed a few weeks later.[14]

1930s–1940s

Ives traveled about the U.S. as an itinerant singer during the early 1930s, earning his way by doing odd jobs and playing his banjo. He was jailed in Mona, Utah, for vagrancy and for singing "Foggy, Foggy Dew," which the authorities decided was a bawdy song.[15] Around 1931 he began performing on WBOW radio in Terre Haute, Indiana. He also went back to school, attending classes at Indiana State Teachers College (now Indiana State University).[16] During the late 1930s Ives also attended The Juilliard School in New York.

In 1940 Ives began his own radio show, titled *The Wayfaring Stranger* after one of his ballads. Over the next decade, he popularized several traditional folk songs, such as "Foggy, Foggy Dew" (an English/Irish folk song), "Blue Tail Fly" (an old Civil War tune), and "Big Rock Candy Mountain" (an old hobo ditty). He was also associated with the 'Almanac Singers' (Almanacs), a folk singing group which at different times included Woody Guthrie, Will Geer and Pete Seeger. The Almanacs were active in the American Peace Mobilization (APM), an anti-war group opposed to American entry into World War II and Franklin Roosevelt's pro-Allied policies. They recorded such songs as 'Get Out and Stay Out of War' and 'Franklin, Oh Franklin'.[17]

In June 1941, promptly after the Germans invaded the Soviet Union, the APM re-organized itself into the pro-war American People's Mobilization. Ives and the Almanacs re-recorded several of their songs to reflect the group's new stance in favor of US entry into the war. Among them were 'Dear Mr. President' and 'Reuben James' (name of a US destroyer sunk by the Germans before US entry into the war).

In early 1942, Ives was drafted into the U.S. Army. He spent time first at Camp Dix, then at Camp Upton, where he joined the cast of Irving Berlin's *This Is the Army.* He attained the rank of corporal. When the show went to Hollywood, he was transferred to the Army Air Force. He was discharged honorably, apparently for medical reasons, in September 1943. Between September and December 1943, Ives lived in California with actor Harry Morgan (who would later go on to play Officer Bill Gannon in the 1960s version of Jack Webb's TV show Dragnet, and Colonel Sherman T. Potter on *M*A*S*H*). In December 1943, Ives went to New York City to work for CBS radio for $100 a week.[18]

On December 6, 1945, Ives married 29-year-old script writer Helen Peck Ehrlich.[19] Their son Alexander was born in 1949.

In 1945 Ives was cast as a singing cowboy in the film *Smoky* (1945).[20]

In 1947, Ives recorded one of many versions of "The Blue Tail Fly (Jimmy Crack Corn)", but paired this time with the incredibly popular Andrews Sisters (Patty, Maxene, and LaVerne). Only Bing Crosby sold more Decca Records than the sisters in the 1940s. The flip side of the record would be a fast-paced "I'm Goin' Down the Road". Ives hoped that the trio's success would help the record sell well, and indeed it did, becoming both a best-selling disc and a Billboard hit.[21] It's unfortunate that the acts never paired again on record, as they well-balanced each other's musical genres for a pleasant blend.

His version of the 17th century English song "Lavender Blue" became his first hit and was nominated for an Academy Award for Best Original Song for its use in the 1949 film, *So Dear to My Heart*.

1950s: Communist blacklisting

Ives was identified in the 1950 pamphlet *Red Channels* and blacklisted as an entertainer with supposed Communist ties.[22] In 1952 he cooperated with the House Committee on Unamerican Activities (HUAC) and agreed to testify. He stated that he was not a member of the Communist Party but that he had attended various union meetings with fellow folk singer Pete Seeger simply to stay in touch with working folk. He stated: "You know who my friends are; you will have to ask them if they are Communists."[23]

Ives's statement to the HUAC ended his blacklisting, allowing him to continue acting in movies. But it also led to a bitter rift between Ives and many folk singers, including Seeger, who accused Ives of betraying them and the cause of cultural and political freedom in order to save his own career. Ives countered by saying he had simply stated what he had always believed. Forty-one years later, Ives reunited with Seeger during a benefit concert in New York City. They sang "Blue Tail Fly" together.[24]

1950s–1960s

Ives expanded his appearances in films during this decade. His movie credits include *East of Eden*, "Big Daddy" in *Cat on a Hot Tin Roof*, *Desire Under the Elms*, *Wind Across the Everglades*, *The Big Country*, for which he won an Academy Award for Best Supporting Actor; *Ensign Pulver*, the sequel to *Mister Roberts*; and *Our Man in Havana*, based on the Graham Greene novel.

Ives (left) with Paul Newman in *Cat on a Hot Tin Roof*.

1960s–1990s

In the 1960s Ives began singing country music with greater frequency. In 1962 he released three songs that were popular with both country music and popular music fans: "A Little Bitty Tear", "Call Me Mister In-Between", and "Funny Way of Laughing".

Ives had several film and television roles during the 1960s and 1970s. In 1962 he starred with Rock Hudson in *The Spiral Road,* which was based on a novel of the same name by Jan de Hartog. In 1964, he played the genie in the movie *The Brass Bottle* with Tony Randall and Barbara Eden.

Ives' "A Holly Jolly Christmas" and "Silver and Gold" became Christmas standards after they were first featured in the 1964 CBS-TV presentation of the Rankin & Bass stop-motion animated family special *Rudolph the Red-Nosed Reindeer*. Johnny Marks had composed the title song (originally an enormous hit for singing cowboy Gene Autry) in 1949, and producers Rankin & Bass retained him to compose the TV special's soundtrack. Ives voiced Sam the Snowman, the banjo-playing "host" and narrator of the story, explaining how Rudolph used his "nonconformity," as

Sam refers to it, to save Christmas from being cancelled due to an impassable blizzard. The following year, Ives re-recorded all three of these Johnny Marks hits, which Ives had sung in the TV special, but with a more "pop" feel than in the TV special. He released them all as singles for the 1965 holiday season, capitalizing on their previous successes.

Ives performed in other television productions, including *Pinocchio* and *Roots*. He starred in two television series: *O.K. Crackerby!* (1965–66), which co-starred Hal Buckley, Joel Davison and Brooke Adams, and *The Bold Ones: The Lawyers* (1969–72). *O.K. Crackerby!*, which was about the presumed richest man in the world, replaced Walter Brennan's somewhat similar *The Tycoon* on the ABC schedule from the preceding year. Ives occasionally starred in macabre-themed productions. In 1970, for example, he played the title role in *"The Man Who Wanted to Live Forever,"* in which his character attempts to harvest human organs from unwilling donors. In 1972, he appeared as old man Doubleday in the episode "The Other Way Out" of Rod Serling's *Night Gallery*, in which his character seeks a gruesome revenge for the murder of his granddaughter.

Ives and Helen Peck Ehrlich were divorced in February 1971.[25] Ives then married Dorothy Koster Paul in London two months later.[26] In their later years, Ives and Dorothy lived in a waterfront home in Anacortes, in the Puget Sound area, and in Galisteo, New Mexico, on the Turquoise Trail. In the 1960s, he had another home just south of Hope Town on Elbow Cay, a barrier island of the Abacos in the Bahamas.

In honor of Ives's influence on American vocal music, on October 25, 1975, he was awarded the University of Pennsylvania Glee Club Award of Merit.[27] This award, initiated in 1964, was "established to bring a declaration of appreciation to an individual each year who has made a significant contribution to the world of music and helped to create a climate in which our talents may find valid expression."

Ives lent his name and image to the U.S. Bureau of Land Management's "This Land Is Your Land – Keep It Clean" campaign in the 1970s. He was portrayed with the program's fictional spokesman, Johnny Horizon.

Burl Ives was seen regularly in television commercials for Luzianne tea for several years during the 1970s and 1980s when he was the company's commercial spokesman.

Death

Ives was a renowned pipe smoker; the cover of his first album depicted a pipe and a fishing hat with the words "Burl Ives" in between. He also smoked cigars. In the summer of 1994 he was diagnosed with oral cancer after being hospitalized for back surgery. After several operations he decided against having further surgery. In April 1995 he fell into a coma. Ives died of complications of oral cancer on April 14, 1995 at the age of 85, at his home in Anacortes, Washington;[28] he is interred in Mound Cemetery in Hunt City Township, Jasper County, Illinois.[29][30]

Broadway roles

Ives's Broadway career included appearances in *The Boys From Syracuse* (1938–39), *Heavenly Express* (1940), *This Is the Army* (1942), *Sing Out, Sweet Land* (1944), *Paint Your Wagon* (1951–52), and *Dr. Cook's Garden* (1967). His most notable Broadway performance (later reprised in a 1958 movie) was as "Big Daddy" Pollitt in *Cat on a Hot Tin Roof* (1955–56).

Author

Ives's autobiography, *The Wayfaring Stranger*, was published in 1948. He also wrote or compiled several other books, including *Burl Ives' Songbook* (1953), *Tales of America* (1954), *Sea Songs of Sailing, Whaling, and Fishing* (1956), and *The Wayfaring Stranger's Notebook* (1962).

Popular culture references

The Ren & Stimpy Show's first season episode "Stimpy's Invention" featured a record, "Happy, Happy, Joy, Joy", which parodied Ives' singing style and re-created some of his crusty dialogue from *The Big Country* and *Summer Magic*. Also, Ren has a little of Ives' tone in his voice, though he's mostly inspired by Kirk Douglas and Peter Lorre.

Ives is known to *Star Wars* fans for his role as the narrator in the 1984 made-for-TV film *Caravan of Courage: An Ewok Adventure*.

The Christmas film *Elf*, starring Will Ferrell, features a snowman resembling the character Ives voiced in *Rudolph the Red-Nosed Reindeer*, voiced by Leon Redbone.

In *The King of Queens* episode "Baker's Doesn't", Arthur (Jerry Stiller) is talking to Spence (Patton Oswalt) and decides not to write a new Christmas song, but a new Hanukkah song instead because "all they have is 'Dreidel, Dreidel' and that Adam Sandler song". He says that their song has nothing new to say that hasn't been said a thousand times by Burl Ives, God rest his soul. Plus I have no idea if he's dead or alive."

Director Wes Anderson included a number of songs (among them "Buckeye Jim") by Ives on the soundtrack for his 2009 film *Fantastic Mr. Fox*.

Popular 1980s British children's album The Runaway Train featured a recording of Ives singing the eponymous song.

Discography

Albums

- *Okeh Presents the Wayfaring Stranger* (1941, Okeh K-3, 4 records, 10 inch, 78 rpm)
- *The Wayfaring Stranger* (1944, Asch 345, 3 records, 10 inch, 78 rpm, reissued in 1947 as Stinson 345 [same catalog number], 10 inch, 78 rpm)
- *The Wayfaring Stranger* (1944, Columbia C-103, 4 records, 10 inch, 78 rpm)
- *BBC Presents The Martins and the Coys* (1944, BBC World, 6 records, 12 inch, 78 rpm)
- *Lonesome Train: A Musical Legend* (1944, Decca A-375, 3 records, 12 inch, 78 rpm, reissued in 1950 as Decca DL 5054, 10 inch, 33⅓ rpm)
- *Sing Out, Sweet Land!* (1945, Decca A-404, 6 records, 10 inch, 78 rpm)
- *A Collection of Ballads and Folk Songs* (1945, Decca A-407, 4 records, 10 inch, 78 rpm, reissued in 1950 as *A Collection of Ballads and Folk Songs, Volume 1*, Decca DL 5080, 10 inch 33⅓ rpm)
- *Ballads and Folk Songs, Volume 2* (1946, Decca A-431, 4 records, 10 inch, 78 rpm, reissued in 1949 as Decca DL 5013, 10 inch, 33⅓ rpm)
- *A Collection of Ballads, Folk and Country Songs, Volume 3* (1949, Decca A-711, 3 records, 10 inch, 78 rpm, reissued in 1950 as Decca DL 5093, 10 inch, 33⅓ rpm)
- *The Wayfaring Stranger* (1949, Stinson SLP 1, 10 inch, 78 rpm, reissued circa 1954 as *Blue Tail Fly and Other Favorites*, Stinson SL 1 [same catalog number], 12 inch, 33⅓ rpm)
- *Animal Fair: Songs for Children* (1949, Columbia MJV 59, 2 records, 10 inch, 78 rpm)
- *Mother Goose Songs* (1949, Columbia MJV 61, 10 inch, 78 rpm)
- *The Return of the Wayfaring Stranger* (1949, C-186, 4 records, 10 inch, 78 rpm, also released as Columbia CL 6058, 10 inch, 33⅓ rpm)
- *The Wayfaring Stranger* (1950, Columbia CL 6109, 10 inch, 33⅓ rpm)
- *Hymns Sung by Burl Ives* (1950, Columbia C-203, 4 records, 10 inch, 78 rpm; Columbia CL 6115, 10 inch, 33⅓ rpm)
- *More Folksongs* (1950, Columbia C-213, 4 records, 10 inch, 78 rpm; Columbia CL 6144, 10 inch, 33⅓ rpm)

- *Burl Ives Sings the Lollipop Tree, The Little Turtle, and The Moon Is the North Wind's Cookie* (1950, Columbia MJV 110, 10 inch, 78 rpm)
- *Tubby the Tuba (Victor Jory)/Animal Fair: Songs for Children* (1950, Columbia JL 8013, 10 inch, 33⅓ rpm)
- *Sing Out, Sweet Land!* (1950, Decca DL 8023, 12 inch, 33⅓ rpm, reissued in 1962 as Decca DL 4304/74304 [simulated stereo])
- *Historical America in Song* (1950, Encyclopædia Britannica Films, 6 albums in 30 records, 12 inch, 78 rpm)
- *Christmas Day in the Morning* (1952, Decca DL 5428, 10 inch, 33⅓ rpm)
- *Folk Songs Dramatic and Humorous* (1953, Decca DL 5467, 10 inch, 33⅓ rpm)
- *Women: Songs About the Fair Sex* (1953, Decca DL 5490, 10 inch, 33⅓ rpm)
- *Coronation Concert* (1954, Decca DL 8080, 12 inch, 33⅓ rpm)
- *The Wayfaring Stranger* (1955, Columbia CL 628, 12 inch, 33⅓ rpm, reissued in 1964 as Columbia CS 9041 [simulated stereo])
- *The Wild Side of Life (album)* (1955, Decca DL 8107, 12 inch, 33⅓ rpm)
- *Men: Songs for and About Men* (1955, Decca DL 8125, 12 inch, 33⅓ rpm)
- *Down to the Sea in Ships* (1956, Decca DL 8245, 12 inch, 33⅓ rpm)
- *Women: Folk Songs About the Fair Sex* (1956, Decca DL 8245, 12 inch, 33⅓ rpm, with 4 additional songs)
- *Burl Ives Sings In the Quiet of the Night* (1956, Decca DL 8247)
- *Burl Ives Sings... For Fun* (1956, Decca DL 8248)
- *Children's Favorites* (1956, Columbia CL 2570, 10 inch, 33⅓ rpm)
- *Burl Ives Sings Songs for All Ages* (1957, Columbia CL 980)
- *Christmas Eve with Burl Ives* (1957, Decca DL 8391)
- *Songs of Ireland* (1958, Decca DL 8444)
- *Captain Burl Ives' Ark* (1958, Decca DL 8587)
- *Old Time Varieties* (1958, Decca DL 8637)
- *Australian Folk Songs* (1958, Decca DL 8749)
- *A Lincoln Treasury* (contains *Lonesome Train: A Musical Legend*) (1959, Decca DL 9065)
- *Cheers* (1959, Decca DL 8886/78886)
- *Burl Ives Sings Little White Duck and Other Children's Favorites* (1959, Harmony HL 9507, reissued circa 1963 as Harmony HS 14507 [simulated stereo], reissued again in 1974 as Columbia C 33183 [simulated stereo])
- *Ballads* (1959, United Artists UAL 3030/UAS 6030)
- *Return of the Wayfaring Stranger* (1960, Columbia CL 1459, 12 inch, 33/13 rpm)
- *Burl Ives Sings Irving Berlin* (1960, United Artists UAL 3117/UAS 6117)
- *Manhattan Troubadour* (1961, United Artists Records UAL 3145/UAS 6145, reissued with two fewer songs as *Burl Ives Favorites*, 1970, Sunset SUS 5280)
- *The Best of Burl Ives* (1961, Decca DX 167/DXS 7167 [simulated stereo], 2 records, reissued in 1973 as MCA 4034 [simulated stereo], 2 records)
- *The Versatile Burl Ives!* (1961, Decca DL 4152/74152)
- *Songs of the West* (1961, Decca DL 4179/74179, reissued as MCA 196)
- *It's Just My Funny Way of Laughin'* (1962, Decca DL 4279/74279)
- *Burl Country Style* (1962, Decca DL 4361/74361)
- *Spotlight on Burl Ives and the Folk Singers Three* (1962, Design DLP/SDLP 156)
- *Sunshine in My Soul* (1962, Decca DL 4329/74329)
- *Songs I Sang in Sunday School* (1963, Word W-3229-LP/ WST-8130-LP)
- *Burl Ives and the Korean Orphan Choir Sing of Faith and Joy* (1963, Word W-3259-LP/WST-8140-LP)
- *Singin' Easy* (1963, Decca DL 4433/74433)
- *The Best of Burl's for Boys and Girls* (1963, Decca DL 4390/74390 [simulated stereo], reissued in 1980 as MCA 98 [simulated stereo])

- *Walt Disney Presents Summer Magic* (1963, Buena Vista BV 3309/STER 4025)
- *Burl Ives Presents America's Musical Heritage* (1963, Longines Symphonette Society LW 194-LW 199, 6 records)
- *Walt Disney Presents Burl Ives' Animal Folk* (1963, Disneyland ST 3920)
- *Walt Disney Presents Burl Ives' Folk Lullabies* (1964, Disneyland ST 3924)
- *Scouting Along with Burl Ives* (1964, Columbia CSP 347)
- *True Love* (1964, Decca DL 4533/74533)
- *Burl Ives Sings Pearly Shells and Other Favorites* (1964, Decca DL 4578/74578, reissued as MCA 102)
- *Chim Chim Cheree and Other Children's Choices* (1964, Disneyland ST 3927)
- *My Gal Sal and Other Favorites* (1965, Decca DL 4606/74606)
- *On the Beach at Waikiki* (1965, Decca DL 4668/74668)
- *Have a Holly Jolly Christmas* (1965, Decca DL 4689/74689, reissued as MCA 237)
- *Shall We Gather at the River?* (1965, Word W-3339-LP/WST-8339-LP)
- *The Lollipop Tree* (1965, Harmony HL 9551/HS 14551)
- *The Daydreamer* (1966, Columbia OL 6540/OS 2940)
- *Burl's Choice* (1966, Decca DL 4734/74734)
- *Something Special* (1966, Decca DL 4789/74789)
- *I Do Believe* (1967, Word W-3391-LP/WST-8391-LP)
- *Burl Ives Sings* (1967, Coronet CXS 271)
- *Rudolph the Red-Nosed Reindeer (album)* (1967, Decca DL 4815/74815)
- *Greatest Hits* (1967, Decca DL 4850/74850)
- *Burl's Broadway* (1967, Decca DL 4876/74876)
- *The Big Country Hits* (1968, Decca DL 4972/74972)
- *Sweet, Sad and Salty* (1968, Decca DL 5028/75028)
- *The Times They Are A-Changin'* (1968, Columbia CS 9675)
- *Christmas Album* (1968, Columbia CS 9728)
- *Got the World by the Tail* (1969, Harmony HS 11275)
- *Time* (1970, Bell 6055, reissued as *The Talented Man*, 1978, Bulldog 1027)
- *How Great Thou Art* (1971, Word WST-8537-LP)
- *Christmas at the White House* (1972, Caedmon TC 1415)
- *Payin' My Dues Again* (1973, MCA 318)
- *Song Book* (1973, MCA Coral CB 20029)
- *Little Red Caboose and Other Children's Hits* (1974, Disneyland 1359)
- *The Best of Burl Ives, Vol. 2* (1975, MCA 4089, 2 records)
- *Hugo the Hippo* (1976, United Artists LA-637-G)
- *Christmas by the Bay* (1977, United States Navy Band)
- *We Americans: A Musical Journey With Burl Ives* (1978, National Geographic Society NGS 07806)
- *Live in Europe* (1979, Polydor 2382094)

Hit Singles

Year	Single	Chart positions				
		US	US AC	US Country	UK	AU
1948	"Blue Tail Fly" (with The Andrews Sisters and Vic Schoen's Orchestra)	24	–	–	–	-
1949	"Lavender Blue (Dilly Dilly)" (with Captain Stubby and The Buccaneers)	16	–	13	–	1
	"Riders In the Sky (A Cowboy Legend)"	21	–	–	–	-
1951	"On Top of Old Smoky" (with Percy Faith and His Orchestra)	10	–	–	–	–
	"The Little White Duck"	-	–	-	–	15
1952	"The Wild Side of Life" (with Grady Martin and The Slewfoot Five)	30	–	6	–	–
1954	"The Parting Song"	-	–	–	–	17
	"True Love Goes On and On" (with Gordon Jenkins and His Orchestra and Chorus)	23	–	–	–	–
1957	"Marianne" (with The Trinidaddies)	84	–	–	–	–
1961	"A Little Bitty Tear" (with The Anita Kerr Singers and Owen Bradley's Orchestra)	9	1	2	9	3
1962	"Funny Way of Laughin'" (with Owen Bradley's Orchestra)	10	3	9	29	7
	"Call Me Mr. In-Between" (with Owen Bradley's Orchestra)	19	6	3	–	18
	"Mary Ann Regrets" (with Owen Bradley's Orchestra and Chorus)	39	13	12	–	15
1963	"The Same Old Hurt" (with Owen Bradley's Orchestra and Chorus)	91	–	–	–	–
	"Baby Come Home To Me"	131	–	–	–	–
	"I'm the Boss" (with Owen Bradley's Orchestra and Chorus)	111	–	–	–	86
	"This Is All I Ask"	67	–	–	–	–
	"It Comes and Goes"	124	–	–	–	94
	"True Love Goes On and On" (second entry)	66	–	–	–	–
1964	"Pearly Shells (Popo O Ewa)" (with Owen Bradley's Orchestra)	60	12	–	–	22
1965	"My Gal Sal" (with Owen Bradley's Orchestra)	122	–	–	–	–
	"Chim Chim Cher-ee"	120	–	–	–	–
1965	"A Holly Jolly Christmas"	–	30	–	–	–
1966	"Evil Off My Mind"	–	–	47	–	–
1967	"Lonesome 7-7203"	–	–	72	–	–
1968	"I'll Be Your Baby Tonight" (with Robert Mersey's Orchestra)	133	35	–	–	28

Singles (selected)

- Foggy, Foggy Dew / Rodger Young (1945, 10 in., 78 rpm, Decca 23405)
- Grandfather Kringle / The Twelve Days of Christmas (1951, 10 in., 78 rpm, Columbia MJV-124)
- Great White Bird / Brighten The Corner Where You Are (1953, 7 in., 45 rpm, Decca 23849)
- That's My Heart Strings / The Bus Stop Song (1956, 7 in., 45 rpm, Decca 30046)
- We Loves Ye Jimmy / I Never See Maggie Alone (1959, 7 in., 45 rpm, Decca 30855)
- A Little Bitty Tear / Shanghied (1961, 7 in., 45 rpm, Decca 31330)
- Funny Way of Laughing / Mother Wouldn't Do That (1962, 7 in., 45 rpm, Decca 31371)
- Call Me Mr. In-Between / What You Gonna Do, Leroy? (1962, 7 in., 45 rpm, Decca 31405)
- Mary Ann Regrets / How Do You Fall Out of Love? (1962, 7 in., 45 rpm, Decca 31433)
- The Twelve Days of Christmas / Indian Christmas Carol (1962, 7 in., 45 rpm, Decca 25585)

- I'm the Boss / The Moon Is High (1963, 7 in., 45 rpm, Decca 31504)
- True Love Goes On and On / I Wonder What's Become of Sally (1963, 7 in., 45 rpm, Decca 31571)
- On The Front Porch / Ugly Bug Ball (1963, 7 in., 45 rpm, Buena Vista 419)
- Four Initials on a Tree /This Is Your Day (1964, 7 in., 45 rpm, Decca 31610)
- Pearly Shells / What Little Tears Are Made Of (1964, 7 in., 45 rpm, Decca 31659)
- Salt Water Guitar / The Story of Bobby Lee Trent (1964, 7 in., 45 rpm, Decca 31811)
- A Holly Jolly Christmas / Snow for Johnny (1965, 7 in., 45 rpm, Decca 31695)
- Evil Off My Mind / Taste of Heaven (c. 1967, 7 in., 45 rpm, Decca 31997)
- Lonesome 7-7203 / Hollow Words (1967, 7 in., 45 rpm, Decca 32078)
- That's Where My Baby Used to Be / Bury the Bottle With Me (1968, 7 in., 45 rpm, Decca 32282)
- I'll Be Your Baby Tonight / Maria, If I Could (1968, 7 in., 45 rpm, Columbia 4-44508)
- Santa Mouse / Oh, What a Lucky Boy I Am (1968, 7 in., 45 rpm, Columbia 4-44711)
- Gingerbread House / Tumbleweed Snowman (c. 1970, 7 in. 45 rpm, Big Tree BT-130)
- The Best Is Yet to Come & Stayin' Song / Blue Tail Fly (1972, 7 in., 45 rpm, MCA 1921)
- Mrs. Johnson's Happiness Emporium / Anytime You Say (1973, 7 in., 45 rpm, Decca 33049)
- The Tail of the Comet Kohoutek / A Very Fine Lady (1974, 7 in., 45 rpm, MCA 40175)
- It's Gonna Be a Mixed Up Xmas / The Christmas Legend of Monkey Joe (1978, 7 in., 45 & 33⅓ rpm, Monkey Joe MJ1)
- The Night Before Christmas / Instrumental (1986, 7 in., 45 rpm, Stillman/Teague STP-1013)

Radio work (selected)[31]

- *Back Where I Came From*, CBS (30 September 1940 – February 28, 1941)
- *The Wayfarin' Stranger*, CBS & WOR (1941–1942, 1946–1948)[32]
- *Burl Ives Coffee Club*, CBS (5 July 1941 – January 24, 1942)
- *The Columbia Workshop*, CBS

  - "Roadside" (March 2, 1941)
  - "The Log of the R-77," second installment of *Twenty-Six by Corwin* (May 11, 1941)
  - "The People, Yes," third installment of *Twenty-Six by Corwin* (May 18, 1941)
  - "A Child's History of Hot Music" (March 15, 1942)
- *G. I. Jive*, military radio (c. 1943)[33]
- *Columbia Presents Corwin*, CBS

  - "The Lonesome Train" (March 21, 1944)
  - "El Capitan and the Corporal" (July 25, 1944)
- *The Theatre Guild on the Air*, ABC

  - "Sing Out, Sweet Land" (October 21, 1945)
- *Hollywood Star Time*, CBS

  - "The Return of Frank James" (March 10, 1946)
- *The Burl Ives Show*, Syndication (1946–1948)
- *Hollywood Fights Back*, ABC (November 2, 1947)
- *The Kaiser Traveler*, ABC (24 July – September 4, 1949)
- *Burl Ives Sings*, Syndication (1950s)

Theater appearances (selected)[34]

- *Pocahontas Preferred* (1935–1936)[35]
- *I Married an Angel* (1938)[32]
- *The Boys from Syracuse* (23 November 1938 – June 10, 1939)
- *Heavenly Express* (18 April – May 4, 1940)
- *This Is the Army* (4 July – September 26, 1942)
- *Sing Out Sweet Land* (December 27, 1944 – March 24, 1945)
- *She Stoops to Conquer* (1950)[36]
- *Knickerbocker Holiday* (1950)[37]
- *The Man Who Came to Dinner* (1951)[38]
- *Paint Your Wagon* (12 November 1951 – July 19, 1952)
- *Show Boat* (1954)[39]
- *Cat on a Hot Tin Roof* (March 24, 1955 – November 17, 1956)
- *Dr. Cook's Garden* (September 25–30, 1967)

Filmography (selected)

Television

- *Playhouse 90: The Miracle Worker* (1957)
- *Rudolph the Red-Nosed Reindeer* (1964)
- *O.K. Crackerby!* (1965–1966)
- *Pinocchio* (1968)
- *Alias Smith and Jones "The McCreedy Bust"* (1971)
- *The Bold Ones: The Lawyers* (1969–1972)
- *Night Gallery "The Other Way Out"* (1972)
- *Roots* (1977)
- *Little House on the Prairie: The Hunters* (1977)
- *The New Adventures of Heidi* (1978)
- The Bermuda Depths (1978)
- *Caravan of Courage: An Ewok Adventure* (1984)

Films

- *Smoky* (1946)
- *Estação West* (1948)
- *So Dear to My Heart* (1948)
- *Sierra* (1950)
- *East of Eden* (1955)
- *The Power and the Prize* (1956)
- *Cat on a Hot Tin Roof* (1958)
- *Desire Under the Elms* (1958)
- *The Big Country* (1958)
- *Wind Across the Everglades* (1958)
- *Day of the Outlaw* (1959)
- *Our Man in Havana* (1959)
- *Let No Man Write My Epitaph* (1960)
- *The Spiral Road* (1962)

- *Summer Magic* (1963)
- *The Brass Bottle* (1964)
- *Ensign Pulver* (1964)
- *Jules Verne's Rocket to the Moon* (1967)
- *The McMasters* (1970)
- *Baker's Hawk* (1976)
- *The Bermuda Depths* (1978)
- *Just You and Me, Kid* (1979)
- *Earthbound* (1981)
- *White Dog* (1982)
- *Caravan of Courage: An Ewok Adventure* (1984)
- *Uphill All the Way* (1986)
- *Two Moon Junction* (1988)
- *Alex Saves Christmas* (2011) (songs)

Concerts (selected)

- Royal Winsor, New York City, April 28, 1939[40]
- Town Hall, New York City, December 1, 1945[35]
- Opera House, San Francisco, February 9, 1949[41]
- Columbia University, New York City, 19 October 1950[42]
- Royal Festival Hall, London, 10 May 1952[43]
- Albert Hall, London, 20 October 1976[44]
- Reuben F. Scarf's house, Sydney, Australia, GROW Party, 1977.[45]
- Royal Philharmonic Hall, Liverpool,1979 accompanying The Spinners.
- Chautauqua, New York, 1982 (VHS [46])
- Eastern Illinois University, Charleston, Illinois, April 27, 1990[47]
- Brodniak Hall, Anacortes, Washington, 1991 (VHS [48])
- Mt. Vernon, Washington, February 1993 (VHS [49])
- Folksong U.S.A., 92nd Street Y, New York City, 17 May 1993[50]

Bibliography

- *The Wayfarin' Stranger: A Collection of 21 Folk Songs and Ballads with Guitar and Piano Accompaniment.* New York: Leeds Music, 1945.
- *Wayfaring Stranger.* New York: Whittlesey House, 1948 (autobiography)
- *Favorite Folk Ballads of Burl Ives: A Collection of 17 Folk Songs and Ballads with Guitar and Piano Accompaniment.* New York: Leeds Music, 1949
- *Burl Ives Song Book.* New York: Ballantine Books, 1953
- *Sailing on a Very Fine Day* [51]. Chicago: Rand McNally, 1954 (Children's picture book)
- *Burl Ives Folio of Australian Songs*, collected and arranged by Percy Jones, 1954.
- *Song in America: Our Musical Heritage*, co-authored with Albert Hague. New York: Duell, Sloan and Pearce, n.d.
- *Tales of America.* Cleveland: World Publishing, 1954
- "Introduction" to Paul Kapp's *A Cat Came Fiddling and Other Rhymes of Childhood*, New York: Harcourt Brace, 1956
- *The Ghost and Hans Van Duin* [excerpt from *Tales of America*]. Pittsburgh: Carnegie Institute of Technology, 1956

- *Sea Songs of Sailing, Whaling, and Fishing*. New York: Ballantine Books, 1956
- *The Wayfaring Stranger's Notebook*. Indianapolis, Bobbs-Merrill, 1962
- *Irish Songs*. New York: Duell, Sloan & Pearce, n.d.
- *The Burl Ives Sing-Along Song Book: A Treasury of American Folk Songs & Ballads*, 1963
- *Albad the Oaf*. London: Abelard-Schuman, 1965
- *More Burl Ives Songs*. New York: Ballantine Books, 1966
- *Sing a Fun Song*. New York: Southern Music Publishing, 1968
- *Burl Ives: Four Folk Song and Four Stories*, co-authored with Barbara Hazen. N.p.: CBS Records, 1969
- *Spoken Arts Treasury of American Ballads and Folk Songs*, co-authored with Arthur Klein and Helen Ives, n.d.
- *Easy Guitar Method*. Dayton, Ohio : Heritage Music Press, 1975
- *We Americans: A Musical Journey with Burl Ives*. Washington, D.C.: National Geographic Society, 1978 (pamphlet)
- "Foreword" to Martin Scot Kosins's *Maya's First Rose*. West Bloomfield, MI: Altweger and Mandel Publishing, 1991

References

[1] John Rockwell, quoted in book review of *Outsider, John Rockwell on the Arts, 1967–2006*, by John Rockwell, the *New York Times* Book Review, 24 December 2006, p. 13.
[2] Burl Ives, *Wayfaring Stranger*, New York: Whittlesey House, 1948, pp. 15–20.
[3] Lone Scout Foundation, "How the Lone Scouts of America Came To Be": link (http://www.lonescouts.net/002_how_lsa_came_2_b.htm).
[4] Guide to the Burl Ives Papers, 1913–1975, New York Public Library for the Performing Arts: link (http://www.nypl.org/research/lpa/the/pdf/THEIVES.pdf).
[5] NNDB: Tracking the Entire World: Silver Buffalo: link (http://www.nndb.com/honors/823/000043694/).
[6] The World of Scouting Museum at Valley Forge: Our Collection: link (http://www.worldofscoutingmuseum.org/collection.html).
[7] John C. Halter, "A Spirit of Time and Place," *Scouting Magazine*, September 2004: link (http://www.scoutingmagazine.org/issues/0409/a-sprt.html).
[8] WorldCat: OCLC No. 28143341: link (http://www.worldcat.org/oclc/28143341&referer=brief_results).
[9] WorldCat: OCLC No. 5641115: link (http://www.worldcat.org/oclc/5641115&referer=brief_results).
[10] Betsy Cole, "Eastern Mourns Burl Ives," *Daily Eastern News*, 17 April 1995.
[11] Ives, *Wayfaring Stranger* pp. 108–109.
[12] Associated Press, "Eastern Illinois University Honors Famed Dropout Burl Ives," *St. Louis Post Dispatch*, 3 May 1990, p. 71. Accessed via NewsBank.
[13] Burl Ives Collection (http://www.scottishrite.org/visitors/gf.html#bic), *Ancient and Accepted Scottish Rite*.
[14] Tony Russell, *Country Music Records: A Discography, 1921–1942*, Oxford: Oxford University Press, 2004, pp. 17, 369.
[15] *Wayfaring Stranger* pp. 129–132.
[16] *Wayfaring Stranger* p. 145.
[17] 'Dupes: How America's Adversaries Have Manipulated Progressives for a Century' by Paul Kengor (2010)
[18] "Testimony of Burl Icle Ives, New York, N.Y. [on May 20, 1952]," *Hearings before the Subcommittee to Investigate the Administration of the Internal Security Act and Other Internal Security Laws of the Committee on the Judiciary, United States Senate, Eighty-Second Congress, Second Session on Subversive Infiltration of Radio, Television, and the Entertainment Industry*. Washington, D.C.: GPO, 1952. Part 2, p. 206.
[19] "Burl Ives Weds Script Writer," *New York Times*, December 8, 1945, p. 24. Accessed via ProQuest Historical Newspapers.
[20] Burl Ives Biography (http://www.sitcomsonline.com/photopost/showphoto.php/photo/43959), *Sitcoms Online*.
[21] Sforza, John: "Swing It! The Andrews Sisters Story;" University Press of Kentucky, 2000; 289 pages
[22] Michael D. Murray, *Encyclopedia of Television News*, Westport, CT: Greenwood, 1998. p 18. Accessed via Ebrary
[23] "Testimony of Burl Icle Ives ...,"*Hearings before the Subcommittee ...*, pp. 205–228.
[24] Dean Kahn, "Ives-Seeger Rift Finally Ended with 'Blue-Tail Fly' Harmony: Skagitonians Ives, Murros Were on Opposite Sides," *Knight Ridder Tribune Business News* [from *Bellingham Herald*, Washington], 19 March 2006, p. 1. Accessed via ProQuest ABI/Inform.
[25] "*Burl Ives Divorced*," *New York Times*, 19 February 1971, p. 27. Accessed via ProQuest Historical Newspapers
[26] UPI, "*Burl Ives Weds*," *Evening Sentinel*, Holland, Michigan, 17 April 1971, p. 3. Accessed via Access NewspaperARCHIVE
[27] "The University of Pennsylvania Glee Club Award of Merit Recipients" (http://www.dolphin.upenn.edu/gleeclub/MEMBERS_merit.html). .
[28] NY Times Ives obituary (http://www.nytimes.com/1995/04/15/obituaries/burl-ives-the-folk-singer-whose-imposing-acting-won-an-oscar-dies-at-85.html?pagewanted=all&src=pm)
[29] Richard Severo, "*Burl Ives, the Folk Singer Whose Imposing Acting Won an Oscar, Dies at 85*," *New York Times*, 15 April 1995, p. 10. Accessed via ProQuest Historical Newspapers

[30] http://www.encyclopedia.com/doc/1S1-9199504150897195.html from encyclopedia.com

[31] Vincent Terrace, *Radio's Golden Years: The Encyclopedia of Radio Programs, 1930–1960*, San Diego: Barnes and Company, 1981, pp. 43, 147; John Dunning, *On the Air: The Encyclopedia of Old-Time Radio*, New York: Oxford University Press, p. 123; Dave Goldin, *RadioGOLDINdex*: link (http://www.radiogoldindex.com/frame1.html). *Unless otherwise noted, the information in this section comes from these sources*

[32] James R. Parish and Michael R. Pitts, *Hollywood Songsters: Singers Who Act and Actors Who Sing*, 2nd ed., Taylor & Francis, 2003, ISBN 0-415-94333-7, p. 403

[33] James R. Parish and Michael R. Pitts, *Hollywood Songsters*, 2nd ed., Taylor & Francis, 2003, p. 404

[34] Internet Broadway Database: Burl Ives Credits on Broadway: link (http://www.ibdb.com/person.asp?ID=46295). *Unless otherwise noted, this database is the source of the information in this section*

[35] *Guide to the Burl Ives Papers, 1913–1975*, New York Public Library for the Performing Arts: link (http://www.nypl.org/research/lpa/the/pdf/THEIVES.pdf)

[36] "Old Play in Manhattan," *Time*, January 9, 1950, link (http://www.time.com/time/magazine/article/0,9171,811683,00.html)

[37] "Along the Straw Hat," *New York Times*, July 30, 1950, p. X3. Includes photo of Ives. Accessed via ProQuest Historical Newspapers

[38] "Along the Straw Hat Trail," *New York Times*, September 2, 1951, p. 54. Includes photo of Ives. Accessed via ProQuest Historical Newspapers

[39] L.F., "The Theatre: 'Show Boat,' *New York Times*, May 6, 1954, p. 44. Includes photograph of Ives and co-stars. Accessed via ProQuest Historical Newspapers

[40] John Martin, "The Dance: Folk Fetes," *New York Times*, April 23, 1939, p. 128. Accessed via ProQuest Historical Newspapers

[41] "Burl Ives to Be in S. F. February 9," *San Mateo Times*, San Mateo, CA, January 29, 1949, p. 5. Accessed via Access NewspaperARCHIVE

[42] Display ad, *New York Times*, October 8, 1950, p. X3. Accessed via ProQuest Historical Newspapers

[43] "Burl Ives Packs London Hall," *New York Times*, May 11, 1952, p. 95. Accessed via ProQuest Historical Newspapers

[44] UPI, "Ives Returns [to London]," *Syracuse Herald Journal*, Syracuse, NY, October 1, 1976, p. 33. Accessed via Access NewspaperARCHIVE

[45] Keogh, C.B. (1979). *GROW Comes of Age: A Celebration and a Vision!* (http://publishing.yudu.com/Freedom/Actiz/GROWcomesofageaceleb/resources/). Sydney, Australia: GROW Publications. ISBN 0-909114-01-3. OCLC 27588634. .

[46] http://www.worldcat.org/oclc/50929161?tab=details

[47] Associated Press, "Eastern Illinois University Honors Famed Dropout Burl Ives," *St. Louis Post-Dispatch*, May 3, 1990, p. 71. Accessed via NewsBank

[48] http://www.burlives.com/Brodniak.htm

[49] http://www.amyhindman.com/amy_history.html

[50] Stephen Holden, "The Cream of Folk, Reunited for a Cause," *New York Times*, May 19, 1993, p. C15. Includes photo of Ives, Seeger, and others. Accessed via ProQuest Historical Newspapers

[51] http://goldengems.blogspot.com/2010/03/burl-ives-sailing-on-very-fine-day.html

External links

- Burl Ives (http://www.imdb.com/name/nm0412322/) at the Internet Movie Database
- Burl Ives (http://www.ibdb.com/person.asp?ID=46295) at the Internet Broadway Database
- Official website for Burl Ives (http://www.burlives.com/)
- Guide to the Burl Ives Papers, 1913–1975 (http://www.nypl.org/research/lpa/the/pdf/THEIVES.pdf) at the New York Public Library for the Performing Arts
- Burl Ives Collection (http://lcweb2.loc.gov/diglib/ihas/loc.natlib.scdb.200033549/default.html) at the Library of Congress
- Burl Ives Profile at the Association for Cultural Equity (http://culturalequity.org/alanlomax/ce_alanlomax_profile_ives.jsp)
- Burl Ives Performance Review (http://www.bigbandsandbignames.com/BurlIves.html)
- Burl Ives – Discography (http://www.akh.se/ives/center.htm)
- Article (http://www.scottishrite.org/what/educ/journal/jan-feb07/ci.html) in *Scottish Rite Journal*
- Burl Ives (http://en.wikipedia.org/wiki/Wikiasite:starwars:burl_ives) on Wookieepedia: a *Star Wars* wiki

Candyman (Christina Aguilera song)

"Candyman"	
Single by Christina Aguilera	
from the album _Back to Basics_	
Released	February 20, 2007
Format	CD single, digital download
Recorded	2006
Genre	Pop, swing, jazz, blues[1]
Length	3:14
Label	RCA
Writer(s)	Christina Aguilera, Linda Perry
Producer	Linda Perry
Christina Aguilera singles chronology	
"Tell Me" (2006) **"Candyman"** (2007) "Slow Down Baby" (2007)	
Music video	
"Candyman" [2] on YouTube	

"**Candyman**" is a song by American recording artist Christina Aguilera. It was written by Aguilera and Linda Perry for Aguilera's fifth studio album, _Back to Basics_. RCA Records released it as the album's third single in early 2007. The song got a positive response from critics, who praised the uptempo beat. "Candyman" had moderate success throughout the charts, peaking at top 20 in most countries. In the US it reached number 25 and sold over 1 million digital copies.[3] The song was highly successful in Australia and New Zealand, peaking at number 2 in both countries.

It received a Grammy Award nomination for Best Female Pop Vocal Performance at 2008 Grammy Awards. The music video was directed by Matthew Rolston and Aguilera herself, and is based on a 1940s World War II theme. The music video received a MTV Video Music Awards nomination for Best Direction at 2007 MTV Video Music Awards.

Background and composition

Aguilera's fifth studio album, _Back to Basics_, is made up of two discs.[4] Aguilera worked with "more beat-driven" producers on the first disc, such as DJ Premier and Mark Ronson, who included samples in the production.[4] The second disc consists solely of collaborations with producer Linda Perry.[4][5] Aguilera sent letters to different producers that she hoped could help her with the direction she was taking for the project, encouraging them to experiment, re-invent and create a modern soul feel.[6] She described the first disc as "kind of a throwback with elements of jazz, blues and soul music combined with a modern-day twist, like hard-hitting beats".[4]

Originally "Candyman" was planned as the second single and even was confirmed by Aguilera during several different interviews. However, RCA felt that, with the holiday season coming up, it would be safer to release "Hurt", as it would become a big holiday power ballad, comparable to how Aguilera's "Beautiful" performed commercially back in late 2002, instead it was released as the album's third single.[7]

Perry and Aguilera have said that the song consists of new lyrics to a melody that borrows from The Andrews Sisters' 1941 hit "Boogie Woogie Bugle Boy".[8] Critics are usually complimentary towards Aguilera for her authentic replication of the old style.[9][10] The song includes the military cadence "Tarzan & Jane Swingin' on a Vine", sampled from the album *Run to Cadence with the United States Marines, Volume 2*.[11] The long belted note at the end of the track is a high "E_5". Aguilera holds the note in full-belt for approximately 8 seconds.

Critical reception

Aguilera performing "Candyman" during her *Back to Basics Tour*.

Most critics reserved high-praise for the single, while commenting on its highly-sexualized lyrics. *Billboard* magazine called the single "right raunchy", but praised it, saying that "Few popular vocalists could pull off such a laudable feat," and that it has such an "irresistible tempo that radio will have no choice but to sweeten airwaves with 'Candyman.'"[12]

Bill with About.com found that "listeners may want to be alerted to the sexual content," but concluded "Aguilera continues to demonstrate she is one of the top female artists in the business", saying: "It's big, bold and brassy just like Christina Aguilera herself. "Candyman" takes us back to 40's USO shows featuring the Andrews Sisters and a crowd ready to jitterbug. Primarily due to possessing some of the strongest vocal chops in the music business, Christina Aguilera pulls it all off with no hint of karaoke or parody", "The entire song amounts to a sexual double entendre. As stated elsewhere on the album Back to Basics, she is "still dirrty." The "Candyman" of the title is identified as "a one stop shop who makes my cherry pop!". "Fortunately, the energy in the song is so focused on dancing and hooks that the sexual content comes off sounding more like a wink than a wallow".[13]

Yahoo! Music called the song "a good-time 1940s big band romp", and gave it eight out of ten stars.[14] A review from blogcritics sad: "This song, inspired by The Andrew Sisters' "Boogie Woogie Bugle Boy," screams "play me" to even the most formulatic radio stations. She sings: "There's nothing more dangerous than a boy with charm/ He's a one stop shop, makes the panties drop/ He's a sweet talkin' sugar coated candy man/A sweet talkin' sugar coated candy man." "The lyrics are cheesy and simple, but that's the whole point to the song!" "It's one of those brainless songs that you can't get out of your head no matter what. It will even appear in your dreams if you try to forget about it".

"Candyman" received a Grammy Award nomination for Best Female Pop Vocal Performance at 2008 Grammy Awards.

Commercial performance

Originally, "Candyman" was to be the second single from the album, but the label pushed for "Hurt" hoping it would have comparable success to 2002's "Beautiful" and would become a holiday hit.[7] The song was released on February 20, 2007 in the US. The song began charting in the US prior to its official release date, appearing on the January 20, 2007 issue of the *Billboard* Hot 100. "Candyman" peaked at #25 in its seventh week on the chart making it Aguilera's 14th top 40 hit on the *Billboard* Hot 100. It was certified Gold and has sold over 1 million digital copies there.[3][15] In the UK it was released on download only, peaking at #17 on the UK main singles chart and staying in the top 75 for 20 weeks[16] while selling over 100,000 digital downloads. The song re-entered the UK iTunes chart in 2008 reaching 60 on the top 100 after Alexandra Burke performed the song on *X-Factor*.

The song performed very well in Oceania, peaking #2 in both Australia (having a platinum certification[17]) and New Zealand, remaining in the Australian Top 10 over 15 weeks[18] and being the eighth most successful single in 2007 in that country.[19] In the rest of Europe, it was a moderate hit, peaking in the top 20, at number 12 in Germany, 14 in Austria, 12 in Netherlands and number 11 in Switzerland.

Music video

The music video for the single "Candyman" was filmed on January 28, 2007. It was directed by Matthew Rolston and co-directed by Aguilera. It is based on a 1940s World War II theme, and Aguilera rented an airport hangar in Southern California to film it. In the music video, she dances and sings in three different hair colors - red, blonde and brown, as if she were in a singing trio, a tribute to the Andrews Sisters.[20] In another scene, she appears as the famous biceps-flexing factory worker from Westinghouse's "We Can Do It!" poster. Finally, she appears in scenes inspired by pin-up girls Judy Garland, Betty Grable, and Rita Hayworth.[7] The video also features product placement for Campari. Benji Schwimmer, 2006 winner of *So You Think You Can Dance*, makes a cameo appearance as Aguilera's GI dance partner. Benji's sister Lacey Schwimmer also appears in the video as a jitterbugger. Aguilera asked Rolston to co-direct the video with her after he worked with her for a photo shoot for the cover of *Rolling Stone*.[21] Shooting the sequences of Aguilera as a singing trio took the longest since they had to be shot for each hair color and camera angle, which was computer controlled for precision.[21] The choreography was carefully arranged so that none of the versions overlapped and the takes could be spliced together.[21] The color scheme is based on Technicolor films, focusing on primary colors and bright secondary colors.[21]

On February 22, 2007, MTV gave the World Premiere of "Candyman" live on *TRL* and later on MTV's *Making The Video*. The video debuted at number six on *TRL*[22] and reached the top of the countdown four times. The video has since gone on to retire at number three, making it Aguilera's ninth video to retire. "Candyman" has garnered Aguilera a MTV Video Music Award nomination for Best Director with co-director Mathew Rolston at the 2007 VMAs.

Aguilera singing "Candyman" with a sailor outfit.

Live performances and covers

"Candyman" has been performed by Aguilera in her Back to Basics Tour and its DVD: Back to Basics: Live and Down Under. In July 2006 Aguilera held two private concerts in Europe, one on July 17 at the Olympia in Paris and the other one on July 20 at the KOKO Club in London. The setlist consisted of four new tracks and two old singles: "Ain't No Other Man", "Understand", "Candyman", "Lady Marmalade". "Oh Mother", "Beautiful" and "Slow Down Baby".[23] On August 16 of the same year she took part at the "Good Morning America" Summer Concert Series and performed there three songs, including "Candyman".[24] Later that year, on September 8 she gave a performance on Fashion Rocks. At the end of 2006 on December 31, she sung "Candyman" on "Dick Clark's New Year's Rockin Eve". The song was also performed live on Sets on Yahoo! Music.[25] Aguilera performed the song live on The Tonight Show with Jay Leno on February 1, 2007. She also executed a performance on *The Ellen DeGeneres Show* and at the 2007 NBA All-Star Game Vegas Half Time.

In 2008, the song was performed in "The X Factor" UK (series 5) by Alexandra Burke. Earlier that same year, the song was covered by "the girls" contestants Niamh Perry, Samantha Barks and Jessie Buckley in round one of The Battle of the Nancys in the BBC series I'd Do Anything. In 2011, the song was also covered in the episode *Pot o' Gold* during the third season of *Glee* by the characters Santana Lopez, Brittany Pierce and Mercedes Jones receiving good reviews by critics. This version peaked the UK charts at 158.[26] "Candyman" was also performed in the second season of the X Factor (Poland) by semifinalist Ewelina Lisowska on the fifth week of the show.[27]

Track listing and formats

Australian CD single

1. "Candyman" (Single Edit) – 3:15
2. "Hurt" (Snowflake Radio Remix) – 4:09
3. "Candyman" (Video)

Versions and remixes

- Album Version
- Video Edit
- Squeaky Clean Edit
- Offer Nissim Club Mix
- Offer Nissim Mix Edit
- Red One Remix
- Ultimix Mixshow

Charts and certifications

Charts

Chart (2007)	Peak position
Australia (ARIA)[28]	2
Austria (Ö3 Austria Top 40)[29]	14
Belgium (Ultratop 50 Flanders)[30]	11
Belgium (Ultratop 40 Wallonia)[31]	13
Canada (Canadian Hot 100)[32]	9
Czech Republic (IFPI)[33]	80
Denmark (Tracklisten)[34]	12
European Hot 100 Singles[35]	15
Germany (Media Control AG)[36]	12
Hungary (Rádiós Top 40)[37]	3
Ireland (IRMA)[38]	12
Italy (FIMI)[39]	4
New Zealand (RIANZ)[40]	2
Netherlands (Mega Single Top 100)[41]	12
Slovakia (IFPI)[42]	45
Sweden (Sverigetopplistan)[43]	24

Switzerland (Schweizer Hitparade)[44]	11
UK Singles (Official Charts Company)[45]	17
US *Billboard* Hot 100[46]	25
US Pop Songs (*Billboard*)[47]	23
US Hot Dance Club Songs (*Billboard*)[48]	18

Certifications

Region	Certification	Sales/shipments
Australia (ARIA)[49]	Platinum	70,000^
Canada (Music Canada)[50]	Gold	40,000^
Denmark (IFPI Denmark)[51]	Gold	7,500^
New Zealand (RIANZ)[52]	Gold	7,500*
United States (RIAA)[53]	Gold	1,000,000^
*sales figures based on certification alone ^shipments figures based on certification alone		

Year-end charts

Year	Country	Position
2007	Australia[54]	8
	Austria[55]	73
	Germany[56]	92
	New Zealand[57]	15
	Netherlands[58]	78
	Switzerland[59]	46
	UK[60]	74

Release history

Country	Date	Format
United States[61]	February 20, 2007	Top 40/Mainstream radio
United Kingdom	March 3, 2007	Digital Download
Germany[62]	April 7, 2007	CD Single
Australia[63]	April 7, 2007	

References

[1] "Candyman - Christina Aguilera - Pandora Internet Radio" (http://www.pandora.com/music/song/christina+aguilera/candyman). Pandora.com. . Retrieved 2010-04-23.

[2] https://www.youtube.com/watch?v=RsQXVJOgvNY

[3] Trust, Gary. "Ask Billboard: Who's The Hot 100's King? Elvis Presley Vs. Lil Wayne" (http://www.billboard.com/#/column/chartbeat/ ask-billboard-who-s-the-hot-100-s-king-elvis-1007955992.story?page=2). Billboard. . Retrieved 2012-09-24.

[4] Moss, Corey (2006-06-06). "Christina Makes Her Comeback Twice As Nice By Expanding Basics Into Double LP" (http://www.mtv.com/ news/articles/1533622/christina-makes-her-comeback-twice-nice.jhtml). MTV News (Viacom). . Retrieved 2011-12-11.

[5] Gitlin, Lauren (2006-03-16). "Christina Aguilera Channels Billie Holiday" (http://www.rollingstone.com/music/news/ christina-aguilera-channels-billie-holiday-20060316). Rolling Stone. Wenner Media. . Retrieved 2011-12-11.

[6] Clarke, Stuart (2006-08-12). "Aguilera takes twin-track approach for new album". Music Week (Intent Media).

[7] Jobling, John (2007-05-24). "Christina Aguilera – Candyman (review)" (http://www.mansized.co.uk/reviews/review.phtml/540/667/). Mansized. . Retrieved 2008-08-25.

[8] Moss, Corey (2007-02-22). "Christina Aguilera Has Multiple-Personality Disorder In Clip" (http://web.archive.org/web/ 20080316013616/http://www.mtvasia.com/News/200702/22014149.html). MTV News (MTV Asia). Archived from the original (http:// www.mtvasia.com/News/200702/22014149.html) on 2008-03-16. . Retrieved 2008-08-25.

[9] Eliscu, Jenny (2006-08-11). "Rolling Stones "Back to Basics" Review" (http://www.rollingstone.com/artists/christinaaguilera/albums/ album/11107200/review/11111609/back_to_basics). Rolling Stone. . Retrieved 2008-08-25.

[10] Sterdan, Darryl. "Xtina loses the chaps & looks for R-E-S-P-E-C-T on new CD" (http://jam.canoe.ca/Music/Artists/A/ Aguilera_Christina/AlbumReviews/2006/08/15/1757059-sun.html). Jam!. . Retrieved 2008-08-25.

[11] Booklet for Back to Basics; Mili Documentary Recordings website (http://www.militaryrecordings.com/product.php?prodID=16)

[12] Taylor, Chuck (2007-03-03), "Candyman". Billboard. 119 (9):46

[13] Lamb, Bill. "Christina Aguilera - Candyman - About.com Review" (http://top40.about.com/od/singles/gr/candyman.htm). About.com. . Retrieved 2008-08-25.

[14] Gennoe, Dan (2006-08-17). "Christina Aguilera - Back To Basics Review" (http://top40.about.com/od/singles/gr/candyman.htm). Yahoo UK. . Retrieved 2008-08-25.

[15] "Gold & Platinum - April 23, 2010" (http://www.riaa.com/goldandplatinumdata.php?table=SEARCH_RESULTS&artist=Christina Aguilera&format=SINGLE&go=Search&perPage=50). RIAA. . Retrieved 2010-04-23.

[16] "Christina Aguilera | Artist" (http://www.theofficialcharts.com/artist/_/christina aguilera). Official Charts. . Retrieved 2012-01-10.

[17] "http://www.aria.com.au/pages/ARIACharts-Accreditations-2007Singles.htm" (http://www.aria.com.au/pages/httpwww.aria.com. aupagesARIACharts-Accreditations-2007Singles.htm). Aria.com.au. 2007-12-31. . Retrieved 2010-04-23.

[18] "Christina Aguilera- Candyman (song)" (http://australian-charts.com/showitem.asp?interpret=Christina+Aguilera&titel=Candyman& cat=s). Australian Charts. . Retrieved 2008-08-25.

[19] "ARIA Top 100 Singles 2007" (http://www.aria.com.au/pages/aria-charts-end-of-year-charts-top-100-singles-2007.htm). Aria.com.au. . Retrieved 2010-04-23.

[20] Vineyard, Jennifer (2007-03-28). "Avril, Christina's Multiple-Personality Clips Copy A Page From Madonna's Handbook" (http://www. mtv.com/news/articles/1555792/20070328/lavigne_avril.jhtml). MTV News (MTV Networks). . Retrieved 2008-08-25.

[21] "Candyman". Making the Video. MTV. February 21, 2007.

[22] "The TRL Archive - Debuts" (http://host17.hrwebservices.net/~atrl/trlarchive/db.html). Popfusion. Retrieved 2007-04-04.

[23] "Christina Aguilera plays surprise London show" (http://www.nme.com/news/christina-aguilera/23680). NME. (July 21, 2006). . Retrieved 2009-01-28.

[24] "Bryant Park: GMA Summer Concert Series - Christina Aguilera" (http://www.nycgovparks.org/sub_things_to_do/upcoming_events/ events_search.php?id=32020). NY Department of Parks & Recreation. . Retrieved 2009-01-28.

[25] "BET.com Christina Aguilera - Candyman (Live Sets on Yahoo! Music)" (http://www.bet.com/video/music/c/christina-aguilera/ candyman-live-sets-on-yahoo-mu.html). Black Entertainment Television. . Retrieved January 25, 2013.

[26] "UK Singles Chart: CLUK Update (12.11.2011 - week 44)" (http://www.zobbel.de/cluk/111112cluk.txt). . Retrieved 2011-12-18.

[27] "Cukiereczek and chocolate with a hint of chilli. Ewelina Lisowska! (In polish)" (http://xfactor.tvn.pl/wideo/
1,1,cukiereczek-i-czekoladka-z-odrobina-chilli-ewelina-lisowska,344721.html). X Factor Poland (Second Edition). May 19, 2012. . Retrieved
january 21, 2013.

[28] " Australian-charts.com – Christina Aguilera – Candyman" (http://www.australian-charts.com/showitem.asp?interpret=Christina+
Aguilera&titel=Candyman&cat=s). ARIA Top 50 Singles. Hung Medien.

[29] " Christina Aguilera – Candyman – Austriancharts.at" (http://www.austriancharts.at/showitem.asp?interpret=Christina+Aguilera&
titel=Candyman&cat=s) (in German). Ö3 Austria Top 40. Hung Medien.

[30] " Ultratop.be – Christina Aguilera – Candyman" (http://www.ultratop.be/nl/showitem.asp?interpret=Christina+Aguilera&
titel=Candyman&cat=s) (in Dutch). Ultratop 50. Ultratop & Hung Medien / hitparade.ch.

[31] " Ultratop.be – Christina Aguilera – Candyman" (http://www.ultratop.be/fr/showitem.asp?interpret=Christina+Aguilera&
titel=Candyman&cat=s) (in French). Ultratop 40. Ultratop & Hung Medien / hitparade.ch.

[32] " Christina Aguilera Album & Song Chart History" (http://www.billboard.com/artist/299251/-/chart?f=793) Canadian Hot 100 for
Christina Aguilera. Prometheus Global Media.

[33] " ČNS IFPI" (http://www.ifpicr.cz/hitparada/index.php?hitp=R) (in Czech). Hitparáda – Radio Top100 Oficiální. IFPI Czech Republic.
Note: insert 200940 into search.

[34] " Christina Aguilera – Candyman Hitlisten.nu (http://www.hitlisterne.dk/default.asp?w=21&y=2007&list=t40)" (in Danish).
Tracklisten. IFPI Danmark & Nielsen Music Control.

[35] " Christina Aguilera Album & Song Chart History" (http://www.billboard.com/artist/299251/-/chart?f=349) European Hot 100 for
Christina Aguilera. Prometheus Global Media.

[36] " Die ganze Musik im Internet: Charts, News, Neuerscheinungen, Tickets, Genres, Genresuche, Genrelexikon, Künstler-Suche,
Musik-Suche, Track-Suche, Ticket-Suche – musicline.de" (http://musicline.de/de/chartverfolgung_summary/title/Aguilera,Christina/
Candyman/single) (in German). Media Control Charts. PhonoNet GmbH.

[37] " Archívum – Slágerlisták – MAHASZ – Magyar Hanglemezkiadók Szövetsége" (http://www.mahasz.hu/?menu=slagerlistak&
menu2=archivum&lista=radios&ev=2007&het=32&submit_=Keresés) (in Hungarian). Rádiós Top 40 játszási lista. Magyar
Hanglemezkiadók Szövetsége.

[38] " Chart Track" (http://www.chart-track.co.uk/index.jsp?c=p/musicvideo/music/archive/index_test.jsp&ct=240001&arch=t&
lyr=2007&year=2007&week=16). Irish Singles Chart. Irish Recorded Music Association.

[39] Classifica settimanale dal 13/04/2007 al 19/04/2007 - Top digital download FIMI-Nielsen Soundscan International (http://www.fimi.it/
classifiche_result_digital.php?anno= 2007&mese=04&id=68)

[40] " Charts.org.nz – Christina Aguilera – Candyman" (http://www.charts.org.nz/showitem.asp?interpret=Christina+Aguilera&
titel=Candyman&cat=s). Top 40 Singles. Hung Medien.

[41] " Dutchcharts.nl – Christina Aguilera – Candyman" (http://www.dutchcharts.nl/showitem.asp?interpret=Christina+Aguilera&
titel=Candyman&cat=s) (in Dutch). Mega Single Top 100. Hung Medien / hitparade.ch.

[42] " SNS IFPI" (http://www.ifpicr.cz/hitparadask/index.php?hitp=R) (in Slovak). Hitparáda – Radio Top100 Oficiálna. IFPI Czech
Republic. *Note: insert 200726 into search.*

[43] " Swedishcharts.com – Christina Aguilera – Candyman" (http://www.swedishcharts.com/showitem.asp?interpret=Christina+Aguilera&
titel=Candyman&cat=s). Singles Top 60. Hung Medien.

[44] " Christina Aguilera – Candyman – swisscharts.com" (http://www.swisscharts.com/showitem.asp?interpret=Christina+Aguilera&
titel=Candyman&cat=s). Swiss Singles Chart. Hung Medien.

[45] " Archive Chart" (http://www.theofficialcharts.com/archive-chart/_/1/2007-04-07/) UK Singles Chart. Official Charts Company.

[46] " Christina Aguilera Album & Song Chart History" (http://www.billboard.com/artist/299251/-/chart?f=379) *Billboard* Hot 100 for
Christina Aguilera. Prometheus Global Media.

[47] " Christina Aguilera Album & Song Chart History" (http://www.billboard.com/artist/299251/-/chart?f=381) *Billboard* Pop Songs for
Christina Aguilera. Prometheus Global Media.

[48] " Christina Aguilera Album & Song Chart History" (http://www.billboard.com/artist/299251/-/chart?f=359) *Billboard* Hot Dance/Club
Play for Christina Aguilera. Prometheus Global Media.

[49] "ARIA Charts – Accreditations – 2007 Singles" (http://www.aria.com.au/pages/httpwww.aria.com.
aupagesARIACharts-Accreditations-2007Singles.htm). Australian Recording Industry Association. . Retrieved 2011-09-16.

[50] "Canadian single certifications – Christina Aguilera – Candyman" (http://www.musiccanada.com/GPSearchResult.aspx?st=Candyman&
sa=Christina+Aguilera&smt=0). Music Canada. .

[51] "Certificeringer I ifpi.dk" (http://www.ifpi.dk/?q=content/guld-og-platin-i-august). IFPI Danmark. . Retrieved 2011-09-16.

[52] "New Zealand single certifications – Christina Aguilera – Candyman" (http://rianz.org.nz/rianz/oldchart.asp?chartNum=1578&
chartKind=S). Recording Industry Association of New Zealand. .

[53] "American single certifications – Christina Aguilera – Candy man" (http://www.riaa.com/goldandplatinumdata.php?artist="Candy+
man"). Recording Industry Association of America. . *If necessary, click* Advanced, *then click* Format, *then select* Single, *then click* SEARCH

[54] Australian Recording Industry Association (2007). "ARIA charts — End of year charts" (http://www.aria.com.au/pages/
aria-charts-end-of-year-charts-top-100-singles-2007.htm). aria.com.au. . Retrieved 2009-01-10.

[55] Steffen Hung (2007-12-21). "Jahreshitparade 2007" (http://austriancharts.at/2007_single.asp). austriancharts.at. . Retrieved 2012-01-10.

[56] (http://www.mtv.de/charts/Single_Jahrescharts_2007)

[57] Record Industry Association of New Zealand (2007). "Annual Top 50 Singles Chart 2007" (http://www.rianz.org.nz/rianz/chart_annual.
asp). RIANZ. . Retrieved 2009-01-10.

[58] Steffen Hung. "Dutch charts portal" (http://dutchcharts.nl/jaaroverzichten.asp?year=2007&cat=s). dutchcharts.nl. . Retrieved
2012-01-10.

[59] Steffen Hung. "Schweizer Jahreshitparade 2007" (http://hitparade.ch/year.asp?key=2007). hitparade.ch. . Retrieved 2012-01-10.

[60] http://www.ukchartsplus.co.uk/ChartsPlusYE2007.pdf

[61] http://www.fmqb.com/Article.asp?id=69239#2007

[62] http://www.amazon.de/Candyman-Premium-Christina-Aguilera/dp/B000NQDDPU/ref=sr_1_3?s=music&ie=UTF8&
qid=1339902654&sr=1-3

[63] http://www.getmusic.com.au/christinaaguilera/store/detail?id=78646

External links

- Full lyrics of this song (http://www.metrolyrics.com/candyman-lyrics-christina-aguilera.html) at MetroLyrics

Capitol Records

Capitol Records	
Parent company	Universal Music Group
Founded	Los Angeles, 1942
Founder	Johnny Mercer Buddy DeSylva Glenn Wallichs
Distributor(s)	Capitol Music Group
Genre	Various
Country of origin	United States
Location	Capitol Records Building Los Angeles, California
Official Website	CapitolRecords.com [1]

Capitol Records is a major American record label which is part of Capitol Music Group. It is a wholly owned subsidiary of Universal Music Group. Founded by a group of industry insiders, the label found immediate success upon formation. Unlike most of the independent labels started in the 1940s, Capitol found financial stability and continued chart success, and over the years has recorded and released important material by such artists as Nat King Cole, Frank Sinatra, The Beach Boys, The Kingston Trio, The Beatles, Exodus, and Megadeth among many others. Eventually acquired by EMI, the label has continued as an American powerhouse. Capitol has released records in pop, rock, classical, jazz, rap, and most other music genres. Its headquarters building has become an internationally recognized landmark.

History

1940s

The Capitol Records Company was founded by songwriter Johnny Mercer in 1942, with the financial help of fellow songwriter and film producer Buddy DeSylva and the business acumen of Glenn Wallichs (1910–1971), owner of Music City, at the time the biggest record store in Los Angeles.

Johnny Mercer first suggested the idea of starting a record company while he was golfing with Harold Arlen and Bobby Sherwood. He told them, "I've got this idea of starting a record company. I get so tired of listening to the way everyone treats music. I keep feeling they're selling out. And I don't like the way artists are treated either. Bing Crosby isn't the only one who can make records. I don't know, I think it would be fun." By 1941, Mercer was not only an experienced songwriter, but a singer with a number of records to his name. Mercer next suggested starting a record company to his friend Glenn Wallichs while Mercer was visiting Wallichs' record store. Wallichs responded, "Fine, you run the record company and find the artists,' and Mercer added, "and you run the business."

On February 2, 1942, they met with Buddy DeSylva at a Hollywood restaurant to ask if Paramount Pictures would invest in the new record company. On the Paramount deal DeSylva said no, but that he himself would, and he gave them a check for $15,000. On March 27 the three men got a statement notarized that they have applied to incorporate "Liberty Records" (later the name of a label which Capitol eventually acquired). In May they amended the application to change the name to Capitol Records. (citations for Feb. 2 to July 25, 1942, see individual day dates at #[2]

On April 6, 1942, Johnny Mercer supervised Capitol's first recording session, recording Martha Tilton singing 'Moon Dreams". On May 5, Bobby Sherwood and his orchestra recorded two tracks. On May 21, Freddie Slack and his orchestra recorded three tracks, one with just the orchestra, one with Ella Mae Morse – "Cow-Cow Boogie', and one with Mercer – "Air-Minded Executive".

On June 4, Capitol Records opened its first office in a second-floor room south of Sunset Boulevard. On the same day, Wallichs presented the first free record to a Los Angeles disc jockey named Peter Potter. Potter was so pleased Wallichs decided to give free records to other DJs, becoming the first in the business to do so.

On June 5, Paul Whiteman and his Orchestra recorded four sides for Capitol. On June 12, the orchestra recorded five more songs, including one side with Billie Holiday. On June 11, Tex Ritter recorded "(I Got Spurs That) Jingle Jangle Jingle" and "Goodbye My Little Cherokee" at his first Capitol recording session. They would become record #110.

On July 1, Capitol Records released its first nine records:

- 101 – "I Found a New Baby"/"The General Jumped at Dawn" – Paul Whiteman and His Orchestra
- 102 – "Cow-Cow Boogie" with Ella Mae Morse and Freddy Slack and His Orchestra/ "Here You Are" – Freddy Slack and His Orchestra
- 103 – "Strip Polka"/"Air-Minded Executive" – both with vocals by Johnny Mercer
- 104 – "Johnny Doughboy Found A Rose In Ireland"/ "Phil, The Fluters Ball" – both with vocals by Dennis Day
- 105 – "The Angels Cried" – vocal Martha Tilton and The Mellowaires/I'll Remember April" – vocal Martha Tilton with Gordon Jenkins and his Orchestra
- 106 – "He Wears A Pair Of Silver Wings" – vocal Connie Haines/"I'm Always Chasing Rainbows" – Gordon Jenkins and his Orchestra
- 107 – "Elk's Parade"/"I Don't Know Why" – Bobby Sherwood and his Orchestra
- 108 – "Serenade In Blue" – Martha Tilton with Paul Whiteman and his Orchestra/"(I've Got a Gal In) Kalamazoo" – The Mellowaires with Paul Whiteman and his Orchestra
- 109 – "Windmill Under The Stars"/"Conchita Lopez" – Johnnie Johnston

By July 25, "Cow Cow Boogie" had gone to #1 on the hit parade. (see dates at #[2]

The earliest recording artists included co-owner Johnny Mercer, Margaret Whiting, Jo Stafford, Paul Whiteman, Martha Tilton, Ella Mae Morse, the Pied Pipers, and Paul Weston and His Orchestra. Capitol's first gold single was Morse's "Cow Cow Boogie" in 1942. Capitol's first record album was *Capitol Presents Songs By Johnny Mercer*, a three 78-rpm record set with recordings by Mercer, Stafford, and the Pied Pipers, all with Paul Weston's Orchestra.

The label's other 1940s artists included Les Baxter, Les Paul, Peggy Lee, Stan Kenton, Les Brown, western swing artists Tex Williams, Merle Travis and Wesley Tuttle, Benny Goodman and Nat King Cole.

Capitol was the first major West Coast label, competing with RCA-Victor, Columbia and Decca, all based in New York. In addition to its Los Angeles recording studio Capitol had a second studio in New York City, and on occasion sent mobile recording equipment to New Orleans, Louisiana and other cities (Nordskog, Sunset and Aamor preceded Capitol on the West Coast).

By 1946, Capitol had sold 42 million records and was established as one of the Big Six record labels. It was also that year that writer-producer Alan W. Livingston created Bozo the Clown for their new children's record library. Some notable music appreciation albums for children by Capitol during that era included *Sparky's Magic Piano* and *Rusty in Orchestraville*.

Capitol also developed a noted jazz line, including the Capitol Jazz Men, and issued the Miles Davis-led sessions called "Birth of the Cool".

Capitol released a few classical albums in the 1940s, some featuring a heavily embossed, leather-like cover. These appeared initially in the 78-rpm format, then on some of Capitol's early LPs (33-1/3 rpm) which first appeared in 1949. Among the recordings was a unique performance of the Brazilian composer Heitor Villa-Lobos' *Choros No.*

10 with a Los Angeles choral group and the Janssen Symphony Orchestra (1940–1952) conducted by Werner Janssen, *Symphony No. 3* by Russian composer Reinhold Moritzovich Glière, and César Franck's *Symphony in D minor* with Willem Mengelberg and the Concertgebouw Orchestra.

In 1949, the Canadian branch was established and Capitol purchased the KHJ Studios on Melrose Avenue next to the Paramount Pictures lot in Hollywood. By the mid-1950s, Capitol had become a huge company, concentrating on popular music.

1950s

The 1950s roster now included Nat King Cole, Frank Sinatra, Stan Kenton, June Christy, Judy Garland, The Andrews Sisters, Jackie Gleason, Jane Froman, Wesley Tuttle, Ray Anthony, Andy Griffith, Shirley Bassey, Merle Travis, The Kingston Trio (who in 1960 would account for 20% of all record sales for Capitol), Dean Martin, The Four Freshmen, Al Martino, Dinah Shore and Nancy Wilson (actually signed in 1960 to Capitol). There were also some notable comedy recordings, including several by Stan Freberg and the Yiddish-dialect parodies of Mickey Katz. The label also began recording rock and roll acts such as The Jodimars and Gene Vincent.

Many children became familiar with Capitol Records through the release of a number of Bozo the Clown albums, which featured 78-rpm discs and full color booklets which the children could follow as they listened to the recorded stories. Although there were a series of Bozo the Clowns on various television stations, Capitol used the voice of Pinto Colvig, who was also the voice for Walt Disney's cartoon character Goofy.

In 1952, *Billboard* magazine presented a multi-page chronicle of the label's first decade—an important source for its early history.[3]

In 1955, the British record company EMI acquired 96% of Capitol Records stock for $8.5 million. Soon afterward, EMI built a new studio at Hollywood and Vine to match its state-of-the-art Abbey Road Studios in London – see the Capitol Tower below. EMI's classical Angel Records label was merged into Capitol in 1957. Some classical recordings were issued in high fidelity and even stereophonic sound on the Capitol label by William Steinberg and the Pittsburgh Symphony Orchestra, Leopold Stokowski with various orchestras (including the Los Angeles Philharmonic Orchestra), and Sir Thomas Beecham and the Royal Philharmonic Orchestra, as well as light classical albums by Carmen Dragon and the Hollywood Bowl Orchestra and a series of albums of film music conducted by leading Hollywood composers such as Alfred Newman. Eventually, most of the classical recordings were re-released exclusively on the Angel and Seraphim labels in the U.S. EMI reissued many of the historic Capitol classical recordings on CD.

In 1959, with the advent of stereo, Capitol changed its LP label design from a large "dome logo" with a gray background, to a smaller "dome logo" in a silver oval with a black background and a colorband around the edge. At first, the oval was on the left side of the label, with a tapering vertical line extending from the top and bottom. Classical labels replaced the vertical line with the words "INCOMPARABLE HIGH-FIDELITY" and added the round "FDS-Full Dimensional Sound" shield. In the early 1960s, the oval was moved to the top of the label, and the colorband was slightly narrower. This design is familiar to Beatles fans.

During the 1950s Capitol Records also introduced its series of "Hi-Q" production music LP's and tapes. Some television and film productions that made use of this extensive library included *Gumby*, *Davey and Goliath*, *The Donna Reed Show*, *The Adventures of Ozzie and Harriet*, and the earliest Hanna-Barbera cartoons.

Capitol released a number of soundtrack recordings in the 1950s, including the film versions of three Rodgers and Hammerstein musicals *Oklahoma!*, *Carousel*, and *The King and I*, as well as excerpts from Dimitri Tiomkin's music from Warner Bros.' *Giant*. All of these were later reissued on CD.

1960s

One of the first groups to get a recording contract with Capitol Records in the early 1960s was The Beach Boys. They started in early 1962 and continued on with Capitol for many years after. As the British music scene was heating up in 1963, Capitol, being an EMI label had first rights of refusal on all EMI artists. After initial resistance to issuing records by The Beatles who were signed to sister EMI label Parlophone, Capitol exercised its option in November 1963, and helped usher in Beatlemania in 1964. (The Beatles' earliest US issues had been on the independent Vee-Jay label and the key "She Loves You" single on the small Swan label.) Capitol's producers significantly altered the content of the Beatles albums (see "Record Altering", below) and, believing the Beatles' recordings were sonically unsuited to the US market, not only added equalization to brighten the sound, but also piped the recordings through the famous Capitol echo chamber, located underneath the parking lots outside the Capitol Tower.

45rpm Beatles single on Capitol

As part of this "first rights of refusal", Capitol passed on such EMI acts as Dave Clark Five, Gerry & The Pacemakers, The Hollies, and Manfred Mann (among others), all of which had their records issued on Canadian Capitol.

As Rock music's influence continued to grow in America, Capitol Records hired Artie Kornfeld, who later went on to co-create and produce the Woodstock Festival, as the vice president of Capitol Records in his early 1920s, making him the youngest to hold the position and the first vice president of rock and roll ever. As Rock music's influence continued to grow in America, Capitol Records hired Artie Kornfeld, who later went on to co-create and produce the Woodstock Festival, as the vice president of Capitol Records in his early 20s, making him the youngest to hold the position and the first vice president of rock and roll ever. Capitol also signed or became American distributors of albums by The Lettermen, Badfinger, The Band, Grand Funk Railroad, If, Bobby Darin, Sandler and Young, Glen Campbell, Cathie Taylor, Steve Miller Band, People, Pink Floyd, Linda Ronstadt, The Human Beinz, Peter Tosh, and various solo albums by members of the Beatles.

The classic "swirl" 45 RPM label design, pictured to the right, first appeared in January 1962. Originally yellow and orange, it had become yellow and red by the mid-1960s. It was brought back briefly 1979 to 1981 for use on 45s by the group The Knack. Before 1968, it also appeared on "Starline" label for reissues, albeit with light and dark green swirls replacing yellow and orange (or red) ones. (Several CD reissues, including an early-1990s version of the Beach Boys' "Pet Sounds," used the "swirl" label.)

In 1968, EMI increased its stake in Capitol Records to 98%; However that same year, Capitol merged with Audio Devices, Inc. A manufacturer of computer tape and recording to form a new holding company called **Capitol Industries, Inc.**, reducing EMI's stake of the company to 68%.

In the summer of 1969, Capitol decided to modernize its logo and replaced its "dome logo" with a "C" logo incorporating a 45 rpm record design. The new logo would be on a light-green label on albums and a red & orange concentric-circle label on 45's. These became known as the "target" label. The target label for LP's had a red background for most albums released during or after May 1971 until November 1972, when both albums and 45's would have an orange label with the word "Capitol" printed at the bottom. (In 1971, Grand Funk Railroad became the first Capitol act to be given custom label designs for all its releases, beginning with the "E Pluribus Funk" album.) Budget albums had the same logos but with a yellow backdrop. (The "dome logo" did not disappear entirely: on many labels of this era it can be seen in the small print at the edge.) In 1978, the "dome" design was brought back, with purple backgrounds for rock and pop releases, and red backgrounds for soul and disco. Budget albums had the same logo but a blue or green label. Between 1964 and 1970, Tower Records was a subsidiary label. Other short-lived subsidiary labels included Uptown, Crazy Horse and Sidewalk.

1970s

In 1972, company changed its name to **Capitol Industries-EMI, Inc.** after EMI increased its holdings to 70.84%. By 1976, EMI purchased the remaining shares of the company. Throughout the seventies, Capitol launched two alternative labels: EMI America Records and EMI Manhattan Records. New artists included Helen Reddy, Anne Murray, Skylark (Canadian band), April Wine, Blondie, Burning Spear, Buzzcocks, David Bowie, Kim Carnes, Rosanne Cash, Max Webster, Natalie Cole, The Goose Creek Symphony, Sammy Hagar, John Hiatt, The Knack, Maze, Raspberries, Minnie Riperton, Diana Ross, Bob Seger, Sweet, The Specials, The Sylvers, Ten Wheel Drive, The Stranglers, Tavares, George Thorogood, Wings and The Persuasions. In 1977, EMI merged with THORN Electrical Industries to form Thorn EMI PLC. In 1979, Capitol was merged into the newly formed EMI Music Worldwide division.

1980s

Capitol added artists in a variety of genres during the 1980s: popular music groups and singers like Richard Marx, The Motels, Tina Turner, George Clinton, Crowded House, Peter Blakeley, Duran Duran (and spinoffs Arcadia and Power Station), Heart, Glass Tiger, Katrina & The Waves, Grace Jones, Lloyd Cole, Pet Shop Boys, Queen, Roxette, Brian Setzer, The Smithereens, Spandau Ballet, and Paul Westerberg; Punk/hard Rock groups such as Butthole Surfers, Concrete Blonde, Billy Idol, and the Red Hot Chili Peppers; thrash metal bands like Megadeth, Exodus and Rigor Mortis, heavy metal bands like Helix, W.A.S.P., Poison, Iron Maiden and Queensrÿche; rap groups like the Beastie Boys, King Tee, Mantronix; individuals like Mellow Man Ace, Robbie Robertson, Smooth Jazz artist Dave Koz, and Soul singer Freddie Jackson; and duo's like BeBe & CeCe Winans, and even a selective industrial/electronic artists such as Skinny Puppy. In 1983, the Beatles-era "colorband" label design was brought back, with white print, for both albums and 45's. The last label Capitol used on records was a return to the old purple design with the "dome logo"; after that, compact discs became the dominant format for recorded music. Since the advent of CD's, labels on the discs have varied greatly.

1990s

Nineties acts include Selena, Los Tucanes de Tijuana, Blind Melon, Garth Brooks, Meredith Brooks, Coldplay, The Dandy Warhols, Dilated Peoples, Doves, Everclear, Foo Fighters, Geri Halliwell, Ice Cube, Idlewild, Jane's Addiction, The Jesus Lizard, Jimmy Eat World, Ras Kass, Kottonmouth Kings, Ben Lee, Less Than Jake, Luscious Jackson, Tara MacLean, Marcy Playground, Mazzy Star, MC Eiht, MC Hammer, MC Ren, The Moffatts, Moist, Liz Phair, Lisa Marie Presley, Radiohead, Bonnie Raitt, Snoop Dogg, Spearhead, Starsailor, STIR, Supergrass, Télépopmusik, Television, Richard Thompson, Butthole Surfers and Robbie Williams. The Ultra-Lounge series of compilation CDs appeared in 1996.

2000s

In 2001, EMI merged the Capitol Records label with the Priority Records label. Capitol lost the deal to Viacom and it was no longer a subsidiary. The combined label manages rap artists including Cee-Lo, Ice Cube, Snoop Dogg, and C-Murder, Lil Romeo, and Lil Zane. Other first decade of the 21st century artists include Katy Perry (whose album, Teenage Dream is the most successful among others as it produced 7 #1 singles), J. Holiday, Jiggolo, LeToya (who had the first #1 album for the label since MC Hammer's 1990 *Please Hammer Don't Hurt Em*), Zay, Red Cafe, Aslyn, Melissa Auf der Maur, Big Moe, Borialis, Chingy, The Decemberists, Dexter Freebish, From First to Last, The F-Ups, Faith Evans, Faultline, Fischerspooner, Interpol, Jonny Greenwood, Kudai, Ed Harcourt, Houston, Van Hunt, Javier, Mae, Matthew Jay, Methrone, Kylie Minogue, Dave Navarro, OK Go, Lisa Marie Presley, Relient K,

Anahí, Belinda Peregrin, Roscoe, RBD, Saosin, Squad Five-O, Otep, The Star Spangles, Steriogram, Supervision, Skye Sweetnam, The Vines, Yellowcard, Young Bleed, Young Life, Don Yute, Cherish, Shout Out Louds, Hurt, Corinne Bailey Rae, The Magic Numbers, Hedley, End of Fashion, Mims, Keith Urban and Morningwood.

In 2001, Robbie Williams released his smash jazz cover album *Swing When You're Winning* on the Capitol label (rather than his native Chrysalis Records) in tribute to his hero Frank Sinatra.

In 2006, the label signed a deal to distribute Fat Joe and his Terror Squad Entertainment. Around the same time, Capitol was able to sign New York phenom Mims. In this deal they also agreed to distribute his American King Music label. Around this time they were also able to add J. Holiday, the main artist for Music Line Group to the label as they have all become frequent collaborators. Now it seems that Capitol has gained ground on some of the more popular labels such as Def Jam, and Interscope Records with these signings. In 2007, they were able to strike up a distribution deal with The Game's The Black Wall Street Records and have signed former Bad Boy Records star Faith Evans. Jermaine Dupri and his So So Def Recordings label were briefly signed on to the label as a result of the Virgin Records merger. Dupri was the head of urban music for the label.

In February 2007, EMI announced the merger of Virgin Records and Capitol Records into the Capitol Music Group, and as part of this restructuring, hundreds of staff from multiple divisions were laid off and many artists were cut from the roster. In September 2006, EMI announced that it had sold the tower and adjacent properties for $50 million to New York-based developer Argent Ventures. Capitol continues to use the building as its West Coast office.

Capitol Records has proceeded to sue Vimeo an online Video sharing website for audio copyright infringement. Capitol filed the claim after users were visibly lip-synching to some of their tracks. The full court filing is available here: http://newteevee.com/2009/12/15/vimeo-sued-over-lip-dubs

2010s

EMI's recorded music operations were sold in 2012 to Universal Music Group which reorganized the Capitol Music Group with world headquarters in the Capitol Tower. Steve Barnett was hired away from Columbia Records to run the division.[4]

Broadway and Films

Capitol Records also released some of the most notable original cast albums and motion picture soundtrack albums ever made. Between 1955 and 1956, they released the soundtrack albums of three now-classic Rodgers and Hammerstein films, *Oklahoma!*, *Carousel*, and *The King and I*. All three films were respectively based on the Rodgers and Hammerstein smash hit stage musicals of the same name. The mono versions of the albums were all released the same year that the films were released. But the films had been made in then state-of-the-art stereophonic sound, and so, Capitol was able to release stereo albums of the three respective soundtracks after stereo LP's became a reality. However, the mono and stereo versions did *not* contain always identical material. Because stereo grooves took up more space at the time than mono grooves, the stereo versions of the soundtracks were always somewhat shorter than the mono ones. This was not much of a problem with *Oklahoma!*, because the album itself as then printed was relatively short, so all that was missing from the stereo version was a few seconds of the overture. With *Carousel*, however, half of the *Carousel Waltz* had to be lopped off for the stereo LP, and with *The King and I*, the instrumental bridge from the song *Getting to Know You* was completely removed from the stereo version of the album. These soundtrack albums (especially *Oklahoma!*) were bestsellers for Capitol for many years, until, in the 1990s, the rights to them were bought by Angel Records. Angel Records not only restored the portions which had been omitted from the stereo LPs and original CD issues, but, in 2001, issued new expanded editions which included all music which had been omitted from every previous edition of these soundtracks, bringing the playing time of each to well over an hour. All three albums continue to be best sellers to this day.

In 1957, Capitol Records issued the original cast album of *The Music Man*, starring Robert Preston, an album which became one of the biggest cast album sellers of all time, even after the highly successful film version of the show was released in 1962. Capitol was also responsible for the original cast and film soundtrack albums of Cole Porter's *Can-Can* and the original cast album of Stephen Sondheim's *A Funny Thing Happened on the Way to the Forum*. In 1962, Capitol issued a studio cast recording of the songs from Lionel Bart's *Oliver!*, in anticipation of its U.S. tour prior to its opening on Broadway.

In 1966, Capitol released the soundtrack album of the documentary tribute, *John F. Kennedy: Years of Lightning, Day of Drums*, a film made by the United States Information Agency, and originally not intended for general viewing. However, the quality of the film was considered so high that the public was eventually allowed to see it. The film featured the voice of Gregory Peck as narrator, with narration written and music composed by Bruce Herschensohn. The album was virtually a condensed version of the film – it included the narration as well as the music.

One spoken word album which was immensely successful for Capitol was that of the soundtrack of Franco Zeffirelli's smash film *Romeo and Juliet*, based on Shakespeare's play. The film became the highest grossing Shakespeare film for years, and the album was also a tremendous hit. It featured not only Nino Rota's score, but large chunks of Shakespeare's dialog. The success of this album in that pre-VHS era spurred Capitol to issue two other *Romeo and Juliet* albums – one a three-disk album containing the entire soundtrack of the film (dialog and music), and another album containing only Nino Rota's score.

However, as Capitol was to be later accused of doing with Beatles albums, there was some tampering with the *Years of Lightning* and *Romeo and Juliet* albums. Extra music was added to some scenes which, in the actual film, contained little or no music, such as the duel between Romeo and Tybalt. Presumably this was done to show off the score – and at the end of both the abridged and complete versions of the *Romeo* albums, the end credits music was omitted, especially unfortunate since virtually all of the film's credits were saved for the end of the picture.

Capitol tried to strike gold again with another spoken word album, one made from the 1970 film *Cromwell*, starring Richard Harris and Alec Guinness, but in this case, both film and album were not successful.

The influence of the *Romeo and Juliet* album spread to other record companies for a brief while. Columbia Records issued an album of dialog and music excerpts from the successful 1970 Dustin Hoffman film, *Little Big Man*, and 20th Century Fox Records included George C. Scott's opening and closing speeches, as well as Jerry Goldsmith's score, in their soundtrack album made from the film *Patton*.

Record altering

Capitol has been criticised many times for the heavy modification of albums being released in other countries before being released in the USA by Capitol. Possibly most infamous is the company's creation of "new" albums by The Beatles. This began with Capitol's release of *Meet the Beatles!*, the first album by the group to be released by Capitol in the USA. It was quite literally the British album *With the Beatles*, with five tracks ("Money", "You've Really Got A Hold On Me", "Devil In Her Heart", "Please Mister Postman", and "Roll Over Beethoven") removed in favor of both sides of the band's first American hit single, which consisted of "I Want To Hold Your Hand" and "I Saw Her Standing There." They also added on the British version of the single's B-Side, "This Boy." Also notable is the issuing of "duophonic" stereo releases of some recordings where the original master was monophonic. Capitol engineers split the single master monaural track into two, boosted the bass on the right channel, boosted treble on the left channel and add a split-second delay between channels to produce a "fake stereo" release. This Duophonic process meant that the Beatles' American fans would often hear a slightly different song from that heard by the rest of the world.[5]

When *With the Beatles* was initially released in Brazil by EMI-Odeon, as well as in Canada, the title was at first modified to *Beatlemania*.

This trend continued through the Beatles' American discography, until the albums had little relation to their original British counterparts. The Beatles' albums were finally released unmodified starting with *Sgt. Pepper's Lonely Hearts Club Band*. This was thanks to a renegotiation of the Beatles' complicated management and recording contracts. Tired of the way Capitol in the US and other companies around the world were issuing their work in almost unrecognizable pieces, beginning in 1967, they had full approval of all album titles and cover art, track listing and running order, worldwide. Their first order of business was to stop the issuing of 45 RPM singles featuring tracks taken from their albums. Instead they would issue non-album tracks as singles in between album releases. This policy changed in late 1969 when a severe cash crunch hit the Beatles company, Apple Corps., and the band was forced (at the urgent behest of new manager Allen B. Klein) to issue a single immediately in conjunction with the *Abbey Road* album ("Something"/"Come Together") in order to pay bills. Four months later Apple allowed Capitol Records to issue the singles compilation *Hey Jude* (aka *The Beatles Again*) to keep cash flowing to the company.

This continued with other bands:

- Pink Floyd's first album, *The Piper at the Gates of Dawn* (on the Tower label), had several tracks removed in favor of their first hit single "See Emily Play". This was criticized because the removed tracks combined ("Flaming", "Bike", and "Astronomy Domine") were much longer than "Emily", making the removal of the three completely unnecessary for reasons of running time.

- Iron Maiden's first two albums, *Iron Maiden* and *Killers*, had additional tracks as opposed to their UK counterparts. Iron Maiden's 1980 self-titled debut was released in the US a few months after its UK release with the track "Sanctuary" added on. Its follow-up, 1981's *Killers*, was also released a few months after later in the US after its initial UK release with the track "Twilight Zone" added to the album.

- Megadeth's "Risk" album was littered with samples and guitar pieces which Dave Mustaine never authorized, causing him to release one final album on Capitol, *Capitol Punishment*, and then move on to a new label Sanctuary Records. As of right now, Megadeth's future with Capitol seems very bright, as they have released all their Remastered discs and their most recent Greatest Hits albums with Capitol. After leaving Sanctuary Records, it was rumoured that Megadeth would return to Capitol, but the rumor turned out to be untrue as Megadeth have recently signed with Roadrunner Records.

The company has also had a history of making mistakes with album releases; the American release of Klaatu's debut album *3:47 EST* had several spelling errors on the track list, and later Capitol pressings of CD versions of Klaatu's albums suffered severe quality problems. The poor sound quality of Duran Duran's May 1982 release *Rio* (on Capitol subsidiary Harvest), contributed to the lag in initial sales, until a remixed version of the album was released in November.

The Capitol Records Building

The Capitol Records Tower is one of the most distinctive landmarks in Hollywood. The 13-story earthquake-resistant tower, designed by Welton Becket, was the world's first circular office building, and is home to several recording studios. Although not originally specifically designed as such,[6] the wide curved awnings over windows on each story and the tall spike emerging from the top of the building combine to give it the appearance of a stack of vinyl 45s on a turntable.

The construction of the building was ordered by British company EMI soon after its 1955 acquisition of Capitol Records, and was completed in April 1956. The building is located just north of the intersection of Hollywood and Vine and is the center of the consolidated West Coast operations of Capitol Records – and was nicknamed "The House That Nat Built" to recognize the enormous financial contributions of Capitol star Nat "King" Cole. The rectangular ground floor is a separate structure, joined to the tower after it was completed.

In mid-2008, a controversy erupted over a plan to build a condominium complex next door, igniting fears that the building's legendary acoustic properties (specifically its renowned underground echo chambers) would be compromised.

The Capitol Records Tower in Hollywood, with mural by **Richard Wyatt** titled *Hollywood Jazz* featuring prominent jazz artists Charlie Parker, Miles Davis, Ella Fitzgerald, Nat King Cole, Billie Holiday and Duke Ellington.

The blinking light atop the tower spells out the phrase "Hollywood" in Morse code, and has done so since the building's opening in 1956. This was an idea of Capitol's then president, Alan Livingston, who wanted to subtly advertise Capitol's status as the first record label with a base on the west coast. The switch activating the light was thrown by Leila Morse, Samuel Morse's granddaughter.[6] In 1992 it was changed to read "Capitol 50" in honor of the label's fiftieth anniversary. It has since returned to spelling "Hollywood".

In the 1974 disaster blockbuster film *Earthquake*, the tower was shown collapsing during a massive tremor. Thirty years later, in an homage to *Earthquake*, the tower was again depicted as being destroyed, this time by a massive tornado, in *The Day After Tomorrow*.

In September 2006, owner EMI announced that it had sold the tower and adjacent properties for $50 million to New York-based developer Argent Ventures.[7]

It was announced in November 2012 that Steve Barnett would become Chairman & CEO of Capitol Music Group and would be based at the Capitol Records Building.[8]

Recently, Capitol Records and artist **Richard Wyatt** joined forces to restore his iconic Hollywood Jazz Mural on the south wall of the Capitol Records building.[9] Restored in hand-glazed ceramic tile, the mural is 26ft. by 88ft.[10] Entitled "Hollywood Jazz: 1945-1972", this masterpiece entails "larger than life" images of: Chet Baker, Gerry Mulligan, Charlie Parker, Tito Puente, Miles Davis, Ella Fitzgerald, Nat King Cole, Shelly Manne, Dizzy Gillespie, Billie Holiday and Duke Ellington. The mural also depicts a stone background upon which names of prominent jazz legends are etched in stone, such as John Coltrane, Sarah Vaughn, Charles Mingus, Buddy Collette, Teddy Edwards, McCoy Tyner, and others.

Artist Richard Wyatt standing in front of jazz mural, 2013

Capitol Studios

Capitol's recording studios were designed by guitarist and sound expert Les Paul to minimize noise and vibration, a newly important goal in the high-fidelity sound era.

The studios feature 10-inch-thick (250 mm) concrete exterior walls, surrounding a one-inch air gap, surrounding an inner wall that floats on layers of rubber and cork – all in an effort to provide complete sound isolation.[11]

The facility also features echo chambers: subterranean concrete bunkers allowing engineers to add real physical reverberation during the recording process. The eight chambers are located 30 feet underground, and are trapezoidal-shaped with 10-inch concrete walls and 12-inch-thick (300 mm) concrete ceilings. The chambers feature speakers on one side and microphones on the other, permitting an echo effect lasting up to five seconds.

Studios A and B can be combined for the recording of orchestral music and symphonic film soundtracks. The first album recorded in the tower was *Frank Sinatra Conducts Tone Poems of Color.*

International operations

Canada

Capitol Records of Canada was established in 1949 by independent businessman W. Lockwood Miller. Capitol Records broke with Miller's company and formed Capitol Record Distributors of Canada Limited in 1954. EMI acquired this company when it acquired Capitol Records. The company was renamed back to Capitol Records of Canada Ltd in 1958 after Miller's rights to the name expired. In 1959, Capitol of Canada picked up distribution rights for sister EMI labels Angel Records, Pathe Records, Odeon Records and Parlophone Records.[12] In 1957, Paul White joined Capitol of Canada and in 1960 established an A&R department independent of the American company to promote talent for the Canadian market.[13] They include home grown Canadian talent (of which Anne Murray is one of the more famous examples) as well as EMI artists from other countries. Canada-only issues bore 6000 series catalog numbers for LPs and 72000 series catalog numbers for singles. Capitol Canada issues of American Capitol recordings bore the same catalog numbers as their American counterparts. Beginning in 1962, Capitol of Canada issued albums by British artists such as Cliff Richard, Helen Shapiro and Frank Ifield. They said yes to The Beatles from day one, even though the American company turned them down during most of 1963. By 1967, they were also distributing non-EMI labels such as Disneyland Records, Buena Vista Records, 20th Century Fox Records and Pickwick Records.[14] The company was renamed Capitol Records-EMI of Canada in 1974 then adopted its present name, EMI Music Canada, in 1993.[15][16][17]

In 1982, Capitol Records-EMI of Canada developed the "SDR", or *Super Dynamic Range*, process of duplicating their cassette releases, which resulted in higher-quality audio. SDR was later adopted by Capitol's American operations that same year and renamed "XDR" (*eXtended Dynamic Range*). SDR/XDR cassette releases are most noted for the short burst of tones ascending in frequency at the beginning and end of the cassette before and after the program material, the tones being a part of the process.

The current headquarters for EMI Music Canada, which operates the Capitol label, are located in Toronto, Ontario.

The Canadian branch of Capitol won two Juno Awards in 1971, the leading music awards in that country. One Juno was for "Top Record Company" and the other was for "Top Promotional Company".

Latin America

EMI Latin / EMI Televisa Music artists are distributed in The United States under Capitol Latin, a Capitol Records division.

Taiwan

Capitol Music Taiwan was established in 2006. It is home to several artists who are megastars in the Chinese music industry. They include Jolin Tsai (蔡依林), Stefanie Sun (孫燕姿), Zhang Hui Mei (張惠妹), Stanley Huang (黃立行) and Show Luo (羅志祥). Even though artistes are signed on with this label, the albums are still released under EMI Music Taiwan. The label is the label with the highest sales among all labels in Taiwan between 2006 and 2008.

In 2008, EMI Music Taiwan is acquired by Paco Wong's Gold Label Records and reformed as Gold Typhoon Entertainment Limited (金牌大風). The name is in reference to Jolin's *Love Exercise* album released after the acquisition. However the label of "Capitol Music" is not part of Gold Typhoon.

United Kingdom

Beginning in 1948, Capitol Records were released in the UK on the Capitol label by Decca Records. After EMI acquired Capitol, they took over distribution directly in 1956.[18] EMI's Parlophone unit handled Capitol label marketing in the UK in recent years.[19] But in 2012, EMI was sold to Universal Music Group. The European Union forced EMI to spin off assets for antitrust reasons including Parlophone. As a result, Universal Music relaunched Capitol as an autonomous label in the UK[20] which has the rights to The Beatles' recorded music catalogue.[21]

References

[1] http://www.capitolrecords.com/

[2] http://www.popculturefanboy.blogspot.com/

[3] "The Record Decade, 1942-42." *Billboard*, 2 August 1952, 49-82.

[4] Brown, August (November 26, 2012). "Steve Barnett to lead Capitol Music Group" (http://articles.latimes.com/2012/nov/26/entertainment/la-et-ms-steve-barnett-capitol-music-group-20121126). *Los Angeles Times*. .

[5] Capitol Albums Finally Coming Out on CD (http://abbeyrd.best.vwh.net/spizeressay.html)

[6] ""Exploring L.A. with Huell" (Howser) clip" (http://kcet.org/explore-ca/huells/pop.php?ID=CAPITOL+RECORDS&Res=High). . Retrieved January 23, 2007. from an 1988 interview of the then vice president of public relations and communications, Sue Satriano.

[7] Vincent, Roger (September 29, 2006). "Capitol Records Tower to Be Sold" (http://www.latimes.com/news/local/la-fi-capitol29sep29,0,5886755.story?coll=la-home-headlines). *Los Angeles Times*. .

[8] Steve Barnett to lead Capitol Music Group (http://www.latimes.com/entertainment/music/posts/la-et-ms-steve-barnett-capitol-music-group-20121126,0,2641587.story)

[9] "Millineum Hollywood" (http://millenniumhollywood.net/2013/01/30/capitol-records-jazz-mural-restored/). . Retrieved 30 January 2013.

[10] http://www.latimes.com/entertainment/arts/culture/la-et-cm-hollywood-jazz-mural-20130219,0,1467048.story

[11] "Plan to build next to Capitol Records studios sounds just awful to music biz," Los Angeles Times, June 17, 2008 (http://www.latimes.com/entertainment/news/la-me-capitol18-2008jun18,0,2972316.story)

[12] Billboard Jul 6, 1959 (http://books.google.com/books?id=2AoEAAAAMBAJ&pg=PA4&dq=angel+++parlophone+++canada&hl=en&ei=W-EzTM-FNNntnQfYjsGCBA&sa=X&oi=book_result&ct=result&resnum=2&ved=0CC4Q6AEwAQ#v=onepage&q=angel +parlophone +canada&f=false)

[13] Billboard Sep 16, 1967 (http://books.google.com/books?id=XygEAAAAMBAJ&pg=RA1-PA42&dq="capitol+records+(canada)"&hl=en&ei=uKgzTL2AH4HhnAfdoqjPBQ&sa=X&oi=book_result&ct=result&resnum=2&ved=0CDMQ6AEwAQ#v=onepage&q="capitol records (canada)"&f=false)

[14] Billboard Sep 16, 1967 (http://books.google.com/books?id=XygEAAAAMBAJ&pg=PA46&dq="growing+with+canada"+++"capitol+record"&hl=en&ei=sOMzTIq2OMr4nAeHmZ3kAw&sa=X&oi=book_result&ct=result&resnum=1&ved=0CCgQ6AEwAA#v=onepage&q="growing with canada" +"capitol record"&f=false)

[15] Capitol Records – EMI of Canada Limited/Disques Capitol – EMI du Canada Limitée – The Canadian Encyclopedia (http://www.thecanadianencyclopedia.com/index.cfm?PgNm=TCE&Params=U1ARTU0000604)

[16] The Capitol 6000 website – The Corporate History of Capitol Records of Canada (http://www.capitol6000.com/corporate_history.html)

[17] Butcher cover, Canadian – Paul White Letter (http://www.rarebeatles.com/album2/discog/pwhite.htm)

[18] http://45-sleeves.com/UK/capitol/capi-uk.htm

[19] http://books.google.com/books?id=UAgEAAAAMBAJ&pg=PA39&lpg=PA39&dq=%22capitol+records%22+%2B+parlophone+%2B+marketing&source=bl&ots=vd4b-vgw3C&sig=yEeUj4046xTAelNjAj75GQJS8yY&hl=en&sa=X&ei=7EwEUd-iLoaVyAGOhYGIBQ&ved=0CDAQ6AEwADgK#v=onepage&q=%22capitol%20records%22%20%2B%20parlophone%20%2B%20marketing&f=false

[20] http://www.thecmuwebsite.com/article/universal-plans-to-launch-capitol-uk/

[21] http://www.musicweek.com/news/read/steve-barnett-named-chairman-of-universal-s-capitol-records/052695

External links

- Capitol Records (http://www.capitolrecords.com)
- Capitol Records, Inc. v. Naxos of America, Inc. legal case (http://www.musicblob.it/archivio-documenti/capitol-records-inc-v-naxos-of-america-inc/)
- Capitol of Canada official site (http://www.capitolmusic.ca)
- A history of Capitol Records (http://www.popculturefanboy.blogspot.com)
- 3D model of the Capitol Tower for use in Google Earth (http://www.googleearthhacks.com/dlfile16719/capitol-records-hollywood.htm)
- The Judy Garland Online Discography "Capitol Records" pages. (http://www.thejudyroom.com/discography/capitol.html)
- Capitol Records's channel (https://www.youtube.com/user/CapitolRecords) on YouTube
- Capitol Records Myspace page. (http://www.myspace.com/capitolrecords)
- Capitol of Canada 72000 series singles discography (http://www.capitol6000.com/72000.html)
- Capitol of Canada 6000 series LP discography (http://www.capitol6000.com/6000.html)
- Swirl Daze – The 1960s Capitol Singles Discography (http://www.eighthavenue.com/capitol.htm)

Carmen Miranda

Carmen Miranda	
 Miranda in the 1943 film *The Gang's All Here*	
Born	Maria do Carmo Miranda da Cunha 9 February 1909 Marco de Canaveses, Portugal
Died	5 August 1955 (aged 46) Beverly Hills, California, U.S.
Cause of death	Heart attack
Resting place	Cemitério São João Batista
Other names	The Brazilian Bombshell The Chiquita Banana Girl
Education	Convent of Saint Therese of Lisieux
Occupation	Singer, dancer, actress
Years active	1928–1955
Spouse(s)	David Alfred Sebastian (m. 1947 – 1955)

Carmen Miranda, GCIH (Portuguese pronunciation: [ˈkaɾmɛ̃j miˈɾɐ̃dɐ], 9 February 1909 – 5 August 1955) was a Portuguese-born Brazilian[1][2] samba singer, dancer, Broadway actress, and film star who was popular in the 1940s and 1950s.

After establishing a successful singing and acting career in Brazil, Lee Shubert signed Miranda and her band to a contract in 1939. She made her American stage debut in July 1939, and later moved to Hollywood to pursue a film career.[3] Nicknamed "The Brazilian Bombshell",[4] Miranda is noted for her signature fruit hat outfit she wore in the 1943 movie *The Gang's All Here*. By 1945, she was the highest paid woman in the United States.

Miranda made a total of fourteen Hollywood films between 1940 and 1953. Though hailed as a talented performer, her popularity waned by the end of World War II. She later grew to resent the stereotypical "Brazilian Bombshell" image she cultivated and attempted to break free of it with limited success.

On 4 August 1955, Miranda unknowingly suffered a mild heart attack while performing during the taping of an episode of *The Jimmy Durante Show*. She finished the show but died the following morning after suffering a second heart attack.

Early life

Carmen Miranda was born **Maria do Carmo Miranda da Cunha** in Várzea da Ovelha e Aliviada, a village in the northern Portuguese municipality of Marco de Canaveses.[1] She was the second daughter of José Maria Pinto da Cunha (17 February 1887 – 21 June 1938) and Maria Emília Miranda (10 March 1886 – Rio de Janeiro, 9 November 1971).[5] In 1909 when she was ten months old, her father emigrated alone to Brazil[6] and settled in Rio de Janeiro, where he opened a barber shop. Her mother followed in 1910 with their daughters Olinda and Maria do Carmo. Maria do Carmo, later *Carmen*, never returned to Portugal, but retained her Portuguese nationality. In Brazil, her parents had four more children: Amaro (1911), Cecília (1913), Aurora (1915–2005) and Óscar (1916).[5]

She was christened Carmen by her father because of his love for the opera comique, and also after Bizet's masterpiece *Carmen*. This passion for opera influenced his children, and Miranda's love for singing and dancing at an early age.[6] She went to school at the Convent of Saint Therese of Lisieux. Her father did not approve of her plans to enter show business. However, her mother supported her and was beaten when her husband discovered Miranda had auditioned for a radio show. She had previously sung at parties and festivals in Rio. Her older sister Olinda contracted tuberculosis and was sent to Portugal for treatment. Miranda went to work in a tie shop at age 14 to help pay her sister's medical bills. She next worked in a boutique, where she learned to make hats and opened her own hat business which became profitable.

Career

Early years

Miranda was discovered when she was first introduced to composer Josué de Barros, who went on to promote and record her first album with Brunswick, a German recording company in 1929. In 1930, she was known to be Brazil's gem singer, and in 1933 went on to sign a two-year contract with Rádio Mayrink Veiga, becoming the first contract singer in the radio industry history of Brazil. In 1934, she was invited as a guest performer in Radio Belgrano in Buenos Aires.[6] Ultimately, Miranda signed a recording contract with RCA Records. She pursued a career as a samba singer for ten years before she was invited to New York City to perform in a show on Broadway.

Carmen Miranda as Chita Chula performing "Chico Chico" in 1946 *Doll Face*.

As with other popular singers of the era, Miranda made her screen debut in the Brazilian documentary *A Voz Do Carnaval* (1933). Two years later, she appeared in her first feature film entitled *Alô, Alô Brasil*. But it was the 1935 film *Estudantes* that seemed to solidify her in the minds of the movie-going public. In the 1936 movie *Alô Alô Carnaval*, she performed the famous song "Cantoras do Rádio" with her sister Aurora, for the first time.[6]

American stage and films

After seeing one of her performances in Rio, theatre owner Lee Shubert signed Miranda and her band, the Bando da Lua, to a contract. She made her American stage debut on July 16, 1939 in *Streets of Paris*, opposite Abbott and Costello. Although her part was small (she only spoke four words), Miranda received good reviews and became a media sensation.[3][7] Her fame grew quickly, having formally been presented to President Franklin D. Roosevelt at a White House banquet shortly after arrival.[6] She was encouraged by the United States government as part of President Roosevelt's Good Neighbor policy, designed to strengthen links with Latin America and Europe; it was believed that in delivering content like hers, the policy would be better received by the American public.

In 1940, 20th Century Fox signed her to a contract for a one-time appearance in *Down Argentine Way*. She received good reviews for her performance prompting Fox to sign her to a long-term film contract.[8]

Criticism

While Miranda's popularity in the United States continued to rise, she began to lose favor with some Brazilians. On July 10, 1940, she returned to Brazil where she was welcomed by cheering fans. Soon after her arrival, however, the Brazilian press began criticizing Miranda for giving in to American commercialism and projecting a negative image of Brazil. Members of the upper class felt her image was "too black" and she was criticized in one Brazilian newspaper for "singing bad-tasting black sambas". Other Brazilians criticized her for playing up the stereotype of a "Latina bimbo" after her first interview upon arriving in the United States. In an interview with the *New York World-Telegram*, Miranda discussed her then limited knowledge of the English language stating, "I say money, money, money. I say twenty words in English. I say money, money, money and I say hot dog!".[9]

On July 15, she appeared at a charity concert organized by Brazilian First Lady Darci Vargas. The concert was attended by members of Brazil's high society. She greeted the audience in English but was met with silence. When Miranda began singing a song from one of her club acts, "The Souse American Way", the audience began to boo her. She attempted to finish her act but gave up and left the stage after the audience continued to boo. The incident deeply hurt Miranda and she later cried in her dressing room. The following day, the Brazilian pressed criticized her for being "too Americanized".[9]

Weeks later, Miranda responded to the criticism with the Portuguese language song "Disseram que Voltei Americanizada" (or "They Say I've Come Back Americanized"). Another song, "Bananas Is My Business," was based on a line in one of her movies and directly addressed her image. She was greatly upset by the criticism and did not return to Brazil again for fourteen years.

Peak years

Upon returning to the United States, Miranda kept up her film career in Hollywood while also appearing on Broadway and performing in clubs and restaurants. In 1941, she shared the screen with Alice Faye and Don Ameche in *That Night in Rio*. Later that same year, she teamed up with Alice Faye again in *Week-End in Havana*. Miranda was now earning $5,000 a week. On March 23, 1941, she became one of the first Latinas to leave her hand and footprints in the sidewalk of the Grauman's Chinese Theater.[8]

In 1943, she appeared in one of her more notable films *The Gang's All Here*. The following year, Miranda made a cameo appearance in *Four Jills in a Jeep*. By 1945, she had become Hollywood's highest-paid entertainer and top female tax payer in the United States,[6] earning more than $200,000 that year ($2.2 million in 2010 adjusted for inflation).[10]

Decline

After World War II ended in 1945, the American public's tastes began to change and musicals began to fall out of favor. Hollywood studio heads and producers also felt that the novelty of Miranda's "Brazilian bombshell" image had worn thin.[11] As a result, Miranda's career declined. She made one last film for Fox, *Doll Face* (1945), before her contract was terminated in January 1946.[12]

She later signed a contract with Universal but at the time, Universal was undergoing a merger with another studio. Due to a change in management, no films for Miranda were planned. Eager to break away from her well established image, Miranda attempted to branch out with different roles. In 1946, she portrayed an Irish American character in *If I'm Lucky*. The following year, she played dual roles opposite Groucho Marx in *Copacabana* for United Artists. While the films were modest hits, film critics and the American public did not accept Miranda's new image.[12]

Though her film career was faltering, Miranda music career remained solid and she was still a popular attraction at nightclubs.[13] From 1948 to 1950, Miranda teamed with The Andrews Sisters to produce and record three Decca singles. Their first collaboration was on radio in 1945 when Miranda guested on ABC's *The Andrews Sisters Show*. The first single, "Cuanto La Gusta", was the most popular (a best-selling record and a number-twelve *Billboard* hit). "The Wedding Samba" (#23) followed in 1950.[14]

In 1948, she co-starred opposite Wallace Beery and Jane Powell in *A Date with Judy*, and *Nancy Goes to Rio* in 1950 for MGM. She made her final film appearance in the 1953 film *Scared Stiff* with Martin and Lewis for Paramount.[15]

Following the release of *Scared Stiff* in April 1953, she embarked on a four month European tour. After collapsing from exhaustion during a club performance in Ohio in October 1953, dates for her future tour were canceled. On the suggestion of her doctor, Miranda returned to Brazil to rest. Miranda was still hurt over the criticism she received there in 1940, but was happy when she received a warm reception upon her return. She remained in Brazil until April 1955.[8]

Personal life

On 17 March 1947, Miranda married American movie producer David Alfred Sebastian.[16] In 1948 she became pregnant, but suffered a miscarriage. The marriage was reportedly rocky and her family claims that Sebastian was abusive.[17] In September 1949, the couple announced their separation, but they later reconciled.[18]

In her later years, in addition to her already heavy smoking and alcohol consumption, Miranda began taking amphetamines and barbiturates, all of which took a toll on her health.[19]

Death

On 4 August 1955, Miranda was taping a segment for the NBC variety series *The Jimmy Durante Show*. According to Durante, Miranda had complained of feeling unwell before taping. Durante offered to get Miranda a replacement but she declined. After completing a song and dance number, "Jackson, Miranda, and Gomez", with Durante, she fell to one knee. Durante later said of the incident, "...I thought she had slipped. She got up and said she was outa [sic] breath. I tells her I'll take her lines. But she goes ahead with 'em. We finished work about 11 o'clock and she seemed happy."[20]

At around 4 a.m. on 5 August 1955, Miranda suffered a second, fatal heart attack at her home in Beverly Hills.[20] The *Jimmy Duarante Show* episode in which Miranda appeared was aired two months after her death.[21] A clip of the episode was also included in the A&E Network's *Biography* episode about Miranda.

Funeral and burial

In accordance with her wishes, Miranda's body was flown back to Rio de Janeiro where the Brazilian government declared a period of national mourning.[22] 60,000 people attended her mourning ceremony at the Rio town hall,[6] and more than half a million Brazilians escorted the funeral cortège to her resting place.[23]

Miranda is buried in the Cemitério São João Batista in Rio de Janeiro.[24]

For her contribution to the motion picture industry, Carmen Miranda has a star on the Hollywood Walk of Fame at 6262 Hollywood Boulevard.

Image

Carmen Miranda in *The Gang's All Here* (1943)

Miranda's Hollywood image was one of a generic Latinness that blurred the distinctions between Brazil, Portugal, Argentina, and Mexico as well as between samba, tango and habanera. It was carefully stylized and outlandishly flamboyant. She was often shown wearing platform sandals and towering headdresses made of fruit, becoming famous as "the lady in the tutti-frutti hat."[25]

Miranda's enormous, fruit-laden hats are iconic visuals recognized around the world. These costumes led to Saks Fifth Avenue developing a line of turbans and jewelry inspired by Carmen Miranda in 1939. Many costume jewelry designers made fruit jewelry also inspired by Carmen Miranda which is still highly valued and collectible by vintage and antique costume jewelry collectors . Fruit jewelry is still popular in jewelry design today. Much of the fruit jewelry seen today is often still called "Carmen Miranda jewelry" because of this.

Her image was much satirized and taken up as camp, and today, the "Carmen Miranda" persona is popular among drag performers. The style was even emulated in animated cartoon shorts. The animation department at Warner Brothers seemed to be especially fond of the actress's image. Animator Virgil Ross used it in his short *Slick Hare*, featuring Bugs Bunny, who escapes from Elmer Fudd by hiding in the fruit hat. Bugs himself mimics Miranda briefly in *What's Cookin' Doc?* Tex Avery also used it in his MGM short *Magical Maestro* when an opera singer is temporarily changed into the persona, fruit hat and all, via a magician's wand.

Legacy

- On 25 September 1998, a city square in Hollywood was named Carmen Miranda Square in a ceremony headed by longtime honorary mayor of Hollywood, Johnny Grant, who was also one of the singer's personal friends dating back to World War II. Brazil's Consul General Jorió Gama was on hand for opening remarks, as were members of Bando da Lua, Carmen Miranda's original band. Carmen Miranda Square is only one of about a dozen Los Angeles city intersections named for historic performers. The square is located at the intersection of Hollywood Boulevard and Orange Drive across from Grauman's Chinese Theater. The location is especially noteworthy not only since Carmen Miranda's footprints are preserved in concrete at Grauman's Chinese Theatre's, but in remembrance of an impromptu performance at a nearby Hollywood Boulevard intersection on V-J Day where she was joined by a throng of servicemen from the nearby USO.[26]
- A museum dedicated to Carmen Miranda is located in Rio de Janeiro in the Flamengo neighborhood on Avenida Rui Barbosa. The museum includes several original costumes, and shows clips from her filmography. There is

also a museum dedicated to her in Marco de Canaveses, Portugal called "Museu Municipal Carmen Miranda", with various photos and one of the famous hats. Outside the museum there is a statue of Carmen Miranda.

In popular culture

Books and films

- Helena Solberg made a documentary of Miranda's life entitled *Carmen Miranda: Bananas Is My Business*, in 1995.
- Brazilian author Ruy Castro wrote a biography of Carmen Miranda entitled *Carmen*, published in 2005 in Brazil. This book has yet to appear in English.
- In the TV-Show *Modern Family* Cameron disguise her 2 years old daughter Lily as Carmen Miranda for a photoshoot.
- In the movie *Gangster Squad*, released in January 2013, Miranda is portrayed by Yvette Tucker performing in Slapsy Maxie's nightclub.

Music

- Brazilian singer Ney Matogrosso's album *Batuque*, brings the period and several of Miranda's early hits back to life in faithful style. Caetano Veloso paid tribute to Miranda for her early samba recordings made in Rio when he recorded "Disseram que Voltei Americanizada" on the live album *Circuladô Vivo* in 1992. He also examined her legacy of both kitsch and sincere samba artistry in an essay in the *New York Times*. Additionally, on one of Veloso's most popular songs, "Tropicalia", Veloso sings "Viva a banda da da da....Carmen Miranda da da da" as the final lyrics of the song.
- Singer/songwriter Jimmy Buffett included a tribute to Carmen Miranda on his 1973 album *A White Sport Coat and a Pink Crustacean*, entitled "They Don't Dance Like Carmen No More."
- In the early 1970s a novelty act known as Daddy Dewdrop had a top 10 hit single in the US titled "Chick-A-Boom," one of Miranda's trademark song phrases, although the resemblance ended there.
- Pink Martini recorded "Tempo perdido" for their 2007 album *Hey Eugene!*.
- Singer Leslie Fish wrote a song called "Carmen Miranda's Ghost Is Haunting Space Station Three", in which a space station is inundated with fresh fruit. A science fiction anthology later had the same title.
- John Cale, a member of the Velvet Underground, issued a song called "The Soul of Carmen Miranda" on his album *Words for the Dying*.

Filmography

Year	Title	Role	Notes
1933	*A Voz do Carnaval*	Herself at Rádio Mayrink Veiga	
1935	*Alô, Alô, Brasil*		
1935	*Estudantes*	Mimi	
1936	*Alô Alô Carnaval*		
1939	*Banana-da-Terra*		
1940	*Laranja-da-China*		
1940	*Down Argentine Way*	Herself	
1941	*That Night in Rio*	Carmen	
1941	*Week-End in Havana*	Rosita Rivas	

1941	*Meet the Stars #5: Hollywood Meets the Navy*	Herself	Short subject
1942	*Springtime in the Rockies*	Rosita Murphy	
1943	*The Gang's All Here*	Dorita	Alternative title: *The Girls He Left Behind*
1944	*Greenwich Village*	Princess Querida	
1944	*Something for the Boys*	Chiquita Hart	
1944	*Four Jills in a Jeep*	Herself	
1945	*The All-Star Bond Rally*	Herself (Pinup girl)	
1945	*Doll Face*	Chita Chula	Alternative title: *Come Back to Me*
1946	*If I'm Lucky*	Michelle O'Toole	
1947	*Copacabana*	Carmen Novarro/Mademoiselle Fifi	
1947	"Slick Hare"	Herself	Voice
1948	*A Date with Judy*	Rosita Cochellas	
1949	*The Ed Wynn Show*	Herself	Episode #1.2
1949 to 1952	*Texaco Star Theater*	Herself	4 episodes
1950	*Nancy Goes to Rio*	Marina Rodrigues	
1951	*Don McNeill's TV Club*	Herself	Episode #1.25
1951	*What's My Line?*	Mystery Guest	November 18, 1951 episode
1951 to 1952	*The Colgate Comedy Hour*	Herself	3 episodes
1951 to 1953	*All-Star Revue*	Herself	2 episodes
1953	*Scared Stiff*	Carmelita Castinha	
1953	*Toast of the Town*	Herself	Episode #7.1
1955	*The Jimmy Durante Show*	Herself	Episode #2.2

Singles

Brazilian singles

1935

- "Anoiteceu"
- "Entre Outras Coisas"
- "Esqueci de Sorrir"
- "Foi Numa Noite Assim"
- "Fogueira Do Meu Coração"
- "Fruto Proibido"
- "Cor de Guiné"
- "Casaco de Tricô"
- "Dia de Natal"
- "Fala, Meu Pandeiro"
- "Deixa Esse Povo Falar"
- "Sonho de Papel" (recorded with Orchestra Odeon on 10 May 1935)
- "E Bateu-Se a Chapa" (recorded with Regional de Benedito Lacerda on 26 June 1935)
- "O Tique-Taque do Meu Coração" (recorded with Regional de Benedito Lacerda on 7 August 1935)

- "Adeus, Batucada" (recorded with Odeon Orchestra on 24 September 1935)
- "Querido Adão" (recorded with Orchestra Odeon on 26 September 1935)

1936

- "Alô, Alô, Carnaval"
- "Duvi-dê-ó-dó"
- "Capelinha do Coração:
- "Cuíca, Pandeiro, Tamborim..."
- "Beijo Bamba"
- "Balancê"
- "Entra no cordão"
- "Como Eu Chorei"
- "Cantores do Rádio" (recorded with Aurora Miranda and Orchestra Odeon on 18 March 1936)
- "No Tabuleiro da Baiana" (recorded with Louis Barbosa and Regional Luperce Miranda on 29 September 1936)
- "Como Vaes" Você?" (recorded with Ary Barroso and Regional Luperce Pixinguinha and Miranda on 2 October 1936)

1937

- "Dance Rumba"
- "Em Tudo, Menos em Ti"
- "Canjiquinha Quente"
- "Cabaret No Morro"
- "Baiana Do Tabuleiro"
- "Dona Geisha"
- "Cachorro Vira-Lata" (recorded with Regional de Benedito Lacerda on 4 May 1937)
- "Me Dá, Me Dá" (recorded with Regional de Benedito Lacerda on 4 May 1937)
- "Camisa Amarela" (recorded with the Odeon Group on 20 September 1937)
- "Eu Dei" (recorded with Regional Odeon on 21 September 1937)

1938

- "Endereço Errado"
- "Falar!"
- "Escrevi um Bilhetinho"
- "Batalhão do amor"
- "E a Festa, Maria?"
- "Cuidado Com a Gaita do Ary"
- "A Pensão Da Dona Stella"
- "A Vizinha Das Vantagens"
- "Samba Rasgado (recorded with Odeon Group on 7 March 1938)
- "E o Mundo Não Se Acabou" ("And the World Would Not End") (recorded with Regional Odeon on 9 March 1938)
- "Boneca de Piche" (recorded with Admiral and Odeon Orchestra on 31 August 1938)
- "Na Baixa do Sapateiro" (recorded with Orchestra Odeon on 17 October 1938)

1939

- "A Preta Do Acarajé"
- "Deixa Comigo"
- "Candeeiro"
- "Amor Ideal"
- "Essa Cabrocha"
- "A Nossa Vida Hoje É Diferente"
- "Cozinheira Grã-fina"
- "O Que É Que a Bahiana Tem?" (recorded with Dorival Caymmi and Regional Assembly on 27 February 1939)
- "Uva de Caminhão" (recorded with Joint Odeon on 21 March 1939)
- "Camisa Listada" (recorded with Bando da Lua on 28 August 1939))

1940

- "Voltei pro Morro" (recorded with Joint Odeon on 2 September 1940)
- "Ela Diz Que Tem"
- "Disso É Que Eu Gosto"
- "Disseram que Voltei Americanizada" (recorded with Odeon Set on 2 September 1940)
- "Bruxinha de Pano"
- "O Dengo Que a Nêga Tem"
- "É Um Quê Que a Gente Tem"
- "Blaque-Blaque"
- "Recenseamento" (recorded with Joint Odeon on 27 September 1940)
- "Ginga-Ginga"

American singles

1939

- "South American Way" (recorded with Bando da Lua and boy on 26 December 1939)
- "Touradas Em Madrid"
- "Marchinha do grande galo"
- "Mamãe Eu Quero"
- "Bambú, Bambú"

1941

- "I, Yi, Yi, Yi, Yi (I Like You Very Much)" (recorded with Bando da Lua on 5 January 1941)
- "Alô Alô"
- "Chica-Chica-Bum-Chic" (recorded with Bando da Lua on 5 January 1941)
- "Bambalê"
- "Cai, Cai" (record with Bando da Lua on 5 January 1941)
- "Arca de Noé"
- "A Weekend In Havana"
- "Diz Que Tem..."
- "When I Love I Love"
- "Rebola, Bola" (recorded with the Bando da Lua on 9 October 1941)
- "The Man With the Lollipop Song"
- "Não Te Dou A Chupeta"
- "Manuelo"

- "Thank You, North America"

1942

- "Chattanooga Choo Choo" (recorded with Bando da Lua and boy on 25 July 1942)
- "Tic-tac do Meu Coração"
- "O Passo Do Kanguru (Brazilly Willy)"
- "Boncea de Pixe"

1945

- "Upa! Upa!"
- "Tico Tico"

1947

- "The Matador (Touradas Em Madrid)" (recorded with The Andrews Sisters and Vic Schoen & his orchestra)
- "Cuanto La Gusta" (recorded with The Andrews Sisters and Vic Schoen & his orchestra)

1949

- "Asi Asi (I See, I See)" (recorded with The Andrews Sisters and Vic Schoen & his orchestra)
- "The Wedding Samba" (recorded with The Andrews Sisters and Vic Schoen & his orchestra)

1950

- "Baião Ca Room' Pa Pa" (recorded with The Andrews Sisters and Vic Schoen & his orchestra)
- "Ipse-A-I-O" (recorded with The Andrews Sisters and Vic Schoen & his orchestra)

References

[1] (McGowan 1998, p. 32)

[2] "Carmen Miranda Dies Following Heart Attack" (http://news.google.com/newspapers?id=FEcNAAAAIBAJ&sjid=A2wDAAAAIBAJ& pg=6451,19260&dq=carmen+miranda+heart+attack&hl=en). *Pittsburgh Post-Gazette*: p. 1. 1955-08-06. . Retrieved 21 November 2012.

[3] Bloom, Stephen G. (1984-08-24). "After 30 years, Carmen Miranda still a bombshell" (http://news.google.com/ newspapers?id=GyhlAAAAIBAJ&sjid=ZogNAAAAIBAJ&pg=1294,2117110&dq=carmen+miranda+heart+attack&hl=en). *Edmonton Journal*: p. B5. . Retrieved 21 November 2012.

[4] (Dennison 2004, p. 112)

[5] (Tompkins 2001, p. 192)

[6] "The century of the Brazilian Bombshell". *It's time for Brazil in Singapore* (Singapore: Sun Media): 63.

[7] (Ruíz 2005, p. 199)

[8] (Parish 2003, p. 606)

[9] (Ruíz 2005, p. 200)

[10] "Large Earnings By Films Stars" (http://news.google.com/newspapers?id=FL5VAAAAIBAJ&sjid=NpcDAAAAIBAJ& pg=5284,5623706&dq=carmen+miranda+highest+earning&hl=en). *The Age*: p. 3. 1946-06-17. . Retrieved 21 November 2012.

[11] (Tompkins 2001, p. 195)

[12] (Parish 2003, p. 607-608)

[13] (Parish 2003, p. 608)

[14] (Sforza 2000, p. 289)

[15] (Hadley-Garcia 1990, p. 123)

[16] "Carmen Miranda Set For Trial Separation" (http://news.google.com/newspapers?id=aelOAAAAIBAJ&sjid=HAAEAAAAIBAJ& pg=2632,5956195&dq=carmen+miranda+marriage&hl=en). *Toledo Blade*: p. 3. 1949-09-27. . Retrieved 21 November 2012.

[17] (Ruíz 2005, p. 206)

[18] "Death Takes Carmen Miranda" (http://news.google.com/newspapers?id=2utKAAAAIBAJ&sjid=BCMNAAAAIBAJ& pg=5989,6744420&dq=carmen+miranda+marriage&hl=en). *Oxnard Press-Courier*: p. 5. 1955-08-06. . Retrieved 21 November 2012.

[19] (Brioux 2007, p. 176)

[20] "Carmen Miranda Of Movies Dies" (http://news.google.com/newspapers?id=PUYxAAAAIBAJ&sjid=6w8EAAAAIBAJ& pg=6067,5271979&dq=carmen+miranda+durante&hl=en). *The Milwaukee Sentinel*. 1955-08-06. . Retrieved 21 November 2012.

[21] (Bakish 2007, p. 136)

[22] (Ruíz 2005, p. 207)

[23] (Ruíz 2005, p. 193)

[24] Lawrence, Sandra (12 August 2003). "Brazil: In search of the queen of samba" (http://www.telegraph.co.uk/travel/destinations/ southamerica/brazil/728105/Brazil-In-search-of-the-queen-of-samba.html). telegraph.co.uk. . Retrieved 2008-10-30.

[25] (Tompkins 2001, p. 191)

[26] Tobar, Hector; Trevino, Joseph (1998-09-26). "Some City Squares Bring Lives, and History, Full Circle" (http://articles.latimes.com/ 1998/sep/26/local/me-26513). . Retrieved 21 November 2012.

Works cited

- Bakish, David (2007). *Jimmy Durante: His Show Business Career, With a Annotated Filmography and Discography*. McFarland. ISBN 0-786-43022-2

- Brioux, Bill (2007). *Truth and Rumors: The Reality Behind TV's Most Famous Myths*. Greenwood Publishing Group. ISBN 0-275-99247-0

- Dennison, Stephanie; Shaw, Lisa (2004). *Popular Cinema in Brazil, 1930–2001*. Manchester University Press. pp. 112. ISBN 0-7190-6499-6

- Hadley-Garcia, George (1990). *Hispanic Hollywood: The Latins in Motion Pictures*. Carol Pub. Group. ISBN 0-8065-1185-0

- McGowan, Chris; Pessanha, Ricardo (1998). *The Brazilian Sound: Samba, Bossa Nova, and the Popular Music of Brazil*. Temple University Press. ISBN 1-56639-545-3

- Parish, James Robert; Pitts, Michael R. (2003). *Hollywood Songsters: Singers Who ACT and Actors Who Sing: A Biographical Dictionary* (2 ed.). Taylor & Francis. ISBN 0-415-94333-7

- Ruíz, Vicki; Sánchez Korrol, Virginia, (2005). *Latina Legacies: Identity, Biography, and Community: Identity, Biography, and Community*. Oxford University Press. ISBN 0-195-15399-5

- Sforza, John (2000). *Swing It! The Andrews Sisters Story*. University Press of Kentucky. ISBN 0-813-12136-1

- Tompkins, Cynthia Margarita; Foster, David William (2001). *Notable Twentieth-Century Latin American Women: A Biographical Dictionary*. Greenwood Publishing Group. ISBN 0-313-31112-9

Bibliography

- Cardoso, Abel. *Carmen Miranda, a Cantora d Brasil*. Sorocaba. 1978. (Portuguese)

- Castro, Ruy. *Carmen: Uma Biografia*. Companhia das Letras. 2005. 8535907602. (Portuguese)

- Gil-Montero, Martha. *Brazilian Bombshell*. Dutton Adult. 1988. 978-1556111280.

External links

- Carmen Miranda (http://www.ibdb.com/person.asp?ID=53252) at the Internet Broadway Database

- Carmen Miranda (http://www.imdb.com/name/nm0000544/) at the Internet Movie Database

- Carmen Miranda (http://tcmdb.com/participant/participant.jsp?participantId=132716) at the TCM Movie Database

- International Jose Guillermo Carrillo Foundation (http://www.fundacionjoseguillermocarrillo.com/sitio/ muspopular_carmen_miranda.php) (**Portuguese**)

- Carmen Miranda (http://www.brightlightsfilm.com/16/carmen.html) at Brightlightsfilm.com

- Carmen Miranda - Brazil (https://www.youtube.com/watch?v=hRz-M30PcEU) on YouTube

- Carmen Miranda on *The Jimmy Durante Show* (Part 2) (https://www.youtube.com/watch?v=blvW39pbLDA) on YouTube

- Carmen Miranda (http://www.findagrave.com/cgi-bin/fg.cgi?page=gr&GRid=1588) at *Find a Grave*

Christina Aguilera

Christina Aguilera	
 Aguilera attending the launch of the Montblanc John Lennon edition, September 2010.	
Background information	
Birth name	Christina María Aguilera
Born	December 18, 1980 Staten Island, New York, U.S.
Origin	Wexford, Pennsylvania, U.S.
Genres	Pop, R&B, soul, dance, electronic
Occupations	Singer-songwriter,[1][2][3] record producer, dancer, television personality,[4] actress
Instruments	Vocals
Years active	1993–present
Labels	RCA
Associated acts	The New Mickey Mouse Club, Linda Perry
Website	www.christinaaguilera.com [5]

Christina María Aguilera (born December 18, 1980) is an American singer-songwriter, television personality, and actress. Born in Staten Island, New York, she appeared in television shows as a child before signing with RCA Records in 1998. Her debut studio album *Christina Aguilera* (1999) became an international success, with singles "Genie in a Bottle", "What a Girl Wants", and "Come On Over Baby (All I Want Is You)" all topping the *Billboard* Hot 100. Despite commercial success with her second and third albums *Mi Reflejo* (2000) and *My Kind of Christmas* (2000) and numerous collaborations, Aguilera was displeased with her lack of input in her music and image. She parted ways with her management and assumed creative control for her fourth album *Stripped* (2002); its second single "Beautiful" helped the album's commercial performance amidst controversy over her image. While Aguilera's jazz, soul and blues-inspired fifth album *Back to Basics* (2006) was met with positive critical and commercial feedback, her sixth album *Bionic* (2010) had trouble maintaining commercial success. Later that year, she made her feature film debut in the musical *Burlesque* which was released to mixed reviews. Aguilera served as the soundtrack's executive producer earning positive reviews and substantial sales. Aguilera's seventh album *Lotus* (2012) garnered mixed reviews and poor sales. She served as a coach and judge for the first three seasons of *The*

Voice from 2011 through 2012.

Aguilera includes themes of dealing with public scrutiny, her childhood, and female empowerment in her music. She has been noted for her vocals, music videos and constantly reinventing her image and music. Aguilera has dedicated much of her time as a philanthropist for charities, human rights and world issues, including her work as a UN ambassador for the World Food Programme. As one of the top selling artists of the early 2000s, *Billboard* named Aguilera as the top female artist of 2000 and 2003.[6][7] Her work has earned numerous awards and accolades, including a star on the Hollywood Walk of Fame, a Golden Globe Award nomination for songwriting, four Grammy Awards and one Latin Grammy Award, amongst seventeen and three nominations respectively. *Rolling Stone* ranked Aguilera number fifty-eight on their list of the 100 Greatest Singers of All Time, ranking as the youngest and only artist on the list under the age of thirty. She has earned five number number one singles on the *Billboard* Hot 100. Among them, her debut single "Genie in a Bottle" and the collaborations "Lady Marmalade" and "Moves like Jagger" are one of the best-selling singles of all time. She was ranked the 20th Artist of the 2000–09 decade by *Billboard*[8] and is the second top selling single artist of the 2000s behind Madonna.[9] Aguilera's albums sales are estimated at over 50 million units worldwide.[10] In 2012, she was ranked #8 in VH1's listing of 100 Greatest Women in Music.[11]

Life and career

Early life and career beginnings

Christina María Aguilera was born in Staten Island, New York in December 18, 1980.[12] Her father, Fausto Xavier Aguilera, was a soldier in the United States Army, while her mother, Shelly Loraine (née Fidler),[13] was a violinist and pianist.[14] Her father is Ecuadorian[15] and her mother, who is American, is of German, Irish, Welsh, and Dutch ancestry.[16] Aguilera has stated that she is "proud of [her] Latino roots and proud of [her] Irish roots."[17] Throughout her father's service in the Army, her family moved to various locations such as New Jersey, Texas, New York, and Japan.[18] Aguilera lived with both her father and mother, up until their divorce when she was six years old. Aguilera then lived with her mother, and her younger sister Rachel, at her grandmother's home in Rochester, Pennsylvania, a town outside Pittsburgh.[15] According to both Aguilera and her mother, her father was very controlling, as well as physically and emotionally abusive, while she used music as an escape from the abuses.[19] Even though he has made several attempts to reconnect with her, Aguilera ruled out any chance of a reunion.[20] Since then, her mother has married again, and has changed her name.[21]

As a child, Aguilera aspired to be a singer. She was known locally as "the little girl with the big voice",[20] singing in local talent shows and competitions. At the age of 8, Aguilera won her first talent show performing Whitney Houston's "I Wanna Dance With Somebody".[18] On March 15, 1990, she appeared on *Star Search* singing "A Sunday Kind of Love", but lost the competition at number 2. Soon after losing on *Star Search*, she returned home and appeared on Pittsburgh's KDKA-TV's *Wake Up With Larry Richert* to perform the same song. Throughout her youth in Pittsburgh, Aguilera sang "The Star-Spangled Banner" before Pittsburgh Penguins hockey, Pittsburgh Steelers football and Pittsburgh Pirates baseball games, including during the 1992 Stanley Cup Finals.[22] She attended Rochester Area School District and Marshall Middle School near Wexford.[20] Her talent was kept a secret to avoid bullying of other children. Following her television appearances Aguilera experienced resentment and bullying including an incident in which her peers slashed the tires on her family's car.[23] She attended North Allegheny Intermediate High School briefly until she was home schooled following several incidents.[20] Aguilera recalls, "doing what I did and maybe being a little smaller, I was definitely picked on and bullied for the attention that I got. It was definitely unwanted attention and there was a lot of unfairness about it."[24]

In 1991, Aguilera auditioned for a role on *The Mickey Mouse Club*; however, she did not meet the age requirements. Two years later, she joined the cast, performing musical numbers and sketch comedy, until the show's cancellation in 1994.[25] Her co-stars included Justin Timberlake, Britney Spears, Ryan Gosling and Keri Russell where they nicknamed her "the Diva"[14] for her performance style and voice. At the age of fourteen, Aguilera recorded her first song, "All I Wanna Do", a hit duet with Japanese singer Keizo Nakanishi.[26] In 1997, she represented the United States at the international Golden Stag Festival with a two-song set.[27] Aguilera entered talent contests on "teen night" at the Pegasus Lounge, a gay and lesbian nightclub in Pittsburgh.[28] In 1998, Aguilera sent in a demo of her Whitney Houston's "Run to You" cover to Disney who were looking for a singer to record the song "Reflection" for their animated feature film *Mulan* (1998).[29] The demo caught the attention of producer and label executive Ron Fair who would later mentor her throughout her career and led to Aguilera earning a contract with RCA Records the same week.[30] "Reflection" peaked within the top twenty on the Adult Contemporary Singles Chart, and was nominated for a Golden Globe Award for Best Original Song.[12][31]

1999–2001: *Christina Aguilera*, *Mi Reflejo* and new management

Aguilera's self-titled debut album was released on August 24, 1999. The album was received to positive reviews from critics; Stephen Thomas Erlewine of Allmusic wrote that the album "remains firmly within the teen-oriented dance-pop genre, but done right", describing it as "lightweight in the best possible sense – breezy, fun, engaging, and enjoyable on each repeated listen."[32] The album reached the top of the *Billboard* 200 and Canadian album charts, shipping eight million copies in the United States[14] and over seventeen million copies worldwide.[33][34][35] The album is also included in the Top 100 Albums of All Time list of The Recording Industry Association of America (RIAA) based on US sales.[36] Her debut single, "Genie in a Bottle", was an instant hit reaching number one on the *Billboard* Hot 100 and several countries worldwide.[37][38] Additionally, "Genie in a Bottle" was the top selling debut single of 1999 with over 1.4 million sold in the US.[39] The follow-up singles, "What a Girl Wants" and "Come On Over Baby (All I Want Is You)" also topped the Hot 100 during 1999 and 2000, while "I Turn to You" reached number three, making Aguilera one of the few artists to have multiple number one singles from a debut album in *Billboard* history.[40][41] "What a Girl Wants" was also the first number one hit of the millennium.[42] Aguilera made a cameo appearence on *Beverly Hills, 90210*,[43] appeared at 1999's Lilith Fair, and performed during the Super Bowl XXXIV halftime show alongside Enrique Iglesias. Aguilera wanted to display the range and audacity in her voice, performing acoustic sets and appeared on television shows accompanied only by a piano.[44] At the 42nd Grammy Awards, Aguilera won the Grammy Award for Best New Artist.[45] On her win Aguilera said she was "in utter and complete shock. I was not expecting it at all, just like I wasn't expecting the nominations, but winning it is actually a different story. So, I had no speech prepared, nothing, and I was trembling like I don't know what, but it feels amazing."[45]

Aguilera performing during her *My Reflection* concert special in 2000.

On September 12, 2000, Aguilera released her second album and first Spanish-language album, *Mi Reflejo*, containing Spanish versions of songs from her previous album and new Spanish material. According to producer Rudy Pérez, with whom Aguilera recorded the album in Miami, Aguilera was only semi-fluent while recording, but understood the language, having grown up with her Ecuadorian father.[46][47] The album peaked at number twenty-seven on the *Billboard* 200 and topped the *Billboard* Latin charts for a record 20 weeks making Aguilera the highest female debut of all time.[48][49] Additionally, it made Aguilera the only artist in history to have back-to-back number one debuts with an English language album followed by a Spanish language album.[49] The album has since sold over 2.2 million copies worldwide,[50] and was certified Gold in the US selling over 480,000 copies.[51][52] Aguilera won the World Music Award and *Billboard* award as the best selling Latin artist that year.[6] In 2001, it won Aguilera a Latin Grammy Award for Best Female Pop Vocal Album.[53] She also released a Christmas album, *My Kind of Christmas*, on October 24, 2000, and performed its only single, "The Christmas Song", at the White House that year.[14] The song made Aguilera one of three artists to take the song into the top twenty on the *Billboard* Hot 100.[54] The album was certified platinum in the US.[55] Her first concert tour, Christina Aguilera in Concert, began in the summer of 2000 in the United States and ended early 2001, where she toured South America and Asia.[56] An ABC concert special, *My Reflection*, was released to DVD and certified Gold in the US.[57] Aguilera was *Billboard*'s top selling female artist of 2000.[6]

Aguilera was rumored to have dated MTV VJ Carson Daly.[58] Rumors of their relationship were fueled after the release of Eminem's song, "The Real Slim Shady", in which he also insinuated a romance between her and rocker Fred Durst. Aguilera responded saying the lyrics were "disgusting, offensive and, above all, not true."[59] Their feud ended two years later backstage at the Video Music Awards after Aguilera presented the rapper an award onstage.[60] Aguilera dated Puerto Rican dancer Jorge Santos, who appeared on her tour and music videos throughout 2000. They dated for nearly two years until the relationship ended on September 11, 2001.[61] He remained her dancer into 2002.[62]

Ricky Martin asked Aguilera to duet with him on "Nobody Wants to Be Lonely" from his album *Sound Loaded*, released in 2001 as the album's second single. The song reached number thirteen in the United States.[12] In 2001, Aguilera, Lil' Kim, Mýa, and Pink remade Labelle's 1975 single "Lady Marmalade" for the film *Moulin Rouge!* and its accompaining soundtrack. The song ultimately peaked at number one on the *Billboard* Hot 100 for five weeks[63] and became the first airplay-only track in history to stay number one for more than one week.[64] It was the year's top selling single worldwide, reaching number one in eleven other countries with over 5.2 million copies sold making it one of the best-selling singles of all time.[65] "Lady Marmalade" earned all four performers a Grammy Award for Best Pop Collaboration with Vocals. The video won two MTV Video Music Awards, including Video of the Year in 2001.[66] Later in 2001, "Just Be Free", a song from one of Aguilera's demos recorded when she was fifteen years old, appeared in record stores. When RCA Records discovered the single, they advised fans not to purchase it.[67] Months later, Warlock Records was set to release *Just Be Free*, an album containing demo material. Aguilera filed a breach of contract and unfair competition suit against Warlock and the album's producers to block the release.[68] The two parties came to a confidential settlement to release the album, where Aguilera lent out her name, likeness, and image for an unspecified amount of damages.[69]

Despite her international success, Aguilera was dissatisfied with the music and image her management had created for her, having been marketed as a bubblegum pop singer because of the genre's upward financial trend.[70] She mentioned plans for her next album to have more musical and lyrical depth.[71] Aguilera's views of Steve Kurtz's influence in matters of the singer's creative direction, the role of being her exclusive personal manager, and over-scheduling had in part caused her to seek legal means of terminating their management contract. In October 2000, Aguilera filed a breach of fiduciary duty lawsuit against her manager Kurtz for improper, undue and inappropriate influence over her professional activities, as well as fraud. According to legal documents, Kurtz did not protect her rights and interests. Instead, he took action that was for his own interest, at the cost of hers. She petitioned the California State Labor Commission to nullify the contract.[72][73] Aguilera revealed while recording her then upcoming album, "I was being overworked. You find out that someone you thought was a friend is stealing money behind your back, and it's heartbreaking. I put faith in the people around me, and unfortunately, it bit me in the butt."[71] After terminating Kurtz's services, Irving Azoff was hired as her new manager.

2002–05: *Stripped*, new image, and marriage

Aguilera's fourth studio album, *Stripped* was released on October 26, 2002. It peaked at number two on the *Billboard* 200, with first-week sales of 330,000 copies.[74] Unlike her previous work, the album showcased Aguilera's raunchier side. She co-wrote much of the album, as Aguilera had recently signed a global music publishing contract with BMG Music Publishing, and was influenced by many different subjects and music styles, including R&B, soul, pop rock and hip hop.[75] The majority of the album was produced by Scott Storch and singer-songwriter Linda Perry, who produced her more personal records. Rockwilder and singer Alicia Keys also contributed a track each. The album was well received by critics, although Aguilera's vocals were overlooked as she began to cultivate a more sexually provocative image,[76] having taken part in nude and semi-nude photoshoots, notably her cover for *Rolling Stone*,[77] featuring Aguilera wearing only boots and an electric guitar. She denied that the change was a matter of publicity, claiming that it better reflected her true personality than her previous image. She dyed her hair black, began referring to herself as "Xtina", got a tattoo of the nickname on the back of her neck, as well as several piercings.[78]

Initially, the raunchy image had a negative effect on Aguilera in the United States, especially after the release of her controversial "Dirrty" music video.[79][80] She defended the video, stating it was about power and control, adding, "I'm also at the forefront. I'm in the power position, in complete command of everything around me."[14] While the video became popular on MTV, it disappointed on the US singles chart.[81] However, the single was a hit worldwide, reaching number one in the UK and Ireland. The second single, classically-influenced ballad "Beautiful", received critical praise, reaching number one in several countries and peaking at number two in the US.[81] The song earned Aguilera the Grammy for Best Female Pop Vocal Performance. Three more singles: "Fighter", "Can't Hold Us Down" featuring Lil' Kim, and "The Voice Within", were released in the following two years, helping the album stay on the charts for the next two years. *Stripped* stayed on the US and UK album charts into 2004, and went on to be certified four-times platinum in the US[51] with over ten million copies sold worldwide.[50] It appeared at number ten on *Billboard*'s year-end album chart and Aguilera was the top female artist for 2003.[7] Kelly Clarkson's second single, "Miss Independent", was co-written by Aguilera, having been half-finished for *Stripped*.

Aguilera performing during Stripped Live... on Tour in 2003

Aguilera performing during Stripped Live... on Tour in 2003

Aguilera joined Justin Timberlake that June on the final leg of his international *Justified* tour in the United States, becoming the Justified & Stripped Tour. In August, an overhead lighting grid collapsed from the ceiling of the Boardwalk Hall in Atlantic City, New Jersey, causing major damage to the sound and video equipment below hours before a show. Few stagehands were injured, though some shows were canceled or postponed.[82] In the fourth quarter of the year, Aguilera continued to tour internationally without Timberlake on the Stripped Live... on Tour. It was one of the top-grossing tours of that year, and sold out most of its venues. *Rolling Stone* readers named it the best tour of the year.[83] That same year, Aguilera hosted the 2003 MTV Europe Music Awards and was a special guest performer with the Pussycat Dolls' dance troupe performing at the Roxy Theatre and Viper Room in Los Angeles. She also appeared on a *Maxim* spread alongside them, her second *Maxim* cover that year set record sales making it the top selling issue to date. By the end of the year, she topped the annual *Hot 100* list, saying, "we had fun working with certain clothes, or the lack thereof."[84][85][86]

Aguilera's first DVD live-recording, *Stripped Live in the U.K.*, was released in November 2004. In light of the tour's success, another U.S. tour was scheduled to begin in mid-2004 with a new theme, though it was scrapped due to vocal cord injuries Aguilera suffered shortly before the opening date.[87] In a tribute to Madonna's performance at the inaugural 2003 MTV Video Music Awards, Aguilera and singer Britney Spears kissed the singer-actress during the ceremony in August, during the opening performance of Madonna's songs "Like a Virgin" and "Hollywood".[14] Also in 2004, she hosted a *Saturday Night Live* episode, which included a *Sex & The City* skit where she portrayed Samantha Jones revealing to everyone she was a man the entire time.[88]

Aguilera later decided to embrace a more mature, Marilyn Monroe-like image, dying her hair flaxen blonde and cutting it short. She is one of the main proponents (along with Dita Von Teese, Gwen Stefani, and Ashley Judd) in bringing back the 1920s–1940s Hollywood glamour look.[89][90] Aguilera later dyed her hair cherry blonde and recorded a jingle, "Hello", for a Mercedes-Benz ad. In late 2004, Aguilera released "Car Wash", a remake of the Rose Royce disco song as a collaboration with rapper Missy Elliott for the soundtrack to the film *Shark Tale*. She voiced a small singing part in the film, playing a Rastafarian jellyfish in the film's closing musical number. She was featured in Nelly's "Tilt Ya Head Back", from his album *Sweat*. Both singles failed commercially in the US, but did considerably better in other parts of the world. Aguilera collaborated with jazz artist Herbie Hancock on a cover of Leon Russell's "A Song for You", recorded for Hancock's album *Possibilities*, released in August 2005. They were later nominated for the Grammy Award for Best Pop Collaboration with Vocals. She helped open the 50th Anniversary for Disneyland performing "When You Wish upon a Star", and also collaborated with Andrea Bocelli on the song "Somos Novios" for his album *Amore*. Aguilera began dating music marketing executive Jordan Bratman in 2002. Their engagement was announced in February 2005,[91] and they married on November 19, 2005, in a Napa Valley estate.[92]

2006–09: *Back to Basics* and motherhood

Aguilera's fifth studio album, *Back to Basics*, was released on August 15, 2006. It debuted at number one in the US, the UK, and eleven other countries. It has since sold 4.5 million units worldwide,[93] with over 1.7 million sold in the US.[94] She described the double CD as "a throwback to the 20s, 30s, and 40s-style jazz, blues, and feel-good soul music, but with a modern twist."[95] It received positive reviews,[96] although many critics commented on the album's length saying, "At one disc, this would have been nothing short of masterful."[97] A review in *AllMusic* adds, "*Back to Basics* also makes clear that *Stripped* was a necessary artistic move for Christina: she needed to get that out of her system in order to create her own style, one that is self-consciously stylized, stylish, and sexy."[98] The critically acclaimed lead single, "Ain't No Other Man", was a substantial success, reaching number two on the World Chart, number six in the US, and number two in the UK. Producers on the album included DJ Premier, Kwamé, Linda Perry, and Mark Ronson. The follow-up singles did well in various regions, "Hurt" in Europe and "Candyman" in the Pacific. She co-directed both music videos, the former with Floria Sigismondi who directed

Aguilera performing during the Sanremo Story festival in 2006

her "Fighter" video, and the latter, "Candyman", with director/photographer Matthew Rolston which was inspired by The Andrews Sisters.[99] "Slow Down Baby" was released as the fourth single in Australia only, while "Oh Mother" was released as the fourth single in selected European countries.

In late 2006, Aguilera collaborated with Diddy on "Tell Me", from his album *Press Play*. She also began the Back to Basics Tour in Europe[100] followed by a 41-date North American tour in early 2007.[101] After this, she toured Asia and Australia, where it was supposed to end on August 3, however she canceled her dates in Melbourne and her final two in Auckland due to an illness.[102] Her extravagant arena tour included cabaret, three-ring circus and juke joint sets and 10 piece costumes designed by Roberto Cavalli.[103] She released her concert DVD *Back to Basics: Live and Down Under* the following year. The tour grossed nearly 50 million by the end of the year in North America and an additional 40 million worldwide in her Europe and Australia dates, grossing almost 90 million by the end of the tour.[104][105] It was the most successful US tour by a female in 2007.[106]

At the 49th Grammy Awards, Aguilera again won the Best Female Pop Vocal Performance for "Ain't No Other Man". She made a noteworthy performance at the ceremony paying tribute to James Brown with her rendition of his song "It's a Man's Man's Man's World".[107] In January 2007, she was named the 19th richest woman in entertainment by *Forbes*, with a net worth of US$60 million.[108] Aguilera performed "Steppin' Out With My Baby" with Tony Bennett on his NBC special *Tony Bennett: An American Classic* and on *Saturday Night Live*. They performed at the 59th Primetime Emmy Awards where both specials received Emmys. "Steppin' Out" was nominated for Best Pop Collaboration with Vocals at the 50th Annual Grammy Awards. Aguilera confirmed she was pregnant on November 4, 2007,[109] though Paris Hilton accidentally revealed her pregnancy several weeks prior during a party Aguilera hosted.[110] She gave birth to her son, Max Liron Bratman, in Los Angeles on January 12, 2008, and held a bris for him with Bratman, who is of Jewish descent, where the baby was circumcised in accordance with Jewish practice.[111] Aguilera was reportedly paid $1.5 million by *People* for her son's baby pictures—the sixth most expensive celebrity baby photos ever taken.[112]

In 2008, Aguilera appeared in the Martin Scorsese documentary *Shine a Light* which chronicles a two day Rolling Stones concert in New York City's Beacon Theatre. The film features Aguilera performing "Live With Me" alongside Mick Jagger. *Shine a Light* premiered at the Berlin Film Festival and was released worldwide on April 4, 2008. She also had a brief cameo in the comedy film *Get Him to the Greek*,[113] and appeared as a guest judge on the sixth season of *Project Runway* on Lifetime Television. She and designer Bob Mackie were the inspiration for the challenge in which they had to design a stage outfit for Aguilera. To commemorate Aguilera's ten years in the music industry, RCA Records released, *Keeps Gettin' Better: A Decade of Hits* on November 11, 2008, exclusively at Target stores in the US. The greatest hits included her first three number one singles, and other songs released from her previous three albums. "Lady Marmalade" and several Spanish singles from *Mi Reflejo* were included in the worldwide releases. The album's only single, "Keeps Gettin' Better", was premiered at the 2008 MTV Video Music Awards, which debuted and peaked at No.7 on the *Billboard* Hot 100, her highest debut on the chart. Following the greatest hits, Aguilera took over a year hiatus in 2009 to work on her then-upcoming album and film. She was one of *Billboard*'s Top 20 Artists of the Decade in their year-end charts.[114]

2010–11: *Bionic*, *Burlesque*, and *The Voice*

Aguilera's sixth studio album *Bionic* was released on June 8, 2010. The album's producers included Tricky Stewart, Samuel Dixon, Polow da Don, Le Tigre, Switch, Ester Dean, songwriters Sam Endicott, Sia Furler, Claude Kelly, Linda Perry and collaborations with M.I.A., Santigold, Nicki Minaj, and Peaches. *Bionic*'s material consisted of many mainstream and pop records along with electronic and dance music. Two of the album's four singles, "Not Myself Tonight" and "You Lost Me" peaked at number one on the *Billboard* Hot Dance Club Play Charts[115] but were unsuccessful elsewhere. "Woohoo", featuring rapper Nicki Minaj, was also released as the album's second single, while "I Hate Boys" was a promotional single. Jon Pareles of *The New York Times* wrote that the singer's new music direction "makes her sound as peer-pressured as a pop singer can be."[116] Allison Stewart of *The Washington Post* described the album as being "noisy, robotic and overstuffed" adding that the disc's "greatest disappointments" is its "virtual abandonment" of Aguilera's voice.[117] She concluded that Aguilera attempts "to do it all," which was to try to "revel in her newfound domesticity, to wrest her crown from Gaga and to reestablish her sex kitten bona fides."[117] Because the album marked her foray into the electropop genre,[118][119][120] *Bionic* was considered "misunderstood" by music journalist Charles Decant. Sales of *Bionic* were underwhelming in the US compared to her previous releases selling 110,000 copies in its first week landing at No.3.[121][122] It has since sold 310,000 copies in the US.[123] Shortly after the album's release, further promotion ended and a scheduled summer tour for the album was canceled due to "inadequate rehearsal time".[124] Responding to the album's performance, Aguilera says,

"I was really proud of that record. I think there was a lot of promotion issues, coming from a standpoint of how everything resulted. Nothing is ever a setback. If anything, it just motivates you for what's next."[125]

Aguilera's star on the Hollywood Walk of Fame, which she received in 2010..

Aguilera announced that she and Bratman had separated, saying in a statement, "Although Jordan and I are separated, our commitment to our son Max remains as strong as ever."[126][127] Aguilera filed for divorce from Bratman on October 14, 2010, seeking joint legal and physical custody of their son, and specifying September 11, 2010, as the date of separation.[128][129] They later reached a settlement agreement and custody deal, details of their agreement were private.[130] Their divorce was finalized on April 15, 2011.[131] The following month, Aguilera appeared as herself on the *Entourage* season seven finale as a client/friend of Ari Gold.[132] On November 15, 2010, Aguilera received a Star on the Hollywood Walk of Fame.[133]

In November 2010, Aguilera appeared in her first feature film, the musical *Burlesque*. She portrayed a small town girl, Ali Rose, who finds love and success in a Los Angeles neo-burlesque club.[134] The film was written and directed by Steve Antin who wrote the part of Ali specifically with Aguilera in mind.[135] Aguilera performed eight of the musical numbers on the film's soundtrack released on November 22, 2010, and co-wrote a number of the tracks working with producers and writers including Tricky Stewart, Sia Furler, Samuel Dixon, Linda Perry, Claude Kelly, Danja, and Ron Fair. The remaining two tracks were sung by Cher, who co-starred alongside Aguilera. The soundtrack debuted in the top 20 in the US and was certified Gold selling over 600,000 copies in the US.[136][137][138] Aguilera's co-stars also included Cam Gigandet, Eric Dane, Kristen Bell and Stanley Tucci. Several critics praised Aguilera's performance. A review in *TIME* states, "Aguilera might not be to your taste, or mine, but in terms of sheer power, she's impressive. If Ali were real, she'd have already been discovered on *American Idol*."[139] While *Variety* wrote, "Aguilera, while undeniably entertaining when her character is onstage, cannot spin the slight backstory into anything resembling a full-blooded person."[140] Though *Burlesque* was released to mixed reviews from critics,[141][142] the film received a Golden Globe nomination for Best Picture – Musical or Comedy and earned Aguilera, writer/producer Sia Furler and Samuel Dixon, a nomination for Best Original Song for the track "Bound to You". The soundtrack also earned Aguilera a Grammy nomination for Best Compilation Soundtrack. *Burlesque* grossed $90 million worldwide.[143]

Aguilera collaborated with rapper T.I. on the track "Castle Walls" from his album *No Mercy*.[144] During Super Bowl XLV, Aguilera performed the U.S. national anthem, "The Star-Spangled Banner", and created embarrassment when she omitted a line of the anthem and messed up the song's lyrics.[145] She later apologized, telling CNN that "I got so caught up in the moment of the song that I lost my place. I can only hope that everyone could feel my love for this country and that the true spirit of its anthem still came through."[146] The following week, Aguilera, alongside Jennifer Hudson, Martina McBride, Yolanda Adams, and Florence Welch opened the 53rd Grammy Awards paying tribute to Aretha Franklin.[147] Aguilera began dating musician and production assistant, Matt Rutler whom she met during the filming of *Burlesque*. Her appearance[148] and personal life were the subject of scrutiny;[149] with reports over out of control behavior, excessive drinking,[150][151] and a reported confrontation with her co-star Julianne Hough.[152][153] On March 1, 2011, Aguilera was arrested for public intoxication in West Hollywood as her boyfriend was arrested for DWI.[154] She was later released on bail and no charges were filed.[155][156] Rutler's DWI charge was dismissed due to insufficient evidence, after his BAC was determined as below the legal limit.[157]

Aguilera signed to be a judge on *The Voice*, which debuted on NBC in April 2011. Aguilera, alongside other musicians Adam Levine, Blake Shelton and Cee Lo Green serve as judges and coaches, with Carson Daly as the show's host. The show's first episode was well-received, and delivered the strongest ratings for a series premiere on a major network since *Undercover Boss* debuted after the Super Bowl in February 2010.[158][159] The show's first season was a ratings success for NBC following its debut.[160][161] Aguilera performed "Moves like Jagger" on *The Voice* – the single with Maroon 5 on which she is featured, from their album *Hands All Over*. The song was an instant hit reaching number two in the UK, and earned Aguilera her fifth number one single on the *Billboard* Hot 100, a decade after her last number one single, "Lady Marmalade".[162] It also made Aguilera the second female artist to achieve number one hits in the 1990s, 2000s and 2010s. The single sold over 8 million copies worldwide, establishing itself among the best-selling singles of all time.[163][164] "Moves like Jagger" marks the first time two former Best New Artist Grammy Award winners have collaborated on a Hot 100 hit[54] and was nominated for Best Pop Duo/Group Performance at the Grammy Awards.

2012–present: *Lotus*

Aguilera's seventh studio album, *Lotus*, was released on November 13, 2012. Producers on the album included Alex da Kid, Max Martin, Lucas Secon, Steve Robson and Shellback, among others and incorporated elements of electropop that Aguilera experimented with on *Bionic*.[118][119][120] The album received mixed reviews from critics. MTV News commented that *Lotus* "was supposed to signify her return to prominence, a high-powered collection of songs penned by the biggest hitmakers in the business", adding, "it wasn't a triumphant comeback album".[165] The album debuted at number seven on the *Billboard* 200 selling just under on 73,000 copies making it her lowest first-week sales in the US[165] and was less successful worldwide.[166] The lead single, "Your Body", debuted and peaked at number 34 on the *Billboard* Hot 100 and was a moderate hit worldwide. "Just a Fool", a country pop duet with Blake Shelton was released as the album's second single.

At the 2012 ALMA Awards, Aguilera was honored with a Special Achievement Award for her career and work in philanthropy. She also recorded her first Spanish-language track in over a decade titled "Casa de Mi Padre" which was released as the title song for the soundtrack and film of the same name.[167] Following the second season and third season of *The Voice*, it was announced that Usher and Shakira will join the show as new coaches for *The Voice*'s fourth season to replace Aguilera and Green, who will take a break from the show. Adam Levine and Blake Shelton will remain for the fourth season, and Aguilera and Green will return for the fifth.[168] Aguilera collaborated with Cee Lo Green on the classic Christmas song "Baby, It's Cold Outside" from his album *Cee-Lo's Magic Moment*, and with rapper Pitbull on the track "Feel This Moment" from his album *Global Warming*.[169][170]

Artistry

Vocal ability

Aguilera, a soprano[171][172] has been referred to as the "voice of her generation" and a blue eyed soul singer.[173][174] She possesses a four octave vocal range[175] and a whistle register.[176] Aguilera also topped COVE's list of the 100 Best Pop Vocalists with a score of 50/50[177][178] and came fifth in MTV's 22 Greatest Voices in Music.[179] Her rendition of "It's A Man's Man's Man's World" at the 49th Grammy Awards ranked third in the Grammy's Greatest Moments List behind Celine Dion's performance of "My Heart Will Go On" and Green Day's performance of "American Idiot". In an interview, Dion described Aguilera as "probably the best vocalist in the world."[180] Aguilera's distinct style of singing has been praised by critics and noted as influential.[181] The People's Choice Awards honored Aguilera with the People's Voice award, recognizing her vocals and "ability to reach millions of people across a number of genres including pop, soul and R&B".[182] *Rolling Stone* ranked Aguilera at 58 as their 100 Greatest Singers of All Time, the youngest singer on the list.[181]

Aguilera performing during her Back to Basics Tour in 2006

Since her debut in 1999, Aguilera has been compared to Mariah Carey and Whitney Houston.[183] David Browne of *The New York Times* writes, "Aguilera has been one of the foremost practitioners of the overpowering, Category 5 vocal style known as melisma. Ms. Carey, Ms. Houston and Ms. Aguilera, to name its three main champions, are most associated with the period from the late '80s through the late '90s."[184] A review in the *Los Angeles Times* compared Aguilera's vocal style to Barbra Streisand, Gladys Knight, and Aretha Franklin adding, "Aguilera's Streisand-esque tendencies are a good thing; they're helping her figure out how to become the "great singer" she's been dubbed since she released her first single, the wise-beyond-its-years "Genie in a Bottle", at 18."[185] Vocal coach Cari Cole, called Aguilera the "Queen of riffing", adding that her vocals are rooted in soul music.[186] Although praised for her vocals, Aguilera has been labeled for oversinging in her songs and concerts.[187] *The Huffington Post* named Aguilera a main proponent for "oversouling", described as the "gratuitous and confected melisma." The term was coined by producer Jerry Wexler who said, "I have found that flagrantly artificial attempts at melisma are either a substitute for real fire and passion or a cover-up for not knowing the melody."[188] The majority of Aguilera's songs are characterized by her loud vocals, though she has used breathy and soft vocals.[189] Aguilera co-wrote "Sing For Me" from her album *Lotus*, a response to critics who labeled her for oversinging. In the song, Aguilera explains why she sings the way she does, saying "I don't even care what the world thinks about how I sound."[190] Aguilera admits to oversinging in her early years adding, "Before, to make up for the kind of music I didn't want to be doing, I would over-riff, to prove that I have talent. It was too much".[191] Longtime producer and writer, Linda Perry, commented on working on the track "Beautiful", saying, "I tried to keep it straight. I told her to get rid of the finger waves. Every time she'd start going into "hoo-ha", I'd stop the tape. I'm like, 'You're doing it again.'" Perry ended up using the first take saying, "She had a hard time accepting that as the final track. It's not a perfect vocal – it's very raw. She knows her voice really well, and she knows what's going on. She can hear things that nobody else would catch."[192]

Themes and musical style

The constant theme in Aguilera's music and lyrics is love, although she has written on other subjects including spirituality, motherhood, female empowerment, and grief. Aguilera has also written about her childhood in two of her records which dealt with domestic abuse. In an interview Aguilera admitted she feels responsible to reveal her most vulnerable feelings and to share the darker sides of her life adding "People that can relate might not feel as alone in the circumstance."[193] Originally marketed as a teen pop singer during the late '90s, Aguilera received commercial success but was displeased with her debut album's musical content.[71] She wrote the hook for "Genie in a Bottle", but did not receive a writing credit[17] and had no input during the album's production. Her fourth single, "Come On Over Baby (All I Want Is You)" was re-recorded with elements of R&B and hip-hop from its original dance pop version. Aguilera was given credit writing the song's sexually suggestive "rap".[194] Wanting to showcase her vocals, Aguilera went on a small venue tour performing acoustic sets for music critics and industry executives across the country. She turned down offers to tour with Backstreet Boys and 'N Sync in order to appear at 1999's Lilith Fair.[44] After leaving her management, Aguilera took creative control of her music and lyrical content; departing into a broad range of musical genres for her follow-up album *Stripped* such as soul, pop rock, R&B, and hip-hop. After recording *Stripped* Aguilera said, "You get signed to a label, people decide what you're going to be, but you're so excited to be doing it, period. Then you realize, 'Man, I don't know if this is what I really want.' Now I'm getting to do my own material and let people know that there's an artist behind the singer".[191] A review in *Billboard* called the album a "creative breakthrough",[75] and was noted as helping distance Aguilera from her then pop contemporaries.[195] Jancee Dunn of *Rolling Stone* writes, "With its lack of gimmickry and a surplus of sweet Seventies soul, Stripped is almost an album for grown-ups."[196] Aguilera co-wrote the majority of the songs on the album and released while the teen pop genre was still prominent on the charts. Music industry executive Clive Davis has praised Aguilera saying, "She has turned into one of today's most cutting-edge artists. She brings a whole fresh look to Top 40 and expands the horizon of what a pop artist can do. Everything from the video to the performance is coming from her."[197]

Marilyn Monroe in the film *Gentlemen Prefer Blondes*. A song of this film, "Diamonds Are A Girl's Best Friend", was performed by Aguilera in *Burlesque*.

Aguilera has often said that she prefers working with producers that are not in popular demand, saying "I don't necessarily go to the main people that are the No.1 chart-toppers in music."[198] Her 2006 release, *Back to Basics* included producer DJ Premier. *The New York Times* exclaims, "Her decision to work with the low-key DJ Premier was also a decision to snub some of the big-name producers on whom pop stars often rely."[199] The album included live instrumentation and samples of past jazz and soul records. Some tracks on the album included non-traditional forms of pop music such as swing jazz and big band, drawing comparisons to Madonna's *I'm Breathless* and the musical film *Cabaret*.[200] Her first feature film, *Burlesque*, influenced by *Cabaret*, featured several established songs that were updated and worked into dance numbers, a style similar to 2001's *Moulin Rouge!* The film included renditions of "A Guy What Takes His Time" introduced by Mae West in 1933 and "Diamonds Are a Girl's Best Friend", a musical number also performed by Nicole Kidman in *Moulin Rouge!*. Aguilera was the soundtrack's executive producer working with well-known producers Tricky Stewart and Danja, many critics compared the film's music to her previous album *Back to Basics*.[201] Additionally, Aguilera's recent albums *Bionic* and *Lotus*, featured mainstream producers including Shellback and Max Martin. On working with Martin, Aguilera added, "He's known about me but we haven't crossed paths. Those records were the kind I wanted to stray apart from. If you look at what I did in the past (after my debut), I always try to do things that will challenge me and challenge the listener, too. Could this have worked 10 years ago? I'm not sure. It's taken us a decade in the same business for us to come together, respect each other's work ethic and how we like to be heard and making a marriage out of it."[195] Both albums however received mixed reviews and criticized Aguilera for the album's material,[117][165] a review in The *Tampa Bay Times* adds, "Aguilera is too talented, and hopefully too smart, to continue down this wasteful path. And yet, it's troubling that she wants to compete with the unworthy Ke$has of the world. Drop the grudges and the desperate party cuts, Christina, and let's get back to basics."[202]

Influences

Aguilera has named Etta James (*left*) and Madonna (*right*) her biggest influences.[203]

Aguilera's major influence and idol is blues singer Etta James, whose classic song "At Last" has been covered by Aguilera throughout her career. Aguilera says, "Etta is my all-time favorite singer. I've said it for the last seven years – since I had my first debut record out – in every interview. I mean, all of Etta's old songs, countless songs I could name, I grew up listening to."[204] Following James' death in 2012, Aguilera was asked to perform "At Last" at her funeral.[205] Prior to performing Aguilera stated, "There's a line in this song that says 'I found a dream that I could speak to.' And for me that dream, all my life, has been Etta James."[206] The majority of her album, *Back to Basics*, pays tribute to James and other pop standard singers who many originated from the 1950s. In her early years she listened to vintage jazz, blues, and soul music.[207] The album includes the song, "Slow Down Baby", which sampled a Gladys Knight & the Pips song. A review in *The Guardian* declared, "Practically everything recorded before Aguilera was born blurs into one amorphous genre, which she categorises, somewhat inadequately, as 'fun music'".[208] Aguilera has also mentioned Whitney Houston as another major influence, having performed many of her songs in her early years during talent shows[18] and adopting her vocal style. Aguilera paid tribute to Houston performing "Run to You" during the 2001 BET Awards. The track was sung by Aguilera and submitted to RCA Records in 1998, which eventually helped in earning her recording contract.[209] Aguilera said early in her career that Mariah Carey was another influence.[210] According to author Pier Dominguez, Aguilera stated that it was Carey and her debut single, "Vision of Love", who had the biggest influence on her vocal style.[211] Aguilera has also named Madonna and Janet Jackson as two of her biggest influences "for being re-inventive and being brave as strong females, to explore whatever, even if they do get bad press. It's just like they were fearless."[203] Her other musical influences include Aretha Franklin,[212] Donna Summer,[213] and Nina Simone.[214]

Aguilera cites the musical *The Sound of Music* and its lead actress, Julie Andrews as her first inspiration for singing and performing.[215] At the age of six, the film helped Aguilera cope with her violent childhood adding, "Bad things happened in my home; there was violence. *The Sound of Music* looked like a form of release. I would open my bedroom window to sing out like Maria. In my own way, I'd be in those hills."[216] She mentioned the "Golden age of Hollywood" as another inspiration in which she says, "I'm referencing Marlene Dietrich, Marilyn Monroe, Carole Lombard, Greta Garbo, Veronica Lake".[217] Her star on the Hollywood Walk of Fame is located near that of Julie Andrews and is next to Greta Garbo's.[218] In her music video for "Ain't No Other Man" she plays her alter ego, "Baby Jane" in reference to the film *Whatever Happened to Baby Jane?*.[219] The film's stars included actresses Bette Davis and Joan Crawford. The third single from *Back to Basics*, "Candyman" was inspired by the 1941 song, "Boogie Woogie Bugle Boy" by The Andrews Sisters which was played during World War II. She was also inspired by pin-up girls and several paintings by Alberto Vargas. Aguilera has expressed interest in cultural icons Nico, Blondie and artists Roy Lichtenstein and Andy Warhol.[220] She has often worked with photographer and close friend, David LaChapelle who once worked with Warhol. Chapelle has shot many of Aguilera's music videos, magazine shoots and advertisements. She is also a fan of graffiti artist Banksy. In 2006, she purchased three of Banksy's works during a private art exhibition; one of them included a pornographic picture of Queen Victoria in a lesbian pose with a prostitute.[221] She has mentioned in several interviews that she is a fan of actress Angelina Jolie,[222] Lucille Ball;[223] and her *Burlesque* co-star, Cher.[125] Fashion has also been a part of Aguilera's music career and image which she has used as a form of expression during performances and music videos. In 2003, she became the muse and inspiration for Donatella Versace's 2003 fall line. Versace also designed pieces for her tour the following year. Aguilera is also a fan of Roberto Cavalli, John Galliano, Marc Jacobs, and Alexander McQueen whose designs she has worn throughout her career.[224][225]

Other ventures

Products and endorsements

In 2000, Aguilera was the face for make-up line *Fetish* where she worked in choosing colors and packaging for the line. She ended her contract the following year.[226] Throughout her career Aguilera has endorsed several brands, including Skechers, Mercedes-Benz, Verizon Wireless, Versace,[227] and soft drink giants Coca-Cola and Pepsi in 2001 and 2006, respectively.[228] In 2004, Aguilera earned £200,000 (about $300,000) for opening the summer sale at London's Harrods store.[229] In 2005, she was reportedly paid $3.6 million[230] to sing a three song set for Russian billionaire Andrey Melnichenko's wedding. Aguilera signed a contract with European cell phone operator Orange to promote the new Sony Ericsson Walkman phone during the 2006 World Cup. In 2010, Aguilera was paid $1 million by investor Charles Brandes to perform at a private party.[231] In 2011, she was paid €2.4 million (around $3.2 million) by a Spanish multi-millionaire for a private four-song concert.[232]

In 2008, jewelry designer Stephen Webster and close friend of Aguilera released "Shattered", a collection of sterling silver pieces, through Neiman Marcus and Bergdorf Goodman. Aguilera, who inspired the collection, was featured as a Hitchcock heroine saying, "Working together on this campaign and collection has been an incredible experience. I am honored to be a part of it all."[233][234] They reprised their work together for Webster's 2009 spring line.[235] In 2011, Aguilera attended São Paulo Fashion Week to premiere her new line of clothing for Brazilian department store C&A which launched in April.[236]

Aguilera released two fragrances throughout Europe, the first one *Xpose*, was released in late 2004 and sold relatively well.[237][238] Through Procter and Gamble Aguilera released her signature fragrance, *Simply Christina* in 2007.[239] In Christmas 2007, the fragrance became the number one perfume in the UK,[240] and later in 2009 it became the 4th best selling perfume in the UK,[241] and Germany where it topped sales for the year.[242] The perfume won as the people's choice for favorite celebrity fragrance at the annual UK Fifi Awards 2008.[243] She released her third fragrance, *Inspire*, accompanied with a body care collection, on September 1, 2008.[244] The perfume hit shelves in the US, Canada, Latin America, Asia and Northern and Eastern Europe. It was Aguilera's first fragrance released outside of Europe.[245] Her worldwide ad campaign included a television ad shot by David LaChapelle and was released in the US through Macy's department stores. The release coincided with Macy's 150th anniversary which featured Aguilera in commemorative photos.[246] She released her fourth fragrance *By Night* in October,[247] which became the third best selling fragrance in the UK in 2009.[241] Both "By Day" and "By Night" were nominated for Best Perfume of the Year at the FIFI Awards 2011.[248] The range was further augmented by *Royal Desire* in 2010[249] and *Secret Potion* the following year.[250]

Philanthropy

Throughout her career, Aguilera has been involved with several charities. She signed a letter from PETA to the South Korean government asking that the country stop its alleged killing of dogs for food.[251] During her 2007 tour she wore a fur stole during the beginning of her tour, which designer Roberto Cavalli provided without informing her. After receiving a video from PETA Vice President Dan Mathews on the treatment of foxes, she replaced the stole with synthetic fur for the remainder of her tour. Aguilera was reportedly upset adding, "I only ever wear fake fur".[252] In 2010, Aguilera auctioned off tickets for her upcoming tour for Christie's A Bid to Save the Earth. Proceeds benefited nonprofit environmental groups Conservation International, Oceana, Natural Resources Defense Council, and The Central Park Conservancy.[253] Aguilera also supports Defenders of Wildlife, Missing Kids, National Alliance of Breast Cancer Organizations,[254] Women's Cancer Research Fund,[255] and Cedars-Sinai Women's Cancer Research Institute.[256] She has also worked alongside nonprofit organization Do Something saying, "Every individual has the power to inspire young people across the country."[257] In 2010, Aguilera was nominated for a VH1 Do Something Award for her work with the organization and her efforts in the response to the 2010 Haiti earthquake.[258] Aguilera is still a major contributor in her hometown of Pittsburgh contributing regularly to the Women's Center & Shelter of Greater Pittsburgh. According to her official website, she toured the center and donated $200,000 to the shelter. She also has auctioned off front row seats and back stage passes for the Pittsburgh-based charity.[259] She has continued her donations and visits to the shelter, and plans to open an additional one.[260] She also supports the National Coalition Against Domestic Violence and Refuge UK.[254] Since then she has worked with Lifetime Television's 'End violence against women' campaign. Her work there included a public service announcement which aired on the network and during her Back to Basics Tour.[261]

Aguilera on a promotional poster for World
Hunger Relief

Regarded as a gay icon, Aguilera was honored at the GLAAD Awards for using gay and transgender images in her music video for "Beautiful". When accepting the award Aguilera said, "My video captures the reality that gay and transgender people are beautiful, even though prejudice and discrimination against them still exists."[262] In 2005, she appeared on a compilation album, *Love Rocks*, proceeds benefit the Human Rights Campaign, an organization dedicated to promoting equal rights for gay, lesbian, bisexual and transgendered people. In 2008, she spoke out against California's Proposition 8 which eliminates same-sex marriage in California saying, "Why you would put so much money behind something [aimed at] stopping people from loving each other and bonding together? I just don't understand it. It's hard for me to grasp. But I would've been out there with my rally sign as well."[263] In 2011, Aguilera was honored at The Abbey, a gay club in West Hollywood, for her contributions to the gay community as the first honoree on their Gay Walk of Fame joining Dame Elizabeth Taylor in being immortalized forever.[264] Aguilera contributes in the fight against AIDS, by participating in AIDS Project Los Angeles' Artists Against AIDS "What's Going On?" cover project. In 2004, Aguilera became the new face for cosmetic company M·A·C and spokesperson for M·A·C AIDS Fund. Aguilera appeared in advertisements of the M·A·C's Viva Glam V lipstick and lipgloss, and was featured on *Vanity Fair* in recognition of her campaign work. In addition, Aguilera contributed to YouthAIDS by posing for a joint YouthAIDS and Aldo Shoes campaign for "Empowerment Tags" in Canada, the U.S. and the UK. She was featured with one of three ubiquitous slogans, "Speak No Evil?" and stated, "HIV is something that people don't want to talk about, hear about, or face."[265][266] Singer Elton John featured Aguilera in his charity book titled *4 Inches* benefiting the Elton John AIDS Foundation.[267] John also picked Aguilera, for his annual "Fashion Rocks" charity concert which accompanies music and fashion to benefit the fight against AIDS/HIV.[268]

In the run-up to the 2004 United States presidential election, Aguilera was featured on billboards for the "Only You Can Silence Yourself" online voter registration drive run by the nonpartisan, non-profit campaign "Declare Yourself". In these political advertisements, shot by David LaChapelle, Aguilera was shown with her mouth sewn shut to symbolize the effects of not voting. She appeared on *The Oprah Winfrey Show* to discuss the importance of voting. In late 2007, Aguilera became the spokesperson for "Rock the Vote" where she urged young people to vote in the 2008 presidential election.[271] In partnership with "Rock the Vote", she appeared in a public service announcement which aired in mid-2008. The advert showed Aguilera with her son, Max Bratman, wrapped

Hillary Clinton (center) and David Novak (right) presented Aguilera (left) with the George McGovern Leadership Award in October 2012 for her outstanding contributions to the United Nations World Hunger Relief effort.[269][270]

in an American flag, while singing "America the Beautiful". In November 2005, all of her wedding gifts were submitted to various charities around the nation in support of Hurricane Katrina victims.[272] That year she also performed at "Unite of the Stars" concert in aid of Unite Against Hunger in Johannesburg, South Africa and at the Nelson Mandela Children's Fund at the Coca-Cola Dome.[273] In March 2007, Aguilera took part in a charity album (remaking Lennon's "Mother"), proceeds benefit Amnesty International's efforts to end genocide in Darfur. The

album, *Instant Karma: The Amnesty International Campaign to Save Darfur*, was released June 12, 2007, and featured various artists.[274] In 2008, she headlined London's Africa Rising charity concert at Royal Albert Hall which raises awareness for finding substantial issues facing the continent.[275] Later that year she appeared on the Turkish version of *Deal or No Deal, Var mısın? Yok musun?*, where proceeds were donated to a charity program for orphans.[276]

In 2009, Aguilera became the global spokesperson for World Hunger Relief appearing in advertisements, online campaigns and a public service announcement.[277] Aguilera and her then-husband traveled to Guatemala with the World Food Programme to bring awareness to issues such as the high malnutrition rate in that country. She met with families of the villages and some of the beneficiaries of WFP's nutrition programs. Aguilera adds, "The people of WFP do such a great job helping hungry children and mothers. I'm thankful for the opportunity to be part of such a wonderful project."[278] Since becoming a global spokeswoman Aguilera has helped raise over $22 million which helped provide over 90 million meals.[279] She was honored at *Variety*'s annual "Power of Women" luncheon in late 2009 alongside other women in entertainment for her contribution to philanthropic and charitable causes.[280] In response to the 2010 Haiti earthquake, Aguilera donated a signed Chrysler 300 which was auctioned for relief efforts.[281] She was one of the many artists who appeared on the *Hope for Haiti* telethon on January 22, 2010, donations directly benefited Oxfam America, Partners In Health, Red Cross and UNICEF. She later appeared on a second public service announcement alongside former boxer Muhammad Ali to raise funds for the World Food Programme's efforts to bring food to survivors of the earthquake.[282] Later that year Aguilera made her first visit to Haiti as an ambassador against hunger where she visited two schools in the town of Léogâne. During her time there she assisted in the ongoing efforts to help the badly damaged town where she served meals and highlighted reconstruction efforts in the country.[283] That year, Aguilera was appointed UN ambassador for the WFP.[149] At the 2012 ALMA Awards, Aguilera was awarded the Special Achievement Award for her career and humanitarian efforts.[284] That year, Hillary Clinton also awarded Aguilera the George McGovern Leadership Award, making her the first singer to receive the award.[285] In 2012, after Hurricane Sandy ripped through New Jersey, New York and other parts of the Northeast, Aguilera performed "Beautiful" to open the *Hurricane Sandy: Coming Together* benefit telethon. She introduced the song by saying that she had been born in the devastated borough of Staten Island; all proceeds went to the American Red Cross.[286]

Discography

- *Christina Aguilera* (1999)
- *Mi Reflejo* (2000)
- *My Kind of Christmas* (2000)
- *Stripped* (2002)
- *Back to Basics* (2006)
- *Bionic* (2010)
- *Lotus* (2012)

Filmography

Year	Title	Role	Notes
Film			
2004	*Shark Tale*	Herself (voice/animated)	Cameo appearance[287]
2008	*Shine a Light*	Herself	Documentary
2010	*Get Him to the Greek*	Herself	Cameo appearance
2010	*Burlesque*	Alice Marilyn "Ali" Rose	Nominated—Golden Globe Award for Best Original Song Nominated—ALMA Award for Favorite Film Leading Actress – Comedy or Musical Nominated—Grammy Award for Best Compilation Soundtrack for Visual Media Also executive music producer
Television			
1993—1995	*The Mickey Mouse Club*	Herself/Various Roles	Season 6–7
1999	*Beverly Hills, 90210*	Herself	"Let's Eat Cake" (Season 10, Episode 2)
2000	*Al salir de clase*	Herself	"El día que no existe" (Season 5, Episode 42) "Augurios" (Season 8, Episode 72)
2000—2006	*Saturday Night Live*	Herself/Various Roles/Host/Musical Guest	"Christopher Walken/Christina Aguilera" (Season 25, Episode 16) "Salma Hayek/Christina Aguilera" (Season 28, Episode 15) "Christina Aguilera/Maroon 5" (Season 29, Episode 13) "Alec Baldwin/Christina Aguilera" (Season 32, Episode 5)
2003	*Player$*	Herself	"Hulk" (Season 2, Episode 10)
2003	*Punk'd*	Herself	"Ryan Pinkston – VH1 Big in 2002 Awards" (Season 1, Episode 1)
2009	*Project Runway*	Herself / Guest Judge	"Sequins, Feathers and Fur, Oh My!" (Season 6, Episode 9)
2010	*Conan*	Herself	"A Prayer for Dick Butkus" (Season 1, Episode 9)
2010	*Entourage*	Herself	"Lose Yourself" (Season 7, Episode 10)
2011—2012	*The Voice*	Herself (Coach and Judge)	Seasons 1—3 Won—ALMA Award for Favorite TV Reality, Variety, or Comedy Personality or Act (2012) Nominated—ALMA Award for Favorite TV Reality, Variety, or Comedy Personality or Act (2011) Nominated—Teen Choice Award for Choice TV: Female Personality (2011, 2012)

Concert tours

- Christina Aguilera in Concert (2000–01)
- Justified & Stripped Tour (2003) (with Justin Timberlake)
- Stripped Live... on Tour (2003)
- Back to Basics Tour (2006–07)

Notes

[1] "Bionic by Christina Aguilera Songfacts" (http://www.songfacts.com/detail.php?id=19834). . Retrieved 2011-06-29.

[2] "Christina Aguilera" (http://www.wfp.org/content/christina-aguilera-ambassador). . Retrieved 2011-06-29.

[3] "Christina Aguilera to Sing the National Anthem at Super Bowl" (http://www.theblogismine.com/2011/01/25/christina-aguilera-to-sing-the-national-anthem-at-super-bowl/). . Retrieved 2011-06-29.

[4] "The Voice Judges: Christina Aguilera, Cee Lo Green, Blake Shelton and Adam Levine" (http://www.starsofreality.com/Voice-Judges-Christina-Aguilera-Cee-Lo-Green-Blake-Shelton-Adam-Levine-16052675). . Retrieved 2011-06-29.

[5] http://www.christinaaguilera.com/

[6] "Christina Aguilera awards" (http://www.bignoisenow.com/christina/awards.html). *Big Noise Now*. 2000. . Retrieved 2012-12-04.

[7] "Top Pop Artists - Female" (http://www1.billboard.biz/bbbiz/charts/yearendcharts/2003/hsitlpfeml.jsp). *Billboard*. 2003-27-12. . Retrieved 2013-08-01.

[8] Staff, Billboard (2010). "Artists of the Decade" (http://www.billboard.com/#/features/artist-of-the-decade-1004053060.story). *Billboard*. Nielsen Company. . Retrieved 2010-05-03.

[9] "Single Sales Artist" (http://www.billboard.biz/bbbiz/charts/decadeendcharts/2009/singles-sales-artists). Billboard.biz. Prometheus Global Media. . Retrieved 2010-12-06.

[10] Levine, Stuart (2011-04-09). "Can 'The Voice' be heard?" (http://www.variety.com/article/VR1118035166). *Variety*. . Retrieved 2012-12-04.

[11] Staff, VH1 (2012). "VH1's 100 Greatest Women in Music (the complete list)" (http://www.vh1.com/music/tuner/2012-02-13/vh1s-100-greatest-women-in-music-complete-list/). *VH1*. VH1. . Retrieved 2012-01-24.

[12] "Christina Aguilera > Biography" (http://www.billboard.com/features/christina-aguilera-billboard-cover-story-1007955332.story#/artist/christina-aguilera/bio/325726). *Billboard*. Prometheus Global Media. . Retrieved 2012-10-01.

[13] "Christina Aguilera - Biography" (http://www.people.com/people/christina_aguilera/biography). *People.com*. Time Inc. . Retrieved 2012-11-02.

[14] "Christina Aguilera Biography" (http://www.people.com/people/christina_aguilera). People.com. . Retrieved 2010-12-08.

[15] Scott Gregory, Sophfronia (1999-09-27). "Uncorking the Genie" (http://www.people.com/people/archive/article/0,,20129327,00.html). People *magazine*. . Retrieved 2012-11-19.

[16] Dominguez, Pier (December 2002). *Christina Aguilera: A Star is Made: The Unauthorized Biography*. Amber Communications Group, Inc.. pp. 1–2. ISBN 978-0-9702224-5-9.

[17] Elaine Rivera (2001-09-15). "What A Woman Wants" (http://www.time.com/time/magazine/article/0,9171,1000774,00.html). *TIME*. . Retrieved 2007-12-03.

[18] Richard Harrington (2000-02-13). "Christina Aguilera's Fast Track" (http://www.washingtonpost.com/wp-srv/WPcap/2000-02/13/003r-021300-idx.html). *Washington Post*. . Retrieved 2012-12-09.

[19] Thompson, Paul (2009-09-23). "Christina Aguilera talks about childhood hell at the hands of her violent father" (http://www.dailymail.co.uk/tvshowbiz/article-1215346/Christina-Aguilera-talks-childhood-hell-hands-violent-father.html). *Daily Mail*. Associated Newspapers Ltd. . Retrieved 2012-12-03.

[20] "Christina Aguilera Biography" (http://movies.yahoo.com/movie/contributor/1800409839/bio). Yahoo!. . Retrieved 2011-02-17.

[21] Helligar, Jeremy; Majewski, Lori (2003-02-03). "Christina's World". *Us Weekly*.

[22] Grupp, John (2009-05-06). "Anthem singer fires up Mellon crowd" (http://www.pittsburghlive.com/x/pittsburghtrib/sports/penguins/s_623827.html). *Pittsburgh Tribune-Review*. . Retrieved 2010-02-05.

[23] USMagazine.com Stars who were bullied (http://www.usmagazine.com/celebritynews/photos/celebs-who-were-bullied-2010510/10466) Retrieved on December 9, 2010.

[24] Goldberg, Lesley (2010-11-17). ""Beautiful," Bullied and "Burlesque" – our interview with Christina Aguilera" (http://www.afterellen.com/people/2010/11/christina-aguilera?page=0,0). After Ellen. . Retrieved 2012-12-04.

[25] Goldstein, Rob (1999-05-15). "Dreaming Of Genie" (http://web.archive.org/web/20070401032341/http://music.yahoo.com/read/interview/12043048). Yahoo! Music. Archived from the original (http://music.yahoo.com/read/interview/12043048) on 2012-12-04. . Retrieved 2012-12-04.

[26] "Christina Aguilera Biography" (http://www.allmusic.com/artist/p357293). Allmusic. Rovi Corporation. . Retrieved 2012-12-04.

[27] Dinca, Alma Boghitoiu. "An Interview with Christina Aguilera" (http://www.brasovtravelguide.ro/en/brasov/events/golden-stag-festival/1997.php). Brasov travel guide. . Retrieved 2007-05-25.

[28] "Pegasus Lounge to close for good" (http://www.pittsburghlive.com/x/pittsburghtrib/news/breaking/s_650758.html). *Tribune-Review*. 2009-10-30. . Retrieved 2009-01-17.

[29] Willman, Chris (2010-10-11). "Club Kid" (http://www.ew.com/ew/article/0,,84715,00.html). *Entertainment Weekly*. Time Inc.. . Retrieved 2012-12-04.

[30] Smith, Andy (1998-08-15). "One talented teen". *The Providence Journal* (The Providence Journal Co.).

[31] Dominguez 2003, p. 45

[32] Erlewine, Stephen Thomas. "Christina Aguilera - Christina Aguilera" (http://www.allmusic.com/album/ christina-aguilera-mw0000244313). Allmusic. Rovi Corporation. . Retrieved 2012-12-04.

[33] "Christina Aguilera Musician Coach of 'The Voice'" (http://www.dutchdailynews.com/christina-aguilera-the-voice/). [Dutch Daily News]. 2011=03-04. .

[34] "Christina Aguilera Net Worth" (http://www.celebritynetworth.com/richest-celebrities/singers/christina-aguilera-net-worth/). [Celebrity Networth]. 2012. .

[35] McLean, Craig (2010-05-07). "Christina Aguilera's 'eye on the prize'" (http://www.telegraph.co.uk/culture/music/rockandpopfeatures/ 7682705/Christina-Aguileras-eye-on-the-prize.html). *The Daily Telegraph* (Telegraph Media Group). . Retrieved 2012-09-11.

[36] Gold and Platinum: Top 100 Albums (http://riaa.com/goldandplatinum.php?content_selector=top-100-albums) Page 2, Retrieved December 5, 2012"

[37] "UK Singles Chart - Number One" (http://www.number-ones.co.uk/Christina-Aguilera-number-ones/Genie-In-The-Bottle.html). Number Ones UK. 1999. . Retrieved 2012-12-07.

[38] "Christina Aguilera - Genie in a Bottle" (http://www.spanishcharts.com/showitem.asp?interpret=Christina+Aguilera&titel=Genie+in+ a+Bottle&cat=s). SpanishCharts.com. 1999. . Retrieved 2012-12-07.

[39] "Best Selling Records of 1999 Singles - (More Than 500,000)" (http://www.billboard.biz/bbbiz/charts/archivesearch/article_display/ 849310). Billboard.*Biz. Billboard*. 1999-12-31. . Retrieved 2007-12-08.

[40] "Stripped for all the world to hear" (http://www.smh.com.au/articles/2003/08/31/1062268467251.html). *Tae Sydney Morning Herald*. Fairfax Media. 2003-09-01. . Retrieved 2007-05-25.

[41] *Billboard* chart beat Fergie Scores Third Solo No. 1 On Hot 100 (http://www.billboard.com/column/chartbeat/ ask-billboard-kylie-fever-1004104865.story#/news/fergie-scores-third-solo-no-1-on-hot-100-1003633227.story) Retrieved on February 16, 2010.

[42] Gelman, Jason (2001-05-15). "'What A Girl Wants' Wins BMI Award" (http://www.bignoisenow.com/christina/bmiaward.html). Daily *Yahoo!* News. . Retrieved 2012-10-12.

[43] IMDB.com Season 10, Episode 2 Let's Eat Cake (http://www.imdb.com/title/tt0522852/) Retrieved on December 5, 2012

[44] Christophe John Farley (2000-03-07). "Christina Aguilera - Building 21st Century Star" (http://articles.chicagotribune.com/2000-03-07/ features/0003070036_1_lilith-fair-electric-artists-rca). *Chicago Tribune*. . Retrieved 2012-12-09.

[45] Rosen, Craig (2000-02-24). "Christina Aguilera Wins Best New Artist" (http://web.archive.org/web/20080528131603/http://music. yahoo.com/read/story/12051721). Yahoo! Music. Archived from the original (http://music.yahoo.com/read/story/12051721) on 2012-12-04. . Retrieved 2012-12-04.

[46] Teri vanHorn (2000-08-16). "Christina Aguilera Delves Into Latin Roots On Spanish LP" (http://www.mtv.com/news/articles/1424794/ 20000816/aguilera_christina.jhtml). MTV News. . Retrieved 2008-08-01.

[47] Colleti, Roger (2000-04-18). "Christina Aguilera To Record With Her Idol" (http://www.mtv.com/news/articles/1424808/20000418/ aguilera_christina.jhtml). MTV News. . Retrieved 2008-08-01.

[48] "Mi reflejo - Christina Aguilera" (http://www.billboard.com/#/album/christina-aguilera/mi-reflejo/443534). *Billboard*. Prometheus Global Media. . Retrieved 2012-12-04.

[49] "Mi Reflejo sales" (http://www.bignoisenow.com/christina/latincdbillboard.html). *Big Noise Now*. November 2000. . Retrieved 2012-12-05.

[50] Newman, Melinda (2006-06-29). "Christina Aguilera Gets Inspired by 30s and 40s Idols for her Upcoming Album" (http://books.google. ca/books?id=JhYEAAAAMBAJ&pg=PA26&lpg=PA26&dq=christina+aguilera+stripped+12+million+worldwide&source=bl& ots=Fy0U0cCXVv&sig=09hOZe7zS7OpOmK876MdC6FjrhI&hl=en&sa=X&ei=NpVQUOOtGKbwyQH41YCgCg& ved=0CDUQ6AEwAjgK#v=onepage&q=christina aguilera stripped 12 million worldwide&f=false). *Billboard (magazine)* (Prometheus Global Media). . Retrieved 2012-09-19.

[51] Gary Trust (September 24, 2012). "Ask Billboard" (http://www.billboard.com/column/chartbeat/ ask-billboard-who-s-the-hot-100-s-king-elvis-1007955992.story?utm_source=most_recent#/column/chartbeat/ ask-billboard-who-s-the-hot-100-s-king-elvis-1007955992.story?page=2). Billboard. . Retrieved 2012-09-24.

[52] "RIAA Mi Reflejo certification" (http://www.riaa.com/goldandplatinumdata.php?artist="Mi+Reflejo"). RIAA. . Retrieved 2012-12-06.

[53] Saraceno, Christina (2001-10-30). "Christina Wins Latin Grammy" (http://www.rollingstone.com/music/news/ christina-wins-latin-grammy-20011030). *Rolling Stone*. Jann S. Wenner. . Retrieved 2012-12-04.

[54] Grein, Paul (2011-10-30). "Week Ending Oct. 30, 2011. Songs: Eleven For Rihanna" (http://music.yahoo.com/blogs/chart-watch/ week-ending-oct-30-2011-songs-eleven-rihanna-002531232.html). Yahoo! Music. . Retrieved 2011-11-06.

[55] RIAA Certifications for Christina Aguilera RIAA Gold and Platinum certifications (http://riaa.com/goldandplatinumdata. php?artist="Aguilera,+Christina") Retrieved on December 4, 2012

[56] "Christina Aguilera Kicks Off Her First Headlining Tour on July 31" (http://www.prnewswire.com/news-releases/
christina-aguilera-kicks-off-her-first-headlining-tour-on-july-31-sears-and-levisr-present-christina-aguilera-in-concert-72584432.html). PR
Newswire. 2000-07-31. . Retrieved 2012-12-07.

[57] Search My Reflection RIAA RIAA Gold and Platinum certifications (http://www.riaa.com/goldandplatinumdata.php?table=SEARCH)
Archived (http://www.webcitation.org/5mr9q5hMa) 17 January 2010 at WebCite

[58] Merin, Jennifer (February 11, 2000). Fleshing out the vital details (http://www.usatoday.com/life/music/lmds924.htm). *USA Today*.
Retrieved on May 25, 2007.

[59] Helling, Steve May 12, 2009 People Magazine Eminem and His Many Feuds (http://www.people.com/people/article/0,,20278448,00.
html) Retrieved on November 9, 2010.

[60] Moss, Corey August 30, 2002 MTV.com Eminem Hugs Christina: Backstage At The VMAs (http://www.mtv.com/news/articles/
1457267/20020830/eminem.jhtml) Retrieved on November 9, 2010.

[61] *USA Today* October 24, 2002 Aguilera's image is 'Stripped' (http://www.usatoday.com/life/music/news/
2002-10-23-christina-aguilera_x.htm) *USA Today* Music Retrieved on July 3, 2009.

[62] US magazine. Christina Aguilera (http://www.usmagazine.com/node/112). Retrieved on May 25, 2007.

[63] "Christina Aguilera Album & Song Chart History" (http://www.billboard.com/#/artist/Christina+Aguilera/chart-history/
325726?f=379&g=Singles). *Billboard*. Prometheus Global Media. . Retrieved 2012-12-04.

[64] "Lady Marmalade chart history" (http://www.bignoisenow.com/christina/ladycharthistory3.html). *Big Noise Now*. . Retrieved
2012-12-08.

[65] Michelle, A. (2001-01-21). ""Lady Marmalade" World's Best-selling single of 2001" (http://www.bignoisenow.com/christina/
ladymarmalade.html). *BigNoiseNow*. . Retrieved 2012-12-27.

[66] Mitchell, John (2011-06-27). "Remaking 'Lady Marmalade' 10 Years Later" (http://newsroom.mtv.com/2011/06/27/
remaking-lady-marmalade-10-years-later/). MTV Newsroom. MTV Networks. . Retrieved 2012-12-04.

[67] "Statement from Aguilera's official site about "Just Be Free" single" (http://web.archive.org/web/20021212142430/http://www.
christinaaguilera.com/rumormill/rumor_0060.html). Archived from the original (http://www.christinaaguilera.com/rumormill/
rumor_0060.html) on December 12, 2002. . (From The Internet Archive). Retrieved on May 25, 2007.

[68] Reid, Shaheem (May 21, 2001). Christina Aguilera Sues to stop release of early recordings (http://www.mtv.com/news/articles/
1443915/20010521/story.jhtml). *MTV*. Retrieved on May 25, 2007.

[69] McGrath, Stephanie (July 3, 2001). "Disputed Aguilera album to be released". *Toronto Sun*. Retrieved on May 25, 2007.

[70] Stitzel, Kim (February 2002). "Christina Aguilera: Not Your Puppet" (http://www.mtv.com/bands/a/aguilera_christina/
news_feature_feb_02/). MTV. . Retrieved January 29, 2009.

[71] *USA Today* October 24, 2002 Aguilera's image is 'Stripped' (http://www.usatoday.com/life/music/news/
2002-10-23-christina-aguilera_x.htm)*USA Today* Music Retrieved on July 3, 2009.

[72] "Aguilera's Ex-Manager Fires Back" (http://abcnews.go.com/Entertainment/story?id=114375&page=1). ABC News. 2000-10-19. .
Retrieved 2012-12-06.

[73] Silverman, Stephen (1997-10-23). "Aguilera Sues Manager" (http://www.people.com/people/article/0,,621366,00.html). *People*
magazine. . Retrieved 2012-12-05.

[74] Jenison, David (November 6, 2002). "Em's "8 Mile" Outstrips Christina" (http://web.archive.org/web/20080210044244/http://www.
eonline.com/news/article/index.jsp?uuid=5e786ebd-a98e-47d7-b61a-0e7e5c8cf9f7). Archived from the original (http://www.eonline.
com/news/article/index.jsp?uuid=5e786ebd-a98e-47d7-b61a-0e7e5c8cf9f7) on February 10, 2008. .. *E! News*. Retrieved on May 25, 2007.

[75] "*Stripped* Review" (http://www.ew.com/ew/article/0,,384149~4~0~stripped,00.html). *Entertainment Weekly*. November 1, 2002. .
Retrieved February 17, 2011.

[76] D'Angelo, Joe (October 18, 2002). 'Dirrty' Christina Aguilera Video Thai-ed To Sex Industry (http://www.mtv.com/news/articles/
1458223/20021018/aguilera_christina.jhtml)". *MTV*. Retrieved on May 25, 2007.

[77] (October 30, 2002). "Aguilera sheds teen pop image, alongside clothes" (http://www.smh.com.au/articles/2002/10/29/1035683410806.
html). *The Sydney Morning Herald*. October 30, 2002. .. *The Sydney Morning Herald*. Retrieved on February 16, 2011.

[78] *People* Magazine: Christina Aguilera August 15, 2006 Christina Aguilera: Five Fun Facts (http://www.people.com/people/
christina_aguilera/0,,,00.html) *People* magazine online Retrieved on August 29, 2008.

[79] Moss, Corey MTV News Online (November 2, 2008) Christina Aguilera Follows Controversial 'Dirrty' With Inspirational 'Beautiful' MTV
News Retrieved on July 5, 2008. (http://www.mtv.com/news/articles/1458506/20021105/story.jhtml)

[80] Scaggs, Austin August 10, 2006 Dirty Girl Cleans Up (http://www.christinamultimedia.com/newssource/index.php?articleID=9603)
RollingStone online Retrieved on February 16, 2010.

[81] "Christina Aguilera Song & Chart History" (http://www.billboard.com/artist/christina-aguilera/chart-history/325726#/artist/
christina-aguilera/chart-history/325726). *Billboard*. . Retrieved 2012-12-07.

[82] "Justin And Christina's Tour Stripped Of Lights, Cameras, Action Due To Accident" (http://www.mtv.com/news/articles/1476581/
justin-christinas-tour-stalled.jhtml). MTV.com. . Retrieved 2012-12-06.

[83] World Entertainment News Network (January 16, 2004). Outkast + Justin Top Rolling Stone Poll (http://www.teenmusic.com/d.
asp?r=57615). Retrieved on May 25, 2007.

[84] "*Maxim* Christina Aguilera" (http://www.maxim.com/slideshow/girls-of-maxim/8565?slide=0#). .. *Maxim* magazine. Retrieved on
February 16, 2011.

[85] Moss, Corey (November 10, 2003) Sing Like Christina And Dance Like Carmen? The Pussycat Dolls Want You (http://www.mtv.com/news/articles/1480321/20031110/aguilera_christina.jhtml?headlines=true). *MTV* Retrieved (February 28, 2008)

[86] PRNewswire *Maxim* Hot 100 2003 (http://www2.prnewswire.com/cgi-bin/stories.pl?ACCT=104&STORY=/www/story/05-16-2003/0001948393&EDATE). *Maxim*. Retrieved on February 16, 2011.

[87] "Christina Calls Off Tour With Chingy Due To Vocal Strain" (http://www.mtv.com/news/articles/1486695/christina-calls-off-tour-with-chingy.jhtml). MTV.com. . Retrieved 2012-12-06.

[88] "Cattrall Praises Aguilera's performance" (http://web.archive.org/web/20090215045115/http://www.sfgate.com/cgi-bin/article.cgi?file=/gate/archive/2004/02/24/ddish.DTL). *San Francisco Gate*. 2004-02-24. Archived from the original (http://www.sfgate.com/cgi-bin/article.cgi?file=/gate/archive/2004/02/24/ddish.DTL) on 2012-12-04. . Retrieved 2012-12-04.

[89] Hello! (October 20, 2004). Christina turns Hollywood pin-up in latest shoot (http://www.hellomagazine.com/music/2004/10/20/christinaaguliera/). Retrieved on May 25, 2007.

[90] Edwards, Tanya L. (November 4, 2004). Christina, Gwen Stefani, Dita Von Teese Help Bring Back Burlesque (http://www.mtv.com/news/articles/1458472/20021101/story.jhtml). *MTV*. Retrieved on May 25, 2007.

[91] BBC (February 13, 2005). Singer Christina Aguilera to wed (http://news.bbc.co.uk/2/hi/entertainment/4261641.stm). Retrieved on May 25, 2007.

[92] "Aguilera ties knot". *Herald Sun (Melbourne)* (Nationwide News Pty Limited): p. 3. November 22, 2005.

[93] Evans, Chris (April 2, 2008). What's Next For Christina Aguilera? (http://blogcritics.org/music/article/whats-next-for-christina-aguilera/). BC. Retrieved on April 2, 2008.

[94] Recording Industry Association of America (November 15, 2006). "U.S. Certification" (http://www.riaa.com/goldandplatinumdata.php?resultpage=1&table=SEARCH_RESULTS&action=&title=Back to Basics&artist=Christina Aguilera&format=&debutLP=&category=&sex=&releaseDate=&requestNo=&type=&level=&label=&company=&certificationDate=&awardDescription=&catalogNo=&aSex=&rec_id=&charField=&gold=&platinum=&multiPlat=&level2=&certDate=&album=&id=&after=&before=&startMonth=1&endMonth=1&startYear=1958&endYear=2009&sort=Artist&perPage=25). . Retrieved July 27, 2009.

[95] Moss, Corey (June 6, 2006). Christina Makes Her Comeback Twice As Nice By Expanding Basics Into Double LP (http://www.mtv.com/news/articles/1533622/20060605/aguilera_christina.jhtml). *MTV*. Retrieved on May 25, 2007.

[96] "Back To Basics Reviews, Ratings, Credits, and More at Metacritic" (http://www.metacritic.com/music/back-to-basics/christina-aguilera). Metacritic. . Retrieved 2008-08-24.

[97] Eliscu, Jenny *Rolling Stone* magazine August 11, 2008 *Back to Basics* review (http://www.rollingstone.com/music/albumreviews/back-to-basics-20100812) Retrieved on September 27, 2008.

[98] Erlewine, Stephen Thomas August 2006 *Back to Basics* review (http://www.allmusic.com/album/r846689) *All Music Guide Retrieved on January 5, 2010.*

[99] Moss, Corety (February 21, 2007). Xtina X Three: Aguilera Has Multiple-Personality Disorder In Clip (http://www.mtv.com/news/articles/1552870/20070220/id_0.jhtml). *MTV*. Retrieved on May 25, 2007.

[100] PRNewswire (September 11, 2006). Aguilera announces Euro tour (http://www.prnewswire.co.uk/cgi/news/release?id=178660). Retrieved on May 25, 2007.

[101] Vineyard, Jennifer (October 12, 2006). Christina Aguilera's Heading Back On Tour For 41 North American Dates (http://www.mtv.com/news/articles/1542894/20061011/aguilera_christina.jhtml). *MTV*. Retrieved on May 25, 2007.

[102] Schulz, Chris (August 2, 2007). Christina Aguilera cancels Auckland shows (http://www.stuff.co.nz/stuff/4150525a10.html). *Stuff New Zealand*. Retrieved on December 11, 2007.

[103] Moss, Corety (February 8, 2007). XChristina's Tour Takes Fans To Circus, Cabaret Club – And Church? (http://www.mtv.com/news/articles/1551861/christinas-tour-gets-spiritual.jhtml). *MTV*. Retrieved on December 11, 2007.

[104] *Billboard.biz* December 13, 2007 The Police Score Top-Grossing Tour Of '07 (http://www.billboard.biz/bbbiz/content_display/industry/e3i7dd5f51b9e62d8922379f7b00b835025) Retrieved on November 16, 2009.

[105] Jamie King's official website Jamie King (http://www.jamiekingofficial.com/) Christina Aguilera *Back to Basics* tour section, video. Retrieved on December 31, 2009.

[106] (December 13, 2007) The Police Score Top-Grossing Tour Of '07 (http://www.billboard.com/bbcom/news/article_display.jsp?vnu_content_id=1003685265). *Billboard*. Retrieved on December 13, 2007.

[107] Micallef, Ken (February 11, 2007). Dixie Chicks Make Nice With Five Grammys (https://www2.grammy.com/GRAMMY_Awards/News/Default.aspx?newsID=2381) *Grammy.com*. Retrieved on May 25, 2007.

[108] Goldman, Lea; Blakeley, Kiri (February 18, 2007). The 20 Richest Women In Entertainment (http://www.forbes.com/2007/01/17/richest-women-entertainment-tech-media-cz_lg_richwomen07_0118womenstars_lander.html). *Forbes*. Retrieved on May 25, 2007.

[109] "Christina Aguilera finally confirms pregnancy" (http://today.msnbc.msn.com/id/21628912/ns/today-entertainment/). NBC.com. November 4, 2007. . Retrieved February 17, 2011.

[110] Fleeman, Mike September 9, 2007 *People* Magazine online Paris Hilton Makes a Baby Announcement – for Christina Aguilera (http://www.people.com/people/package/article/0,,20053775_20055465,00.html) Retrieved on November 18, 2010.

[111] "Christina Aguilera's baby Bris" (http://www.femalefirst.co.uk/celebrity/Christina+Aguilera-19321.html). Female First. January 21, 2008. . Retrieved February 7, 2011.

[112] Rose, Lacey (July 1, 2009). "Jackson Pic Won't Make List of Priciest Celeb Photos" (http://www.forbes.com/2009/07/01/michael-jackson-magazine-business-media-jackson.html). *Forbes*. . Retrieved July 30, 2011.

[113] IMDB.com page *Get Him to the Greek* Get Him to the Greek (2009) Retrieved on October 22, 2008.

[114] Billboard's Best of the 2000s December 2009. Artists of the Decade (http://www.billboard.com/charts-year-end/ hot-100-songs?year=2009#/charts-decade-end/artists-of-the-decade?year=2009&begin=11&order=position) Billboard.com Retrieved on December 11, 2009.

[115] "allmusic (((Bionic > Charts & Awards > Billboard Singles)))" (http://www.allmusic.com/album/r1801137). Allmusic. . Retrieved June 10, 2010.

[116] Pareles, Jon (2010-06=06). "New CDs" (http://www.nytimes.com/2010/06/07/arts/music/07choice.html?pagewanted=1& sq=bionic&st=cse&scp=1). *New York Times*. . Retrieved June 10, 2010.

[117] Stewart, Allison (June 7, 2010). "Christina Aguilera's new album 'Bionic' is a mish-mash of Gaga and blah" (http://www.washingtonpost. com/wp-dyn/content/article/2010/06/04/AR2010060402181.html). *The Washington Post* (The Washington Post Company). . Retrieved June 7, 2010.

[118] Bain, Becky. "The Top 10 Worst Lyrics On 'Bionic'" (http://idolator.com/5529861/ the-top-10-worst-lyrics-on-bionic-christina-aguilera). Idolator. Buzz Media. . Retrieved 2 November 2012.

[119] Young, Matt. "Reviewed: Christina Aguilera, Bionic" (http://balmain-village-voice.whereilive.com.au/lifestyle/story/ reviewed-christina-aguilera-bionic/). *Village Voice*. Village Voice Media. . Retrieved 2 November 2012.

[120] Lamb, Bill. "Christina Aguilera - Bionic A Great: Album Buried In Here" (http://top40.about.com/od/albums/fr/ christinaaguilerabionic.htm). *About.com*. IAC. . Retrieved 2 November 2012.

[121] Grein, Paul Yahoo! Music News June 16, 2010 Where's That "Genie" When You Need Her? (http://new.music.yahoo.com/blogs/ chart_watch/55237/week-ending-june-13-2010-wheres-that-genie-when-you-need-her/) Retrieved on June 16, 2010.

[122] "Week of July 10, 2010" (http://www.billboard.com/charts/billboard-200?begin=21&order=position). *Billboard*. Prometheus Global Media. . Retrieved July 1, 2010.

[123] Elber, Lynn (August 28, 2012). "Christina Aguilera Says 'Feel-Good' New Album Is a 'Rebirth'" (http://www.billboard.com/news/ christina-aguilera-says-feel-good-new-album-1007904422.story?utm_source=most_recent#/news/ christina-aguilera-says-feel-good-new-album-1007904422.story?utm_source=most_recent). Billboard. . Retrieved August 29, 2012.

[124] "Christina Aguilera Cancels Summer Tour Pilot" (http://www.tvguide.com/News/Aguilera-Cancels-Tour-1018919.aspx). TVGuide.com. .

[125] Radish, Christina November 16, 2010 Collider.com Christina Aguilera Interview BURLESQUE (http://www.collider.com/2010/11/16/ christina-aguilera-interview-burlesque/?_r=true) Retrieved on December 3, 2010.

[126] Fleeman, Mike, and Ulrica Wihlborg. "Christina Aguilera Speaks Out About Separation" (http://www.people.com/people/article/ 0,,20433693,00.html), *People*, October 12, 2010

[127] "Exclusive: Christina Aguilera Splits From Husband" (http://www.usmagazine.com/celebritynews/news/ christina-aguilera-splits-from-husband-20101210), *Us*, October 12, 2010

[128] Fleeman, Mike, and Ulrica Wihlborg. "Christina Aguilera Files for Divorce" (http://www.people.com/people/article/0,,20434117,00. html), *People*, October 14, 2010

[129] ""Christina Aguilera Files for Divorce", "TMZ", October 14, 2010" (http://www.tmz.com/2010/10/14/ christina-aguilera-files-for-divorce-jordan-bratman/). Tmz.com. 2010-10-14. . Retrieved 2011-11-05.

[130] "Christina Aguilera and Jordan Bratman reach a divorce deal" (http://www.glamourmagazine.co.uk/celebrity/celebrity-news/2011/02/ 10/christina-aguilera-jordan-bratman-divorce-deal). Glamour *magazine*. February 10, 2011. . Retrieved February 9, 2011.

[131] "Christina Aguilera, Jordan Bratman Finalize Their Divorce" (http://www.usmagazine.com/healthylifestyle/news/ christina-aguilera-jordan-bratman-finalize-their-divorce-2011112). *US magazine.com*. .

[132] "Eminem, Aguilera to Appear on Entourage Season Finale" (http://www.tvguide.com/News/Eminem-Aguilera-Entourage-1020000. aspx). TVGuide.com. .

[133] "Welcome − Hollywood Chamber of Commerce" (http://www.hollywoodchamber.net/index.php?module=blogs&blog_id=25). Hollywoodchamber.net. . Retrieved 2011-11-05.

[134] Fleming, Michael (May 4, 2009). "Christina Aguilera going 'Burlesque'" (http://www.variety.com/article/VR1118003172. html?categoryid=16&cs=1). *Variety*. . Retrieved September 26, 2009.

[135] Radish, Christina Collider.com November 22, 2010 Writer/Director Steven Antin Exclusive Interview Burlesque (http://www.collider. com/2010/11/22/steven-antin-interview-burlesque/) Retrieved on November 22, 2010.

[136] Trust, Gary *Billboard* online September 24, 2012 Ask Billboard: Who's The Hot 100's King? (http://www.billboard.com/#/column/ chartbeat/ask-billboard-who-s-the-hot-100-s-king-elvis-1007955992.story?page=2) Retrieved on November 28, 2012.

[137] Grein, Paul *Yahoo!* November 28, 2010 Week Ending Nov. 28, 2010: The King And Queen Of Hip-Hop (http://music.yahoo.com/blogs/ chart-watch/week-ending-nov-28-2010-the-king-and-queen-of-hip-hop.html) Retrieved on January 27, 2012.

[138] RIAA "Burlesque" soundtrack (http://www.riaa.com/goldandplatinumdata.php?artist=Burlesque) Retrieved December 17, 2011.

[139] Pols, Mary *TIME* November 24, 2010 *Burlesque* Review: Dances with Divas (http://www.time.com/time/arts/article/ 0,8599,2033004,00.html) Retrieved on December 7, 2010.

[140] DeBruge, Peter *Variety* magazine November 18, 2010 Burlesque (http://www.variety.com/review/VE1117944072?refcatid=31) Retrieved on December 7, 2010.

[141] "Burlesque Reviews, Ratings, Credits, and More at Metacritic" (http://www.metacritic.com/movie/burlesque). Metacritic.com. . Retrieved 2011-11-05.

[142] "Burlesque Movie Reviews, Pictures − Rotten Tomatoes" (http://www.rottentomatoes.com/m/burlesque/). Rottentomatoes.com. . Retrieved 2011-11-05.

[143] Box Office Mojo, January 2011 *Burlesque* box office (http://boxofficemojo.com/movies/?id=burlesque.htm)

[144] Bain, Becky (2010-11-29). "Christina Aguilera Soars On T.I.'s "Castle Walls"" (http://idolator.com/5702242/ christina-aguilera-soars-on-t-i-s-castle-walls). Idolator. Buzz Media. . Retrieved 2012-12-04.

[145] Yahoo! Sports February 6, 2011 Aguilera Goofs Up the National Anthem (http://sports.yahoo.com/nfl/blog/shutdown_corner/post/ Video-Christina-Aguilera-goofs-up-the-National-?urn=nfl-317568) Retrieved on February 6, 2011

[146] By Wenn.Com (December 12, 2010). "Aguilera sorry for Super Bowl fumble | Music | Entertainment" (http://www.torontosun.com/ entertainment/music/2011/02/07/17179721-wenn-story.html). *Toronto Sun*. . Retrieved February 7, 2011.

[147] Semigran, Aly (2011-02-13). "Christina Aguilera, Jennifer Hudson Belt Out Aretha Franklin Grammy Tribute" (http://www.mtv.com/ news/articles/1657852/christina-aguilera-jennifer-hudson-aretha-franklin-grammy-tribute.jhtml). *MTV News. MTV Networks*. . Retrieved 2012-12-04.

[148] "Christina Aguilera on her curvy, controversial figure" (http://www.nydailynews.com/entertainment/gossip/ christina-aguilera-fat-girl-article-1.1171905). *New York Daily News*. October 1, 2012. . Retrieved December 5, 2012.

[149] "Christina Aguilera Goes Solo" (http://www.redbookmag.com/fun-contests/celebrity/christina-aguilera-news-interview). *Redbook magazine*. . Retrieved February 24, 2011.

[150] ""Wasted" Christina Aguilera Passes Out in Jeremy Renner's Bed" (http://www.usmagazine.com/celebritynews/news/ wasted-christina-aguilera-passes-out-in-jeremy-renners-bed--2011191). US *Online*. January 19, 2011. . Retrieved February 6, 2011.

[151] "Is Christina Aguilera Spiraling Out of Control?" (http://omg.yahoo.com/news/is-christina-aguilera-spiraling-out-of-control/54821). *Yahoo.com*. January 24, 2011. . Retrieved February 6, 2011.

[152] "Catfight Alert! Christina Aguilera Goes After Julianne Hough" (http://www.eonline.com/uberblog/ b220917_catfight_alert_christina_aguilera_goes.html). *E! Online*. January 17, 2011. . Retrieved February 6, 2011.

[153] "Julianne Hough, Christina Aguilera Clash at Globes Party" (http://www.cbsnews.com/8301-31749_162-20028757-10391698.html). *CBS News*. January 18, 2011. . Retrieved February 6, 2011.

[154] *The Los Angeles Times* (March 1, 2011). "Christina Aguilera arrested, released;" (http://latimesblogs.latimes.com/gossip/2011/03/ christina-aguilera-arrested-boyfriend-matthew-rutler-dui.html). *The Los Angeles Times*. . Retrieved March 1, 2011.

[155] Camille Mann (March 1, 2011). "Christina Aguilera arrested for public drunkenness" (http://www.cbsnews.com/ 8301-504083_162-20037700-504083.html). CBS News. . Retrieved March 1, 2011.

[156] Erin Skarda (March 1, 2011). "Christina Aguilera Arrested and Jailed for Public Intoxication" (http://newsfeed.time.com/2011/03/01/ christina-aguilera-arrested-and-jailed-for-public-intoxication/). *TIME magazine*. . Retrieved March 1, 2011.

[157] "Christina Aguilera's Boyfriend's DUI Charges Dropped" (http://www.usmagazine.com/celebritynews/news/ christina-aguileras-boyfriends-dui-charges-dropped-2011174). UsMagazine.com. . Retrieved July 7, 2011.

[158] *The Voice* posts solid ratings for premiere, encore" (http://marquee.blogs.cnn.com/2011/04/28/ the-voice-posts-solid-ratings-for-premiere-encore/). CNN. April 28, 2011. . Retrieved May 2, 2011.

[159] Sanger, Craig (May 2, 2011). "You're going to want to turn around for *The Voice*" (http://communities.washingtontimes.com/ neighborhood/tv-den/2011/may/2/youre-going-want-turn-around-voice/). *The Washington Times*. . Retrieved May 2, 2011.

[160] Seidman, Robert (May 4, 2011). "Tuesday Final Ratings: 'The Voice,' 'NCIS,' 'Dancing With The Stars,' 'Glee,' 'The Biggest Loser,' 'Hellcats' Adjusted Up; 'Raising Hope,' 'Traffic Light' Adjusted Down − Ratings | TVbytheNumbers" (http://tvbythenumbers.zap2it.com/ 2011/05/04/ tuesday-final-ratings-the-voice-ncis-dancing-with-the-stars-the-biggest-loser-adjusted-up-raising-hope-traffic-light-adjusted-down/91583). Tvbythenumbers.zap2it.com. . Retrieved July 7, 2011.

[161] "The Voice beats NCIS, Dancing With The Stars and Glee in ratings war!" (http://www.unrealitytv.co.uk/reality-tv/ the-voice-beats-ncis-dancing-with-the-stars-and-glee-in-ratings-war/). Unreality TV. May 4, 2011. . Retrieved July 7, 2011.

[162] "Maroon 5 and Christina Aguilera's 'Moves Like Jagger' Struts To No. 1 on Billboard Hot 100" (http://www.billboard.biz/bbbiz/ industry/record-labels/maroon-5-and-christina-aguilera-s-moves-1005334872.story). *Billboard*. August 31, 2011. . Retrieved August 31, 2011.

[163] "Week Ending July 1, 2012. Songs: Jepsen Does Canada Proud" (http://music.yahoo.com/blogs/chart-watch/ week-ending-july-1-2012-songs-jepsen-does-035518750.html). Yahoo!. . Retrieved 4 July 2012.

[164] "Bruno Mars claims 2 best-selling digital songs of 2011" (http://www.musicweek.com/story.asp?sectioncode=1&storycode=1048221& c=1). Music Week. . Retrieved 2012-03-08.

[165] "Christina Aguilera's Lotus: Why Her 'Comeback' Album Wasn't A Comeback At All" (http://www.mtv.com/news/articles/1697829/ christina-aguilera-lotus-review.jhtml). MTV News. MTV Networks. 2012-11-21. . Retrieved 2012-11-21.

[166] "What happened to Christina Aguilera?" (http://www.digitalspy.com/music/thesound/a439874/what-happened-to-christina-aguilera. html). Digital Spy. Hachette Filipacchi Médias. . Retrieved 2012-11-21.

[167] "Christina Aguilera Returns to Latin Roots on Soundtrack Song" (http://www.billboard.com/news/ christina-aguilera-returns-to-latin-roots-1006392352.story#/news/christina-aguilera-returns-to-latin-roots-1006392352.story). Billboard.com. March 7, 2012. . Retrieved March 10, 2012.

[168] "Usher and Shakira join 'The Voice'" (http://insidetv.ew.com/2012/09/17/the-voice-usher-shakira/). Entertainment Weekly. . Retrieved 17 September 2012.

[169] "New Music: CeeLo Green f/ Christina Aguilera – 'Baby, It's Cold Outside' [Snippet (http://www.rap-up.com/2012/10/02/ new-music-ceelo-green-f-christina-aguilera-baby-its-cold-outside-snippet/)"]. Rap-Up. October 2, 2012. . Retrieved November 21, 2012.

[170] Corner, Lewis (October 23, 2012). "Christina Aguilera, Pitbull on new track 'Feel This Moment' - listen" (http://www.digitalspy.co.uk/ music/news/a432643/christina-aguilera-pitbull-on-new-track-feel-this-moment-listen.html). Digital Spy. Hachette Filipacchi Médias. . Retrieved November 21, 2012.

[171] Beale, Lauren (2011-08-26). "Christina's Home moving plans 'The LA Times'" (http://articles.latimes.com/2011/aug/26/home/ la-hm-hotprop-christina-aguilera-20110826). Articles.latimes.com. . Retrieved 2011-11-05.

[172] Hermione Hoby (June 13, 2010). "Christina Interview with The Guardian Newspaper" (http://www.guardian.co.uk/music/2010/jun/ 13/christina-aguilera-interview-bionic). London: Guardian. . Retrieved 2011-11-05.

[173] Holder, Peter; Jo Casamento (March 10, 2000). "Genie out of a bottle". *The Daily Telegraph (Sydney)*: p. 16.

[174] Farber, Jim (March 24, 2007). "Christina glitzes up Garden". *New York Daily News*: p. 16.

[175] Gayles, Contessa (2011). "10 Things You Didn't Know About *The Voice* Coach and "Dirrty" Pop Star Christina Aguilera" (http://blog. music.aol.com/2011/05/24/10-things-you-didnt-know-about-the-voice-christina-aguilera/). AOL.com. . Retrieved December 22, 2012.

[176] Stacey, Wendy (2011). "Pop Divas, Vocal Range and Whistle Tones" (http://www.wendystacey.com/pop_divas.html). WendyStacey.com. . Retrieved February 3, 2013.

[177] Cove magazine. The 100 Outstanding Pop Vocalists (http://popdirt.com/top-100-vocalists-list-from-cove-magazine/17649/). Retrieved on May 25, 2007.

[178] PopSugar.com (sourced from Cove magazine) The 100 Outstanding Pop Vocalists (http://celebrities-group.popsugar.com/ 100-Outstanding-Pop-Vocalists-1659579).

[179] MTV 22 Greatest Voices (http://www.amiannoying.com/(S(vtymyb55th2lstnmhecdqsny))/collection.aspx?collection=534)". *Am I Annoying*. Retrieved on December 11, 2007.

[180] Simon Gage (December 2007). "Queen of the World". *Gay Times Magazine*. "Next day, Celine very much likes the mention of Christina. "Oh, thank you", she says, beaming. "That's a real compliment. I love her. She's probably the best vocalist in the world"."

[181] "100 Greatest Singers of All Time" (http://www.rollingstone.com/music/lists/6027/32782/33774). *Rolling Stone*. . Retrieved November 11, 2008.

[182] Vena, Jocelyn (December 20, 2012). "Christina Aguilera Goes From *The Voice* To People's Choice" (http://www.mtv.com/news/ articles/1699242/christina-aguilera-peoples-choice-awards.jhtml). MTV.com. . Retrieved December 22, 2012.

[183] Lamb, Bill Top About.com 40/Pop The Bottom Line (http://top40.about.com/od/singles/gr/caguilaintman.htm) About.com Top 40 Retrieved on August 4, 2008.

[184] Browne, David *The New York Times* December 24, 2010 Trilling Songbirds Clip Their Wings (http://www.nytimes.com/2010/12/26/ arts/music/26browne.html?_r=1) Retrieved on January 4, 2010.

[185] Powers, Ann *Los Angeles Times* August 15, 2006 Old-school? Her? (http://articles.latimes.com/2006/08/15/calendar/et-christina15) *Los Angeles Times* Music archives Retrieved on August 4, 2008.

[186] "How to Sing Like Christina Aguilera" (http://on.aol.com/video/how-to-sing-like-christina-aguilera-517292989). *AOL.com*. . Retrieved December 4, 2012.

[187] William, Chris *EW.com* December 11, 2001 Genie at Full Throttle (http://www.ew.com/ew/article/0,,91277,00.html) *Entertainment Weekly* Music Retrieved on August 4, 2008.

[188] Eskow, John (February 8, 2011). "Christina Aguilera and the Hideous Cult of Oversouling" (http://www.huffingtonpost.com/ john-eskow/christina-aguilera-and-th_b_819979.html). *Huffington Post*. . Retrieved December 5, 2012.

[189] Davies, Luvy BBC News August 14, 2006 Christina Aguilera – Back to Basics (http://www.bbc.co.uk/music/release/4g25/) BBC Online Pop/Chart Music Review Retrieved on December 16, 2008.

[190] Copsey, Robert (November 2, 2012). "Christina Aguilera's new album 'Lotus': First listen" (http://www.digitalspy.co.uk/music/ thesound/a435214/christina-aguileras-new-album-lotus-first-listen.html). *Digital Spy*. . Retrieved November 2, 2012.

[191] Watson, Courtney (April 16, 2002). "Christina Comes Clean : The Allure Interview" (http://www.bignoisenow.com/christina/ allure02interview.html). Allure *magazine* (Big Noise Now). . Retrieved December 9, 2012.

[192] Hiatt, Brian *EW.com* October 29, 2002 'Dirrty' Work (Continued) (http://www.ew.com/ew/article/0,,385297_2,00.html) *Entertainment Weekly* Music Retrieved on August 4, 2008.

[193] "'Basic' Instinct" (http://web.archive.org/web/20090114034718/http://www.billboard.com/bbcom/esearch/article_display. jsp?vnu_content_id=1002985896). *Billboard* (Prometheus Global Media). 2006-08-13. Archived from the original (http://www.billboard. com/bbcom/esearch/article_display.jsp?vnu_content_id=1002985896) on 2012-12-04. . Retrieved 2009-01-03.

[194] "This Day In Music - 8th October" (http://mtv.in.com/thebuzz/parent/This Day in Music/this-day-in-music-8th-october-12030.html). *MTV India*. 2012-10-30. . Retrieved 2012-12-29.

[195] Hampp, Andrew *Billboard* Magazine September 21, 2012 Christina Aguilera: Billboard Cover Story (http://www.billboard.com/ features/christina-aguilera-billboard-cover-story-1007955332.story#/features/christina-aguilera-billboard-cover-story-1007955332. story?page=2) Retrieved on November 28, 2012

[196] "Christina Aguilera *Stripped* review" (http://www.rollingstone.com/music/albumreviews/stripped-20021105). *Rolling Stone*. 2013-11-05. . Retrieved 2013-02-19.

[197] Ogunnaike, Lola (2006-07-31). "Aguilera Aims For Edgy, But Richer, Sound" (http://www.christina-aguilera.net/pastnews/jul06. html). *The Christina Connection, taken from original article by The* New York Times. . Retrieved 2013-02-19.

[198] Cohen, Jonathan (2006-06-11). "New Aguilera Album Set For August" (http://web.archive.org/web/20090114030752/http://www.
       billboard.com/bbcom/esearch/article_display.jsp?vnu_content_id=1002501406). *Billboard*. Prometheus Global Media. Archived from the
       original (http://www.billboard.com/bbcom/esearch/article_display.jsp?vnu_content_id=1002501406) on 2012-12-04. . Retrieved
       2012-12-04.

[199] Sanneh, Kelefa *The New York Times* August 17, 2006 Honey They've Shrunk the Pop Stars (http://www.nytimes.com/2006/08/17/arts/
       music/17sann.html?_r=1) Critic's Notebook Music review Retrieved on July 8, 2009.

[200] Fleming, Michael *Variety* October 15, 2007 Screen Gems enlists Antin for 'Burlesque' (http://www.variety.com/article/VR1117974104.
       html?categoryid=13&cs=1) *Variety*.com Retrieved on January 5, 2010.

[201] Mason, Kerri *Billboard* December 11, 2010 Burlesque: Original Motion Picture Soundtrack (http://www.billboard.biz/bbbiz/
       content_display/magazine/reviews/albums/e3ibde532c77149bc3146237ecd8761e87d) *Billboard* album review Retrieved on November 28,
       2012.

[202] Daly, Sean *Tampa Bay Times* November 22, 2012 Review: Christina Aguilera's *Lotus* is a waste of her robust talent (http://www.
       tampabay.com/features/music/review-christina-aguileras-lotus-is-a-waste-of-her-robust-talent/1262622) Retrieved on November 28, 2012.

[203] Sculley, Alan (September 8, 2000). "What Christina wants". *The Patriot Ledger*: p. 17.

[204] Vineyard, Jennifer (June 28, 2006). Christina Aguilera Can Die Happy — She's Bonded With 'Bad Girl' Idol Etta James (http://www.mtv.
       com/news/articles/1535359/20060628/aguilera_christina.jhtml)". *MTV*. Retrieved on May 25, 2007.

[205] Martinez, Michael (January 28, 2012). "Etta James remembered as an authentic voice at funeral" (http://edition.cnn.com/2012/01/28/
       showbiz/etta-james-funeral/index.html). *CNN*. . Retrieved January 29, 2012.

[206] Farley, Christopher *The Wall Street Journal* online January 29, 2012 Christina Aguilera Sings "At Last" at Etta James Funeral (http://
       blogs.wsj.com/speakeasy/2012/01/29/christina-aguilera-sings-at-last-at-etta-james-funeral/) Retrieved on January 29, 2012.

[207] "Christina Aguilera" (http://web.archive.org/web/20090114080605/http://www.muchmusic.com/music/artists/bio.asp?artist=64).
       Much Music. Archived from the original (http://www.muchmusic.com/music/artists/bio.asp?artist=64) on 2012-12-04. . Retrieved
       2012-12-04.

[208] Lyskey, Dorian *The Guardian* August 4, 2006 Christina Aguilera, Back to Basics (http://www.guardian.co.uk/music/2006/aug/04/
       popandrock.shopping4) *The Guardian* online album review Retrieved on August 27, 2008.

[209] Billboard Magazine; Al Gomes (June 19, 2001). Christina performs on the 2001 BET Awards in a special tribute to Whitney Houston
       (http://www.bignoisenow.com/christina/betawards.html). *BigNoiseNow*. Retrieved on May 25, 2007.

[210] Catlin, Roger (2000-08-31). "A Matter of Time Christina Aguilera Says She'll Leave The Pack" (http://pqasb.pqarchiver.com/courant/
       access/59339487.html?dids=59339487:59339487&FMT=ABS&FMTS=ABS:FT&type=current&date=Aug+31,+2000&
       author=ROGER+CATLIN;+Courant+Rock+Critic&pub=Hartford+Courant&desc=A+MATTER+OF+TIME+CHRISTIANA+
       AGUILERA+SAYS+SHE'LL+LEAVE+THE+PACK,+INCLUDING+BRITNEY+SPEARS+IN+THE+DUST&pqatl=google).
       Hartford Courant (Tribune Company). . Retrieved 2011-07-21.

[211] Dominguez, Pier (2003). *Christina Aguilera: a star is made : the unauthorized biography*. Amber Books Publishing. p. 134.
       ISBN 0-9702224-5-9.

[212] Moss, Corey MTV News online April 28, 2006 Christina's New Split-Personality Album Is Mature And 'Dirrty' (http://www.mtv.com/
       news/articles/1529698/04272006/id_0.jhtml?headlines=true) MTV.com Retrieved on August 7, 2008.

[213] Pedersen, Erik (2013-01-23). "Dave Grohl, Christina Aguilera Among Rock and Roll Hall of Fame Presenters" (http://www.
       hollywoodreporter.com/news/dave-grohl-christina-aguilera-rock-414673). *Hollywood Reporter*. . Retrieved 2013-02-07.

[214] Vineyard, Jennifer MTV News August 2007 Christina Aguilera's old soul (http://www.mtv.com/bands/a/aguilera_christina/
       news_feature_080906/) MTV.com News Retrieved on August 7, 2008

[215] Rosen, Craig (2000-09-29). "Christina Aguilera Climbs Every Mountain For 'My Kind Of Christmas'" (http://web.archive.org/web/
       20110524205307/http://music.yahoo.com/read/story/12058962). *Yahoo! Music*. Archived from the original (http://music.yahoo.com/
       read/story/12058962) on 2012-12-04. . Retrieved 2012-12-04.

[216] Hirschberg, Lynn July 2011 *W Magzine* Christina Finds Her Voice (http://www.wmagazine.com/celebrities/2011/07/
       christina-aguilera-cover-story) Retrieved on November 21, 2012.

[217] Araya, Eric MTV.com June 29, 2006 Christina Channels Marilyn Monroe For Intimate Album Cover (http://www.mtv.com/news/
       articles/1535431/20060629/aguilera_christina.jhtml?headlines=true) MTV online Retrieved on August 25, 2008.

[218] ABC News Radio November 16, 2010 (http://abcnewsradioonline.com/entertainment-news/tag/christina-aguilera) Retrieved on
       February 1, 2011.

[219] Vineyard, Jennifer MTV.com June 19, 2006 'Ain't No Other Man' Video Has Christina Singing The Blues (http://www.mtv.com/news/
       articles/1534591/20060619/aguilera_christina.jhtml?headlines=true) MTV Online Retrieved on October 31, 2008.

[220] Vena, Jocelyn November 10, 2009 MTV News Christina Aguilera Looks Back — And Forward — With New LP, Next LP (http://www.
       mtv.com/news/articles/1599011/20081110/aguilera_christina.jhtml) MTV.com Retrieved on November 22, 2009.

[221] Beard, Matthew *The Independent* October 20, 2009 Banksy's 'Mona Lisa' breaks auction price record (http://www.independent.co.uk/
       news/uk/this-britain/banksys-mona-lisa-breaks-auction-price-record-420836.html) *Independent UK* online Retrieved on November 20,
       2009.

[222] Reiter, Amy (December 9, 2002). Dirrty flicks (http://archive.salon.com/people/col/reit/2002/12/09/nprcon/index.html). *Salon.com*.
       Retrieved on May 25, 2007.

[223] Anderson Minshall Diane November 28, 2012 Christina Aguilera Says LGBT Fans Held Her Up When She Couldn't Stand (http://www.advocate.com/arts-entertainment/music/2012/11/28/christina-aguilera-says-lgbt-fans-held-her-when-she-could-not) *The Advocate* Retrieved on December 1, 2012.

[224] Alexander, Hilary July 7, 2005 *Telegraph* Galliano celebrates 100 years of Dior with his own 'new look' (http://www.telegraph.co.uk/fashion/catwalkdiaries/paris/3342005/Galliano-celebrates-100-years-of-Dior-with-his-own-new-look.html) Retrieved on November 20, 2009.

[225] Morley-Cartner, Jess June 4, 2004 *The Guardian* The old black McQueen in London for charity (http://www.guardian.co.uk/uk/2004/jun/04/jesscartnermorleyonfashion.arts) Retrieved on November 20, 2009.

[226] Christina Aguilera: Inside Beauty (September 15, 2002) Christina's Personal Stylist Steve Sollitto: Inside Beauty with Christina 2 (http://www.bignoisenow.com/christina/lifebeat/stylist2.html) Big Noise Now Retrieved on (March 17, 2008).

[227] Susman, Gary (March 5, 2003). Beautiful: Designer signs new muse and model. (http://www.ew.com/ew/article/0,,429223~10~0~versacesignschristinaaguilera,00.html). *EW*. Retrieved on May 25, 2007.

[228] MTV Online; MTV Staff Writer (October 2005). Quick News: Christina shoots ad for Pepsi (http://www.mtv.com/news/articles/1511468/20051013/aguilera_christina.jhtml?headlines=true) Retrieved on January 30, 2007.

[229] Christina Aguilera Opens Harrods (http://www.femalefirst.co.uk/celebrity/Christina+Aguilera-21.html) Female First Retrieved on (March 18, 2008).

[230] Noon, Chris Forbes.com September 9, 2005 Celebrity Singers Headline Billionaire's Wedding (http://www.forbes.com/2005/09/06/melnichenko-aguilera-billionaire-cx_cn_0906autofacescan01.html) Retrieved on December 7, 2010.

[231] Cina, Mark (March 5, 2011). "The Shocking Amounts of Money a Singer Can Make Off a Private Performance" (http://www.hollywoodreporter.com/news/shocking-amounts-money-a-singer-163861). *The Hollywood Reporter*. . Retrieved March 5, 2011.

[232] "2,4 millones por escuchar a Christina Aguilera (In spanish)" (http://www.elmundo.es/elmundo/2011/08/23/cultura/1314096117.html). *El Mundo (Spain)*. . Retrieved February 2, 2013.

[233] Conti, Samantha (February 19, 2008). Women's Wear Daily Christina Aguilera Inspires Stephen Webster Silver Line (http://www.wwd.com/fashion-news/christina-aguilera-inspires-stephen-webster-silver-line-465346) Retrieved on February 19, 2008.

[234] Celebrities and music (March 10, 2008) Christina Aguilera Talks Shedding Her Baby Weight (http://www.accesshollywood.com/article/8720/christina-aguilera-talks-shedding-her-baby-weight/) *Access Hollywood* Online Retrieved on (March 18, 2008).

[235] Brown, Rachel (December 18, 2008) Women's Wear Daily Aguilera Goes Retro... Pamela Meets Vivienne (http://www.wwd.com/media-news/fashion-memopad/aguilera-goes-retro-pamela-meets-vivienne-stella-goes-moblie-1897710?full=true) Retrieved on January 16, 2009.

[236] Daily Mail Reporter February 3, 2011 All eyes are on Miss Aguilera's ample cleavage at Sao Paulo launch of her clothing line (http://www.dailymail.co.uk/tvshowbiz/article-1352815/Christina-Aguileras-ample-cleavage-Sao-Paulo-launch-new-clothing-line.html?ito=feeds-newsxml) Retrieved on February 8, 2011.

[237] "Showbiz Gossip". *The Evening Chronicle* (Newcastle Chronicle & Journal Ltd): p. 35. January 18, 2007.

[238] Hazlett, Courtney MSN.com (May 8), (2008) Aguilera's new scent (http://www.msnbc.msn.com/id/24525545/) MSNBC News online Retrieved on (May 9), (2008).

[239] Christina Aguilera's New Perfume Ad (http://www.hollyscoop.com/christina-aguilera/christina-aguileras-new-perfume-ad_12195.aspx). www.hollyscoop.com (http://www.hollyscoop.com/). August 8, 2007. Retrieved on October 2, 2007. Archived (http://www.webcitation.org/5tnn1EVvi) 27 October 2010 at WebCite

[240] "Christina Tops Fragrance Charts" (http://www.sonybmgmusic.co.uk/artists/christina_aguilera/8020/). Sony BMG UK. December 17, 2007. . Retrieved August 9, 2008.

[241] "All Star Perfumes (Vogue.com UK)" (http://www.vogue.co.uk/blogs/the-vogue-beauty-blog/articles/100114-all-star-perfumes.aspx). Vogue.co.uk. January 15, 2010. . Retrieved September 18, 2010.

[242] "Ein Grund Zum Feiern: Christina Aguilera" (http://www.anziehungskraft.de/index.php?idx=aguilera_duft_des_jahres). Anziehungskraft. . Retrieved August 9, 2008. (in German)

[243] "Marc Jacobs, Tom Ford, and Christina Aguilera Win Top Fragrance Awards" (http://nymag.com/daily/fashion/2008/04/marc_jacobs_tom_ford_christina_1.html). New York Mag. April 24, 2008. . Retrieved August 9, 2008.

[244] Fragantica (May 23, 2008) Christina Aguilera will present her new perfume Inspire (http://www.fragrantica.com/news/Christina-Aguilera-Presents-her-New-Perfume-Inspire-269.html) Fragrantica news Retrieved (May 24, 2008).

[245] Stephanie Epiro (July 24, 2008 accessdate=2008-08-27). "P&G Hopes Aguilera Will 'Inspire' Its Fragrance Fortunes". WWD Beauty.

[246] Business Wire – Macy's July 31, 2008 Mark Seliger Captures Macy's "Stars" for Commemorative 150th Birthday Images (http://www.businesswire.com/portal/site/google/?ndmViewId=news_view&newsId=20080731005593&newsLang=en) Macy's press release Retrieved on July 31, 2008.,

[247] Fragrantica Christina Aguilera by Night (for women) (http://www.fragrantica.com/perfume/Christina-Aguilera/Christina-Aguilera-by-Night-6714.html) Perfume description Retrieved on August 20, 2009.

[248] Raičević Petrović, Sandra (2011-03-27). "FIFI Awards Nominations 2011" (http://www.fragrantica.com/news/FIFI-Awards-Nominations-2011-2109.html). Fragrantica. . Retrieved 2012-12-04.

[249] Fragrance Direct February 22, 2010 Christina Aguilera range (http://www.fragrancedirect.co.uk/c/christina-aguilera/icat/christinaaguilera/) featuring Royal Desire eau de toilette Retrieved February 23, 2010

[250] "Secret Potion Christina Aguilera for women" (http://www.fragrantica.com/perfume/Christina-Aguilera/Secret-Potion-11722.html). Fragrantica. . Retrieved December 13, 2011.

[251] Travis, Neal (September 13, 2001). "Terror Attack Blows D.A.'s Timing". *New York Post*, p. 67. Retrieved on April 21, 2007.

[252] The PETA Files December 12, 2006 Christina Aguilera's Costume Change (http://blog.peta.org/archives/christina_aguilera/) PETA.org Archives Retrieved on December 2, 2009.

[253] Ju, Siel Mother Nature Network February 3, 2010 Christie's celeb-studded Earth Day auction (http://www.mnn.com/lifestyle/ecollywood/blogs/christies-celeb-studded-earth-day-auction) MNN.com Retrieved on February 4, 2010

[254] Christina Aguilera Charities (http://www.christinaaguilera.com/). Retrieved on May 25, 2007. Archived (http //www.webcitation.org/5msW5DKaM) 18 January 2010 at WebCite

[255] Berliner, Alex (March 3, 2004) Nicole Kidman fashions fight against women's cancers (http://www.usatoday.com/news/health/spotlighthealth/2004-03-03-nicole_x.htm) *USA Today Health* Retrieved on (March 6, 2008).

[256] Peden, Lauren David (October 12, 2006) Celebrities Sign On To Help Fight Breast Cancer (http://www.fashionwiredaily.com/first_word/news/article.weml?id=668) *Fashion Wire Daily* Retrieved on (March 12, 2008).

[257] Press Release (April 27, 2000). Christina Aguilera, Sears and Levi's Launch 'Come On Over and Do... – re> HOFFMAN ESTATES, Ill., April 27 /PRNewswire/ -- (http://www.prnewswire.com/cgi-bin/stories.pl?ACCT=104&STORY=/www/story/04-27-2000/0001202754&EDATE=) Christina Aguilera, Sears and Levi's Launch "Come On Over and Do Something". *PR Newswire*. Retrieved on February 27, 2008.

[258] "DO SOMETHING Music Artist" (http://www.vh1.com/shows/events/do_something_awards/2010/music-artist/). VH1. . Retrieved 2012-12-04.

[259] Post Gazette (July 15, 2003). Aguilera auction to aid battered women (http://www.post-gazette.com/ae/20030715christina0715fnp6.asp). Retrieved on May 25, 2007.

[260] MTV News staff (July 27, 2006). Aguilera wants to open domestic-abuse shelter (http://www.mtv.com/news/articles/1537268/20060727/aguilera_christina.jhtml) *MTV*. Retrieved on May 25, 2007.

[261] Yahoo! Finance (April 3, 2007). Multi-Grammy Winner Aguilera Takes Campaign on 'Back to Basics' Concert Tour (http://uk.us.biz.yahoo.com/prnews/070403/nytu011.html?.v=73). Retrieved on May 25, 2007.

[262] Gelman, Jason (2003-03-07). "Christina Aguilera Video Recognized By Gay & Lesbian Alliance" (http://web.archive.org/web/20110629150744/http://music.yahoo.com/read/story/12027755). *Yahoo! Music*. Archived from the original (http://music.yahoo.com/read/story/12027755) on 2012-12-04. . Retrieved 2012-12-04.

[263] Harris, Chris MTV.com November 7, 2008 Christina Aguilera Speaks Out Against Proposition 8 (http://www.mtv.com/news/articles/1598837/20081107/aguilera_christina.jhtml) MTV online Retrieved on November 7, 2008.

[264] "Christina Aguilera honored at debut of The Abbey's Gay Walk of Fame" (http://chicago.gopride.com/news/article.cfm/articleid/18110025/christina-aguilera-honored-at-debut-of-the-abbeys-gay-walk-of-fame-photos). ChicagoPride.com. April 21, 2011. . Retrieved April 21, 2011.

[265] Hear No Evil? (http://www.christinamultimedia.com/statistics/images/charities_youthaids.jpg). Retrieved on May 25, 2007.

[266] Christina Multimedia (http://www.christinamultimedia.com/picturearchive/index.php?catID=16&subcatID=7064). Retrieved on May 25, 2007.

[267] "Paris and Nicky Hilton, Kimora Lee Simmons, Christina Aguilera, Rebecca Romijn, Elle Macpherson, Heidi Klum Among 44 Celebrities To Bare All For New Book To Benefit The Elton John AIDS Foundation" (http://www.prnewswire.com/news-releases/paris-and-nicky-hilton-kimora-lee-simmons-christina-aguilera-rebecca-romijn-elle-macpherson-heidi-klum-among-44-celebrities-to-bare-all-for-new-book-to-ben html). PR Newswire. United Business Media. 2005-06-05. .

[268] Cohen, Jonathan (July 6, 2006). Elton Curating Fashion Rocks, Busy With New CD (http://www.billboard.com/bbcom/news/article_display.jsp?vnu_content_id=1002800867). *Billboard*. Retrieved on May 25, 2007.

[269] "Hillary Clinton Busted Staring At Christina Aguilera's Chest In Photo" (http://www.ibtimes.com/hillary-clinton-busted-staring-christina-aguileras-chest-photo-815195). *International Business Times*. Etienne Uzac, Johnathan Davis. . Retrieved 2 November 2012.

[270] "Christina Aguilera honoured by Hilary[sic (http://www.ok.co.uk/celebrity-news/view/54686/Christina-Aguilera-honoured-by-Hilary-Clinton-for-hunger-relief-work/) Clinton for hunger relief work"]. *OK'*. Northern & Shell. . Retrieved 2 November 2012.

[271] Channel 4 News(November 14, 2007). Aguilera back voting campaign with Rock the Vote (http://www.channel4.com/news/articles/arts_entertainment/aguilera+backs+voting+campaign/1047562). Retrieved on November 14, 2007.

[272] Watson, Donna (October 21, 2005). Chrissie Presents (http://www.dailyrecord.co.uk/news/tm_objectid=16275053&method=full&siteid=66633&headline=chrissie-presents--name_page.html). *Daily Record*. Retrieved on May 25, 2007.

[273] MTV News staff (October 26, 2005). For The Record: Quick News On Christina Aguilera (http://www.mtv.com/news/articles/1512314/20051026/aguilera_christina.jhtml). *MTV*. Retrieved on May 25, 2007.

[274] USA Today (March 11, 2007). Aguilera takes part in All-Star charity project. (http://blogs.usatoday.com/listenup/2007/03/allstar_darfur_.html). Retrieved on May 25, 2007.

[275] Virgin Media August 22, 2008 Christina's mother of a performance (http://musicnews.virginmedia.com/news/?news_id=83415) Virgin music Retrieved on August 22, 2008.

[276] Altinsas, E. Baris (2008-10-26). "A loving family for children in need of protection" (http://web.archive.org/web/20110520083051/ http://www.todayszaman.com/newsDetail_getNewsById.action?load=detay&link=156957&bolum=101). *Today's Zaman.* Archived from the original (http://www.todayszaman.com/tz-web/detaylar.do?load=detay&link=156957&bolum=101) on 2012-12-04. . Retrieved 2008-10-31.

[277] Business Wire Christina Aguilera Lends Powerful Voice in Fight to End Hunger as Global Spokesperson Aguilera Raises Awareness of Hunger Issue by Appearing in PSA, Advertising, Posters (http://www.businesswire.com/portal/site/google/?ndmViewId=news_view& newsId=20090715006146&newsLang=en) July 15, 2009 Retrieved on July 15, 2009.

[278] Relief Web September 23, 2009 Christina Aguilera sees hunger first hand in Guatemala (http://www.reliefweb.int/rw/rwb.nsf/ db900SID/EGUA-7W6MTE?OpenDocument) Relief Web press release Retrieved on September 23, 2009.

[279] World Food Programme official site Christina and the World Food Programme (http://www.wfp.org/christina-aguilera) Retrieved on May 13, 2010.

[280] McNiece, Mia *Variety* online September 1, 2009 Variety to celebrate Power of Women (http://www.variety.com/article/ VR1118007957.html?categoryId=13&cs=1) Retrieved on September 10, 2009.

[281] PRNewswire January 17, 2010 The Chrysler Brand Joins Forces With 'The 67th Annual Golden Globe Awards' to Contribute Relief Efforts to Haiti (http://www.prnewswire.com/news-releases/ the-chrysler-brand-joins-forces-with-the-67th-annual-golden-globe-awards-to-contribute-relief-efforts-to-haiti-81918812.html) Retrieved on January 18, 2010.

[282] WFO (http://www.wfp.org/content/sneak-peek-christina-aguilera-and-muhammad-alis-haiti-psa) Retrieved on January 31, 2010

[283] *World Food Programme* May 12, 2010 Haiti Is First Stop For New WFP Ambassador Christina Aguilera (http://www.wfp.org/stories/ haiti-first-stop-new-ambassador-against-hunger-christina-aguilera) Retrieved on May 12, 2010.

[284] "Tributo y entrega de Premio a Christina Aguilera - (ALMA Awards 2012)" (http://www.youtube.com/watch?v=WfLRhDx9cuA). YouTube. . Retrieved 2012-11-01.

[285] Posted: 10/04/2012 1:17 pm Updated: 10/04/2012 3:00 pm. "Hillary Clinton Honors Christina Aguilera At United Nations Ceremony, Stares At Her Breasts (PHOTO)" (http://www.huffingtonpost.com/2012/10/04/ hillary-clinton-christina-aguilera-world-food-programme-boobs-breasts-photo_n_1939733.html). Huffingtonpost.com. . Retrieved 2012-11-01.

[286] "Stars perform to help victims of Sandy" (http://entertainment.nbcnews.com/_news/2012/11/02/ 14888295-stars-perform-to-help-victims-of-sandy?lite). 2012-11-02. . Retrieved 2012-12-07.

[287] Jennifer Vineyard September 24, 2004 Christina Aguilera Is Poisonous In Video With Missy Elliott: Singer animated as jellyfish in 'Car Wash' clip from 'Shark Tale.' (http://www.mtv.com/news/articles/1491393/x-tina-soaking-wet-car-wash-clip.jhtml) MTV Networks Retrieved on November 08, 2012.

References

- Dominguez, Pier (2002). *Christina Aguilera: A Star is Made: The Unauthorized Biography*. Amber Communications Group, Inc. ISBN 978-0-9702224-5-9.

External links

- ChristinaAguilera.com (http://www.christinaaguilera.com/) – Christina Aguilera official website
- Twitter (http://www.twitter.com/TheRealXtina) – Official Twitter account
- Christina Aguilera (http://www.myspace.com/christinaaguilera) on Myspace
- Christina Aguilera (http://www.imdb.com/name/nm4694/) at the Internet Movie Database
- Christina Aguilera (https://www.facebook.com/christinaaguilera) on Facebook

Ciribiribin

"Ciribiribin" is a merry Italian ballad in three quarter time, composed by Alberto Pestalozza in 1898 with lyrics by Carlo Tiochet. It quickly became popular and has been recorded by many artists. The distinguishing feature of the song is repeated use of the five note phrase that forms the song name. In the sheet music the name is indicated to be enunciated "chiribiribee", to allows singers to hold the vowel at the end as long as they like.

The song was a favorite of Harry James, who chose it as his theme song when he formed his band in 1939. Frank Sinatra worked with James' band for a while before going to work for Tommy Dorsey. On the James/Sinatra recording of the song, Sinatra enuciated the trailing "n".

Grace Moore made a live recording accompanied by a pianist, Gibner King, as an encore after presenting some pieces with Willem Mengelberg and the Concertgebouw Orchestra on June 23, 1936.

Artists who have recorded the song in Italian include Mario Lanza, Claudio Villa, The Andrews Sisters with Bing Crosby, and Renato Carosone.

Warren Beatty's character in the 1978 film *Heaven Can Wait* plays the song on saxophone.

The song "Java Jive", a hit song for The Ink Spots in 1940, originally featured the couplet "I'm not keen about a bean / Unless it is a 'cheery beery bean'", as a pun on Ciribiribin, but the Ink Spots' lead singer inadvertently sang it as "cheery cheery bean", and recordings by subsequent artists have generally either followed suit or changed it to "chili chili bean".

An earlier play on the "chili" joke came in a comic song written by Albert Von Tilzer and recorded by Billy Murray in 1921. The song, "Chili Bean", is about an exotic woman named Chili Bean. A bar of 'Ciribiribin" appears in a brief instrumental segment in the middle of the song.

A rock 'n' roll adaptation, "Gotta Lotta Love", sung by Steve Alaimo, was mildly successful in late 1963.

References

• George T. Simon, "In the Beginning." Booklet of Columbia's Harry James disk, 1995.

Civilization (song)

"Civilization" is a pop song. It was written by Bob Hilliard and Carl Sigman, published in 1947 and introduced in the 1947 Broadway musical *Angel in the Wings*, sung by Elaine Stritch. The song is sometimes also known as "Bongo, Bongo, Bongo (I Don't Want to Leave the Congo)" from its first line of the chorus.

Concept

The song is considered satire and is sung from the perspective of a native "savage", whose village has recently been settled by a missionary and other "civilized" people who have been trying to make the tribe into a civilized place. However, the savage thinks differently and sings about the major flaws in civilized society, ultimately deciding that he will stay where he lives (presumably the Congo, as it is referenced in the song lyrics).

Recordings

Many recorded versions made the *Billboard* charts: by The Andrews Sisters and Danny Kaye, by Louis Prima, by "Smilin'" Jack Smith, by Ray McKinley, and by Woody Herman.

The Andrews Sisters and Danny Kaye recording was recorded September 27, 1947 and released by Decca Records as catalog number 24462. The record first reached the *Billboard* magazine charts on November 14, 1947 and lasted 10 weeks on the chart, peaking at #3.[1] The Louis Prima recording was recorded July 24, 1947 and released by RCA Victor Records as catalog number 20-2400. The record first reached the *Billboard* magazine charts on November 7, 1947 and lasted eight weeks on the chart, peaking at #8.[1] The Jack Smith recording was released by Capitol Records as catalog number 465. The record first reached the *Billboard* magazine charts on December 26, 1947 and lasted two weeks on the chart, peaking at #14.[1] The Ray McKinley recording was released by Majestic Records as catalog number 7274. The record first reached the *Billboard* magazine charts on December 26, 1947 and lasted one week on the chart, at #14.[1] The Woody Herman recording was released by Columbia Records as catalog number 37885. The record first reached the Billboard magazine charts on December 26, 1947 and lasted one week on the chart, at #15.[1]

A recording by Joe Loss and his Orchestra with vocal by Elizabeth Batey was made in London on March 11, 1948. It was released by EMI on the His Master's Voice label BD 6007. Dyan Cannon performed the song on *The Muppet Show* along with several Muppet jungle animals.

In popular culture

"Civilization", performed by Danny Kaye and the Andrews Sisters, is featured on the in-game Galaxy News Radio in the 2008 game *Fallout 3* on PC, PlayStation 3 and Xbox 360, which takes place in a post-apocalyptic, retro-futurist United States in the year 2277.[2]

Louis Prima's recording of "Civilization" is heard playing on the radio in Adrian Lyne's 1997 film *Lolita*.

References

[1] Whitburn, Joel (1973). *Top Pop Records 1940–1955*. Record Research.
[2] *Fallout* FAQ (http://fallout.bethsoft.com/eng/info/faq.html) at bethsoft.com

Dan Dailey

Dan Dailey

Born	Daniel James Dailey December 14, 1915 New York, New York, USA
Died	October 16, 1978 (aged 62) Los Angeles, California, USA
Years active	1940-1977
Spouse(s)	Esther Rodier (?-1941) Elizabeth Hofert (1942-1951) 1 child Gwen Carter O'Connor (1955-1960)
Children	Dan Dailey III, died 1975

Daniel James Dailey Jr. (December 14, 1915 – October 16, 1978) was an American dancer and actor.

Early life and career

Born in New York City on December 14, 1915,[1] to James J. and Helen Dailey, both born in New York City. He appeared in a minstrel show when very young, and appeared in vaudeville before his Broadway debut in 1937 in *Babes in Arms*. In 1940, he was signed by MGM to make movies and, although his past career had been in musicals, he was initially cast as a Nazi in *The Mortal Storm* and a mobster in *The Get Away*.[2] However, the people at MGM realized their mistake quickly and cast him in a series of musical films.

He served in the United States Army during World War II, was commissioned as an Army officer after graduation from Signal Corps Officer Candidate School at Fort Monmouth, NJ.[3] He then returned Hollywood to more musicals. Beginning with *Mother Wore Tights* (1947) Dailey became the frequent and favorite co-star of movie legend Betty Grable. His performance in their film *When My Baby Smiles at Me* in 1948 garnered him an Academy Award nomination for Best Actor.

In 1949, he showcased his singing abilities by recording four songs for Decca Records with the enormously popular Andrews Sisters (Patty, Maxene, and LaVerne). Two of the songs were Irish novelties ("Clancy Lowered the Boom!" and "I Had a Hat (When I Came In)"). The other songs, "Take Me Out to the Ballgame" and "In the Good Old Summertime" capitalized on the success of two MGM blockbuster films of the same names from that same year, starring Gene Kelly and Frank Sinatra, and Judy Garland and Van Johnson, respectively. Dailey and The Andrews Sisters were an excellent match, and their vocal stylings on these selections were full of gaeity and fun.[4]

In 1950, he starred in *A Ticket to Tomahawk*, often noted as one of the first screen appearances of Marilyn Monroe, in a very small part as a dance-hall girl. He portrayed baseball pitcher Dizzy Dean in a 1952 biopic, *Pride of St.*

Louis.

One of his most notable roles came in *There's No Business Like Show Business* (1954), which featured Irving Berlin's music and also starred Ethel Merman, Marilyn Monroe, Johnnie Ray, and Donald O'Connor, whose wife Gwen divorced O'Connor and married Dailey at about the same period.

As the musical genre began to wane in the mid-1950s, he moved on to various comedic and dramatic roles, including appearing as one of *The Four Just Men* (1959) in the Sapphire Films TV series for ITV, his television series, *The Governor & J.J.* and the NBC Mystery Movie series "Faraday & Company".

In the late 1960s, Dailey toured as Oscar Madison in a road production of *The Odd Couple*. co-starring Elliott Reid as Felix Unger and also featuring Peter Boyle as Murray the cop.

His sister was *Another World* actress Irene Dailey.

Filmography

Features:

- *Susan and God* (1940)
- *The Mortal Storm* (1940)
- *The Captain Is a Lady* (1940)
- *Dulcy* (1940)
- *Hullabaloo* (1940)
- *Keeping Company* (1940)
- *The Wild Man of Borneo* (1941)
- *Washington Melodrama* (1941)
- *Ziegfeld Girl* (1941)
- *The Getaway* (1941)
- *Down in San Diego* (1941)
- *Lady Be Good* (1941)
- *Moon Over Her Shoulder* (1941)
- *Mokey* (1942)
- *Sunday Punch* (1942)
- *Timber!* (1942)
- *Give Out, Sisters* (1942)
- *Panama Hattie* (1942)
- *This Is the Army* (1943)
- *Mother Wore Tights* (1947)
- *You Were Meant for Me* (1948)
- *Give My Regards to Broadway* (1948)
- *When My Baby Smiles at Me* (1948)
- *Chicken Every Sunday* (1948)
- *You're My Everything* (1949)
- *When Willie Comes Marching Home* (1950)
- *My Blue Heaven* (1950)
- *I'll Get By* (1950) (cameo appearance)
- *A Ticket to Tomahawk* (1950)
- *Call Me Mister* (1951)
- *I Can Get It for You Wholesale* (1951)
- *The Pride of St. Louis* (1952)
- *What Price Glory?* (1952)

- *Meet Me at the Fair* (1953)
- *Taxi* (1953)
- *The Girl Next Door* (1953)
- *The Kid from Left Field* (1953)
- *There's No Business Like Show Business* (1954)
- *It's Always Fair Weather* (1955)
- *Meet Me in Las Vegas* (1956)
- *The Best Things in Life Are Free* (1956)
- *The Wings of Eagles* (1957)
- *Oh, Men! Oh, Women!* (1957)
- *The Wayward Bus* (1957)
- *Underwater Warrior* (1958)
- *Pepe* (1960)
- *Hemingway's Adventures of a Young Man* (1962)
- *Four Nights of the Full Moon* (1963)
- *The Private Files of J. Edgar Hoover* (1977)

Short Subjects:

- *Tournament of Roses* (1954) (narrator)

References

[1] The 1920 census and Dailey's official enlistment record shows that he was born December 14, 1915, not 1913 as is sometimes reported.

[2] Donna Reed Foundation for the Performing Arts. "The Get Away" (http://www.donnareed.org/html/templates/dr_detail. php?dr_detail=f01_tga). .

[3] Dailey enlisted in the Army shortly after Pearl Harbor and attended Signal Corps Officer Candidate School at Fort Monmouth, NJ starting in September 1942. He was commissioned on Dec 12, 1942 and served until late 1946, when he was discharged as a captain.

[4] Sforza, John: "Swing It! The Andrews Sisters Story;" University Press of Kentucky, 2000; 289 pages

External links

- Dan Dailey (http://www.imdb.com/name/nm197314/) at the Internet Movie Database
- Dan Dailey (http://www.ibdb.com/person.asp?ID=37108) at the Internet Broadway Database

Danny Kaye

Danny Kaye	
Born	David Daniel Kaminsky January 18, 1913[1] Brooklyn, New York, U.S.
Died	March 3, 1987 (aged 74) Los Angeles, California, U.S.
Occupation	Actor, singer, comedian
Years active	1933–1986
Spouse(s)	Sylvia Fine (m. 1940-1987; his death) 1 daughter
Children	Dena Kaye (b. 1946)

Danny Kaye (born **David Daniel Kaminsky**; January 18, 1913 − March 3, 1987)[2] was a celebrated American actor, singer, dancer, and comedian. His best known performances featured physical comedy, idiosyncratic pantomimes, and rapid-fire nonsense songs.

Kaye starred in 17 movies, notably *The Kid from Brooklyn* (1946), *The Secret Life of Walter Mitty* (1947), *The Inspector General* (1949), *Hans Christian Andersen* (1952), *White Christmas* (1954), and − perhaps his most accomplished performance − *The Court Jester* (1956). His films were extremely popular, especially his bravura performances of patter songs and children's favorites such as "Inchworm" and "The Ugly Duckling". He was the first ambassador-at-large of UNICEF in 1954 and received the French Legion of Honor in 1986 for his many years of work with the organization.[3]

Early years

David Daniel Kaminsky was born to Ukrainian Jewish immigrants in Brooklyn. Jacob and Clara Nemerovsky Kaminsky and their two sons, Larry and Mac, left Ekaterinoslav two years before his birth; he was the only one of their sons born in the United States.[4] He spent his early youth attending Public School 149 in East New York, Brooklyn—which eventually would be re-named to honor him[5]—where he began entertaining his classmates with songs and jokes,[6] before moving to Thomas Jefferson High School, but he never graduated.[7] His mother died when he was in his early teens. Clara had enjoyed the impressions and humor of her youngest son and always had words of encouragement for them; her death was a great loss for the young Kaye.

Not long after his mother's death, Kaye and his best friend ran away to Florida. Kaye sang while his friend Louis played the guitar; the pair eked out a living like this for a while. When Kaye did return to New York, his father did not pressure him to return to school or to get a job, giving his son the chance to mature and discover his own abilities.[8] Kaye said he had wanted to become a surgeon as a young boy, but there was no chance of the family being able to afford a medical school education for him.[4][9] He held a succession of jobs after leaving school: a soda jerk, insurance investigator, office clerk. Most of them ended with him being fired. He lost the insurance job when he made an error that cost the insurance company $40,000. The dentist who had hired him to look after his office during his lunch hour did the same when he found Kaye using his drill to create designs in the office woodwork.[4][10] He learned his trade in his teenage years in the Catskills as a tummler in the Borscht Belt.,[6] especially for four seasons at The White Roe resort.[11]

Kaye's first break came in 1933 when he was asked to become one of the "Three Terpsichoreans", a vaudeville dance act. He opened with them in Utica, New York using the name **Danny Kaye** for the first time.[6] The act toured the United States, then signed on to perform in the Orient with the show *La Vie Paree*.[12] The troupe left for six months in the Far East on February 8, 1934. While the group was in Osaka, Japan, a typhoon hit the city. The hotel Kaye and his colleagues stayed in suffered heavy damage; a piece of the hotel's cornice was hurled into Kaye's room by the strong wind, nearly killing him. By performance time that evening, the city was still in the grip of the storm. There was no power and the audience had become understandably restless and nervous. To keep everyone calm, Kaye went on stage, his face lit by a flashlight, and sang every song he could recall as loudly as he was able.[4] The experience of trying to entertain audiences who did not speak English is what brought him to the pantomimes, gestures, songs and facial expressions which eventually made him famous.[6][10] Sometimes it was necessary just to try to get a meal. Kaye's daughter, Dena, tells a story her father related about being at a restaurant in China and trying to order chicken. Kaye flapped his arms and clucked, giving the waiter his best imitation of a chicken. The waiter nodded his understanding, bringing Kaye two eggs. His interest in cooking began on the tour.[6][12]

When he returned to the United States, jobs were in short supply; Kaye struggled for bookings. One of the jobs was working in a burlesque revue with fan dancer Sally Rand. After the dancer dropped one of her fans while trying to chase away a fly, Kaye was hired to be in charge of the fans so they were always held in front of her.[6][10]

Career

Danny Kaye made his film debut in a 1935 comedy short *Moon Over Manhattan*. In 1937 he signed with New York–based Educational Pictures for a series of two-reel comedies. Kaye usually played a manic, dark-haired, fast-talking Russian in these low-budget shorts, opposite young hopefuls June Allyson or Imogene Coca. The Kaye series ended abruptly when the studio shut down permanently in 1938. He was still working in the Catskills at times in 1937, using the name **Danny Kolbin**.[13][14] Kaye's next venture was a short-lived Broadway show, where Sylvia Fine was the pianist, lyricist and composer. The *Straw Hat Revue* opened on September 29, 1939, and closed after ten weeks, but it was long enough for critics to take notice of Kaye's work in it.[4][15] The glowing reviews brought an offer for both Kaye and his new bride, Sylvia, to work at La Martinique, an upscale New York City nightclub. Kaye performed with Sylvia as his accompanist. At La Martinique, playwright Moss Hart saw Danny perform, which led to Hart casting him in his hit Broadway comedy *Lady in the Dark*.[4][10]

Kaye scored a personal triumph in 1941 in *Lady in the Dark*. His show-stopping number was "Tchaikovsky", by Kurt Weill and Ira Gershwin, in which he sang the names of a whole string of Russian composers at breakneck speed, seemingly without taking a breath.[16][17] By the next Broadway season, he was the star of his own show about a young man who is drafted called *Let's Face It!*.[18]

His feature film debut was in producer Samuel Goldwyn's Technicolor 1944 comedy *Up in Arms*,[19] a remake of Goldwyn's Eddie Cantor comedy *Whoopee!* (1930).[20] Kaye's rubber face and fast patter were an instant hit, and rival producer Robert M. Savini cashed in almost immediately by compiling three of Kaye's old Educational Pictures shorts into a makeshift feature, *The Birth of a Star* (1945).[21] Studio mogul Goldwyn wanted Kaye to have his prominent nose fixed so it would look less Jewish,[11][22] but Kaye refused. However, he did allow his natural red hair to be dyed blonde, apparently because it looked better that way in Technicolor.[22]

Kaye starred in a radio program of his own, *The Danny Kaye Show*, on CBS in 1945–1946.[23] Its cast included Eve Arden, Lionel Stander, and Big Band leader Harry James, and it was scripted by radio notable Goodman Ace and respected playwright-director Abe Burrows.

The radio program's popularity rose quickly. Before Kaye had been on the air a year, he tied with Jimmy Durante for fifth place in the *Radio Daily* popularity poll.[10] Kaye was asked to participate in a USO tour following the end of World War II. It meant he would be absent from his radio show for close to two months at the beginning of the season. Kaye's friends filled in for him, with a different guest host each week.[24] Kaye was the first American actor to visit postwar Tokyo; it was his first time there after touring there some ten years before with the vaudeville troupe.[25][26] When Kaye asked to be released from his radio contract in mid-1946, he agreed not to accept another regular radio show for one year and also to limit his guest appearances on the radio programs of others.[24][27] Many of the show's episodes survive today, and are notable for Kaye's opening "signature" patter.[10]

> "Git gat gittle, giddle-di-ap, giddle-de-tommy, riddle de biddle de roop, da-reep, fa-san, skeedle de woo-da, fiddle de wada, reep!"

Kaye was sufficiently popular that he inspired imitations:

Danny Kaye on USO tour at Sasebo, Japan, 25 October 1945. Kaye and his friend, Dodgers manager Leo Durocher, made the trip.[25]

- The 1946 Warner Bros. cartoon *Book Revue* had a lengthy sequence with Daffy Duck impersonating Kaye singing "Carolina in the Morning" with the Russian accent that Kaye would affect from time to time.

- Satirical songwriter Tom Lehrer's 1953 song "Lobachevsky" was based on a number that Kaye had done, about the Russian director Constantin Stanislavski, again with the affected Russian accent. Lehrer mentioned Kaye in the opening monologue, citing him as an "idol since childbirth".

- Superman creators Jerry Siegel and Joe Shuster also fashioned a short-lived superhero title, *Funnyman*, taking inspiration from Kaye's persona.

Kaye starred in several movies with actress Virginia Mayo in the 1940s, and is well known for his roles in films such as *The Secret Life of Walter Mitty* (1947), *The Inspector General* (1949), *On the Riviera* (1951) co-starring Gene Tierney, *Knock on Wood* (1954), *White Christmas* (1954, in a role originally intended for Fred Astaire, then Donald O'Connor),*The Court Jester* (1956), and *Merry Andrew* (1958). Kaye starred in two pictures based on biographies, *Hans Christian Andersen* (1952) about the Danish story-teller, and *The Five Pennies* (1959) about jazz pioneer Red Nichols. His wife, writer/lyricist Sylvia Fine, wrote many of the witty, tongue-twisting songs Danny Kaye became famous for.[9][28] She was also an associate producer.[29] Some of Kaye's films included the theme of doubles, two people who look identical (both played by Danny Kaye) being mistaken for each other, to comic effect.

White Christmas trailer

Kaye teamed with the very popular Andrews Sisters (Patty, Maxene, and LaVerne) on Decca Records in 1947, producing the number-three Billboard smash hit "Civilization (Bongo, Bongo, Bongo)". The success of the pairing prompted both acts to record repeatedly through 1950, producing such rhythmically comical fare as "The Woody Woodpecker Song" (based on the frisky bird from the Walter Lantz cartoons, and another *Billboard* hit for the quartet), "Put 'em in a Box, Tie 'em with a Ribbon (And Throw 'em in the Deep Blue Sea)," "The Big Brass Band from Brazil," "It's a Quiet Town (In Crossbone County)," "Amelia Cordelia McHugh (Mc Who?)," "Ching-a-ra-sa-sa", and a duet by Danny and Patty of "Orange Colored Sky". The acts also teamed for two yuletide favorites: a frantic, melodious, harmonic rendition of "A Merry Christmas at Grandmother's House (Over the River and Through the Woods)", and another duet by Danny & Patty, "All I Want for Christmas Is My Two Front Teeth"[30]

While his wife wrote Kaye's material, there was much of it that was unwritten, springing from the mind of Danny Kaye, often while he was performing. Kaye had one character he never shared with the public; Kaplan, the owner of an Akron, Ohio rubber company, came to life only for family and friends. His wife Sylvia described the Kaplan character:[31]

> He doesn't have any first name. Even his wife calls him just Kaplan. He's an illiterate pompous character who advertises his philanthropies. Jack Benny or Dore Schary might say, "Kaplan, why do you hate unions so?" If Danny feels like doing Kaplan that night, he might be off on Kaplan for two hours.

When he appeared at the London Palladium music hall in 1948, he "roused the Royal family to shrieks of laughter and was the first of many performers who have turned English variety into an American preserve." *Life* magazine described his reception as "worshipful hysteria" and noted that the royal family, for the first time in history, left the royal box to see the show from the front row of the orchestra.[32][33][34] He later related that he had no idea of the familial connections when the Marquess of Milford Haven introduced himself after one of the shows and said he would like his cousins to see Kaye perform.[17] Kaye also later stated that he never returned to the venue because there was no way to re-create the magic of that time.[35] Kaye had an invitation to return to London for a *Royal Variety Performance* in November of the same year.[36] When the invitation arrived, Kaye was busy at work on *The Inspector General* (which had a working title

Kaye in 1955

of *Happy Times* for a while). Warners stopped work on the film to allow their star to attend.[37] When his Decca co-workers The Andrews Sisters began their engagement at the London Palladium directly on the heels of Kaye's incredibly successful 1948 appearance there, the trio was so well received that David Lewin of the *Daily Express* declared, "The audience gave The Andrews Sisters the Danny Kaye roar!"[30]

He hosted the 24th Academy Awards in 1952. The program was broadcast only on radio. Telecasts of the Oscar ceremony would come later. During the 1950s, Kaye visited Australia, where he played "Buttons" in a production of *Cinderella* in Sydney. In 1953, Kaye started his own production company, Dena Pictures, named for his daughter. *Knock on Wood* was the first film produced by his firm. The firm expanded into television in 1960 under the name Belmont Television.[38][39]

Singer Nancy Wilson appearing on his show in 1965

Kaye entered the world of television in 1956 through the CBS show *See It Now* with Edward R. Murrow.[40] *The Secret Life of Danny Kaye* combined his 50,000-mile, ten-country tour as UNICEF ambassador with music and humor.[41][42] His first solo effort was in 1960 with an hour-long special produced by Sylvia and sponsored by General Motors; there were similar specials in 1961 and 1962.[4] He hosted his own variety hour on CBS television, *The Danny Kaye Show*, from 1963 to 1967, which won four Emmy awards and a Peabody award.[43][44] During this period, beginning in 1964, he acted as television host to the annual CBS telecasts of MGM's *The Wizard of Oz*. Kaye also did a stint as one of the *What's My Line?* Mystery Guests on the popular Sunday night CBS-TV quiz program. Kaye later served as a guest panelist on that show. He also appeared on the NBC interview program *Here's Hollywood*.

In the 1970s Kaye tore a ligament in his leg during the run of the Richard Rodgers musical *Two by Two*, but went on with the show, appearing with his leg in a cast and cavorting on stage from a wheelchair.[43][45] He had done much the same on his television show in 1964 when his right leg and foot were seriously burned from an at-home cooking accident. The camera shots were planned so television viewers did not see Kaye in his wheelchair.[46]

In 1976, he played the role of Mister Geppetto in a television musical adaptation of *Pinocchio* with Sandy Duncan in the title role. Kaye also portrayed Captain Hook opposite Mia Farrow in a musical version of *Peter Pan* featuring songs written by Anthony Newley and Leslie Bricusse. It was shown on NBC-TV in December 1976 as part of the *Hallmark Hall of Fame* series. He guest-starred much later in his career in episodes of *The Muppet Show*, *The Cosby Show*[47] and in the 1980s revival of *The Twilight Zone*.

In many of his movies, as well as on stage, Kaye proved to be a very able actor, singer, dancer and comedian. He showed quite a different and serious side as Ambassador for UNICEF and in his dramatic role in the memorable TV movie *Skokie*, in which he played a Holocaust survivor.[43] Before his death in 1987, Kaye demonstrated his ability to conduct an orchestra during a comical, but technically sound, series of concerts organized for UNICEF fundraising. Kaye received two Academy Awards: an Academy Honorary Award in 1955 and the Jean Hersholt Humanitarian Award in 1982.[16] Also that year he received the Screen Actors Guild Annual Award.[16]

Kaye was enamored of music. While he often claimed an inability to read music, he was quite the conductor and was said to have perfect pitch. Kaye's ability with an orchestra was brought up by Dimitri Mitropoulos, who was then the conductor of the New York Philharmonic Orchestra. After Kaye's guest appearance, Mitropoulos remarked, "Here is a man who is not musically trained, who cannot even read music, and he gets more out of my orchestra than I ever have."[7] Kaye was often invited to conduct symphonies as charity fundraisers[9][16] and was the conductor of the all-city marching band at the season opener of the Los Angeles Dodgers in 1984. Over the course of his career he raised over US$5,000,000 in support of musicians pension funds.[48]

In 1980, Kaye hosted and sang in the 25th Anniversary of Disneyland celebration, and hosted the opening celebration for Epcot in 1982 (EPCOT Center at the time), both of which were aired on prime-time American television.

Other projects

Cooking

In his later years he took to entertaining at home as chef – he had a special stove installed in his patio – and specialized in Chinese and Italian cooking.[16] The specialized stove Kaye used for his Chinese dishes was fitted with special metal rings for the burners to allow the heat from them to be highly concentrated. Kaye needed to install a trough with circulating ice water so he could use the burners.[49] Kaye also taught Chinese cooking classes at a San Francisco Chinese restaurant in the 1970s.[50] The theater and demonstration kitchen underneath the library at the Culinary Institute of America in Hyde Park, New York is named for him.[51]

Danny referred to his kitchen as "Ying's Thing". While filming *The Madwoman of Chaillot* in France, he phoned home to ask his family if they would like to eat at "Ying's Thing" that evening; Kaye then flew home for dinner.[12] Not all of his efforts in the kitchen turned out well. After flying to San Francisco for a recipe for sourdough bread, he came home and spent hours preparing loaves. When his daughter asked about the bread, Kaye tried showing her by hitting the bread on the kitchen table. His bread was hard enough to chip it.[12] Kaye approached his kitchen work with enthusiasm, making his own sausages and other items needed for his cuisine.[49][52] His work as a chef earned him the "Les Meilleurs Ouvriers de France" cuilinary award; Kaye was the only non-professional to achieve this honor.[7]

Flying

Like many in the film business, Danny was an aviation enthusiast. He became seriously interested in learning how to fly in 1959. An enthusiastic and accomplished golfer, Kaye gave up golf in favor of flying.[53] When Kaye went for his first written pilot's exam, he brought a liverwurst sandwich in case he was there for hours. The first plane Kaye owned was a Piper Aztec.[54][55] Kaye got his first license as a private pilot of multi-engine aircraft, not getting certified for operating a single engine plane until six years later.[54] He was an accomplished pilot, rated for airplanes ranging from single-engine light aircraft to multi-engine jets.[16] Kaye held a commercial pilot's license and had flown every type of aircraft except military planes.[7][54][56] A vice-president of Learjet, Kaye owned and operated a Learjet 24.[54] He supported many flying projects. In 1968, he was Honorary Chairman of the Las Vegas International Exposition of Flight, a major show that utilized most facets of the city's entertainment industry while presenting a major air show. The operational show chairman was well-known aviation figure Lynn Garrison. Kaye flew his own plane to 65 cities in five days on a mission designed to help UNICEF.[7]

Danny Kaye was very fond of the legendary arranger Vic Schoen. Schoen had arranged for him on *White Christmas*, *The Court Jester*, and albums and concerts with the Andrews Sisters. In the 1960s Vic Schoen was working on a show in Las Vegas with Shirley Temple. He was injured in a car accident. When Danny Kaye heard about the accident, he immediately flew his own plane to McCarran Airport to pick up Schoen and bring him back to Los Angeles to guarantee the best medical attention.

Baseball

Kaye was part-owner of baseball's Seattle Mariners along with his partner Lester Smith from 1977 to 1981.[16][57] Prior to that, the lifelong fan of the Brooklyn/Los Angeles Dodgers recorded a song called "The D-O-D-G-E-R-S Song (Oh really? No, O'Malley!)", describing a fictitious encounter with the San Francisco Giants, which was a hit during the real-life pennant chase of 1962. That song is included on *Baseball's Greatest Hits* compact discs. A good friend of Leo Durocher, he would often travel with the team.[10] In addition to being an owner, Kaye had an encyclopedic knowledge of the game.[16]

Medicine

He was an honorary member of the American College of Surgeons and the American Academy of Pediatrics.[16]

Charity

Throughout his life, Kaye donated to various charities. Working alongside UNICEF's Halloween fundraiser founder, Ward Simon Kimball Jr., the actor educated the public on impoverished children in deplorable living conditions overseas and assisted in the distribution of donated goods and funds. His involvement with UNICEF came about in a very unusual way. Kaye was flying home from an appearance in London in 1949 when one of the plane's four engines lost its propeller and caught fire. The problem was initially thought to be serious enough that it might need to make an ocean landing; life jackets and life rafts were made ready. The plane was able to head back over 500 miles to make a landing in Shannon, Ireland. On the way back to Shannon, the head of the Children's Fund, Maurice Pate, had the seat next to Danny

Danny Kaye on a promotion tour for UNICEF in the Netherlands, 1955

Kaye and spoke at length to him about the need for recognition for the Fund. Their discussion continued on the flight from Shannon to New York; it was the beginning of the actor's long association with UNICEF.[58][59]

Death

Kaye died of a heart attack in March 1987, following a bout of hepatitis. Kaye had quadruple bypass heart surgery in February 1983; he contracted hepatitis from a blood transfusion he received at that time.[16][47] He left a widow, Sylvia Fine, and a daughter, Dena.[60] He is interred in Kensico Cemetery in Valhalla, New York. His grave is adorned with a bench that contains friezes of a baseball and bat, an aircraft, a piano, a flower pot, musical notes, and a glove. Kaye's name, birth and death dates are inscribed on the glove.[61] The United Nations held a memorial tribute to him at their New York headquarters.[62][63]

Personal life

Kaye and his wife, Sylvia, both grew up in Brooklyn, living only a few blocks apart, but they did not meet until they were both working on an off-Broadway show in 1939.[64] Sylvia was an audition pianist at the time.[9][28][65] Sylvia discovered that Danny had once worked for her father, dentist Samuel Fine.[10] They were married on January 3, 1940.[60][66] Kaye, working in Florida at the time, proposed on the telephone; the couple was married in Fort Lauderdale.[67] Their daughter, Dena, was born on December 17, 1946.[15][68]

Both Kaye and his wife raised their daughter without any parental hopes or aspirations for her future. Kaye said in a 1954 interview, "Whatever she wants to be she will be without interference from her mother nor from me."[8][52] When she was very young, Dena did not like seeing her father perform because she did not understand that people were supposed to laugh at what he did.[69] On January 18, 2013,

Kaye in 1986, by Allan Warren.

during a 24-hour salute to Kaye on Turner Classic Movies in celebration of his 100th birthday, Kaye's daughter Dena revealed to TCM host Ben Mankiewicz that Kaye was actually born in 1911.

During World War II, the Federal Bureau of Investigation investigated rumors that Kaye dodged the draft by manufacturing a medical condition to gain 4-F status and exemption from military service. FBI files show he was also under investigation for supposed links with Communist groups. The allegations were never substantiated, and he was never charged with any associated crime.[70]

After Kaye and his wife became estranged,[15][71][72] he was allegedly involved with a succession of women, though he and Fine never divorced.[73][74] The best-known of these women was actress Eve Arden.[75][76]

There are persistent claims that Kaye was homosexual or bisexual, and some sources assert that Kaye and Laurence Olivier had a ten-year relationship in the 1950s while Olivier was still married to Vivien Leigh.[77] A biography of Leigh states that their love affair caused her to have a breakdown.[78] The affair has been denied by Olivier's official biographer, Terry Coleman.[79] Joan Plowright, Olivier's third wife and widow, has dealt with the matter in different ways on different occasions: she deflected the question (but alluded to Olivier's "demons") in a BBC interview.[80] She is reputed to have referred to Danny Kaye on another occasion, in response to a claim that it was she who broke up Olivier's marriage to Leigh. However, in her own memoirs, Plowright denies that there had been an affair between the two men.[81] Producer Perry Lafferty reported: "People would ask me, 'Is he gay? Is he gay?' I never saw anything to substantiate that in all the time I was with him."[75] Kaye's final girlfriend, Marlene Sorosky, reported that he told her, "I've never had a homosexual experience in my life. I've never had any kind of gay relationship. I've had opportunities, but I never did anything about them."[75]

Honors, awards, tributes

- Jean Hersholt Humanitarian Award (1981)
- Asteroid 6546 Kaye
- Danny Kaye has three stars on the Hollywood Walk of Fame for his work in music, radio, and films.[82]
- Danny Kaye was knighted by Queen Margrethe II of Denmark in 1983 for his 1952 portrayal of Hans Christian Andersen in the film of the same name.[60]
- Kennedy Center Honor (1984)
- Grand Marshal of the Tournament of Roses Parade (1984)
- French Legion of Honor (Chevalier of the Légion d'honneur) on 24 February 1986 for his UNICEF work.[3]
- The song "I Wish I Was Danny Kaye" on Miracle Legion's 1996 album *Portrait of a Damaged Family*
- On June 23, 1987, Kaye was posthumously presented with the Presidential Medal of Freedom by President Ronald Reagan. The award was received by his daughter Dena.[83][84]
- UNICEF's New York Visitor's Centre is named to honor Danny Kaye.[85]
- In December 1996, the PBS series, *American Masters*, aired a special on the life of Danny Kaye.[35]

Filmography

Film

#	Title	Year	Role	Director	Co-stars	Filmed in
1.	*Moon Over Manhattan*[86]	1935	Himself	Al Christie	Sylvia Froos, Marion Martin	Black and white
2.	*Dime a Dance*[87]	1937	Eddie	Al Christie	Imogene Coca, June Allyson	Black and white
3.	*Getting an Eyeful*[88]	1938	Russian	Al Christie	Charles Kemper, Sally Starr	Black and white
4.	*Cupid Takes a Holiday*[89]	1938	Nikolai Nikolaevich (bride-seeker)	William Watson	Douglas Leavitt, Estelle Jayne	Black and white
5.	*Money on Your Life*[90]	1938	Russian	William Watson	Charles Kemper, Sally Starr	Black and white
6.	*Up in Arms*	1944	Danny Weems	Elliott Nugent	Dinah Shore, Dana Andrews	Technicolor
7.	*I Am an American*[91]	1944	Himself	Crane Wilbur	Humphrey Bogart, Gary Gray, Dick Haymes, Joan Leslie, Dennis Morgan, Knute Rockne, Jay Silverheels	Black and white
8.	*Wonder Man*	1945	Edwin Dingle / Buzzy Bellew	H. Bruce Humberstone	Virginia Mayo, Vera-Ellen, Steve Cochran	Technicolor
9.	*The Kid from Brooklyn*	1946	Burleigh Hubert Sullivan	Norman Z. McLeod	Virginia Mayo, Vera-Ellen, Steve Cochran, Eve Arden	Technicolor
10.	*The Secret Life of Walter Mitty*	1947	Walter Mitty	Norman Z. McLeod	Virginia Mayo, Boris Karloff, Fay Bainter, Ann Rutherford	Technicolor
11.	*A Song Is Born*	1948	Professor Hobart Frisbee	Howard Hawks	Virginia Mayo, Benny Goodman, Hugh Herbert, Steve Cochran	Technicolor
12.	*It's a Great Feeling*	1949	Himself	David Butler	Dennis Morgan, Doris Day, Jack Carson	Technicolor
13.	*The Inspector General*	1949	Georgi	Henry Koster	Walter Slezak, Barbara Bates, Elsa Lanchester, Gene Lockhart	Technicolor
14.	*On the Riviera*	1951	Jack Martin / Henri Duran	Walter Lang	Gene Tierney, Corinne Calvet	Technicolor
15.	*Hans Christian Andersen*	1952	Hans Christian Andersen	Charles Vidor	Farley Granger, Zizi Jeanmaire	Technicolor
16.	*Knock on Wood*	1954	Jerry Morgan / Papa Morgan	Norman Panama Mevin Frank	Mai Zetterling, Torin Thatcher	Technicolor
17.	*White Christmas*	1954	Phil Davis	Michael Curtiz	Bing Crosby, Rosemary Clooney, Vera-Ellen, Dean Jagger	VistaVision Technicolor
18.	*The Court Jester*	1956	Hubert Hawkins	Norman Panama Mevin Frank	Glynis Johns, Basil Rathbone, Angela Lansbury	VistaVision Technicolor
19.	*Merry Andrew*	1958	Andrew Larabee	Michael Kidd	Salvatore Baccaloni, Pier Angeli	CinemaScope Metrocolor
20.	*Me and the Colonel*	1958	Samuel L. Jacobowsky	Peter Glenville	Curt Jürgens, Nicole Maurey, Françoise Rosay, Akim Tamiroff	Black and white
21.	*The Five Pennies*	1959	Red Nichols	Melville Shavelson	Barbara Bel Geddes, Louis Armstrong, Tuesday Weld	VistaVision Technicolor
22.	*On the Double*	1961	Pfc. Ernie Williams	Melville Shavelson	Dana Wynter, Margaret Rutherford, Diana Dors	Panavision Technicolor
23.	*The Man from the Diner's Club*	1963	Ernest Klenk	Frank Tashlin	Cara Williams, Martha Hyer	Black and white

24.	The Madwoman of Chaillot	1969	The Ragpicker	Bryan Forbes	Katharine Hepburn, Charles Boyer	Technicolor

Television

- *Autumn Laughter* (1938) (experimental telecast)
- *The Secret Life of Danny Kaye* (1956) (*See It Now* special)
- *An Hour With Danny Kaye* (1960 and 1961) (specials)
- *The Danny Kaye Show with Lucille Ball* (1962) (special)
- *The Danny Kaye Show* (1963–1967) (series)
- *The Lucy Show:* "Lucy Meets Danny Kaye" (1964) (guest appearance)
- *Here Comes Peter Cottontail* (1971) (voice)
- *The Dick Cavett Show* (1971) (interview guest)
- *The Enchanted World of Danny Kaye: The Emperor's New Clothes* (1972) (special)
- *An Evening with John Denver* (1975) (special)
- *Pinocchio* (1976 TV-musical) (1976) (special), live television musical adaptation starring Sandy Duncan and Danny Kaye
- *Peter Pan* (1976) (special)
- *The Muppet Show* (1978) (guest appearance)
- *Disneyland's 25th Anniversary* (1980) (special guest appearance)
- *An Evening with Danny Kaye* (1981) (special)
- *Skokie* (1981)
- *The New Twilight Zone:* "Paladin of the Lost Hour" (1985) (guest appearance)
- *The Cosby Show:* "The Dentist" (1986) (guest appearance)

Stage Work

- *The Straw Hat Revue* (1939)
- *Lady in the Dark* (1941)
- *Let's Face It!* (1941)
- *Two by Two* (1970)

Discography

Studio Albums

- *The Five Pennies* [92] with Louis Armstrong (1959)
- *Mommy, Gimme a Drinka Water* (Orchestration by Gordon Jenkins) (Capitol Records, 1959)

Soundtracks

- *Hans Christian Andersen* [93] (1980)

Story Albums

- *Danny Kaye tells 6 stories from faraway lands* [94] (1960)

Compilations

- *Selections From Irving Berlin's White Christmas* [95] (1954)

References

[1] Dena Kaye interview on TCM January 18, 2013. Her father was actually born in 1911 but, for reasons unknown to her, changed it to 1913

[2] Tony Woolway (4 March 1987). "Danny Kaye Dies, Age 74" (http://icwales.icnetwork.co.uk/news/feature-news/2008/03/04/danny-kaye-dies-aged-74-91466-20552911/). *icWales.* . Retrieved 14 May 2008.

[3] "French Honor Danny Kaye" (http://news.google.com/newspapers?id=njEuAAAAIBAJ&sjid=q9YFAAAAIBAJ&pg=3376,2978120&dq=danny+kaye+french+legion+of+honor&hl=en). The Modesto Bee. 26 February 1986. . Retrieved 18 January 2011.

[4] Adir, Karen, ed. (2001). *The Great Clowns of American Television* (http://books.google.com/books?id=5jr9L--C4tMC&pg=PA247&dq=danny+kaye+cooking#v=onepage&q=danny kaye&f=false). McFarland & Company. pp. 270. ISBN 0-7864-1303-4. . Retrieved 18 January 2011.

[5] "Welcome P.S. 149 Danny Kaye" (http://schools.nyc.gov/schoolportals/19/k149/default.htm). NY City Dept of Education. . Retrieved 8 January 2013.

[6] "World-renown comedian dies" (http://news.google.com/newspapers?id=kO5VAAAAIBAJ&sjid=dOEDAAAAIBAJ&pg=7184,629748&dq=danny+kaye&hl=en). Eugene Register-Guard. 4 March 1987. . Retrieved 15 December 2010.

[7] Goodman, Mark (23 December 1979). "A Conversation With Danny Kaye" (http://news.google.com/newspapers?id=LIUwAAAAIBAJ&sjid=pfoDAAAAIBAJ&pg=4058,2842167&dq=sylvia+fine+dena&hl=en). Lakeland Ledger. . Retrieved 10 March 2011.

[8] Perry, Lawrence (9 May 1954). "Danny Kaye Looks At Life" (http://news.google.com/newspapers?id=jGIaAAAAIBAJ&sjid=7iQEAAAAIBAJ&pg=6234,4925619&dq=sylvia+fine+dena&hl=en). The Milwaukee Journal. . Retrieved 10 March 2011.

[9] Battelle, Phyllis (8 May 1959). "Mrs. Danny Kaye Proves a Genius" (http://news.google.com/newspapers?id=jGxQAAAAIBAJ&sjid=4g8EAAAAIBAJ&pg=7347,4079273&dq=sylvia+fine+dena&hl=en). The Milwaukee Sentinel. . Retrieved 10 March 2011.

[10] "Git Gat Gittle" (http://www.time.com/time/magazine/article/0,9171,776720-1,00.html). Time. 11 March 1946. . Retrieved 14 January 2011.

[11] Kanfer, Stefan (1989). *A summer world : the attempt to build a Jewish Eden in the Catskills from the days of the ghetto to the rise and decline of the Borscht Belt* (http://www.amazon.com/Summer-World-Attempt-Catskills-Decline/dp/0374271801) (1st ed. ed.). New York: Farrar, Straus & Giroux. pp. 157. ISBN 978-0374271800. .

[12] Kaye, Dena (19 January 1969). "Life With My Zany Father-Danny Kaye" (http://news.google.com/newspapers?id=OwBKAAAAIBAJ&sjid=LB4NAAAAIBAJ&pg=2332,3334403&dq=danny+kaye&hl=en). Tri City Herald. . Retrieved 15 January 2011.

[13] ""Highlights and Shadows"-front of program" (http://www.loc.gov/exhibits/bobhope/images/vc53ap1.jpg). The President Players. 4 July 1937. . Retrieved 25 February 2011.

[14] ""Highlights and Shadows"-inside of program" (http://www.loc.gov/exhibits/bobhope/images/vc53ap2.jpg). The President Players. 4 July 1937. . Retrieved 25 February 2011.

[15] "Who Is Sylvia?" (http://news.google.com/newspapers?id=T9paAAAAIBAJ&sjid=uWwDAAAAIBAJ&pg=5291,8225005&dq=sylvia+fine&hl=en). Pittsburgh Post-Gazette. 30 October 1960. . Retrieved 18 January 2011.

[16] "Danny Kaye, comedian who loved children, dead at 74" (http://news.google.com/newspapers?id=A-EyAAAAIBAJ&sjid=2RMEAAAAIBAJ&pg=3090,1636996&dq=danny+kaye&hl=en). Star-News. 4 March 1987. . Retrieved 15 December 2010.

[17] Remington, Fred (12 January 1964). "Danny Kaye: King of Comedy" (http://news.google.com/newspapers?id=rkIqAAAAIBAJ&sjid=_E4EAAAAIBAJ&pg=3849,3453774&dq=sylvia+fine+dena&hl=en). *The Pittsburgh Press.* . Retrieved 10 March 2011.

[18] Edel, Leon (8 November 1941). "Danny Kaye as Musical Draftee Brightens the Broadway Scene" (http://news.google.com/newspapers?id=X7EtAAAAIBAJ&sjid=ppgFAAAAIBAJ&pg=4949,1337710&dq=eve+arden+danny+kaye&hl=en). . Retrieved 19 January 2011.

[19] *Up In Arms* (http://www.imdb.com/title/tt0037420/) at the Internet Movie Database

[20] Whittaker, Herbert (20 May 1944). "Danny Kaye Makes Successful Debut in 'Up In Arms'" (http://news.google.com/newspapers?id=aX8uAAAAIBAJ&sjid=IJkFAAAAIBAJ&pg=5349,3577434&dq=danny+kaye&hl=en). *The Montreal Gazette.* . Retrieved 22 January 2011.

[21] "The Birth of a Star" (http://www.imdb.com/title/tt0218051/). Internet Movie Database. . Retrieved 19 January 2011.

[22] Nolan, J. Leigh. "Danny! Danny Kate F.A.Q.s" (http://www.dannykaye.net/dkfaq.htm#hair). J. Leigh Nolan. . Retrieved 8 January 2013.

[23] Foley, Roy L. (2 February 1946). "Helen and Danny: O-Kaye! Crowd Howls" (http://news.google.com/newspapers?id=SatYAAAAIBAJ&sjid=Aw4EAAAAIBAJ&pg=5953,2615111&dq=danny+kaye&hl=en). The Milwaukee Sentinel. . Retrieved 14 January 2011.

[24] "Danny Kaye" (http://www.digitaldeliftp.com/DigitalDeliToo/dd2jb-Danny-Kaye-Show.html). DigitalDeli. . Retrieved 14 January 2011.

[25] BCL (12 November 1945). "Riding the Airwaves" (http://news.google.com/newspapers?id=u6kaAAAAIBAJ&sjid=LyMEAAAAIBAJ&pg=2305,5825718&dq=danny+kaye&hl=en). *The Milwaukee Journal*. . Retrieved 14 January 2011.

[26] "Lily Pons the Guest Star Tonight Of Danny Kaye, Back From Tour" (http://news.google.com/newspapers?id=6C8rAAAAIBAJ&sjid=OJkFAAAAIBAJ&pg=2576,3628988&dq=danny+kaye&hl=en). *The Montreal Gazette*. 23 November 1945. . Retrieved 15 January 2011.

[27] "Hollywood" (http://news.google.com/newspapers?id=xEAxAAAAIBAJ&sjid=Lw0EAAAAIBAJ&pg=7284,4219513&dq=danny+kaye&hl=en). *The Milwaukee Sentinel*. 2 May 1946. . Retrieved 14 January 2011.

[28] Boyle, Hal (27 August 1959). "Composer Sylvia Fine Can Write Anywhere Anytime" (http://news.google.com/newspapers?id=pfxTAAAAIBAJ&sjid=-zgNAAAAIBAJ&pg=538,1883597&dq=sylvia+fine&hl=en). The Sunday News-Press. . Retrieved 27 November 2010.

[29] Brady, Thomas F. (13 November 1947). "Danny Kaye Film Set at Warners" (http://news.google.com/newspapers?id=AH4tAAAAIBAJ&sjid=8pgFAAAAIBAJ&pg=5142,2228369&dq=sylvia+fine&hl=en). The Montreal Gazette. . Retrieved 18 January 2011.

[30] Sforza, John: *Swing It! The Andrews Sisters Story*. University Press of Kentucky, 2000; 289 pages.

[31] Wilson, Earl (4 July 1959). "It Happened Last Night" (http://news.google.com/newspapers?id=4T01AAAAIBAJ&sjid=FGUEAAAAIBAJ&pg=7384,576802&dq=sylvia+fine&hl=en). *Sarasota Herald-Tribune*. . Retrieved 18 January 2011.

[32] Young, Andrew (4 March 1987). "Kaye: everyone's favourite" (http://news.google.com/newspapers?id=ci41AAAAIBAJ&sjid=_KULAAAAIBAJ&pg=2305,591697&dq=danny+kaye&hl=en). The Glasgow Herald. . Retrieved 15 December 2010.

[33] Januzzi, Gene (23 October 1949). "Danny Kaye Won't Talk of Royalty" (http://news.google.com/newspapers?id=TtQMAAAAIBAJ&sjid=QGoDAAAAIBAJ&pg=1357,1943058&dq=danny+kaye&hl=en). Pittsburgh Post-Gazette. . Retrieved 15 January 2011.

[34] Handsaker, Gene (11 October 1948). "Danny Kaye Is a Real Showoff" (http://news.google.com/newspapers?id=s-orAAAAIBAJ&sjid=XmcFAAAAIBAJ&pg=1385,2017653&dq=danny+kaye&hl=en). Kentucky New Era. . Retrieved 12 March 2011.

[35] Bianculli, David (10 December 1996). "The Many Lives of Danny Kaye" (http://www.nydailynews.com/archives/entertainment/1996/12/10/1996-12-10_the_many_lives_of_danny_kaye.html). New York Daily News. . Retrieved 10 March 2011.

[36] "Royal Variety Performance" (http://www.eabf.org.uk/royal-variety-performance/archive/1940s/1948). Entertainment Artistes Benenevolent Fund. 1948. . Retrieved 22 January 2011.

[37] "Royal Invitation for Danny Kaye" (http://news.google.com/newspapers?id=824rAAAAIBAJ&sjid=kJkFAAAAIBAJ&pg=4316,3809280&dq=danny+kaye&hl=en). *The Montreal Gazette*. 20 October 1948. . Retrieved 22 January 2011.

[38] Goldie, Tom (10 July 1953). "Friday Film Notes-Danny--Producer" (http://news.google.com/newspapers?id=nAlBAAAAIBAJ&sjid=EqgMAAAAIBAJ&pg=3858,794217&dq=sylvia+fine+dena&hl=en). Evening Times. . Retrieved 10 March 2011.

[39] "Danny Kaye Founds Film Firm" (http://news.google.com/newspapers?id=GWscAAAAIBAJ&sjid=404EAAAAIBAJ&pg=2662,2550219&dq=sylvia+fine+dena&hl=en). *The Pittsburgh Press*. 6 December 1960. . Retrieved 10 March 2011.

[40] McManus, Margaret (23 September 1956). "Found at Last: A Happy Comedian" (http://news.google.com/newspapers?id=UFIaAAAAIBAJ&sjid=sSUEAAAAIBAJ&pg=4120,1727656&dq=sylvia+fine+dena&hl=en). The Milwaukee Journal. . Retrieved 10 March 2011.

[41] Mercer, Charles (5 December 1956). "Danny Kaye Gives TV Its Finest 90 Minutes" (http://news.google.com/newspapers?id=AqIyAAAAIBAJ&sjid=BewFAAAAIBAJ&pg=3770,1889642&hl=en). *The Miami News*. . Retrieved 19 January 2011.

[42] Pearson, Howard (3 December 1956). "Color Shows, Danny Kaye, Draw Attention" (http://news.google.com/newspapers?id=7_YvAAAAIBAJ&sjid=bUkDAAAAIBAJ&pg=7030,339720&dq=danny+kaye&hl=en). The Deseret News. . Retrieved 19 January 2011.

[43] Drew, Mike (4 March 1987). "Danny Kaye always excelled as an entertainer and in life" (http://news.google.com/newspapers?id=V2MaAAAAIBAJ&sjid=lSoEAAAAIBAJ&pg=6902,3612185&dq=danny+kaye&hl=en). *The Milwaukee Journal*. . Retrieved 15 December 2010.

[44] "The Danny Kaye Episode Guide" (http://www.mateas.com/DannyKaye/TV1963Season.htm). Mateas Media Consulting. . Retrieved 2 February 2011.

[45] Raidy, William A. (17 February 1971). "Real people go to matinees and Danny Kaye loves 'em" (http://news.google.com/newspapers?id=u64tAAAAIBAJ&sjid=iKAFAAAAIBAJ&pg=2126,4385316&dq=eve+arden+danny+kaye&hl=en). *The Montreal Gazette*. . Retrieved 19 January 2011.

[46] Lowry, Cynthia (17 April 1964). "Accident Confines Danny Kaye to Chair" (http://news.google.com/newspapers?id=sgBWAAAAIBAJ&sjid=-uIDAAAAIBAJ&pg=3155,3543465&dq=danny+kaye&hl=en). *Eugene Register-Guard*. . Retrieved 15 January 2011.

[47] "Actor-comedian Danny Kaye dies" (http://news.google.com/newspapers?id=9dQ0AAAAIBAJ&sjid=6C0DAAAAIBAJ&pg=5772,634574&dq=danny+kaye&hl=en). Pittsburgh Post-Gazette. 3 March 1987. . Retrieved 15 December 2010.

[48] "Biography of Danny Kaye" (http://www.kennedy-center.org/calendar/index.cfm?fuseaction=showIndividual&entitY_id=3748&source_type=A). The Kennedy Center. . Retrieved 14 May 2008.

[49] "Marcella Hazan: Memoir of a classic Italian chef" (http://today.msnbc.msn.com/id/27054074). *Today*. 7 October 2008. . Retrieved 10 March 2011.

[50] "Danny Kaye Teaches Chinese Cooking" (http://news.google.com/newspapers?id=O2QtAAAAIBAJ&sjid=Y4kFAAAAIBAJ&pg=2509,4246744&hl=en). Tri City Herald. 22 January 1974. . Retrieved 15 January 2011.

[51] Culinary Institute of America, ed. (1995). *Cooking secrets of the CIA* (http://books.google.com/booksid=Au1XKfGD3kUC&pg=PA7&dq=danny+kaye+cooking#v=onepage&q&f=false). Chronicle Books. pp. 131. ISBN 0-8118-1163-8. . Retrieved 18 January 2011.

[52] Boyd, Joseph G. (23 May 1980). "Travel writer attends party saluting hotel" (http://news.google.com/newspapers?id=AnlQAAAAIBAJ&sjid=AhIEAAAAIBAJ&pg=6402,4316845&dq=sylvia+fine+dena&hl=en). The Milwaukee Sentinel. . Retrieved 10 March 2011.

[53] Scott, Vernon (14 July 1962). "Kaye Likes Air" (http://news.google.com/newspapers?id=gk4_AAAAIBAJ&sjid=v1AMAAAAIBAJ&pg=3103,2142968&dq=danny+kaye+plane&hl=en). The Windsor Star. . Retrieved 18 March 2011.

[54] Kaye, Danny (January 1967). *If I Can Fly, You Can Fly* (http://books.google.com/books?id=CSEDAAAAMBAJ&pg=PA76&dq=danny+kaye#v=onepage&q=danny kaye&f=false). Popular Science. . Retrieved 11 March 2011.

[55] Thomas, Bob (21 September 1965). "Danny Kaye Likes Flying, TV, Dodgers" (http://news.google.com/newspapers?id=TSgmAAAAIBAJ&sjid=S_4FAAAAIBAJ&pg=990,3305946&dq=danny+kaye&hl=en). Gettysburg Times. . Retrieved 15 January 2011.

[56] Smith, Red (12 June 1976). "American League's a new act for Danny Kaye" (http://news.google.com/newspapers?id=oKAyAAAAIBAJ&sjid=bOoFAAAAIBAJ&pg=1197,1151876&dq=danny+kaye&hl=en). The Miami News. . Retrieved 21 January 2011.

[57] "Major League Baseball Returns To Seattle" (http://news.google.com/newspapers?id=BDZVAAAAIBAJ&sjid=-D0NAAAAIBAJ&pg=3564,1956170&dq=danny+kaye&hl=en). The Leader-Post. 9 February 1976. . Retrieved 15 January 2011.

[58] "Crippled Transport Limps to Safety" (http://news.google.com/newspapers?id=jUIjAAAAIBAJ&sjid=O2gFAAAAIBAJ&pg=2884,742737&dq=danny+kaye&hl=en). The Lewiston Daily Sun. 8 July 1949. . Retrieved 19 January 2011.

[59] "Danny Kaye" (http://www.unicef.org/people/people_danny_kaye.html). UNICEF. . Retrieved 19 January 2011.

[60] "Movie producer, songwriter Sylvia Fine Kaye dies at 78" (http://news.google.com/newspapers?id=Cw4bAAAAIBAJ&sjid=C0gEAAAAIBAJ&pg=4302,6871133&dq=sylvia+fine&hl=en). Daily News. 29 October 1991. . Retrieved 27 November 2010.

[61] "Photo of Bench-Danny Kaye" (http://www.findagrave.com/cgi-bin/fg.cgi?page=pv&GRid=1316&PIpi=78925). Find a Grave. . Retrieved 27 November 2010.

[62] Taylor, Clarke (23 October 1987). "UN and Friends Pay Tribute to Kaye" (http://articles.latimes.com/1987-10-23/entertainment/ca-10800_1). LA Times. . Retrieved 19 January 2011.

[63] Lewis, Paul (22 October 1987). "U.N. Praises Danny Kaye at Tribute" (http://www.webcitation.org/5xHnXWIAm). New York Times. Archived from the original (http://www.nytimes.com/1987/10/22/arts/un-praises-danny-kaye-at-tribute.html) on 18 March 2011. . Retrieved 18 March 2011.

[64] "A team grew in Brooklyn" (http://news.google.com/newspapers?id=JeAbAAAAIBAJ&sjid=2lEEAAAAIBAJ&pg=2702,4987848&dq=sylvia+fine+dena&hl=en). The Dispatch. 25 April 1975. . Retrieved 10 March 2011.

[65] "Kaye at the Met" (http://news.google.com/newspapers?id=27pGAAAAIBAJ&sjid=9TMNAAAAIBAJ&pg=4524,4626774&dq=sylvia+fine&hl=en). The Evening News. 25 April 1975. . Retrieved 27 November 2010.

[66] Wilson, Earl (4 July 1959). "Danny Kaye To End TV Holdout; Wife To Write Script" (http://news.google.com/newspapers?id=3b8VAAAAIBAJ&sjid=JxAEAAAAIBAJ&pg=6918,1273346&dq=danny+kaye&hl=en). The Milwaukee Sentinel. . Retrieved 15 January 2011.

[67] Raymer, Dorothy (6 November 1945). "Who Is Sylvia? What Is She?-Danny Kaye's Inspiration" (http://news.google.com/newspapers?id=yk8yAAAAIBAJ&sjid=H-gFAAAAIBAJ&pg=6116,1463811&dq=danny+kaye&hl=en). The Miami News. . Retrieved 14 January 1945.

[68] Parsons, Louella (28 July 1946). "Danny Kaye Awaits Christmas Bulletin On Maternity Front" (http://news.google.com/newspapers?id=pCxaAAAAIBAJ&sjid=JkwNAAAAIBAJ&pg=6459,3561608&dq=danny+kaye&hl=en). The News and Courier. . Retrieved 14 January 2011.

[69] Hughes, Alice (28 January 1953). "A Woman's New York" (http://news.google.com/newspapers?id=ywwrAAAAIBAJ&sjid=gZsFAAAAIBAJ&pg=6191,2517594&dq=sylvia+fine+dena&hl=en). Reading Eagle. . Retrieved 10 March 2011.

[70] Freedom of Information/Privacy Act Section. "Subject: Danny Kaye" (http://foia.fbi.gov/foiaindex/dannykaye.htm). Federal Bureau of Investigation. . Retrieved 14 May 2008.

[71] Cheney, Carlton (26 October 1947). "The Secret Life of Danny Kaye" (http://news.google.com/newspapers?id=tzQaAAAAIBAJ&sjid=CCUEAAAAIBAJ&pg=4207,5865807&dq=danny+kaye&hl=en). The Milwaukee Journal. . Retrieved 15 January 2011.

[72] Handsaker, Gene (11 December 1947). "Like Peas In Pod Are Film Married Duos" (http://news.google.com/newspapers?id=X0wdAAAAIBAJ&sjid=CVgEAAAAIBAJ&pg=6751,1682189&dq=sylvia+fine&hl=en). The Deseret News. . Retrieved 18 January 2011.

[73] Thomas, Bob (13 January 1948). "Opportunities Galore In Films For Women" (http://news.google.com/newspapers?id=ZmhaAAAAIBAJ&sjid=CE0NAAAAIBAJ&pg=6885,647268&dq=danny+kaye&hl=en). Waycross Journal-Herald. . Retrieved 22 January 2011.

[74] MacPherson, Virginia (9 February 1948). "Hollywood Report" (http://news.google.com/newspapers?id=M8ZdAAAAIBAJ&sjid=V14NAAAAIBAJ&pg=6725,4893317&dq=danny+kaye&hl=en). Oxnard Press-Courier. . Retrieved 22 January 2011.

[75] Gottfried, Martin (1994). *Nobody's Fool: The Lives of Danny Kaye*. New York; London: Simon & Schuster. ISBN 0-671-86494-7.

[76] Parsons, Louella (21 February 1948). "Movie Comedy Is Easy for Eve Arden" (http://news.google.com/ newspapers?id=vVEwAAAAIBAJ&sjid=8lQDAAAAIBAJ&pg=6251,2922582&dq=eve+arden+danny+kaye&hl=en). The Deseret News. . Retrieved 19 January 2011.

[77] Spoto, Donald (1992). *Laurence Olivier: A Biography*. New York: HarperCollins. ISBN 0-06-018315-2.

[78] Capua, Michelangelo (2003). *Vivien Leigh: A Biography*. McFarland & Company. ISBN 0-7864-1497-9.

[79] Coleman, Terry (2006). "Author's Note: The Androgynous Actor". *Olivier*. Macmillan. pp. 478–481. ISBN 0-8050-8136-4.

[80] "Olivier Had 'Demons', Says Widow Answering Gay Question" (http://www.contactmusic.com/news.nsf/story/ olivier-had-demons-says-widow-answering-gay-question_1006512). Contactmusic.com. 26 August 2006. . Retrieved 25 July 2011.

[81] Christiansen, Rupert (13 October 2001). "Tending the sacred flame" (http://www.spectator.co.uk/the-magazine/books/19685/part_2/ tending-the-sacred-flame.thtml). The Spectator. . Retrieved 10 February 2009.

[82] "Danny Kaye-Hollywood Star Walk" (http://projects.latimes.com/hollywood/star-walk/danny-kaye/). LA Times. . Retrieved 19 January 2011.

[83] "Kaye, Willson to Get Medal of Freedom" (http://articles.latimes.com/1987-04-22/news/mn-287_1). LA Times. 22 April 1987. . Retrieved 19 January 2011.

[84] "Remarks at the Presentation Ceremony for the Presidential Medal of Freedom" (http://www.reagan.utexas.edu/archives/speeches/ 1987/062387j.htm). University of Texas. 23 June 1987. . Retrieved 10 March 2011.

[85] "Danny Kaye Visitor's Centre Virtual Tour" (http://www.unicef.org/virtualtour/). UNICEF. . Retrieved 19 January 2011.

[86] "Moon Over Manhattan" (http://www.imdb.com/title/tt0026728/). Internet Movie Database. . Retrieved 19 January 2011.

[87] "Dime a Dance" (http://www.imdb.com/title/tt0254280/). Internet Movie Database. . Retrieved 19 January 2011.

[88] "Getting an Eyeful" (http://www.imdb.com/title/tt0214716/). Internet Movie Database. . Retrieved 19 January 2011.

[89] "Cupid Takes a Holiday" (http://www.imdb.com/title/tt0292484/). Internet Movie Database. . Retrieved 19 January 2011.

[90] "Money on Your Life" (http://www.imdb.com/title/tt0344078/). Internet Movie Database. . Retrieved 19 January 2011.

[91] The 16 minute film, *I Am an American*, was featured in American theaters as a short feature in connection with "I Am an American Day" (now called Constitution Day). *I Am an American* was produced by Gordon Hollingshead, also written by Crane Wilbur. See: *I Am An American* (http://tcmdb.com/title/title.jsp?stid=730264) at the TCM Movie Database and *I Am an American* (http://www.imdb.com/ title/tt0198551/) at the Internet Movie Database.

[92] http://www.discogs.com/Danny-Kaye-2-Louis-Armstrong-The-Five-Pennies/master/143201

[93] http://www.discogs.com/Danny-Kaye-Hans-Christian-Andersen/master/361156

[94] http://wayoutjunk.blogspot.com/2008/05/danny-kaye-tells-six-stories-from.html

[95] http://www.discogs.com/Irving-Berlin-Bing-Crosby-Danny-Kaye-2-And-Peggy-Lee-Selections-From-Irving-Berlins-White-Christmas/ master/369880

Sources

- *Remarks at the Presentation Ceremony for the Presidential Medal of Freedom, 23 June 1987* (http://www. reagan.utexas.edu/archives/speeches/1987/062387j.htm)

External links

- Danny Kaye (http://www.imdb.com/name/nm1414/) at the Internet Movie Database
- Danny Kaye tribute and fan website (http://www.dannykaye.org)
- Tribute to Danny Kaye in The Court Jester (http://www.thevesselwiththepestle.com)
- Danny! – The Definitive Danny Kaye Fan Site (http://www.dannykaye.net)
- Royal Engineers Museum (http://www.remuseum.org.uk/on_line/rem_online_korea.htm#kaye) Danny Kaye in Korea 1952
- Literature on Danny Kaye (http://www.virtual-history.com/movie/person/2666/danny-kaye)

Listen

- *The Danny Kaye Show* (http://www.archive.org/details/DannyKayeShows) on radio at Internet Archive.
- *The Danny Kaye Show* (http://www.archive.org/details/otr_dannykayeshow) more radio episodes at Internet Archive.

Watch

- *The Inspector General* (http://www.archive.org/details/inspector_general_ipod_version) for iPod at Internet Archive.
- *The Inspector General* (http://www.archive.org/details/TheInspectorGeneral) at Internet Archive.

Dick Haymes

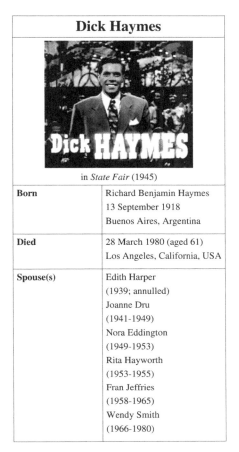

Dick Haymes	
in *State Fair* (1945)	
Born	Richard Benjamin Haymes 13 September 1918 Buenos Aires, Argentina
Died	28 March 1980 (aged 61) Los Angeles, California, USA
Spouse(s)	Edith Harper (1939; annulled) Joanne Dru (1941-1949) Nora Eddington (1949-1953) Rita Hayworth (1953-1955) Fran Jeffries (1958-1965) Wendy Smith (1966-1980)

Richard Benjamin "Dick" Haymes (September 13, 1918 − March 28, 1980) was an actor and singer. He was one of the most popular male vocalists of the 1940s and early 1950s. He was the older brother of Bob Haymes, who was an actor, television host, and songwriter.

Biography

Haymes was born in Buenos Aires, Argentina in 1918.[1][2] His mother, whom Haymes predeceased, was Irish-born Marguerite Haymes (1894–1987), a well-known vocal coach and instructor. Dick Haymes became a vocalist in a number of big bands, worked in Hollywood, on radio, and in films throughout the 1940s/1950s.

Though never achieving the immensely popular status of fellow baritone crooners like Bing Crosby, Frank Sinatra, or Perry Como, Haymes was nonetheless just as respected for his musical ability. He teamed with female vocalist Helen Forrest for many hit duets during World War Two, including "Together," "I'll Buy That Dream," and "Long Ago and far Away"; he sang with Judy Garland on two Decca recordings of songs from a film "The Shocking Miss Pilgrim" in which he appeared with Betty Grable; and he paired repeatedly with the famous Andrews Sisters (Patty, Maxene, and LaVerne) on a dozen or so Decca collaborations, including the Billboard hit "Teresa," "Great Day," "My Sin," and a masterful 1952 rendering of the dramatic ballad "Here in My Heart,' backed by the sisters and Nelson Riddle's lush strings. His duets with Patty Andrews were also well received, both on Decca vinyl and on radio's "Club Fifteen" with the sisters, which he hosted in 1949 and 1950. He also joined Bing Crosby and The Andrews Sisters for an historic session in 1947 producing the Billboard hit "There's No Business Like Show

Business", as well as "Anything You Can Do (I Can Do Better)". His popular renditions of tender ballads such as "Little White Lies" and "Maybe It's Because" were recorded with mood master and exceptional arranger Gordon Jenkins and his orchestra and chorus. Jenkins achieved a haunting beauty in several recordings with Decca artists which set them apart from most musical fare of the day, including The Andrews Sisters' "I Can Dream, Can't I?" and The Weavers' "Goodnight, Irene" (both million-selling, number-one hits).[3]

World War II

Haymes's birth in Argentina to non-U.S. citizens meant he was not an American citizen. In order to avoid military service during World War II, Haymes asserted his non-belligerent status as a citizen of Argentina, which was neutral at that time. Hollywood-based columnists Louella Parsons and Hedda Hopper seized upon this at the time, questioning Haymes' patriotism, but the story had little effect on Haymes' career. About that time, he was classified 4-F by the draft board because of hypertension. As part of his draft examination, he was confined for a short period to a hospital at Ellis Island, which confirmed his hypertension.[4] However, Haymes' decision would come back to haunt him in 1953 when he went to Hawaii (then a territory and, technically, not part of the United States) without first notifying immigration authorities. On trying to return to the mainland United States, Haymes was nearly deported to Argentina, but won his battle to remain in the United States.

Later years

He experienced serious financial problems later in life and at one point was forced into bankruptcy.[5]

He appeared as unscrupulous doctor Elroy Gantman in a 1974 episode of *Adam-12*.

Marriages

Haymes was married six times. His more notable marriages were to film actresses Joanne Dru (1941–1949), Rita Hayworth (1953–1955), and Fran Jeffries (1958–1964). He was also married to Nora Eddington, a former wife of Errol Flynn. Haymes' wives bore him a total of six children.

Death

Dick Haymes died in Los Angeles from lung cancer in 1980. He was 61 years old.

Discography

78rpm albums

Dick Haymes Sings - Carmen Cavallaro at the Piano - Irving Berlin Songs (1948 Decca Record)

Original LPs

* *Rain or Shine* (1955)
* *Moondreams* (1957)
* *Look at Me Now!* (1956 or 1957)
* *Richard the Lion-Hearted - Dick Haymes that is!* (1960)

LP compilations

- *Dick Haymes* (1950s)
- *Little White Lies* (1958)
- *Dick Haymes - Maury Laws Orchestra / Featuring Cy Coleman* (1960s)
- *Love Letters* (1960s)
- Spotlight On -- *Dick Haymes Sings Romantic Ballads - Featuring Johnny Kay* (1960s)
- *Easy* (1973)
- *Imagination* (1982) (also available on CD)

Live LP albums

- *Dick Haymes Comes Home!* (1973)

Selected CD compilations

- (1990) *Richard the Lion-Hearted - Dick Haymes that is!* (1990) re-issue of the vinyl album
- *Imagination* (1992)
- *The Very Best of Dick Haymes, Vol. 1* (1997)
- *The Very Best of Dick Haymes, Vol. 2* (1997)
- *The Complete Columbia Recordings - with Harry James and Benny Goodman* (1998)
- *Little White Lies: 25 Original Mono Recordings 1942-1050. Living Era. ASV Mono. CD AJA 5387 (2001)*
- *Christmas Wishes* (2002, radio transcriptions)
- *Golden Years of Dick Haymes* (2003)
- *The Complete Capitol Collection* (2006)

Filmography

- *Dramatic School* (1938)
- *Du Barry Was a Lady* (1943)
- *Four Jills in a Jeep* (1944)
- *Irish Eyes Are Smiling* (1944)
- *I Am an American* (1944)[6]
- *State Fair* (1945)
- *Diamond Horseshoe* (1945)
- *Do You Love Me* (1946)
- *The Shocking Miss Pilgrim* (1947)
- *Carnival in Costa Rica* (1947)
- *Up in Central Park* (1948)
- *One Touch of Venus* (1948)
- *St. Benny the Dip* (1951)
- *Hollywood Fun Festival* (1952)
- *All Ashore* (1953)
- *Cruisin' Down the River* (1953)
- *Betrayal* (1974) (TV)
- *Won Ton Ton, the Dog Who Saved Hollywood* (1976)

Hit records

Year	Single	Chart positions	
		U.S.	U.S. R&B
1941	"A Sinner Kissed an Angel"(with Harry James)	15	
1942	"The Devil Sat Down and Cried"(with Harry James & Helen Forrest)	15	
	"Idaho"(with Benny Goodman)	4	
	"Take Me"(with Benny Goodman)	10	
	"Serenade In Blue"(with Benny Goodman)	17	
1943	"It Can't Be Wrong"	1	2
	"In My Arms"	3	
	"You'll Never Know"	1	1
	"Wait For Me, Mary"	6	
	"I Never Mention Your Name"	11	
	"I Heard You Cried Last Night"	13	8
	"Put Your Arms Around Me, Honey"	5	
	"For the First Time"	13	
1944	"I'll Get By"(with Harry James)	1	
	"Long Ago (and Far Away)"(with Helen Forrest)	2	
	"How Many Times Do I Have To Tell You"	27	
	"How Blue the Night"	11	
	"It Had To Be You"(with Helen Forrest)	4	
	"Together"(with Helen Forrest)	3	
	"Janie"	26	
1945	"Laura"	9	
	"The More I See You"	7	
	"I Wish I Knew"	6	
	"Till the End of Time"	3	
	"Love Letters"	11	
	"I'll Buy That Dream"(with Helen Forrest)	2	
	"Some Sunday Morning"(with Helen Forrest)	9	
	"That's For Me"	6	
	"It Might As Well Be Spring"	5	

1946	"I'm Always Chasing Rainbows"(with Helen Forrest)	7	
	"It's a Grand Night For Singing"	21	
	"Oh! What It Seemed To Be"(with Helen Forrest)	4	
	"Slowly"	12	
	"Come Rain or Come Shine"(with Helen Forrest)	23	
	"In Love In Vain"(with Helen Forrest)	12	
	"You Make Me Feel So Young"	21	
	"Why Does It Get So Late So Early"(with Helen Forrest)	22	
	"On the Boardwalk"	21	
1947	"For You, For Me, Forevermore"(with Judy Garland)	19	
	"How Are Things In Glocca Mora"	9	
	"Mam'selle"	3	
	"There's No Business Like Show Business"(with Bing Crosby & Andrew Sisters)	25	
	"Ivy"	19	
	"Naughty Angeline"	21	
	"I Wish I Didn't Love You So"	9	
	"And Mimi"	15	
1948	"Teresa"(with Andrews Sisters)	21	
	"Little White Lies"(gold record)	2	
	"You Can't Be True, Dear"	9	
	"Nature Boy"	11	
	"It's Magic"	9	
	"Ev'ry Day I Love You"	24	
1949	"Bouquet of Roses"	22	
	"Room Full of Roses"	6	
	"Maybe It's Because"	5	
	"The Old Master Painter"	4	
1950	"Roses"	29	
	"Count Every Star"(with Artie Shaw)	10	
	"Can Anyone Explain"	23	
1951	"You're Just In Love"(with Ethel Merman)	30	
	"And So To Sleep Again"	28	
1956	"Two Different Worlds"	80	

Musical theatre

- *Miss Liberty* (1951, Dallas Theatre)

References

[1] Prigozy, Ruth (June 2006). *The Life of Dick Haymes: No More Little White Lies*. University Press of Mississippi. (http://books.google.com/ books?id=q1YLv__iXW0C&printsec=frontcover&dq=dick+haymes&ei=wRC2S4K5ApKCyASjuKE7&cd=1#v=onepage&q=&f=false)

[2] See also Social Security Death Index (http://www.ancestry.com/ssdi) for Richard Haymes (SS#113-05-9919). His birthdate is frequently incorrectly given as 1916

[3] Sforza, John: "Swing It! The Andrews Sisters Story;" University Press of Kentucky, 2000; 289 pages

[4] Prigozy, *The Life of Dick Haymes, op cit*, p. 48

[5] Prigorzy, *The Life of Dick Haymes, op cit*, p. 177. "By the early sixties I was a desperate alcholic [*sic?*]. I had been forced into bankruptcy with a half million dollars in debts and no assets."

[6] The 16 minute film, *I Am an American*, was featured in American theaters as a short feature in connection with "I Am an American Day" (now called Constitution Day). *I Am an American* was produced by Gordon Hollingshead, written and directed by Crane Wilbur. Besides Haymes, it featured Humphrey Bogart, Gary Gray, Danny Kaye, Joan Leslie, Dennis Morgan, Knute Rockne, and Jay Silverheels. See: *I Am An American* (http://tcmdb.com/title/title.jsp?stid=730264) at the TCM Movie Database and *I Am an American* (http://www.imdb.com/ title/tt0198551/) at the Internet Movie Database.

Further reading

- Prigozy, Ruth (June 2006). *The Life of Dick Haymes: No More Little White Lies*. University Press of Mississippi.

External links

- Dick Haymes (http://www.imdb.com/name/nm0371376/) at the Internet Movie Database
- Dick Haymes (http://www.allrovi.com/name/p31269) at AllRovi
- Dick Haymes (http://www.allmusic.com/artist/p13157) at Allmusic
- Homepage of: 'The Dick Haymes Society' (http://www.dickhaymes.com/)
- Haymes' entry (http://www.parabrisas.com/d_haymesd.php) at Solid! - The encyclopedia of big band, lounge, classic jazz and space-age sounds (http://www.parabrisas.com/index.php)
- Dick Haymes: Hollywood's Balladeer Supreme (http://www.classicimages.com/1997/july97/haymes.html) article by Laura Wagner at Classic Images - Films of the Golden Age (http://www.classicimages.com/index. html) (online magazine)
- "Dick Haymes" (http://www.findagrave.com/cgi-bin/fg.cgi?page=gr&GRid=6001207). Find a Grave. Retrieved August 30, 2010.

Don't Fence Me In (song)

Don't Fence Me In is a popular American song with music by Cole Porter and lyrics by Robert Fletcher and Cole Porter.

Origins

Originally written in 1934 for *Adios, Argentina,* an unproduced 20th Century Fox film musical, "**Don't Fence Me In**" was based on text by a poet and engineer with the Department of Highways in Helena, Montana, Robert (Bob) Fletcher. Cole Porter, who had been asked to write a cowboy song for the 20th Century Fox musical, bought the poem from Fletcher for $250. Porter reworked Fletcher's poem, and when the song was first published, Porter was credited with sole authorship. Porter had wanted to give Fletcher co-authorship credit, but his publishers did not allow that. After the song became popular, however, Fletcher hired attorneys who negotiated his being given co-authorship credit in subsequent publications. Although it was one of the most popular songs of its time, Porter claimed it was his least favorite of his own compositions.[1]

In 1934, Robert Fletcher sent Porter his song, titled "Don't Fence Me In," which he had written at film producer Lou Brock's suggestion, with the film "Adios, Argentina" in mind; Porter bought the rights, with the agreement that he would use the title, could re-work the lyrics if he chose, and could write his own music.

Porter's revision of the song retained quite a few segments of Fletcher's lyrics, such as "Give me land, lots of land," "... breeze ... cottonwood trees," "turn me loose, let me straddle my old saddle," "mountains rise ... western skies," "cayuse," "where the west commences," and "... hobbles ... can't stand fences,"[2] but in some places modified to give them "the smart Porter touch".[3] Porter substituted some whole lines, rearranged lyric phrases, added two verses, and composed his own music for it. (Porter's exact verse, about Wildcat Kelly, was not included in any of the hit recordings of the song or used in either of the movies in which the song was actually used, although Roy Rogers referred to "Wildcat Willy" when he performed it in 1944's "Hollywood Canteen (film)".).[4][5]

Cover versions

Ten years later, in 1944, Warner Bros. resurrected "Don't Fence Me In" for Roy Rogers to sing in the movie, *Hollywood Canteen*. Many people heard the song for the first time when Kate Smith introduced it on her radio broadcast of October 8, 1944. "Don't Fence Me In" was also recorded by Bing Crosby and The Andrews Sisters in 1944. Crosby entered the studio on July 25, 1944, without having seen or heard the song. Within 30 minutes, he and The Andrews Sisters had made the recording, which later sold over a million copies and topped the *Billboard* charts for eight weeks in 1944–45.

Ella Fitzgerald recorded this on her Verve Cole Porter Songbook album, it was also released on her Verve release "Ella Fitzgerald Sings More Cole Porter."

Covers of the song were also made by the original "Singin' Cowboy" Gene Autry. Eddy Arnold included it on his [RCA] release "A Dozen Hits". Willie Nelson recorded his cover with Leon Russell.

Roy Rogers and Don't Fence Me In

The following year, the song was sung again as the title tune of another Roy Rogers film, *Don't Fence Me In* (1945), in which Dale Evans plays a magazine reporter who comes to Roy Rogers' and George "Gabby" Hayes' ranch to research a story which she is writing about a legendary late gunslinger. When it's revealed that Gabby Hayes is actually the supposedly dead outlaw, Roy must clear his name. Rogers and The Sons of the Pioneers also find time to perform some songs, including the Cole Porter title tune.

The next year (1946), a biopic about Cole Porter titled *Night and Day* used a clip from *Hollywood Canteen* of Rogers singing "Don't Fence Me In."

Pop culture

- David Byrne did a cover of this song in 1990 for a Cole Porter tribute album entitled *Red Hot + Blue*. Byrne performed what he describes as his "Brazilian" version of the song during his 2004 tour for the *Grown Backwards* album.[6]
- Steve Goodman performed the song, including on his album *The Easter Tapes* recorded during one of his annual visits with New York radio personality Vin Scelsa.
- Lynn Anderson recorded the song for her album *Cowboy's Sweetheart* in 1992.
- Chumbawamba recorded a version of the song with lead vocals by Danbert Nobacon. A segment of the song featured on the unreleased album *Jesus H. Christ* that was later reworked to become *Shhh!* (1992), but "Don't Fence Me In" did not feature on the final album cut.
- The first verse of the song was sung by Apu in The Simpsons episode "The Lastest Gun in the West".
- The song was sung in the 1954 action movie "Hell and High Water" Starring Richard Widmark.
- The song was featured in the 1999 film *The Bachelor*, which follows a sworn bachelor who is reluctant to marry.
- The song was used in the opening credits of the 2000 film *Chopper*.
- Cary-Hiroyuki Tagawa's character Eddie Sakamura sings it at a karaoke bar in the opening scene of the 1993 film Rising Sun. It is also played while the end credits roll.
- Shortly after the Berlin Wall was erected in 1961, a communist-run East Berlin radio station called Ops used "Don't Fence Me In" as the theme song for its nightly propaganda broadcast aimed at Allied soldiers based in West Berlin.[7]
- Australian male voice choir The Spooky Men's Chorale have recorded this on their DVD album "Deep".
- Black Iris covered the song in a wildly popular Nokia commercial for the Nokia C7. Despite public response, the song was never released as a full-track mp3.

References

[1] "Don't Fence Me In." *Spotlight*. Turner Classic Movies. 2008. Turner Sports and Entertainment Digital Network. Accessed 3 June 2008. (http://www.tcm.com/thismonth/article.jsp?cid=161339).

[2] The Complete Lyrics of Cole Porter (http://mudcat.org/thread.cfm?threadid=34307#462556), (http://books.google.com/books?id=AJWKS3w0BNAC&q=Don't+Fence#v=snippet&q=Don't Fence&f=false) (http://books.google.com/books?ei=J4dpT_PNMIi0iwKq_On7BA&id=cLNdRXpSFssC&dq=The+Complete+Lyrics+of+Cole+Porter,+Robert+Kimball,&q=Don't+Fence+Me+In#v=snippet&q=Don't Fence Me In&f=false).

[3] "Cole Porter: A revival is under way." Tom Prideaux (http://www.spiegel.de/spiegel/print/d-45138058.html) Life Magazine, 25.02.1972, p.71 (http://books.google.com/books?id=cVIEAAAAMBAJ&pg=PA71&dq="Don't+Fence+Me+In"+-+"Robert+Fletcher"&hl=en&sa=X&ei=dYBpT6vuK4XbiAKEs-T8BA&ved=0CFIQ6AEwBA#v=onepage&q="Don't Fence Me In" - "Robert Fletcher"&f=false)

[4] The Complete Lyrics of Cole Porter (http://mudcat.org/thread.cfm?threadid=34307#462556).

[5] America's Songs: The Stories Behind The Songs Of Broadway (http://books.google.com/books?id=-ENtazHbVc4C&printsec=frontcover#v=onepage&q&f=false)

[6] David Byrne Journal Entry, davidbyrne.com, accessed 2008-02-29, webpage:

9.21.04: Town Hall with Gilberto Gi (http://journal.davidbyrne.com/2004/09/index.html).

[7] (http://www.spiegel.de/spiegel/print/d-45138058.html) Der Spiegel, 24.01.1962, in German

Don't Rob Another Man's Castle

"Don't Rob Another Man's Castle"	
Single by Eddy Arnold	
Released	1949
Genre	Country music
Length	2:34
Writer(s)	Jenny Lou Carson
Eddy Arnold singles chronology	
"Then I Turned and Walked Slowly Away" (1948) "**Don't Rob Another Man's Castle**" (1949) "The Echo of Your Footsteps" (1949)	

"**Don't Rob Another Man's Castle**" is a song written by Jenny Lou Carson. The song was first performed by Eddy Arnold who reached #1 on the Folk Best Seller charts in 1949.[1] Later that same year, Ernest Tubb and The Andrews Sisters along with The Texas Troubadors, took their version of the song to #10 on the Folk Best Seller List.[2] Guy Mitchell released a version of the song in 1952.

References

[1] Whitburn, Joel (2004). *The Billboard Book Of Top 40 Country Hits: 1944-2006, Second edition*. Record Research. p. 29.

[2] Whitburn, Joel (2004). *The Billboard Book Of Top 40 Country Hits: 1944-2006, Second edition*. Record Research. p. 28.

External links

- Full lyrics of this song (http://www.metrolyrics.com/dont-rob-another-mans-castle-lyrics-eddy-arnold.html) at MetroLyrics

Dot Records

Dot Records	
Parent company	Independent (1950-57) Paramount Pictures (1957-74) Gulf+Western (1966-74) Famous Music Group (1968-74) ABC Records (1974-78)
Founded	1950
Founder	Randy Wood
Status	Defunct, absorbed into ABC Records in 1978, catalog now owned by Universal Music Group
Distributor(s)	Self-distributed (1950-68) Famous Music Group (1968-74) ABC Records (1974-78)
Genre	Various (early) Country (later)
Country of origin	United States
Location	Nashville, Tennessee

Dot Records was an American record label and company that was active between 1950 and 1977. It was founded by Randy Wood. In Gallatin, Tennessee, Wood had earlier started a mail order record shop, known for its radio ads on WLAC in Nashville and its R&B (later black gospel) air personality Bill "Hoss" Allen. The label was known to hire artists to record remakes of their previous hits.

History

The early years

The original headquarters of Dot Records were in Gallatin, Tennessee, in fact many of the older recording were recorded in radio station WHIN, which Wood owned at the time. WHIN was a daytime only radio station so recording sessions were held at night when the station was off the air.[1] In 1956, the company moved to Hollywood, California.

In its early years, the label specialized in artists from around Tennessee. Then it branched out to include musicians and singers from across the United States. It recorded a variety of country music, rhythm & blues, polkas & waltzes, gospel music, rockabilly, pop music, and early rock & roll. After the move to Hollywood, Dot Records bought up many recordings by small local independent labels and issued them nationally.

Paramount ownership

In 1957, Wood sold ownership of the label to Paramount Pictures, but he remained the president of the company for another decade. Dot Records then began to release soundtrack albums, including Elmer Bernstein's score for *The Ten Commandments* (1956),[2] a 2-LP set that played longer than the usual record album.

In 1958, Dot Records started a subsidiary label, Hamilton Records, for rockabilly and rhythm & blues. They distributed Jeff Barry's Steed Records and also distributed the only record from Carnival Records. In addition, Dot Records created two other subsidiary labels: Crystalette and Acta. In 1967, Dot Records picked up distribution of Bob Crewe's DynoVoice label from Bell Records. In 1967, Randy Wood left to co-found the Ranwood Records label with Lawrence Welk.

Pat Boone recorded his most popular songs for the label. Both Boone's albums and singles were very successful. Dot recordings were distributed in the United Kingdom on the London label.

Eddie Fisher recorded some of his later albums for the label. *Eddie Fisher Today* was the most popular and included popular standards of the day, but he did not have a substantial hit single in his time with them.

Later years

In 1968, two years after Paramount was purchased by Gulf and Western, the Dot Records label was rebranded as a country music label under the umbrella of Famous Music Group. This included the Paramount, Stax (until 1970) and Blue Thumb labels, along with distribution of Sire Records (now owned by Warner Music Group) and Melanie Safka's Neighborhood Records (which later moved to Arista Records). By 1968, Lawrence Welk had acquired his Dot catalog which was reissued on his Ranwood Records label.[3]

In 1974, the label (along with the rest of the Famous Music Group) was bought by ABC Records (which ironically had tried to purchase Dot years before) and discontinued the label at the start of 1978.[4] The ABC/Dot headquarters became the Nashville office of ABC Records, a division of the American Broadcasting Company, which coincidentally had been bought by Paramount's old theater chain in 1953 (which helped the network catch up to its rivals CBS and NBC), and had started a good relationship with Paramount's TV division (wherein Paramount produced a number of hit series on ABC).

ABC Records was sold to MCA Records in 1979. The Dot/Paramount catalog is now owned by Universal Music Group, with Geffen Records (which absorbed MCA Records, and was founded by David Geffen, who become a co-founder of Paramount's one-time sister studio DreamWorks) managing the pop/rock back catalog, and MCA Nashville Records managing the country back catalog.

Family members report that Randy Wood died in La Jolla, California on April 9, 2011 after a fall in his home at age 94.

Dot Records artists

This list is incomplete.

(** indicates a master purchase (or lease) from another record company)

- Jim Doval and the Gauchos
- Hal Aloma
- Arthur Alexander
- Steve Allen
- American Breed (Acta)
- The Andrews Sisters
- Louis Armstrong
- Gene Austin
- Jack Barlow
- Count Basie
- The Baskerville Hounds
- Danny Boy (Danny Wahlquist)
- Al Bollington (British organist)
- Pat Boone
- Barbara Eden
- Jimmy Boyd
- Walter Brennan
- The Blenders

- Browning Bryant
- Rusty Bryant
- Jerry Burke
- Jo Ann Castle
- The Chantays**
- Children of Rain
- Roy Clark
- Sanford Clark**
- Colours[5]
- Don Cornell
- Eddie Costa
- The Counts
- Bob Crosby
- Mac Curtis
- Velva Darnell
- The Dartells**
- Jimmy Dee
- Lonnie Donegan**
- Jimmy Dorsey
- The Fairmount Singers
- Donna Fargo
- Fear Itself
- Freddy Fender
- Jack Fina
- The Fireballs
- Eddie Fisher
- Myron Floren
- The Fontane Sisters
- The Four Lads
- William Frawley
- Bob Gaddy
- Jimmy Gilmer & The Fireballs
- Bonnie Guitar
- The Jack Halloran Singers
- Hamilton Streetcar
- Roy Head[6]
- Milt Herth (organist)
- The Hilltoppers
- Tab Hunter
- Gunilla Hutton
- The Illusion (Steed)
- Tommy Jackson
- Denise Jannah
- Carol Jarvis
- Danny Kaye
- Sandra Kaylor
- Sylvia and the Five Panthers

- Dr. Charles Kendall
- The Kendalls
- Gary Usher
- Jack Kerouac[7]
- Anita Kerr
- Andy Kim (Steed)
- Sonny Knight
- The Lennon Sisters
- Liberace
- Jim Lowe
- Robin Luke**
- Johnny Maddox
- Barbara Mandrell
- Tony Martin
- Wink Martindale
- Robin McNamara (Steed)
- The Mills Brothers
- Mike Minor
- Mint Tattoo
- Vaughn Monroe
- Tiny Morrie
- Mount Rushmore
- Leonard Nimoy
- Ken Nordine
- Nervous Norvus**
- Larry Novak
- Tommy Overstreet
- Eddie Peabody
- Nancy Priddy
- Louis Prima
- Jimmie Rodgers
- Mitch Ryder (DynoVoice)
- John Wesley Ryles
- Lalo Schifrin
- John Serry, Sr.
- Ray Sharpe
- Six Fat Dutchmen
- Keely Smith
- Jo-El Sonnier
- The Split Level
- Dodie Stevens
- Val Stöecklein
- Gale Storm
- The String-A-Longs
- The Sunshine Boys
- The Surfaris**
- Diana Trask

- Helen Traubel
- Leroy Van Dyke
- Billy Vaughn
- Robin Ward
- Lawrence Welk
- The Lawrence Welk Glee Club
- Margaret Whiting
- Don Williams
- Easy Williams
- Lew Williams
- Mac Wiseman
- George Wright
- Dr. Norman Wright
- Yankee Dollar
- Barry Young

References

[1] http://www.bsnpubs.com/dot/dotstory.html
[2] "demillegenlrelease1.htm" (http://www.widescreenmuseum.com/widescreen/demillegenlrelease1.htm). Widescreenmuseum.com. . Retrieved 2010-09-20.
[3] http://books.google.com/books?id=qwoEAAAAMBAJ&pg=PA3&dq=%22ranwood+to+release+21+Welk+top+sallers%22&hl=en& ei=LePuTbT7BISFtgft1PyqCQ&sa=X&oi=book_result&ct=result&resnum=1&ved=0CDMQ6AEwAA#v=onepage&q&f=false
[4] *Billboard - Google Books* (http://books.google.com/books?id=piQEAAAAMBAJ&pg=PT2&dq="abc+records"+++diener& cd=1#v=onepage&q="abc records" +diener&f=false). Books.google.com. 1978-01-14. . Retrieved 2010-09-20.
[5] Unterberger, Richie. "Allmusic.com" (http://www.allmusic.com/artist/p12588). Allmusic.com. . Retrieved 2010-09-20.
[6] "The Story of Roy Head and The Traits" (http://myspace.com/royheadandthetraits). Myspace.com. . Retrieved 2010-09-20.
[7] Birmingham, Jed (2006-03-22). "Beat Vinyl: Reports from the Bibliographic Bunker" (http://realitystudio.org/bibliographic-bunker/ beat-vinyl). *Realitystudio.org*. Supervert. . Retrieved 2007-11-14. "The ultimate Beat Generation collectible on vinyl might be Jack Kerouac's *Poetry of the Beat Generation* on Dot Records."

External links

- The Dot Records Story (http://www.bsnpubs.com/dot/dotstory.html)
- Singles discography (http://www.globaldogproductions.com/)
- Velva Darnell Electronics (http://www.velvadarnell.com/about.htm)
- Billy Vaughn & Dot recording stars (http://digital.library.unt.edu/ark:/67531/metadc19752/m1/) (interviewed 2.22.1968) on the Pop Chronicles (audio).

Down in the Valley (folk song)

"Down in the Valley" ("Birmingham Jail")	
Written by	Traditional
Language	English
Form	Ballad

"Down in the Valley", also known as **"Birmingham Jail"**, is a traditional American folk song.[1][2][3] It has been recorded by many artists, and is included in the *Songs of Expanding America* recordings in the Burl Ives six-album set *Historical America in Song*.

Lyrics

Down in the valley, the valley so low

Hang your head over, hear the wind blow

Hear the wind blow, dear, hear the wind blow;

Hang your head over, hear the wind blow.

Roses love sunshine, violets love dew,

Angels in Heaven know I love you,

Know I love you, dear, know I love you,

Angels in Heaven know I love you.

Build me a castle, forty feet high;

So I can see her as she rides by,

As she rides by, dear, as she rides by,

So I can see her as she rides by.

"If you don't love me, love whom you please,"

"Throw your arms round me, give my heart ease,"

"Give my heart ease, dear, give my heart ease,"

"Throw your arms round me, give my heart ease,"

Write me a letter, send it by mail;

Send it in care of the Birmingham jail,

Birmingham jail, dear, Birmingham jail,

Send it in care of the Birmingham jail.

Roses love sunshine, violets love dew,

Angels in Heaven know I love you,

Know I love you, dear, know I love you,

Angels in Heaven know I love you.

Lyrics vary, as with most folk songs and it is a ballad played in the 3/4 time signature. The most notable change in lyrics, and title, is Lead Belly's performance of the tune as Birmingham Jail. For example, sometimes the line "Hang your head over, hear the wind blow" is replaced by "Late in the evening, hear the train blow".

Pop culture

The song is performed on The Andy Griffith Show when Andy Griffith and actress Joanna Moore sing the song.

In the original *Friday the 13th* (1980) a group of camp councilors sing the song while the killer stalks.

Alvin and the Chipmunks covered the song for their 1962 album *The Chipmunk Songbook*.

This song is sung by Erland Van Lidth De Jeude in the 1980 comedy movie Stir Crazy starring Richard Pryor and Gene Wilder in which they are sent to prison after being wrongfully convicted of a bank robbery.

The song was recorded by The Andrews Sisters.

In the Star Trek: The Next Generation episode "Dark Page", an illusion of Deanna Troi's father sings the song in the form of a lullaby.

The 1982 film *Safari 3000* features a scene where Eddie Miles (David Carradine) and J.J. Dalton (Stockard Channing) sing a verse of the song.

The author/songwriter David M Pierce used selected lyrics from the song as titles for a series of detective novels written between 1989 and 1996 - "Down In The Valley", "Hear The Wind Blow, Dear", "Roses Love Sunshine", "Angels In Heaven", "Write Me A Letter" and "As She Rides By".

References

[1] Ken and Janice Tate, *Favorite Songs of the Good Old Days* (http://books.google.com/books?isbn=159217034X) (p. 29). Berne, Indiana: DRG (Dynamic Resource Group), 2005. ISBN 1-59217-034-X.

[2] Lyrics. "Down In The Valley" (http://www.bluegrasslyrics.com/flatt_song.cfm-recordID=sp394.htm). *Bluegrass Lyrics.Com.* .

[3] MIDI file. "Down In The Valley" (http://www.contemplator.com/tunebook/america/downvaly.htm). *Popular Songs in American History.*
        .

External links

- The free score on www.traditional-songs.com (http://www.traditional-songs.com/download_score. php?name=Down in the valley)

Bibliography

- Boas, Frank (ed.). *The Journal of American Folk-Lore* Vol. XXX (July–September 1917) No. CXVII. Lancaster, Pennsylvania: American Folk-Lore Society.

Ernest Tubb

Ernest Tubb	
Background information	
Birth name	Ernest Dale Tubb
Also known as	The Texas Troubadour
Born	February 9, 1914 Crisp, Texas, United States
Died	September 6, 1984 (aged 70) Nashville, Tennessee, United States
Genres	country, honky tonk
Occupations	singer-songwriter, bandleader
Instruments	guitar
Years active	1936–1982
Labels	Bluebird, Decca, First Generation

Ernest Dale Tubb (February 9, 1914 – September 6, 1984), nicknamed the Texas Troubadour, was an American singer and songwriter and one of the pioneers of country music. His biggest career hit song, "Walking the Floor Over You" (1941), marked the rise of the honky tonk style of music.[1] In 1948, he was the first singer to record a hit version of "Blue Christmas", a song more commonly associated with Elvis Presley and his mid-1950s version. Another well-known Tubb hit was "Waltz Across Texas" (1965), which became one of his most requested songs and is often used in dance halls throughout Texas during waltz lessons. Tubb recorded duets with the then up-and-coming Loretta Lynn in the early 1960s, including their hit "Sweet Thang". Tubb is a member of the Country Music Hall of Fame.

Biography

Early years

Tubb was born on a cotton farm near Crisp, in Ellis County, Texas (now a ghost town). His father was a sharecropper, so Tubb spent his youth working on farms throughout the state. He was inspired by Jimmie Rodgers and spent his spare time learning to sing, yodel, and play the guitar. At age 19, he took a job as a singer on San Antonio radio station KONO-AM. The pay was low so Tubb also dug ditches for the Works Progress Administration and then clerked at a drug store. In 1939 he moved to San Angelo, Texas and was hired to do a 15-minute afternoon live show on radio station KGKL-AM. He drove a beer delivery truck in order to support himself during this time, and during World War II he wrote and recorded a song titled "Beautiful San Angelo".[2]

Recording career

In 1936, Tubb contacted Jimmie Rodgers's widow (Rodgers died in 1933) to ask for an autographed photo. A friendship developed and she was instrumental in getting Tubb a recording contract with RCA. His first two records were unsuccessful. A tonsillectomy in 1939 affected his singing style so he turned to songwriting. In 1940 he switched to Decca records to try singing again and it was his sixth Decca release with the single "Walking the Floor Over You" that brought Tubb to stardom.[3]

Tubb (3rd from left, back row) at Carnegie Hall in 1947

Tubb joined the Grand Ole Opry in February 1943 and put together his band, the Texas Troubadours.[4] Tubb's first band members were from Gadsden, Alabama. They were, Vernon "Toby" Reese, Chester Studdard, and Ray "Kemo" Head. He remained a regular on the radio show for four decades, and hosted his own *Midnight Jamboree* radio show each Saturday night after the Opry. Tubb headlined the first Grand Ole Opry show presented in Carnegie Hall in New York City in September 1947.

Tubb always surrounded himself with some of Nashville's best musicians. Jimmy Short, his first guitarist in the Troubadours, is credited with the Tubb sound of single-string guitar picking. From about 1943 to 1948, Short featured clean, clear riffs throughout Tubb's songs. Other well-known musicians to either travel with Tubb as band members or record on his records were steel guitarist Jerry Byrd and Tommy "Butterball" Paige, who replaced Short as Tubb's lead guitarist in 1947. Billy Byrd joined the Troubadours in 1949 and brought jazzy riffs to the instrumental interludes, especially the four-note riff at the end of his guitar solos that would become synonymous with Tubb's songs. Actually a jazz musician, Byrd—no relation to Jerry—remained with Tubb until 1959.

Another Tubb musician was actually his producer, Owen Bradley. Bradley played piano on many of Tubb's recordings from the 1950s, but Tubb wanted him to sound like Moon Mullican, the honky tonk piano great of that era. The classically trained Bradley tried, but couldn't quite match the sound, so Tubb said Bradley was "half as good" as Moon. When Tubb called out Bradley's name at the start of one of the piano interludes the singer always referred to him as "Half-Moon Bradley."

In 1949, Tubb helped the famed boogie-woogie Andrews Sisters crossover to the country charts when they teamed on Decca Records to record a cover of Eddy Arnold's "Don't Rob Another Man's Castle" and the western-swing flavored "I'm Bitin' My Fingernails and Thinking of You." Tubb was impressed by the enormous success of Patty, Maxene, and LaVerne, and he remembered that their 1947 recording of "The Blue Tail Fly (Jimmy Crack Corn)" with folk legend Burl Ives produced a Top-10 Billboard hit,[5] and he was therefore eager to repeat that success. He brought the upbeat "Fingernails" tune to the session, hoping that the trio would like it, and they did. Not realizing how tall the Texas Troubador was, the recording technicians at Decca had the sisters stand on a wooden box on one side of the one microphone they shared with Tubb so that the audio would balance. The rhythm trio also wasn't used to Tubb's vocal style, as Maxene once remembered, "He sang different than anybody I've ever heard. He sang the melody of the song, but the timing was different. It wasn't like we were used to...you sing eight bars, and then you sing eight bars, and then you sing eight bars. Not with him. He just sang eight bars, ten bars, eleven bars, and then stopped, whatever it was. So, we'd just start to follow him, and then got paid on 750,000 records sold that never came above the Mason-Dixon Line!"[6]

Tubb never possessed the best voice and actually mocked his own singing. He told an interviewer that 95 percent of the men in bars would hear his music on the juke box and say to their girlfriends, "I can sing better than him," and Tubb added they would be right. In fact, he missed some notes horribly on some recordings. When Tubb was recording "You Don't Have to Be a Baby to Cry" in 1949 and tried to hit a low note, Red Foley, his duet partner at the time, was sitting in the booth when somebody said, "I bet you wish you could hit that low note." Foley replied, "I bet Ernest wishes *he* could hit that note." The two, who released seven albums together, maintained a friendly on-air "feud" over the years, and Tubb appeared on Foley's *Ozark Jubilee* on ABC-TV.

In 1957, he walked into the National Life building's lobby in Nashville and fired a .357 magnum, intending to shoot music producer Jim Denny. Tubb shot at the wrong man but did not hit anyone. He was arrested and charged with public drunkenness.[7]

In the 1960s, Tubb was well known for having one of the best bands in country music history. The band included lightning-fingered Leon Rhodes, who later appeared on TV's *Hee Haw* as the guitarist in the show's band. Buddy Emmons, another pedal steel guitar virtuoso, began with Tubb in about 1958 and lasted through the early 1960s. Emmons went on to create a steel-guitar manufacturing company that bears his name.

Beginning in the fall of 1965, he hosted a half-hour TV program, *The Ernest Tubb Show*, which aired in first-run syndication for three years.[8] That same year, he was inducted into the Country Music Hall of Fame; and in 1970, Tubb was inducted into the Nashville Songwriters Hall of Fame.[9][10]

Later years

Tubb inspired some of the most devoted fans of any country artist — and his fans followed him throughout his career, long after the chart hits dried up. He remained, as did most of his peers, a fixture at the Grand Ole Opry where he continued to appear. He continued to host his *Midnight Jamboree* radio program a few blocks away from the Opry at his record shop. A notable release in 1979, *The Legend and the Legacy* paired Tubb with a who's who of country singers on the Cachet Records label, a label which Tubb was connected to financially. This long out of print duets album was re-released in 1999 as a CD on the First Generations label, on the 20th anniversary of its release, and it quickly went out of print again.[3]

In 1980, he appeared as himself in Loretta Lynn's autobiographical film, *Coal Miner's Daughter* with Roy Acuff and Minnie Pearl.

His singing voice remained intact until late in life, when he fell ill with emphysema. Even so, he continued to make over 200 personal appearances a year, carrying an oxygen tank on his bus. After each performance he would shake hands and sign autographs with every fan who wanted to stay. Health problems finally halted his performances in 1982.[11]

He died of the illness in 1984 at Baptist Hospital in Nashville, Tennessee.[3] He is buried in Nashville's Hermitage Memorial Gardens.

Legacy

Current fans may know Tubb primarily for the Ernest Tubb Record Shop [12] in Nashville, which opened in May 1947. There are also Ernest Tubb Record Shops in Pigeon Forge, Tennessee and Fort Worth, Texas. The record shops have been meeting places for country music stars and fans for decades.

He was inducted into the Texas Country Music Hall of Fame in 1999, and he ranked No. 21 in *CMT's 40 Greatest Men of Country Music* in 2003.

One of Tubb's sons, Justin Tubb, made a minor splash on the country music scene in the 1950s; and Justin's sons, Carey and Zachary Tubb, also became musicians. Tubb's nephew, Billy Lee Tubb, was his lead guitarist briefly (fall 1959–April 1960). He also had solo careers under several pseudonyms (Ronny Wade, X. Lincoln) and played with John Anderson, writing several songs with him.[13] Tubb's great nephew, Lucky Tubb, has toured with Hank Williams III.

Original sign from the Nashville, Tennessee store on Broadway. On temporary exhibit at the Tennessee State Museum on the roots of country music March 22, 2006.

Cal Smith, who played guitar for the Texas Troubadours during the 1960s, went on to a successful country music career of his own in the 1970s, recording hits such as "Country Bumpkin". Jack Greene, who played drums for the Texas Troubadours, also went on to become a successful country music star following his departure from Tubb's band, recording the hits "There Goes My Everything" and "Statue of a Fool".

Ernest Tubb nephew Glenn Douglas Tubb {www.glenndouglastubb.webs.com/}wrote his 1st hit song for his Uncle Ernest Tubb in 1952 then went on to write over 50 hits songs for more than 2 dozen different country and rock music super stars including Bob Dylan Johnny Cash B J Thomas George Jones Kentucky Headhunters Charlie Pride Ann Murray Kitty Wells Ernest Tubb winning a Grammy for Skip A Rope Glenn currently performs The Ernest Tubb Tribute Show at The Texas Troubadour Theater broadcast on WSM Radio and Theaters across America

Notes

[1] Vinopal, David. "Ernest Tubb Biography" (http://www.allmusic.com/artist/p24900/biography). Allmusic. . Retrieved January 9, 2010.

[2] Pugh, Ronnie (1998). *Ernest Tubb: The Texas Troubadour* (http://books.google.com/books?id=m_cDTOIdVRcC&pg=PA4&dq=Ernest+ Tubb+Crisp+Texas&cd=1#v=onepage&q=Ernest Tubb Crisp Texas&f=false). Duke University Press. pp. 5. ISBN 978-0-8223-2190-3. .

[3] Vinopal, David. "Ernest Tubb Biography" (http://www.allmusic.com/artist/p24900). Allmusic. . Retrieved January 9, 2010.

[4] Pugh, Ronnie. *Ernest Tubb: The Texas Troubadour*, p. 84

[5] Sforza, John: "Swing It! The Andrews Sisters Story;" University Press of Kentucky, 2000; 289 pages

[6] Sforza, John: "Swing It! The Andrews Sisters Story;" University Press of Kentucky, 2000; 289 pages

[7] Cusic, Don *Eddy Arnold: I'll Hold You in My Heart* (1997), Rutledge Hill Press, ISBN 1-55853-492-X, p. 137

[8] Gross, Mike "Country Television Programs Enjoying Coast-to-Coast Hayride" (November 13, 1965) *Billboard*, p.1

[9] Country Music Association Hall of Fame list of members. (http://www.CMAworld.com/hall_of_fame/current_members.asp) Retrieved January 9, 2010.

[10] Nashville Songwriters Hall of Fame entry for Ernest Tubb. (http://www.nashvillesongwritersfoundation.com/t-z/ernest-tubb.aspx) Retrieved January 9, 2010.

[11] "Ernest Tubb" Texas Country Music Hall of Fame (http://www.carthagetexas.com/HallofFame/inductees_99.htm) Retrieved March 20, 2011

[12] http://www.ernesttubb.com

[13] Pugh, Ronnie. *Ernest Tubb: The Texas Troubadour*, p. 240

References

- "Ernest Tubb". Country Music Hall of Fame (http://www.countrymusichalloffame.org/full-list-of-inductees/ view/ernest-tubb). Retrieved Apr. 21, 2005.

- Pugh, Ronnie (1998). "Ernest Tubb". In *The Encyclopedia of Country Music*. Paul Kingsbury, Editor. New York: Oxford University Press. pp. 547–8.

- Pugh, Ronnie (1996). "First Year In Nashville". In *Ernest Tubb - The Texas Troubadour*. Durham, London: Duke University Press. pp. 88.

External links

- Ernest Tubb Record Shop (http://www.etrecordshop.com/)

- Ernest Tubb at the Country Music Hall of Fame (http://www.countrymusichalloffame.org/ full-list-of-inductees/view/ernest-tubb)

- Ernest Tubb (http://www.allmusic.com/artist/p24900) at Allmusic

- Ernest Tubb at Find A Grave (http://www.findagrave.com/cgi-bin/fg.cgi?page=gr&GRid=8444)

Fallout 3

Fallout 3	
Developer(s)	Bethesda Game Studios
Publisher(s)	Bethesda Softworks
Producer(s)	Todd Howard (executive)
Designer(s)	Emil Pagliarulo (lead)
Artist(s)	Istvan Pely (lead)
Composer(s)	Inon Zur
Series	*Fallout*
Engine	Gamebryo[1] Havok Physics
Version	1.7.0.3 (as of July 31, 2009)[2]
Platform(s)	Windows,[3] PlayStation 3, Xbox 360[4]
Release date(s)	• NA October 28, 2008[5] • EU October 30, 2008[5] • AUS October 30, 2008[5] • UK October 31, 2008[5] • JP December 4, 2008
Genre(s)	Action role-playing, open world[6]
Mode(s)	Single-player
Media/distribution	Blu-ray Disc, DVD, Steam

Fallout 3 is an action role-playing open world video game developed by Bethesda Game Studios. It is the third major installment in the *Fallout* series. The game was released in North America, Europe and Australia in October 2008, and in Japan in December 2008 for Microsoft Windows, PlayStation 3 and Xbox 360. *Fallout 3* takes place in the year 2277, 36 years after the setting of *Fallout 2* and 200 years after the nuclear apocalypse that devastated the game's world in a future where international conflicts between the USA and China culminated in a Sino-American war in 2077, due to the scarcity of petroleum reserves that ran the economies of both countries.

The player character is an inhabitant of Vault 101, a survival shelter designed to protect up to 1,000 humans from the nuclear fallout. When the player character's father disappears under mysterious circumstances, the Overseer, or the leader of the vault, goes insane, and sends security forces after the player, who is forced to escape from the Vault and journey into the ruins of Washington, D.C. to track him down. Along the way the player is assisted by a number of human survivors and must battle a myriad of enemies that inhabit the area now known as the "Capital Wasteland". The game has an attribute and combat system typical of an action strategy game.

Following its release, *Fallout 3* was well received by critics and received a number of Game of the Year awards, praising the game's open-ended gameplay and flexible character-leveling system. The NPD Group estimated that *Fallout 3* sold over 610,000 units during its initial month of release in October 2008, performing better than Bethesda Softworks' previous game *The Elder Scrolls IV: Oblivion*, which sold nearly 500,000 units in its first month. The game has also received post-launch support with Bethesda releasing five downloadable add-ons. The game received controversy upon release, including the use of morphine in the game for Australia, religious and cultural sentiments in India, and sensitivity in Japan due to a mission involving the detonation of an atomic bomb.

Gameplay

Attributes

The game starts with the main character as a newborn, whereupon the player determines the race, the gender, and the general appearance of their character. As a one year-old baby, the infant reads a child's book titled *You're SPECIAL*, where the player can set the character's starting S.P.E.C.I.A.L. primary attributes: Strength, Perception, Endurance, Charisma, Intelligence, Agility, and Luck. The character gains a set of Skills with base levels determined by these attributes. At age 16, the player takes the Generalized Occupational Aptitude Test (G.O.A.T.) to determine the three Skills they wish the character to focus on.[7]

As the character progresses through the game, experience points are earned that are used to achieve levels of accomplishment. Upon achieving a new level, the player receives a set of skill points that can be assigned to improve any of the Skill percentages. For instance, increasing the lock pick skill grants the player the ability to pick harder locks to unlock doors and supply crates. A Perk is granted at each level, which offers advantages of varying quality and form. Many Perks have a set of prerequisites that must be satisfied, and new Perks are unlocked every two levels.[7]

An important statistic tracked in the game is karma. Each character has an aggregate amount of karma that can be affected by the decisions and actions made in the game. Positive karmic actions include freeing captives and helping others. Negative karmic actions include killing good characters and stealing. Beyond acting as flavor for the game's events, karma can have tangible effects to the player, primarily affecting the game's ending. Other effects include altered dialogue with non-player characters (NPCs), or unique reactions from other characters. Actions vary in the level of karma change they cause; thus, pickpocketing produces less negative karma than the killing of a good character. However, the player's relationships with the game's factions are distinct, so any two groups or settlements may view the player in contrasting ways, depending on the player's conduct. Some Perks require specific karma levels.[8]

Health and weapons

Health is separated into two types: general and limb. General health is the primary damage bar, and the player will die if it is depleted. Limb health is specific to each portion of the body, namely the arms, legs, head, and torso. Non-human enemies will sometimes have additional appendages. When a limb's health bar is depleted, that limb is rendered "crippled" and induces a negative status effect, such as blurred vision from a crippled head or reduced movement speed from a crippled leg. Health is diminished when damage is taken from being attacked, falling from great distances, and/or accidental self injury. General health can be replenished by sleeping, using medical equipment (stimpaks), eating food, or drinking water. Limbs can be healed directly by injecting them with stimpaks, by sleeping, or by being healed by a doctor.[9] Along with the health, there are 20 bobbleheads that can be found throughout the game that will give the player bonuses to attributes and skills. Each bobblehead is an iconic Vault-Tec Boy figurine with a different pose. Three of them have to be found in different time periods in the gameplay; otherwise they will be lost.[10]

There are secondary health factors that can affect performance. Chief among these is radiation poisoning: most food is irradiated to a small degree, and parts of the world have varying levels of background radiation. As the player is exposed to radiation, it builds up, causing negative effects and eventually death if left untreated. Radiation sickness must be healed by special medicine or a doctor. The player can become addicted to drugs and alcohol, and then go through withdrawal symptoms if denied those substances. Both afflictions can blur the player's vision for a few seconds and have a negative effect on SPECIAL attributes until the problem is corrected.[11]

Items can become degraded and become less effective. Firearms do less damage and may jam during reloading, and apparel becomes gradually less protective.[12] This will eventually result in the item breaking altogether. Items can be repaired for a price from special vendors, or, when the player has two of the same item (or a comparable item), one can be repaired using salvage parts from the other. Players have the option to create their own weaponry using various scavenged items found in the wasteland. These items can only be created at workbenches, and only if the player possesses the necessary schematics or Perk. These weapons usually possess significant advantages over other weapons of their type. Each schematic has three copies that can be found. Each copy improves the condition (or number) of items produced at the workbench. A higher repair skill will result in a better starting condition for the related weapon. Weapon schematics can be found lying in certain locations, bought from vendors, or received as quest rewards.[13]

V.A.T.S.

The Vault-Tec Assisted Targeting System, or V.A.T.S., plays an important part in combat. While using V.A.T.S., real-time combat is paused, and action is played out from varying camera angles in a computer graphics version of "bullet time", creating a combat system that the Bethesda developers have described as a hybrid between turn-based and real-time combat. Various actions cost action points, limiting the actions of each combatant during a turn, and the player can target specific body areas for attacks to inflict specific injuries; head shots can be used for quick kills or blinding, legs can be targeted to slow enemies' movements, opponents can be disarmed by shooting at their weapons, and players can drive certain enemies into a berserker rage by shooting out things like antennae on various overgrown insects and combat inhibitors on armored robots. However, the use of V.A.T.S. also eliminates most of the first-person shooter elements of the game; aiming is taken over by the computer, and the player is unable to move as a means of avoiding attacks. Each body part has a percentage of hit chance, and generally the closer the player character is to an enemy the higher that percentage. The higher level the character using V.A.T.S is, the more likely that character will hit their enemy.[14]

Companions

The player can have a maximum party of three, consisting of the player's character, a dog named Dogmeat, and a single non-player character. Dogmeat can be killed during the game if the player misuses him or places him in a severely dangerous situation and he cannot be replaced (this was changed with the introduction of *Broken Steel*: the level 22 "Puppies!" perk allows the player to gain a puppy follower if Dogmeat dies);[15][16] it is possible to not encounter Dogmeat at all depending on how the game is played.[17] One other NPC can travel with the player at any time, and in order to get another NPC to travel, the first one must be dismissed (either voluntarily by the player or as a consequence of other events) or die in combat.

Plot

Setting

Fallout 3 takes place in the year 2277, 200 years after a war over resources that ended in nuclear holocaust in 2077. The setting is a post-apocalyptic, retro-future, covering a region that includes Washington, D.C., Northern Virginia and parts of Maryland.[18] The game's landscape includes war-ravaged variants of numerous real-life landmarks such as the White House, the Jefferson and Lincoln Memorials, Arlington National Cemetery and the Washington Monument. The area that the game is set in, known in-game as the Capital Wasteland, holds a number of small settlements of the descendants of survivors from the Great War. Many inhabitants were killed during the nuclear holocaust and the Wasteland is now little more than a barren land nearly devoid of healthy water, food, plant and animal life due to the extreme radiation levels. However, there is a small settlement in the north part of the Capital Wasteland where plant life is abundant.[19]

The player begins the game inside Vault 101, where they believe they were originally born, before venturing out into the Capital Wasteland and facing its many dangers. The Capital Wasteland is home to a number of mutated species of creatures such as two-headed cattle called Brahmin, radscorpions, molerats, and mirelurks. Many of these creatures are generally hostile to the player and will attack on sight. The Wasteland and the city proper is home to several hostile groups, including super mutants, feral ghouls, raiders, slavers, mercenaries, and robots. Of note are the various Vaults—underground structures designed as shelters to protect inhabitants from the dangers of nuclear war (and also for more sinister purposes). In the Washington, D.C. area, many of the roads are blocked off with giant piles of rubble. The player can navigate around the city using a system of underground metro tunnels that connect with other locations (loosely based on the real-life Washington Metro).[20]

Because the game takes place following a nuclear war, cultural advancements have stagnated and, as a result, the game contains a 1950s utopian theme as evidenced in-game through posters and billboards with music from the time period.[21]

Story

The introductory sequence introduces the player to their character's father James, a doctor and scientist in Vault 101. James frequently makes comments about the player character's deceased mother Catherine, and her favorite Bible passage, Revelation 21:6, which speaks of "the waters of life".

The main quest begins after the player is forced to flee Vault 101 when James leaves the vault, throwing it into anarchy and causing the paranoid Overseer to send his security force after the player. The search for James takes the character on a journey through the Wasteland, first to the nearby town of Megaton, named for the undetonated atomic bomb at the center of town, then the Galaxy News Radio station, whose enthusiastic DJ, Three Dog, gives the player the moniker of "The Lone Wanderer". The player travels to Rivet City, a derelict aircraft carrier now serving as a fortified human settlement. Here the player meets Doctor Li, a scientist who worked alongside the player's father. Doctor Li informs the player of Project Purity, a plan conceived by Catherine and James to purify all the water in the Tidal Basin and eventually the entire Potomac River with a giant water purifier built in the Jefferson Memorial. However, continued delays and Catherine's death during childbirth put an end to the project, and James took the player's character as a newborn to raise them in the safety of Vault 101.

After investigating the Jefferson Memorial, the Lone Wanderer tracks James to Vault 112, and frees him from a virtual reality program being run by the Vault's sadistic Overseer, Dr. Braun. James and the player return to Rivet City, and James reveals he sought out Braun for information on the Garden of Eden Creation Kit (G.E.C.K.), a device that contains the components needed to finally activate Project Purity. James and Doctor Li lead a team of Rivet City scientists to the memorial with intent to restart the project, but the memorial is invaded by the Enclave, a powerful military organization formed from the remnants of the pre-War United States government. James floods the project's control room with radiation to stop the Enclave military leader, Colonel Augustus Autumn, from taking control of it, killing himself, his last words urging his child to run. The Lone Wanderer and Dr. Li flee to the ruins of the Pentagon, now a base for the Brotherhood of Steel and now known as the Citadel. With Project Purity still inoperational even with the Enclave occupying the site, the player travels to Vault 87 to find a G.E.C.K. and finish James's work. The player finds the Vault to be a testing site for the FEV (Forced Evolutionary Virus), and the source of the Super Mutants in the Capital Wasteland. After the player acquires the G.E.C.K., the Wanderer is ambushed by the Enclave and captured.

At the Enclave base at Raven Rock, the player is freed from their cell by the Enclave leader, President John Henry Eden, who requests a private audience with them. En route to his office however, Colonel Autumn defies Eden's orders and takes command of the Enclave military, ordering them to kill the player. Fighting their way to Eden's office, the player discovers Eden is actually a sentient supercomputer who took control of the Enclave after their defeat in *Fallout 2* on the West Coast thirty years ago. Eden wishes to repeat the plan of then-President Dick Richardson using Project Purity, infecting the water with a modified strain of FEV that will make it toxic to any mutated life. This plan will kill most life in the wasteland including humans, but the Enclave, due to their genetic "purity" as a result of their isolation, will be immune and free to take control of the area. The Wanderer, provided with a sample of the new F.E.V., is given a choice to either leave peacefully or convince Eden to self-destruct the entire base. The Lone Wanderer escapes Raven Rock and returns to the Citadel.

With the knowledge they possess the G.E.C.K. and the means to activate Project Purity, the Brotherhood assault the Jefferson Memorial, spearheaded by a giant robot named Liberty Prime. In the control room of Project Purity the player confronts Colonel Autumn, and has the choice to persuade him to give up or kill him. Dr. Li informs the player that the purifier is ready to be activated, but the activation code must be input manually, and also that the control room is flooded with lethal amounts of radiation. The Lone Wanderer is forced to choose between sending Sarah Lyons of the Brotherhood inside the extremely irradiated purifier or entering themselves. Whoever enters into the chamber inputs the code hinted at through the game, that being 21:6, and immediately dies from a radiation spike. If the "Broken Steel" DLC is installed, the player survives if they activate it themselves, but they also have the option of sending one of their radiation-immune companions to enter the code and start the purifier with no casualties. The player also has the possibility to enter the F.E.V. sample into the water prior to activation, having adverse effects on the games side quests post-ending.

Development

Interplay Entertainment

Fallout 3 was initially under development by Black Isle Studios, a studio owned by Interplay Entertainment, under the working title *Van Buren*. Black Isle Studios was the developer of the original *Fallout* and *Fallout 2*. When Interplay Entertainment went bankrupt and closed down Black Isle Studios before the game could be completed, the license to develop *Fallout 3* was sold for a $1,175,000 minimum guaranteed advance against royalties to Bethesda Softworks, a studio primarily known as the developer of *The Elder Scrolls* series.[22] Bethesda's *Fallout 3*, however, was developed from scratch, using neither Van Buren code, nor any other materials created by Black Isle Studios.[23] In May 2007, a playable technology demo of the canceled project was released to the public.[24]

Leonard Boyarsky, art director of the original *Fallout*, when asked about Interplay Entertainment's sale of the rights to Bethesda Softworks, said:

> To be perfectly honest, I was extremely disappointed that we did not get the chance to make the next *Fallout* game. This has nothing to do with Bethesda, it's just that we've always felt that *Fallout* was ours and it was just a technicality that Interplay happened to own it. It sort of felt as if our child had been sold to the highest bidder, and we had to just sit by and watch. Since I have absolutely no idea what their plans are, I can't comment on whether I think they're going in the right direction with it or not.[25]

Bethesda Softworks

System requirements

	Minimum	Recommended
Windows[26]		
Operating system	Windows XP or Windows Vista	
CPU	Intel Pentium 4 2.4 GHz or AMD equivalent	Intel Core 2 Duo or AMD equivalent
Memory	1 GB RAM (2 GB for Vista)	2 GB RAM
Hard drive space	7 GB free hard disk space	
Graphics hardware	NVIDIA GeForce 6800 256 MB or ATi Radeon X850 Pro 256 MB	NVIDIA GeForce 8800 512 MB or ATi Radeon HD 3850 512 MB
Network	Online play requires log-in to Game for Windows - Live	

Bethesda Softworks started working on *Fallout 3* in July 2004,[27] but principal development did not begin until after *The Elder Scrolls IV: Oblivion* and its related extras and plug ins were completed.[28] Bethesda Softworks decided to make *Fallout 3* similar to the previous two games, focusing on non-linear gameplay, story, and black comedy. Bethesda also chose to pursue an ESRB rating of M (for mature) by including the adult themes, violence, and depravity characteristic of the *Fallout* series. They also decided to shy away from the self-referential gags of the game's predecessors that broke the illusion that the world of *Fallout* is real. *Fallout 3* uses a version of the same Gamebryo engine as *Oblivion*,[1] and was developed by the team responsible for that game.[29] Liam Neeson was cast as the voice of the player's father.[30]

In February 2007, Bethesda stated that the game was "a fairly good ways away" from release, but that detailed information and previews would be available later in the year.[29] Following a statement made by Pete Hines that the team wanted to make the game a "multiple platform title",[31] the game was announced by *Game Informer* to be in development for Windows, Xbox 360 and PlayStation 3.[4]

During a March 21, 2008 *Official Xbox Magazine* podcast interview, Todd Howard revealed that the game had expanded to nearly the same scope as *Oblivion*. There were originally at least 12 versions of the final cutscene, but with further development this expanded to over 200 possible permutations in the final release, all of which are determined by the actions taken by the player.[16] Bethesda Softworks attended E3 2008 to showcase *Fallout 3*. The first live demo of the Xbox 360 version of the game was shown and demonstrated by Todd Howard, taking place in downtown Washington, D.C. The demo showcased various weapons such as the Fat Man nuclear catapult, the V.A.T.S. system, the functions of the Pip-Boy 3000, as well as combat with several enemies. The demo concluded as the player neared the Brotherhood of Steel-controlled Pentagon and was attacked by an Enclave patrol.[32]

Audio

Several actors of film and video games lent their voices to *Fallout 3*, including Liam Neeson as James,[30] Ron Perlman as the game's narrator, Malcolm McDowell as President John Henry Eden, Craig Sechler as Butch DeLoria and Odette Yustman as Amata Almodovar. Veteran voice actors Dee Bradley Baker, Wes Johnson, Paul Eiding and Stephen Russell also provided voice overs for the game. The *Fallout 3* soundtrack continued the series' convention of featuring sentimental 1940s big band American popular music, the main theme, and few other side songs recorded by The Ink Spots and The Andrews Sisters; in addition to a score written by composer Inon Zur.[33] The soundtrack of the game included artists such as Roy Brown, Billie Holiday, Billy Munn, Cole Porter, and Bob Crosby.[34]

Marketing and release

Trailers

A teaser site for the game appeared on May 2, 2007, and featured music from the game and concept art, along with a timer that counted down to June 5, 2007. The artists and developers involved later confirmed that the concept art, commissioned before *Oblivion* had been released, did not reveal anything from the actual game.[35] When the countdown finished, the site hosted the first teaser trailer for the game, and unveiled a release date of "Fall 2008".[36]

On June 5, 2007, Bethesda released the *Fallout 3* teaser trailer.[37] The press kit released with the trailer indicated that Ron Perlman would be on board with the project, and cited a release date of Fall 2008. The trailer featured The Ink Spots song "*I Don't Want to Set the World on Fire*", which the previous *Fallout* developer Black Isle Studios originally intended to license for use in the first *Fallout* game. The trailer, which was completely done with in-engine assets, closed with Ron Perlman saying his trademark line which he also spoke in the original *Fallout*: "War. War never changes". The trailer showed a devastated Washington, D.C., evidenced by the partially damaged Washington Monument in the background as well as the crumbling buildings that surrounded a rubble-choked city thoroughfare.[38]

A second trailer was first shown during a GameTrailers TV E3 special on July 12, 2008. The trailer zoomed out from a ruined house in the Washington, D.C. suburbs, and provided a wider view of the capital's skyline including the Capitol Building and Washington Monument in the distance.[39] On July 14, 2008, an extended version of this trailer was made available, which besides the original content, included a Vault-Tec advertisement and actual gameplay. Both versions of the trailer featured the song "Dear Hearts and Gentle People" as recorded by Bob Crosby and the Bobcats.[40]

Film festival

On July 11, 2008, as a part of promoting *Fallout 3*, Bethesda Softworks partnered with American Cinematheque and *Geek Monthly magazine* to sponsor "A Post-Apocalyptic Film Festival Presented by *Fallout 3*". The festival took place on August 22–23 at Santa Monica's Aero Theater. Six post-apocalyptic movies were shown which depict life and events that could occur after a world-changing disaster, including *Wizards*, *Damnation Alley*, *A Boy and His Dog*, *The Last Man on Earth*, *The Omega Man*, and *Twelve Monkeys*.[41]

Retail versions

Features	Edition				
	Standard	**Collector's**	**Limited**	**Survival**	**Game of the Year**
Game disc & manual	Yes	Yes	Yes	Yes	Yes
Bonus DVD	No	Yes	No	Yes	No
Concept artbook	No	Yes	No	Yes	No
Vault Boy Bobblehead	No	Yes	No	Yes	No
Lunchbox case	No	Yes	No	Yes	No
Power Armor figurine	No	No	Yes	No	No
PIP-Boy 3000 clock	No	No	No	Yes	No
Downloadable content	No	No	No	No	Yes

Fallout 3 was released in five separate versions, only three of which were made available worldwide:

- The Standard Edition includes the game disc and instruction manual with no extras.
- The Collector's Edition includes the game disc, manual, a bonus "making of" disc, a concept artbook, and a 5" Vault Boy Bobblehead, all of which is contained in a Vault-Tec lunchbox.[42] In Australia, the Collector's Edition is exclusive to Gametraders and EB Games.[43]
- The Limited Edition includes the game disc and manual, as well as a Brotherhood of Steel Power Armor figurine. This edition is available only in the UK through the retailer Game.
- The Survival Edition includes everything from the Collector's Edition, as well as a model of the PIP-Boy 3000 from the game which functions as a digital clock.[42] The Survival Edition is available exclusively from Amazon.com to U.S. customers only.[44]
- The Game of the Year Edition, which includes the original *Fallout 3* game as well as all 5 of the downloadable content packs, was released on October 13, 2009 in North America and October 16, 2009 in Europe. It was released in Australia on October 22, 2009, and in Japan on December 3, 2009.[45] It was made available on Steam on December 17, 2009.[46]

An Xbox 360 version of *Fallout 3* and *Oblivion* double pack was announced for release in North America on April 3, however it was not mentioned whether the bundled games include any of the downloadable content released for either game.[47]

Downloadable content

Bethesda's Todd Howard first confirmed during E3 2008 that downloadable content (DLC) would be prepared for the Xbox 360 and Windows versions of *Fallout 3*.[48][49][50] There are five DLCs: *Operation: Anchorage*, *The Pitt*, *Broken Steel*, *Point Lookout*, and *Mothership Zeta*, released in that order. Of the five, *Broken Steel* has the largest effect on the game, altering the ending and allowing the player to continue playing past the end of the main quest line.[51]

Originally, there was no downloadable content announced for the PlayStation 3 version of the game.[48] Although Bethesda had not offered an official explanation as to why the content was not released for PlayStation 3, Lazard Capital Markets analyst Colin Sebastian speculated that it may have been the result of a money deal with Bethesda by Sony's competitor, Microsoft.[49] When asked if the PlayStation 3 version would receive an update that would enable gameplay beyond the main quest's completion, Todd Howard responded, "Not at this time, no."[52] However, in May 2009, Bethesda announced that the existing DLC packs (*Operation: Anchorage*, *The Pitt* and *Broken Steel*) would be made available for the PlayStation 3; the later two (*Point Lookout* and *Mothership Zeta*) were released for all platforms.[53]

On October 1, 2009, a New Xbox Experience premium theme for the game was released for the Xbox 360. Consumers could pay 240 Microsoft Points, or by having downloaded all other downloadable content. The PlayStation 3 received a free theme, featuring a Brotherhood of Steel Knight in the background, and includes symbols from the game as icons on the PS3 home menu.[54][55][56] In December 2008 the official editor, known as the G.E.C.K. (Garden of Eden Creation Kit) was made available for the Windows version of the game as a free download from the *Fallout 3* website.[57][58]

Reception

Reviews

Reception	
Aggregate scores	
Aggregator	**Score**
GameRankings	92.79% (X360)[59] 90.69% (PC)[60] 90.60% (PS3)[61]
Metacritic	93/100 (X360)[62] 91/100 (PC)[63] 90/100 (PS3)[64]
Review scores	
Publication	**Score**
1UP.com	A[65]
Edge	7/10[66]
Electronic Gaming Monthly	A, B+, A+[67]
Eurogamer	10/10[68]
Famitsu	38/40[69]
Game Informer	9.5/10[70]

GameSpot	9/10 (X360/PC)[71][72] 8.5/10 (PS3)[73]
GameSpy	★ ★ ★ ★ ★ [7]
IGN	9.6/10 (X360/PC)[74] 9.4/10 (PS3)[75]
Official Xbox Magazine	10/10[76]
PC Gamer US	91%[77]

Awards	
Entity	**Award**
9th Annual Game Developers Choice Awards	Game of the Year 2008[78] Best Writing[78]
IGN Best of 2008[79]	Game of the Year 2008[80] Best Xbox 360 Game[81] Best RPG[82] Best Use of Sound[82]
GameSpot Best of 2008	Best PC Game[82] Best RPG[82]
Golden Joystick Award 2009	Ultimate Game of the Year 2009[83] PC Game of the Year 2009[83]

Fallout 3 received critical acclaim from many reviewers, with an average GameRankings score of 92.79% for the Xbox 360,[59] 90.69% for the PC[60] and 90.60% for the PlayStation 3.[61] 1UP.com's Demian Linn praised its open-ended gameplay and flexible character-leveling system. While the V.A.T.S. system was called "fun", enemy encounters were said to suffer from a lack of precision in real-time combat and little variety in enemy types. The review concluded, *Fallout 3* is a "hugely ambitious game that doesn't come around very often".[65] IGN editor Erik Brudvig praised the game's "minimalist" sound design, observing, "you might find yourself with nothing but the sound of wind rustling through decaying trees and blowing dust across the barren plains ... *Fallout 3* proves that less can be more". The review noted that the "unusual amount of realism" combined with the "endless conversation permutations" produces "one of the most truly interactive experiences of the generation".[74] In a review of the game for Kotaku, Mike Fahey commented that "While Inon Zur's score is filled with epic goodness, the real stars of *Fallout 3*'s music are the vintage songs from the 1940s".[84] Will Tuttle of GameSpy commended the game for its "engaging storyline, impeccable presentation, and hundreds of hours of addictive gameplay".[85] Although *Edge* awarded the game 7 out of 10, in a later anniversary issue it placed the game 37th in a "100 best games to play today" list, saying "*Fallout 3* empowers, engages and rewards to extents that few games have ever achieved".[86]

Some criticisms were the bugs in regards to the physics and crashes—some of which broke quests and even prevented progression.[74] The AI and stiff character animations are another common point of criticism,[87][88][89] as is the ending.[87][90] *Edge* stated that "the game is cumbersome in design and frequently incompetent in the details of execution", taking particular issue with the nakedness of the HUD, the clarity of the menu interface, and that the smaller problems are carried over from *Oblivion*. *Edge* liked the central story but said "the writing isn't quite as consistent as the ideas that underpin" and that the "voice-acting is even less reliable".[66]

Sales

From its release in October through the end of 2008, *Fallout 3* shipped over 4.7 million units.[91] According to NPD Group the Xbox 360 version has sold 1.14 million units and the PlayStation 3 version has sold 552,000 units as of January 2009.[92] The Xbox 360 version was the 14th best-selling game of December 2008 in the United States, while the PlayStation 3 version was the eighth best-selling PlayStation 3 game in that region and month.[93]

Awards

Fallout 3 won several awards following its showcasing at E3 2007. IGN gave it the "Game of E3 2007" award, and GameSpot gave it the "Best Role-Playing Game of E3 2007" award.[94][95] Following the game's demonstration at E3 2008, IGN also gave it "Best Overall RPG", "Best Overall Console Game", and "Overall Game of the Show" for E3 2008.[96] Game Critics Awards gave the game "Best Role-Playing Game" and "Best of Show" for E3 2008.[97]

After its release, *Fallout 3* won numerous awards from gaming journalists and websites. At the 2009 Game Developer's Choice Awards, it won overall "Game of the Year" along with "Best Writing."[78] It was also awarded "Game of the Year" by IGN,[80] GamesRadar,[98] GameSpy,[99] UGO Networks,[100] Gamasutra[101] and the Golden Joystick Awards.[83] The game also won "Xbox 360 Game of the Year" from *Official Xbox Magazine*,[82] GameSpy[82] and IGN,[81] while winning "PC Game of the Year" from *GamePro*,[102] GameSpy,[103] GameTrailers[104] and GameSpot,[82] with the latter two also awarding it "Best RPG."[82][105]

At the end of 2009, *Fallout 3* was featured in IGN's "Best Video and Computer Games of the Decade" (2000–2009), with the game being placed top game of 2008[106] and seventh overall game of the decade.[107] In 2012, *Fallout 3* was also exhibited at the Smithsonian Art Exhibition in America. *Fallout 3* was voted for and won the "Adventure" section for the platform "Modern Windows."[108] That same year, G4tv ranked it as the 75th top video game of all time.[109]

Technical issues

Shortly before the game's release, IGN posted a review of the game citing numerous bugs and crashes in the PlayStation 3 release.[110] The game also contained a bug causing the game to freeze and the screen to blur when friends signed out of and into the PlayStation Network.[110] The IGN review was edited shortly thereafter, removing all references to the PS3 version's bugs, causing controversy in the PlayStation communities.[110][111] In reviewing the PlayStation 3 Game of the Year edition, reviewers found that most bugs remained, citing occasional freezes, several animation and scripting issues, and other bugs requiring a restart of the game.[112][113] Even IGN recursively cited bugs with the original release, as well as the Game of the Year edition, calling it "a fantastic game", but warning players to "be aware that you might have to deal with some crashes and bugs".[114]

Controversies

Drug references

On July 4, 2008, *Fallout 3* was refused classification by the ACB in Australia, thus making it illegal to distribute or purchase the game in the country. In order for the game to be reclassified, the offending content in the Australian version of the game would have had to be removed by Bethesda Softworks and the game resubmitted to the ACB.[115][116] According to the ACB board report, the game was refused classification due to the "realistic visual representations of drugs and their delivery method [bringing] the 'science-fiction' drugs in line with 'real-world' drugs."[117]

A revised version of the game was resubmitted to the ACB and reclassified as MA 15+ on August 7, 2008, or not suitable for people under the age of 15 unless accompanied by a parent or adult guardian; this new rating ensured that the game could retail legally in Australia.[115][118] According to the ACB board report, the drug content was not removed entirely from the revised version of the game, but the animation showing the actual usage of the drugs was removed; the minority view on the decision stated that the drug content was still enough to warrant a refused classification rating, despite the admission that the portrayal of the drugs was appropriate within the context of the game.[119]

In a later interview with UK gaming magazine *Edge*, Bethesda Softworks revealed that there would be only one version of *Fallout 3* released worldwide, and that this version would have all real world drug references removed. It was later clarified that the only change made would be that morphine, a real world drug that would have appeared in the game, would instead be renamed to the more generic "Med-X."[120]

Release in India

On October 22, 2008, Microsoft announced that the game would not be released in India on the Xbox 360 platform.[121] Religious and cultural sentiments were cited as the reason. Microsoft stated, "Microsoft constantly endeavors to bring the best games to Indian consumers in sync with their international release. However, in light of cultural sensitivities in India, we have made the business decision to not bring *Fallout 3* into the country."[122] Although the specific reason was not revealed in public, it is possible that it is because the game contains two-headed mutated cows called Brahmin, or that Brahmin is also the name of an ancient, powerful hereditary caste of Hindu priests and religious scholars in India, or its similarity to the spelling of brahman, a type of cow that originated in India. Brahman, a breed of Zebu, are revered by Hindus.[123]

Sensitivity to Japan

Bethesda Softworks changed the side quest "The Power of the Atom" in the Japanese version of *Fallout 3* to relieve concerns about depictions of atomic detonation in inhabited areas. In non-Japanese versions, players are given the option of either defusing, ignoring, or detonating the dormant atomic bomb in the town of Megaton. In the Japanese version, the character Mr. Burke has been taken out of this side quest, making it impossible to detonate the bomb.[124] Also in the Japanese release, the "Fat Man" nuclear catapult weapon was renamed "Nuka Launcher", as the original name was a reference to the bomb used on Nagasaki.[124][125] According to Tetsu Takahashi, responsible for localizing *Fallout 3* to Japan under his company Zenimax Asia, the available actions prior to localizing "The Power of the Atom" and the ability to kill civilians almost got the game banned by CERO before it got an Adult Only Rating.[126]

References

[1] "Bethesda Speaks On Gamebryo Engine, Final Fallout 3 DLC" (http://games.slashdot.org/story/09/07/09/1655222/ Bethesda-Speaks-On-Gamebryo-Engine-Final-emFallout-3em-DLC). Slashdot. 2009-07-09. . Retrieved 2009-11-19.

[2] "Fallout 3 Patches" (http://fallout.bethsoft.com/eng/downloads/updates-v1.5updatenotes-US.html). Bethesda Softworks. . Retrieved 2009-01-13.

[3] "Fallout 3 is in Windows 7 Not Compatible List" (http://www.microsoft.com/windows/compatibility/windows-7/en-us/Details. aspx?type=Software&p=Fallout 3&v=Bethesda Games&uid=&l=en&pf=0&pi=0&s=fallout&os=64-bit). Microsoft. . Retrieved 2010-10-02.

[4] Berghammer, Billy (2007-06-05). "Game Informer's July Cover Revealed!" (http://web.archive.org/web/20070607222938/http://www. gameinformer.com/News/Story/200706/N07.0605.1221.21984.htm). *Game Informer*. Archived from the original (http://www. gameinformer.com/News/Story/200706/N07.0605.1221.21984.htm) on 2007-06-07. . Retrieved 2007-06-05.

[5] "Fallout 3 Has Gone Gold" (http://fallout.bethsoft.com/eng/home/pr-100908.php). Bethesda Softworks. Retrieved 2009-11-11.

[6] "Fallout 3". *Game Informer* (171): 52. June 2007.

[7] Tuttle, Will (2008-10-27). "Fallout 3 Review" (http://au.xbox360.gamespy.com/xbox-360/fallout-3/924342p1.html). GameSpy. . Retrieved 2008-10-28.

[8] Clayman, David (2008-09-23). "Fallout 3 Week: Skills and Perks" (http://au.xbox360.ign.com/articles/912/912469p1.html). IGN. . Retrieved 2008-11-23.

[9] Lewis, Cameron (2008-10-27). "11 Tips For Surviving Fallout 3" (http://web.archive.org/web/20100129212821/http://www.gamepro. com/article/features/207651/11-tips-for-surviving-fallout-3/). GamePro. Archived from the original (http://www.gamepro.com/article/ features/207651/11-tips-for-surviving-fallout-3/) on 2010-01-29. . Retrieved 2011-08-14.

[10] Woodland, Barney (2011-09-01). "Fallout 3 Bobbleheads" (http://www.fallout3bobbleheads.com). Fallout 3 Bobbleheads. . Retrieved 2011-09-01.

[11] "Fallout 3 Radiation" (http://www.mahalo.com/fallout-3-radiation/). Mahalo. . Retrieved 2011-08-14.

[12] Amrich, Dan (March 2008). "Fallout 3" (http://web.archive.org/web/20080405181101/http://www.oxmonline.com/article/previews/ a-f/fallout-3-0). *Official Xbox Magazine*. Archived from the original (http://www.oxmonline.com/article/previews/a-f/fallout-3-0) on 2008-04-05. . Retrieved 2008-04-03.

[13] Halas, Jacek. "Fallout 3 Game Guide Unique Weapon Schematics" (http://guides.gamepressure.com/fallout3/guide.asp?ID=5791). Game Pressure. . Retrieved 2011-08-14.

[14] Brudvig, Erik (2008-09-22). "Fallout 3 Week: Tools of Survival" (http://uk.ps3.ign.com/articles/912/912254p1.html). IGN. . Retrieved 2011-08-01.

[15] Lopez, Miguel (2008-03). "Fallout 3 Preview" (http://xbox360.gamespy.com/xbox-360/fallout-3/865671p1.html). GameSpy. . Retrieved 2008-04-16.

[16] "OXM Podcast #107" (http://web.archive.org/web/20080327192729/http://www.oxmpodcast.com/?p=134). *Official Xbox Magazine*. 2008-03-21. Archived from the original (http://www.oxmpodcast.com/?p=134) on 2008-03-27. . Retrieved 2008-08-26.

[17] DeSanto, Mark (2008-10). "Ars Reviews Fallout 3" (http://arstechnica.com/gaming/reviews/2008/10/fallout-3-review.ars/3). Ars Technica. . Retrieved 2008-10-29.

[18] "FAQ" (http://fallout.bethsoft.com/eng/info/faq.html). Bethesda Softworks. 2008-05-05. . Retrieved 2011-08-14.

[19] "50 Things to Do in the Capital Wasteland" (http://www.crispygamer.com/features/2009-08-10/ 50-things-to-do-in-the-capital-wasteland.aspx). Crispy Gamer. 2009-08-10. . Retrieved 2011-08-18.

[20] Halas, Jacek. "Fallout 3 Game Guide" (http://guides.gamepressure.com/fallout3/guide.asp?ID=5694). Game Pressure. . Retrieved 2011-08-18.

[21] Halas, Jacek. "Fallout 3 Game Guide" (http://guides.gamepressure.com/fallout3/guide.asp?ID=5698). Game Pressure. . Retrieved 2011-08-18.

[22] Caen, Herve (2004-10-13) (Form 10-Q). *Interplay* (http://web.archive.org/web/20070927215630/http://yahoo.brand.edgar-online. com/fetchFilingFrameset.aspx?FilingID=3222135&Type=HTML). Q2 2004. SEC EDGAR. Archived from the original (http://yahoo. brand.edgar-online.com/fetchFilingFrameset.aspx?FilingID=3222135&Type=HTML) on 2007-09-27. . Retrieved 2006-10-30.

[23] Thorsen, Tor (2008-10-04). "Video Q&A: Fallout 3's Endgame" (http://uk.gamespot.com/pc/rpg/fallout2/news/6198577/ video-qanda-fallout-3s-endgame). GameSpot. . Retrieved 2011-09-04.

[24] "Van Buren Tech Demo" (http://www.fileplanet.com/176640/170000/fileinfo/Van-Buren-Tech-Demo-[Cancelled-Fallout-3-Project]). FilePlanet. . Retrieved 2011-08-14.

[25] Blancato, Joe (2006-12-26). "The Rise and Fall of Troika" (http://www.escapistmagazine.com/articles/view/issues/issue_77/ 440-The-Rise-and-Fall-of-Troika). *The Escapist*. . Retrieved 2007-06-05.

[26] Faylor, Chris (2008-10-09). "Fallout 3 PC System Requirements Released" (http://www.shacknews.com/article/55221/ fallout-3-pc-system-requirements). Shacknews. . Retrieved 2008-10-09.

[27] "Bethesda Softworks to Develop and Publish Fallout 3" (http://web.archive.org/web/20061004195839/http://www.bethsoft.com/ news/pressrelease_071204.htm) (Press release). Bethesda Softworks. 2004-07-12. Archived from the original (http://www.bethsoft.com/ news/pressrelease_071204.htm) on 2006-10-04. . Retrieved 2006-10-30.

[28] "Fallout 3 360-bound?" (http://uk.gamespot.com/news/6236061.html). GameSpot. 2007-01-24. . Retrieved 2009-11-11.

[29] Hines, Pete (2007-02-08). *Interview: Bethesda Softworks' Pete Hines* (http://web.archive.org/web/20070210053336/http://www. shacknews.com/extras/2007/020807_petehines_2.x). (Interview). Shacknews. Archived from the original (http://www.shacknews.com/ extras/2007/020807_petehines_2.x) on 2007-02-10. .

[30] "Bethesda Softworks Announces Award-Winning Actor Liam Neeson to Play Lead Role in Fallout 3" (http://web.archive.org/web/ 20070710175056/http://bethsoft.com/news/pressrelease_050807.htm). Archived from the original (http://bethsoft.com/news/ pressrelease_050807.htm) on 2007-07-10. . Retrieved 2007-07-11.

[31] Adams, David (2007-07-12). "Talking Fallout 3" (http://pc.ign.com/articles/529/529773p1.html). IGN. . Retrieved 2009-11-25.

[32] "*Fallout 3* Xbox 360 Gameplay" (http://xbox360.ign.com/dor/objects/882301/fallout-3/videos/fallout3demo1_071408.html). IGN. . Retrieved 2009-11-11.

[33] Peckham, Matt (2008-10-31). "Gadget review: *Fallout 3*" (http://web.archive.org/web/20110720063107/http://www.digitalartsonline. co.uk/news/index.cfm?NewsID=11669). *DigitalArts*. Archived from the original (http://www.digitalartsonline.co.uk/news/index. cfm?NewsID=11669) on 2011-07-20. . Retrieved 2011-08-14.

[34] Good, Owen (2008-11-09). "All the Songs of Fallout 3" (http://kotaku.com/5081270/all-the-songs-of-fallout-3). Kotaku. . Retrieved 2011-08-14.

[35] Klepek, Patrick (2007-05-02). "Bethesda Launches Teaser Site For Real *Fallout 3*" (http://www.1up.com/news/ bethesda-launches-teaser-site-real). 1UP.com. . Retrieved 2007-06-05.

[36] Graft, Kris (2007-06-05). "*Fallout 3* Coming Fall '08" (http://www.next-gen.biz/index.php?option=com_content&task=view& id=5864&Itemid=2). *Next Generation*. . Retrieved 2007-06-05.

[37] "*Fallout 3* teaser trailer" (http://fallout.bethsoft.com/teaser/teaser.html). Bethesda Softworks. 2007-06-05. . Retrieved 2009-11-11.

[38] Rausch, Allen 'Delsyn' (2007-06-05). "Fallout 3 Trailer Released" (http://pc.gamespy.com/pc/fallout-3/794187p1.html). GameSpy. . Retrieved 2007-07-11.

[39] "E3 2008: Microsoft Press Conference Cam Walkthrough" (http://www.gametrailers.com/video/e3-2008-fallout-3/36197).
      GameTrailers. 2008-07-14. . Retrieved 2009-11-11.

[40] "*Fallout 3* Extended E3 Teaser (Requires membership)" (http://xbox360.ign.com/dor/objects/882301/fallout-3/videos/
      fallout3_security_071408.html). IGN. . Retrieved 2009-11-11.

[41] "A Post-Apocalyptic Film Festival Presented by Fallout 3" (http://fallout.bethsoft.com/eng/home/pr-071108.php). . Retrieved
      2008-07-12.

[42] Hines, Pete (2008-06-06). "Bethesda Softworks Blog: Creating Collectibles" (http://blogs.ign.com/Bethesda_Softworks/2008/06/06/
      92163/). IGN. . Retrieved 2009-11-11.

[43] "Fallout 3 Collector's Edition Only A Retailer Exclusive In Australia?" (http://www.kotaku.com.au/2008/06/
      fallout_3_collectors_edition_only_a_retailer_exclusive_in_australia/). Kotaku. 2008-07-23. . Retrieved 2009-11-11.

[44] "Bethesda Softworks and Amazon.com Announce Fallout 3 Survival Edition" (http://xbox360.ign.com/articles/879/879836p1.html).
      IGN. 2008-06-06. . Retrieved 2009-11-11.

[45] "Fallout 3 (Game of the Year Edition)" (http://uk.xbox360.ign.com/objects/143/14351019.html). IGN. . Retrieved 2011-09-01.

[46] "Fallout 3 on Steam" (http://store.steampowered.com/app/22370). Steam. . Retrieved 2010-05-19.

[47] "Fallout 3 & Oblivion double pack drops April 3" (http://asia.gamespot.com/news/
      fallout-3-and-oblivion-double-pack-drops-april-3-6350639). Gamespot. . Retrieved 19 February 2012.

[48] DeVries, Jack (2008-07-14). "E3 2008: *Fallout 3* to Have Console Exclusive Downloadable Content" (http://xbox360.ign.com/articles/
      888/888898p1.html). IGN. . Retrieved 2009-11-11.

[49] Graft, Kris (2008-07-21). "Bethesda Mum on Fallout 3 DLC Exclusivity Deal" (http://www.next-gen.biz/news/
      bethesda-mum-fallout-3-dlc-exclusivity-deal). Edge Online. . Retrieved 2009-11-11.

[50] Beaumont, Claudine (2008-11-25). "Fallout 3 downloadable content announced" (http://www.telegraph.co.uk/technology/video-games/
      3520398/Fallout-3-downloadable-content-announced.html). The Telegraph. . Retrieved 2011-09-04.

[51] Frushtick, Russ (2008-12-11). "EXCLUSIVE: Fallout 3's "Broken Steel" to Change the End of the Game: Games: UGO" (http://www.ugo.
      com/games/exclusive-fallout-3s-broken-steel-to-change-the-end-of-the-game). UGO Networks. . Retrieved 2009-11-11.

[52] Klepek, Patrick (2009-01-23). "Bethesda Won't Commit To PS3 'Fallout 3' Getting Ability To Play Post-Ending » MTV Multiplayer" (http:/
      /multiplayerblog.mtv.com/2009/01/23/no-ending-update-ps3-fallout/). MTV. . Retrieved 2009-11-11.

[53] Purchese, Robert (2009-05-19). "Bethesda doing more Fallout 3 DLC" (http://www.eurogamer.net/articles/
      bethesda-doing-more-fallout-3-dlc). Eurogamer. . Retrieved 2009-11-11.

[54] Sliwinski, Alexander (2009-09-17). "Fallout 3 premium theme available now, free to loyal DLC buyers" (http://www.joystiq.com/2009/
      09/17/fallout-3-premium-theme-available-now-free-to-loyal-dlc-buyers/). Joystiq. . Retrieved 2009-11-11.

[55] Edwards, Andru (2009-10-01). "Bethesda gives free Fallout 3 premium theme to DLC buyers" (http://games gearlive.com/playfeed/
      article/q309-free-fallout-3-premium-theme-dlc/). Playfeed. . Retrieved 2009-11-11.

[56] Fahey, Mike (2009-09-16). "Free Fallout 3 Premium 360 Theme For DLC Fans" (http://kotaku.com/5360741/
      free-fallout-3-premium-360-theme-for-dlc-fans). Kotaku. . Retrieved 2009-11-11.

[57] "Bethesda's blog announces the release of the G.E.C.K." (http://bethblog.com/index.php/2008/12/11/the-geck-is-here/). Beth Blog.
      2008-12-11. . Retrieved 2011-09-04.

[58] Peckham, Matt (2008-12-11). "Fallout 3 G.E.C.K. Editor Available Now" (http://www.pcworld.com/article/155382/
      fallout_3_geck_editor_available_now.html). PC World. . Retrieved 2011-09-04.

[59] "Fallout 3 Xbox 360 Reviews at GameRankings" (http://www.gamerankings.com/xbox360/939933-fallout-3/index.html).
      GameRankings. . Retrieved 2012-04-09.

[60] "Fallout 3 PC Reviews at GameRankings" (http://www.gamerankings.com/pc/918428-fallout-3/index.html). GameRankings. .
      Retrieved 2012-04-09.

[61] "Fallout 3 PS3 Reviews at GameRankings" (http://www.gamerankings.com/ps3/939932-fallout-3/index.html). GameRankings. .
      Retrieved 2012-04-09.

[62] "Fallout 3 Xbox 360 Reviews at Metacritic" (http://www.metacritic.com/game/xbox-360/fallout-3). Metacritic. . Retrieved 2008-11-07.

[63] "Fallout 3 PC Reviews at Metacritic" (http://www.metacritic.com/game/pc/fallout-3). Metacritic. . Retrieved 2008-11-07.

[64] "Fallout 3 PS3 Reviews at Metacritic" (http://www.metacritic.com/game/playstation-3/fallout-3). Metacritic. . Retrieved 2008-11-07.

[65] Linn, Demian (2008-10-27). "Fallout 3 Review" (http://www.1up.com/reviews/fallout-3). 1UP.com. . Retrieved 2008-10-28.

[66] Staff, Edge (2008-11-28). "Edge Review: Fallout 3" (http://www.next-gen.biz/reviews/edge-review-fallout-3). Edge Online. . Retrieved
      2009-07-31.

[67] Linn; Thierry "Scooter" Nguyen, Philip Kollar (December 2008). "Fallout 3 review". *Electronic Gaming Monthly* (235): 69.

[68] Reed, Kristan (2008-10-28). "Fallout 3 Review" (http://www.eurogamer.net/articles/fallout-3-review). Eurogamer. . Retrieved
      2008-10-28.

[69] Gifford, Kevin (2008-11-26). "Japan Review Check: Fallout 3" (http://www.1up.com/news/japan-review-check-fallout-3). 1UP.com. .
      Retrieved 2011-08-14.

[70] Bertz, Matt (2009-09-22). "If the End of the World Looks This Sweet, Then Bring On the Apocalypse - Fallout 3 - Xbox 360" (http://www.
      gameinformer.com/games/fallout_3/b/xbox360/archive/2009/09/23/review.aspx). www.GameInformer.com . Retrieved 2012-04-21.

[71] Van Ord, Kevin (2008-10-28). "Fallout 3 Review" (http://www.gamespot.com/pc/rpg/fallout3/review.html?om_act=convert&
      om_clk=gssummary&tag=summary;read-review). GameSpot. . Retrieved 2009-11-11.

[72] Van Ord, Kevin (2008-10-28). "Fallout 3 Review" (http://www.gamespot.com/xbox360/rpg/fallout3/review.html). GameSpot. . Retrieved 2008-10-28.

[73] Van Ord, Kevin (2008-10-28). "Fallout 3 Review" (http://uk.gamespot.com/ps3/rpg/fallout3/review.html). GameSpot. . Retrieved 2008-10-28.

[74] Brudvig, Erik (2008-10-27). "Fallout 3 Review A bleak, twisted, yet utterly wonderful game." (http://xbox360.ign.com/articles/924/924165p1.html). IGN. p. 5. . Retrieved 2009-06-23. "The difference in looks between the two console versions is small compared to the leap that comes with a top of the line PC".

[75] Brudvig, Erik (2008-10-27). "IGN: Fallout 3 Review" (http://uk.ps3.ign.com/articles/924/924345p1.html). IGN. . Retrieved 2008-11-01.

[76] Curthoys, Paul (2008-10-28). "Fallout 3 OXM Review" (http://web.archive.org/web/20090126075121/http://oxmonline.com/article/reviews/xbox-360/a-f/fallout-3). *Official Xbox Magazine*. Archived from the original (http://www.oxmonline.com/article/reviews/xbox-360/a-f/fallout-3) on 2009-01-26. . Retrieved 2008-10-28.

[77] Desslock (2008). "Fallout 3: Your life in the wasteland is just beginning". *PC Gamer* (182): 54–65. ISSN 1080-4471.

[78] "Game Developers Choice Awards: Nominees and Awards Recipients" (http://www.gamechoiceawards.com/archive/gdca_9th.html). GDC. . Retrieved 2009-12-20.

[79] "IGN Best of 2008" (http://bestof.ign.com/2008/xbox360/). IGN. . Retrieved 2009-11-11.

[80] "IGN Game of the Year 2008" (http://games.ign.com/dor/articles/944244/ign-game-of-the-year-2008-revealed/videos/igngoty2008_winner_011609.html). IGN. 2009-01-16. . Retrieved 2009-01-16.

[81] "Xbox 360 Game of the Year" (http://uk.bestof.ign.com/2008/xbox360/21.html). IGN. . Retrieved 2011-08-18.

[82] "Fallout 3 Awards" (http://fallout.bethsoft.com/eng/links/fallout3-awards.php). Fallout: Welcome to the Official Site. . Retrieved 2011-08-18.

[83] Fahey, Mike (2009-10-30). "Fallout 3 Wins The Golden Joysticks - golden joystick awards - Kotaku" (http://kotaku.com/5393592/fallout-3-wins-the-golden-joysticks). Kotaku. . Retrieved 2009-11-11.

[84] Fahey, Mike (2008-10-29). "Fallout 3 Review: Wasting Away Again In Radiationville" (http://kotaku.com/5070394/fallout-3-review-wasting-away-again-in-radiationville). Kotaku. . Retrieved 2011-08-14.

[85] "Fallout 3" (http://uk.xbox360.gamespy.com/xbox-360/fallout-3/924342p3.html). GameSpy. 2008-10-27. . Retrieved 2011-09-04.

[86] "100 Best Games to Play Today" (http://www.next-gen.biz/features/100-best-games-play-today). Edge Online. 2009-09-03. . Retrieved 2009-05-09.

[87] Breckon, Nick (2008-10-27). "Fallout 3 Review: An Old PC Game at Heart" (http://www.shacknews.com/article/55595/fallout-3-review-an-old). Shacknews. . Retrieved 2009-11-11.

[88] Buckland, Jeff (2008-10-29). "Fallout 3 Review" (http://www.atomicgamer.com/articles/672/fallout-3-review). AtomicGamer. . Retrieved 2009-11-11.

[89] Kelly, Andy. "Fallout 3 Review". *PlayStation Magazine 3* (107). October 2008.

[90] Gerstmann, Jeff (2008-11-27). "Fallout 3 Review" (http://www.giantbomb.com/fallout-3/61-20504/reviews/). Giant Bomb. . Retrieved 2009-11-11.

[91] Thang, Jimmy (2008-12-30). "Fallout 3 Expanding to More Markets" (http://pc.ign.com/articles/941/941189p1.html). IGN. . Retrieved 2008-12-30.

[92] "NPD: January 2009 Life to Date Numbers" (http://web.archive.org/web/20090325011912/http://www.n4g.com/News-298592.aspx). N4G. 2009-03-22. Archived from the original (http://www.n4g.com/News-298592.aspx) on 2009-03-25. . Retrieved 2009-03-28.

[93] "Top 10 Games of December 2008, By Platform" (http://www.wired.com/gamelife/2009/01/top-10-games-of/). *Wired*. 2009-01-18. . Retrieved 2009-01-19.

[94] Thang, Jimmy (2008-06-11). "IGN Pre-E3 2008: Fallout 3 Confirmed for Show" (http://ps3.ign.com/articles/881/881180p1.html). IGN. . Retrieved 2009-11-11.

[95] "GameSpot E3 2007 Editor's Choice Awards" (http://www.gamespot.com/special_features/editorschoicee307/genre/index.html?page=6). GameSpot. . Retrieved 2009-11-11.

[96] IGN Editorial Staff (2008-07-25). "IGN's Overall Best of E3 2008 Awards" (http://games.ign.com/articles/893/893833p1.html). IGN. . Retrieved 2009-11-11.

[97] "Game Critics Awards 2008 Winners" (http://www.gamecriticsawards.com/winners.html). Game Critics. . Retrieved 2009-11-11.

[98] "Games Radar's Officially Annual Platinum Chalice Awards 2008" (http://www.gamesradar.com/gamesradars-officially-annual-platinum-chalice-awards-2008/). GamesRadar. . Retrieved 2009-11-11.

[99] "GameSpy's Game of the Year" (http://goty.gamespy.com/2008/overall/10.html). GameSpy. . Retrieved 2009-12-27.

[100] Plante, Chris (2008-12-18). "UGO's Game of the Year Awards 2008" (http://www.ugo.com/games/ugos-game-of-the-year-awards-2008). UGO Networks. . Retrieved 2011-08-18.

[101] "Gamasutra's Best Of 2008: Top 10 Games Of The Year" (http://gamasutra.com/php-bin/news_index.php?story=21377). Gamasutra. 2008-12-23. . Retrieved 2011-08-18.

[102] "The Best (and Worst) of 08: The GamePro Awards" (http://web.archive.org/web/20110721211704/http://www.gamepro.com/article/features/208404/the-best-and-worst-of-08-the-gamepro-awards/). GamePro. 2008-12-17. Archived from the original (http://www.gamepro.com/article/features/208404/the-best-and-worst-of-08-the-gamepro-awards/) on 2011-07-21. . Retrieved 2011-08-18.

[103] "PC Awards Recap" (http://goty.gamespy.com/2008/pc/12.html). GameSpy. . Retrieved 2011-08-18.

[104] "GameTrailers Best PC Game of 2008" (http://www.gametrailers.com/player/43920.html). GameTrailers. 2008-12-31. . Retrieved 2009-11-11.

[105] "Gametrailers Best RPG of 2008" (http://www.gametrailers.com/video/best-role-playing-gt-goty/43842). GameTrailers. 2008-12-24. . Retrieved 2009-11-11.

[106] IGN Staff. "IGN's Best Video and Computer Games of the Decade - 2008" (http://uk.ign.com/decade/best-games-2008.html). IGN. . Retrieved 2010-06-08.

[107] IGN Staff. "IGN's Best Video and Computer Games of the Decade - Overall" (http://uk.ign.com/decade/best-games-decade.html). IGN. . Retrieved 2010-06-08.

[108] "Winning Games" (http://www.americanart.si.edu/exhibitions/archive/2012/games/winninggames.pdf). American Art. . Retrieved 2011-08-01.

[109] Top 100 Video Games of All Time #75 - Fallout 3 – G4tv.com (http://www.g4tv.com/videos/59223/top-100-video-games-of-all-time-75-fallout-3/)

[110] Spiess, Kevin (2008-10-29). "IGN edits Fallout 3 review to remove mention of "major issue" bug found in PS3 version" (http://www.neoseeker.com/news/9108-ign-edits-fallout-3-review-to-remove-mention-of-major-issue-bug-found-in-ps3-version/). Neoseeker. . Retrieved 2009-11-18.

[111] Barlow, Anthony (2008-10-29). "IGN Fallout 3 Review–There's Been Some Changes" (http://www.theplaystationnetwork.com/ign-fallout-3-review-theres-been-some-changes/). The PlayStation Network. . Retrieved 2009-11-18.

[112] Stevens, Nathaniel (2009-10-27). "Fallout 3: Game of the Year Edition" (http://www.digitalchumps.com/game-reviews/35-ps3/3990-fallout-3-game-of-the-year-edition.html). Digital Chumps. . Retrieved 2009-11-18.

[113] "Review: Fallout 3 Game of the Year Edition" (http://spawnkill.com/review-fallout-3-game-of-the-year-edition/). Spawn Kill. 2009-11-02. . Retrieved 2009-11-18.

[114] Brudvig, Erik (2009-10-15). "Fallout 3 Game of the Year Edition Review" (http://ps3.ign.com/articles/103/1035569p5.html). IGN. . Retrieved 2009-11-18.

[115] "OFLC listing for *Fallout 3*" (http://www.classification.gov.au/www/cob/find.nsf/d853f429dd038ae1ca25759b0003557c/ae87cbba1093d4b0ca25767100791a27?OpenDocument). Classification by Australian Government. 2008-07-08. . Retrieved 2011-09-04.

[116] Thang, Jimmy (2008-07-09). "*Fallout 3* Officially Refused Classification in Australia" (http://xbox360.ign.com/articles/887/887547p1.html). IGN. . Retrieved 2009-11-11.

[117] Booker, Logan (2008-07-10). "OFLC Report: Why Fallout 3 Was Banned In Australia" (http://www.kotaku.com.au/2008/07/olfc_report_why_fallout_3_was_banned_in_australia/). Kotaku. . Retrieved 2009-11-11.

[118] Hill, Jason (2008-08-12). "Fallout 3 ban lifted in Australia" (http://www.smh.com.au/news/articles/fallout-3-ban-lifted-in-australia/2008/08/12/1218306838907.html). The Sydney Morning Herald. . Retrieved 2011-09-04.

[119] Kolan, Patrick (2008-08-12). "Fallout 3 Censorship Report" (http://xbox360.ign.com/articles/898/898386p1.html). IGN. . Retrieved 2009-11-11.

[120] Ellison, Blake (2008-09-09). "Fallout 3 Censorship Goes Global" (http://www.shacknews.com/article/54651/fallout-3-censorship-goes-global). Shacknews. . Retrieved 2009-11-11.

[121] Fahey, Mike (2008-10-22). "Fallout 3 Not Coming To India" (http://kotaku.com/5067039/fallout-3-not-coming-to-india). Kotaku. . Retrieved 2010-04-20.

[122] Lee, Jason (2008-10-22). "Fallout 3 withheld from India" (http://www.gamesindustry.biz/articles/fallout-3-withheld-from-india). Games Industry. . Retrieved 2009-12-01.

[123] Haas, Pete (2008-10-22). "Are Brahmin The Reason For Fallout 3's Cancellation in India?" (http://www.cinemablend.com/games/Are-Brahmin-The-Reason-For-Fallout-3-s-Cancellation-in-India-12947.html). Gaming Blend. . Retrieved 2011-09-04.

[124] "Bethesda Softworks Statement of Fallout 3 Censorship" (http://www.bethsoft.com/jpn/news/20081110a.html) (in Japanese). Bethesda Softworks. . Retrieved 2009-12-02.

[125] Snow, Jean (2008-11-11). "Fallout 3 Pulls Nuke References for Japan" (http://www.wired.com/gamelife/2008/11/japanese-fallou/). *Wired*. . Retrieved 2009-11-11.

[126] "Interview: Zenimax Asia's Takahashi on Bringing Western Games to Japan" (http://gamecareerguide.com/news/25670/interview_zenimax_asias_.php). Game Career Guide. 2009-11-24. . Retrieved 2009-12-02.

External links

- Official website (http://fallout.bethsoft.com/)
- *Fallout 3* (http://www.imdb.com/title/tt1073664/) at the Internet Movie Database
- *Fallout 3* (http://www.mobygames.com/game/fallout-3) at MobyGames
- Fallout 3 Portal (http://www.falloutwiki.com/Portal:Fallout_3) on The Vault, a *Fallout* wiki

Follow the Boys

Follow the Boys *AKA Three Cheers for the Boys*	
Original film poster	
Directed by	A. Edward Sutherland
Produced by	Charles K. Feldman
Written by	Lou Breslow Gertrude Purcell
Starring	George Raft Vera Zorina
Music by	Fred E. Ahlert Billy Austin Dick Charles Kermit Goell Leigh Harline Inez James Louis Jordan Larry Markes Jimmy McHugh Phil Moore Buddy Pepper Frank Skinner Roy Turk Oliver Wallace
Cinematography	David Abel
Editing by	Fred R. Feitshans Jr.
Distributed by	Universal Pictures
Release date(s)	April 25, 1944
Running time	122 minutes
Country	United States
Language	English

Follow the Boys (1944), also known as *Three Cheers for the Boys*, is a musical film made by Universal Pictures as an all-star cast morale booster to entertain the troops abroad and the civilians at home. The film was directed by A. Edward "Eddie" Sutherland and produced by Charles K. Feldman. The movie stars George Raft and features Vera Zorina, Grace McDonald, Charles Grapewin, Regis Toomey and George Macready.

Making appearances are virtually the entire roster of contracted players at Universal, including Walter Abel, Carmen Amaya, The Andrews Sisters, Evelyn Ankers, Louise Beavers, Noah Beery, Jr., Turhan Bey, Steve Brodie, Nigel Bruce, Lon Chaney, Jr., the Delta Rhythm Boys, Andy Devine, Marlene Dietrich, W. C. Fields, Susanna Foster, Thomas Gomez, Louis Jordan and His Orchestra, Ted Lewis and His Band, Jeanette MacDonald, Maria Montez, Clarence Muse, Donald O'Connor, Slapsie Maxie Rosenbloom, Artur Rubinstein, Peggy Ryan, Randolph Scott, Dinah Shore, Freddie Slack and His Orchestra, Gale Sondergaard, Sophie Tucker, Orson Welles, among many others.

Cast

- George Raft as Tony West
- Vera Zorina as Gloria Vance
- Charles Grapewin as Nick West
- Grace McDonald as Kitty
- Charles Butterworth as Louie West
- George Macready as Bruce
- Elizabeth Patterson as Annie
- Theodore von Eltz as Barrett
- Regis Toomey as Doctor Henderson
- Ramsay Ames as Laura
- Spooks as Junior
- And Molly Lamont, Doris Lloyd, Nelson Leigh, Lane Chandler, Cyril Ring, Emmett Vogan, Addison Richards, Stanley Andrews, Frank Jenks, Ralph Dunn, Billy Benedict, Howard C. Hickman, Edwin Stanley, Wallis Clark, Richard Crane, Frank Wilcox, Clyde Cook, Bobby Barber, Walter Tetley, Anthony Warde, William Forrest, Dennis Moore, Duke York, Carlyle Blackwell, Edwin Stanley, Charles King[1]

References

[1] Deschner, Donald (1966). *The Films of W.C. Fields*. New York: Cadillac Publishing by arrangement with The Citadel Press. p. 164. Introduction by Arthur Knight

External links

- *Follow the Boys* (http://www.imdb.com/title/tt0036832/) at the Internet Movie Database
- *Follow the Boys* (http://www.allrovi.com/movies/movie/v91862) at AllRovi

Frank Sinatra

Frank Sinatra	
 Sinatra in 1947, at the Liederkrantz Hall in New York.	
Background information	
Birth name	Francis Albert Sinatra
Also known as	Ol' Blue Eyes[1] The Chairman of the Board The Voice
Born	December 12, 1915 Hoboken, New Jersey, U.S.[2]
Died	May 14, 1998 (aged 82) West Hollywood, California, U.S.
Genres	Traditional pop, jazz, swing, big band, vocal[3]
Occupations	Singer,[1] actor, producer,[1] director,[1] conductor[4]
Instruments	Vocals
Years active	1935-1971, 1973–1995[5]
Labels	Columbia, Capitol, Reprise, Apple Records
Associated acts	Rat Pack, Bing Crosby, Nancy Sinatra, Judy Garland, Quincy Jones, Antonio Carlos Jobim, Frank Sinatra, Jr., Dean Martin, Count Basie, Sammy Davis, Jr.
Website	[sinatra.com sinatra.com]

Francis Albert "Frank" Sinatra, pron.: /sɪˈnɑːtrə/, (December 12, 1915 – May 14, 1993)[6] was an American singer and film actor. Beginning his musical career in the swing era with Harry James and Tommy Dorsey, Sinatra found unprecedented success as a solo artist from the early to mid-1940s after being signed to Columbia Records in 1943. Being the idol of the "bobby soxers", he released his first album, *The Voice of Frank Sinatra* in 1946. His professional career had stalled by the 1950s, but it was reborn in 1953 after he won the Academy Award for Best Supporting Actor for his performance in *From Here to Eternity*.

He signed with Capitol Records in 1953 and released several critically lauded albums (such as *In the Wee Small Hours*, *Songs for Swingin' Lovers!*, *Come Fly with Me*, *Only the Lonely* and *Nice 'n' Easy*). Sinatra left Capitol to found his own record label, Reprise Records in 1961 (finding success with albums such as *Ring-a-Ding-Ding!*, *Sinatra at the Sands* and *Francis Albert Sinatra & Antonio Carlos Jobim*), toured internationally, was a founding member of the Rat Pack and fraternized with celebrities and statesmen, including John F. Kennedy. Sinatra turned 50 in 1965, recorded the retrospective *September of My Years*, starred in the Emmy-winning television special *Frank Sinatra: A Man and His Music*, and scored hits with "Strangers in the Night" and "My Way".

With sales of his music dwindling and after appearing in several poorly received films, Sinatra retired for the first time in 1971. Two years later, however, he came out of retirement and in 1973 recorded several albums, scoring a Top 40 hit with "(Theme From) New York, New York" in 1980. Using his Las Vegas shows as a home base, he toured both within the United States and internationally, until a short time before his death in 1998.

Sinatra also forged a highly successful career as a film actor. After winning Best Supporting Actor in 1953, he also garnered a nomination for Best Actor for *The Man with the Golden Arm*, and critical acclaim for his performance in *The Manchurian Candidate*. He also starred in such musicals as *High Society*, *Pal Joey*, *Guys and Dolls* and *On the Town*. Sinatra was honored at the Kennedy Center Honors in 1983 and was awarded the Presidential Medal of Freedom by Ronald Reagan in 1985 and the Congressional Gold Medal in 1997. Sinatra was also the recipient of eleven Grammy Awards, including the Grammy Trustees Award, Grammy Legend Award and the Grammy Lifetime Achievement Award.

Early life

Born December 12, 1915, in Hoboken, New Jersey, Sinatra was the only child of Italian immigrants Natalie Della (Garaventa) and Antonino Martino Sinatra,[7] and was raised Roman Catholic.[8] In his book Try and Stop Me (p. 218), American publisher and writer Bennett Cerf says that Sinatra's father was a lightweight boxer who fought under the name Marty O'Brien and was a member of the Hoboken fire brigade. Sinatra left high school without graduating,[9]:38 having attended only 47 days before being expelled because of his rowdy conduct. Sinatra's father, often referred to as Marty, served with the Hoboken Fire Department as a Captain. His mother, known as Dolly, was influential in the neighborhood and in local Democratic Party circles, but also ran an illegal abortion business from her home; she was arrested several times and convicted twice for this offense.[9]:16 During the Great Depression, Dolly nevertheless provided money to her son for outings with friends and expensive clothes.[10] In 1938, Sinatra was arrested for carrying on with a married woman, a criminal offense at the time.[11] For his livelihood, he worked as a delivery boy at the *Jersey Observer* newspaper,[9]:44 and later as a riveter at the Tietjan and Lang shipyard,[9]:47 but music was Sinatra's main interest, and he listened carefully to big band jazz.[12] He began singing for tips at the age of eight, standing on top of the bar at a local nightclub in Hoboken. Sinatra began singing professionally as a teenager in the 1930s,[9]:48 although he learned music by ear and never learned how to read music.[12]

Career

1935–40: Start of career, work with Harry James and Tommy Dorsey

Sinatra got his first break in 1935 when his mother persuaded a local singing group, The Three Flashes, to let him join. With Sinatra, the group became known as the Hoboken Four,[5] and they sufficiently impressed Edward Bowes. After appearing on his show, *Major Bowes Amateur Hour*, they attracted 40,000 votes and won the first prize – a six-month contract to perform on stage and radio across the United States.

Sinatra left the Hoboken Four and returned home in late 1935. His mother secured him a job as a singing waiter and MC at the Rustic Cabin in Englewood Cliffs, New Jersey, for which he was paid $15 a week.[13]

On March 18, 1939, Sinatra made a demo recording of a song called "Our Love", with the Frank Mane band. The record has "Frank Sinatra" signed on the front. The bandleader kept the original record in a safe for nearly 60 years.[9] In June, Harry James hired Sinatra on a one-year contract of $75 a week.[14] It was with the James band that Sinatra released his first commercial record "From the Bottom of My Heart" in July 1939[15]— US Brunswick No. 8443 and UK Columbia #DB2150.[16]

Fewer than 8,000 copies of "From the Bottom of My Heart" (Brunswick No. 8443) were sold, making the record a very rare find that is sought after by record collectors worldwide. Sinatra released ten commercial tracks with James through 1939, including "All or Nothing At All" which had weak sales on its initial release but then sold millions of copies when re-released by Columbia at the height of Sinatra's popularity a few years later.[17]

In November 1939, in a meeting at the Palmer House in Chicago, Sinatra was asked by bandleader Tommy Dorsey to join his band as a replacement for Jack Leonard (the vocalist, not to be confused the comedian Jack E. Leonard), who had recently left to launch a solo career. This meeting was a turning point in Sinatra's career. By signing with Dorsey's band, one of the hottest at the time, he greatly increased his visibility with the American public. Though Sinatra was still under contract with James, James recognized the opportunity Dorsey offered and graciously released Sinatra from his contract. Sinatra recognized his debt to James throughout his life and upon hearing of James' death in 1983, stated: "he [James] is the one that made it all possible."[18]

On January 26, 1940, Sinatra made his first public appearance with the Dorsey band at the Coronado Theater in Rockford, Illinois.[19] In his first year with Dorsey, Sinatra released more than forty songs, with "I'll Never Smile Again" topping the charts for twelve weeks beginning in mid-July.[9]:91

Sinatra's relationship with Tommy Dorsey was troubled, because of their contract, which awarded Dorsey one-third of Sinatra's lifetime earnings in the entertainment industry. In January 1942, Sinatra recorded his first solo sessions without the Dorsey band (but with Dorsey's arranger Axel Stordahl and with Dorsey's approval). These sessions were released commercially on the Bluebird label. Sinatra left the Dorsey band in late 1942 in an incident that started rumors of Sinatra's involvement with the Mafia. A story appeared in the Hearst newspapers that mobster Sam Giancana coerced Dorsey to let Sinatra out of his contract for a few thousand dollars, and was fictionalized in the book and movie *The Godfather*.[12] According to Nancy Sinatra's biography, the Hearst rumors were started because of Frank's Democratic politics. In fact, the contract was bought out by MCA founder Jules Stein for $75,000.[18]

1940–50: Sinatramania and decline of career

In May 1941, Sinatra was at the top of the male singer polls in the *Billboard* and *Down Beat* magazines.[9]:94 His appeal to bobby soxers, as teenage girls of that time were called, revealed a whole new audience for popular music, which had been recorded mainly for adults up to that time.[20]

On December 30, 1942, Sinatra made a "legendary opening" at the Paramount Theater in New York. Jack Benny later said, "I thought the goddamned building was going to cave in. I never heard such a commotion... All this for a fellow I never heard of." When Sinatra returned to the Paramount in October 1944, 35,000 fans caused a near riot outside the venue because they were not allowed in.[12]

During the musicians' strike of 1942–44, Columbia re-released Harry James and Sinatra's version of "All or Nothing at All" (music by Arthur Altman and lyrics by Jack Lawrence), recorded in August 1939 and released before Sinatra had made a name for himself. The original release did not even mention the vocalist's name. When the recording was re–released in 1943 with Sinatra's name prominently displayed, the record was on the best–selling list for 18 weeks and reached number 2 on June 2, 1943.[21]

Sinatra being interviewed for American Forces Network during World War II.

Sinatra signed with Columbia on June 1, 1943, as a solo artist, and he initially had great success, particularly during the 1942–44 musicians' strike. Although no new records had been issued during the strike, he had been performing on the radio (on *Your Hit Parade*), and on stage. Columbia wanted to get new recordings of their growing star as fast as possible, so Sinatra convinced them to hire Alec Wilder as arranger and conductor for several sessions with a vocal group called the Bobby Tucker Singers. These first sessions were on June 7, June 22, August 5, and November 10, 1943. Of the nine songs recorded during these sessions, seven charted on the best–selling list.[22]

Sinatra did not serve in the military during World War II. On December 11, 1943, he was classified 4-F ("Registrant not acceptable for military service") for a perforated eardrum by his draft board. Additionally, an FBI report on Sinatra, released in 1998, showed that the doctors had also written that he was a "neurotic" and "not acceptable material from a psychiatric standpoint." This was omitted from his record to avoid "undue unpleasantness for both the selectee and the induction service."[23][24] Active-duty servicemen, like journalist William Manchester, said of Sinatra, "I think Frank Sinatra was the most hated man of World War II, much more than Hitler", because Sinatra was back home making all of that money and being shown in photographs surrounded by beautiful women.[10]:91[25] His exemption would resurface throughout his life and cause him grief when he had to defend himself.[23][26] There were accusations, including some from noted columnist Walter Winchell,[27] that Sinatra paid $40,000 to avoid the service – but the FBI found no evidence of this.[24][28]

In her book "Over Here, Over There" with Bill Gilbert, Maxene Andrews recalled when Sinatra entertained the troops during an overseas USO tour with comedian Phil Silvers during the war, observing, "I guess they just had a wing-ding, whatever it was. Sinatra demanded his own plane. But Bing [Crosby] said, 'Don't demand anything. Just go over there and sing your hearts out.' So, we did."[29] Sinatra worked frequently with the very popular Andrews Sisters, both on radio in the 1940s, appearing as guests on each other's shows, as well as on many shows broadcast to troops via the Armed Forces Radio Service (AFRS). He appeared as special guest on a rare pilot episode of the sisters' ABC Eight-to-the-Bar Ranch series at the end of 1944, and returned for another much funnier guest stint a few months later, while the trio in turn guested on his Songs By Sinatra series on CBS, to the delight of an audience filled with screaming bobby-soxers. Patty, Maxene, and LaVerne also teamed with Frankie when they appeared three times as guests on Sinatra's CBS television show in the early-1950s. Maxene once told Joe Franklin during a 1979 WWOR-AM Radio interview that Sinatra was "a peculiar man," with the ability to act indifferent towards her at times.[30]

In 1945, Sinatra co-starred with Gene Kelly in *Anchors Aweigh*. That same year, he was loaned out to RKO to star in a short film titled *The House I Live In*. Directed by Mervyn LeRoy, this film on tolerance and racial equality earned a special Academy Award shared among Sinatra and those who brought the film to the screen, along with a special Golden Globe for "Promoting Good Will". 1946 saw the release of his first album, *The Voice of Frank Sinatra*, and the debut of his own weekly radio show. By the end of 1948, Sinatra felt that his career was stalling, something that was confirmed when he slipped to No. 4 on *Down Beat*'s annual poll of most popular singers (behind Billy Eckstine, Frankie Laine, and Bing Crosby).[9]:149

The year 1949 saw an upswing, as Frank co-starred with Gene Kelly in *Take Me Out to the Ball Game*. It was well received critically and became a major commercial success. That same year, Sinatra teamed up with Kelly for a third time in *On the Town*.

1950–60: Rebirth of career, Capitol concept albums

After two years' absence, Sinatra returned to the concert stage on January 12, 1950, in Hartford, Connecticut. His voice suffered and he experienced hemorrhaging of his vocal cords on stage at the Copacabana on April 26, 1950.[10] Sinatra's career and appeal to new teen audiences declined as he moved into his mid-30s.

This was a period of serious self-doubt about the trajectory of his career. In February 1951, he was walking through Times Square, past the Paramount Theatre, keystone venue of his earlier phenomenal success. The Paramount marquee glowed in announcement of Eddie Fisher in concert. Swarms of teen-age girls had gathered in frenzy, swooning over the current singing idol. For Sinatra this public display of enthusiasm for Fisher validated a fear he had harbored in his own mind for a long time. The Sinatra star had fallen; the shouts of "Frankieee" were echoes of the past. Agitated and disconsolate he rushed home, closed his kitchen door, turned on the gas and laid his head on the top of the stove. A friend returned to the apartment not long after to find Sinatra lying on the floor sobbing out the melodrama of his life, proclaiming his failure was so complete he could not even commit suicide.[31]:*458*

In September 1951, Sinatra made his Las Vegas debut at the Desert Inn. A month later, the second season of *The Frank Sinatra Show* began on CBS Television. Ultimately, Sinatra did not find the success on television for which he had hoped. The persona he presented to the TV audience was not that of a performer easily welcomed into homes. He projected an arrogance not compatible with the type of cozy congeniality that played well on the small screen.[31]:439

Columbia and MCA dropped him in 1952.

The rebirth of Sinatra's career began with the eve-of-Pearl Harbor drama *From Here to Eternity* (1953), for which he won an Academy Award for Best Supporting Actor. This role and performance marked a turnaround in Sinatra's career: after several years of critical and commercial decline, becoming an Oscar-winning actor helped him regain his position as the top recording artist in the world.[32]

Also in 1953, Sinatra starred in the NBC radio program *Rocky Fortune*. His character, Rocko Fortunato (aka Rocky Fortune) was a temp worker for the Gridley Employment Agency who stumbled into crime-solving by way of the odd jobs to which he was dispatched. The series aired on NBC radio Tuesday nights from October 1953 to March 1954, following the network's crime drama hit *Dragnet*. During the final months of the show, just before the 1954 Oscars, it became a running gag that Sinatra would manage to work the phrase "from here to eternity" into each episode, a reference to his Oscar-nominated performance.[33]

In 1953, Sinatra signed with Capitol Records, where he worked with many of the finest musical arrangers of the era, most notably Nelson Riddle,[15] Gordon Jenkins, and Billy May. With a series of albums featuring darker emotional material, Sinatra reinvented himself, including *In the Wee Small Hours* (1955)—Sinatra's first 12" LP and his second collaboration with Nelson Riddle—*Where Are You?* (1957) his first album in stereo, with Gordon Jenkins, and *Frank Sinatra Sings For Only The Lonely* (1958). He also incorporated a hipper, "swinging" persona into some of his music, as heard on *Swing Easy!* (1954), *Songs for Swingin' Lovers!* (1956), and *Come Fly With Me* (1957).

By the end of the year, Billboard had named "Young at Heart" Song of the Year; *Swing Easy!*, with Nelson Riddle at the helm (his second album for Capitol), was named Album of the Year; and Sinatra was named "Top Male Vocalist" by *Billboard*, *Down Beat* and *Metronome*.

A third collaboration with Nelson Riddle, *Songs for Swingin' Lovers!*, was both a critical and financial success, featuring a recording of "I've Got You Under My Skin".

Frank Sinatra Sings for Only the Lonely, a stark collection of introspective saloon songs and blues-tinged ballads, was a mammoth commercial success, spending 120 weeks on Billboards album chart and peaking at No. 1. Cuts from this LP, such as "Angel Eyes" and "One for My Baby (and One More for the Road)", would remain staples of Sinatra's concerts throughout his life.

Through the late fifties, Sinatra frequently criticized rock and roll music, much of it being his reaction to rhythms and attitudes he found alien. In 1958 he lambasted it as "sung, played, and written for the most part by cretinous goons. It manages to be the martial music of every sideburned delinquent on the face of the earth."[34]

Sinatra's 1959 hit "High Hopes" lasted on the Hot 100 for 17 weeks, more than any other Sinatra hit did on that chart, and was a recurring favorite for years on *Captain Kangaroo*.

1960–70: *Ring-A-Ding Ding!*, Reprise records, Basie, Jobim, "My Way"

Sinatra started the 1960s as he ended the 1950s. His first album of the decade, *Nice 'n' Easy*, topped *Billboard*'s chart and won critical plaudits. Sinatra grew discontented at Capitol and decided to form his own label, Reprise Records. His first album on the label, *Ring-A-Ding Ding!* (1961), was a major success, peaking at No.4 on *Billboard* and No.8 in the UK.

Frank Sinatra at Girl's Town Ball in Florida,
March 12, 1960

His fourth and final Timex TV special was broadcast in March 1960, and earned massive viewing figures. Titled *It's Nice to Go Travelling*, the show is more commonly known as *Welcome Home Elvis*. Elvis Presley's appearance after his army discharge was somewhat ironic; Sinatra had been scathing about him in the mid fifties, saying: "His kind of music is deplorable, a rancid smelling aphrodisiac. It fosters almost totally negative and destructive reactions in young people."[35] Presley had responded: "... [Sinatra] is a great success and a fine actor, but I think he shouldn't have said it... [rock and roll] is a trend, just the same as he faced when he started years ago."[36] Later, in efforts to maintain his commercial viability, Sinatra recorded Presley's hit "Love Me Tender" as well as works by Paul Simon ("Mrs. Robinson"), The Beatles ("Something", "Yesterday"), and Joni Mitchell ("Both Sides Now").[37]

Following on the heels of the film *Can Can* was *Ocean's 11*, the movie that became the definitive on-screen outing for "The Rat Pack," a group of entertainers led by Sinatra who worked together on a loose basis in films and casino shows featuring Dean Martin, Sammy Davis, Jr., Peter Lawford, and Joey Bishop. Subsequent pictures together included *Sergeants 3* and *Robin and the 7 Hoods*, although the movies' rosters of actors varied slightly according to whom Sinatra happened to be angry with when casting any given film; he replaced Sammy Davis, Jr. with Steve McQueen in *Never So Few* and Peter Lawford with Bing Crosby in *Robin and the 7 Hoods*.

From his youth, Sinatra displayed sympathy for African Americans and worked both publicly and privately all his life to help them win equal rights. He played a major role in the desegregation of Nevada hotels and casinos in the 1960s. On January 27, 1961, Sinatra played a benefit show at Carnegie Hall for Martin Luther King, Jr. and led his fellow Rat Pack members and Reprise label mates in boycotting hotels and casinos that refused entry to black patrons and performers. He often spoke from the stage on desegregation and repeatedly played benefits on behalf of Dr. King and his movement. According to his son, Frank Sinatra, Jr., King sat weeping in the audience at a concert in 1963 as Sinatra sang *Ol' Man River*, a song from the musical *Show Boat* that is sung by an African-American stevedore.

On September 11 and 12, 1961, Sinatra recorded his final songs for Capitol.

In 1962, he starred with Janet Leigh and Laurence Harvey in the political thriller, *The Manchurian Candidate*, playing Bennett Marco. That same year, Sinatra and Count Basie collaborated for the album *Sinatra-Basie*. This popular and successful release prompted them to rejoin two years later for the follow-up *It Might as Well Be Swing*, which was arranged by Quincy Jones. One of Sinatra's more ambitious albums from the mid-1960s, *The Concert Sinatra*, with a 73-piece symphony orchestra led by Nelson Riddle, was recorded on a motion picture scoring stage with the use of multiple synchronized recording machines that employed 35mm magnetic film (multi-track master tape machines were not yet a reality in the recording studio).

Sinatra's first live album, *Sinatra at the Sands*, was recorded during January and February 1966 at the Sands Hotel and Casino in Las Vegas.

Dean Martin and Frank Sinatra

In June 1965, Sinatra, Sammy Davis, Jr., and Dean Martin played live in Saint Louis to benefit Dismas House. The Rat Pack concert was broadcast live via satellite to numerous movie theaters across America. Released in August 1965 was the Grammy Award–winning album of the year, *September of My Years*, containing the single "It Was A Very Good Year", which won the Grammy Award for Best Vocal Performance, Male in 1966. A career anthology, *A Man and His Music*, followed in November, winning Album of the Year at the Grammys in 1966. The TV special, *Frank Sinatra: A Man and His Music*, garnered both an Emmy award and a Peabody Award.

In the spring, *That's Life* appeared, with both the single and album becoming Top Ten hits in the US on *Billboard*'s pop charts. *Strangers in the Night* went on to top the *Billboard* and UK pop singles charts, winning the award for Record of the Year at the Grammys. The album of the same name also topped the *Billboard* chart and reached number 4 in the UK.

Sinatra started 1967 with a series of important recording sessions with Antônio Carlos Jobim. Later in the year, a duet with daughter Nancy, "Somethin' Stupid", topped the *Billboard* pop and UK singles charts. In December, Sinatra collaborated with Duke Ellington on the album *Francis A. & Edward K.*.

During the late 1960s, press agent Lee Solters would invite columnists and their spouses into Sinatra's dressing room just before he was about to go on stage. *The New Yorker* recounted that "the first columnist they tried this on was Larry Fields of the *Philadelphia Daily News*, whose wife fainted when Sinatra kissed her cheek. 'Take care of it, Lee,' Sinatra said, and he was off." The professional relationship Sinatra shared with Solters focused on projects on the west coast while those focused on the east coast were handled by Solters' partner, Sheldon Roskin of Solters/Roskin/Friedman, a well-known firm at the time.[38]

Back on the small-screen, Sinatra once again worked with Jobim and Ella Fitzgerald on the TV special, *A Man and His Music + Ella + Jobim*.

With Sinatra in mind, singer-songwriter Paul Anka wrote the song "My Way", inspired from the French "Comme d'habitude" ("As Usual"), composed by Claude François and Jacques Revaux. (The song had been previously commissioned to David Bowie, whose lyrics did not please the involved agents.) "My Way" would, ironically, become more closely identified with him than any other song over his seven decades as a singer even though he reputedly did not care for it.

Watertown (1970) was one of Sinatra's most acclaimed concept albums[39] with music by Bob Gaudio (of the Four Seasons) and lyrics by Jake Holmes, but it was all but ignored by the public. Selling a mere 30,000 copies in 1970 and reaching a peak chart position of 101, its failure put an end to plans for a television special based on the album. Watertown [40] was one of the only recording sessions having Sinatra sing against pre-recorded tracks vs. a live orchestra

1970–80: Retirement and comeback

On June 13, 1971 – at a concert in Hollywood to raise money for the Motion Picture and TV Relief Fund – at the age of 55, Sinatra announced that he was retiring, bringing to an end his 36-year career in show business.

In 1973, Sinatra came out of retirement with a television special and album, both entitled *Ol' Blue Eyes Is Back*. The album, arranged by Gordon Jenkins and Don Costa, was a great success, reaching number 13 on *Billboard* and number 12 in the UK. The TV special was highlighted by a dramatic reading of "Send in the Clowns" and a song and dance sequence with former co-star Gene Kelly.

In January 1974, Sinatra returned to Las Vegas, performing at Caesars Palace despite vowing in 1970 never to play there again after the manager of the resort, Sanford Waterman, pulled a gun on him during a heated argument.[10]:436 In Australia, he caused an uproar by describing journalists there – who were aggressively pursuing his every move and pushing for a press conference – as "fags", "pimps", and "whores". Australian unions representing transport workers, waiters, and journalists went on strike, demanding that Sinatra apologize for his remarks.[10]:464 Sinatra instead insisted that the journalists apologize for "fifteen years of abuse I have taken from the world press".[10]:464 The future Prime Minister of Australia, Bob Hawke, then the Australian Council of Trade Unions (ACTU) leader, also insisted that Sinatra apologize, and a settlement was eventually reached to the apparent satisfaction of both parties,[10]:464 Sinatra's final show of his Australian tour was televised to the nation.

Empress Farah Diba of Persia (Iran) and Frank Sinatra, Tehran, 1975.

In October 1974, Sinatra appeared at New York City's Madison Square Garden in a televised concert that was later released as an album under the title *The Main Event – Live*. Backing him was bandleader Woody Herman and the Young Thundering Herd, who accompanied Sinatra on a European tour later that month. The TV special garnered mostly positive reviews while the album – actually culled from various shows during his comeback tour – was only a moderate success, peaking at No.37 on *Billboard* and No.30 in the UK.

Frank Sinatra, with Giulio Andreotti (left) and Richard Nixon at the White House, 1973.

In August 1975, Sinatra held several back-to-back concerts together with the newly-risen singer, John Denver. Soon they became friends with each other. John Denver later appeared as a guest in the *Sinatra and friends* TV Special, singing "September Song" together with Sinatra. Sinatra covered the John Denver hits "My Sweet Lady" and "Leaving on a Jet Plane". And, according to Denver, his song "A Baby Just Like You" was written at Sinatra's request.

In 1979, in front of the Egyptian pyramids, Sinatra performed for Anwar Sadat. Back in Las Vegas, while celebrating 40 years in show business and his 64th birthday, he was awarded the Grammy Trustees Award during a party at Caesars Palace.

1980–90: *Trilogy, She Shot Me Down, L.A. Is My Lady*

In 1980, Sinatra's first album in six years was released, *Trilogy: Past Present Future*, a highly ambitious triple album that found Sinatra recording songs from the past (pre-rock era) and present (rock era and contemporary) that he had overlooked during his career, while 'The Future' was a free-form suite of new songs linked à la musical theater by a theme, in this case, Sinatra pondering over the future. The album garnered six Grammy nominations – winning for best liner notes – and peaked at number 17 on *Billboard*'s album chart, while spawning yet another song that would become a signature tune, "Theme from New York, New York", as well as Sinatra's much lauded (second) recording of George Harrison's "Something" (the first was not officially released on an album until 1972's *Frank Sinatra's Greatest Hits, Vol. 2*).

Sinatra sings with then First Lady Nancy Reagan at the White House.

The following year, Sinatra built on the success of *Trilogy* with *She Shot Me Down*, an album that revisited the dark tone of his Capitol years, and was praised by critics as a vintage late-period Sinatra. Sinatra would comment that it was "A complete saloon album... tear-jerkers and cry-in-your-beer kind of things".[41]

Also in 1981, Sinatra was embroiled in controversy when he worked a ten-day engagement for $2 million in Sun City, in the internationally unrecognized "independent" bantustan Bophuthatswana, breaking a cultural boycott against apartheid-era South Africa. (See Artists United Against Apartheid) Bophuthatswana's president, Lucas Mangope, awarded Sinatra with Bophuthatswana's highest honor, the Order of the Leopard, and made him an honorary tribal chief.[42]

He was selected as one of the five recipients of the 1983 Kennedy Center Honors, alongside Katharine Dunham, James Stewart, Elia Kazan, and Virgil Thomson. Quoting Henry James in honoring his old friend, President Reagan said that "art was the shadow of humanity" and that Sinatra had "spent his life casting a magnificent and powerful shadow".[10]:544

In 1984, Sinatra worked with Quincy Jones for the first time in nearly two decades on the album, *L.A. Is My Lady*, which was well received critically. The album was a substitute for another Jones project, an album of duets with Lena Horne, which had to be abandoned. (Horne developed vocal problems and Sinatra, committed to other engagements, could not wait to record.)

1990s: *Duets*, final performances

In 1990, Sinatra did a national tour,[43] and was awarded the second "Ella Award" by the Los Angeles–based Society of Singers. At the award ceremony, he performed for the final time with Ella Fitzgerald.[44]

In December, as part of Sinatra's birthday celebrations, Patrick Pasculli, the Mayor of Hoboken, made a proclamation in his honor, declaring that "no other vocalist in history has sung, swung, crooned, and serenaded into the hearts of the young and old... as this consummate artist from Hoboken."[44]:407 The same month Sinatra gave the first show of his Diamond Jubilee Tour at the Brendan Byrne Arena in East Rutherford, New Jersey.

In 1993 Sinatra made a surprise return to Capitol and the recording studio for *Duets*, which was released in November.

The other artists who added their vocals to the album worked for free, and a follow-up album (*Duets II*) was released in 1994 that reached No.9 on the *Billboard* charts.

Still touring despite various health problems, Sinatra remained a top concert attraction on a global scale during the first half of the 1990s. At times during concerts his memory failed him and a fall onstage in Richmond, Virginia, in March 1994, signaled further problems.

Sinatra's final public concerts were held in Japan's Fukuoka Dome in December, 1994. The following year, on February 25, 1995, at a private party for 1200 select guests on the closing night of the Frank Sinatra Desert Classic golf tournament, Sinatra sang before a live audience for the very last time. *Esquire* reported of the show that Sinatra was "clear, tough, on the money" and "in absolute control". His closing song was "The Best is Yet to Come".

Sinatra was awarded the Legend Award at the 1994 Grammy Awards, where he was introduced by Bono, who said of him, "Frank's the chairman of the bad attitude... Rock 'n roll plays at being tough, but this guy is the boss—the chairman of boss... I'm not going to mess with him, are you?"[45] Sinatra called it "the best welcome...I ever had", but his acceptance speech ran too long and was abruptly cut off, leaving him looking confused and talking into a dead microphone.[46] Later in the telecast, Billy Joel protested the decision to cut Sinatra off by leaving a long pause in the middle of his song "The River of Dreams" in order to waste "valuable advertising time".[47]

In 1995, to mark Sinatra's 80th birthday, the Empire State Building glowed blue. A star-studded birthday tribute, *Sinatra: 80 Years My Way*, was held at the Shrine Auditorium in Los Angeles. At the end of the program Sinatra graced the stage for the last time to sing the final notes of "New York, New York" with an ensemble. It was Sinatra's last televised appearance.

In recognition of his many years of association with Las Vegas, Frank Sinatra was elected to the Gaming Hall of Fame in 1997.[48]

Film career

Sinatra enjoyed a huge film career and began making movies almost as soon as his singing career took off. His most important pictures include *The Manchurian Candidate* with Angela Lansbury, *From Here to Eternity* with Burt Lancaster, *Suddenly* with Sterling Hayden, *The Man With the Golden Arm* with Arnold Stang, *Kings Go Forth* with Natalie Wood, *Guys and Dolls* with Marlon Brando, *High Society* with Bing Crosby, *Pal Joey* with Rita Hayworth, *Some Came Running* with Dean Martin, *Never So Few* with Steve McQueen, *A Hole in the Head* with Edward G. Robinson, *Meet Danny Wilson*, *On the Town* with Gene Kelly, *Robin and the 7 Hoods* with Bing Crosby, *Ocean's 11* and *Sergeants 3* with the Rat Pack (Dean Martin, Sammy Davis, Jr., Peter Lawford, and Joey Bishop), *Step Lively*, *None But the Brave* (directed by Sinatra), *The Detective* with Lee Remick, *Come Blow Your Horn* with Lee J. Cobb and Barbara Rush, and *The Pride and the Passion* starring Cary Grant, among many others spanning most of his lengthy career.

Personal life

Sinatra had three children, Nancy, Frank Jr., and Tina, all with his first wife, Nancy Sinatra (née Barbato) (m. 1939–1951). He was married three more times, to actresses Ava Gardner (m. 1951–1957), Mia Farrow (m. 1966–1968), and finally to Barbara Marx (m. 1976-1998; his death).

Throughout his life, Sinatra had mood swings and bouts of depression. Avoiding solitude and unglamorous surroundings at all cost, he struggled with the conflicting need "to get away from it all, but not too far away."[31]:485 He acknowledged this, telling an interviewer in the 1950s: "Being an 18-karat manic depressive, and having lived a life of violent emotional contradictions, I have an over-acute capacity for sadness as well as elation."[9]:218 In her memoirs *My Father's Daughter*, his daughter Tina wrote about the "eighteen-karat" remark: "As flippant as Dad could be about his mental state, I believe that a Zoloft a day might have kept his demons away. But that kind of medicine was decades off."[49]

Although beloved as a hero by his hometown of Hoboken, Frank Sinatra rarely visited it. According to one account, Sinatra returned once in 1948 to celebrate the election of Hoboken's first Italian mayor and was not well received by the crowd. He stated he would never come back, and in fact did not return until 1984, to appear with Ronald Reagan.[50]

Alleged organized crime links

Sinatra garnered considerable attention due to his alleged personal and professional links with organized crime,[51] including figures such as Carlo Gambino,[52] Sam Giancana,[52] Lucky Luciano,[52] and Joseph Fischetti.[52] The Federal Bureau of Investigation kept records amounting to 2,403 pages on Sinatra. With his alleged Mafia ties, his ardent New Deal politics and his friendship with John F. Kennedy, he was a natural target for J. Edgar Hoover's FBI.[53] The FBI kept Sinatra under surveillance for almost five decades beginning in the 1940s. The documents include accounts of Sinatra as the target of death threats and extortion schemes. They also portray rampant paranoia and strange obsessions at the FBI and reveal nearly every celebrated Sinatra foible and peccadillo.[54]

For a year Hoover investigated Sinatra's alleged Communist affiliations, but found no evidence. The files include his rendezvous with prostitutes, and his extramarital affair with Ava Gardner, which preceded their marriage. Celebrities mentioned in the files are Dean Martin, Marilyn Monroe, Peter Lawford, and Giancana's girlfriend, singer Phyllis McGuire.

The FBI's secret dossier on Sinatra was released in 1998 in response to Freedom of Information Act requests.

The released FBI files reveal some tantalizing insights into Sinatra's lifetime consistency in pursuing and embracing seemingly conflicting affiliations. But Sinatra's alliances had a practical aspect. They were adaptive mechanisms for behavior motivated by self-interest and inner anxieties. In September 1950 Sinatra felt particularly vulnerable. He was in a panic over his moribund career and haunted by the continual speculations and innuendos in circulation regarding his draft status in World War II. Sinatra "was scared, his career had sprung a leak." In a letter dated September 17, 1950, to Clyde Tolson, Deputy FBI Director, Sinatra offered to be of service to the FBI as an informer. An excerpted passage from a memo in FBI files states that Sinatra "feels he can be of help as a result of going anywhere the Bureau desires and contacting any people from whom he might be able to obtain information. Sinatra feels as a result of his publicity he can operate without suspicion...he is willing to go the whole way." The FBI declined his assistance.[31]:446–47

Political views

Sinatra held differing political views throughout his life.

Sinatra's parents had immigrated to the United States in 1895 and 1897 respectively. His mother, Dolly Sinatra (1896–1977), was a Democratic Party ward leader.[55]

Sinatra remained a supporter of the Democratic Party until the early 1970s when he switched his allegiance to the Republican Party.

Eleanor Roosevelt and Sinatra in 1947; Sinatra named his son after her husband.

Political activities 1944–68

In 1944, after sending a letter to President Franklin D. Roosevelt, Sinatra was invited to meet Roosevelt at the White House, where he agreed to become part of the Democratic party's voter registration drives.[56]:40

Sinatra, pictured here with Eleanor Roosevelt in 1960, was an ardent supporter of the Democratic Party until 1970

He donated $5,000 to the Democrats for the 1944 presidential election and by the end of the campaign was appearing at two or three political events every day.[56]:40

After World War II, Sinatra's politics grew steadily more left wing,[56]:41 and he became more publicly associated with the Popular Front. He started reading liberal literature and supported many organizations that were later identified as front organizations of the Communist Party by the House Un-American Activities Committee in the 1950s, though Sinatra was never brought before the committee.

Sinatra spoke at a number of New Jersey high schools in 1945, where students had gone on strike in opposition to racial integration. Later that year Sinatra would appear in *The House I Live In*, a short film that stood against racism. The film was scripted by Albert Maltz, with the title song written by Earl Robinson and Abel Meeropol (under the pseudonym of Lewis Allen).

In 1948, Sinatra actively campaigned for President Harry S. Truman.[57] In 1952 and 1956, he also campaigned for Adlai Stevenson.[57] In 1956 and 1960, Sinatra sang the National Anthem at the Democratic National Convention.[]

Of all the U.S. Presidents he associated with during his career, he was closest to John F. Kennedy.[] In 1960, Sinatra and his friends Peter Lawford, Dean Martin, and Sammy Davis Jr. actively campaigned for Kennedy throughout the United States;[57] On the campaign trail, Sinatra's voice was heard even if he wasn't physically present.[57] The campaign's theme song, played before every appearance, was a newly recorded version of "High Hopes," specially recorded by Sinatra with new lyrics saluting JFK.[]

In January 1961, Sinatra and Peter Lawford organized the Inaugural Gala in Washington, DC, held on the evening before President Kennedy was sworn into office.[] The event, featuring many big show business stars, was an enormous success, raising a large amount of money for the Democratic Party. Sinatra also organized an Inaugural Gala in California in 1962 to welcome second term Democratic Governor Pat Brown.[10]

Sinatra's move toward the Republicans seems to have begun when he was snubbed by President Kennedy in favor of Bing Crosby,[58] a rival singer and a Republican, for Kennedy's visit to Palm Springs, in 1962. Kennedy had planned to stay at Sinatra's home over the Easter holiday weekend, but decided against doing so because of Sinatra's alleged connections to organized crime.[58] Kennedy stayed at Crosby's house instead.[58] Sinatra had invested a lot of his own money in upgrading the facilities at his home in anticipation of the President's visit.[59] At the time, President Kennedy's brother, Attorney General Robert F. Kennedy, was intensifying his own investigations into organized crime figures such as Chicago mob boss Sam Giancana, who had earlier stayed at Sinatra's home.

Despite his break with Kennedy, however, he still mourned over Kennedy after he learned he was assassinated.[57] According to his daughter Nancy, he learned of Kennedy's assassination while filming a scene of *Robin and the Seven Hoods* in Burbank.[] After he learned of the assassination, Sinatra quickly finished filming the scene, returned to his Palm Springs home, and sobbed in his bedroom for three days.[]

The 1968 election illustrated changes in the once solidly pro-JFK Rat Pack: Peter Lawford, Sammy Davis, Jr., and Shirley MacLaine all endorsed Robert Kennedy in the spring primaries; Sinatra, Dean Martin, and Joey Bishop backed Vice-President Hubert Humphrey. In the fall election, Sinatra appeared for Humphrey in Texas at the Houston Astrodome with President Lyndon Johnson and in a television commercial soliciting campaign contributions.[60] He also re-stated his support for Humphrey on a live election-eve national telethon.

Political activities 1970–84

In 1970, the first sign of Sinatra's break from the Democratic Party came when he endorsed Ronald Reagan for a second term as Governor of California;[44][57] Sinatra, however, remained a registered Democrat and encouraged Reagan to become more moderate.[57] In July 1972, after a lifetime of supporting Democratic presidential candidates, Sinatra announced he would support Republican U.S. President Richard Nixon for re-election in the 1972 presidential election. His switch to the Republican Party was now official;[57] he even told his daughter Tina, who had actively campaigned for Nixon's Democratic opponent George McGovern,[] "the older you get, the more conservative you get."[] Sinatra said he agreed with the Republican Party on most positions, except that of abortion.[56]

During Nixon's Presidency, Sinatra visited the White House on several occasions.[] Sinatra also became good friends with Vice President Spiro Agnew. In 1973, Agnew was charged with corruption and resigned as Vice President; Sinatra helped Agnew pay some of his legal bills.[10]:458

Sinatra is awarded the Presidential Medal of Freedom by President Ronald Reagan.

In the 1980 presidential election, Sinatra supported Ronald Reagan, and donated $4 million to Reagan's campaign. Sinatra said he supported Reagan as he was "the proper man to be the President of the United States... it's so screwed up now, we need someone to straighten it out."[44]:395 Reagan's victory gave Sinatra his closest relationship with the White House since the early 1960s.[57] Sinatra arranged Reagan's Presidential gala,[10]:503 as he had done for Kennedy 20 years previously.

In 1984, Sinatra returned to his birthplace in Hoboken, bringing with him President Reagan, who was in the midst of campaigning for the 1984 presidential election. Reagan had made Sinatra a fund-raising ambassador as part of the Republican National Committee's "Victory '84 Get-Out-The-Vote" (GOTV) drive.[10]:550[61] On January 19, 1985, Sinatra hosted the 50th Presidential Inaugural Gala, the day before the second inauguration of Ronald Reagan.

Death

Sinatra began to show signs of dementia in his last years. After a heart attack in February 1997, he made no further public appearances. After suffering another heart attack,[62] he died at 10:50 p.m. on May 14, 1998, at the Cedars-Sinai Medical Center, with his wife, Barbara, by his side.[62] He was 82 years old.[62] Sinatra's final words, spoken after Barbara encouraged him to "fight" as attempts were made to stabilize him, were, "I'm losing."[63] The official cause of death was listed as complications from dementia, heart and kidney disease, and bladder cancer.[64] His death was confirmed by the Sinatra family on their website with a statement accompanied by a recording of the singer's version of "Softly As I Leave You." The next night the lights on the

Sinatra's gravestone

Las Vegas Strip were dimmed for 10 minutes in his honor and the lights on the Empire State Building in New York were turned blue. President Bill Clinton, an amateur saxophonist and musician, led the world's tributes to Sinatra, saying that after meeting and getting to know the singer as president, he had "come to appreciate on a personal level what millions of people had appreciated from afar".[65] Elton John stated that Sinatra, "was simply the best – no one else even comes close".[65]

On May 20, 1998, at the Roman Catholic Church of the Good Shepherd in Beverly Hills, Sinatra's funeral was held, with 400[66] mourners in attendance and hundreds of fans outside.[66]Gregory Peck, Tony Bennett, and Frank, Jr., addressed the mourners, among whom were Jill St. John, Tom Selleck, Joey Bishop, Faye Dunaway, Tony Curtis, Liza Minnelli, Kirk Douglas, Robert Wagner, Bob Dylan, Don Rickles, Nancy Reagan, Angie Dickinson, Sophia Loren, Bob Newhart, Mia Farrow, and Jack Nicholson.[63][66] A private ceremony was held later that day at St. Theresa's Catholic Church in Palm Springs. Sinatra was buried following the ceremony next to his parents in section B-8 of Desert Memorial Park[6] in Cathedral City, a quiet cemetery on Ramon Road where Cathedral City meets Rancho Mirage and near his compound, located on Rancho Mirage's tree-lined Frank Sinatra Drive.[63] His close friends, Jilly Rizzo and Jimmy Van Heusen, are buried nearby in the same cemetery. The words "The Best Is Yet to Come" are imprinted on Sinatra's grave marker.[67]

Legacy

"Sinatra was... the first modern pop superstar... Following his idol Bing Crosby, who had pioneered the use of the microphone, Sinatra transformed popular singing by infusing lyrics with a personal, intimate point of view that conveyed a steady current of eroticism... Almost singlehandedly, he helped lead a revival of vocalized swing music that took American pop to a new level of musical sophistication... his 1950s recordings... were instrumental in establishing a canon of American pop song literature."

--Stephen Holden[62]

Philadelphia radio DJ Sid Mark has hosted a Frank Sinatra show (Friday with Frank, Saturday with Sinatra, Sunday with Sinatra) for over 50 years.

The U.S. Postal Service issued a 42-cent postage stamp in honor of Sinatra on May 13, 2008.[68] The design of the stamp was unveiled Wednesday, December 12, 2007 – on what would have been his 92nd birthday – in Beverly Hills, California, with Sinatra family members on hand.[69] The design shows a 1950s-vintage image of Sinatra, wearing a hat. The design also includes his signature, with his last name alone.[69] The Hoboken Post Office was renamed in his honor in 2002.[69] The Frank Sinatra School of the Arts in Astoria, Queens and the Frank Sinatra Park in Hoboken were named in his honor.

The U.S. Congress passed a resolution on May 20, 2008, designating May 13 as Frank Sinatra Day to honor his contribution to American culture. The resolution was introduced by Representative Mary Bono Mack.[70]

To commemorate the anniversary of Sinatra's death, Patsy's Restaurant in New York City, which Sinatra frequented, exhibited in May 2009 fifteen previously unseen photographs of Sinatra taken by Bobby Bank.[71] The photos are of his recording "Everybody Ought to Be in Love" at a nearby recording studio.[71]

Stephen Holden wrote for the 1983 *Rolling Stone Record Guide*:

> Frank Sinatra's voice *is* pop music history. [...] Like Presley and Dylan – the only other white male American singers since 1940 whose popularity, influence, and mythic force have been comparable – Sinatra will last indefinitely. He virtually invented modern pop song phrasing.

Wynn Resorts dedicated a signature restaurant to Sinatra inside Encore Las Vegas on December 22, 2008.[72] Memorabilia in the restaurant includes his Oscar for "From Here to Eternity", his Emmy for "Frank Sinatra: A Man and His Music", his Grammy for "Strangers in the Night", photographs and a gold album he received for "Classic Sinatra".

There is a residence hall at Montclair State University named for him in recognition of his status as an iconic New Jersey native.[73]

The Frank Sinatra International Student Center at Israel's Hebrew University, Mt. Scopus campus, was dedicated in 1978 in recognition of Sinatra's charitable and advocacy activities on behalf of the State of Israel.

In 1999 Huell Howser Productions, in association with KCET/Los Angeles, featured Frank Sinatra's Palm Springs home in *California's Gold*; the 49 minute program is available on VHS.[74]

Film and television portrayals

- In *The Godfather*, fictional singer Johnny Fontane, whose career was helped by organized crime boss Vito Corleone, was recognized by many, even Sinatra, as being based on his life.[75]
- In 1992, CBS aired a TV mini-series about the entertainer's life titled, *Sinatra*, directed by James Steven Sadwith and starred Philip Casnoff as Sinatra. Opening with his childhood in Hoboken, New Jersey, the film follows Sinatra's rise to the top in the 1940s, through the dark days of the early 1950s and his triumphant re-emergence in the mid-1950s, to his status as pop culture icon in the 1960s, 1970s and 1980s. In between, the film hits all of the main events, including his three marriages, his connections with the Mafia and his notorious friendship with the Rat Pack. Tina Sinatra was executive producer. Casnoff received a Golden Globe nomination for his performance.
- In 1998, Ray Liotta portrayed Sinatra in the HBO movie *The Rat Pack*, alongside Joe Mantegna as Dean Martin and Don Cheadle as Sammy Davis, Jr. It depicted their contribution to John F. Kennedy's election as U.S. president in 1960.
- Episode 4 of the Areana Series was issued in 1998 and dedicated to the life and work of Frank Sinatra, entitled "The Voice of a Century"
- Joe Piscopo and the late Phil Hartman spoofed Sinatra on *Saturday Night Live*.
- In 2003, Sinatra was portrayed by James Russo in *Stealing Sinatra*, which revolved around the kidnapping of Frank Sinatra Jr. in 1963.
- Also in 2003, he was portrayed by Dennis Hopper in *The Night We Called It a Day*, based upon events that occurred during a tour of Australia where Frank had called a member of the news media a "two-bit hooker" and all the unions in the country came crashing down on him.
- Sinatra was also portrayed by Sebastian Anzaldo in the film *Tears of a King*, who also impersonated Sinatra in a TV episode of *The Next Best Thing*.
- In the Emmy Award Winning 2011 miniseries, *The Kennedys*, Sinatra was depicted by Canadian actor Chris Diamantopoulos.
- Martin Scorsese is developing a biopic of Sinatra's life to be scripted by Phil Alden Robinson and produced by Scott Rudin.[76] When the film was first announced, three actors were said to be in contention for the part: Leonardo DiCaprio was Scorsese's preference, Johnny Depp was the studio's, and the Sinatra estate preferred George Clooney.[77] Scorsese later mentioned that he wanted Al Pacino for Sinatra and Robert De Niro as Dean Martin.[78] The film covers his whole life, so three or more actors will be playing him at different ages.[79] Billy Ray has been linked to write the screenplay for the film.[80]

References

[1] "Frank Sinatra" (http://www.hollywood.com/celebrity/Frank_Sinatra/192093#fullBio). *Hollywood.com*. . Retrieved May 15, 2008.
[2] "Frank Sinatra obituary" (http://news.bbc.co.uk/2/hi/special_report/1998/05/98/sinatra/67911.stm). *BBC News*. May 16, 1998. . Retrieved May 15, 2008.
[3] Music Genre: Vocal music (http://www.allmusic.com/explore/genre/d131). AllMusic. Retrieved October 23, 2008.
[4] Gigliotti, Gilbert L. *A Storied Singer: Frank Sinatra as Literary Conceit*
[5] Ruhlmann, William. "Frank Sinatra" (http://www.mtv.com/music/artist/sinatra_frank/artist.jhtml#bio). MTV. . Retrieved May 15, 2008.
[6] "Palm Springs Cemetery District "Interment Information" (http://www.pscemetery.com/pdfs/interments.pdf) (PDF). . Retrieved 2012-08-20.
[7] "Frank Sinatra Biography (1915–1998)" (http://www.filmreference.com/film/39/Frank-Sinatra.html). Film reference. . Retrieved July 18, 2009.
[8] "Frank Sinatra Has a Cold" (http://www.esquire.com/features/ESQ1003-OCT_SINATRA_rev_?click=main_sr). Esquire (magazine). October 8, 2007. . Retrieved October 12, 2010.
[9] Summers, Anthony; Swan, Robbyn (2005). *Sinatra: The Life*. New York: Alfred A. Knopf. ISBN 0-375-41400-2.
[10] Kelley, Kitty (1986). *His Way: Frank Sinatra, the Unauthorized Biography*. ISBN 978-0-553-05137-7.
[11] "Sinatra" (http://www.thesmokinggun.com/mugshots/sinatramug1.html). *Mug Shots of the Week*. The Smoking Gun. .
[12] O'Brien, Geoffrey (February 10, 2011). "Portrait of the Artist as a Young Man" (http://www.nybooks.com/articles/archives/2011/feb/10/portrait-artist-young-man/?pagination=false). *The New York Review of Books*. . Retrieved January 24, 2011.

[13] Nelson, Michael (Autumn 1999). *Frank Sinatra: the Loneliness of the Long Distance Singer* (http://www.vqronline.org/articles/1999/autumn/nelson-frank-sinatra/). VQR online. .

[14] Ingham, Chris. *The Rough Guide to Frank Sinatra*. Rough Guides. June 30, 2005. ISBN 1-84353-414-2, p. 9.

[15] Gilliland, John (June 8, 1969). "Part 1" (http://digital.library.unt.edu/ark:/67531/metadc19775/m1/). *Pop Chronicles*. UNT Digital Library. .

[16] Ridgeway, John (1991) [1978]. *The SinatraFile*. **Part 2** (2nd ed.). John Ridgway Books. ISBN 978-0-905808-08-6.

[17] "Frank Sinatra" (http://www.rollingstone.com/music/artists/frank-sinatra/biography). *Artists* (Rolling Stone). . Retrieved September 19, 2011.

[18] Sinatra, Nancy (1986). *Frank Sinatra, My Father*. Doubleday. ISBN 978-0-385-23356-9.

[19] Ridgeway, John (1977). *The SinatraFile*. **Part 1** (1st ed.). John Ridgway Books. ISBN 0-905808-00-2.

[20] "Frank Sinatra and the 'bobby-soxers'" (http://century.guardian.co.uk/1940-1949/Story/0,,127764,00.html). *The Guardian* (London). January 10, 1945. Retrieved June 2, 2012.

[21] Peters, Richard (1982). *Frank Sinatra Scrapbook*. New York: St. Martins Press. pp. 123, 157.

[22] (CD booklet) *Frank Sinatra: The Columbia Years: 1943–1952, The Complete Recordings*. **1**. 1993.

[23] Santopietro, Tom (2008). *Sinatra in Hollywood*. New York: Macmillan/Thomas Dunne Books. p. 45. ISBN 978-0-312-36226-3.

[24] Newton, Michael (2003). *The FBI Encyclopedia*. Jefferson, North Carolina: McFarland & Co. p. 314. ISBN 978-0-7864-1718-6.

[25] Erenberg, Lewis A. (1999). *Swing-in' the Dream*. Chicago, Illinois: University of Chicago Press. p. 197. ISBN 978-0-226-21517-4.

[26] Fuchs, Jeanne, and Ruth Prigozy (2007). *Frank Sinatra: The Man, the Music, the Legend*. Rochester, New York: University of Rochester Press. p. 136. ISBN 978-1-58046-251-8.

[27] Holland, Bill (December 19, 1998). *Billboard*. Volume 110, Number 51. p. 10.

[28] "Frank Sinatra" (http://vault.fbi.gov/Frank Sinatra). *Vault*. USA: FBI. , 2 403 pp.

[29] Andrews, Maxene and Bill Gilbert: "The Andrews Sisters and the USO Stars in World War Two;" New York, Kensington, Zebra Books, 1993, 260 pages.

[30] Sforza, John: "Swing It! The Andrews Sisters Story;" University Press of Kentucky, 2000; 289 pages.

[31] Kaplan, James (2010). *Frank the Voice*. Doubleday.

[32] Schmidt, M.A. "Best Pictures: *From Here to Eternity*" (http://www.nytimes.com/packages/html/movies/bestpictures/eternity-ar.html). The New York Times. May 9, 1954.

[33] *Rocky Fortune* (http://www.archive.org/details/OTRR_Rocky_Fortune_Singles) Old Time Radio Researchers Group, Archive.org. Retrieved April 9, 2009.

[34] *5 Enemies of Rock 'n' Roll* (http://www.ew.com/ew/article/0,,318545,00.html) Entertainment Weekly. Retrieved March 31, 2009.

[35] Khurana, Simran. "Quotes About Elvis Presley" (http://quotations.about.com/od/stillmorefamouspeople/a/elvispresley3.htm). *about.com*. Retrieved on October 14, 2007.

[36] Hopkins, J. (2007). *Elvis. The Biography*, Plexus. p. 126

[37] *The TIME 100* (http://www.time.com/time/time100/artists/profile/sinatra2.html). Retrieved March 31, 2009.

[38] Martin, Douglas. "Lee Solters, Razzle-Dazzle Press Agent, Dies at 89" (http://www.nytimes.com/2009/05/22/theater/22solters.html), *The New York Times*, May 21, 2009. Accessed May 22, 2009.

[39] Erlewine, Stephen Thomas. *Watertown* (http://www.allmusic.com/album/r187805). allmusic.com. Retrieved December 19, 2006.

[40] http://www.watertownology.com

[41] " *She Shot Me Down* (http://www.allmusic.com/album/r26337). Allmusic.com. Retrieved November 28, 2006.

[42] Lamb, David. *The Africans*, p. 328

[43] "Frank Sinatra: He held the 'patent' for the popular song" (http://www.cnn.com/fyi/school.tools/profiles/Frank.Sinatra/student.storypage.html). *Profiles* (CNN). . Retrieved November 5, 2011.

[44] Freedland, Michael. *All the Way: A biography of Frank Sinatra*. St Martin's Press, 2000. ISBN 0-7528-1662-4.

[45] *Bono On Sinatra's Legacy* (http://www.mtv.com/news/articles/1434089/19980515/sinatra_frank.jhtml). MTV.com. May 15, 1998.

[46] Bono at Grammy's 1994(Sinatra) (http://www.trilulilu.ro/beugen2001/83ee4ac391fbe8?video_google_com=) – Trilulilu Video TV. Retrieved March 5, 2009.

[47] Pareles, Jon (March 2, 1994). "Top Grammy to Houston; 5 for 'Aladdin'" (http://www.nytimes.com/1994/03/02/movies/top-grammy-to-houston-5-for-aladdin.html?pagewanted=all). *The New York Times*. . Retrieved February 15, 2012.

[48] "The Gaming Hall of Fame" (http://gaming.unlv.edu/hof/index.html). University of Nevada Las Vegas. . Retrieved August 30, 2009.

[49] Sinatra, Tina; Coplon, Jeff (2000). *My Father's Daughter: A Memoir*. New York: Simon & Schuster. p. 47. ISBN 0-684-87076-2.

[50] Stahl, Jason (2010-05-12). "Why Sinatra Hated Hobokenites - Hoboken, NJ Patch" (http://hoboken.patch.com/articles/remembering-sinatra). Hoboken.patch.com. . Retrieved 2012-04-25.

[51] "Frank Sinatra" (http://foia.fbi.gov/foiaindex/sinatra.htm). *Federal Bureau of Investigation*. . Retrieved May 12, 2008.

[52] "Mafia reports dogged Sinatra" (http://news.bbc.co.uk/2/hi/special_report/1998/05/98/sinatra/94360.stm). *News* (BBC). May 15, 1998. . Retrieved May 15, 2008.

[53] "Sinatra: The FBI Files" (http://www.npr.org/templates/story/story.php?storyId=1075739). NPR. . Retrieved June 14, 2008.

[54] "AKA Frank Sinatra" (http://www.washingtonpost.com/wp-srv/national/daily/march99/sinatra7.htm). The Washington Post Magazine. March 6, 1999. . Retrieved June 14, 2008.

[55] Sinatra: The Life, Anthony Summers and Robbyn Swan, p. 16

[56] Smith, Martin (2005). *When Ol' Blue Eyes was a Red*. Redwords. ISBN 1-905192-02-9.

[57] Steve Pond (1991-07-04). "Frank Sinatra and Politics" (http://web.archive.org/web/20110515000915/http://www.sinatra.com/legacy/frank-sinatra-and-politics). *Legacy*. Sinatra.com. Archived from the original (http://www.sinatra.com/legacy/frank-sinatra-and-politics) on 2011-05-15. . Retrieved 2011-07-04.

[58] "Peter Lawford's grave" (http://www.hollywoodusa.co.uk/WestwoodObituaries/peterlawford.htm). UK: Hollywood, USA. . Retrieved 2011-07-04.

[59] "Frank Sinatra Turned Violent After Kennedy Snub" (http://www.contactmusic.com/new/xmlfeed.nsf/story/sinatra-turned-violent-after-kennedy-snub). Contact Music. . Retrieved 2011-07-04.

[60] *Humphrey campaign ad* (http://www.livingroomcandidate.org/commercials/1968/frank-sinatra). Livingroom candidate. 1968.

[61] "Victory (year)" and "Get-Out-The-Vote" is a specific proper name for a particular campaign/election activity.

[62] Holden, Stephen (May 16, 1998). "Frank Sinatra Dies at 82; Matchless Stylist of Pop" (http://www.nytimes.com/learning/general/onthisday/bday/1212.html). *On This Day*. . Retrieved March 29, 2011.

[63] *Hollywood bids Sinatra last farewell* (http://www.cnn.com/SHOWBIZ/Music/9805/20/sinatra.funeral.early/index.html). CNN.com. Retrieved November 24, 2006.

[64] "Frank Sinatra Pictures, Biography, Profile, Facts, Discography, Filmography, more" (http://www.numberonestars.com/musiclegends/franksinatra.htm). Numberonestars.com. . Retrieved 2011-07-04.

[65] "Clinton leads Sinatra tributes" (http://news.bbc.co.uk/2/hi/special_report/1998/05/98/sinatra/94559.stm). *BBC News*. May 16, 1998. . Retrieved November 24, 2006.

[66] "Special Report: Final curtain for Sinatra" (http://news.bbc.co.uk/2/hi/special_report/1998/05/98/sinatra/97196.stm). *BBC News*. May 20, 1998. . Retrieved May 15, 2008.

[67] "Frank Sinatra" (http://www.findagrave.com/cgi-bin/fg.cgi?page=gr&GRid=2953). *singer, actor, entertainer*. Find a Grave. January 01, 2001. . Retrieved June 29, 2011.

[68] Fusilli, Jim (May 13, 2008). "Sinatra as Idol — Not Artist" (http://online.wsj.com/article/SB121063311685686579.html?mod=googlenews_wsj). *Wall Street Journal*. . Retrieved May 15, 2008.

[69] "Postal Service to immortalize 'Ol' Blue Eyes'" (http://www.reuters.com/article/2007/12/05/idUS202395-05-Dec-2007+PRN20071205) (Press release). United States Postal Service. December 5, 2007. . Retrieved January 29, 2012. "Frank Sinatra, one of the most iconic entertainers of the 20th century, will be commemorated on a postage stamp next spring, Postmaster General John Potter announced today."

[70] Bono Mack, Mary (May 20, 2008). "Frank Sinatra Day" (http://bono.house.gov/News/DocumentSingle.aspx?DocumentID=91885). .

[71] "Why Sinatra Liked Patsy's Restaurant" (http://cityroom.blogs.nytimes.com/2009/05/11/why-sinatra-liked-patsys-restaurant/). *The New York Times*. May 11, 2009. .

[72] "Opening of Sinatra" (http://www.wynnpressroom.com/index.php?s=23&cat=27). Wynn Resorts. n.d.. . Retrieved December 1, 2009.

[73] "'Montclair State University Campus Map'" (http://www.montclair.edu/map/index.php?FontSize=10&w=950&h=494&x=2369.33333333&y=335&Zoom=0&Building=CLR). Montclair State University. August 18, 2010. . Retrieved August 18, 2010.

[74] OCLC 61398698

[75] Santopietro, Tom (2012). *The Godfather Effect: Changing Hollywood, America, and Me* (http://books.google.com/books?id=YhdU8thA6eEC&pg=PT148). Macmillan. pp. 148–153. ISBN 1-4299-5262-8. .

[76] Merchan, George (2011-03-08). "Super-producer Scott Rudin to inject new life in Martin Scorsese's Sinatra biopic? - Movie News" (http://www.joblo.com/movie-news/super-producer-scott-rudin-to-inject-new-life-in-martin-scorseses-sinatra-biopic). JoBlo.com. . Retrieved 2011-07-04.

[77] Gallagher, Paul (October 25, 2009). "George Clooney, Leonardo DiCaprio and Johnny Depp battle to play Frank Sinatra their way" (http://www.guardian.co.uk/film/2009/oct/25/george-johnny-leo-scorsese-sinatra). *The Guardian* (London). .

[78] "'Content has taken a backseat'" (http://www.hindu.com/fr/2010/05/21/stories/2010052150020100.htm). *The Hindu* (Chennai, India). May 21, 2010. .

[79] "Scorsese Speaks" (http://www.shortlist.com/entertainment/scorsese-speaks). Shortlist.com. . Retrieved 2011-07-04.

[80] "Martin Scorsese's Frank Sinatra Movie Hires 'Hunger Games' Writer Billy Ray For Screenplay" (http://www.huffingtonpost.com/2012/08/13/martin-scorseses-frank-sinatra-movie_n_1774204.html?utm_hp_ref=entertainment). *The Huffington Post*. 2012-08-13. . Retrieved 2012-08-20.

Further reading

Biographies

- De Stefano, Gildo, *The Voice - Vita e italianità di Frank Sinatra*, Coniglio Press, Roma 2011 ISBN 9788860632593
- Freedland, Michael (2000) *All the Way: A Biography of Frank Sinatra*. St Martins Press. ISBN 0-7528-1662-4
- Grudens, Richard (2010) *Sinatra Singing*. Celebrity Profiles Publishing. ISBN 978-0-9763877-8-7
- Havers, Richard (2004) *Sinatra*. Dorling Kindersley. ISBN 1-4053-1461-3
- Kaplan, James (2010) *Frank: The Voice*. Doubleday. ISBN 978-0-385-51804-8
- Kelley, Kitty (1986) *His Way: The Unauthorized Biography of Frank Sinatra*. Bantam Press. ISBN 0-553-26515-6
- Lahr, John (1987) *Sinatra*. Random House. ISBN 0-7538-0842-0
- Munn, Michael (2002) *Sinatra: The Untold Story*. Robson Books Ltd. ISBN 1-86105-537-4
- Rockwell, John (1984) *Sinatra: An American Classic*. Rolling Stone. ISBN 0-394-53977-X
- Rojek, Chris (2004) *Frank Sinatra*. Polity. ISBN 0-7456-3090-1
- Santopietro, Tom (2008) *Sinatra In Hollywood*. Thomas Dunne Books. ISBN 978-0-312-36226-3
- Summers, Antony and Swan, Robbyn (2005) *Sinatra: The Life*. Doubleday. ISBN 0-552-15331-1
- Taraborrelli, J. Randall (1998) *Sinatra: The Man Behind the Myth*. Mainstream Publishing. ISBN 1-84018-119-2
- Wilson, Earl (1976) *Sinatra*.

Memoirs

- Ash, Vic. (2006) *I Blew it My Way: Bebop, Big Bands and Sinatra*. Northway Publications. ISBN 0-9550908-2-2
- Jacobs, George and Stadiem, William. (2003) *Mr. S.: The Last Word on Frank Sinatra*. HarperCollins. ISBN 0-330-41229-9
- Falcone, Vincent (2005). *Frankly – Just Between Us: My Life Conducting Frank Sinatra's Music*. Hal Leonard. ISBN 978-0-634-09498-9.

Criticism

- Fuchs, J. & Prigozy, R., ed. (2007) *Frank Sinatra: The Man, the Music, the Legend*. The Boydell Press. ISBN 1-58046-251-0
- Granata, Charles L. (1999) *Sessions with Sinatra: Frank Sinatra and the Art of Recording*. Chicago Review Press. ISBN 978-1-55652-509-4
- Hamill, Pete (2003) *Why Sinatra Matters*. Back Bay Books. ISBN 0-316-73886-7
- Mustazza, Leonard, ed. (1998) *Frank Sinatra and Popular Culture*. Praeger. ISBN 0-275-96495-7
- Petkov, Steven and Mustazza, Leonard, ed. (1997) *The Frank Sinatra Reader*. Oxford University Press. ISBN 0-19-511389-6
- Pugliese, S., ed. (2004) *Frank Sinatra: "History, Identity, and Italian American Culture "*. Palgrave. ISBN 1-4039-6655-9
- Smith, Martin (2005) *When Ol' Blue Eyes Was a Red*. Redwords. ISBN 1-905192-02-9
- Zehme, Bill (1997) *The Way You Wear Your Hat: Frank Sinatra and the Lost Art of Livin'*. Harper Collins. ISBN 0-06-093175-2
- "Frank Sinatra – Through the Lens of Jazz" (http://www.jazzsingers.com/FrankSinatra/), *Jazz Times Magazine*, May 1998
- Friedwald, Will (1999) *Sinatra! The Song Is You: A Singer's Art*. Da Capo Press. ISBN 0-684-19368-X
- Granata, Charles L. (1999) *Sessions with Sinatra: Frank Sinatra and the Art of Recording*. Chicago Review Press. ISBN 1-55652-509-5

- McNally, Karen (2008) *When Frankie Went to Hollywood: Frank Sinatra and American Male Identity* University of Illinois Press. ISBN 0-252-03334-5
- Pignone, Charles, with foreword by Sinatra, Frank Jr. and Jones, Quincy (2004) *The Sinatra Treasures*. Virgin Books. ISBN 1-85227-184-1
- Pignone, Charles, with foreword by Sinatra, Amanda (2007) *Frank Sinatra: The Family Album* Little Brown and Company. ISBN 0-316-00349-2
- Sinatra, Julie (2007) *Under My Skin: My Father, Frank Sinatra The Man Behind the Mystique* iuniverse.com, ISBN 0-595-43478-9
- Sinatra, Nancy (1986) *Frank Sinatra, My Father*. Doubleday. ISBN 978-0-385-23356-9
- Sinatra, Nancy (1998) *Frank Sinatra 1915–1998: An American Legend*. Readers Digest. ISBN 0-7621-0134-2
- Sinatra, Tina (2000) *My Father's Daughter*. Simon & Schuster. ISBN 0-684-87076-2

Cultural criticism

- Gigliotti, Gilbert L. *A Storied Singer: Frank Sinatra as Literary Conceit*. Greenwood Press, 2002.
- Hamill, Pete. *Why Sinatra Matters*. Back Bay Books, 2003.
- Mustazza, Leonard, ed. *Frank Sinatra and Popular Culture*. Praeger, 1998.
- Petkov, Steven and Mustazza, Leonard, ed. *The Frank Sinatra Reader*. Oxford University Press, 1997.
- Pugliese, S., ed. *Frank Sinatra: "History, Identity, and Italian American Culture "*. Palgrave, 2004.
- Smith, Martin. *When Ol' Blue Eyes was a red*. Redwords, 2005.
- Zehme, Bill. *The Way You Wear Your Hat: Frank Sinatra and the Lost Art of Livin'*. Harper Collins, 1997.

Other

- Gigliotti, Gilbert L., ed. (2008) *Sinatra: But Buddy I'm a Kind of Poem*. Entasis Press ISBN 978-0-9800999-0-4
- Giordmaina, Diane [McCue] (2009) "Sinatra and The Moll". iUniverse. ISBN 978-0-595-53234-6
- Havers, Richard (2004) *Sinatra*. Dorling Kindersley. ISBN 1-4053-1461-3
- Ingham, Chris (2005) *The Rough Guide to Frank Sinatra*. Rough Guides. ISBN 1-84353-414-2
- Knight, Timothy (2010) *Sinatra – Hollywood His Way*. Running Press. ISBN 978-0-7624-3743-6
- Kuntz, Tom; Kuntz, Phil (2000) *The Sinatra Files: The Secret FBI Dossier*. Three Rivers Press ISBN 0-8129-3276-5
- Lloyd, David (2003) *The Gospel According to Frank*. New American Press. ISBN 1-930907-19-2
- O'Neill, Terry, ed. Morgan, Robert (2007) *Sinatra: Frank and Friendly*. Evans Mitchell Books. ISBN 1-901268-32-2
- Phasey, Chris (1995) *Francis Albert Sinatra: Tracked Down* (Discography). Buckland Publications. ISBN 0-7212-0935-1
- *The New Rolling Stone Record Guide*, Rolling Stone Press, 1983.

External links

- Official website (http://www.sinatra.com)
- Frank Sinatra (http://www.discogs.com/artist/Frank+Sinatra) discography at Discogs
- Frank Sinatra (http://www.ibdb.com/person.asp?ID=79640) at the Internet Broadway Database
- Frank Sinatra (http://www.imdb.com/name/nm69/) at the Internet Movie Database
- Frank Sinatra (http://www.dmoz.org/Arts/People/S/Sinatra,_Frank/) at the Open Directory Project
- The House I Live In (1945) (http://www.archive.org/details/TheHouseILiveIn)
- The Frank Sinatra Show (1950–1952) (http://www.archive.org/details/Lbines-RetroVisionTheaterPresentsTheFrankSinatraShow870)

- Frank Sinatra (http://digital.library.unt.edu/explore/partners/UNTML/browse/?start=21& fq=untl_collection:JGPC) interviewed on *the Pop Chronicles* (1969).
- FBI file on Frank Sinatra (http://vault.fbi.gov/Frank Sinatra)
- Archival Television Audio on Frank Sinatra (http://www.atvaudio.com/ata_search_qs.php?QS=Y& keywords=frank sinatra)
- Unofficial Fansite on Frank Sinatra (http://www.franksinatras.com)

Freddie Slack

Frederick Charles Slack (August 7, 1910 – August 10, 1965) was an American swing and boogie-woogie pianist and bandleader.

Life and career

Born in Viroqua, Wisconsin, he learned to play drums as a boy. Later he took up xylophone and at 13 changed to piano. He studied with a local teacher throughout high school. At 17 his parents moved to Chicago where he continued his musical training. He met Rosy McHargue, a well known clarinetist, who took him to hear many leading musicians including Bix Beiderbecke and Earl Hines. His first job was with Johnny Tobin at the Beach View Gardens. He later moved to Los Angeles where he worked with Henry Halstead, Earl Burtnett and Lennie Hayton, before joining Ben Pollack in 1934.

He played with the Jimmy Dorsey Band in the 1930s and was a charter member of the Will Bradley Orchestra when it formed in 1939. Known to bandmates as "Daddy Slack," he played the piano solo on Bradley's recording of "Beat Me Daddy, Eight to the Bar", one of the early white boogie-woogie hits and a classic of the Big Band era.

After forming his own band in 1942 and signing with the newly-founded Capitol Records, he recorded three songs at the third Capitol recording session on May 21, 1942. His recording of "Cow Cow Boogie," sung by the 17-year-old Ella Mae Morse, was the second record Capitol issued on July 1, and by July 25 it had reached number 1 on the hit parade. It was Capitol's first gold single.[1]

T-Bone Walker was a member of Slack's band from 1942 to 1944 and Slack later accompanied Walker on his first solo recording for Capitol, Mean Old World.[2] This band also had a hit with "Strange Cargo."

Slack continued to record with Capitol until at least 1950, recording some 80 tracks for the label.[3]

Slack also recorded as an accompanist for Big Joe Turner, Johnny Mercer, Margaret Whiting, and Lisa Morrow.

In the original version of the song "Down the Road a Piece", recorded in 1940 by the Will Bradley Orchestra, Slack is mentioned in the lyrics:

> If you wanna' hear some boogie then I know the place
> It's just an old piano and a knocked-out bass.
>
> The drummer-man's a guy they call 8-beat Mack
> You remember Doc and old "Beat Me Daddy" Slack.
>
> Man it's better than chicken fried in bacon grease
> Come along with me boys, it's just down the road a piece.

"Eight Beat Mack" refers to drummer Ray McKinley, and "Doc" refers to the band's bass player, Doc Goldberg.

His 1955 album *Boogie Woogie on the 88* featured a horn section including jazz musicians Shorty Sherock and Herbie Harper among others, and with arrangements by Benny Carter.

He also co-wrote the 1945 classic "The House of Blue Lights" first recorded with singer Ella Mae Morse, and later by Chuck Miller, The Andrews Sisters, Chuck Berry, and Jerry Lee Lewis.

References

[1] Ella Mae Morse's biography at allmusic (http://www.allmusic.com/artist/p3133/biography)

[2] T-Bone Walker biography at Tunegenie (http://www.tunegenie.com/bio/MN0000003829/t-bone-walker/?b=waal)

[3] Mosaic Records (http://www.mosaicrecords.com/prodinfo.asp?number=MS-018)

External links

- Freddie Slack (http://www.imdb.com/name/nm0805134/) at the Internet Movie Database
- All Music Guide (http://www.allmusic.com/artist/p9676/biography)

George Martin Lane

George Martin Lane (December 24, 1823–June 30, 1897),[1] American scholar, was born at Charlestown, Massachusetts.

He graduated in 1846 at Harvard, and in 1847-1851 studied at the universities of Berlin, Bonn, Heidelberg and Göttingen. In 1851 he received his doctor's degree at Göttingen for his dissertation *Smyrnaeorum Res Gestae et Antiquitates*, and on his return to America he was appointed University Professor of Latin in Harvard College.[1]

From 1869 until 1894, when he resigned and became professor emeritus, he was Pope Professor of Latin in the same institution.[1] His *Latin Pronunciation*, which led to the rejection of the English method of Latin pronunciation in the United States, was published in 1871.

His *Latin Grammar*, completed and published by Professor Morris H. Morgan in the following year, is of high value. Lane's assistance in the preparation of Harper's Latin lexicons was also invaluable. He wrote English light verse with humour and fluency, and his song "*Jonah and the Ballad of the Lone Fishball*" was famous.

Lane c. 1868-1875

Upon Lane's retirement in 1894, Harvard granted him an honorary degree as well as the first pension it had ever granted a faculty member; which, according to Lane, was enough to support him for the rest of his life.[1]

"The Lone Fish Ball"

In 1855 while living at Cloverden in Cambridge, Massachusetts, Lane wrote the song "The Lone Fish Ball"; after decades as a staple of Harvard undergraduates, it was modernized into the popular hit "**One Meat Ball**".[1]

According to Morgan, the song is based upon an actual experience of Lane's at a restaurant in Boston, although the reality involved a half-portion of macaroni, rather than a fish ball. The song goes on to relate the impoverished diner's embarrassment at the hands of a disdainful waiter. After becoming popular among Harvard undergraduates, it was translated into a mock Italian operetta, "*Il Pesceballo*", by faculty members Francis James Child, James Russell Lowell and John Knowles Paine, set to a pastiche of grand opera music, and performed in Boston and Cambridge to raise funds for the Union army.,[1][2]

In 1944, the song was revived by Tin Pan Alley songwriters Hy Zaret and Lou Singer in a more bluesy format as "One Meat Ball", and the recording by Josh White became one of the biggest hits of the early part of the American folk music revival.[1] Over the years, it was recorded by The Andrews Sisters, Bing Crosby, Jimmy Savo,[3] Lightnin' Hopkins, Lonnie Donegan, Dave Van Ronk, Ry Cooder, Washboard Jungle, Tom Paxton, Shinehead, and

Ann Rabson, among many others.

References

[1] "Song for Hard Times" (http://harvardmagazine.com/2009/05/song-hard-times), Harvard Magazine, May–June 2009

[2] Il pesceballo, opera in one act (http://books.google.com/books?hl=en&id=NGIRAAAAYAAJ&dq=Il+pesceballo+&
     printsec=frontcover&source=web&ots=ZMVzxZygUW&sig=zzCh6DbA_INiQDXs-7EFblLzmXQ&sa=X&oi=book_result&resnum=1&
     ct=result#PPA55,M1) History and libretto of *Il Pesceballo*, including history, lyrics, and music of "The Lay of the One Fishball"

[3] "100-Year-Old Hit" *Time Magazine* April 8, 1945 (http://www.time.com/time/magazine/article/0,9171,933491,00.html)

• This article incorporates text from a publication now in the public domain: Chisholm, Hugh, ed. (1911). *Encyclopædia Britannica* (11th ed.). Cambridge University Press.

Hollywood Canteen

For the 1944 Warner Bros. motion picture, see Hollywood Canteen (film)

The **Hollywood Canteen** operated at 1451 Cahuenga Boulevard in Hollywood, California between October 3, 1942, and November 22, 1945 (Thanksgiving Day), as a club offering food, dancing and entertainment for servicemen, usually on their way overseas. Even though the majority of visitors were U.S servicemen, the canteen was open to servicemen of allied countries as well as women in all branches of service. A serviceman's ticket for admission was his uniform and everything at the canteen was free of charge.

The driving forces behind its creation were Bette Davis and John Garfield, along with Jules Stein, President of Music Corporation of America, who headed up the finance committee. Bette Davis devoted an enormous amount of time and energy to the project and served as its president. The various guilds and unions of the entertainment industry donated the labor and money for the building renovations. The Canteen was operated and staffed completely by volunteers from the entertainment industry. By the time the Canteen opened its doors, over 3000 stars, players, directors, producers, grips, dancers, musicians, singers, writers, technicians, wardrobe attendants, hair stylists, agents, stand-ins, publicists, secretaries, and allied craftsmen of radio and screen had registered as volunteers.

Stars volunteered to wait on tables, cook in the kitchen and clean up. One of the highlights for a serviceman was to dance with one of the many female celebrities volunteering at the Canteen. The other highlight was the entertainment provided by some of Hollywood's most popular stars, ranging from radio stars to big bands to novelty acts. On September 15, 1943, the one millionth guest walked through the door of the Hollywood Canteen. The lucky soldier, Sgt. Carl Bell, received a kiss from Betty Grable and was escorted in by another beautiful star, including Marlene Dietrich.

A Hall of Honor at the Hollywood Canteen had a wall of photos which honored the film actors who served in the military.

By 1944, the Canteen had become so popular that Warner Bros. made a movie titled *The Hollywood Canteen*. Starring Joan Leslie and Robert Hutton, the film had scores of stars playing themselves. It was directed by Delmar Daves, who also wrote the screenplay. At the time the Canteen closed its doors, it had been host to almost three million servicemen.

Canteen site today

Today, the site of the Original Hollywood Canteen is occupied by Amoeba Music.

Reuse of the name

Fifty years after the closure of the Hollywood Canteen, a private business opened under the same name as a private restaurant and night club. It does not cater to military servicemen and women.

Volunteers

Among the many celebrities who donated their services at the Hollywood Canteen were:

- Bud Abbott and Lou Costello
- June Allyson
- Don Ameche
- Eddie 'Rochester' Anderson
- The Andrews Sisters
- Dana Andrews
- Eve Arden
- Louis Armstrong
- Jean Arthur
- Fred Astaire
- Mary Astor
- Lauren Bacall
- Lucille Ball
- Tallulah Bankhead
- Theda Bara
- Lynn Bari
- Diana Barrymore
- Ethel Barrymore
- Lionel Barrymore
- Count Basie
- Anne Baxter
- Louise Beavers
- Wallace Beery
- William Bendix
- Constance Bennett
- Joan Bennett
- Jack Benny
- Edgar Bergen
- Ingrid Bergman
- Milton Berle
- Mel Blanc
- Ann Blyth
- Humphrey Bogart
- Ray Bolger
- Beulah Bondi
- William Boyd
- Charles Boyer
- Clara Bow
- Walter Brennan

- Gloria DeHaven
- Dolores Del Rio
- William Demarest
- Olivia de Havilland
- Cecil B. DeMille
- Marlene Dietrich
- Walt Disney
- Jimmy Dorsey
- Tommy Dorsey
- Irene Dunne
- Jimmy Durante
- Deanna Durbin
- Nelson Eddy
- Duke Ellington
- Faye Emerson
- Dale Evans
- Jinx Falkenburg
- Alice Faye
- Louise Fazenda
- Gracie Fields
- Barry Fitzgerald
- Errol Flynn
- Kay Francis
- Jane Frazee
- Joan Fontaine
- Susanna Foster
- Eva Gabor
- Ava Gardner
- Judy Garland
- Greer Garson
- Lillian Gish
- James Gleason
- Betty Grable
- Cary Grant
- Kathryn Grayson
- Sydney Greenstreet
- Paulette Goddard
- Samuel Goldwyn
- Benny Goodman

- Veronica Lake
- Hedy Lamarr
- Dorothy Lamour
- Carole Landis
- Frances Langford
- Angela Lansbury
- Charles Laughton
- Peter Lawford
- Gertrude Lawrence
- Peggy Lee
- Pinky Lee
- Mervyn LeRoy
- Vivien Leigh
- Joan Leslie
- Ted Lewis
- Beatrice Lillie
- Mary Livingston
- June Lockhart
- Anita Loos
- Peter Lorre
- Myrna Loy
- Keye Luke
- Bela Lugosi
- Ida Lupino
- Diana Lynn
- Marie McDonald
- Jeanette MacDonald
- Fred MacMurray
- Irene Manning
- The Marx Brothers
- Herbert Marshall
- Victor Mature
- Elsa Maxwell
- Louis B. Mayer
- Hattie McDaniel
- Roddy McDowall
- Frank McHugh
- Victor McLaglen
- Butterfly McQueen

- Claude Rains
- Basil Rathbone
- Martha Raye
- Donna Reed
- Bill "Bojangles" Robinson
- Edward G. Robinson
- Ginger Rogers
- Roy Rogers
- Cesar Romero
- Mickey Rooney
- Jane Russell
- Rosalind Russell
- Ann Rutherford
- Peggy Ryan
- S.Z. Sakall
- Olga San Juan
- Ann Savage
- Hazel Scott
- Lizabeth Scott
- Randolph Scott
- Toni Seven
- Norma Shearer
- Ann Sheridan
- Dinah Shore
- Sylvia Sidney
- Phil Silvers
- Ginny Simms
- Frank Sinatra
- Red Skelton
- Alexis Smith
- Kate Smith
- Ann Sothern
- Jo Stafford
- Barbara Stanwyck
- Craig Stevens
- Leopold Stokowski
- Lewis Stone
- Gloria Swanson
- Elizabeth Taylor

- Fanny Brice
- Joe E. Brown
- Les Brown
- George Burns & Gracie Allen
- Spring Byington
- James Cagney
- Cab Calloway
- Rod Cameron
- Eddie Cantor
- Judy Canova
- Kitty Carlisle
- Jack Carson
- Adriana Caselotti
- Charlie Chaplin
- Marguerite Chapman
- Cyd Charisse
- Charles Coburn
- Claudette Colbert
- Jerry Colonna
- Ronald Colman
- Perry Como
- Chester Conklin
- Gary Cooper
- Joseph Cotten
- Noël Coward
- James Craig
- Bing Crosby
- Joan Crawford
- George Cukor
- Xavier Cugat
- Cass Daley
- Dorothy Dandridge
- Linda Darnell
- Bette Davis
- Doris Day
- Yvonne De Carlo

- Jack Haley
- Margaret Hamilton
- Phil Harris
- Moss Hart
- Helen Hayes
- Dick Haymes
- Susan Hayward
- Rita Hayworth
- Sonja Henie
- Paul Henreid
- Katharine Hepburn
- Darla Hood
- Bob Hope
- Hedda Hopper
- Lena Horne
- Edward Everett Horton
- Ruth Hussey
- Betty Hutton
- Harry James
- Gloria Jean
- Van Johnson
- Al Jolson
- Jennifer Jones
- Marcia Mae Jones
- Boris Karloff
- Danny Kaye
- Buster Keaton
- Ruby Keeler
- Evelyn Keyes
- Andrea King
- Gene Krupa
- Kay Kyser
- Alan Ladd
- Bert Lahr
- Elsa Lanchester
- Angela Lansbury

- Lauritz Melchior]
- Adolphe Menjou
- Una Merkel
- Ray Milland
- Ann Miller
- Glenn Miller
- Carmen Miranda
- Robert Mitchum
- Maria Montez
- Jackie Moran
- Dennis Morgan
- Ken Murray
- The Nicholas Brothers
- Ramon Novarro
- Jack Oakie
- Margaret O'Brien
- Virginia O'Brien
- Donald O'Connor
- Maureen O'Hara
- Oona O'Neill
- Maureen O'Sullivan
- Merle Oberon
- Eugene Pallette
- Eleanor Parker
- Louella Parsons
- John Payne
- Gregory Peck
- Mary Pickford
- Walter Pidgeon
- Cole Porter
- Dick Powell
- Eleanor Powell
- Jane Powell
- William Powell
- Anthony Quinn
- George Raft

- Shirley Temple
- Danny Thomas
- Gene Tierney
- Lawrence Tibbett
- Martha Tilton
- Claire Trevor
- Sophie Tucker
- Lana Turner
- Spencer Tracy
- Gloria Vanderbilt
- Beryl Wallace
- Nancy Walker
- Ethel Waters
- John Wayne
- Clifton Webb
- Virginia Weidler
- Johnny Weissmuller
- Orson Welles
- Mae West
- Alice White
- Paul Whiteman
- Margaret Whiting
- Esther Williams
- Chill Wills
- Marie Wilson
- Jane Withers
- Teresa Wright
- Anna May Wong
- Jane Wyman
- Rudy Vallee
- Lupe Vélez
- Loretta Young
- Robert Young
- Darryl F. Zanuck
- Vera Zorina

References

External links

- *Hollywood Canteen* (http://www.imdb.com/title/tt0036922/) at the Internet Movie Database
- Current Hollywood Canteen (http://www.hollywoodcanteenla.com)

Hollywood Canteen (film)

Hollywood Canteen	
Original theatrical poster	
Directed by	Delmer Daves
Produced by	Alex Gottlieb
Written by	Delmer Daves
Starring	Joan Leslie Robert Hutton Dane Clark
Music by	**Musical Director:** Leo F. Forbstein **Musical Adaptation:** Ray Heindorf
Cinematography	Bert Glennon
Editing by	Christian Nyby
Distributed by	Warner Bros.
Release date(s)	• December 15, 1944
Running time	124 minutes
Country	United States
Language	English
Box office	$4.2 million (US/ Canada rentals) [1]

Hollywood Canteen is a 1944 Warner Bros. film starring Joan Leslie, Robert Hutton, and Dane Clark. The film was written and directed by Delmer Daves, and is notable for featuring many stars (appearing as themselves) in cameo roles. The film received three Academy Award nominations.

Plot and cast

Two soldiers on leave spend three nights at the Hollywood Canteen before returning to active duty in the South Pacific. Slim Green (Hutton) is the millionth G.I. to enjoy the Canteen, and consequently wins a date with Joan Leslie. The other G.I., Sergeant Nolan, (Clark) gets to dance with Joan Crawford. Canteen founders Bette Davis and John Garfield give talks on the history of the Canteen. The soldiers enjoy a variety of musical numbers performed by a host of Hollywood stars.

Historical note

The film's setting is the Hollywood Canteen, a free entertainment club open to servicemen. The Canteen was created as a G.I. morale-booster by movie stars Bette Davis and John Garfield during World War II. Many of those cameoing in the film had previously volunteered to work there or provide entertainment. They include: The Andrews Sisters, Jack Benny, Joe E. Brown, Eddie Cantor, Kitty Carlisle, Jack Carson, Joan Crawford, Faye Emerson, Sydney Greenstreet, Alan Hale, Sr., Paul Henreid, Joan Leslie, Peter Lorre, Ida Lupino, Dorothy Malone, Dennis Morgan, Janis Paige, Eleanor Parker, Roy Rogers (with Trigger), S.Z. Sakall, Zachary Scott, Alexis Smith, Barbara Stanwyck, Jane Wyman, Jimmy Dorsey and The Golden Gate Quartet.

The East Coast counterpart was the "Stage Door Canteen" also celebrated in an RKO film.

Reception

Variety noted, "There isn't a marquee big enough to hold all the names in this one, so how can it miss? Besides, it's basically solid. It has story, cohesion, and heart."

Kate Cameron in *The New York Times* commented, "It is an elaborate show, but it is presented by author-director Delmar Daves in such a patronizing manner as to make one blush for its complete lack of reserve in singing the praises of Hollywood." [2]

Awards and nominations

Hollywood Canteen received Academy Award nominations for Best Original Song: "Sweet Dreams Sweetheart", by M. K. Jerome and Ted Koehler; Scoring of a Musical Picture: Ray Heindorf; and Sound Recording: Nathan Levinson.[3]

References

[1] "All-Time Top Grossers", *Variety*, 8 January 1964 p 69
[2] Quirk, Lawrence J.. *The Films of Joan Crawford*. The Citadel Press, 1968.
[3] "The 17th Academy Awards (1945) Nominees and Winners" (http://www.oscars.org/awards/academyawards/legacy/ceremony/17th-winners.html). *oscars.org*. . Retrieved 2011-08-14.

External links

- *Hollywood Canteen* (http://tcmdb.com/title/title.jsp?stid=618) at the TCM Movie Database
- *Hollywood Canteen* (http://www.allrovi.com/movies/movie/v22745) at AllRovi
- *Hollywood Canteen (film)* (http://www.imdb.com/title/tt0036922/) at the Internet Movie Database

I, Yi, Yi, Yi, Yi (I Like You Very Much)

"I, Yi, Yi, Yi, Yi (I Like You Very Much)" is a 1941 song. It was written for the 1941 film, *That Night in Rio*, and was popularized by Carmen Miranda. The lyrics were written by Mack Gordon and the music by Harry Warren.

Covers and performances

- The song was recorded by The Andrews Sisters on January 7, 1941.[1]
- Alvin and the Chipmunks covered this song along with "Cunato Le Gusta" for their 1987 film *The Chipmunk Adventure* and its soundtrack.
- Carol Channing sang this song when she appeared on "The Muppet Show".

Other appearances in pop culture

- The song makes an appearance in the series finale of the 1967-68 British television series, *The Prisoner*, then in an advert for Kellogg's Fruit 'n Fibre in 1996, and was used in a sequence for the *Futurama* movie *The Beast with a Billion Backs* (2008).

External links

- List of recordings [2] at AllMusic

References

[1] Rust, Brian (1973). *The Complete Entertainment Discography*. New Rochelle, New York: Arlington House. p. 8. ISBN 0-87000-150-7.

[2] http://www.allmusic.com/cg/amg.dll?p=amg&sql=17:777667

I Don't Know Why (I Just Do)

"**I Don't Know Why (I Just Do)**" is a popular song.

The music was written by Fred E. Ahlert, the lyrics by Roy Turk. The song was published in 1931. It had three periods of great popularity: in 1931, right after its publication; in 1946; and in 1961.[1] into 1962.

In 1931, the biggest-selling version was either by Russ Columbo[1] or by Wayne King;[2] both versions and recordings by Bennie Krueger's orchestra (with a vocal by Smith Ballew) and by Kate Smith all had significant popularity.[1]

In 1946, three versions, by Tommy Dorsey's orchestra (with a vocal by Stuart Foster), by Frank Sinatra, and by Skinnay Ennis, all contended for popularity.[1]

In 1961, a US hit recording was issued by Linda Scott. It reached a peak position #12 in 8 weeks on the Billboard chart;[3][4] in early 1962, Eden Kane reached the British Top 10 with his version.

The song has been recorded by many artists (ranging from country-blues legends like Moon Mullican and Jerry Lee Lewis, to swing legends Frank Sinatra and Dean Martin) and is now a standard.

Recorded versions

- The Andrews Sisters and Vic Schoen's orchestra (recorded May 8, 1946, released by Decca Records as catalog number 18899A, with the flip side "Azusa"[5])
- The Aristocrats (recorded September 1, 1931, released by Romeo Records as catalog number 1711, with the flip side "Let's Drift Away on Dreamer's Bay"[6])
- Georgie Auld and his orchestra (recorded April 30, 1946, released by Musicraft Records as catalog number 15078, with the flip side "Just You, Just Me"[7])
- Hoagy Carmichael and his orchestra (released by ARA Records as catalog number 148, with the flip side "I Can't Get Started"[8])
- Larry Clinton and his orchestra (released by Cosmo Records as catalog number 704, with the flip side "More Than You Know"[9])
- King Cole Trio (released by Capitol Records as catalog number 1030, with the flip side "You're the Cream in My Coffee"[10])
- Russ Columbo (recorded September 3, 1931, released by Victor Records as catalog number 22801,[1] with the flip side "Guilty"[11])
- Eddie Davis Trio (recorded August 16, 1955, released by King Records as catalog number 4832, with the flip side "It's a Pity to Say Goodbye"[12])

- Jimmie Davis (recorded March 6, 1953, released by Decca Records as catalog number 29157, with the flip side "Just Between You and Me"[13])
- The Deep River Boys (featuring Harry Douglass) (released October 1959 by Top Rank Records as catalog number JAR174, with the flip side "Timbers Gotta Roll"[14])
- The Delicates (released 1961 by Roulette Records as catalog number 4387, with the flip side "Strange Love"[15])
- DeMarco Sisters with Bud Freeman (recorded October 1945, released by Majestic Records as catalog number 7194, with the flip side "Chiquita Banana"[16])
- Hal Denman and his orchestra (recorded November 27, 1931, released by Supertone Records as catalog number 2768, with the flip side "How's Your Uncle?"[17])
- Lou Donaldson on his 1995 album *Caracas*
- Tommy Dorsey and his orchestra (vocal: Stuart Foster; recorded April 16, 1946, released by RCA Victor Records as catalog number 20-1901, with the flip side "Remember Me"[18])
- Skinnay Ennis and his orchestra (released by Signature Records as catalog number 15033B, with the flip side "Got a Date with an Angel"[19])
- Erroll Garner Trio (recorded June 28, 1950, released by Columbia Records as catalog numbers 39038, with the flip side "When Johnny Comes Marching Home,"[20] and 39168, with the flip side "It Could Happen to You"[20])
- Ken Griffin (recorded April 1953, released by Columbia Records as catalog number 40101, with the flip side "It Had to Be You"[21])
- Annette Hanshaw (recorded September 22, 1931, released by Harmony Records as catalog number 1376-H, with the flip side "Guilty"[22])
- Eddie Heywood (recorded May 29, 1946, released by Decca Records as catalog number 23590, with the flip side "Loch Lomond"[23])
- Eden Kane (recorded 1961, released by Decca Records in Britain as catalog number F 11460, with the flip side "Music For Strings")
- Lloyd Keating and his orchestra (recorded August 20, 1931, released by Clarion Records as catalog number 11002, with the flip side "Love Letters in the Sand"[24])
- Wayne King (recorded September 3, 1931, released by Victor Records as catalog number 22817,[1][2] with the flip side "Guilty"[11])
- Bennie Krueger and his orchestra (vocal: Smith Ballew; recorded September 14, 1931, released by Brunswick Records as catalog number 6185,[1] with the flip side "I Idolize My Baby's Eyes"[25])
- Tony Martin with Al Sack's Starlight Orchestra (recorded April 1946, released by Mercury Records as catalog numbers 3019[26] and 5034,[27] both with the flip side "Without You"[26][27])
- Kenzie Moore with Joe Dyson's Band (recorded January 1953, released by Specialty Records as catalog number 456, with the flip side "Let It Lay"[28])
- Leon Payne (released by Capitol Records as catalog number 1405, with the flip side "If I Could Only Live My Life Over"[10])
- The RadioLites (recorded September 18, 1931, released by Columbia Records as catalog number 2540-D, with the flip side "Love Letters in the Sand"[29])
- The Ravens (recorded September 1947, released by National Records as catalog number 9059, with the flip side "How Could I Know?"[30])
- Linda Scott (released by Canadian American Records as catalog number 129[3][4])
- Bobby Sherwood and his orchestra (recorded May 5, 1942, released by Capitol Records as catalog number 107, with the flip side ""[31])
- Frank Sinatra (recorded July 30, 1945, released by Columbia Records as catalog number 36918, with the flip side "You Go to My Head"[32])
- Kate Smith (recorded September 15, 1931, released by Columbia Records as catalog number 2539-D,[1] with the flip side "You Call It Madness"[29])

- Claude Thornhill and his orchestra (recorded July 25, 1942, released by Columbia Records as catalog number 36858, with the flip side "Buster's Last Stand"[32])
- Al Trace's Silly Symphonists (released by Hit Records as catalog number 8081A, with the flip side "Sugar Blues"[33])
- Billy Williams Quartet (released by Mercury Records as catalog number 70012, with the flip side "Mad About Cha"[34])

References

[1] Gardner, Edward Foote (2000). *Popular Songs of the 20th Century: Chart Detail & Encyclopedia, 1900-1949*. St. Paul, Minnesota: Paragon House. ISBN 1-55778-789-1.
[2] Whitburn, Joel (1999). *Joel Whitburn Presents a Century of Pop Music*. Menomonee Falls, Wisconsin: Record Research. ISBN 0-89820-135-7.
[3] Whitburn, Joel (2000-11-01). *The Billboard Book of Top 40 Hits* (7th Rev. edition ed.). New York: Watson-Guptill Publications. ISBN 978-0-8230-7690-1.
[4] Lonergan, David (2004-01-28). *Hit Records 1950-1975*. Lanham, Maryland: Scarecrow Press. ISBN 978-0-8108-5129-0.
[5] Decca Records in the 18500 to 18999 series (http://78discography.com/Dec18500.htm)
[6] Romeo Records in the 1500 to 1999 series (http://78discography.com/ROM1500.htm)
[7] Musicraft Records in the 15000 to 15130 series (http://78discography.com/Musicraft15000.htm)
[8] ARA Records in the 100 to 162 series (http://78discography.com/ARA100.htm)
[9] Cosmo Records listing (http://78discography.com/Cosmo.htm)
[10] Capitol Records in the 1000 to 1499 series (http://78discography.com/Capitol1000.htm)
[11] Victor Records in the 22500 to 22999 series (http://78discography.com/vic22500.html)
[12] King Records in the 4100 to 4997 series (http://78discography.com/King4000.htm)
[13] Decca Records in the 29000 to 29499 series (http://78discography.com/Dec29000.htm)
[14] Top Rank Records listing (http://www.globaldogproductions.info/t/top-rank-uk.html)
[15] Roulette Records listing (http://www.globaldogproductions.info/r/roulette.html)
[16] Majestic Records listing (http://78discography.com/Majestic.htm)
[17] Supertone Records in the 2500 to 2839 series (http://78discography.com/Superior.htm)
[18] RCA Victor Records in the 20-1500 to 20-1999 series (http://78discography.com/RCA201500.htm)
[19] Signature Records listing (http://78discography.com/Signiature.htm)
[20] Columbia Records in the 39000 to 39499 series (http://78discography.com/COL39000.htm)
[21] Columbia Records in the 40000 to 40499 series (http://78discography.com/COL40000.htm)
[22] Harmony Records in the 1000-H to 1428-H series (http://78discography.com/Har1000.htm)
[23] Decca Records in the 23500 to 23999 series (http://78discography.com/Dec23500.htm)
[24] Clarion Records in various series (http://78discography.com/ClarionSP.htm)
[25] Brunswick Records in the 6000 to 6499 series (http://78discography.com/BRN6000.htm)
[26] Mercury Records in the 3000 to 3072 series (http://78discography.com/Merc030.htm)
[27] Mercury Records in the 5000 to 5497 series (http://78discography.com/Merc050.htm)
[28] Specialty Records listing (http://78discography.com/Specialty.htm)
[29] Columbia Records in the 2500-D to 2999-D series (http://78discography.com/COL2500D.htm)
[30] National Records listing (http://78discography.com/NationalLate.htm)
[31] Capitol Records in the 100 to 499 series (http://78discography.com/Capitol100.htm)
[32] Columbia Records in the 36500 to 36999 series (http://78discography.com/COL36500.htm)
[33] Hit Records in the 8001 to 8090 series (http://78discography.com/Hit8000.htm)
[34] Mercury Records in the 70000 to 71696 series (http://78discography.com/Merc700.htm)

I Wanna Be Loved

"I Wanna Be Loved"	
Music by	Johnny Green
Lyrics by	Edward Heyman, Billy Rose
Published	1933
Recorded by	Billy Eckstine, Maria Muldaur, The Andrews Sisters, George Maharis, Mina

"**I Wanna Be Loved**" is a popular song with music by Johnny Green and lyrics by Edward Heyman and Billy Rose, published in 1933.

The song is a standard, with many recorded versions.

*   Billy Eckstine - *Passing Strangers* (2009)
*   Grant Green plays on the song on his album Am I Blue.
*   Maria Muldaur performs the song on her 1999 album *Meet Me Where They Play The Blues*.
*   The song was recorded by The Andrews Sisters in 1950.
*   George Maharis covered the song on his 1963 album "Just Turn Me Loose!"
*   Mina covered the song on her 1969 album "Mina for you"

Is You Is or Is You Ain't My Baby

"Is You Is or Is You Ain't My Baby"	
Single by Louis Jordan	
A-side	"G.I. Jive"
Released	1944
Genre	Rhythm and blues
Label	Decca

"Is You Is Or Is You Ain't My Baby" is a 1944 Louis Jordan song, released as the B-side of single with "G.I. Jive". "Is You Is or Is You Ain't My Baby" reached #1 on the US folk/country charts.[1] The Louis Jordan recording also peaked at number two for three weeks on the pop chart and peaked at number three on the R&B charts.[2]

It was co-written by Jordan and Billy Austin. Austin (March 6, 1896 - July 24, 1964) was a songwriter and author, born in Denver, Colorado. The phrase "Is you is or is you ain't" is dialect, apparently first recorded in a 1921 story by Octavus Roy Cohen, a Jewish writer from South Carolina who wrote humorous black dialect fiction. Glenn Miller recorded this song on a radio broadcast from Europe during World War II.

Cover versions

- The tune has become something of a jazz standard with versions recorded by artists including The Andrews Sisters, June Christy, Bing Crosby, Nat "King" Cole, Buster Brown, Glenn Miller, Renee Olstead, Dinah Washington, Woody Herman, Anita O'Day, Joe Williams, B.B. King, Vic Damone, Screamin' Jay Hawkins, Diana Krall, Joe Jackson and Emilie-Claire Barlow. There was also a cover of this on Tom and Jerry by Ira "Buck" Woods sung by a character of Tom Cat.
- A remix of the Dinah Washington version by Rae & Christian appeared on the Verve Remixed (2002) album.

In popular culture

- The song was featured in the film "Follow the Boys", starring Marlene Dietrich.
- The title of the song is used by Bugs Bunny in the 1944 Warner Brothers short, "The Unruly Hare".
- In 1946, the song was sung in a more upbeat fashion by Tom in the Tom and Jerry short "Solid Serenade" as well as *Smitten Kitten*.
- A remix by DJ Shark, credited to Dinah Washington vs. DJ Shark appeared in the Michael Douglas film *It Runs in the Family*.
- The song was featured in the 2009 film "World's Greatest Dad", starring Robin Williams. It was performed by Bruce Hornsby.
- The song is featured at the end of Series 1, Episode 7 of Spaced.
- The song is featured in the opening credits of the John Cameron Mitchell film Shortbus.

References

[1] Whitburn, Joel (2004). *The Billboard Book Of Top 40 Country Hits: 1944-2006, Second edition*. Record Research. p. 184.
[2] Whitburn, Joel (2004). *Top R&B/Hip-Hop Singles: 1942-2004*. Record Research. p. 309.

Leon Belasco

Leon Belasco (11 October 1902 – 1 June 1988), born **Leonid Simeonovich Berladsky**, was a Russian-American musician and actor who had a 60-year career in film and television from the 1920s to the 1980s, appearing in more than 100 films.

Musical career

Born in Odessa, Ukraine, Belasco attended St. Joseph College in Yokohama, Japan, and trained as a musician in Japan and Manchuria. For several years he appeared as the first violinist with the Tokyo Symphony.[1]

When his family moved to California, Belasco found occasional work in Hollywood. He made his film debut in 1926 in the silent film *The Best People*. To supplement his income, he played the violin. Later he formed his own band, which mainly performed in hotels in and around New York City. The Andrews Sisters were introduced through his band.[2]

Film career

During a season break from a hotel engagement, he returned to Hollywood, first appearing in *Broadway Serenade* and *Topper Takes a Trip* (1938). He acted in 13 films in 1942, including *Holiday Inn*, *Casablanca*, *Yankee Doodle Dandy*, and *Road to Morocco*.[2]

He appeared with the Marx Brothers in their last film together, *Love Happy* (1949).[3] Being able to speak Russian, he was a dialogue director in Norman Jewison's 1966 comedy *The Russians Are Coming, the Russians Are Coming*.

Belasco often played eccentric or befuddled European and ethnic characters.[2] He also played heavier roles in World War II and Cold War espionage dramas. On radio he played a thieving informant in *The Man Called X*. His best-known television role was as Appopoplous the landlord in *My Sister Eileen* (1960).[1] His last film was *Superdad* (1973), and his final television movie was *Woman of the Year* (1976).[2]

Television career

Beginning in 1953,[2] Belasco appeared in a variety of television shows. These included: *Maverick* (1961), *Twilight Zone* (1963), *The Lucy Show* (1963), *The Beverly Hillbillies* (1964-1967), *My Three Sons* (1966), *The Dick Van Dyke Show* (1966), *The Man from U.N.C.L.E.* (1966), *Little House on the Prairie* (1978) and *Trapper John, M.D.* (1980).

On his death in 1988 in Orange, California, Belasco was cremated, and his ashes scattered.

References

[1] "Leon Belasco - Full Biography" (http://movies.nytimes.com/person/5065/Leon-Belasco/biography). The New York Times. . Retrieved 13 September 2010.
[2] "Leon Belasco as a Dealer" (http://mcgady.net/Casab/evenmore/even_more_minor_characters.html). mcgady.net. . Retrieved 13 September 2010.
[3] "Leon Belasco" (http://movies.nytimes.com/person/5065/Leon-Belasco/filmography). The New York Times. . Retrieved 13 September 2010.

External links

- Leon Belasco (http://www.imdb.com/name/nm0067589/) at the Internet Movie Database

Les Paul

Les Paul	
 Les Paul playing a Gibson Les Paul in a live show at Iridium Jazz Club in New York City, 2008.	
Background information	
Birth name	Lester William Polsfuss[1]
Born	June 9, 1915 Waukesha, Wisconsin, United States
Died	August 13, 2009 (aged 94) White Plains, New York, United States[2]
Genres	Jazz, country, blues, rock and roll
Occupations	Innovator, Inventor, Musician, Songwriter
Instruments	Guitar, Banjo, Harmonica
Years active	1928–2009
Website	lespaulfoundation.org [3]
Notable instruments	
Gibson Les Paul	

Lester William Polsfuss (June 9, 1915 – August 13, 2009)[4][5][6]—known as **Les Paul**—was an American jazz, country and blues guitarist, songwriter, luthier and inventor. He was one of the pioneers of the solid-body electric guitar, which made the sound of rock and roll possible.[7] He is credited with many recording innovations. Although he was not the first to use the technique, his early experiments with overdubbing (also known as sound on sound),[8] delay effects such as tape delay, phasing effects and multitrack recording were among the first to attract widespread attention.[9]

His innovative talents extended into his playing style, including licks, trills, chording sequences, fretting techniques and timing, which set him apart from his contemporaries and inspired many guitarists of the present day.[10][11][12][13] He recorded with his wife Mary Ford in the 1950s, and they sold millions of records.

Among his many honors, Paul is one of a handful of artists with a permanent, stand-alone exhibit in the Rock and Roll Hall of Fame.[14] He is prominently named by the music museum on its website as an "architect" and a "key inductee" along with Sam Phillips and Alan Freed.[15]

Biography

Early life

Les Paul was born **Lester William Polsfuss** outside Milwaukee, in Waukesha, Wisconsin, to George and Evelyn (1888–1989) (née Stutz) Polsfuss. His family was of German ancestry.[16] Paul's mother was related to the founders of Milwaukee's Valentin Blatz Brewing Company and the makers of the Stutz automobile.[17] His parents divorced when he was a child.[18] The Prussian family name was first simplified by his mother to Polfuss before he took his stage name of **Les Paul**. He also used the nicknames **Red Hot Red**[19] and **Rhubarb Red**.[20]

While living in Wisconsin, he first became interested in music at age eight when he began playing the harmonica. After an attempt at learning the banjo, he began to play the guitar. It was during this time that he invented a neck-worn harmonica holder, which allowed him to play the harmonica hands-free while accompanying himself on the guitar. Paul's device is still manufactured using his basic design.[21] By age thirteen, Paul was performing semi-professionally as a country-music singer, guitarist and harmonica player. While playing at the Waukesha area drive-ins and roadhouses, Paul began his first experiment with sound. Wanting to make himself heard by more people at the local venues, he wired a phonograph needle to a radio speaker, using that to amplify his acoustic guitar.[22] At age seventeen, Paul played with Rube Tronson's Texas Cowboys, and soon after he dropped out of high school to join Wolverton's Radio Band in St. Louis, Missouri, on KMOX.

Early career

Paul migrated to Chicago in 1934, where he continued to perform on radio, and met pianist Art Tatum, whose playing influenced him to a career devoted to guitar rather than original plans of taking on the piano.[23] His first two records were released in 1936. One was credited to "Rhubarb Red", Paul's hillbilly *alter ego*, and the other was as an accompanist for blues-artist Georgia White. It was during this time that he began playing jazz and adopted his stage name.[24]

Paul's jazz-guitar style was strongly influenced by the music of Django Reinhardt, whom he greatly admired. Following World War II, Paul sought out and befriended Reinhardt. After Reinhardt's death in 1953, Paul furnished his headstone. One of Paul's prize possessions was a Selmer Maccaferri acoustic guitar given to him by Reinhardt's widow.[19]

 **External video**

🎞 *Oral History, Les Paul shares moments of his life story and career.* interview date November 13, 2001, NAMM (National Association of Music Merchants) Oral History Library [25]

Paul formed a trio in 1937 with singer/rhythm guitarist Jim Atkins[26] (older half-brother of guitarist Chet Atkins) and bassist/percussionist Ernie "Darius" Newton. They left Chicago for New York in 1939, landing a featured spot with *Fred Waring's Pennsylvanians* radio show. Chet Atkins later wrote that his brother, home on a family visit, presented the younger Atkins with an expensive Gibson archtop guitar that had been given to Jim Atkins by Les Paul. Chet recalled that it was the first professional-quality instrument he ever owned.[27]

Paul was dissatisfied with acoustic-electric guitars and began experimenting at his apartment in Queens, NY with a few designs of his own. Famously, he created several versions of "The Log", which was nothing more than a length of common 4x4 lumber with a bridge, guitar neck and pickup attached. For the sake of appearance, he attached the body of an Epiphone hollow-body guitar, sawn lengthwise with The Log in the middle. This solved his two main problems: feedback, as the acoustic body no longer resonated with the amplified sound, and sustain, as the energy of the strings was not dissipated in generating sound through the guitar body. These instruments were constantly being improved and modified over the years, and Paul continued to use them in his recordings long after the development of his eponymous Gibson model. In 1945, Richard D. Bourgerie made an electric guitar pickup and amplifier for professional guitar player George Barnes. Bourgerie worked through World War II at Howard Radio Company making electronic equipment for the American military. Barnes showed the result to Les Paul, who then arranged for Bourgerie to have one made for him.

While experimenting in his apartment in 1940, Paul nearly succumbed to electrocution. During two years of recuperation, he relocated to Hollywood, supporting himself by producing radio music and forming a new trio. He was drafted into the US Army shortly after the beginning of World War II, where he served in the Armed Forces Network, backing such artists as Bing Crosby, the Andrews Sisters, and performing in his own right.[28]

Les Paul, ca. January 1947 (Photograph by William P. Gottlieb)

As a last-minute replacement for Oscar Moore, Paul played with Nat King Cole and other artists in the inaugural Jazz at the Philharmonic concert in Los Angeles, California, on July 2, 1944. The recording, still available as Jazz at the Philharmonic- the first concert- shows Paul at the top of his game, both in his solid four to the bar comping in the style of Freddie Green and for the originality of his solo lines. Paul's solo on 'Blues' is an astonishing tour de force and represents a memorable contest between himself and Nat 'King' Cole. Much later in his career, Paul declared that he had been the victor and that this had been conceded by Cole. His solo on Body and Soul is a fine demonstration both of his admiration for and emulation of the playing of Django Reinhardt, as well as his development of some very original lines.

Also that year, Paul's trio appeared on Bing Crosby's radio show. Crosby went on to sponsor Paul's recording experiments. The two also recorded together several times, including a 1945 number-one hit, "It's Been a Long, Long Time." In addition to backing Crosby, The Andrews Sisters and other artists, Paul's trio also recorded a few albums of their own on the Decca label in the late 1940s. Paul was particularly enamored by the famous Andrews Sisters, who hired The Les Paul Trio as their opening act while they toured in 1946. Lou Levy, the sisters' manager and a music publishing giant of the big band era and beyond, once said, "Watching his fingers work was like watching a locomotive go."[29] The trio's longtime conductor, Vic Schoen, said of Les, "You could always count on him to come up with something no one else had thought of,"[29] while Maxene Andrews once remembered, "It was wonderful having him perform with us. He'd tune into the passages we were singing and lightly play the melody, sometimes in harmony. We'd sing these fancy licks and he'd keep up with us note for note in exactly the same rhythm...almost contributing a fourth voice. But he never once took the attention away from what we were doing. He did everything he could to make us sound better."[29] Two Decca recordings from 1946 pairing Paul with The Andrews Sisters ("Rumors Are Flying" and "It's a Pity to Say Goodnight") exist today to well affirm such comments. Paul's many hits with wife Mary Ford recording her vocals in triplicate in the 1950s produced a sound eerily similar to the harmonious blend of The Andrews Sisters.[29] As Les Paul biographer Mary Alice Shaughnessy noted of Paul's association with The Andrews Sisters, "Les welcomed the opportunity to study them in full flight."[29]

In January 1948, Paul shattered his right arm and elbow in a near-fatal automobile accident on an icy Route 66 just west of Davenport, Oklahoma. Mary Ford was driving the Buick convertible, which rolled several times down a creek bed; they were on their way back from Wisconsin to Los Angeles after performing at the opening of a restaurant owned by Paul's father. Doctors at Oklahoma City's Wesley Presbyterian Hospital told him that they could not rebuild his elbow so that he would regain movement; his arm would remain permanently in whatever position they placed it in. Their other option was amputation. Paul instructed surgeons, brought in from Los Angeles, to set his arm at an angle—just under 90 degrees—that would allow him to cradle and pick the guitar. It took him nearly a year and a half to recover.[30]

Guitar builder

Paul's innovative guitar, "The Log", built after-hours in the Epiphone guitar factory in 1940, a 4" × 4" chunk of pine with strings and a pickup, was one of the first solid-body electric guitars.[31][32] Paul Tutmarc of Audiovox Manufacturing Co. built a solid body electric bass in 1935 and Adolph Rickenbacker had marketed a solid-body guitar in the 1930s and Paul A. Bigsby had built one for Merle Travis in 1948 and Leo Fender also independently created his own (the Fender "Esquire," a single pickup model) in 1948. Although Paul approached the Gibson Guitar Corporation with his idea of a solid body electric guitar, they showed no interest until Fender began marketing its Esquire which later had a second pick-up added and became known as the Broadcaster (Renamed Telecaster in 1952).

The Gibson Les Paul, one of the world's most popular electric guitars, was named after the man who invented it.

The arrangement persisted until 1961, when declining sales prompted Gibson to change the design without Paul's knowledge, creating a much thinner, lighter and more aggressive-looking instrument with two cutaway "horns" instead of one. Paul said he first saw the "new" Gibson Les Paul in a music-store window, and disliked it. Although his contract required him to pose with the guitar, he said it was not "his" instrument and asked Gibson to remove his name from the headstock. Others claimed that Paul ended his endorsement contract with Gibson during his divorce to avoid having his wife get his endorsement money.[33] At Paul's request, Gibson renamed the guitar "Gibson SG", which stands for "Solid Guitar", and it also became one of the company's best sellers.

The original Gibson Les Paul-guitar design regained popularity when Eric Clapton began playing the instrument a few years later, although he also played an SG and an ES-335. Paul resumed his relationship with Gibson and endorsed the original Gibson Les Paul guitar from that point onwards. His personal Gibson Les Pauls were much modified by him—Paul always used his own self-wound pickups and customized methods of switching between pickups on his guitars. To this day, various models of Gibson Les Paul guitars are used all over the world by both novice and professional guitarists. A less-expensive version of the Gibson Les Paul guitar is also manufactured for Gibson's lower-priced Epiphone brand.[34]

On January 30, 1962, the US Patent and Trademark Office issued Paul a patent, Patent No. 3,018,680, for an "Electrical Music Instrument."[35]

Multitrack-recording innovations

Paul had never been happy with the way his records sounded. During a post-recording session talk with Bing Crosby, the crooner suggested Paul try building his own recording studio so he might be able to get the sound he wanted. At first Paul discounted the idea only to give it a few more minutes thought before deciding Crosby was right. Paul started his own studio in the garage of his home on Hollywood's North Curson Street. The studio drew many other famous vocalists and musicians who wanted the benefit of Paul's expertise. The home and studio are still standing, but both had been moved to Pasadena at some point after Paul no longer owned the home.[36]

In 1948, Les Paul was given one of the first Ampex Model 200A reel-to-reel audio tape recording decks by Crosby and went on to use Ampex's eight track "Sel-Sync" machines for Multitrack recording. Capitol Records released a recording that had begun as an experiment in Paul's garage, entitled "Lover (When You're Near Me)", which featured Paul playing eight different parts on electric guitar, some of them recorded at half-speed, hence "double-fast" when played back at normal speed for the master. ("Brazil", similarly recorded, was the B-side.) This was the first time that Les Paul used multitracking in a recording (Paul had been shopping his multitracking technique, unsuccessfully, since the '30s. Much to his dismay, Sidney Bechet used it in 1941 to play half a dozen instruments on "Sheik of Araby"). These recordings were made not with magnetic tape, but with acetate discs. Paul would record a track onto a disk, then record himself playing another part with the first. He built the multitrack recording with overlaid tracks, rather than parallel ones as he did later. By the time he had a result he was satisfied with, he had discarded some five hundred recording disks.

Paul even built his own disc-cutter assembly, based on automobile parts. He favored the flywheel from a Cadillac for its weight and flatness. Even in these early days, he used the acetate-disk setup to record parts at different speeds and with delay, resulting in his signature sound with echoes and birdsong-like guitar riffs. When he later began using magnetic tape, the major change was that he could take his recording rig on tour with him, even making episodes for his fifteen-minute radio show in his hotel room. He later worked with Ross Snyder in the design of the first eight-track recording deck (built for him by Ampex for his home studio.)[36][37]

Electronics engineer Jack Mullin had been assigned to a U.S. Army Signal Corps unit stationed in France during World War II. On a mission in Germany near the end of the war, he acquired and later shipped home a German Magnetophon (tape recorder) and fifty reels of I.G. Farben plastic recording tape. Back in the U.S., Mullin rebuilt and developed the machine with the intention of selling it to the film industry, and held a series of demonstrations which quickly became the talk of the American audio industry.

Within a short time, Crosby had hired Mullin to record and produce his radio shows and master his studio recordings on tape. Crosby invested US$50,000 in a Northern California electronics firm, Ampex. With Crosby's backing, Mullin and Ampex created the Ampex Model 200, the world's first commercially produced reel-to-reel audio tape recorder. Crosby gave Les Paul the second Model 200 to be produced.

Les Paul invented **Sound on Sound** recording using this machine by placing an additional playback head, located before the conventional erase/record/playback heads. This allowed Paul to play along with a previously recorded track, both of which were mixed together on to a new track. This was a mono tape recorder with just one track across the entire width of quarter-inch tape; thus, the recording was "destructive" in the sense that the original recording was permanently replaced with the new, mixed recording. He eventually enhanced this by using one tape machine to play back the original recording and a second to record the combined track. This preserved the original recording[38]

Les Paul bought the first Ampex 8-track recorder in 1957.[38] Rein Narma built a custom 8-channel mixing console for Les Paul.[39] The mixing board included in-line equalization and vibrato effects The recorder was named "the octopus" and the mixing console was named "the monster".[40] The name octopus was inspired by W. C. Fields who was the first person Les Paul played a multi-track recording to. Upon hearing the recording W. C. Fields said: 'My boy, you sound like an octopus."[41]

Les Paul & Mary Ford

Paul met country-western singer Colleen Summers in 1945. They began working together in 1948, at which time she adopted the stage name Mary Ford. They were married in 1949. The couple's hits included "How High the Moon", "Bye Bye Blues", "Song in Blue", "Don'cha Hear Them Bells", "The World Is Waiting for the Sunrise", and "Vaya con Dios". These songs featured Ford harmonizing with herself.

Like Crosby, Paul and Ford used the now-ubiquitous recording technique known as close miking,[36] where the microphone is less than 6 inches (15 cm) from the singer's mouth. This produces a more-intimate, less-reverberant sound than is heard when a singer is 1 foot (30 cm) or more from the microphone. When implemented using a cardioid-patterned microphone, it emphasizes low-frequency sounds in the voice due to a cardioid microphone's proximity effect and can give a more relaxed feel because the performer isn't working so hard. The result is a singing style which diverged strongly from unamplified theater-style singing, as might be heard in musical comedies of the 1930s and 1940s.

Radio and television programs

Paul had hosted a fifteen-minute radio program, *The Les Paul Show*, on NBC radio in 1950, featuring his trio (himself, Ford and rhythm player Eddie Stapleton) and his electronics, recorded from their home and with gentle humor between Paul and Ford bridging musical selections, some of which had already been successful on records, some of which anticipated the couple's recordings, and many of which presented re-interpretations of such jazz and pop selections as "In the Mood", "Little Rock Getaway", "Brazil" and "Tiger Rag". Over ten of these shows survive among old-time radio collectors today.[42]

The show also appeared on television a few years later with the same format, but excluding the trio and retitled *The Les Paul & Mary Ford Show* (also known as *Les Paul & Mary Ford at Home*) with "Vaya Con Dios" as a theme song. Sponsored by Warner Lambert's Listerine mouthwash, it was widely syndicated during 1954–1955, and was only five minutes (one or two songs) long on film, therefore used as a brief interlude or fill-in in programming schedules. Since Paul created the entire show himself, including audio and video, he maintained the original recordings and was in the process of restoring them to current quality standards until his death.[43]

During his radio shows, Paul introduced the fictional "Les Paulverizer" device, which multiplies anything fed into it, like a guitar sound or a voice. Paul has stated that the idea was to explain to the audience how his single guitar could be multiplied to become a group of guitars. The device even became the subject of comedy, with Ford multiplying herself and her vacuum cleaner with it so she could finish the housework faster.

Later career

Les Paul, May 2004

In 1965, Paul went into semi-retirement, although he did return to the studio occasionally. He and Ford had divorced in December 1962, as she could no longer cope with the traveling lifestyle their act required of them. Paul's most-recognizable recordings from then through the mid-1970s were an album for London Records/Phase 4 Stereo, *Les Paul Now* (1968), on which he updated some of his earlier hits; and, backed by some of Nashville's celebrated studio musicians, a meld of jazz and country improvisation with fellow guitar virtuoso Chet Atkins, *Chester and Lester* (1976), for RCA Victor.

In 1987, Paul underwent heart surgery. He then returned to active live performance, continuing into his 80s even though he often found it painful to play the guitar because of arthritis in his hands. In 2006, at age 90, he won two Grammys at the 48th Annual Grammy Awards for his album *Les Paul & Friends: American Made World Played*. He also performed every Monday night, accompanied by a trio which included guitarist Lou Pallo, bassist Paul Nowinksi (and later, Nicki Parrott) and pianist John Colaianni, originally at Fat Tuesdays, and later at the Iridium Jazz Club on Broadway in the Times Square area of New York City.[44][45][46]

Les and his trio held court at the Iridium Jazz Club in midtown Manhattan for many years, playing every Monday night. Often, a wide array of other artists would appear and sit in with or sing in front of the trio. A tribute trio still plays the Monday dates.

Composer Richard Stein (1909–1992) sued Paul for plagiarism, charging that Paul's "Johnny (Is the Boy for Me)" was taken from Stein's 1937 song "Sanie cu zurgălăi" (Romanian for "Sleigh with Bells"). A 2000 cover version of "Johnny" by Belgian musical group Vaya Con Dios that credited Paul prompted another action by the Romanian Musical Performing and Mechanical Rights Society.[47]

For many years Les Paul would sometimes surprise radio hosts Steve King and Johnnie Putman with a call to the "Life After Dark Show" on WGN (AM) in Chicago. These calls would take place in the wee hours of Tuesday Morning following his long-running Monday evening show at the Iridium Jazz Club in Manhattan. Until they ended their show on WGN, Steve and Johnnie continued to honor Les on Tuesday Mornings at 2:35 AM with their segment "A Little More Les" drawing from around 30 hours of recorded conversations with Les.

Death

On August 13, 2009,[5][6] Paul died of complications from pneumonia at White Plains Hospital in White Plains, New York.[48] His family and friends were by his side.[49] Paul is survived by his four children and his companion Arlene Palmer.[50] His attorney told the media that he had made several hospital stays over the previous few months.[51] His last concert took place a few weeks before his death.

Upon learning of his death many artists and popular musicians paid tribute by publicly expressing their sorrow. After learning of Paul's death, former Guns N' Roses guitarist Slash called him "vibrant and full of positive energy.", while Richie Sambora, lead guitarist of Bon Jovi, referred to him as "revolutionary in the music business". U2 guitarist The Edge said, "His legacy as a musician and inventor will live on and his influence on rock and roll will never be forgotten." [52][53][54]

On August 21, 2009, he was buried near Milwaukee in Waukesha, Wisconsin at Prairie Home Cemetery which indicated that his plot would be in an area where visitors can easily view it.[55][56] Like his funeral in New York on August 19, the burial was private, but earlier in the day a public memorial viewing of the closed casket was held in

Milwaukee at Discovery World with 1,500 attendees who were offered free admission to the Les Paul House of Sound exhibit for the day.[57]

Awards and honors

Paul was initiated into the Gamma Delta chapter of the Tau Kappa Epsilon fraternity at the University of Miami in 1952.[58] He has earned the Presidential award from the Tau Kappa Epsilon fraternity.[59]

In 1979, Paul and Ford's 1951 recording of "How High the Moon" was inducted into the Grammy Hall of Fame.[60] Paul received a Grammy Trustees Award for his lifetime achievements in 1983, and in 2001 the Special Merit/Technical Grammy Award.[61]

In 1988, Paul was inducted into the Rock and Roll Hall of Fame by Jeff Beck, who said, "I've copied more licks from Les Paul than I'd like to admit." In 1991, the Mix Foundation established an annual award in his name; the Les Paul Award which honors "individuals or institutions that have set the highest standards of excellence in the creative application of audio technology".[62] In 2005, he was inducted into the National Inventors Hall of Fame for his development of the solid-body electric guitar.[63] In 2006, Paul was inducted into the National Association of Broadcasters Hall of Fame. He was named an honorary member of the Audio Engineering Society.[64] In 2007, he was awarded the National Medal of Arts.[65]

A one-hour biographical documentary film *The Wizard of Waukesha* was shown at the Los Angeles International Film Exposition (FILMEX) March 4–21, 1980, and later on PBS television. A biographical, feature-length documentary titled *Chasing Sound: Les Paul at 90* made its world première on May 9, 2007, at the Downer Theater in Milwaukee, Wisconsin. Paul appeared at the event and spoke briefly to the enthusiastic crowd. The film is distributed by Koch Entertainment and was broadcast on PBS on July 11, 2007, as part of its American Masters series[66][67] and was broadcast on October 17, 2008, on BBC Four as part of its Guitar Night. The première coincided with the final part of a three-part documentary by the BBC broadcast on BBC One *The Story of the Guitar*.

In June 2008, an exhibit showcasing his legacy and featuring items from his personal collection opened at Discovery World in Milwaukee.[68] The exhibit was facilitated by a group of local musicians under the name Partnership for the Arts and Creative Excellence (PACE).[69] Paul played a concert in Milwaukee to coincide with the opening of the exhibit.[70]

Paul's hometown of Waukesha is planning a permanent exhibit to be called "The Les Paul experience."[71]

In July 2005, a 90th-birthday tribute concert was held at Carnegie Hall in New York City. After performances by Steve Miller, Peter Frampton, Jose Feliciano and a number of other contemporary guitarists and vocalists, Paul was presented with a commemorative guitar from the Gibson Guitar Corporation.[72]

On November 15, 2008, he received the American Music Masters award through the Rock and Roll Hall of Fame at a tribute concert at the State Theater in Cleveland, Ohio. Among the many guest performers were Duane Eddy, Eric Carmen, Lonnie Mack, Jennifer Batten, Jeff "Skunk" Baxter, Dennis Coffey, James Burton, Billy Gibbons, Lenny Kaye, Steve Lukather, Barbara Lynn, Katy Moffatt, Alannah Myles, Richie Sambora, The Ventures and Slash.

In February 2009, only months prior to his death, Les Paul sat down with Scott Vollweiler of Broken Records Magazine, in which would be one of Les Paul's final interviews. His candid answers were direct and emotional. Broken Records Magazine had planned to run that cover feature the following month but due to delays was held until the summer. 3 days before the release, Les Paul died. The issue would be his final cover feature of his storied career.[73]

In April 2009, Gerbren Deves did an extensive interview with him, which was published in the English Guitar Magazine just after his death.

In August, 2009, Paul was named one of the ten best electric guitar players of all-time by *Time* magazine.[74]

On June 9, 2010, which would have been Les Paul's 95th birthday, a tribute concert featuring Jeff Beck, Imelda May, Gary U.S. Bonds and Brian Setzer among others, was held at the Iridium Jazz Club where Les Paul played nearly every week almost to the end of his life. The concert was released on the live album Rock 'n' Roll Party (Honoring Les Paul) in 2011.

On June 9–10, 2011 Google celebrated what would have been Paul's 96th birthday with a Google doodle of an interactive guitar.[75]

On November 23, 2011, Paul was ranked at #18 on *Rolling Stone*'s "100 Greatest Guitarists of All Time".[76]

In 2010, Paul was inducted into the New Jersey Hall of Fame.[77]

Personal life

Paul married Virginia Webb in 1938. They had two children, Gene (Lester Jr.), born in 1941 and named after actor-songwriter Gene Lockhart, and Russell (Rusty), born 1944, before divorcing in 1949. Later that year, Paul and Mary Ford (born Iris Colleen Summers) were married. They adopted a girl, Colleen, in 1958 and their son Robert (Bobby) was born the following year. They had also lost a child, who was born prematurely and died only four days old. Les Paul and Mary Ford divorced in 1963.[78]

Les Paul with pianist John Colianni.

Paul was the instructor of rock guitarist Steve Miller of the Steve Miller Band, to whom Paul gave his first guitar lesson.[79] Miller's father was best man at Paul's 1949 wedding to Mary Ford.

Paul resided for many years in Mahwah, New Jersey.

Discography

Hit singles

Year	Single	Chart positions			
		US	US R&B	US Country	UK[80]
1945	"It's Been a Long, Long Time"(with Bing Crosby)	1			
1946	"Rumors Are Flying"(with Andrews Sisters)	4			
1948	"Lover"	21			
	"Brazil"	22			
	"What Is This Thing Called Love?"	11			
1950	"Nola"	9			
	"Goofus"	21			
	"Little Rock Getaway"	18			
	"Tennessee Waltz"	6			
1951	"Jazz Me Blues"	23			
	"Mockin' Bird Hill"(gold record)	2		7	
	"How High the Moon"(gold record)	1	2		
	"Josephine"	12			

	"I Wish I Had Never Seen Sunshine"	18			
	"The World Is Waiting for the Sunrise"(gold record)	2			
	"Whispering"	7			
	"Just One More Chance"	5			
	"Jingle Bells"	10			
1952	"Tiger Rag"	2			
	"I'm Confessin'"	13			
	"Carioca"	14			
	"In the Good Old Summertime"	15			
	"Smoke Rings"	14			
	"Meet Mr. Callahan"	5			
	"Take Me In Your Arms and Hold Me"	15			
	"Lady of Spain"	8			
	"My Baby's Comin' Home"	7			
1953	"Bye Bye Blues"	5			
	"I'm Sittin' On Top of the World"	10			
	"Sleep"	21			
	"Vaya Con Dios"(gold record)	1			7
	"Johnny"	15			
	"The Kangaroo"	25			
	"Don'cha Hear Them Bells"	13			
1954	"I Really Don't Want To Know"	11			
	"I'm a Fool To Care"	6			
	"Wither Thou Goest"	10			
	"Mandolino"	19			
1955	"Hummingbird"	7			
	"Amukiriki"	38			
	"Magic Melody"	96			
1956	"Texas Lady"	91			
	"Moritat"	49			
	"Nuevo Laredo"	91			
1957	"Cinco Robles"	35			
1958	"Put a Ring On My Finger"	32			
1961	"Jura"	37			
	"It's Been a Long Long Time"	105			

Albums

- *Feedback* (1944)—compilation
- *Les Paul Trio* (1946)—compilation
- *Hawaiian Paradise* (1949)
- *The New Sound* (1950)
- *Les Paul's New Sound, Volume 2* (1951)
- *Bye Bye Blues!* (1952)
- *Gallopin' Guitars* (1952)—compilation
- *The Hit Makers!* (1953)
- *Les and Mary* (1955)
- *Time to Dream* (1957)

- *Lover's Luau* (1959)
- *The Hits of Les and Mary* (1960)—compilation
- *Bouquet of Roses* (1962)

- *Warm and Wonderful* (1962)
- *Swingin' South* (1963)
- *Fabulous Les Paul and Mary Ford* (1965)
- *Les Paul Now!* (1968)
- *Guitar Tapestry*
- *Lover*
- *The Guitar Artistry of Les Paul* (1971)
- *The World is Still Waiting for the Sunrise* (1974)—compilation

- *The Best of Les Paul with Mary Ford* (1974)—compilation
- *Chester and Lester* (1976)—with Chet Atkins
- *Guitar Monsters* (1977)—with Chet Atkins
- *Les Paul and Mary Ford* (1978)—compilation
- *Multi Trackin'* (1979)
- *All-Time Greatest Hits* (1983)—compilation
- *The Very Best of Les Paul with Mary Ford'*
- *Famille Nombreuse* (1992)—compilation
- *The World Is Waiting* (1992)—compilation
- *The Best of the Capitol Masters: Selections From "The Legend and the Legacy" Box Set* (1992)—compilation
- *All-Time Greatest Hits* (1992)—compilation
- *Their All-Time Greatest Hits* (1995)—compilation
- *Les Paul: The Legend and the Legacy* (1996; a four-CD box set chronicling his years with Capitol Records)
- *16 Most Requested Songs* (1996)—compilation
- *The Complete Decca Trios—Plus (1936–1947)* (1997)—compilation
- *California Melodies* (2003)
- *Les Paul – The Legendary Fred Waring Broadcasts (2004)*
- *Les Paul & Friends: American Made World Played* (2005)
- *Les Paul And Friends: A Tribute To A Legend* (2008)

Singles

- "It's Been a Long, Long Time"—Bing Crosby & The Les Paul Trio (1945), #1 on Billboard Pop singles chart, 1 week, December 8
- "Rumors Are Flying"—Andrews Sisters & Les Paul (1946)
- "Guitar Boogie" (1947)
- "Lover (When You're Near Me)" (1948)
- "Brazil" (1948)
- "What Is This Thing Called Love?" (1948)
- "Nola" (1950)

- "Goofus" (1950)

- "Little Rock 69 Getaway" (1950/1951)

- "Tennessee Waltz"—Les Paul & Mary Ford (1950/1951), #1, Cashbox
- "Mockingbird Hill"—Les Paul & Mary Ford (1951), #1, Cashbox
- "How High The Moon"—Les Paul & Mary Ford (1951), #1, Billboard Pop singles chart, 9 weeks, April 21 – June 16; #1, Cashbox, 2 weeks; #2, R&B chart
- "I Wish I Had Never Seen Sunshine"—Les Paul & Mary Ford (1951)

- "Take Me In Your Arms and Hold Me"—Les Paul & Mary Ford (1952)
- "Lady of Spain" (1952)
- "My Baby's Coming Home"—Les Paul & Mary Ford (1952)
- "Bye Bye Blues"—Les Paul & Mary Ford (1953)
- "I'm Sitting on Top of the World"—Les Paul & Mary Ford (1953)
- "Sleep" (Fred Waring's theme song) (1953)
- "Vaya Con Dios"—Les Paul & Mary Ford (1953), #1, Billboard Pop singles chart, 11 weeks, August 8 – October 3, November 7–14; #1, Cashbox, 5 weeks
- "Johnny (Is The Boy for Me)"—Les Paul & Mary Ford (1953), #15, Billboard; #25, Cashbox
- "Don'cha Hear Them Bells"—Les Paul & Mary Ford (1953), #13, Billboard; #32, Cashbox
- "The Kangaroo" (1953), #25, Billboard; #23, Cashbox
- "I Really Don't Want To Know"—Les Paul & Mary Ford (1954)
- "I'm A Fool To Care"—Les Paul & Mary Ford (1954)

- "Whither Thou Goest"—Les Paul & Mary Ford (1954)

- "The World Is Waiting for the Sunrise"—Les Paul & Mary Ford (1951), #2, Billboard; #3, Cashbox
- "Just One More Chance"—Les Paul & Mary Ford (1951)
- "Jazz Me Blues" (1951)
- "Josephine" (1951)
- "Whispering" (1951)
- "Jingle Bells" (1951)
- "Tiger Rag"—Les Paul & Mary Ford (1952), #2, Billboard; #8, Cashbox
- "I'm Confessin' (That I Love You)"—Les Paul & Mary Ford (1952)
- "Carioca" (1952)
- "In the Good Old Summertime"—Les Paul & Mary Ford (1952)
- "Smoke Rings"—Les Paul & Mary Ford (1952)
- "Meet Mister Callaghan" (1952), #5, Billboard

- "Mandolino"—Les Paul & Mary Ford (1954), #19, Billboard
- "Song in Blue"—Les Paul & Mary Ford (1954), #17, Cashbox
- "Hummingbird"—Les Paul & Mary Ford (1955)
- "Amukiriki (The Lord Willing)"—Les Paul & Mary Ford (1955)
- "Magic Melody"—Les Paul & Mary Ford (1955)
- "Texas Lady"—Les Paul & Mary Ford (1956)
- "Moritat" (Theme from "Three Penny Opera") (1956)
- "Nuevo Laredo"—Les Paul & Mary Ford (1956)
- "Cinco Robles (Five Oaks)"—Les Paul & Mary Ford (1957)
- "Put a Ring On My Finger"—Les Paul & Mary Ford (1958)
- "Jura (I Swear I Love You)"—Les Paul & Mary Ford (1961)
- "Love Sneakin' Up On You"-Les Paul, Joss Stone & Sting (2005)

Compositions

Paul was also a prolific composer. Some of the songs he wrote were "Song in Blue", "Cryin'", "Hip-billy Boogie", "Suspicion", "Mandolino", "Magic Melody", "Don'cha Hear Them Bells", "The Kangaroo", "Big-Eyed Gal", "All I Need is You", "Mammy's Boogie", "Pacific Breeze", "Mountain Railroad", "Move Along, Baby (Don't Waste My Time)", "Five Alarm Fire", and "Walkin' and Whistlin' Blues".

References

[1] Farber, Jim (August 13, 2009). "Electric Guitar Hero Les Paul Dead at 94: Hit-Maker, Musical Designer, Pioneer" (http://www.nydailynews.com/entertainment/music/2009/08/14/2009-08-14_electric_guitar_hero_les_paul_dead_at_94_career_spanned_from_hitmaker_to_musical.html). *Daily News)*. Accessed August 24, 2009.

[2] "Les Paul Obituary" (http://www.nytimes.com/2009/08/14/arts/music/14paul.html?_r=1&pagewanted=1). *New York Times.* . Retrieved 2009-09-29.

[3] http://www.lespaulfoundation.org/

[4] "Guitar legend Les Paul dies at 94 - Entertainment - Music - TODAY.com" (http://today.msnbc.msn.com/id/32403755/ns/today-entertainment/t/guitar-legend-les-paul-dies/#.Tx9MCG_OXQg). Today.msnbc.msn.com. 2009-08-13. . Retrieved 2012-03-26.

[5] "the site of LES PAUL – The Wizard of Waukesha" (http://www.lespaulonline.com/indexo.html). Lespaulonline.com. . Retrieved March 27, 2011.

[6] "In Pictures: 'Les Paul Memorial Service'" (http://www.monstersandcritics.com/people/features/article_1496730.php/In-Pictures-Les-Paul-Memorial-Service?page=4). Monsters and Critics. August 21, 2009. . Retrieved March 27, 2011.

[7] Voices from the Smithsonian Associates. *Les Paul, Musician and Inventor.* (http://web.archive.org/web/20071020014312/http://smithsonianassociates.org/programs/paul/paul.asp) Archived at www.archive.org.

[8] Guitarist and recording pioneer Les Paul dies, aged 94 (http://www.list.co.uk/article/19914-guitarist-and-recording-pioneer-les-paul-dies-aged-94/). The List. August 12, 2009.

[9] "The Wizard Of Waukesha" (http://www.pbs.org/wnet/americanmasters/episodes/les-paul/chasing-sound/100/). Pbs.org. .

[10] Houston, Frank (July 8, 1999). "Father of invention" (http://archive.salon.com/people/feature/1999/07/08/paul/print.html). *Salon.com.* . Retrieved August 14, 2009.

[11] Staff writer (October 12, 2005). "Les Paul, 90, Releases Tribute Album" (http://www.cbc.ca/arts/story/2005/10/12/lespaul_20051012.html). *CBC.* Accessed August 24, 2009.

[12] Swing Licks for C6th Lap Steel (http://steelguitarforum.com/Forum8/HTML/001019.html). The Steel Guitar Forum.

[13] Benson, John (November 12, 2008). Rock hall to honor Les Paul (http://www.vindy.com/news/2008/nov/12/rock-hall-to-honor-les-paul/). Vindy.com.

[14] "Exhibits | The Rock and Roll Hall of Fame and Museum" (http://rockhall.com/exhibits). Rockhall.com. . Retrieved March 27, 2011.

[15] "The Architects of Rock and Roll featuring Les Paul, Alan Freed and Sam Phillips | The Rock and Roll Hall of Fame and Museum" (http://rockhall.com/exhibits/the-architects/). Rockhall.com. . Retrieved 2011-08-19.

[16] "Book Excerpt: The Early Years of the Les Paul Legacy 1915–1963" (http://www.gibson.com/en-us/Lifestyle/Features/the-les-paul-legacy/). Gibson.com. . Retrieved March 27, 2011.

[17] Masino, Susan; Paul, Les (2003). *Famous Wisconsin Musicians*. Oregon, Wisconsin: Badger Books. pp. 9–11. ISBN 1-878569-88-0.

[18] Henry, David (August 12, 2009). "Les Paul, Pioneer of Electric Guitar, Inventor, Dies at 94" (http://www.bloomberg.com/apps/ news?pid=20601088&sid=aD_WpRVvFQwk). *Bloomberg*. Accessed August 24, 2009.

[19] American Masters (2007 Season)—"Les Paul: Chasing Sound" (http://www.thirteen.org/pressroom/release.php?get=2539)—thirteen WNET New York

[20] "Articles" (http://classicjazzguitar.com/articles/article.jsp?article=25). Classic Jazz Guitar. . Retrieved March 27, 2011.

[21] (August 14, 2009). (http://www.nytimes.com/2009/08/14/arts/music/14paul.html) *The New York Times* (website registration required).

[22] Ladd, Patty (22 October 2009). "Cinemax to honor 'Edison' of music" (http://news.google.com/newspapers?id=CfNYAAAAIBAJ& sjid=doUMAAAAIBAJ&pg=1140,3217614&dq=grammy+hall+of+fame+jo+stafford&hl=en). The Vindicator. . Retrieved 4 May 2011.

[23] "ClassicJazzGuitar.com" (http://www.classicjazzguitar.com/articles/article.jsp?article=25). ClassicJazzGuitar.com. . Retrieved 2012-09-10.

[24] Kaufman, Gil. "Paul Les" (http://www.mtv.com/news/articles/1618673/20090813/paul_les.jhtml). MTV News. .

[25] http://www.namm.org/library/oral-history/les-paul

[26] liner notes from Chet Atkins/Jim Atkins 1963 RCA Camden LP #CAL-753, "The Guitar Genius"

[27] Atkins, Chet; Neely, Bill (1974). *Country Gentleman*. Chicago: H. Regnery. ISBN 978-0-8092-9051-2

[28] Tianen, Dave (2009-08-26). "The Wizard of Waukesha" (http://www.pbs.org/wnet/americanmasters/episodes/les-paul/chasing-sound/ 100/). Milwaukee Journal Sentinel. .

[29] Sforza, John: "Swing It! The Andrews Sisters Story;" University Press of Kentucky, 2000; 289 pages.

[30] Fresh Air from WHYY. "Guitar Hero: Les Paul, 1915–2009" (http://www.npr.org/templates/story/story.php?storyId=111888401). Npr.org. . Retrieved March 27, 2011.

[31] "The Log" (http://www.dkimages.com/discover/Home/Performing-Arts/Music/Instruments/String/Guitars/Electric-Guitar/Les-Paul/ Les-Paul-01.html). DK Images. . Retrieved March 27, 2011.

[32] "Epiphone: A History" (http://www.epiphone.com/History.aspx). Epiphone.com. . Retrieved 23 February 2012.

[33] "Interview I July 19, 1999, at the Iridium jazz club, New York City" (http://www.jinxmagazine.com/les_paul.html). Jinx Magazine. July 19, 1999. . Retrieved March 27, 2011.

[34] "Epiphone Les Paul Standard" (http://www.epiphone.com/Products/Les-Paul/Les-Paul-Standard.aspx). Epiphone.com. . Retrieved 23 February 2012.

[35] "Patents" (http://www.google.com/patents/about?id=Ce9TAAAAEBAJ&dq=3,018,680). Google. . Retrieved March 27, 2011.

[36] Lawrence, Robb, ed. (2008). *The Early Years of the Les Paul Legacy: 1915–1963* (http://books.google.com/?id=NqIgLrXaA6QC& pg=PA19&lpg=PA19&dq=les+paul+recorded+andrews+sisters#v=onepage&q=les paul recorded andrews sisters&f=false). Hal Leonard Corporation. pp. 20–21. ISBN 978-0-634-04861-6. . Retrieved 10 May 2011.

[37] "Sel-sync and the 'Ocotpus': How Came to be the First Recorder to Minimize Successive Copying in Overdubs" (http://www.aes.org/ aeshc/docs/sel-sync/snyder_sel-sync.pdf) (PDF). *ARSC Journal*. . Retrieved March 27, 2011.

[38] "Sel-sync and the 'Octopus': How Came to be the First Recorder to Minimize Successive Copying in Overdubs" (http://www.aes.org/ aeshc/docs/sel-sync/snyder_sel-sync.pdf) (PDF). *ARSC Journal*. . Retrieved March 27, 2011.

[39] http://www.mixonline.com/ms/aes2007/2007aes-web-report/Where Audio Comes Alive

[40] http://www.soundonsound.com/sos/jan07/articles/classictracks_0107.htm CLASSIC TRACKS: Les Paul & Mary Ford 'How High The Moon'

[41] http://www.puremusic.com/61les.html THE BEST OF THE CAPITOL MASTERS

[42] "The Les Paul Show" (http://www.archive.org/details/TheLesPaulShow). Archive.org. . Retrieved March 27, 2011.

[43] Cellini, Joe (undated). "Les Paul: Invented Here" (http://www.apple.com/pro/profiles/lespaul/index.html). Apple Inc.. . Retrieved August 24, 2009.

[44] "Iridium Jazz Club" (http://www.iridiumjazzclub.com/). Iridium Jazz Club. . Retrieved March 27, 2011.

[45] Milicia, Joe, "Guitar hero Les Paul ready for Rock Hall tribute," *The Associated Press via Times Union*, p. C8, November 10, 2008, see AP Google website (http://ap.google.com/article/ALeqM5iBP-_uehMM5Ls2dPdOoGf008DWcgD94A6G600). Retrieved November 10, 2008.

[46] Foster, D.R. (June 1, 2009). "Les is more: 93 years old and cooler than you—A Night with the Longstanding Guitar Great" (http://newyork. decider.com/articles/les-is-more-93-years-old-and-cooler-than-you,28498/). *The A.V. Club*. Accessed August 15, 2009

[47] Nicoleanu, Anca (February 2, 2007). "Zici că n-ai plagiat şi, gata, ai scăpat" (http://www.cotidianul.ro/ zici_ca_n_ai_plagiat_si_gata_ai_scapat-22511.html). . Retrieved June 19, 2009. (non-English language)

[48] Newels, Eric (August 17, 2009). "Music Great Les Paul Dies at 94" (http://www.idiomag.com/peek/97288/les_paul). *idiomag*. . Retrieved August 21, 2009.

[49] Caine, Paul (August 13, 2009). "R.I.P. Les Paul: pioneering guitarist, inventor, New York character" (http://newyork.decider.com/ articles/rip-les-paul-pioneering-guitarist-inventor-new-yor,31640/). The A.V. Club. . Retrieved August 14, 2009.

[50] Russell, Tony (August 13, 2009). "Les Paul Guitarist and inventor with huge influence on pop and jazz" (http://www.guardian.co.uk/ music/2009/aug/13/obituary-les-paul). *The Guardian*. Accessed August 24, 2009.

[51] Tourtellotte, Bob (August 13, 2009). "Legendary guitarist, inventor Les Paul dies, age 94" (http://www.reuters.com/article/topNews/ idUSTRE57C3TI20090813). *Reuters*. . Retrieved August 13, 2009.

[52] Staff writer (August 13, 2009). "Les Paul Remembered: Guitar Greats on Their True Hero" (http://www.rollingstone.com/rockdaily/ index.php/2009/08/13/les-paul-remembered-guitar-greats-on-their-true-hero/). *Rolling Stone*. . Retrieved August 13, 2009.

[53] Jack Malvern (August 13, 2009). "Musicians pay tribute to the 'original guitar hero' Les Paul" (http://entertainment.timesonline.co.uk/tol/arts_and_entertainment/music/article6795384.ece). London: *The Times*. . Retrieved August 13, 2009.

[54] Sheridan, Luke (August 14, 2009). "Les Paul, 94: Guitar legend" (http://www.thestar.com/news/obituary/article/681159). *The Associated Press via Toronto Star*. . Retrieved August 15, 2009.

[55] Itzkoff, Dave (August 18, 2009). "Funeral Plans Announced for Les Paul" (http://artsbeat.blogs.nytimes.com/2009/08/18/funeral-plans-announced-for-les-paul/). *The New York Times*. . Retrieved May 7, 2010.

[56] "Les Paul comes home to his mother" (http://www.jsonline.com/news/waukesha/54027427.html). JSOnline. . Retrieved March 27, 2011.

[57] "Saying goodbye to Les Paul" (http://www.jsonline.com/news/milwaukee/53940442.html). JSOnline. August 21, 2009. . Retrieved March 27, 2011.

[58] "University of Miami TKE" (http://www.tke-miami.com/lespaul.php). Tke-miami.com. . Retrieved March 27, 2011.

[59] "TKE News 105" (http://www.tke.org/news/105). Tke.org. . Retrieved 2011-08-19.

[60] "Grammy Hall of Fame Award Past Recipients" (http://www.grammy.org/recording-academy/awards/hall-of-fame#h). grammy.com. . Retrieved August 19, 2009.

[61] "Technical GRAMMY Award" (http://www.grammy.org/recording-academy/producers-and-engineers/awards). grammy.com. . Retrieved January 29, 2012.

[62] Mix Foundation. *Les Paul Award Winners* (http://www.mixfoundation.org/tec/lespaul_winners.html).

[63] "Inventor Profile, National Inventors Hall of Fame" (http://www.invent.org/hall_of_fame/225.html). Invent.org. . Retrieved March 27, 2011.

[64] List of Awardees of the AES (http://www.aes.org/info/awards.cfm).

[65] "Lifetime Honors – National Medal of Arts" (http://www.nea.gov/honors/medals/medalists_year.html#07). Nea.gov. . Retrieved March 27, 2011.

[66] *Les Paul: Chasing Sound* (http://www.lespaulfilm.com/).

[67] *American Masters—Les Paul* (http://www.pbs.org/wnet/americanmasters/database/paul_l.html).

[68] Williams, Scott (April 30, 2008). "Discovery World Lands Les Paul Exhibit—Guitar Wiz Sees No Effect on Waukesha Museum" (http://www.jsonline.com/story/index.aspx?id=745264) *Milwaukee Journal Sentinel*. Accessed August 24, 2009.

[69] Williams, Scott (May 5, 2008). "Their Role is Instrumental—Musicians' Connections Help bring Les Paul Exhibit to Milwaukee" (http://www.jsonline.com/news/waukesha/29512884.html). *Milwaukee Journal Sentinel*. . Retrieved August 24, 2009.

[70] Tianen, Dave (June 23, 2008). "Paul Brings Bit of Manhattan to the Pabst" (http://www.jsonline.com/story/index.aspx?id=764817). *Milwaukee Journal Sentinel*. Accessed August 24, 2009.

[71] Farabaugh, Kane (December 27, 2007). "At 92, Music Pioneer Les Paul Still Performing" (http://voanews.com/english/archive/2007-12/2007-12-26-voa47.cfm). *Voice of America*. . Retrieved August 24, 2009.

[72] Landers, Rick (July 3, 2005). "Les Paul Tribute Concert at Carnegie Hall" (http://www.modernguitars.com/archives/000877.html). Modern Guitars Magazine. . Retrieved August 14, 2009.

[73] "Broken Records Magazine, Les Paul Issue" (http://brokenrecordsonline.com/lespaul_issue_digital.pdf/). Brokenrecordsonline.com. . Retrieved March 27, 2011.

[74] by Dave on August 24, 2009 (August 24, 2009). "Fretbase, Time Magazine Picks the 10 Best Electric Guitar Players" (http://www.fretbase.com/blog/2009/08/time-magazine-picks-the-10-best-electric-guitar-players-including-yngwie/). Fretbase.com. . Retrieved March 27, 2011.

[75] Jemima Kiss (June 9, 2011). "Les Paul: Google's best doodle yet?" (http://www.guardian.co.uk/technology/pda/2011/jun/09/google-doodle-les-paul). The Guardian. . Retrieved June 9, 2011.

[76] "100 Greatest Guitarists: Les Paul" (http://www.rollingstone.com/music/lists/100-greatest-guitarists-20111123/les-paul-19691231). Rolling Stone. November 23, 2011. .

[77] *The Newark Star Ledger*.

[78] "Les Paul and Mary Ford Marriage Profile" (http://marriage.about.com/od/entertainmen1/p/lespaulmaryford.htm). Marriage.about.com. . Retrieved March 27, 2011.

[79] Steve Miller (http://www.allmusic.com/artist/p106068) at Allmusic

[80] Roberts, David (2006). *British Hit Singles & Albums* (19th ed.). London: Guinness World Records Limited. p. 420. ISBN 1-904994-10-5.

External links

- Official website (http://www.lespaulfoundation.org)
- History of Les Paul (http://opportunity.ditudo.com/les_paul.html)
- Les Paul (http://www.imdb.com/name/nm666904/) at the Internet Movie Database
- With Mary Ford, early stereo from 1958: Zing (http://www.youtube.com/watch?v=z2nfgAYeJqU)
- Les Paul: Chasing Sound (http://www.hulu.com/watch/91100/les-paul---chasing-sound) (may require subscription) PBS Documentary on the life of Les Paul, including extended interviews with Paul.
- Remembering Les Paul (http://www.wgnradio.com/shows/stevejohnnie/ wgnam-steve-johnnie-remembering-les-paul,0,6975991.story) Photos and extended interviews with Les on WGN Chicago's Steve & Johnnie early morning show
- Staff writer (August 13, 2009). "Les Paul" (http://www.telegraph.co.uk/news/obituaries/culture-obituaries/ music-obituaries/6024055/Les-Paul.html), obituary at *The Daily Telegraph* (Accessed August 24, 2009)
- "Les Paul, 'The Wizard of Waukesha'" (http://www.wisconsinhistory.org/topics/paul/index.asp), a biography (undated) at the Wisconsin Historical Society's official website
- *Les Paul – Discovery World 2005* (http://www.discoveryworld.org/) video (requires Adobe Flash) at Discovery World's (museum) official website
- *The Les Paul Show* (http://www.archive.org/details/TheLesPaulShow), archive of Paul's NBC radio show at the Internet Archive's official website (includes MP3 files (free) of eleven of their radio shows including their audition show)
- "Les Paul: Legacy of a Guitar Hero" (http://www.life.com/gallery/32122/ les-paul-legacy-of-a-guitar-hero#index/0) at LIFE
- *The Wizard of Waukesha* (http://www.allmovie.com/work/the-wizard-of-waukesha-55022) (1980) at Allmovie's official website
- *Les Paul – 'Miles of Music'* (http://milesofmusic.tv/lespaul.html), two video interviews of and performances by Paul (5–6 minutes each; requires Adobe Flash) with Bob Miles on *Miles of Music* (milesofmusic.tv (http:// milesofmusic.tv/)), a Public-access television cable TV program
- CLASSIC TRACKS: Les Paul & Mary Ford 'How High The Moon' (http://www.soundonsound.com/sos/ jan07/articles/classictracks_0107.htm)
- Photo Library from performances at Iridium (http://www.redhotred.com/photo_main.htm)
- Les Paul's final interview (http://www.performing-musician.com/pm/oct09/articles/lespaul.htm)
- Les Paul - The Man Who Changed it All (http://live4guitar.com/article/les-paul-the-man-who-changed-it-all)
- Les Paul (http://www.findagrave.com/cgi-bin/fg.cgi?page=gr&GRid=40622216) at *Find a Grave*

Lou Levy (publisher)

Lou Levy (1912–1995)[1] was a music publisher during the Tin Pan Alley era of American popular music.

Levy established Leeds Music in 1935 with his friends, lyricist Sammy Cahn and composer Saul Chaplin. He is credited with the discoveries of Cahn and Chaplin, Bob Dylan, Charles Strouse, Richard Adler and Jerry Ross, and Henry Mancini. He also either discovered, managed, or developed the careers of such artists as the Ames Brothers, Petula Clark, Bobby Darin, Eddie Fisher, Connie Francis, Woody Herman, Steve Lawrence, Les Paul, The Andrews Sisters, Buddy Rich, Woody Herman and Charles Aznavour

Levy supplied numerous other singers with hit material: Frank Sinatra with "All or Nothing At All," "Strangers in the Night," and "I'll Never Smile Again"; Petula Clark with "Downtown" and "Call Me"; The Everly Brothers with "Let It Be Me"; Tom Jones with "It's Not Unusual". He published the Beatles' first American hit, "I Want to Hold Your Hand."

Levy served on the Board of Directors of ASCAP from 1958 to 1970 and was honored by ASCAP in 1986 for "outstanding contributions as a major force in music publishing." In 1987 he received the Songwriters Hall of Fame Abe Olman Award for Excellence in Music Publishing.

References

[1] LOU LEVY PUBLISHERS ROUND TABLE 1998 (http://www.ascap.com/musicbiz/loulevy1a.html)

Mafia II

Mafia II	
Developer(s)	2K Czech Massive Bear Studios (Optimisation)[1] Feral Interactive (Mac OS X)[2]
Publisher(s)	2K Games 1C Company Feral Interactive (Mac OS X)[2] Connect2Media (mobile)[3]
Designer(s)	Daniel Vávra Pavel Brzák
Composer(s)	Matus Siroky Adam Kuruc
Engine	Illusion Engine PhysX
Version	1.4 1.03 (PlayStation 3)
Platform(s)	Microsoft Windows, Mac OS X, PlayStation 3, Xbox 360
Release date(s)	• NA 24 August 2010 • AUS 26 August 2010 • EU 27 August 2010[4]
Genre(s)	Third-person shooter, action-adventure
Mode(s)	Single-player
Media/distribution	Optical disc, digital distribution, cloud computing

Mafia II is a third-person action-adventure video game, the sequel to *Mafia: The City of Lost Heaven*. It is developed by 2K Czech, previously known as Illusion Softworks, and is published by 2K Games.[5] Originally announced in August 2007 at the Leipzig Games Convention, it was released on Microsoft Windows, PlayStation 3 and Xbox 360 in August 2010.[4][6] The Mac OS X edition of the game was published by Feral Interactive in December 2011.[2] A version of the game for mobile platforms[7] was developed by Twistbox Entertainment and released in 2010 by Connect2Media.

Gameplay

The game is set in the 1940s-1950s era of Empire Bay, a fictional city based on New York City, Chicago, Los Angeles, Boston and Detroit.[8][9] There are 30-40 vehicles in the game (45 with DLC) as well as licensed music from the era.[10]

Many firearms from the previous game return, such as the Thompson submachine gun and Colt 1911, as well as a pump-action shotgun (though it was changed from a Winchester Model 12 to a Remington 870). New WWII-era weapons like the MP 40, the M3 submachine gun, the MG 42 and the Beretta Model 38 also appear in the game.

Interacting with objects in the environment involves two action buttons- a standard action and a "violent" action (for example, when stealing a car, the player may choose to either pick its lock or break the window glass), used in context-sensitive situations. A map is included as in the original *Mafia* game. The checkpoint system has been completely overhauled.[11] New controls include a cover system that allows the player to hide behind objects (such as generators, walls and large crates) to shoot enemies, rather than just using a crouch while behind an object.

It has been stated by 2K Czech that the game's cutscenes are created by the game engine, in real-time, rather than pre-rendered cutscenes. For example, if the player is riding in a car and a cut scene starts, the player will be driving the same car and if the car is damaged, that too will appear in the cut scene.[12] Certain scenes, however, such as the opening sequence and the Empire Arms Hotel explosion, were presented as pre-rendered Bink videos.

The game has three different in game radio stations, Empire Central Radio, Empire Classic Radio and Delta Radio, with licensed music, news, and commercials. The radio stations includes music from different genres including rock and roll, big band, rhythm and blues, doo-wop, among others with licensed songs by Chuck Berry, The Everly Brothers, Dean Martin, Little Richard, Muddy Waters, Buddy Holly & The Crickets, Bing Crosby, Bill Haley & His Comets, The Chordettes, Bo Diddley, Ricky Nelson, Eddie Cochran, The Champs, The Drifters, The Fleetwoods, Screamin' Jay Hawkins, The Andrews Sisters, among others.

Backstory

Vito Scaletta was born in Sicily in 1925 to a poor family. He was with his father, his mother and his older sister Francesca. His father decides that it is time to move away, and he arranges for his family to immigrate to the Empire Bay area in America, (specifically Little Italy), where they arrive in the early spring of 1931. As fate would have it, the family would end up even worse off in their new home than they had been in Sicily. His father gets a small-time job at the dockyards, eventually turning to alcohol as a release. As he gets older, Vito gets involved with a local criminal named Joe Barbaro, who has been his best friend from a young age. They form a partnership. In 1943, his father drowns on the dockyards during his shift, and left his family struggling for money. Unbeknownst to Vito, his father took out a large loan from a loan-shark before he died, and his mother and sister find out about it shortly after Vito is shipped overseas. This unfortunate event is what turned Vito to crime.

Plot

Army

Vito chose the army, and he ends up in the 504th Parachute Infantry as a paratrooper. He is dispatched to Sicily in July 1943 in Operation Husky, and helps liberate citizens in a small village rebelling against the fascists, but the rest of his squad are killed in the process. He defends the town square from several Italian soldiers with an MG-42 on the balcony, but a tank almost kills him. Just then, Don Calogero Vizzini, head of the Sicilian Mafia, arrives with the US Army. Vito is shot by German troops. He is sent to hospital, and is discharged with two months leave.

February 1945

Vito returns to Empire Bay in February 1945, where Joe awaits him. He takes him for a drink at Freddy's Bar and hears about his situation, makes a call and tells him to stop by tomorrow. At home, his mother and Francesca await him. Next morning, he leaves for Joe's apartment, but a thug threatens Francesca on the street. Vito knocks him off, but he tells him to watch his back. Francesca explains him that before he died, his father borrowed $2000 from a local loan shark, and the thug arrived to collect the debt. He meets Joe, who takes him to Giuseppe, a local shop owner, who gives him discharge papers so he can stay permanently. Joe also introduces him to Mike Bruski, a junkyard owner. After couple of small-time jobs, Vito and Joe start making serious money. In the same time, Vito's mother tells him to work at the docks, where he becomes a loan shark for Derek Pappalardo, a corrupt mafioso and the dock owner, along with Steve Coyne, his personal henchmen.

Serious jobs start with Joe introducing Vito to Henry Tomassino, a made man for a local crime boss, Don Alberto Clemente. Henry instructs Vito to steal precious gas stamps from OPA (Office of Price Administration) and bring them back to him. Although Vito is successful, Henry realizes that the gas stamps expire tomorrow, and orders Vito to resell them all to the gas stations. Vito succeeds in this, and gets a large sum of cash for the job. Vito and Joe also rob a jewelry store, where they are ambushed by the O'Neil Gang, an Irish mob family led by Brian O'Neil, but they manage to escape from him and the police, while Brian and his crew are arrested and sentenced.

After the job, Luca Gurino, Clemente's Capo, orders Henry to assassinate Sidney "Fat Man" Pen, a local loan shark who took large sum of money from Clemente to start his own business, but he didn't return the money and managed to evade Clemente's assassins, and after that, they could become the part of the family, but only if they pay $5000 fee to enter the family, which they reluctantly accept. On the job, Vito is instructed to go to Harry, a black market arms dealer, to get an MG-42 from him. He takes the gun to a rented apartment next to Fat Man's warehouse. They find him and blaze his men with the 'Hitler's Buzzsaw', but are forced to go after him as they are discovered on the scene. They manage to find him, but he shoots Henry in the leg just as he is prepared to shoot him, and Vito and Joe take him to El Greco, a local doctor who treats injured mobsters. At his place, Henry gives Vito $2000 for the successful job, and he takes it to Francesca to repay his father's debt, but the next day, Vito is cornered by the police, and he is arrested for stealing gas stamps from the OPA. As he sold worthless gas stamps to the station, one of the workers sold Vito to the police. Vito is placed on trial, given a lawyer by Clemente (to make sure he wouldn't rat out his business). After two months, Vito is sentenced to 10 years.

Prison

Inside the prison, Vito has an unpleasant surprise when he finds Brian O'Neil, who tries to beat him up to revenge him for sending him to prison. Although Vito manages to defend himself a little bit, he is placed in a solitary confinement, but he catches attention of Leo Galante, local mafioso. He takes Vito to his gym, where he learns to fight and beats up couple good fighters around. Leo's fighter, Pepe, is also injured by the thugs while he was scheduled to fight with O'Neil, so he is instructed to beat him up and break couple of his bones while he is alone in the gym, but Vito is forced to kill O'Neil after he pulls a knife. Vito is relocated to Galante's cell, where he explains that besides Clemente, there are also two families in the Empire Bay; Falcone and Vinci crime Family. Leo himself is consigliere for Frank Vinci, Don of the Vinci Family, while there is also Carlo Falcone, Don of the Falcone Family. Vito tells him about Luca's fee, and Leo tells him that Clemente and Luca will have to speak in front of the Commission, which monitors the Three Families, about this. Under Leo's wing, Vito's sentence is shortened by 4 years. During a visit, Vito's sister Francesca tells him that she is getting married, but also that their mother is ill and isn't getting better. Although Vito leaves all his money for Francesca to get their mother a good doctor and to keep any leftovers as a wedding gift, all of the money instead goes toward their mother's funeral, as she died while Francesca was visiting Vito.

April–September 1951

Vito returns in April 1951. Once out, Vito meets up with Joe, who now works for Eddie Scarpa, Falcone's underboss, and he is welcomed by them, who takes him to Scarpa's cathouse, and they have a wild night of fun. After that, Scarpa remembers that he needs to drop the body of Frankie Potts, that is in the trunk of his car, and Vito is assigned to bury him, ruining his evening. He also goes with Joe to sell cigarettes on Eddie's orders, and they manage to earn plenty of cash, but the truck and the loads are stolen by The Greasers, a local hot rod racing gang, and Joe kills their leader, but Eddie is furious and wants his $2000 back for the truck. Joe and Vito arrive with Steve and Joe's 17-year old neighbour Marty to their hangout and kill the rest of the gang, and Joe and Vito sell their hot rods to Derek and manage to get the cash back to Eddie.

Eddie informs Vito that Harvey "Beans" Epstein, Falcone's accountant, and Antonio "Tony Balls" Balsamo, his bodyguard, have been kidnapped, and they suspect Luca Gurino. Vito goes to Freddy's and finds Luca, he follows him to Clemente's slaughterhouse. Vito manages to get in through the sewers, and he battles through Luca's henchmen and rescues Tony and Beans. Tony helps Vito through the rest of Luca's men and they abduct Luca. Vito leaves, while Tony and Beans kill Luca. The same day, Vito arrives at the Maltese Falcon restaurant to meet Eddie, and he and Joe meet Carlo Falcone, with Frank Vinci, who is here with Galante. Joe and Vito take a bit of their blood and swear the oath, holding the picture of a burning saint, becoming made men for Falcone. Galante is happy because of Vito, but he is disappointed that Vito didn't became a member of the Vinci Family.

Vito, arriving in the family and finally becoming somebody, becomes a wealthy mafioso along with Joe, taking jobs and making money. They frequently arrive at Scarpa's cathouse and buy new clothes, cars and hook up with girls. Vito also manages to get his own house in a wealthy neighbourhood, feeling happy about his new position along with Joe.

As an official member of Falcone Family, Vito's biggest job comes when he is sent to kill Clemente, who has participated in the drug trade against the commission's wishes. Vito and Joe head to the Empire Bay hotel with Marty. At the hotel, Joe tells Marty to stay in the car inside the parking lot to be their getaway driver, while Vito and Joe head into the hotel disguised as hotel staff. They head into the conference room where Clemente and his men plan to have a meeting and set a bomb under the table. During the meeting, the bomb goes off and the conference room explodes, killing everybody inside. Vito and Joe inspect the scene only to find out that Clemente was in the bathroom and didn't get killed in the explosion. They give chase, and after shooting their way through many of Clemente's men in the hotel, they reach the parking lot where they find Marty shot dead. Vito and Joe pursue Clemente in a car chase, with Joe infuriated at Marty's death. During the chase, Clemente's car becomes inoperable after taking many bullets and crashes. Joe approaches the car, angrily mumbles to an injured Clemente "this is for Marty..." and personally executes him at point blank range with a Tommy Gun. Later in the day, Joe becomes deeply depressed over Marty's death and gets himself heavily drunk at a bar in Sand Island, a neighborhood owned by The Bombers. The bartender at the bar calls Vito and urges him to pick Joe up before he hurts someone. When Vito gets there, Joe accidentally shoots and kills the bartender while he is waving his gun around, forcing Vito to put dump the bartender's body after dropping Joe off home.

Soon after, Vito is approached by Henry, who wants to defect to Falcone's crew. Vito recommends Henry himself to Eddie, and Henry is ordered by Eddie to kill Galante. Vito, overcome with emotions, races to Galante's mansion and convinces Henry to let Galante simply disappear. Vito drives Galante to the train station, and he escapes to Lost Heaven. After Vito returns home, he finds Francesca there, crying. She explains that her husband, Eric Reilly, is constantly beating her up. Vito goes to an apartment of Eric's friend, beats him up and forces him to be a good husband to Francesca, or he will kill him. Francesca calls him, and Vito tells her that he will kill Eric if he touches her again. Francesca, horrified, tells Vito to stay away from her and Eric. Vito becomes depressed and goes to bed.

During the night, the O'Neil gang pulls up at Vito's house with their new leader, Mickey Desmond, and burns the house to the ground in revenge for Brian O' Neil's murder. Vito narrowly escapes, and left with no money, clothes or house, he turns to Joe who helps him get revenge. They both head to the gang's bar and take out everyone there. During the shootout, Mickey attempts to escape, but Vito and Joe chase him down in a car chase and kill him. While driving home, Vito expresses grief and depression over losing everything he had worked for, but Joe reassures him that he will earn it all back in the future and gives him Marty's apartment to stay in for the time being.

Henry hears about Vito's situation, and the trio meet at the Lincoln Park, Henry tells Vito and Joe that Clemente was in the drug business, and Falcone is also going in, which is against the rules of the Commission. Henry suggests that he can arrange a deal with one family which is out of the Commission and supplies the drugs, The Triads. Vito is initially hesitant because, "drugs kill people", but he agrees to the proposition. They first arrive to Bruno Levine, the biggest loan shark in town, and they loan $35 000 from him in the orders of returning $55 000 till the end of the week. Henry, Joe, and Vito depart for Chinatown, where they buy the merchandise from Mr. Wong, the local Triad leader gang called The Tongs. As they are leaving The Tong's fish factory, they are ambushed by cops who order them to hand over the merchandise. After Joe compliments one of the officer's shoes, Henry notices that the shoes are not part of the EBPD's uniform, and warns Vito and Joe that they are not real cops. A large shootout erupts within the factory between the trio and the disguised gangsters, with Henry, Vito and Joe escaping with the merchandise. They plan and sell small portions of the drugs, and they sell drugs to The Bombers, The Greasers, The Irish, etc. They earn over $100.000 dollars.

The next day, Henry calls Vito, telling him that Falcone has found out about the deal, and Eddie took $60,000 as a cut, leaving them without enough money to pay Bruno. Vito and Joe head to Lincoln Park to meet up with Henry and try to solve the problem, but when they get there, they witness Henry in the distance being brutally hacked to death with meat cleavers by The Tongs. After killing his attackers and grieving over Henry's body, they notice Mr. Wong drive past and they follow him to his base at a Chinese restaurant, which they raid and totally demolish in revenge for Henry's death, killing all of his men and also witnesses. During the raid, they arrive at Mr. Wong's office, where they force him to tell them why he killed Henry and why he ordered gangsters disguised as cops to ambush them after the exchange. Mr. Wong denies that the gangsters dressed as cops where his men as he would never destroy his own factory, but he tells them that he had Henry killed because he is actually a "rat"; an informant for the Bureau Of Narcotics. Neither Vito nor Joe believe him and force him to tell him where he stashed the money. Mr. Wong refuses to tell them the location as "he is dead anyway", resulting in Joe shooting him in the head. Vito and Joe escape the scene with the cops on their tail.

Back at Joe's apartment, Vito and Joe realize that they are now in bigger trouble than ever before; the incident with the Chinese has caused too much tension between Falcone and Vinci, as both believe the other was responsible for the attack on the Chinese restaurant, and at the same time the Chinese pin both Falcone and Vinci as the suspects. On top of this, Vito and Joe begin to doubt their justification for the attack, opening up to the possibility that Henry really was a rat.

Vito and Joe eventually manage to get the money back; in the process, they kill Thomas "Tommy" Angelo, the Salieri informant from Lost Heaven on Eddie's orders, and Vito finds out that his father was actually murdered by Derek and Steve from one of the workers at the port, resulting in Vito killing them both in revenge and taking Derek's $25 000 retirement fund. He checks over at Maltese Falcon, where he lies to Eddie about his involvement with Henry and pretends to be shocked over his death, and then goes at Giusseppe's place, where he learns that Vinci's men took Joe. He goes to Vinci's bar, the Mona Lisa, where he is cornered by Vinci's men. They tell him that

Joe only went here to talk with Vinci about the incident, and that he could join Joe in the talk, but as he goes, they knock him out.

Vito wakes up on a construction site for a new hotel, tied up on the pipe next to badly beaten Joe. Frank Vinci himself is in front of them, who demands to know who was behind the attack on The Triads. Joe swears that he doesn't know, and Vinci's men start to repeatedly hit both Vito and Joe. Vinci leaves the site, and Vito and Joe manage to escape the site, but Joe is badly injured and Vito takes him to El Greco's place, where Joe gives Vito the money he earned, leaving enough to pay back the debt. Vito visits Bruno and pays back, and Bruno asks for Vito's name, and he tells him that he is Vito Scaletta, which reminds Bruno on an other Scaletta who borrowed $2000 from him, and Vito realizes that Bruno is the loan shark who loaned his father the money. He leaves Bruno's office in anger, and goes home.

The next day, Eddie calls Vito, who tells him that Falcone wants to meet Vito at the observatory just outside town. Vito leaves on foot, but just then, a limo arrives with Leo inside, who angrily demands Vito to get in. Inside the car, Leo introduces Vito to Mr. Chu, a head of The Triad organization, and he tells him that both the Commission, The Triads, and even Falcone want him dead. He offers Vito a last chance to spare his life; to kill Carlo Falcone. Vito leaves the limo and goes to the observatory.

As Leo assumed, Falcone really wants Vito dead; Falcone's henchmen order Vito to discharge his guns, but he manages to fight them off and forces his way in the observatory, killing loads of Falcone's men before he finally reaches the main observation room, where Carlo awaits. Carlo tells him that it is an insult that he was sent to kill him, and tells him that there is no friendships in the mob, revealing Joe, who puts his gun to Vito's forehead. Carlo orders Joe to kill Vito, but Joe hints Vito to shoot, and they battle last of his henchmen. After killing all of his men, Vito steps out to the wounded Carlo, who is crawling around the floor. Vito shoots him three more times while telling him; *"You know something, Carlo? For the last 10 years of my life all what I ever done was kill. I killed for my country. I killed for my family. I killed anyone who got in my way. But this one, this one is for me."*. He finally shoots Carlo in the head, killing him.

Vito goes away with Joe, questioning him as to why he was there with Falcone. Joe explains to him that he promised to make him very wealthy and give him his own crew, something that he always wanted, but he couldn't go over their friendship. When they go outside, Leo Galante awaits them with his men, and they go out to celebrate, but Leo insists that Vito should come with him to talk. Joe departs in the other car. Breaking the suspicious silence, Vito asks what Leo wanted to talk to him about, and sees the car that Joe is in quickly turning and going in another direction. Vito angrily asks Leo where they are taking him, to which he responds; "Sorry, kid. Joe wasn't the part of our deal." Vito angrily looks at Leo, realizing that Joe was the price that he paid for his path, the path of Mafia, as the camera rises showing panoramic view of Empire Bay.

Soundtrack

1. Riverboat Shuffle - Frankie Trumbauer & his Orchestra (1927)
2. Clarinet Marmalade - Frankie Trumbauer & his Orchestra (1927)
3. Come On and Stomp, Stomp, Stomp - Johnny Dodds (1928)
4. Good Little Bad Little You - Cliff Edwards (1928)
5. Beating the Dog - Joe Venuti & Eddie Lang (1929)
6. Gangster's Blues - Peetie Wheatstraw (1929)
7. Going Places - Joe Venuti & Eddie Lang (1929)
8. Stringin' the Blues - Joe Venuti & Eddie Lang (1929)
9. Happy Feet - Cab Calloway (1930)
10. By the Light of the Silvery Moon - Bing Crosby (1932)
11. It Don't Mean a Thing (If It Ain't Got That Swing) - Duke Ellington (1932)
12. Pennies from Heaven - Bing Crosby (1936)

13. The Pessimistic Character - Bing Crosby (1936)

14. I haven't Time to be a Millionaire - Bing Crosby (1936)

15. Sing, Sing, Sing (With a Swing) - Benny Goodman (1937)

16. You're Driving Me Crazy - Django Reinhardt (1937)

17. The Dipsy Doodle - Tommy Dorsey (1938)

18. Belleville - Django Reinhardt (1940)

19. Boogie Woogie Bugle Boy - The Andrews Sisters (1941)

20. Strip Polka - The Andrews Sisters (1942)

21. Praise the Lord and Pass the Ammunition - Kay Kyser & his Orchestra (1942)

22. Why Don't You Do Right - Benny Goodman & Peggy Lee (1943)

23. Vict'ry Polka - Bing Crosby & The Andrews Sisters (1943)

24. Straighten Up and Fly Right - The Andrews Sisters (1944)

25. G.I. Jive - Louis Jordan & his Tympany Five (1944)

26. There'll Be a Hot Time in the Town of Berlin - Bing Crosby & The Andrews Sisters (1944)

27. I've Got a Pocketful of Dreams - Bing Crosby (1944)

28. Rum and Coca-Cola - The Andrews Sisters (1945)

29. Caldonia Boogie - Louis Jordan & his Tympany Five (1945)

30. Ain't That Just Like a Woman - Louis Jordan & his Tympany Five (1946)

31. Choo Choo Ch'Boogie - Louis Jordan & his Tympany Five (1946)

32. That Chick's Too Young to Fry - Louis Jordan & his Tympany Five (1946)

33. Did you Ever Love a Woman - Gatemouth Moore (1947)

34. Friendship - Louis Jordan & his Tympany Five (1947)

35. Inflation Blues - Jack McVea (1947)

36. Open the Door, Richard - Louis Jordan & his Tympany Five (1947)

37. Everybody Eats When They Come to My House - Cab Calloway (1947)

38. Buttons and Bows - Dinah Shore (1948)

39. Happiness is a Thing called Joe - Peggy Lee (1948)

40. The Best Things in Life are Free - The Ink Spots (1948)

41. Auf Wiedersehn, Sweetheart - Les Baxter (1949)

42. Baby, It's Cold Outside - Dinah Shore & Buddy Clark (1949)

43. That'll Get It - Floyd Dixon (1949)

44. The Fat Man - Fats Domino (1949)

45. After the Lights Go Down Low - Albert Hibbler (1950)

46. Count Every Star - Albert Hibbler (1950)

47. Rock Around the Clock - Harold Singer (1950)

48. Jezebel - Frankie Laine (1951)

49. Pachuko Hop - Ike Carpenter Orchestra (1951)

50. Makin' Whoopee - Doris Day (1952)

51. I Can't Lose With the Stuff I Use - Lester Williams (1952)

52. Chow Mein - The Gaylords (1953)

53. Mercy Mr. Percy - Varetta Dillard (1953)

54. Rags to Riches - Jackie Wilson (1953)

55. That's Amore - Dean Martin (1953)

56. Che la Luna - Louis Prima & Keely Smith (1954)

57. Oh, Marie - Louis Prima (1954)

58. Closer to the Bone - Louis Prima (1954)

59. Pennies from Heaven - Louis Prima (1954)

60. Honey Love - The Drifters (1954)
61. Ling Ting Tong - The Five Keys (1954)
62. Mambo Italiano - Rosemary Clooney (1954)
63. Mr. Sandman - The Chordettes (1954)
64. Rock Around the Clock - Bill Haley & his Comets (1954)
65. Sh-Boom (Life Could Be a Dream) - The Crew-Cuts (1954)
66. When You're Smiling - Louis Prima (1954)
67. Ain't That a Shame - Fats Domino (1955)
68. Bo Diddley - Bo Diddley (1955)
69. In the Still of the Night - The Five Satins (1955)
70. Mannish Boy - Muddy Waters (1955)
71. Held for Questioning - Farell Draper (1955)
72. I Put a Spell on You - Screamin' Jay Hawkins (1956)
73. 900 Miles - Billy Merman (1956)
74. Springtime in Monaco - Billy Merman (1956)
75. Long Tall Sally - Little Richard (1956)
76. One Kiss Led to Another (Brazil) - The Coasters (1956)
77. Smokestack Lightnin' - Howlin' Wolf (1956)
78. Speedo - The Cadillacs (1956)
79. Why do Fools fall in Love - Frankie Lymon & The Teenagers (1956)
80. Keep A-Knockin' - Little Richard (1957)
81. Nadine - Chuck Berry (1957)
82. Not Fade Away - Buddy Holly (1957)
83. Stood Up - Ricky Nelson (1957)
84. All I Have To Do Is Dream - The Everly Brothers (1958)
85. At the Hop - Danny & The Juniors (1957)
86. Book of Love - The Monotones (1958)
87. C'mon Everybody - Eddie Cochran & Jerry Capehart (1958)
88. Don't Let Go - Roy Hamilton (1958)
89. Donna - Ritchie Valens (1958)
90. Forty Miles of Bad Road - Duane Eddy (1958)
91. Framed - The Coasters (1958)
92. Got My Mojo Working - Muddy Waters (1958)
93. Let the Good Times Roll - Sam Butera & The Witnesses (1958)
94. Lucille - Little Richard (1957)
95. Maybe - The Chantels (1958)
96. Moovin 'n' Groovin - Duane Eddy (1958)
97. Ooh, Baby, Ooh - Dave Appell & The Applejacks (1958)
98. Rave On - Buddy Holly (1958)
99. Rebel Rouser - Duane Eddy (1958)
100. Return to Me - Dean Martin (1958)
101. Summertime Blues - Eddie Cochran (1958)
102. Tequila - The Champs (1958)
103. That'll Be the Day - Buddy Holly (1958)
104. The Peanut Vendor - Perez Prado (1958)
105. Who Do You Love - Bo Diddley (1956)
106. You Can Have Her - [Roy Hamilton] (1958)

107. Cannonball - Duane Eddy (1959)
108. Come On, Let's Go - Ritchie Valens (1959)
109. Come Softly to Me - The Fleetwoods (1959)
110. Let It Snow - Dean Martin (1959)
111. Manhattan Spiritual - Reg Owen Orchestra (1959)
112. Money (That's What I Want) - Barret Strong (1959)
113. My Guardian Angel - Jim Breedlove (1959)
114. Ain't That a Kick in the Head - Dean Martin (1960)
115. Teen Beat - Sandy Nelson (1960)
116. Boom Boom - John Lee Hooker (1962)
117. Java - Al Hirt (1963)
118. No Particular Place to Go - Chuck Berry (1964)

Cast

Vito Scaletta - Rick Pasqualone

Joe Barbaro - Robert Costanzo

Henry Tomasino - Sonny Marinelli

Eddie Scarpa - Joe Hanna

Carlo Falcone - Andre Sogliuzzo

Leo Galante - Frank Ashmore

Luca Gurino - Andre Sogliuzzo

Frederico 'Derek' Pappalardo - Robert Costanzo

Alberto Clemente - Nolan North

Frank Vinci - Larry Kenney

Steve Coyne - Mark Mintz

Francesca Scaletta - Jeannie Elias

Marketing and release

System requirements

	Minimum	Recommended
Windows[13][14]		
Operating system	Windows XP SP2/Vista/7	Windows XP SP2/Vista/7
CPU	Intel Pentium D 3 GHz or AMD Athlon 64 X2 3600+ (Dual Core) or higher	Intel Core 2 Quad 2.4 GHz
Memory	1.5 GB	2.0 GB
Hard drive space	8 GB of free space	10 GB of free space
Graphics hardware	Nvidia 8600 / ATI Radeon HD 2600	Nvidia GeForce 9800 GTX / ATI 3870
Sound hardware	DirectX 9.0c	DirectX 9.0c
Network	Internet connection required (STEAM) for online activation and installation	

A promotional trailer was released for the game in August 2007. A second trailer was released on the Spike VGA show on 14 December 2008.[15] An extended version of the trailer was released on 15 January with an extra 30 seconds of cut scene footage.[16]

The first gameplay footage debuted on GameSpot on 17 April 2009 as part of an interview with *Mafia II*'s producer, Denby Grace.[17] The video shows driving and gunplay aspects to gameplay as well as portraying the physics engine. The interview was later removed.

A third trailer was uploaded to the website on 28 May 2009. From 1 June 2009, four short videos are to be added to the *Mafia II* website. The first of these is called "The Art Of Persuasion" and features the song "Mercy, Mr Percy" by the female singer Varetta Dillard.

Another video was released featuring footage from the mission "The Buzzsaw". The video reveals the fate of "The Fat Man" who appeared in the earlier trailers.[18] On 27 March 2010, a new trailer was released showcasing the PhysX-based cloth and physics system used in the game.[19]

On 3 August 2010, Sheridyn Fisher, the face of Playboy Swim 2010, became the official ambassador for *Mafia II*. Sheridyn's involvement with *Mafia II* highlights the agreement between 2K Games and *Playboy* magazine to use 50 of their vintage covers and Centerfolds in *Mafia II* as part of the in-game collectibles integration.[20] A demo for the game was released on 10 August 2010 on Steam, Xbox Live Marketplace and PlayStation Network.[21]

Pre-order bonuses

On 26 May 2010 four content packs were offered as pre-order bonus's in America and European countries, each one available through different retailers. The *Vegas Pack* containing two additional cars and suits for Vito and the *War Hero Pack* containing two military-style vehicles and suits was available from GameStop and EBGames. The *Renegade Pack* containing two sports cars and two jackets was available from Amazon and the *Greaser Pack* featuring two hot-rods and two suits were available to Best Buy customers.[22] These pre-order packs are now available for purchase as game add-ons on the PlayStation Network, Xbox Live and Steam. On 26 May 2010 a collector's edition was announced for *Mafia II*.[23]

PlayStation 3 version

The PlayStation 3 version became subject to controversy on 2K's *Mafia II* forums when 2K's interactive marketing manager Elizabeth Tobey stated that the PlayStation 3 version would be missing certain graphical details that were present in the Windows and Xbox 360 versions including three dimensional grass, pools of blood forming under dead bodies and realistic cloth physics.[24] These details were said to be present in earlier builds of the game, but had to be removed to increase the game's frame rate.

Upon release, the PS3 version received the same or higher review scores than the Xbox 360 version from Destructoid and Nowgamer (sites that review the game on multiple platforms rather than the normal practice of reviewing a single platform) due to additional content.[25][26] Metacritic gave both versions the same score of 74/100,[27][28] while GameRankings has the Xbox 360 version 4 points ahead of the PS3 version based on more reviews.[29][30]

Downloadable content

Three downloadable content packs have been announced for the game. The first, titled "The Betrayal of Jimmy" is a PlayStation 3 exclusive episode that was a free download upon release to users who purchase the game new. This was announced by Sony on 15 June 2010 at E3 2010.[31]

The second installment of downloadable content, "Jimmy's Vendetta", was released on PlayStation Network, Xbox Live Marketplace, and Steam on 7 September 2010.[32] "Joe's Adventures", the third and final DLC was released on 23 November 2010. "Joe's Adventures" focuses on the events that occur in Empire Bay during the years that Vito is imprisoned in the main Mafia II storyline while playing as Vito's best friend Joe Barbaro and seeing his perspective. The DLC combines standard missions with score-based, open world missions. It is estimated to provide eight hours of gameplay.[33]

The Russian company 1C officially announced *Mafia II: Extended Edition* for the Russian market. It will include the game, 4 DLC (Vegas Pack, Renegade Pack, Greaser Pack, and War Hero Pack), and "The Betrayal of Jimmy", which was previously available as a PlayStation 3 exclusive addon, as well as the 2 other addons (Jimmy's Vendetta and Joe's Adventures). It was released on 3 December 2010 for PS3 and Windows. It will be released for Xbox 360 later. The same package is released for Western markets as *Mafia II: Director's Cut* on PC, Mac OS X[2] and their respective budget labels on consoles.[34]

Mobile version

A version of *Mafia II* was also released for mobile phones and smartphones by Connect2Media. The game features a different storyline and follows the exploits of Marco Russetto, a soldato for the Salieri crime family.

Controversy

Sonia Alfano, a member of the European Parliament and president of Italy's association for the families of Mafia victims, called for the game to be banned.[35] Alfano's father Beppe, was murdered by the Mafia in January 1993.

Take-Two Interactive quickly responded to the issue, stating that the game's depiction of the American Mafia was no different from organised crime films such as *The Godfather*. They also responded to allegations of racism from Unico National, who claimed that the game portrayed Italian-Americans unfairly and "indoctrinating" the youth into the violent stereotype.[36]

Reception

Reception	
Aggregate scores	
Aggregator	**Score**
GameRankings	PC: 76.48%[37] 360: 75.80%[29] PS3: 75.05%[30]
Metacritic	PC: 77/100[38] 360: 74/100[27] PS3: 75/100[28]
Review scores	
Publication	**Score**
1UP.com	B[39]

Edge	6/10[40]
Eurogamer	4/10[41]
Game Informer	9/10[42]
GamePro	★ ★ ★ ★ ★ [43]
GameSpot	8.5/10[44]
GamesTM	8/10[45]
IGN	7.0/10[46]
Official Xbox Magazine	7/10[47]
PC Gamer UK	78%[48]
X-Play	★ ★ ★ ★ ★ [49]

Mafia II received mostly positive to average reviews from critics. IGN gave the game 7/10, saying "*Mafia II* is a solid little game that'll give you a fun ride − just don't expect the world." IGN AU gave it a 8.0/10 and said that *Mafia II* is "A deeply flawed game, where the story is the highlight - and far more engaging than most. I certainly enjoyed my 11-12 hours with *Mafia II*, and those looking for an authentic-feeling mob tale should definitely check it out. This one is more than the sum of its parts." Gamespot gave it 8.5 and stated "*Mafia II*'s exciting action and uncompromising mob story make for an impressive and violent adventure." Game Informer gave it a 9.0/10 and said "In an era when video games are moving away from relying on cinematics for storytelling, *Mafia II* draws on the rich mobster film history to weave a gripping drama about family, friendship, loyalty, betrayal, and pragmatism."

The most negative review came from Eurogamer who gave the game a 4/10 and said that "*Mafia II* gets the last word by destroying the myth that the mafia is interesting at all. It contends that the mob world is a hell of boredom populated by aggressively stupid automatons. These drones wake up each morning, carry out a series of repetitious tasks, and return home." The A.V. Club gave the game a D+, praising the game's attention to detail but criticising that "aging gameplay mechanics and weak plot turns make the game's magic peel away faster than a bank-job getaway car." Zero Punctuation's Ben Croshaw called the game "generic", and noted the main characters' similarities with the main characters of *Grand Theft Auto IV*, but criticised the lack of features prevalent in other sandbox games. He also criticised the mundane parts of the game, such as driving, making the game feel "unnecessarily padded."[50]

It has the most profanity in a video game, particularly the word "fuck", which is spoken over 200 times, beating previous record holder, *The House of the Dead: Overkill*.[51]

The game was also criticised by fans of the series for omitting a significant amount of content in the final build of the game, with some being released (albeit altered to a certain extent) as downloadable content. Melee weapons, which were present in the previous game, such as a baseball bat and brass knuckles, were found to be stored in the game's archives, and was also announced by producer Denby Grace in a developer podcast,[52] but were left unused.[53] Jack Scalici, 2K Director of Creative Production, later denied their existence from the game, stating that they were only "a test bed for a work-in-progress melee weapon combat system", and was never been added in the game. Mafia II also lacked the "Freeride" sandbox mode, which was also a point of criticism among fans. Similar functionality, however, can be added through third-party modifications.[54]

The map's size was also put into question,[55] contrary to claims made by 2K Games that Empire Bay took up 10 square miles.

References

[1] "Massive Bear Studios" (http://massivebear.com/portfolio.php). Massivebear.com. . Retrieved 24 August 2010.

[2] "Feral Interactive: Mafia II: Director's Cut release announcement" (http://www.feralinteractive.com/?section=news&article=303). .

[3] "Mafia II" (http://www.connect2media.com/index.php/index.php?option=com_content&view=article&Itemid=2&id=221:mafia-ii). Connect2Media. . Retrieved 21 March 2012.

[4] "*Announcing Mafia II's Release Date*" (http://mafia2game.com/community/us/home.php). 2K Games. .

[5] Robinson, Martin (8 January 2008). "Take -Two Takes Mafia Dev" (http://pc.ign.com/articles/844/844122p1.html). IGN. . Retrieved 27 September 2008.

[6] "2K Games Announces Mafia 2" (http://2kgames.com/index.php?p=news&ID=232). 2K Games. 21 August 2008. . Retrieved 27 September 2008.

[7] "Mafia II Mobile review - Mobile reviews" (http://www.pocketgamer.co.uk/r/Mobile/Mafia+II+Mobile/review.asp?c=23535). Pocket Gamer. . Retrieved 21 March 2012.

[8] Ivan, Tom (19 October 2008). "First Mafia 2 details roll in" (http://www.computerandvideogames.com/article.php?id=199532). Computer and Video Games. . Retrieved 4 November 2008.

[9] "GC09: Mafia II interview" (http://www.gamereactor.de/grtv/?id=5423). Gamereactor Deutschland. 25 August 2009. . Retrieved 26 September 2009.

[10] "Mafia II GamesCom 2009 Preview" (http://www.gamingunion.net/news/mafia-ii-gamescom-2009-preview--384.html). Gaming Union. 27 August 2009. . Retrieved 27 August 2009.

[11] "*Mafia II Preview*" (http://www.psxextreme.com/ps3-previews/196.html). PSXExtreme. 26 April 2008. . Retrieved 25 March 2010.

[12] Hrebicek, Tomas (15 January 2009). "Mafia II Holiday Confessions interview" (http://uk.pc.ign.com/articles/944/944987p1.html). IGN. . Retrieved 15 January 2009.

[13] "Mafia 2: System Requirements, Check Requirements for Mafia 2" (http://www.strategyinformer.com/pc/system/mafia2/systemrequirements.html). Strategyinformer.com. . Retrieved 21 August 2010.

[14] "Mafia 2: GPU & CPU Performance" (http://www.techspot.com/review/312-mafia2-performance/). TechSpot.com. . Retrieved 31 August 2010.

[15] "*Spike Shows Off Mafia 2 Trailer*" (http://www.1up.com/do/newsStory?cId=3171850). 1UP. 14 December 2008. . Retrieved 21 June 2010.

[16] "Extended trailer" (http://uk.pc.ign.com/dor/objects/957839/mafia-ii/videos/mafia2_trailer_011409.html;jsessionid=117d6i9tdbni3). Uk.pc.ign.com. . Retrieved 24 August 2010.

[17] Park, Andrew (16 April 2009). "Mafia II Impressions - Exclusive First Preview" (http://uk.gamespot.com/ps3/action/mafia2/news.html?sid=6208079). GameSpot. . Retrieved 27 April 2009.

[18] "Mafia II Walk-Through Video 1" (http://www.gamespot.com/xbox360/action/mafia2/video/6213414/mafia-ii-walk-through-video-1?hd=1&tag=topslot;img;1). Gamespot.com. . Retrieved 24 August 2010.

[19] "Mafia II: first PhysX Trailer" (http://physxinfo.com/news/2514/mafia-ii-first-physx-trailer/). 27 March 2010. . Retrieved 7 April 2010.

[20] Ferry (24 August 2010). "Mafia 2 Playboy Magazines Locations" (http://www.videogamesblogger.com/2010/08/24/mafia-2-playboy-magazines-locations-guide-xbox-360-ps3-pc.htm). VideoGamesBlogger. . Retrieved 26 August 2010.

[21] "Mafia II Demo" (http://www.mafia2game.com/demo/). Mafia2game.com. . Retrieved 21 August 2010.

[22] "Mafia II Pre-order" (http://www.mafia2game.com/preorder/). Mafia2game.com. . Retrieved 21 August 2010.

[23] "Mafia II - Official Community" (http://www.2kgames.com/mafia2/community/us/features_collectors.php). 2kgames.com. 26 May 2010. . Retrieved 21 August 2010.

[24] Robert Purchese (17 August 2010). "2K: Mafia II loses some detail on PS3 PlayStation 3 News - Page 1" (http://www.eurogamer.net/articles/2010-08-17-2k-mafia-ii-loses-some-detail-on-ps3). Eurogamer.net. . Retrieved 21 August 2010.

[25] "Review: Mafia II" (http://www.destructoid.com/review-mafia-ii-181950.phtml). Destructoid. . Retrieved 27 August 2010.

[26] "Mafia II (PS3) review | NowGamer" (http://ps3.nowgamer.com/reviews/ps3/9347/mafia-ii). Ps3.nowgamer.com. . Retrieved 27 August 2010.

[27] "Mafia II for Xbox 360" (http://www.metacritic.com/game/xbox-360/mafia-ii). Metacritic. . Retrieved 24 August 2010.

[28] "Mafia II for PlayStation 3" (http://www.metacritic.com/game/playstation-3/mafia-ii). Metacritic. . Retrieved 24 August 2010.

[29] "Mafia II for Xbox 360 - GameRankings" (http://www.gamerankings.com/xbox360/942955-mafia-ii/index.html). GameRankings. . Retrieved 24 August 2010.

[30] "Mafia II for PlayStation 3 - GameRankings" (http://www.gamerankings.com/ps3/942954-mafia-ii/index.html). GameRankings. . Retrieved 24 August 2010.

[31] Tom Bramwell (15 June 2010). "Sony ties up DLC/pack-in exclusives PlayStation 3 News - Page 1" (http://www.eurogamer.net/articles/sony-ties-up-dlc-pack-in-exclusives). Eurogamer.net. . Retrieved 21 August 2010.

[32] "Mafia II Upcoming DLC Packs A Vendetta" (http://kotaku.com/5626249/mafia-ii-upcoming-dlc-packs-a-vendetta/gallery). *Kotaku*. . Retrieved 31 August 2010.

[33] Adam Pavlacka (12 November 2010). "PS3/X360/PC Preview - 'Mafia II: Joe's Adventures'" (http://worthplaying.com/article/2010/11/12/previews/78184/). WorthPlaying. . Retrieved 12 November 2010.

[34] by JC Fletcher on 30 March 2011 3:55PM (30 March 2011). "$30 Mafia 2 re-release includes all DLC, available now" (http://www. joystiq.com/2011/03/30/30-mafia-2-re-release-includes-all-dlc-available-now/). Joystiq. . Retrieved 27 October 2011.

[35] "Mob violence victim calls for Mafia II ban News • News • Eurogamer.net" (http://www.eurogamer.net/articles/ 2010-12-17-mob-violence-victim-calls-for-mafia-ii-ban). *Eurogamer*. . Retrieved 9 January 2013.

[36] "Take-Two rubbishes Mafia II racism claims News • News • Eurogamer.net" (http://www.eurogamer.net/articles/ 2010-08-19-take-two-rubbishes-mafia-ii-racism-claims). *Eurogamer*. . Retrieved 9 January 2013.

[37] "Mafia II for PC - GameRankings" (http://www.gamerankings.com/pc/942953-mafia-ii/index.html). GameRankings. . Retrieved 24 August 2010.

[38] "Mafia II for PC" (http://www.metacritic.com/game/pc/mafia-ii). Metacritic. . Retrieved 24 August 2010.

[39] (http://www.1up.com/do/reviewPage?cId=3181020&p=1)

[40] "Mafia II Review | Edge Magazine" (http://www.next-gen.biz/reviews/mafia-ii-review). Next-gen.biz. . Retrieved 27 August 2010.

[41] John Teti. "Mafia II Review - Page 1" (http://www.eurogamer.net/articles/2010-08-23-mafia-ii-review). Eurogamer.net. . Retrieved 24 August 2010.

[42] Helgeson, Matt (20 August 2010). "Mafia II Review: Jump Into This Thing Of Ours - Mafia II - Xbox 360" (http://gameinformer.com/ games/mafia_ii/b/xbox360/archive/2010/08/20/mafia-ii-review-jump-into-this-thing-of-ours.aspx). GameInformer.com. . Retrieved 27 August 2010.

[43] Hayward, Andrew (23 August 2010). "Mafia 2 Review from" (http://web.archive.org/web/20100825080543/http://www.gamepro. com/article/reviews/216220/mafia-2/). GamePro. Archived from the original (http://www.gamepro.com/article/reviews/216220/ mafia-2/) on 25 August 2010. . Retrieved 27 August 2010.

[44] "Mafia II Review for PC - GameSpot" (http://uk.gamespot.com/pc/action/mafia2/review.html?om_act=convert& om_clk=gssummary&tag=summary;read-review). Uk.gamespot.com. 23 August 2010. . Retrieved 27 August 2010.

[45] "Mafia II Review | Videogames Magazine - gamesTM - Official Website" (http://www.gamestm.co.uk/reviews/mafia-ii-review/). gamesTM. . Retrieved 27 August 2010.

[46] Greg Miller (7 July 2010). "Mafia II Review - PlayStation 3 Review at IGN" (http://uk.ps3.ign.com/articles/111/1114635p2.html). Uk.ps3.ign.com. . Retrieved 24 August 2010.

[47] "Xbox Review: Mafia 2 - Official Xbox 360 Magazine" (http://www.oxm.co.uk/article.php?id=21898). Oxm.co.uk. 23 August 2010. . Retrieved 27 August 2010.

[48] "Mafia 2 review" (http://www.pcgamer.com/2010/08/24/mafia-2-review/). PC Gamer. . Retrieved 27 August 2010.

[49] Sessler, Adam (23 August 2010). "X-Play Mafia II review" (http://www.g4tv.com/games/xbox-360/47821/Mafia-II/review/). G4. . Retrieved 23 February 2011.

[50] by Ben "Yahtzee" Croshaw, 15 September 2010 16:00 (15 September 2010). "The Escapist : Video Galleries : Zero Punctuation : Mafia II" (http://www.escapistmagazine.com/videos/view/zero-punctuation/1988-Mafia-II). Escapistmagazine.com. . Retrieved 27 October 2011.

[51] "Guinness Gives Mafia II The F-Bomb Record" (http://kotaku.com/5640174/guinness-gives-mafia-ii-the-f+bomb-record). Kotaku.com. 16 September 2010. . Retrieved 27 October 2011.

[52] "Empire Times - Mafia II Behind the Scenes : Melee Combat" (http://www.game-archivist.com/empirebay/bts_melee-combat.php). . Retrieved 5 July 2012.

[53] "Mafia 2 [Beta / Unused - Xbox 360 / PS3 / PC (http://www.unseen64.net/2011/09/19/mafia-2-beta-xbox-360-ps3-pc/)"]. . Retrieved 5 July 2012.

[54] "Mafia II 'Free Ride' mode released" (http://n4g.com/news/594042/mafia-ii-free-ride-mode-released). . Retrieved 5 February 2013.

[55] "Empire Times - Mafia II Articles : Empire Bay Map" (http://www.game-archivist.com/empirebay/article_empire-bay-map.php). . Retrieved 5 July 2012.

External links

- *Mafia II* official website (http://www.2kgames.com/mafia2/)
- *Mafia II* (http://www.imdb.com/title/tt1181833/) at the Internet Movie Database
- *Mafia II* at [[Feral Interactive (http://www.feralinteractive.com/?game=mafia2)]]

Make Mine Music

Make Mine Music	
Original theatrical release poster	
Directed by	Jack Kinney Clyde Geronimi Hamilton Luske Joshua Meador Robert Cormack
Produced by	Walt Disney
Written by	Walt Disney James Bordrero Homer Brightman Erwin Graham Eric Gurney T. Hee Sylvia Holland Dick Huemer Dick Kelsey Jesse Marsh Tom Oreb Cap Palmer Erdman Penner Harry Reeves Dick Shaw John Walbridge Roy Williams
Starring	Nelson Eddy Dinah Shore Benny Goodman The Andrews Sisters Jerry Colonna Sterling Holloway Andy Russell David Lichine Tania Riabouchinskaya The Pied Pipers The King's Men The Ken Darby Chorus
Studio	Walt Disney Productions
Distributed by	RKO Radio Pictures, Inc.
Release date(s)	August 15, 1946
Running time	76 minutes
Country	United States
Language	English

Make Mine Music is an animated feature produced by Walt Disney and released to theatres on August 15, 1946. It is the 8th animated feature in the Walt Disney Animated Classics series.

During the Second World War, much of Walt Disney's staff was drafted into the army, and those that remained were called upon by the U.S. government to make training and propaganda films. As a result, the studio was littered with unfinished story ideas. In order to keep the feature film division alive during this difficult time, the studio released six package films including this one, made up of various unrelated segments set to music. This is the third package film, following *Saludos Amigos* and *The Three Caballeros*.

The musical director was Al Sack.[1]

The film was entered into the 1946 Cannes Film Festival.[2]

Film segments

This particular film has ten such segments.

The Martins and the Coys

This segment featured popular radio vocal group, King's Men singing the story of a Hatfields and McCoys-style feud in the mountains broken up when two young people from each side fell in love. It was edited out in the NTSC home media version because it had parts too intense for children, while in the PAL version, it was kept.

Blue Bayou

This segment featured animation originally intended for *Fantasia* using the Claude Debussy musical composition *Clair de Lune*. However, by the time *Make Mine Music* was released *Clair de Lune* was replaced by the new song *Blue Bayou*, performed by the Ken Darby Singers. However, the original version of the segment still survives.

All the Cats Join In

This segment was one of two segments to which Benny Goodman contributed: an innovative shot in which a pencil drew the action as it was happening, and in which 1940s teens were swept away by popular music.

Without You

This segment was a ballad of lost love, sung by Andy Russell.

Casey at the Bat

This segment featured Jerry Colonna, reciting the poem also titled "Casey at the Bat" by Ernest Thayer, about the arrogant ballplayer whose cockiness was his undoing.

Two Silhouettes

This segment featured two live-action ballet dancers, David Lichine and Tania Riabouchinskaya, moving in silhouette with animated backgrounds and characters. Dinah Shore sang the title song.

Peter and the Wolf

This segment was an animated dramatization of the 1936 musical composition by Sergei Prokofiev, with narration by actor Sterling Holloway. A Russian boy named Peter set off into the forest to hunt the wolf with his animal friends: a bird named Sasha, a duck named Sonia, and a cat named Ivan. Each character is represented with a specific musical accompaniment as follows:

Peter: String Quartet
Sasha the Bird: Flute
Sonia the Duck: Oboe
Ivan the Cat: Clarinet
Grandpapa: Bassoon

Hunters: Kettle Drums

The Wolf: Primarily horns and cymbals.

After You've Gone

This segment again featured Benny Goodman and his orchestra as four anthropomorphized instruments who paraded through a musical playground.

Johnny Fedora and Alice Blue Bonnet

This segment told the romantic story of two hats who fell in love in a department store window. When Alice was sold, Johnny devoted himself to finding her again. They eventually, by pure chance, meet up again and live happily ever after together, side by side.The Andrews Sisters provided the vocals. Like the other segments, it was later released theatrically. It was released as such on May 21, 1954.[3]

The Whale Who Wanted to Sing at the Met

The bittersweet finale about a Sperm Whale with incredible musical talent and his dreams of singing Grand Opera. A legend is spread throughout the city that there is an opera-singing whale, but as it is seemingly disproven, it is assumed that the whale has swallowed an opera singer who is the one the sailors are actually hearing sing. The short-sighted impresario Tetti-Tatti believes this and sets out to destroy Willy, the newspapers announcing that he was going to see. Whitey, Willy's seagull friend, excitedly brings Willy the newspaper, all of his friends believing that this is his big chance, so he goes out to meet the boat and sing for Tetti-Tatti. Of course he finds them, and upon hearing Willy sing, Tetti-Tatti comes to believe that Willy has swallowed not one, but THREE singers (due to his having three uvulae), and chases him with a harpoon on a boat with three crewmen. Upon hearing the whale sing, the crewmen try to stop Tetti-Tatti from killing the whale, as they want to continue listening to him sing, even to the point of tying up Tetti-Tatti and sitting on him, however he still manages to escape and fire the harpoon gun. In the end, Willie was harpooned and killed, but the narrator then explains that Willy's voice will sing on in Heaven. Nelson Eddy narrated and performed all the voices in this segment. As Willie the Whale, Eddy sang all three male voices in the first part of the Sextet from Donizetti's opera, Lucia di Lammermoor.

Cast

Actor	Role(s)
Nelson Eddy	Narrator; characters (*The Whale Who Wanted to Sing at the Met*)
Dinah Shore	Singer (*Two Silhouettes*)
Benny Goodman	Musician (*All the Cats Join In*/*After You've Gone*)
The Andrews Sisters	Singers (*Johnny Fedora and Alice Bluebonnet*)
Jerry Colonna	Narrator (*Casey at the Bat*)
Sterling Holloway	Narrator (*Peter and the Wolf*)
Andy Russell	Singer (*Without You*)
David Lichine	Dancer (*Two Silhouettes*)
Tania Riabouchinskaya	Dancer (*Two Silhouettes*)
The Pied Pipers	Singers
The King's Men	Singers (*The Martins and the Coys*)
The Ken Darby Chorus	Singers (*Blue Bayou*)

Home video

Make Mine Music was originally released on laserdisc in Japan on October 21, 1985, and on VHS and DVD on June 6, 2000 under the Walt Disney Gold Classic Collection title. This release was edited to remove "The Martins and the Coys", because it had "graphic gunplay not suitable for children." Before, two of its segments (Willie the Operatic Whale, and Peter and the Wolf) were released on home video indepent of the original feature, in company with original animated shorts in the 1980s and 1990s. The Japanese laserdisc includes all the cuts made to the VHS/DVD versions. Europan Region 2 DVDs also include the unedited feature. No unedited release has been scheduled in America. It is the only film in the Disney Animated Classics canon never to see a release on Region 4 DVD in Australia.

References

[1] "Al Sack and Disney" (http://news.google.com/newspapers?id=iBxPAAAAIBAJ&sjid=1U4DAAAAIBAJ&pg=4028,2916329& dq=al-sack+tony+martin&hl=en). *St. Petersburg Times* (Times Publishing Company): p. 38. 19 May 1946. . Retrieved 13 July 2012.

[2] "Festival de Cannes: Make Mine Music" (http://www.festival-cannes.com/en/archives/ficheFilm/id/4280/year/1946.html). *festival-cannes.com*. . Retrieved 2009-01-03.

[3] "Johnny Fedora and Alice Blue Bonnet" (http://affichesdisney.canalblog.com/archives/johnny_fedora___alice_bluebonnet/index.html) (in French). . Retrieved 2010-12-03.

External links

- *Make Mine Music* (http://www.imdb.com/title/tt0038718/) at the Internet Movie Database
- *Make Mine Music* (http://www.bcdb.com/bcdb/cartoon.cgi?film=22) at the Big Cartoon DataBase
- *Make Mine Music* (http://www.rottentomatoes.com/m/make_mine_music/) at Rotten Tomatoes

Mel Tormé

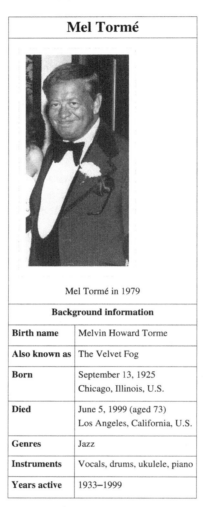

Mel Tormé	
Mel Tormé in 1979	
Background information	
Birth name	Melvin Howard Torme
Also known as	The Velvet Fog
Born	September 13, 1925 Chicago, Illinois, U.S.
Died	June 5, 1999 (aged 73) Los Angeles, California, U.S.
Genres	Jazz
Instruments	Vocals, drums, ukulele, piano
Years active	1933–1999

Melvin Howard Tormé (September 13, 1925 – June 5, 1999), nicknamed **The Velvet Fog**, was an American musician, known for his jazz singing. He was also a jazz composer and arranger, drummer, pianist, and actor in radio, film, and television, and the author of five books. He composed the music for the classic holiday song "The Christmas Song" ("Chestnuts Roasting on an Open Fire") and co-wrote the lyrics with Bob Wells.

Early years

Melvin Howard Tormé was born in Chicago, Illinois, to immigrant Russian Jewish parents,[1] whose surname had been **Torma**. However, the name was changed at Ellis Island to "Torme." A child prodigy, he first sang professionally at age 4 with the Coon-Sanders Orchestra, singing "You're Driving Me Crazy" at Chicago's Blackhawk restaurant.[2]

Between 1933 and 1941, he acted in the network radio serials *The Romance of Helen Trent* and *Jack Armstrong, the All-American Boy*. He wrote his first song at 13, and three years later, his first published song, "Lament to Love," became a hit recording for Harry James. He played drums in Chicago's Shakespeare Elementary School drum and bugle corps in his early teens. While a teenager, he sang, arranged, and played drums in a band led by Chico Marx of the Marx Brothers. His formal education ended in 1944 with his graduation from Chicago's Hyde Park High School.

Early career

Tormé works with the most beautiful voice a man is allowed to have, and he combines it with a flawless sense of pitch... As an improviser he shames all but two or three other scat singers and quite a few horn players as well.

—Will Friedwald, Jazz Singing

In 1943, Tormé made his movie debut in Frank Sinatra's first film, the musical *Higher and Higher*. He went on to sing and act in many films and television episodes throughout his career, even hosting his own television show in 1951–52. His appearance in the 1947 film musical *Good News* made him a teen idol for several years.

In 1944 he formed the vocal quintet "Mel Tormé and His Mel-Tones," modeled on Frank Sinatra and The Pied Pipers. The Mel-Tones, which included Les Baxter and Ginny O'Connor, had several hits fronting Artie Shaw's band and on their own, including Cole Porter's "What Is This Thing Called Love?" The Mel-Tones were among the first jazz-influenced vocal groups,[3] blazing a path later followed by The Hi-Lo's, The Four Freshmen, and The Manhattan Transfer.

Later in 1947, Tormé went solo. His singing at New York's Copacabana led a local disc jockey, Fred Robbins, to give him the nickname "The Velvet Fog," thinking to honor his high tenor and smooth vocal style, but Tormé detested the nickname. (He self-deprecatingly referred to it as "this Velvet Frog voice".[4] As a solo singer, he recorded several romantic hits for Decca (1945), and with the Artie Shaw Orchestra on the Musicraft label (1946–48). In 1949, he moved to Capitol Records, where his first record, "Careless Hands," became his only number one hit. His versions of "Again" and "Blue Moon" became signature tunes. His composition "California Suite," prompted by Gordon Jenkins' "Manhattan Tower," became Capitol's first 12-inch LP album. Around this time, he helped pioneer cool jazz.

Tormé on drums performing with Benny Goodman and Teddy Wilson.

In his 1994 book "My Singing Teachers," Torme cited Patty Andrews, lead singer of The Andrews Sisters, the most successful show business act of the 1940s (second only to Bing Crosby), as one of his favorite vocalists, saying, "They had more hit records to their credit than you could count, and one of the main reasons for their popularity was Patty Andrews. She stood in the middle of her sisters, planted her feet apart, and belted out solos as well as singing the lead parts with zest and confidence. The kind of singing she did cannot be taught, it can't be studied in books, it can't be written down. Long experience as a singer and wide-open ears were her only teachers, and she learned her lessons well."[5]

From 1955 to 1957, Tormé recorded seven jazz vocal albums for Red Clyde's Bethlehem Records, all with groups led by Marty Paich, most notably *Mel Tormé with the Marty Paich Dektette*. When rock and roll music (which Tormé called "three-chord manure")[6] came on the scene in the 1950s, commercial success became elusive. During the next two decades, Tormé often recorded mediocre arrangements of the pop tunes of the day, never staying long with any particular label. He was sometimes forced to make his living by singing in obscure clubs. He had two minor hits, his 1956 recording of "Mountain Greenery," which did better in the United Kingdom where it reached No. 4 in May that year; and his 1962 R&B song "Comin' Home, Baby," arranged by Claus Ogerman. The latter recording led the jazz and gospel singer Ethel Waters to say that "Tormé is the only white man who sings with the soul of a black man." It was later covered instrumentally by Quincy Jones and Kai Winding.

In 1960, he appeared with Don Dubbins in the episode "The Junket" in NBC's short-lived crime drama *Dan Raven*, starring Skip Homeier and set on the Sunset Strip of West Hollywood. He also had a significant role in a cross-cultural western entitled *Walk Like a Dragon* starring Jack Lord. Tormé played 'The Deacon', a bible-quoting gunfighter who worked as an enforcer for a lady saloon-owner and teaches a young Chinese, played by James

Shigeta, the art of the fast draw. In one scene, he tells a soon-to-be victim: 'Say your prayers, brother Masters. You're a corpse.' And then delivers on the promise. Tormé, like Sammy Davis Jr. and Robert Fuller was a real-life fast-draw expert. He also sang the title song.[7]

In 1963–64, Tormé wrote songs and musical arrangements for *The Judy Garland Show*, where he made three guest appearances. However, he and Garland had a serious falling out, and he was fired from the series, which was canceled by CBS not long afterward. A few years later, after Garland's death, his time with her show became the subject of his first book, "The Other Side of the Rainbow with Judy Garland on the Dawn Patrol" (1970). Although the book was praised, some felt it painted an unflattering picture of Judy, and that Tormé had perhaps over-inflated his own contributions to the program; it led to an unsuccessful lawsuit by Garland's family.[8]

Tormé befriended Buddy Rich, the day Rich left the Marine Corps in 1942. Rich became the subject of Tormé's book *Traps — The Drum Wonder: The Life of Buddy Rich* (1987). Tormé also owned and played a drum set that drummer Gene Krupa used for many years. George Spink, treasurer of the Jazz Institute of Chicago from 1978 to 1981, recalled that Tormé played this drum set at the 1979 Chicago Jazz Festival with Benny Goodman on the classic "Sing, Sing, Sing."[9] Tormé had a deep appreciation for classical music; especially that of Frederick Delius and Percy Grainger.[10]

Later career and death

The resurgence of vocal jazz in the 1970s resulted in another artistically fertile period for Tormé, whose live performances during the 1960s and 1970s fueled a growing reputation as a jazz singer. He found himself performing as often as 200 times a year around the globe. In 1976, he won an Edison Award (the Dutch equivalent of the Grammy) for best male singer, and a Down Beat award for best male jazz singer.[11] For several years around this time, his September appearances at Michael's Pub on the Upper East Side would unofficially open New York's fall cabaret season. Tormé viewed his 1977 Carnegie Hall concert with George Shearing and Gerry Mulligan as a turning point. Shearing later said:

> "It is impossible to imagine a more compatible musical partner… I humbly put forth that Mel and I had the best musical marriage in many a year. We literally breathed together during our countless performances. As Mel put it, we were two bodies of one musical mind."[12]

Starting in 1982, Tormé recorded several albums with Concord Records, including:

- Five albums with pianist George Shearing;
- His big band work with Rob McConnell and his Boss Brass orchestra (see *Mel Tormé, Rob McConnell and the Boss Brass*);
- A reunion with Marty Paich, resulting in a live recording in Tokyo (*In Concert Tokyo*) and a studio album (*Reunion*).

In the 80s and 90s, Mel's trio often included pianist John Colianni, bassist Jennifer Leitham, drummer Donny Osborne, as well as famed New Zealand pianist Carl Doy.

In 1993, Verve Records released the classic "Blue Moon" album featuring the Velvet voice and the Rodgers and Hart Songbook. His version of Blue Moon performed live at the "Sands" in November that year earned him a new nickname from older audiences: "The Blue Fox." The nickname was used to describe Tormé's performance after spending an extra hour with pianist Bill Butler cracking jokes and answering queries from a throng of more "mature" women who turned out to see the show. Under the shimmering blue lights at the Sands, he gained a new nickname that would endure for every future performance in Las Vegas and his last performance at Carnegie Hall. Tormé would develop other nicknames later in life, but none seemed as popular as the Velvet Fog (primarily on the East Coast) and the Blue Fox.

Tormé made nine guest appearances as himself on the 1980s situation comedy *Night Court* whose main character, Judge Harry Stone (played by Harry Anderson), was depicted as an unabashed Tormé fan (an admiration that

Anderson shared in real-life; Anderson would later deliver the eulogy at Tormé's funeral) which led to a following among Generation Xers along with a series of Mountain Dew commercials and on an episode of the sitcom *Seinfeld* ("The Jimmy"), in which he dedicates a song to the character Kramer. Tormé also recorded a version of Nat King Cole's "Straighten up and Fly Right" with his son, alternative/adult contemporary/jazz singer Steve March Tormé.[13] Tormé was also able to work with his other son, television writer-producer Tracy Tormé on *Sliders*. The 1996 episode, entitled "Greatfellas," sees Tormé playing an alternate version of himself: a country-and-western singer who is also an FBI informant.[14]

In a scene in the 1988 Warner Bros. cartoon *Night of the Living Duck*, Daffy Duck has to sing in front of several monsters, but lacks a good singing voice. So, he inhales a substance called "Eau de Tormé" and sings like Mel Tormé (who in fact provided the voice during this one scene, while Mel Blanc provided Daffy's voice during most of the cartoon).[4]:p. 176

On August 8, 1996, a stroke abruptly ended his 65-year singing career. In February 1999, Tormé was awarded the Grammy Lifetime Achievement Award. Another stroke in 1999 ended his life. Torme is buried at the Westwood Village Memorial Park cemetery in Los Angeles. In his eulogistic essay, John Andrews wrote about Tormé:[15]

Mel Torme's grave

> "Tormé's style shared much with that of his idol, Ella Fitzgerald. Both were firmly rooted in the foundation of the swing era, but both seemed able to incorporate bebop innovations to keep their performances sounding fresh and contemporary. Like Sinatra, they sang with perfect diction and brought out the emotional content of the lyrics through subtle alterations of phrasing and harmony. Ballads were characterized by paraphrasing of the original melody which always seemed tasteful, appropriate and respectful to the vision of the songwriter. Unlike Sinatra, both Fitzgerald and Tormé were likely to cut loose during a swinging up-tempo number with several scat choruses, using their voices without words to improvise a solo like a brass or reed instrument."

Accomplishments

Tormé also made a guest vocal appearance on the 1983 album *Born to Laugh at Tornadoes* from the progressive pop band Was (Not Was). Tormé sang the black comedic cocktail jazz song "Zaz Turned Blue" about a teenager who is choked as part of an asphyxiophiliac turn-on in a park ("Steve squeezed his neck/He figured what the heck") − and who may or may not have suffered brain damage as a result ("Now he plays lots of pool/And as a rule/He wears a silly grin/On his chin").[16]

The Writer

Tormé's other books include *My Singing Teachers: Reflections on Singing Popular Music* (1994), a biography of Buddy Rich, *Traps, the Drum Wonder* (1997), and his autobiography *It Wasn't All Velvet* (1988). He also published the novel *Wynner* in 1977.

The songwriter

Tormé wrote more than 250 songs, several of which became jazz standards. He also often wrote the arrangements for the songs he sang. He often collaborated with Bob Wells, and the best known Tormé-Wells song is "The Christmas Song," often referred to by its opening line "Chestnuts roasting on an open fire." The song was recorded first by Nat King Cole. Tormé said that he wrote the music to the song in only 45 minutes,[17] and that it was not one of his personal favorites, calling it, somewhat dismissively, "my annuity".[4]

For a partial Mel Tormé discography, see the Mel Tormé discography.

Bibliography

- *The Other Side of the Rainbow* (1970), about his time as musical adviser to Judy Garland's television show
- *Wynner* (1978), a novel
- *It Wasn't All Velvet* (1988), the autobiography
- *Traps — The Drum Wonder: The Life of Buddy Rich* (1991)
- *My Singing Teachers: Reflections on Singing Popular Music* (1994)

Filmography

- *Higher and Higher* (1943)
- *Ghost Catchers* (1944)
- *Pardon My Rhythm* (1944)
- *Resisting Enemy Interrogation* (1944) (documentary)
- *Let's Go Steady* (1945)
- *Junior Miss* (1945)
- *The Crimson Canary* (1945) (drums dubber)
- *Janie Gets Married* (1946)
- *Good News* (1947)
- *Words and Music* (1948)
- *Duchess of Idaho* (1950)
- *The Fearmakers* (1958)
- *The Big Operator* (1959)
- *Girls Town* (1959)
- *Walk Like a Dragon* (1960)
- *The Private Lives of Adam and Eve* (1960)
- *The Patsy* (1964) (Cameo)
- *A Man Called Adam* (1966) (Cameo)
- *Land of No Return* (1978)
- *Artie Shaw: Time Is All You've Got* (1985) (documentary)
- *The Night of the Living Duck* (1988) (short subject) (voice)
- *Daffy Duck's Quackbusters* (1988) (voice)
- *The Naked Gun 2½: The Smell of Fear* (1991) (Cameo)

Television work

- *The Mel Tormé Show* (1951–1952)
- *TV's Top Tunes* (host in 1951)
- *Faye Emerson's Wonderful Town* (1 episode, 1952)
- *Summertime U.S.A.* (1953) (Summer replacement series)
- *The Nat King Cole Show* (July 9, 1957)
- *The Comedian* (1957) (live drama written by Rod Serling and directed by John Frankenheimer)
- *The Pat Boone Chevy Showroom* (January 7, 1960)
- *To Tell the Truth (panelist, 1964)*
- *The Lucy Show* as Mel Tinker (3 episodes, 1965–1967)
- *The Sammy Davis Jr. Show* (March 11, 1966)
- *Run for Your Life*, with Ben Gazzarra (episode writer)

- *You Don't Say!* (guest, 1967)
- *The Virginian* (special guest 1968)
- *It Was a Very Good Year* (1971) (Summer replacement series)
- *Pray TV* (1982) (Cameo)
- *Hotel* (1983) (pilot for series) (Cameo)
- *Night Court* (guest appearances 1986–1992)
- *A Spinal Tap Reunion: The 25th Anniversary London Sell-Out* (1992)
- *Pops Goes the Fourth* (1995)
- *Seinfeld* — episode "The Jimmy" (1995)
- *Sliders* — episode "Greatfellas" (1996)

Family

Spouses:

- Candy Toxton (February 1949–1955) (divorced) 2 children.
- Arlene Miles (1956–1965) (divorced) 1 child.
- Janette Scott (1966–1977) (divorced) 2 children.
- Ali Severson (June 5, 1984–1999, his death).

Tormé was survived by five children and two stepchildren, including:

- Steve (b. 1953), an alternative adult contemporary singer/guitar player.
- Melissa (Melissa Torme-March).
- Tracy (b. 1959), a screenwriter and film producer.
- Daisy, a broadcaster.
- James, a singer.

References

[1] Bloom, Nate (2006-12-19). "The Jews Who Wrote Christmas Songs" (http://www.interfaithfamily.com/site/apps/nl/content2. asp?c=ekLSK5MLIrG&b=297399&ct=3303147). InterfaithFamily. . Retrieved 2006-12-19.

[2] Knack, Bob (2002). "Bringing Down The Blackhawk" (http://www.jazzinchicago.org/educates/journal/articles/ bringing-down-blackhawk). Jazz Institute of Chicago. . Retrieved 2009-12-15.

[3] "Mel Torme & The Mel-Tones" (http://www.singers.com/group/Mel-Torme/). *Primarily A Cappella*. Singers.com. . Retrieved 2 September 2012.

[4] Hemming, Roy and David Hajdu (1991). *Discovering Great Singers of Classic Pop: A New Listener's Guide to the Sounds and Lives of the Top Performers* (http://books.google.com/books?id=zbYtmOIHvfcC&printsec=frontcover#v=onepage&q&f=false). New York: Newmarket Press. pp. 177. ISBN 1-55704-072-9. .

[5] Sforza, John: "Swing It! The Andrews Sisters Story;" University Press of Kentucky, 2000; 289 pages.

[6] "Mel Tormé – A Series of Odd Jobs" (http://www.legacy.com/ns/news-story.aspx?t=mel-torm--a-series-of-odd-jobs&id=97). *The Obit Report*. Legacy.com. . Retrieved 2 September 2012.

[7] Mateas, Lisa. "Walk Like a Dragon" (http://www.tcm.com/this-month/article/196853|0/Walk-Like-a-Dragon.html). *Turner Classic Movies Film Article*. Turner Entertainment Networks. . Retrieved 2 September 2012.

[8] Spadoni, Mike. "The Judy Garland Show" (http://www.televisionheaven.co.uk/judy_garland_show.htm). Television Heaven. . Retrieved 2 September 2012.

[9] George Spink (2007-03-23). "The Chicago Jazz Festival" (http://web.archive.org/web/20070810191239/http://www.tuxjunction.net/ chicagojazzfestival.htm). Archived from the original (http://www.tuxjunction.net/chicagojazzfestival.htm) on 2007-08-10. . Retrieved 2007-08-26.

[10] Hulme, George (2008). *Mel Tormé: A Chronicle of His Recordings, Books and Films* (http://books.google.com/ books?id=PZCG4zlFpqMC&printsec=frontcover#v=onepage&q&f=false). Jefferson NC: McFarland. pp. 3. ISBN 978-0-7864-3743-6. .

[11] Holden, Stephen (6 June 1999). "Mel Torme, Velvet Voice of Pop and Jazz, Dies at 73" (http://www.nytimes.com/1999/06/06/us/ mel-torme-velvet-voice-of-pop-and-jazz-dies-at-73.html?pagewanted=3). *New York Times*. . Retrieved 2 September 2012.

[12] "Sir George Shearing Jazz pianist dies at 91" (http://www.tributes.com/show/George-Shearing-90810957). Tributes, Inc.. . Retrieved 2 September 2012.

[13] "Tormé, Steve March" (http://kbflfm.com/personality-steve-march-torme.aspx). *KBFL Music of Your Life*. Meyer Communications. .
      Retrieved 2 September 2012.

[14] Truman, Mike. "Review: Greatfellas" (http://earthprime.com/reviews/greatfellas-review.html). Earth Prime. . Retrieved 2 September
      2012.

[15] Mel Torme, an appreciation (http://www.wsws.org/articles/1999/jun1999/tor-j10.shtml)

[16] Carlin, Marcello (2011). *The Blue in the Air* (http://books.google.com/books?id=OHZCro5YV48C&printsec=frontcover#v=onepage&
      q&f=false). Ropley Hants: Zero Books. pp. 66. ISBN 978-1-84694-0. .

[17] Furia, Philip and Michael Lasser (2006). *America's Songs: The Stories Behind the Songs of Broadway, Hollywood, and Tin Pan Alley* (http:/
      /books.google.com/books?id=-ENtazHbVc4C&printsec=frontcover#v=onepage&q&f=false). New York: Routledge. pp. 207.
      ISBN 0-415-97246-9. .

External links

- Biography and discography from vh1.com (http://www.vh1.com/artists/az/torme_mel/bio.jhtml)
- Biography and discography from theiceberg.com (http://www.theiceberg.com/artist/556/mel_torme.html)
- *Fuller Up* Obituary (http://elvispelvis.com/meltorme.htm)
- Mark Evanier on Tormé and "The Christmas Song" (http://www.povonline.com/cols/COL245.htm)
- 1976 interview with Tormé (http://www.jazzprofessional.com/interviews/Mel Torme_1.htm)
- Mel Tormé (http://www.imdb.com/name/nm0868123/) at the Internet Movie Database
- Smooth As Velvet The Mel Torme Discography (http://home.ica.net/~blooms/tormehome.html)
- "Mel Tormé and the Marty Paich Dek-tette" (http://www.jazz.com/features-and-interviews/2008/8/21/
  mel-marty-dek-tette) by Thomas Cunniffe (Jazz.com (http://www.jazz.com))
- Radio interview with Steve March Torme WSLR (http://dougmilesinterview.milestonebroadcasting.com/2009/
  07/14/doug-miles-interviews-singermusician-steve-march-torme-wslr-radio.aspx)

Melody Time

Melody Time	
Original theatrical release poster	
Directed by	Jack Kinney Clyde Geronimi Hamilton Luske Wilfred Jackson
Produced by	Walt Disney
Written by	Winston Hibler Harry Reeves Ken Anderson Erdman Penner Homer Brightman Ted Sears Joe Rinaldi William Cottrell Jesse Marsh Art Scott Bob Moore John Walbridge
Starring	Roy Rogers Trigger Dennis Day The Andrews Sisters Fred Waring and the Pennsylvanians Freddy Martin Ethel Smith Frances Langford Buddy Clark Bob Nolan Sons of the Pioneers The Dinning Sisters Bobby Driscoll Luana Patten Jerry Colonna The King's Men
Music by	Eliot Daniel Paul J. Smith
Editing by	Donald Halliday Thomas Scott Ken Darby
Studio	Walt Disney Productions
Distributed by	RKO Radio Pictures, Inc.
Release date(s)	May 27, 1948
Running time	75 minutes
Language	English

Melody Time (working title *All in Fun*), a 1948 film, is the 10th theatrically released animated feature produced by Walt Disney and released to theatres by RKO Radio Pictures on May 27, 1948. Made up of several sequences set to popular music and folk music, the film is, like *Make Mine Music* before it, the popular music version of *Fantasia* (an ambitious film that proved to be a commercial disappointment upon its original theatrical release). *Melody Time*, while not meeting the artistic accomplishments of *Fantasia*, was a mildly successful film in its own right. It is the tenth animated feature in the Walt Disney Animated Classics series and the fifth package film following *Saludos Amigos*, *The Three Caballeros*, *Make Mine Music*, and *Fun and Fancy Free*.

Production

In late 1947, Disney announced he would be releasing a "regrouping of various cartoons at his studio under two titles, 'Melody Time' and 'Two Fabulous Characters'", to be released in August 1948 and 1949, respectively.[1]Melody Time ended up being a released a few month earlier than planned, in May.

Melody Time is considered to be the last anthology feature made by the Walt Disney Animation Studios (the next film to be released was The Adventures of Ichabod and Mr. Toad, which featured two stories). These package features were "little-known short-film compilations that Disney produced and released as feature films during World War II". They were "financially (and artistically) lightweight productions meant to bring in profits [to allow the studio to] return to fairy tale single-narrative feature form", a endevour which they successfully completed two years later with Cinderlla. While each of the shorts "contrast in length, form, and style", a common thread throughout is that each one "is accompanied by song[s] from musicians and vocalists of the '40s"[2] - both popular and folk music.[3] This sets it apart from the similarly structured Fantasia, whose segments were set to classical music instead. [4] As opposed to Fun and Fancy Free, whose story was bound to the tales of Bongo and Jack and the Beanstalk, in this film "Walt Disney has let his animators and his color magicians have free rein".[5]

The entire film was produced at the Walt Disney Studios, in Burbank, California.

It was made with 35 mm film negatives, through the spherical cinematographic process, in Technicolor, and had an aspect ratio of 1.37:1.

Melody Time was the last film The Andrew Sisters ever took part in. They sang throughout the 10 minutes segment known as *Little Toot*. Andrew Sisters member Maxine described the experience as follows: "In was quite an experience. On the wall at the studio they had the whole story in picture form. Two songwriters played the score and Walk Disney explained it to us. It was a new thing for Disney. We sang the narrative. It was very exciting to work with Disney-he was such a gentleman".[6]

The two children who hear the story of Pecos Bill, Bobby Driscoll and Luana Patten, also appear together in Song of the South and So Dear to My Heart.[7]

Melody Time was the last feature film to include Donald Duck until the 1988 movie Who Framed Roger Rabbit.[7]

Marketing

The various taglines of the film were: "*For Your All-Time Good Time !*", "*7 HIT SONGS! 11 MUSICAL STARS!*", and "*Walt Disney's GREAT NEW MUSICAL COMEDY*".

Collectible items for the film include books, figures, and posters.[4]

Plot and background information of film segments

According to Disney, the film's plot is as follows: "In the grand tradition of Disney's greatest musical classics such as FANTASIA, MELODY TIME features seven classic stories, each enhanced with high-spirited music and unforgettale characters...[A] feast for the eyes and ears [full of] wit and charm...a delightful Disney classic with something for everyone".[8]. Rose Pelswick, in a 1948 review for The News-Sentinel, described the film as an 'adventure into the intriguing make-believe world people by Walk Disney's Cartoon characters". It also explains that "with the off-screen voice of Buddy Clack doing the introductions, the...episodes include fantasy, folklore, South American rhythms, poetry, and slapstick".[9] A 1948 review by the Pittsburgh Post-Gazette described it as a "mixture of fantasy, abstraction, parable, music, color, and movement".[10]

The seven "mini-musical"[7] stories are outlined below:

Once Upon a Wintertime

This segment features Frances Langford singing the title song about two romantic young lovers in December. The boy shows off on the ice for his lover, and near-tragedy and a timely rescue ensues. Like several other segments of these package films, *Once Upon a Wintertime* was later released theatrically as an individual short, in this case on September 17, 1954.[11] This short is also featured in *Very Merry Christmas Songs*. which is part of *Disney Sing Along Songs*, as a background movie for the song Jingle Bells.

Bumble Boogie

This segment presents a surrealistic battle for a solitary bumble bee as he tries to ward a visual and musical frenzy off. The music is courtesy of Freddy Martin and his orchestra (with Jack Fina playing the piano) and is a swing-jazz variation of Rimsky-Korsakov's *Flight of the Bumblebee*, which was one of the many pieces considered for inclusion in *Fantasia*.

The Legend of Johnny Appleseed

This segment is a retelling of the story of John Chapman, who spent most of his life roaming Mid-Western America (mainly Illinois and Indiana) in the pioneer days, and planting apple trees, thus earning his famous nickname. Dennis Day narrates and provides all the voices, except for the angel, who is voiced by Dallas McKennon (uncredited). This segment was released independently on December 25, 1955 as just *Johnny Appleseed*.[12] The piece has a running time of "17 minutes [making it] the film's second-longest piece".[2] Before being adapted as a segment in Melody Time, the story of Johnny Appleseed was "first immortali[s]ed around campfires", then later turned into "storybook form".[13]

Little Toot

This segment is based on the story also titled *Little Toot* by Hardie Gramatky, in which the title protagonist, a small tugboat, wanted to be just like his father Big Toot, but couldn't seem to stay out of trouble. The Andrews Sisters provide the vocals.

Trees

This segment is a recitation of the famous Alfred Joyce Kilmer poem by Fred Waring and the Pennsylvanians with the lyrical setting seen through the seasons.

Blame It on the Samba

This segment has Donald Duck and José Carioca meeting with the Aracuan Bird, who introduces them to the pleasures of the samba. The accompanying music is the 1914 polka *Apanhei-te, Cavaquinho* by Ernesto Nazareth, fitted with English lyrics. The Dinning Sisters provide the vocals while organist Ethel Smith plays the organ.

Donald Duck, Jose Carioca, and the Aracuan bird reprise their roles from The Three Caballeros. The animated short includes some live-action footage.[14]

Pecos Bill

The film's final segment is about Texas' famous hero Pecos Bill, he was raised by coyotes (similar to how Mowgli was raised by wolves in The Jungle Book) the biggest and best cowboy that ever lived. It also features his horse Widowmaker, and recounts how Pecos was brought back down to earth by a woman named Slue-Foot Sue. This retelling of the story features Roy Rogers, Bob Nolan, and the Sons of the Pioneers to Bobby Driscoll and Luana Patten. This segment was later edited on the film's NTSC video release (but not the PAL release) to remove all scenes of Bill smoking a cigarette. The entire scene with Bill rolling the smoke and lighting it with a lightning bolt was cut and all other shots of the offending cigarette hanging from his lips were digitally removed.[15] With a total running time of "22 minutes, [it] is the lengthiest piece".[2]

Cast

The cast is listed below[8]:

- Roy Rogers - Himself; Narrator; Singer (*Pecos Bill*)
- Trigger, the Smartest Horse in the Movies - Himself
- Dennis Day - Narrator; Singer; Characters (*Johnny Appleseed*)
- The Andrews Sisters - Singers (*Little Toot*)[6]
- Fred Waring and the Pennsylvanians - Singers (*Trees*)
- Freddy Martin - Music composer (*Bumble Boogie*)
- Ethel Smith - Organist (*Blame It On the Samba*)
- Frances Langford - Singer (*Once Upon a Wintertime*)
- Buddy Clark - Singer; Narrator
- Bob Nolan - Himself; Singer; Narrator (*Pecos Bill*)
- Sons of the Pioneers - Themselves; Singers; Narrators (*Pecos Bill*)
- The Dinning Sisters - Singers (*Blame It On the Samba*)
- Bobby Driscoll - Himself (*Pecos Bill*)
- Luana Patten - Herself (*Pecos Bill*)
- Dallas McKennon - Himself; Narrator; Character (*Johnny Appleseed*)

Songs

The songs in Melody Time were all "largely based around (then) contemporary music and musical performances".[16]

Song	Writer(s)	Performer(s)
Melody Time	George David Weiss and Bennie Benjamin	Buddy Clark
Once Upon a Wintertime	Bobby Worth and Ray Gilbert	Frances Langford
Bumble Boogie	Nikolai Rimsky-Korsakov (arranged by Jack Fina)	Freddy Martin and His Orchestra (with Jack Fina on piano)
Johnny Appleseed	Kim Gannon and Walter Kent	Dennis Day
Little Toot	Allie Wrubel	The Andrews Siste
Trees	Joyce Kilmer (poem) and Oscar Rasbach (music)	Fred Waring and His Pennsylvanians
Blame It on the Samba	Ernesto Nazareth and Ray Gilbert	Ethel Smith and The Dinning Sisters
Pecos Bill	Eliot Daniel and Johnny Lange	Roy Rogers and the Sons of the Pioneers
Blue Shadows on the Trail	Eliot Daniel and Johnny Lange	Roy Rogers and the Sons of the Pioneers

Release

The film was originally released in USA, Brazil, and Argentina in 1948, and later in 1950 in Mexico. From 30 January 1951 (UK) to 15 September 1954 (Denmark) the film was released across Europe. The film was known by a variety of names including *Време за музика* in Bulgaria, *Mélodie cocktail* in France, *Musik, Tanz und Rhythmus* in Germany, and *Säveltuokio* in Finland.

Disney later released a package film entitled *Music Land*, a nine-segment film which "recycled sequences from both Make Mine Music and Melody Time". Five selections were from Melody Time while another was the short *Two For the Record*, which consisted of two segments produced under Benny Goodman's direction. [17]

Melody Time was unique in that, up until 1998, 50 years after its initial release, it was "one of the handful of Disney's animated features yet to be released on videocassette". Some of the segments "have been re-released as featurettes", and *Once Upon a Wintertime* has "been included on other Disney video cartoon compilations".[18]

Critical reception

At the time of its release, the film received "generally unfavorable reviews".[19] However, *Disney Discourse: Producing the Magic Kingdom* notes that an article in Time Magazine around that time "celebrated the global scope of the Disney product"[19], and a 1948 review for The News-Sentinel said the "charm and skill" that one had to to expect from Disney is "delightful entertainment" for all children.[9] A 1940 review of the film for The Los Angeles Times said the "acts" *Johnny Appleseed* and *Pecos Bill*, which the "new variety show from Walt Disney [gave] special attention to" are "'human' sagas" and as a result "more endearing" than the rest of the segments.[20] *The Andrews Sisters: A Biography and Career Record* notes that "the public liked the film and it was a box-office success".[6]

A 1948 review by the Pittsburgh Post-Gazette said the film was a "visual and auditory delight" and added that if Disney was able to reached his audiences other senses, "there's no doubt he'd be able to please them too". It says a "tuneful and functional soundtrack rounds out the Disney art". It said that Bumble Boogie "reverted back to fantasia-like interpretive technique. *It also notes that the abstraction ends after* Trees, *and the final three shorts after that are "story-sequences". It says the simple story of Johnny Appleseed is done with "touching perception". It said* Little Toot *"is destined to become a fable of our time" and adds "the Andrew Sisters tell the story in lilting song". The review ended with the author saying "deserving accolades will go to [Walt Disney] and his whole production staff, as well as to the staff whose voices he has used as well".* [10]

A 1948 review of the film for The News-Sentinel described Pecos Bill as the best segment, and said it "caused a stir among the small fry in the audience".

Contemporary reviews are more mixed, picking up the film's faults, but also praising it for various technical achievements.

DVDizzy notes that in regard to the mix of shorts and 1940s music, "the marriage often does not work, and the melodies are not particularly the film's forte", however itadds that this is a modern day opinion, and that paying audiences at the time the film was released probably "felt better about the music". The site then reviewed each segment in turn, saying: *Once Upon a Wintertime* is "physical slapstick" that doesn't match the "dramatic singing by Frances Langford", *Bumble Boogie* is "fun but forgettable", *The Legend of Johnny Appleseed* is the "most enjoyable" of the segments, *Little Toot* is "rather generic", *Trees* features "some nice imagery", *Blame it on the Samba* "involve[s] Latin dancing and nothing more", and *Pecos Bill* has "Disney...go[ing] back and us[ing] today's technology to alter [Bill's smoking,] what admittedly is a minor point in one short of a film that's predominantly going to be watched and purchased by animation enthusiasts/historians". It explains the "video quality is consistently satisfying" and that the "audio has the dated feel of other '40s Disney films". [2]

The film received a score of 77.06 out of 100 based on 50 votes, on the site Disney Movies Guide.[21]

In his book *The Animated Movie Guide*, Jerry Beck gave Melody Time a rating of 2/5 stars, and described the film as "odds and ends from a studio geared up towards revival". He said that by this time the post-war formula of releasing anthologies had become "tired", with only a few of the segments being interesting, and the feeling as if the animators kept "pushing for something more creative to do". He commented that the film, a "vast underachievement" for Disney, felt dated like its predecessor Make Mine Music, and added that he found it hard to believe that the artists that made this film also made Pinocchio eight years before. He praised the "exceptional designs and palettes" by stylist Mary Blair, including the "flat styli[s]ed backgrounds" of *Wintertime*, and the Impressionist painting/folk art look of The Legend of Johnny Appleseed. He highlighted the "slapstick...impressive montage of Bill's impressive feats" as a "true treat". He described the "manic interpretation" of Flight of the Bumblebee known as *Bumble Boogie*, in which a bee terrorised by musical instruments and notes "change[s] colo[u]rs and outlines from one moment to the next as the backgrounds seamlessly dissolve, change or morph around him", as "Disney's best piece of surealism since the 'Pink Elephant on Parade' sequence in Dumbo". He also spoke about the "stellar special effects" involved in the dynamite exploding Ethel Smith's organ instrument, in the segment *Blame it on the Samba*. However, he added that the rest of Melody time was "sad[ly]...forgettable".[14]

As part of a series of videos collectively known as Disneycember, internet reviewer Doug Walker reviewed Melody Time, along with the other traditionally animated Disney movies throughout December 2011. He noted its similarities to Make Mine Music (stories mixed with variations of modern songs and some poetry), and said a suitable name to the "almost identical" film would have been Make Mine Music 2. He said that just like the former package film, this one "works pretty good too". He says that some of the narratives are "more forgettable than others", and cites *Tress* (which he describes as the animators "drawing what they hear when the poem is read") as "especially nice". He compared Bumble Boogie to the Elephant sequence and said it had some "fun imagery". He said The Legend of Johnny Appleseed "st[ood] out the most" with its "really heavy atmosphere and really heavy visuals", and its "incredible" backgrounds. He complimented its "size and scope", although also described it as "corny", and also praised the surreal "apple trees becoming...clouds" sequence. He says the short is "gripping" and should have stood on its own as a short rather than being "tucked away in here". He calls Pecos Bill "fun" and "really creative" although questions why it was chosen to finish the film as opposed to the "far superior" Johnny Appleseed short (adding that it ends on a bizarre tone). He said that as a whole, Melody Time has both good shorts, music, and animation, and that there are some points thorough the film where the animation hits the "real Disney charm" that was featured throughout Fantasia. His closing statement was that one should "definitely check it out".[22]

In *The Magic Kingdom: Walt Disney and the American Way of Life*, Steven Watts explains that while *Pecos Bill* "recaptured some of the old magic", the film as a whole, along with the other "halfhearted...pastiche[s] of short subjects" came across as "animated shorts surrounded with considerable filler and stuff into a concocted package", He adds that as a result they "never caught fire" due to them "varying wildly in quality", with moments of creativity being outweighed by the "insipid, mediocre, stale stretches of work".[23]

The authors of *The Cartoon Music Book* said Melody Time was "much better" than the other pose-Fantasia Disney package films of the era, adding that it was "beautifully designed and scored", paving the way for the "'populuxe' style" of Disney's first renaissance (starting with Cinderella in 1950). They stated that *Trees* and *Blame it on the Samba* (which they described as a "psychedelic Latin American sequence") are "charming, if still obscure, entries in the Disney pop song catalog[ue].[24]

The Andrews Sisters: A Biography and Career Record author H. Arlo Nimmo said "in general, [the Andrew Sisters-sung] Melody Time holds up well, and the story of 'Little Toot' is as appealing to today as when it originally appeared fifty-some years ago". He described the singing as "unremarkable but narrat[ing] the...story cleverly". He adds Variety's quote: "'Little Toot,'...is colorful and engrossing. Andrew Sisters give it popular vocal interpretation", and said that although The New York Times preferred the film to make Mine Music, the magazine added "The Andrew Sisters sing the story...not very excitingly". He also included Metronome's indifferent comment: "The Andrew Sisters sing a silly song about a tugboat". The article *The Walt Disney Classics Collection Gets*

"Twitterpatted" For Spring deemed *Little Toot* one of Melody time's highlights.[25]

In a review of the 2004 Disney film Home on the Range, the article *Frisky 'Range' doesn't measure up Disney delivers fun* said that the "sendup of the Wild West...has some fitful comic vitality and charm - [but] it can't hold a candle to the 'Pecos Bill' segment of the studio's late-'40s anthology, 'Melody Time'".[26]

A 1998 Chicago Tribute review of the film, in honour of its VHS release, described the film as a "sweet, old-fashioned delight and one of the few Disney animated films preschoolers can watch alone without danger of being traumatized", but also added that the younger generation might be bored by it But older due to them being "attuned to the faster, hipper rhythms of the post-'Mermaid' era".[18]

Controversy

Due to the controversy surrounding the appearance in "Pecos Bill", when the film was released onto DVD in 1998 the segment was "heavily edited". While the character of Bill is supposed to be shown "smoking a cigarette in several sequences", in the edited version these scenes were removed, "resulting in the removal of almost the entire tornado sequence and some odd hand and mouth movements for Bill throughout". In a review at DVDizzy, it is noted that is one has an interested in the shorts, they'd "probably be upset to know that Disney has decided to digitally edit out contents of the 50-plus-year-old frames of animation".[2] In the Melody Time section of the *Your Guide To Disney's 50 Animated Features* feature at Empire Online said "at least, it was for the US releases, but not for the rest of the world. Go figure."[16] The scenes are removed on the *Golden Collection* DVD release[14] although the Japanese laserdisc and the version of the DVD released in the United Kingdom are uncut during the Pecos Bill segment.

According to a source, upon reviewing the music that Ken Darby had composed for "Johnny Appleseed", Walt Disney "scorned the music", describing it as "like New Deal music". Darby, "enraged", said to Disney "THAT is just a cross-section of one man's opinion!". Darby was only employed at The Walt Disney Company Darby for a short while after this supposed incident.

Jerry Beck, in his book *The Animated Movie Guide*, comments on a risque joke in Pecos Bill that somehow made it passed the censors, when Bill kisses Sue and his guns rise from their holsters and begin to fire by themselves, simulating ejaculation. He adds jokingly that "perhaps Roy Rogers was covering the eyes of Bobby Driscoll and Luana Patten during this scene".[14]

Legacy

Many of the seven segments were later released as shorts, and some of them became "more successful than the original film". "Bumble Boogie" was among the few segments to receive huge popularity upon individual release.[21] The article *The Walt Disney Classics Collection Gets "Twitterpatted" For Spring* notes that "the 'Little Toot' segment of the film was so popular that it was re-released on its own as a short cartoon in 1954, and was subsequently featured on Walt Disney's popular weekly television series".[25]

There are many references to the Pecos Bill segment in the Frontierland themed land at part of Magic Kingdom: there is a sign of Bill outside the *Pecos Bill Tall Tale Inn and Cafe*, as well as various images of him, the other characters, and their accessories around the cafe. A pair of gloves with the inscription "To Billy, All My Love, Slue Foot Sue" is located in a glass display case. In the World of Disney, Jose Carioca from *Blame it on the Samba* appears in a mural on the ceiling among many other characters. In a glass case, behind the windows of the All-Star Movies, there is a script for Melody Time. [7]

Home video and DVD

Melody Time was first released in Japan on laserdisc on January 25, 1987, and on VHS on June 2, 1998, under the Walt Disney Masterpiece Collection title.[27]

Its latest release was on June 6, 2000 on VHS and DVD under the Walt Disney Gold Classic Collection, released by Buena Vista Home Entertainment.

The DVD has bonus features in the form of the following 3 cartoons: "Casey Bats Again", "Lambert The Sheepish Lion", and "Donald Applecore".[8]

References

[1] "DISNEY ANNOUNCES TWO NEW PROJECTS; ' Melody Time' to Be Released in August and Two Fabulous Characters' in 1949" (http:// select.nytimes.com/gst/abstract.html?res=F50F11FB3A5E17738DDDAE0994D9415B8788F1D3). . Retrieved January 12, 2013.

[2] "Melody Time" (http://www.dvdizzy.com/melodytime.html). DVDizzy. . Retrieved January 11, 2013.

[3] "World War II and the Postwar Years in America: Volume 1" (http://books.google.com.au/books?id=YjbR9EXABPEC&pg=PA163& dq="Melody+Time"+disney&hl=en&sa=X&ei=WWLwUJ6LCMa_kgWJ_YHgDg&ved=0CFoQ6AEwBzgK#v=onepage&q="Melody Time" disney&f=false). pp. 276. . Retrieved January 12, 2013.

[4] Farrell, Ken (2006). "Warman's Disney Collectibles Field Guide: Values and Identification" (http://books.google.com.au/ books?id=qE7kN8OvJD8C&pg=PA171&dq="Melody+Time"+disney&hl=en&sa=X&ei=gu3uUPf9MsWqkgWxjYHICQ& ved=0CD4Q6AEwAw#v=onepage&q="Melody Time" disney&f=false). Kreuse Publications. pp. 171–3. . Retrieved January 12, 2013.

[5] Crowther, Bosley (May 28, 1948,). "Disney's Newest Cartoon Array, 'Melody Time,' Opens at Astor -- Seven Scenes Featured" (http:// select.nytimes.com/gst/abstract.html?res=F40F13FD3954177A93CAAB178ED85F4C8485F9). The New York Times. . Retrieved January 12, 2013.

[6] Nimmo, H. Arlo (2004). "The Andrews Sisters: A Biography and Career Record" (http://books.google.com.au/ books?id=9mE2-RxDyZsC&pg=PA251&dq="Melody+Time"+disney&hl=en&sa=X&ei=WWLwUJ6LCMa_kgWJ_YHgDg& ved=0CFQQ6AEwBjgK#v=onepage&q="Melody Time" disney&f=false). pp. 150–1. . Retrieved January 12, 2013.

[7] Dodge, Brent (2010). "From Screen to Theme" (http://books.google.com.au/books?id=Ax6PzlpRgNkC&pg=PA46&dq="Melody+ Time"+disney&hl=en&sa=X&ei=WWLwUJ6LCMa_kgWJ_YHgDg&ved=0CDEQ6AEwADgK#v=onepage&q="Melody Time" disney& f=false). pp. 46–9. . Retrieved January 12, 2013.

[8] "Walt Disney Studios Home Entertainment: Melody Time" (http://disneydvd.disney.go.com/melody-time.html). . Retrieved January 10, 2013.

[9] Pelswick, Rose (July 20, 1948). "Walk Disney's "Melody Time" Better Than Ever" (http://news.google.com/ newspapers?id=kipjAAAAIBAJ&sjid=-XMNAAAAIBAJ&pg=3448,628931&dq=melody-time+disney&hl=en). The News-Sentinel. . Retrieved January 12, 2013.

[10] E. F. J. (July 26, 1948). "Melody Time" (http://news.google.com/newspapers?id=TuYMAAAAIBAJ&sjid=X2oDAAAAIBAJ& pg=3155,5097171&dq=melody-time+disney&hl=en). Pittsburgh Post-Gazette. . Retrieved January 12, 2013.

[11] "Melody Time" (http://affichesdisney.canalblog.com/archives/c_est_un_souvenir_de_decembre/index.html) (in French). . Retrieved 2010-12-03.

[12] "Johnny Appleseed" (http://affichesdisney.canalblog.com/archives/johnny_pepin_de_pomme/index.html) (in French). . Retrieved 2010-12-03.

[13] Susan Veness and Simon Veness (2012). "The Hidden Magic of Walt Disney World Planner" (http://books.google.com.au/ books?id=G_g4MfaemmQC&pg=PA118&dq="Melody+Time"+disney&hl=en&sa=X&ei=gu3uUPf9MsWqkgWxjYHICQ& ved=0CEgQ6AEwBQ#v=onepage&q="Melody Time" disney&f=false). pp. 118. . Retrieved January 12, 2013.

[14] Beck, Jerry (2005). "The Animated Movie Guide" (http://books.google.com.au/books?id=fTI1yeZd-tkC&pg=PA165&dq="Melody+ Time"+disney&hl=en&sa=X&ei=gu3uUPf9MsWqkgWxjYHICQ&ved=0CE4Q6AEwBg#v=onepage&q="Melody Time" disney& f=false). pp. 165–6. . Retrieved January 12, 2013.

[15] http://www.ultimatedisney.com/melodytime.html

[16] "Your Guide To Disney's 50 Animated Features: Melody Time" (http://www.empireonline.com/features/50-disney-films/default. asp?film=10). Empire Online. . Retrieved January 11, 2013.

[17] Daniel Goldmark and Yuval Taylor (2002). "The Cartoon Music Book" (http://books.google.com.au/books?id=5rfRdOMfTqsC& pg=PA33&dq="Melody+Time"+disney&hl=en&sa=X&ei=gu3uUPf9MsWqkgWxjYHICQ&ved=0CFQQ6AEwBw#v=onepage& q="Melody Time" disney&f=false). A Capella Books. pp. 126–9. . Retrieved January 12, 2013.

[18] Liebenson, Donald (June 11, 1998). "THE FULL COMPOSITION DISNEY'S 50-YEAR-OLD 'MELODY TIME' FINALLY RELEASED IN WHOLE ON VIDEO" (http://pqasb.pqarchiver.com/chicagotribune/access/30116463.html?dids=30116463:30116463&FMT=ABS& FMTS=ABS:FT&type=current&date=Jun+11,+1998&author=Donald+Liebenson.+Special+to+the+Tribune.&pub=Chicago+ Tribune&desc=THE+FULL+COMPOSITION+DISNEY'S+50-YEAR-OLD+`MELODY+TIME'+FINALLY+RELEASED+IN+ WHOLE+ON+VIDEO&pqatl=google). Chicago Tribute. . Retrieved January 12, 2013.

[19] Smoodin, Eric Loren (1994). "Disney Discourse: Producing the Magic Kingdom" (http://books.google.com.au/books?id=WPXZl1lcR30C&pg=PA11&dq="Melody+Time"+disney&hl=en&sa=X&ei=WWLwUJ6LCMa_kgWJ_YHgDg&ved=0CEIQ6AEwAzgK#v=onepage&q="Melody Time" disney&f=false). Routledge. pp. 11. . Retrieved January 12, 2013.

[20] Scheuer, Philip K. (July 30, 1948). "Disney's 'Melody Time' Diverting Show" (http://pqasb.pqarchiver.com/latimes/access/416715191.html?dids=416715191:416715191&FMT=ABS&FMTS=ABS:AI&type=historic&date=Jul+30,+1948&author=&pub=Los+Angeles+Times&desc=Disney's+'Melody+Time'+Diverting+Show&pqatl=google). The Los Angeles Times. . Retrieved January 12, 2013.

[21] "Melody Time" (http://www.disneymovieslist.com/movies/details.asp?mov=melody-time). Disney Movies Guide. . Retrieved January 10, 2013.

[22] Walker, Doug (December 08 2011). "Disneycember! Part 4" (http://thatguywiththeglasses.com/videolinks/thatguywiththeglasses/specials/33511-disneycember-part-4). That Guy With The Glasses. . Retrieved January 12, 2013.

[23] Watts, Steven (1997). "The Magic Kingdom: Walt Disney and the American Way of Life" (http://books.google.com.au/books?id=NgARIndAbjAC&pg=PA483&dq="Melody+Time"+disney&hl=en&sa=X&ei=gu3uUPf9MsWqkgWxjYHICQ&ved=0CFsQ6AEwCA#v=onepage&q="Melody Time" disney&f=false). First University of Missouri Press. pp. 249. . Retrieved January 12, 2013.

[24] Daniel Goldmark and Yuval Taylor (2002). "The Cartoon Music Book" (http://books.google.com.au/books?id=5rfRdOMfTqsC&pg=PA33&dq="Melody+Time"+disney&hl=en&sa=X&ei=gu3uUPf9MsWqkgWxjYHICQ&ved=0CFQQ6AEwBw#v=onepage&q="Melody Time" disney&f=false). A Capella Books. pp. 32–3. . Retrieved January 12, 2013.

[25] "The Walt Disney Classics Collection Gets "Twitterpatted" For Spring" (http://www.laughingplace.com/News-ID10009210.asp). . Retrieved January 12, 2013.

[26] "Frisky 'Range' doesn't measure up: Disney delivers fun, but it won't fulfill fans of old 'Pecos Bill'" (http://rl.newsbank.com/nl-search/we/Archives?p_product=WT&p_theme=wt&p_action=search&p_maxdocs=200&p_topdoc=1&p_text_direct-0=101C758A8454481C&p_field_direct-0=document_id&p_perpage=10&p_sort=YMD_date:D&s_trackval=GooglePM). . Retrieved January 12, 2013.

[27] "NEW DISNEY VIDEO IN STORES TUESDAY" (http://nl.newsbank.com/nl-search/we/Archives?p_product=LB&p_theme=lb&p_action=search&p_maxdocs=200&p_topdoc=1&p_text_direct-0=0EAE92495BCD6794&p_field_direct-0=document_id&p_perpage=10&p_sort=YMD_date:D&s_trackval=GooglePM). . Retrieved January 12, 2013.

External links

- *Melody Time* (http://www.bcdb.com/bcdb/cartoon.cgi?film=25) at the Big Cartoon DataBase
- *Melody Time* (http://www.imdb.com/title/tt0040580/) at the Internet Movie Database
- *Melody Time* (http://www.rottentomatoes.com/m/melody_time/) at Rotten Tomatoes
- Various Melody Time posters (http://www.learnaboutmovieposters.com/posters/db/release.asp?rid=18097)
- cornel1801 review (http://www.cornel1801.com/disney/Melody-Time-1948/movie-film.html)
- DVD movie guide review (http://www.dvdmg.com/melodytime.shtml)
- Disney Screen Caps (http://disneyscreencaps.com/caps/melody-time-1948/)

Mound, Minnesota

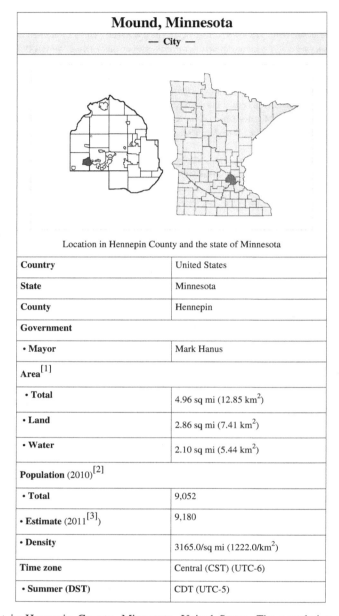

Mound, Minnesota	
— City —	
Location in Hennepin County and the state of Minnesota	
Country	United States
State	Minnesota
County	Hennepin
Government	
• **Mayor**	Mark Hanus
Area[1]	
• **Total**	4.96 sq mi (12.85 km^2)
• **Land**	2.86 sq mi (7.41 km^2)
• **Water**	2.10 sq mi (5.44 km^2)
Population (2010)[2]	
• **Total**	9,052
• **Estimate** (2011[3])	9,180
• **Density**	3165.0/sq mi (1222.0/km^2)
Time zone	Central (CST) (UTC-6)
• **Summer (DST)**	CDT (UTC-5)

Mound is a settlement in Hennepin County, Minnesota, United States. The population was 9,052 at the 2010 census.[4] Mound is the birthplace of the Tonka truck, named after Lake Minnetonka. The Tonka Toys headquarters was originally in Mound, but moved when business picked up and they needed a better place for supplies to be delivered to.

Geography

According to the United States Census Bureau, the city has a total area of 4.96 square miles (12.85 km^2), of which, 2.86 square miles (7.41 km^2) is land and 2.1 square miles (5.44 km^2) is water.[1] County roads 15 and 110 are two of the main arterial routes.

Lakes in Mound include Black Lake, Dutch Lake, Lake Langdon, Saunders Lake, Seton Lake. Lake Minnetonka encompasses these and many others in the area.

Lake Langdon lies immediately west of Mound, between an old Great Northern railroad line and Lake Minnetonka. One of its most notable places is an old ice house and grocery store at the east side of the lake. The store for many years in the 1940s and '50s was owned and operated by Ed and Pete Sollie, uncles of the Andrews Sisters. Other historic places on the east shore of Lake Langdon are Our Lady of the Lake parochial school and the Mound Baptist Church, long cared for by Ulrich Eugster, an immigrant to the United States from Reute, Switzerland.

According to Melvin Gimmestad's *Historical Backgrounds of Mound, Minnesota*, "Mound derived its name from the Indian mounds once found within the present-day limits. They were not built by the Dakota Indians but were made by prehistoric Indians".[5]

City Hall

The Mound Public Safety Facility houses both the city's Fire and Police Departments.

Mound has more than 1,000 docks on its various lakes. The lakes geographically define the town's areas, such as Three Points, The Island, The Highlands, Grandview Boulevard and Shirley Hills.

Education

Because the Westonka School District encompasses Mound, the city is also connected to Spring Park, Orono, St. Bonifacious, and Minnetrista. Mound schools include Grandview Middle School, Hilltop Primary School, Mound-Westonka High School, and Shirley Hills Elementary. The school mascot is the Whitehawk, which was changed from the Mohawk in 1997. Some students attend public schools in other school districts chosen by their families under Minnesota's open enrollment statute.

Local sites

The Mound City Council has been working for a number of years on a project called "Mound Visions". One of the project's goals is to improve business traffic in the city. Some of its recent accomplishments are the Mound Marketplace, the realignment of County Road 15, the Lost Lake Greenway, and the Villas on Lost Lake townhouses.

Demographics

Historical populations			
Census	Pop.		%±
2000	9,435		—
2010	9,052		–4.1%
U.S. Decennial Census [6]			

2010 census

As of the census[2] of 2010, there were 9,052 people, 3,974 households, and 2,444 families residing in the city. The population density was 3,165 inhabitants per square mile (1,222 /km^2). There were 4,379 housing units at an average density of 1,531.1 per square mile (591.2 /km^2). The racial makeup of the city was 95.8% White, 0.9% African American, 0.3% Native American, 1.3% Asian, 0.4% from other races, and 1.4% from two or more races. Hispanic or Latino of any race were 1.8% of the population.

There were 3,974 households out of which 27.8% had children under the age of 18 living with them, 48.1% were married couples living together, 8.6% had a female householder with no husband present, 4.9% had a male householder with no wife present, and 38.5% were non-families. 30.7% of all households were made up of individuals and 7.9% had someone living alone who was 65 years of age or older. The average household size was 2.28 and the average family size was 2.85.

The median age in the city was 42.6 years. 21.3% of residents were under the age of 18; 6.4% were between the ages of 18 and 24; 25.9% were from 25 to 44; 35% were from 45 to 64; and 11.5% were 65 years of age or older. The gender makeup of the city was 51.5% male and 48.5% female.

2000 census

As of the census[7] of 2000, there were 9,435 people, 3,982 households, and 2,560 families residing in the city. The population density was 3,203.8 people per square mile (1,239.1/km²). There were 4,118 housing units at an average density of 1,398.3 per square mile (540.8/km²). The diverse racial makeup of the city was 96.24% White, 0.64% African American, 0.19% Native American, 1.30% Asian, 0.04% Pacific Islander, 0.45% from other races, and 1.14% from two or more races. Hispanic or Latino of any race were 0.96% of the population. 32.4% were of German, 14.1% Norwegian, 11.8% Irish, 7.7% Swedish and 6.1% English ancestry according to Census 2000.

There were 3,982 households out of which 30.2% had children under the age of 18 living with them, 53.5% were married couples living together, 7.4% had a female householder with no husband present, and 35.7% were non-families. 28.3% of all households were made up of individuals and 7.0% had someone living alone who was 65 years of age or older. The average household size was 2.37 and the average family size was 2.93.

In the city the population was spread out with 23.9% under the age of 18, 6.2% from 18 to 24, 35.6% from 25 to 44, 25.4% from 45 to 64, and 9.0% who were 65 years of age or older. The median age was 38 years. For every 100 females there were 108.3 males. For every 100 females age 18 and over, there were 106.9 males.

The median income for a household in the city was $60,671, and the median income for a family was $68,396. Males had a median income of $44,437 versus $34,125 for females. The per capita income for the city was $30,309. About 0.9% of families and 2.7% of the population were below the poverty line, including 1.7% of those under age 18 and 5.1% of those age 65 or over.

Fictional natives

Mound is the birthplace and childhood home of the fictional character S. "Jonesy" Jones from *Reno 911!* (actor Cedric Yarbrough is actually from Burnsville, Minnesota). It is also the hometown of Larry Sanders, main character of *The Larry Sanders Show*.

Famous residents

- Sheldon Beise - All-American fullback on Bernie Bierman's undefeated national championship football teams at the University of Minnesota, 1934–1935
- The Andrews Sisters, Patty, Maxene and LaVerne grew up in Mound as children from 1918 through 1931 and always came back to visit at least one week each July. They visited their uncles Pete and Ed Sollie at their small grocery store, enjoy themselves at the Mound Casino and relax at the Mound swimming beach, reminiscing about their childhood.
- Actor Kevin Sorbo was born and raised in Mound.
- Kris Humphries - Professional basketball player and ex-husband of Kim Kardashian has a home in Mound on the shores of Lake Minnetonka which was featured on the wedding special of Keeping up with the Kardashians.
- Author Lisa Wysocky was born and raised in Mound.
- Henning Linden was born in Mound.

References

[1] "US Gazetteer files 2010" (http://www.census.gov/geo/www/gazetteer/files/Gaz_places_national.txt). United States Census Bureau (http://en.wikipedia.org/wiki/United_States_Census_Bureau). . Retrieved 2012-11-13.
[2] "American FactFinder" (http://factfinder2.census.gov/faces/nav/jsf/pages/index.xhtml). United States Census Bureau (http://en.wikipedia.org/wiki/United_States_Census_Bureau). . Retrieved 2012-11-13.
[3] "Population Estimates" (http://www.census.gov/popest/data/cities/totals/2011/files/SUB-EST2011-IP.csv). United States Census Bureau (http://en.wikipedia.org/wiki/United_States_Census_Bureau). . Retrieved 2013-01-03.
[4] "2010 Census Redistricting Data (Public Law 94-171) Summary File" (http://factfinder2.census.gov/faces/tableservices/jsf/pages/productview.xhtml?pid=DEC_10_PL_GCTPL2.ST13&prodType=table). *American FactFinder*. U.S. Census Bureau, 2010 Census. . Retrieved 23 April 2011.
[5] Upham, Warren (2001). *Minnesota Place Names* (http://shop.mnhs.org/moreinfo.cfm?Product_ID=137). Minnesota Historical Society Press. pp. 231. ISBN 0-87351-396-7. .
[6] http://www.census.gov/prod/www/abs/decennial/
[7] "American FactFinder" (http://factfinder.census.gov). United States Census Bureau. . Retrieved 2008-01-31.

- (http://maps.google.com/maps?hl=en&tab=wl)

External links

- Official City of Mound Homepage (http://www.cityofmound.com/)
- Mound Dock Program Administration (http://www.mounddocks.com/)
- Mound Police Department (http://www.moundpolice.com/)
- Mound Fire Department (http://www.moundfire.com/)
- Mound Westonka Public Schools (http://www.westonka.k12.mn.us/)
- Mound Westonka Regional Site (http://www.MoundWestonka.com/)
- Mound/Westonka Hockey Association (http://www.westonkahockey.org/)
- Mound Hockey Program Coverage (http://www.moundhockey.com/)
- Mound Westonka Public Library (http://www.hclib.org/AgenciesAction.cfm?agency=Wt/)
- Westonka Historical Society (http://www.llbrustad.com/historicalsociety/index.html)

- U.S. Geological Survey Geographic Names Information System: Mound Maps (http://geonames.usgs.gov/pls/gnispublic/f?p=gnispq:3:::NO::P3_FID:648143)

Near You

"Near You"	
Single by George Jones and Tammy Wynette	
from the album *Golden Ring*	
Released	November 1976 (US)
Format	7"
Recorded	December 12, 1974
Genre	Country
Length	2:21
Label	Epic 50314
Writer(s)	Francis Craig, Kermit Goell
Producer	Billy Sherrill
George Jones and Tammy Wynette singles chronology	

"Golden Ring" (1976)	"Near You" (1976)	"Southern California" (1977)

"**Near You**" is a popular song written by Francis Craig with lyrics by Kermit Goell. The song was published in 1947.

The recording by Francis Craig (the song's composer) was released by Bullet Records as catalog number 1001. It first reached the *Billboard* Best Sellers chart on August 30, 1947, and lasted 21 weeks on the chart, peaking at number one. On the "Most Played By Jockeys" chart, the song spent 17 consecutive weeks at number one, setting a record for both the song and the artist with most consecutive weeks in the number-one position on a music chart.[1] In 2009, hip-hop group The Black Eyed Peas surpassed Craig's record for artist with most consecutive weeks in the number-one position with the songs "Boom Boom Pow" and "I Gotta Feeling". However, their record was accomplished with combined weeks of two #1 songs - one succeeding the other in the top position.

Other notable versions

Other recordings of the song that charted on the *Billboard* best seller in 1947 include:[1]

- The Andrews Sisters (Decca Records catalog number 24171) entered the chart on October 3 and peaked at number four.
- *Near You* became the closing theme song for Milton Berle's TV comedy shows.[2]
- Elliot Lawrence (Columbia Records catalog number 37838) entered the chart on October 3 and peaked at number nine. This was Lawrence's only charting hit.
- Larry Green (RCA Victor Records catalog number 20-2421) entered the chart on October 10 and peaked at number three.
- Alvino Rey (Capitol Records catalog number 452) entered the chart on October 17 and peaked at number nine in its only week on the chart. This was Rey's last charting hit.

Roger Williams recorded the song in 1958, and it charted on the Billboard Hot 100 singles chart, peaking at number ten. Jerry Lee Lewis recorded an instrumental version of the song in 1959. It has also been recorded by Marlene Dietrich and Andy Williams.

In 1977, it was a number-one country hit for the duo of George Jones and Tammy Wynette. The Jones-Wynette version was recorded on December 12, 1974.

"Near You" was used by Milton Berle as the closing song on his Texaco Star Theater, and became his theme song for many years thereafter.[3]

References

[1] Whitburn, Joel (1973). *Top Pop Records 1940-1955*. Record Research.
[2] Texaco Star Theater (comedy-variety hosted by Milton Berle) (http://www.classicthemes.com/50sTVThemes/themePages/texacoStarTheater.html)
[3] Classic Themes' Texaco Star Theater page (http://www.classicthemes.com/50sTVThemes/themePages/texacoStarTheater.html)

External links

* Full lyrics of this song (http://www.metrolyrics.com/near-you-lyrics-george-jones.html) at MetroLyrics

Nice Work If You Can Get It (song)

"Nice Work If You Can Get It" is a popular song.

The music was written by George Gershwin, the lyrics by Ira Gershwin. It was one of nine songs George Gershwin wrote for the movie *A Damsel in Distress*, in which it was performed by Fred Astaire with backing vocals provided by The Stafford Sisters. The song was published in 1937.

A version of this song was used during the opening credits of the 1995 to 1998 CBS sitcom *Cybill*, starring Cybill Shepherd, who performed the song herself.

The song was included in the Tony Award-winning Broadway musical *Crazy for You* and lent its name to the musical *Nice Work If You Can Get It*.

Notable recordings

* Fred Astaire
* The Andrews Sisters (1938)
* Bing Crosby on his 1956 album "Bing Sings Whilst Bregman Swings."
* Doris Day - *Hooray For Hollywood* (1958)
* Ella Fitzgerald - *Ella Fitzgerald Sings the George and Ira Gershwin Songbook* (1959)
* *Nice Work If You Can Get It: Ella Fitzgerald and Andre Previn do Gershwin*, Pablo Records, 1983
* The Hi-Lo's - *A Musical Thrill* (2006)
* Billie Holiday - *Quintessential Billie Holiday: Vol. V* (1944)
* Stan Kenton - *At The Rendezvous: Vol 2* (2000) (vocal by Ann Richards)
* Thelonious Monk
* Georges Guetary - *An American in Paris* (1951)
* Frank Sinatra - *A Swingin' Affair!* (1957) and *Sinatra-Basie: An Historic Musical First* (1962)
* Johnny Smith - *Moonlight in Vermont*
* Jeri Southern - *Jeri Southern At the Crescendo* (1960)
* Maxine Sullivan and Her Orchestra (recorded October 22, 1937; released November 20, 1937) - 2:49
* Majestic 12- *Red Hot + Rhapsody* (1998)
* Mel Tormé

Over Here!

Over Here!	
Original Cast Recording	
Music	Richard M. Sherman Robert B. Sherman
Lyrics	Robert B. Sherman Richard M. Sherman
Book	Will Holt
Productions	1974 Broadway

Over Here! is a musical with a score by Richard M. Sherman and Robert B. Sherman and book by Will Holt. The original Broadway production was directed by Tom Moore and choreographed by Patricia Birch, with scenic design by Douglas W. Schmidt and costumes by Carrie F. Robbins.

Over Here! was a follow-up to the Sherman brothers' World War II musical *Victory Canteen*, an off-Broadway production that featured 1940s icon Patty Andrews. The setting is a cross-country train trip in the United States during World War II (hence the name of the play, in contrast to the popular patriotic war anthem entitled *Over There*). The show begins as a nostalgic look at 1940s America (where fashion, music, big bands and swing dance dominates) but, quickly evolves into a social commentary about the fear of dying in battle, prejudice, and discrimination.

Production history

After thirteen previews, the show opened on March 6, 1974 at the Shubert Theatre, where it ran for 341 performances and became the top-grossing production of the 1974 Broadway season. It is largely credited as the Broadway musical which launched many careers. [1] The opening night cast included Patty and Maxene Andrews (of the Andrews Sisters) and newcomers John Travolta, Treat Williams, Marilu Henner, Samuel E. Wright, and Ann Reinking, all of whom went on to achieve successful careers. Despite still playing to capacity audiences, the show closed on January 4, 1975 under controversial conditions. "The producers blamed Patty and Maxine, claiming they wanted more money and made unreasonable demands, and cancelled the national tour. The Andrews sisters blamed the producers, claiming they had mismanaged the show from the beginning and were now using them as scapegoats."[2] According to an article in *The New York Times*, the tour was cancelled due to a "salary dispute" between the Andrews sisters and the producers.[3]

Radar online and the Official site reports that Cody Linley will be starring in an all new production of *Over Here!* set to launch early in 2010 at the Saban Theatre, Beverly Hills and an official website shows open auditions. In an interview, Linley confirmed that he will play the role of Bill.[4]

The postponed 2010 production is an "all-new" production with a modified book by original playwright Will Holt, choreographed by Tony Stevens, designed by Royal Court designer Mark Walters with associate designer Christopher Hone and Costume Designer David Toser, featuring Music Supervision by David Barber. Dick Van Dyke had agreed to head an all-star cast however he was forced to withdraw days before the start date when his partner Michelle's illness became terminal. Unable to find an immediate replacement for Van Dyke at such short notice, the producers rescheduled the production to premiere in California in 2012, following which a US tour is being planned.

Song list

Act I	Act II
• The Beat Begins (Overture) - The Big Band • Since You're Not Around - Makeout, Rankin, Mother, Father, Sarge and Company • Over Here! - Paulette and Pauline de Paul • Buy a Victory Bond - Company • My Dream for Tomorrow - June and Bill • Charlie's Place - Pauline de Paul, Maggie, Lucky, The Big Band and Company • Hey Yvette/The Grass Grows Green - Spokesman, Rankin and Father • The Good-Time Girl (later called "The V.D. Polka") - Paulette de Paul and Company • Wait for Me Marlena - Mitzi and Company • We Got It - Paulette de Paul, Pauline de Paul, Mitzi and Company	• The Beat Continues (Entr'acte) - The Big Band and Company • Wartime Wedding - Paulette de Paul, Pauline de Paul and Company • Don't Shoot the Hooey to Me, Louie - Sam • Where Did the Good Times Go? - Paulette de Paul • Dream Drummin'/Soft Music - Misfit, The Big Band and Company • The Big Beat - Paulette de Paul, Pauline de Paul and Mitzi • No Goodbyes - Paulette de Paul, Pauline de Paul and Company

Awards and nominations

Original Broadway production

Year	Award	Category	Nominee	Result
1974	Tony Award	Best Musical		Nominated
		Best Performance by a Featured Actress in a Musical	Janie Sell	Won
		Best Direction of a Musical	Tom Moore	Nominated
		Best Choreography	Patricia Birch	Nominated
		Best Costume Design	Carrie F. Robbins	Nominated
	Drama Desk Award	Outstanding Set Design	Douglas W. Schmidt	Won
		Outstanding Costume Design	Carrie F. Robbins	Won
	Theatre World Award		John Driver	Won
			Ann Reinking	Won
			Janie Sell	Won

References

[1] Paddock, Terri. Sherman Bros' Over Here Confirms Delay" (http://www.whatsonstage.com/news/theatre/london/E8821166463525/Update:+Sherman+Bros☐+Over+Here+Confirms+Delay.html) whatsonstage.com, 19 December 2006

[2] Nimmo, Harry. *The Andrews Sisters* (2004), McFarland, ISBN 0-7864-1731-5, pp 366-371

[3] Calta, Louis. " *Over Here!* Tour is Off in Dispute", *The New York Times*, December 21, 1974, p. 18

[4] Snider, Mike. Cody Linley: Goodbye 'Hannah,' hello Broadway" (http://whosnews.usaweekend.com/2010/02/cody-linley-goodbye-hannah-hello-broadway/) usaweekend.com, February 4, 2010

External links

• *Over Here!* (http://www.ibdb.com/production.php?id=3706) at the Internet Broadway Database
• The Sherman Brothers (http://www.shermanmusic.com/)

Private Buckaroo

Private Buckaroo	
Film poster	
Directed by	Edward F. Cline
Produced by	Ken Goldsmith
Written by	Edward James (writer) Edmond Kelso (writer) Paul Girard Smith (story)
Cinematography	Elwood Bredell
Editing by	Milton Carruth
Distributed by	Universal Studios
Release date(s)	28 May 1942
Running time	68 minutes
Country	United States
Language	English

Private Buckaroo (1942) is an American musical film directed by Edward F. Cline and starring The Andrews Sisters, Dick Foran, Harry James, Shemp Howard, Joe E. Lewis, and Jennifer Holt. The film tells the story of army recruits following basic training, with the Andrews Sisters attending USO dances.

Plot summary

Entertainer Lon Prentice initially is keen to enlist in the US Army but is prevented due to have one flat foot. Having the flat fixed, he is accepted for enlistment. Soon after basic training begins, Private Prentice informs his commanding officer he finds most military training useless, unnecessary and beneath him. His commander orders all the men that Private Prentice is exempt from doing things he doesn't want to do, which turns the entire camp against him.

Cast

- The Andrews Sisters (Maxene Andrews, Patty Andrews and Laverne Andrews)
- Dick Foran as Lon Prentice
- Joe E. Lewis as Lancelot Pringle McBiff
- Ernest Truex as Col. Elias Weatherford
- Jennifer Holt as Joyce Mason
- Shemp Howard as First Sgt. 'Muggsy' Shavel
- Harry James as Himself (Harry James and His Music Makers)
- Richard Davies as Lt. Howard Mason
- Mary Wickes as Bonnie-Belle Schlopkiss
- Donald O'Connor as Donny
- Peggy Ryan as Peggy
- Huntz Hall as Cpl. Anemic
- Susan Levine as Tagalong
- Jivin' Jacks and Jills (vocal group)

Eddie Acuff, Wade Boteler, Eddie Bruce, George Chandler, Jimmy Conlin, Pat Flaherty, Bess Flowers, Helen Forrest, Edmund Glover, Grace Hayle, Robert Emmett Keane, Harold Miller, Sidney Miller, Edmund Mortimer, William H. O'Brien, Gene O'Donnell, Eddie Parker, Tommy Rall, Joey Ray, Addison Richards, Jeffrey Sayre, Edwin Stanley and Billy Wayne appears uncredited.

Soundtrack

- Dick Foran - "Private Buckaroo" (written by Charles Newman and Allie Wrubel)
- The Andrews Sisters - "Three Little Sisters" (written by Irving Taylor and Vic Mizzy)
- Dick Foran - "I'm in the Army Now"
- The Andrews Sisters - "Six Jerks in a Jeep" (written by Sid Robin)
- The Andrews Sisters - "Don't Sit Under the Apple Tree" (written by Sam H. Stept and Charles Tobias)
- The Andrews Sisters - "James Session" danced by Donald O'Connor, Peggy Ryan and The Jivin' Jacks and Jills
- The Andrews Sisters - "Steppin' Out Tonight" based on the song "That's The Moon, My Son" (written by Art Kassel and Sammy Gallop.
- Dick Foran and Helen Forrest - "Nobody Knows the Trouble I've Seen"
- Harry James and His Music Makers - "Concerto for Trumpet"
- The Andrews Sisters - "Johnny Get Your Gun Again" (written by Don Raye and Gene de Paul)
- Dick Foran and The Andrews Sisters - "We've Got a Job To Do" (written by Vickie Knight)
- Joe E. Lewis - "I Love the South"
- Helen Forrest with Harry James and His Music Makers - "You Made Me Love You" (written by Joseph McCarthy and James V. Monaco)

External links

- *Private Buckaroo* [1] at the Internet Movie Database
- *Private Buckaroo* [2] is available for free download at the Internet Archive [*more*]

References

[1] http://www.imdb.com/title/tt0035218/
[2] http://www.archive.org/details/private_buckaroo

Road to Rio

Road to Rio	
Theatrical release poster	
Directed by	Norman McLeod
Produced by	Daniel Dare
Written by	• Edmund Beloin • Jack Rose
Based on	title by author
Starring	• Bing Crosby • Bob Hope • Dorothy Lamour
Music by	Robert Emmett Dolan
Cinematography	Ernest Laszlo
Editing by	Ellsworth Hoagland
Studio	Paramount Pictures
Distributed by	Paramount Pictures
Release date(s)	• December 25, 1947 (USA)
Running time	100 minutes
Country	United States
Language	English
Box office	$4.5 million (US/ Canada rentals) [1]

Road to Rio is a 1947 American comedy film directed by Norman Z. McLeod and starring Bing Crosby, Bob Hope, and Dorothy Lamour.[2] Written by Edmund Beloin and Jack Rose, the film is about two inept vaudevillians who stow away on a Brazilian-bound ocean liner and foil a plot by a sinister hypnotist to marry off her niece to a greedy fortune hunter. *Road to Rio* was the fifth of the "*Road to …*" series.

Plot

Scat Sweeney, and Hot Lips Barton, two out of work musicians, travel the US trying to find work and stay away from girls. After running from state to state, each time running because of a girl, they try their luck in Louisiana.

They stow away on board a Rio-bound ship, after accidentally starting some fires at a circus. They then get mixed up with the distraught Lucia, who first thanks them, then unexpectedly turns them over to the ship's captain. Unbeknownst to both of them, Lucia is being hypnotized by her crooked guardian, Catherine Vail. Vail plans to marry Lucia to her brother so she can control her and a set of 'papers'.

After a series of misadventures including sneaking off the boat, recruiting a few local musicians, and the boys trying to escape with Lucia only to have Vail hypnotize her again and slap them both, Vail decides to do away with the boys permanently. She hypnotizes both of them and tries to get them to kill each other in a duel, but it fails. Scat and Hot Lips finally figure things out and the boys head for the ceremony in order to stop the wedding and to help catch the crooks. Upon finding the 'papers', which Scat reads, when Hot Lips asks what they are about, Scat tears them up and looks into the camera saying "The world must NEVER know."

Later on, Scat is dismayed to see that Lucia loves Hot Lips and not him. But upon peaking through a keyhole, he sees Hot Lips hypnotizing her.

Hope's frequent sidekick Jerry Colonna has a cameo as the leader of a cavalry charging to the rescue of Bing and Bob, as the film cuts away to the galloping horses periodically. All is resolved before Colonna can arrive. "Exciting, though... *was*n't it?!"

This movie also has the distinction of being the only film that Bing Crosby and the Andrew Sisters appeared in together.

Cast

- Bing Crosby as Scat Sweeney
- Bob Hope as Hot Lips Barton
- Dorothy Lamour as Lucia Maria de Andrade
- Gale Sondergaard as Catherine Vail
- Frank Faylen as Trigger
- Joseph Vitale as Tony
- George Meeker as Sherman Mallory
- Frank Puglia as Rodrigues
- Nestor Paiva as Cardoso
- Robert Barrat as Johnson
- Stanley Andrews as Capt. Harmon
- Harry Woods as Ship's Purser
- The Wiere Brothers as Three Musicians
- The Andrews Sisters as Themselves
- Jerry Colonna as Himself[3]

Production

Soundtrack

All songs were written by Johnny Burke (lyrics) and Jimmy Van Heusen (music).

- "You Don't Have to Know the Language", performed by Bing Crosby and The Andrews Sisters
- "Experience", by Dorothy Lamour
- "But Beautiful", Bing Crosby
- "Apalachicola, Fla.", Bing Crosby and Bob Hope
- "For What?", Bing Crosby and Bob Hope
- "Diz Que Tem", performed by Marquita Rivera[4]

For the commercial recordings, Bing Crosby recorded the song "Experience" with big band vocalist Nan Wynn. Bing Crosby also recorded the songs "You Don't Have to Know The Language" and "Apalachicola, Fla" with the Andrews Sisters. Bing did not record any of the songs from the film with Bob Hope or Dorothy Lamour.

Copyright

The film's copyright was renewed in a timely manner by an associate of the film's owner. Originally registered for copyright as LP1171 with a declared publication date of August 25, 1947, the continuation of copyright was contingent upon renewal between the 27th and 28th anniversaries of that date. Renewal occurred July 25, 1975, number R610335. The film opened February 19, 1948, so the renewal is still timely even if that later date were considered publication date.

The copyright is now scheduled to run until 95 years after the publication date (2042). The renewal form names as authors Hope Enterprises and Bing Crosby Enterprises, which were partners when the film was produced. As it turned out, the copyright (which never expired, and thus the film never entered the public domain) was re-assigned to Columbia Pictures Television—Columbia and LBS Communications (which formed the joint venture Colex Enterprises) assumed the rights to this film from Hope Enterprises, and re-released the film to television in the 1980s.

Today, CPT and what is now FremantleMedia hold ancillary rights, with FremantleMedia holding the video license. Any DVD release from a company not licensed by FremantleMedia violates the copyright, which continues to credit CPT as the copyright holder, as evidenced by recent video releases by BCI Eclipse, and now, as of the present, Shout! Factory (under Fremantle's license).

References

[1] "All-Time Top Grossers", *Variety*, 8 January 1964 p 69
[2] "Road to Rio" (http://www.imdb.com/title/tt0039776/). *Internet Movie Database*. . Retrieved September 3, 2012.
[3] "Full cast and crew for Road to Rio" (http://www.imdb.com/title/tt0039776/fullcredits). *Internet Movie Database*. . Retrieved September 3, 2012.
[4] "Soundtracks for Road to Rio" (http://www.imdb.com/title/tt0039776/soundtrack). *Internet Movie Database*. . Retrieved September 3, 2012.

External links

- *Road to Rio* (http://www.imdb.com/title/tt0039776/) at the Internet Movie Database
- *Road to Rio* (http://www.allrovi.com/movies/movie/v41580) at AllRovi

Route 66 (song)

"Route 66" also known as "(Get Your Kicks on) Route 66"	
Sheet music cover featuring Nat King Cole Trio	
Written by	Bobby Troup
Published	1946
Recorded by	Chuck Berry, Glenn Frey,[1] Nat King Cole Trio, Pappo (Spanish version), Perry Como, The Rolling Stones and numerous others

"**(Get Your Kicks on) Route 66**", often rendered simply as "**Route 66**", is a popular song and rhythm and blues standard, composed in 1946 by American songwriter Bobby Troup. It was first recorded in the same year by Nat King Cole, and was subsequently covered by many artists including Chuck Berry in 1961, The Rolling Stones in 1964, Depeche Mode in 1987, Pappo's Blues in 1995, John Mayer in 2006, and Glenn Frey in 2012.[1] The song's lyrics follow the path of the U.S. Route 66 highway, which used to run a long distance across the U.S., going from Chicago, Illinois, to Los Angeles, California.

Composition and lyrics

Location of U.S. Route 66

Troup conceived the idea for the song while driving west from Pennsylvania to Los Angeles, California, and the lyrics—which include references to the U.S. Highway of the title and many of the cities it passes through—celebrate the romance and freedom of automobile travel. In an interview he once said the tune for the song, as well as the lyric "Get your kicks on Route 66," came to him easily, but the remainder of the lyrics eluded him. More in frustration than anything else he simply filled up the song with the names of towns and cities on the highway.

The lyrics read as a mini-travelogue about the major stops along the route, listing several cities and towns that Route 66 passes through, viz. St Louis; Joplin, Missouri; Oklahoma City, Oklahoma; Amarillo, Texas; Gallup, New Mexico; Flagstaff, Arizona; Winona, Arizona; Kingman, Arizona; Barstow, California; and San Bernardino, California. Winona is the only town out of sequence: it was a very small settlement east of Flagstaff, and might indeed have been forgotten if not for the lyric "Don't forget Winona," written to rhyme with "Flagstaff, Arizona." Many artists who have covered the tune over the years have changed the initial lyrics, usually to "It goes to St. Louis, down through Missouri..." then continuing on with Oklahoma City and so on. Of the eight states that the actual route passes through, only Kansas and its cities are not mentioned by the song.

Recording history

"Route 66" was first recorded in 1946 by Nat King Cole, whose rendition became a hit on both the U.S. R&B and pop record charts. Cole would later re-record the tune in 1956 (on the album *After Midnight*) and 1961 (on the album *The Nat King Cole Story*).

The version recorded by Perry Como in 1959 (on the album *Como Swings*) is more lyrically complete, including the seldom-heard second verse and also the introductory verse.

The song has become a pop standard and has since been covered by numerous other vocal and instrumental artists, including:

• Acoustix	• The Manhattan Transfer
• Aerosmith	• John Mayer[2]
• Asleep at the Wheel	• Eddie Meduza
• Chuck Berry	• The Outlaws
• Patrick Burns	• Brad Paisley
• The Cheetah Girls	• Pappo (in Spanish)
• Natalie Cole	• Ariel Deam (in Spanish)
• Chris Connor	• Wes Paul (The Wes Paul Band)
• The Cramps	• Tom Petty and the Heartbreakers (*Fack Up the Plantation: Live!* VHS only)
• The Lamont Cranston Band	• John Pizzarelli
• Bing Crosby & The Andrews Sisters	• Jane Powell
• The Dead Boys	• Louis Prima
• Depeche Mode (one of only three cover songs ever released by the band)	• The Replacements
• The Doughboys	• Rockfour
• Dr. Feelgood	• The Rolling Stones
• E-Type Jazz	• Scatman John
• Four Freshmen	• The Brian Setzer Orchestra[3]
• Guitar Wolf	• Nancy Sinatra
• Wayne Hancock	• Skrewdriver
• Hot Zex	• The Strypes
• Jason & the Scorchers[4]	• Hans Teeuwen
• Juggernaut Jug Band[5]	• Téléphone
• The Jolt	• Them featuring Van Morrison
• The Legendary Tigerman	• Mel Tormé
• Jerry Lee Lewis	• U.K. Subs
• George Maharis	• Buckwheat Zydeco
	• Yo La Tengo

Re-worked version by Billy Bragg

Essex-born English singer-songwriter Billy Bragg also recorded an "anglicised" version of the song called "A13 (Trunk Road to the Sea)" for a John Peel session. In the song—strummed and sung to the same tune as the original—the landmark cities are replaced with English ones along the route of the A13, with Bragg inviting listeners to "Go motoring, on the A-thirteen".

Re-worked version by Cantabile - The London Quartet

The British vocal group, Cantabile - The London Quartet perform another "anglicised" version of the song, A66, describing this road in the north of England; it is part of their Funny Side of the Street show, and includes the immortal line 'Braithwaite, Thornthwaite, Embleton and Cockermouth'.

Appearances in other media

In films

(Chronological)

- Jane Powell performed the song in the 1948 movie *Three Daring Daughters*; an apparently umimpressed José Iturbi responded with a virtuoso piano rendition of the song.[6]
- The Manhattan Transfer recording of the song appears on the soundtrack of the 1981 film *Sharky's Machine*.
- Depeche Mode's (The Nile Rodgers Mix) version also appears in the 1988 *Earth Girls Are Easy* movie.
- The 2006 Disney/Pixar film *Cars* depicts Route 66 as a forgotten and faded piece of America, rediscovered by the main character. The film was originally to have been called *Route 66*, and the film's soundtrack includes the popular Chuck Berry version and the Grammy nominated "update version" by modern blues rock artist John Mayer.
- The song is performed by the cast of the 2006 Columbia Pictures film *RV*.

In games

- Depeche Mode's (Beatmasters Mix) version appears in the video game *Burnout Paradise*.

In radio

- The song was performed by Ray Ellington and his Quartet on *The Goon Show* "King Solomon's Mines", first broadcast by the BBC on December 2, 1957.

In television

- Mountain Dew had an extreme sports-themed television commercial in the mid-1990s reworking the song to mention various cities across the world.
- The producers of television show *Route 66* commissioned a new theme song because they wanted to avoid making royalty payments for Troup's song.
- Performance artist Kalup Linzy performed the song while guest starring on the daytime soap opera *General Hospital*.
- Glenn Frey performed his version of "Route 66" on the *Today Show* [7] on May 7, 2012.

Notes

[1] Today, Show. "Glenn Frey on the Today Show" (http://today.msnbc.msn.com/id/3041478/vp/47321575#47321575). . Retrieved 7 May
     2012.
[2] (nominated for Best Solo Rock Vocal Performance for the 49th Annual Grammys, also used in the soundtrack for the 2006 Pixar film *Cars*)
[3] (includes part of Nelson Riddle's theme song from *Route 66*)
[4] (as a bonus track on the 2002 CD release of the 1986 album *Still Standing*)
[5] "Kentucky's Other Roots Music", music column, Scott Harrell, Sarasota Weekly Planet, Sarasota, 2–8 March 2005
[6] *Three Daring Daughters* at IMDb (http://www.imdb.com/title/tt0040875/soundtrack)
[7] http://today.msnbc.msn.com/id/3041478/vp/47321575#47321575

External links

- De Lisle, Tim (August 25, 2006). " Drive-time blues (http://arts.guardian.co.uk/filmandmusic/story/
  0,,1857188,00.html)". *The Guardian*

Rumors Are Flying

"Rumors Are Flying" is a popular song.

It was written by Bennie Benjamin and George David Weiss and published in 1946.

It was popularized in 1946 by Frankie Carle and by Les Paul. It was a number-one hit in America for eight weeks from late October that year.

Harry Cool also recorded the song for Signature Records, catalog #15043.

In 1946, the song was recorded by The Andrews Sisters with Les Paul.

Sabre Dance

Aram Khachaturian circa 1960

🎬 External video

The "Sabre Dance" [1] by the Berlin Philharmonic orchestra, conducted by Seiji Ozawa

The "**Sabre Dance**" (Armenian: Սուսերով պար *Suserov par*) is a movement in the final act of the ballet *Gayane*, written by Armenian composer Aram Khachaturian and completed in 1942.

Overview

It evokes a whirling war dance in an Armenian dance, where the dancers display their skill with sabres. Its middle section incorporates an Armenian folk song from Gyumri.[2][3] Due to its exceptionally exciting rhythm, the "Sabre Dance" established a place for itself in common concert practice, leading also to various adaptations in popular music. Its recognizable ostinato and popular melodies have made it a popular concert band piece.

The orchestral version is written in the key of G major. It starts out with a recognizable motif ostinato with the timpani and strings that can be heard throughout much of the piece. The upper woodwinds and keyboard percussion take an exciting dance melody, later accompanied by the low brass. Then the strings come in with a folk song melody. The first melody is then briefly recapitulated. Descending chromatic eighth notes bring the piece down to straight eighth notes on the note G in the low strings. The piece ends on ascending quarter notes in a F♯ pentatonic scale (against the G bass) to an open G octave.

Notable performers

- 1948 – Oscar Levant in the film *The Barkleys of Broadway* (US)
- 1948 – Benno Moiseiwitsch (UK) audio [4]
- 1948 – Woody Herman (US) from album *The Second Herd* (1948) audio [5]
- 1954 – Liberace (US)[6] video [7]
- 1955 – Lester Metcalf in the film *Little Boy Lost* (UK)
- 1958 – Les Baxter (US) in album *Space Escapade* (1958) video [8]
- 1962 – Jerry Murad's Harmonicats (US) from album *Stereo Party Volume Two* (1962) audio [9]
- 1999 – Budapest Gypsy Symphony Orchestra/100 Violins (Hungary) video [10]
- 2006 – James Galway (Northern Ireland) from album *The Essential James Galway* (2006) audio [11]
- 2007 – Georges Cziffra (Hungary) video [12]
- 2008 – André Rieu (Netherlands) in the film *Andre Rieu - In Wonderland* video [13]
- Jascha Heifetz (Lithuania) audio [14]

Covers

Recorded

- 1948 – The Andrews Sisters (US) video [15]
- 1949 – Chick Rooster and The Barnyarders (US) audio [16]
- 1964 – Steve Miller Band video [17]
- 1968 – Love Sculpture with Dave Edmunds (Wales) video [18]
- 1973 – Spontaneous Combustion (US) audio [19]
- 1974 – Ekseption (Netherlands) from album *Bingo* (1974) audio [20]
- 1979 – The Boys (UK) from album *To Hell with the Boys* (1979) audio [21]
- 1979 – Pretenders (US/UK) covered it during 1979 live shows, a recording appears on the two disc 2006 reissue of their eponymous debut album audio [22]
- 1985 – *The Lord's Prayer* by Nina Hagen (Germany) from album *In Ekstase* (1985) audio [23]
- 1988 – U.K. Subs (UK) from album *Killing Time* (1988) audio [24]
- 1989 – Toy Dolls (UK) from album *Wakey Wakey* (1989) audio [25]
- 1992 – Mekong Delta (Germany) from album *Kaleidoscope* (1992) video [26]
- 1994 – "Sodom and Gomorrah" by band Accept (Germany) from album *Death Row* (1994)[27] audio [28]
- 1996 – Skyclad (UK) from album *Irrational Anthems* (1996) audio [29]
- 2004 – Vanessa-Mae (UK) from album *Choreography* (2004) video [30]
- 2004 – "Highly Strung" by Bond (UK) from album *Classified* (2004) [31] audio [32]
- 2006 – Tony Levin (US) from album *Resonator* (2006) audio [33]
- 2007 – The Brian Setzer Orchestra (US) from album *Wolfgang's Big Night Out* (2007) audio [34]
- 2009 – "Sabre Dance" by Sonya Kahn (Germany) video [35]
- 2010 – Les Fradkin (US) from album *Hyper Midi Guitar* (2010)
- 2011 – Michał Jelonek (Poland) from album *Revenge* (2011) video [36]

Live

- Ivan Rebroff (Germany) performed the song in a concert in Sydney, Australia in 1982 video [37]
- The Disco Biscuits (US) sometimes cover "Sabre Dance" at their live shows, often mixing in elements of rock and trance. No recorded version is available. live audio [38]

In popular culture

The "Sabre Dance" has been used in numerous films, animated films, TV series, video games and commercials over the years.[39] Some notable TV shows that have used it include *The Jack Benny Program* (1961), *A Piano in the House* from *The Twilight Zone* (1962), *The Onedin Line* (1971 and 1972), *The Benny Hill Show* (1985), *The Simpsons* (1991-2011), *Two and a Half Men* (2004), *What's New, Scooby-Doo?* (2004), "Peterotica" from the *Family Guy* (2006), *SpongeBob SquarePants* (2007),[40] *The Big Bang Theory* (2009).[41]

The piece's popular familiarity has been enhanced by its traditional use as accompaniment by travelling circuses and on television variety shows such as *The Ed Sullivan Show* when novelty acts such as plate spinners appeared.[42]

News program Teleprensa from El Salvador used a modern version of the song as intro for their newscasts in the 1980s during the Salvadoran Civil War.

The "Sabre Dance" is used in Road Runner (1985) from Atari Games and *Aero the Acro-Bat* (1993) video game in each of one of the game's soundtracks. It is also featured in the Classical Music radio station in Sleeping Dogs.

The National Hockey League team Buffalo Sabres uses the piece as a theme song.[43]

Films in which the "Sabre Dance" was used include:[39]

- *The Barkleys of Broadway* (US, 1949) - pianist Oscar Levant plays a piano transcription of the piece
- *One, Two, Three* (US, 1961) - the piece reinforces James Cagney's energetic performance in the final act of the film as he plays a troubled executive making snap decisions to save his career.
- *The System* (UK, 1964)
- *Amarcord* (Italy, 1973)
- *Nu, pogodi!* 6th episode "Countryside" (Soviet Union, 1973) - a portion was used in the train scene when the Wolf is trying to catch the Hare
- *Jumpin' Jack Flash* (US, 1986)
- *Muuttolinnun aika* (Finland, 1991)
- *Radioland Murders* (US, 1994)
- *The Hudsucker Proxy* (US/UK, 1994) - in a scene in which a newly-invented hula hoop is picked up and used by a young boy for the first time. The piece was arranged and integrated into the wider score by Carter Burwell, who also made use of Khachaturian's other well-known piece, the Adagio from Spartacus, as the movie's main theme.[44]
- *Don't Drink the Water* (US, 1994)
- *I Married a Strange Person!* (US, 1997)
- *Vegas Vacation* (US, 1997)
- *A Simple Wish* (US, 1997)
- 'The Blues Brothers 2000 *(US, 1998) - when the main heroes encounter Russians in the grave and run, "Sabre Dance" can be heard for several seconds.*
- *Kung Fu Hustle* (Hong Kong, 2004) - the Sabre Dance plays in the background as Sing (Stephen Chow) infiltrates a mental institution to spring an assassin known as the Beast
- *Scoop* (US/UK, 2006)
- *Sicko* (US, 2007)
- *Ghost Town* (US, 2008) - when the character of Ricky Gervais Bertram Pincus runs from a horde of ghosts through tunnel in the park, a violin version of "Sabre Dance" could be heard, performed by a ghost musician in tunnel.
- *Witless Protection* (US, 2008)
- *Le Concert* (France, 2009)
- *Paper Birds* (in Spanish) (Spain, 2010)

Charts

In 1948, two versions of the "Sabre Dance": one directed by Artur Rodziński and played by the Chicago Symphony Orchestra and another one directed by Efrem Kurtz and played by the New York Philharmonic peaked number one on *Billboard* Best-Selling Records by Classical Artists.[45]

References

[1] http://www.youtube.com/watch?v=ejIk_Za-q4Y

[2] Randel, Don Michael (1996). *The Harvard Biographical Dictionary of Music*. Harvard University Press. ISBN 0-674-37299-9.

[3] Studwell, William Emmett (1997). *The Americana Song Reader*. Haworth Press. ISBN 0-7890-0150-0.

[4] http://www.youtube.com/watch?v=j-Z9_TE8J1c

[5] http://www.youtube.com/watch?v=lCC6aWmEgtU

[6] "Liberace Plays the Saber Dance ..." (http://archive.evtv1.com/player.aspx?itemnum=403&aid=19). EVTV1. . Retrieved September 22, 2012.

[7] http://www.youtube.com/watch?v=J2t6SWG1vgo

[8] http://www.youtube.com/watch?v=H4dn0e5Hwr8

[9] http://www.youtube.com/watch?v=sBVRc6bi2O4

[10] http://www.youtube.com/watch?v=3KzUe7I4UHA

[11] http://www.youtube.com/watch?v=TEUoCXE9k_Y

[12] http://www.youtube.com/watch?v=JFP2AWoGqWo

[13] http://www.youtube.com/watch?v=CkfY6_FKrQQ

[14] http://www.youtube.com/watch?v=N4g7Qhq74UM

[15] http://www.youtube.com/watch?v=Sl3KCcU_08I

[16] http://www.madmusic.com/song_details.aspx?SongID=8994

[17] http://www.youtube.com/watch?v=ZoshUXOvLgM

[18] http://www.youtube.com/watch?v=0IBgRPUcwt4

[19] http://www.youtube.com/watch?v=yEWcJWeJarY

[20] http://www.youtube.com/watch?v=HU0hRvKL0a4

[21] http://www.youtube.com/watch?v=byNfL1M4Cv8

[22] http://www.myspace.com/music/player?sid=10830&ac=now

[23] http://www.youtube.com/watch?v=ki0wmI4-KOY

[24] http://www.youtube.com/watch?v=IG3065i786k

[25] http://www.youtube.com/watch?v=oM5PUlZCPnI

[26] http://www.youtube.com/watch?v=mfEMnjGMEwY

[27] "Wolf Hoffmann" (http://www.dinosaurrockguitar.com/new/node/25). Dinosaur Rock Guitar. May 28, 2008. . Retrieved September 22, 2012.

[28] http://www.youtube.com/watch?v=aCL9ry7VvP4

[29] http://www.youtube.com/watch?v=tXjK_q4zwww

[30] http://www.youtube.com/watch?v=rxtKeYBQdr0

[31] "Bond Classified review" (http://www.allmusic.com/album/classified-mw0000337970). allmusic. . Retrieved September 22, 2012.

[32] http://www.youtube.com/watch?v=kZjB5qzsBtY

[33] http://www.youtube.com/watch?v=XGyxAcQx5iw

[34] http://www.youtube.com/watch?v=wB8jnEyp4uY

[35] http://www.youtube.com/watch?v=oS4Xr7CrW5U

[36] http://www.youtube.com/watch?v=Jhm_lL1bzAo

[37] http://www.youtube.com/watch?v=xFW0NrmhBys

[38] http://www.youtube.com/watch?v=JjnB19DRm6Y

[39] "Aram Khachaturyan" (http://www.imdb.com/name/nm0006154/#Composer). IMDb. . Retrieved September 19, 2012.

[40] "Slimy Dancing" (http://spongebob.wikia.com/wiki/Slimy_Dancing). The SpongeBob SquarePants. . Retrieved September 22, 2012.

[41] "The Work Song Nanocluster" (http://www.imdb.com/title/tt1256028/). IMDb. . Retrieved September 22, 2012.

[42] Tom Huizenga (June 5, 2003). "The 'Sabre Dance' Man" (http://www.npr.org/templates/story/story.php?storyId=1287262). NPR Music. . Retrieved September 21, 2012.

[43] "*Amusement business*, Volume 83, Issue 1". 1971. " The Buffalo Sabres have a new old wrinkle. Miss Sandae Bafo, a smooth lass on the blades entertains between periods with her special rendition of Khachaturian's fiery Sabre Dance. (http://books.google.com/books?id=4s47AQAAIAAJ&q="Buffalo+Sabres"+khachaturian&dq="Buffalo+Sabres"+khachaturian&source=bl&ots=TEPAiftsoz&sig=ursS3alLyl5qR3OWpTxxELuRdUU&hl=en&sa=X&ei=YVNeUM3SLsXv0gGg3oGgDQ&ved=0CDAQ5AEwAA)"

[44] Eddie Robson (2003). *Coen Brothers*. London: Virgin Books. pp. 139–142. ISBN 1-57488-273-2.

[45] "Retail Record Sales: Best-Selling Records by Classical Artists". *Billboard*. June 26, 1948. p. 27 (http://books.google.com/books?id=d_UDAAAAMBAJ&pg=PA27&lpg=PA27&dq=khachaturian+sabre+dance&source=bl&ots=LJQD3HTx8M&sig=H-ruO2eps3IracRvCfFZykacxn8&hl=en&sa=X&ei=mVReUI-bJOn10gG15oDICw&ved=0CFEQ6AEwCQ#v=onepage&q=khachaturian sabre dance&f=false).

External links

- Article with several recordings (http://www.npr.org/templates/story/story.php?storyId=1287262), NPR

Sailor (song)

Sailor (original title: *Seemann (Deine Heimat ist das Meer)*) is a song written by Werner Scharfenberger and Fini Busch which via a 1960 recording by Lolita became an international hit, with its #5 peak on the Hot 100 chart in *Billboard* making "Sailor" the most successful American hit sung in German until *99 Luftballons* by Nena in 1984.

With English lyrics written by Norman Newell (credited as "David West") the song also provided a comeback vehicle for two veteran UK vocalists: Petula Clark and Anne Shelton whose respective versions of "Sailor" were both musical milestones for each singer marking Clark's first #1 on the UK Singles chart and Shelton's final chart appearance.

Northern European versions

The Lolita version - originally entitled "Seemann (Deine Heimat ist das Meer)" - entered the German Top 20 in March 1960; peaking at #2 in June. Lolita's single was in the Top 20 for ten months and was the fourth biggest German hit of the year.[1] In December 1960 the single's B-side "La Luna" also became a chart hit reaching #30. It was also featured in the film "Schick deine Frau nicht nach Italien".[2] Estimate for global sales of "Seemann (Deine Heimat Ist Das Meer)"/ "Sailor (Your Home is the Sea)" by Lolita is two million units.

There was immense US media interest in Germany in 1960 due to the political situation in Berlin and also Elvis Presley's being stationed on a West German airbase: this likely factored into Kapp Records' decision to release Lolita's German hit in the US. [3]

Re-entitled "Sailor (Your Home is the Sea)" the US single - which augmented Lolita's original German vocal with a spoken word translation by British actress Maureen Renée - reached #5 on the Hot 100 chart in *Billboard* in December 1960. One of only two German language songs to become a Top 10 hit in the United States (See *99 Luftballons* by Nena), "Sailor..." also afforded Lolita a hit in Australia (#14), Japan (Top 20) and New Zealand reaching #8 in the latter territory despite the #1 ranking achieved there by the Petula Clark English rendering "Sailor".

"Seemann..." also provided Lolita with a hit in Norway where it spent nine weeks at #1 in the spring of 1961 with sales of 50,000 units recognized that October with the awarding of a Gold Disc.[4] A Norse rendering by Jan Høiland ([[no) entitled "Sjømann" concurrently charted spending two weeks at #2. In Sweden "Seemann..." reached #5 sharing the charts with a translated cover version by Towa Carson who in Jun 1961 reached #9 with "Sjöman" (a double A-sided hit with "Sista Dansen" ie. "Save the Last Dance for Me").[5] "Sjöman" had first been recorded by Thory Bernhards (sv) in a 12 October 1960 session, the Swedish lyrics being the work of Åke Gerhard whose composition "Ann-Caroline" - first sung by Benhards - had coincidentally developed into "Lay Down Your Arms" the career record of Anne Shelton who would have a Top Ten UK hit with "Sailor".[6]

Caterina Valente covered Lolita's hit for the Dutch market: in the autumn of 1960 her version - entitled "Zeeman" - charted in the Netherlands and reached #10 on the charts for the Flemish region of Belgium. Even so the Lolita original itself reached the Dutch Top Ten and in Flemish Belgium - co-ranked with Petula Clark's English rendition - Lolita's "Seemann" reached #12.[7] "Zeeman" was also recorded by the Fouryo's (nl) and a 1981 remake by Ciska

Peters (nl) - as "Zeeman, Je Verlangen Is Dezee" - reached #19 in the Netherlands.

The original German version of the song has also been recorded by the Günter Kallmann (de) Chor as "Seemann" for their 1965 album *Serenade am Meer* and by Géraldine Olivier (de) as "Seemann, deine Heimat ist das Meer" for her 2009 album *Maritime Welthits der 50er und 60er*.

English version

Composition

Lyricist Norman Newell would recall that his publisher phoned him on a Friday requesting he write English lyrics for Lolita's hit ""Seemann...": although Newell agreed to prepare the lyrics over the weekend the assignment slipped his mind until a messenger arrived Monday morning to pick up Newell's work. "I sent [the messenger] to the canteen and wrote the lyric 'Sailor' in ten minutes."[8]

Petula Clark

Alan A. Freeman, who regularly produced Petula Clark, suggested she record "Sailor" and produced Clark's recording in a session which featured guitarists Vic Flick and Big Jim Sullivan.[9] Freeman was assisted with the production of "Sailor" by Tony Hatch marking the first collaboration between Clark and her future hitmaking mentor.

"Sailor" debuted at #18 in the UK Top 50 dated 28 January 1961, becoming Clark's first UK chart entry since "Baby Lover", #12 in March 1958, an intermittent ten single releases having failed to chart. [10] A sales total of 250,000 units for Clark's "Sailor" was announced by Pye Records the week of 18 February 1961 when the single was in its second week at #2: on the chart for the following week: that of 23 February 1961, Clark's "Sailor" moved to the #1 position of the UK chart, besting Clark's previous strongest UK charter: the #4 "With All My Heart" (1957). Although "Downtown" was to become Clark's signature song its UK chart peak would be #2: the second Petula Clark single to reach #1 UK would be "This is My Song" in 1967.[11]

Clark's "Sailor" became the third hit version of the song in the Netherlands (#13) and - in a tandem ranking with ""Seemann (Deine Heimat Ist Das Meer)" by Lolita - reached #12 on the chart for the Flemish Region of Belgium.[12] "Sailor" was #1 in New Zealand and Israel in respectively March and September 1961. A hit in Denmark (#9) and Spain (Top 20), "Sailor" reached #2 in South Africa in 1961 and when re-released there as the follow-up to "This is My Song" in 1968 reached #9.[10]

[13] Both of Clark's UK #1 hits would compete with rival versions: "Sailor" would be a #10 hit for Anne Shelton[14] while Harry Secombe's version of "This is My Song" would rise as high as #2. [15] (The relevant recordings by both Shelton and Secombe have Wally Stott perform arranging and conducting duties.)[16][17]

Anne Shelton

Another veteran British vocalist: Anne Shelton, also utilized "Sailor" as a comeback vehicle. Like Clark's version, Shelton's featured guitarist Big Jim Sullivan.[18]

Shelton had spent four weeks at #1 UK with "Lay Down Your Arms" in 1956 but had since only had one further chart record: " The Village Of St. Bernadette" #27 in 1959, when her version of "Sailor" reached #10 in January 1961. Although she'd been recording since 1943 "Sailor" was only her fifth UK chart appearance as her most intense period of popularity had pre-dated regulated record-sales chart formatting in the UK (which began in 1952, prior to this sales of music sheets with or without record sales were common marker of a tune's popularity [19]).

Shelton's strongest association was as an entertainer of the forces in World War II:[16] while this made "Sailor" a good thematic choice for her this association also probably made her seem outmoded (despite only being four years Clark's senior) and although Shelton's version of "Sailor" and Clark's both debuted on the UK Top 50 for 28 January

1961 there was immediate preference apparent for Clark's version at #18 over Shelton's at #27. The 4 February chart had Clark rise to #4 for the first of six weeks in the Top Five three of them at #2 and one at #1, while Shelton's version in its second week rose to #19 and in its third week to #10 which proved to be its peak as it subsequently descended the charts over the next five weeks for a total eight week chart span: Clark's version had almost double the chart span at fifteen weeks.[11][14] After "Sailor" Shelton had eleven subsequent single releases, the last in 1965.[16]

Other versions

"Sailor" was also recorded by the Andrews Sisters who were in London for an engagement at the Talk of the Town and made a one-off single for Decca Records (UK) comprising "Sailor" backed by "Goodnight and Sweet Dreaming"; the tracks featured Bernard Ebbinghouse conducting his orchestra were recorded 29 December 1960.[20]

Louise Morrissey[21] recorded "Sailor" for her 2008 album release *The Gift*.

Anica Zubović (hr) recorded the Croatian rendering "Mornar" in 1968.

French version: Petula Clark: "Marin"

Although absent from the UK charts through the late 1950s and the year 1960, Clark did during the same period enjoy a string of hit singles in France and "Sailor" - recorded with French lyric by Jean Broussolle as "Marin" - was to reach #2 on the French charts in May 1961. Clark's eighth French chart hit, "Marin" matched her previous #2 chart peak of "Java Pour Petula" in 1959: the follow-up to "Marin": "Roméo" would be the first of Clark's five French #1's.[22] "Marin" reached #10 on the charts for the French speaking sector of Belgium and the single also entered the Montreal charts (as "Sailor") in January 1961 peaking at #13 marking Clark's first appearance on an accredited North American chart almost four years before her breakout hit "Downtown".[23]

References

[1] "German Top 20" (http://ki.informatik.uni-wuerzburg.de/~topsi/deu1960). . Retrieved 26 February 2009.
[2] *Schick deine Frau nicht nach Italien* (http://www.imdb.com/title/tt0054275/) at the Internet Movie Database
[3] *That Old Time Rock & Roll by Richard Aquila* (http://books.google.com/books?id=pGN7fPeEYSEC&pg=PA265&lpg=PA265& dq=that+old+time+rock+&+roll+richard+aquila+lolita&source=bl&ots=jWBwnxK2yK&sig=0MmnHC3fS4HKv9KmvevA70WStgs). . Retrieved 26 February 2009.
[4] *Billboard* vol 73 #18 (3 April 1961) p.38
[5] *Billboard* vol 73 #22 (5 June 1961) p.10
[6] "Thory Bernhards - Biografi" (http://hem.passagen.se/sihmon/Thory). . Retrieved 28 February 2009.
[7] "Sixties Hit Parade - Belgium" (http://www.rock-ola.be). . Retrieved 28 February 2009.
[8] "Norman Newell" (http://www.independent.co.uk/news/obituaries/norman-newell-678793.html). *The Independent* (London). 7 December 2004. .
[9] http://www.overzeal.co.uk/
[10] "RPM/Petula Clark" (http://www.45-rpm.org.uk/dirp/petulac.htm). . Retrieved 26 February 2009.
[11] "Chartstats/Petula Clark" (http://www.chartstats.com/artistinfo.php?id=1052). . Retrieved 26 February 2009.
[12] "PClark/ChartsEuro" (http://petulaclark.net/chartseuropean.html). . Retrieved 26 February 2009.
[13] "PClark/ChartsSAfrica" (http://petulaclark.net/chartsafricanasian.html#safrica). . Retrieved 26 February 2009.
[14] "Chartstats/Anne Shelton" (http://www.chartstats.com/artistinfo.php?id=1119). . Retrieved 26 February 2009.
[15] "Chartstats/Harry Secombe" (http://www.chartstats.com/artistinfo.php?id=1118). . Retrieved 26 February 2009.
[16] "RPM/Anne Shelton" (http://www.45-rpm.org.uk/dira/annes.htm). . Retrieved 26 February 2009.
[17] "Philips Discography" (http://www.discogs.com/label/Philips). . Retrieved 2 March 2009.
[18] http://www.bigjimsullivan.com/Pamra.html
[19] http://www.everyhit.com/searchsec.php
[20] Nimmo, H. Arlo (2004). *The Andrews Sisters: a biography and career record*. Jefferson NC: McFarland & Company, Inc. pp. 338. ISBN 0-7864-1731-5.
[21] http://www.louisemorrissey.com/Louise Morrissey
[22] "PClark/ChartsFrench" (http://petulaclark.net/chartsfrench.html). . Retrieved 26 February 2009.
[23] "PClark/ChartsCdn" (http://petulaclark.net/chartscanadian.html). . Retrieved 26 February 2009.

Say "Si Si"

"Say 'Si Si'" is a popular song.

The music was written by Ernesto Lecuona, the original Spanish lyrics by Francia Luban (its original title is Para Vigo Me Voy), with English lyrics written by Al Stillman. The song was published in 1935.

The song appeared in various movies, among them "It Comes Up Love" (sung by Gloria Jean and The Guadalajara Trio, accompanied by Leon Belasco and his orchestra).

The song has been recorded by The Andrews Sisters and by Glenn Miller and his orchestra.

Shoo Shoo Baby (song)

"Shoo Shoo Baby" is a popular song made famous by The Andrews Sisters. They sang it in the 1943 film *Three Cheers for the Boys* and it became a big hit for them in 1944, reaching No. 6 in the chart. Their version features a jazzy vocal pop arrangement typical of the time, with a key hook provided by the horns. It was written by Phil Moore and has appeared on many albums of 1940's music.

Ella Mae Morse also recorded this song in 1943, released on CAPITOL label 143, with Dick Walters Orchestra. This version went to number four on the pop chart and number one on the R&B charts for 2 weeks in Dec, 1943.[1] It was also recorded by Glenn Miller with the vocals performed by the Crew Chiefs. Frank Sinatra recorded the song in the fifties, as did Nat King Cole.

In 1984 the Norwegian swing/pop duo Bobbysocks! covered the song on their LP *Bobbysocks!*.

R&B Girlband Mis-Teeq, covered the song for the soundtrack to the Disney film *Valiant* in 2005. It was the last track Mis-Teeq ever recorded before they split up to pursue solo careers.

References

[1] Whitburn, Joel (2004). *Top R&B/Hip-Hop Singles: 1942-2004*. Record Research. p. 415.

Sonny Boy (song)

"Sonny Boy" is a song written by Ray Henderson, Bud De Sylva, and Lew Brown. The hyper-sentimental tearjerker was featured in the 1928 talkie *The Singing Fool*. Sung by Al Jolson, the 1928 recording was a hit and stayed at #1 for 12 weeks in the charts and was a million seller. [1]

Singer Eddie Fisher was always called "Sonny Boy" by his family because of the popularity of this song, which was recorded the same year as Fisher's birth. In his autobiography, Fisher wrote that even after he was married to Elizabeth Taylor in 1959, earning $40,000 a week performing in Las Vegas, spending time with Frank Sinatra and Rocky Marciano, and had songs at the top of the charts, his family still called him "Sonny Boy".[2]

Arild Andresen, piano with guitar and bass recorded it in Oslo on March 11, 1955 as the first melody of the medley "Klaver-Cocktail Nr. 4" along with "Top Hat, White Tie and Tails" and "Ain't Misbehavin'. The medley was released on the 78 rpm record His Master's Voice A.L. 3514.

The song has also been recorded by The Andrews Sisters and Mandy Patinkin.

The song is used repeatedly in the film *Jacob's Ladder* where it is used to convey a link between Jacob and his dead son Gabe.

References

[1] CD liner notes: Chart-Toppers of the Twenties, 1998 ASV Ltd.
[2] Fisher, Eddie; Fisher, David (Sept. 1999). *Been There, Done That*. New York: St. Martin's Press. p. 2. ISBN 0-312-20972-X.

According to the British TV documentary, "The Real Jolson Story," "Sonny Boy" was written in a single sitting in a hotel room in Atlantic City as a joke.

Sparrow in the Treetop

"Sparrow in the Treetop"	
Single by Guy Mitchell	
Released	1951
Length	3:17
Writer(s)	Bob Merrill
Guy Mitchell singles chronology	

"You're Just in Love" (1951)	**"Sparrow in the Treetop"** (1951)	"Christopher Columbus" (1951)

"Sparrow in the Treetop" is a popular song written by Bob Merrill. The song was published in 1951.

Charting versions of the song were made by Guy Mitchell[1] (the most popular version, reaching #8 on the Billboard chart), Bing Crosby and The Andrews Sisters (also reaching #8 on the Billboard chart), and Rex Allen[2] (reaching #28 on the Billboard chart). The Allen version crossed to Billboard's C/W chart.

References

[1] Guy Mitchell, *Great Guy Mitchell* (http://www.allmusic.com/album/great-guy-mitchell-r431005)
[2] Rex Allen, *Versatile* (http://www.allmusic.com/album/versatile-r1825264)

Summer of '42

Summer of '42	
Theatrical release poster	
Directed by	Robert Mulligan
Produced by	Richard A. Roth
Written by	Herman Raucher
Narrated by	Robert Mulligan
Starring	Jennifer O'Neill Gary Grimes Jerry Houser Oliver Conant
Music by	Michel Legrand
Cinematography	Robert Surtees
Editing by	Folmar Blangsted
Distributed by	Warner Bros. Pictures
Release date(s)	• April 9, 1971
Running time	104 minutes[1]

Country	United States
Language	English
Budget	$1 million
Box office	$32,063,634[2]

Summer of '42 is a 1971 American coming-of-age comedy-drama film based on the memoirs of screenwriter Herman Raucher. It tells the story of how Raucher, in his early teens on his 1942 summer vacation on Nantucket Island, off the coast of New England, embarked on a one-sided romance with a woman, Dorothy, whose husband had gone off to fight in World War II.

The film was directed by Robert Mulligan, and starred Gary Grimes as Hermie, Jerry Houser as his best friend Oscy, Oliver Conant as their nerdy young friend Benjie, Jennifer O'Neill as Hermie's mysterious love interest, and Katherine Allentuck and Christopher Norris as a pair of girls whom Hermie and Oscy attempt to seduce. Mulligan also has an uncredited role as the voice of the adult Hermie. Maureen Stapleton (Allentuck's real-life mother) also appears in a small, uncredited voice role (calling after Hermie as he leaves the house in an early scene, and after he enters his room in a later scene).

Raucher's novelization of his screenplay of the same name was released prior to the film's release and became a runaway bestseller, to the point that audiences lost sight of the fact that the book was based on the film and not vice-versa. Though a pop culture phenomenon in the first half of the 1970s, the novelization went out of print and slipped into obscurity throughout the next two decades until a Broadway adaptation in 2001 brought it back into the public light and prompted Barnes & Noble to acquire the publishing rights to the book.

Synopsis

The film opens with a series of still photographs appearing over melancholic music, representing the abstract memories of the unseen Herman Raucher, now a middle-aged man. We then hear Raucher recalling the summer he spent on the island in 1942. The film flashes back to a day that then 15-year-old "Hermie" and his friends — jock Oscy and introverted nerd Benjie — spent playing on the beach. They spot a young soldier carrying his new bride into a house on the beach and are struck by her beauty, especially Hermie, who is unable to get her out of his mind.

They continue spending afternoons on the beach where, in the midst of scantily-clad teenage girls, their thoughts invariably turn to sex. All of them are virgins: Oscy is obsessed with the act of sex, while Hermie finds himself developing romantic interest in the bride, whose husband he spots leaving the island on a water taxi one morning. Later that day, Hermie finds her trying to carry bags of groceries by herself, and helps get them back to her house. They strike up a friendship and he agrees to return to help her with chores.

Meanwhile, Oscy and Hermie, thanks to a sex manual discovered by Benjie, become convinced they know everything necessary to lose their virginity. Led by Oscy, they test this by going to the cinema and picking-up a trio of high-school girls. Oscy stakes out the most attractive one, Miriam, "giving" Hermie her less attractive friend, Aggie, and leaving Benjie with Gloria, a heavyset girl with braces. Frightened by the immediacy of sex, Benjie runs off, and is not seen by Hermie or Oscy again that night. Hermie and Oscy spend the entirety of the evening's film attempting to "put the moves" on Miriam and Aggie. Oscy pursues Miriam, eventually making out with her during the movie, and later learns her ways are well-known on the island. Hermie finds himself succeeding with Aggie, who allows him to grope what he thinks is her breast; Oscy later points out Hermie was fondling her arm.

The next morning, Hermie helps the bride move boxes into her attic and she thanks him by giving him a kiss on the forehead. Later, in preparation for a marshmallow roast on the beach with Aggie and Miriam, Hermie goes to the local drugstore. In a painfully humorous sequence he builds up the nerve to ask for condoms.

That night, Hermie roasts marshmallows with Aggie while Oscy succeeds in having sex with Miriam between the dunes. He is so successful he sneaks over to Hermie and Aggie to ask for more condoms. Confused as to what's happening, Aggie follows Oscy back, where she sees him having sex with Miriam and runs home, upset.

The next day, Hermie comes across the bride sitting outside her house, writing to her husband. Hermie offers to keep her company that night and she says she looks forward to seeing him, revealing her name is Dorothy. An elated Hermie goes home and puts on a suit, dress shirt and heads back to Dorothy's house, running into Oscy on the way; Oscy relates that Miriam's appendix burst and she's been rushed to the mainland. Hermie, convinced he is at the brink of adulthood because of his relationship with Dorothy, brushes Oscy off.

He heads to her house, which is eerily quiet. Going in, he discovers a bottle of whiskey, several cigarette butts, and a telegram from the government. Dorothy's husband is dead, his plane shot down over France. Dorothy comes out of her bedroom, crying, and Hermie tells her "I'm sorry." The sense of empathy triggers her to channel to Hermie some of her loneliness. She turns on the record player and invites Hermie to dance with her. They kiss and embrace, tears on both their faces. Without speaking, and to the sound only of the waves, they move to the bedroom, where she draws him into bed and gently makes love with him. Afterward, withdrawing again into her world of hurt, Dorothy retires to the porch, leaving Hermie alone in her bedroom. He approaches her on the porch, where she can only quietly say "Good night, Hermie." He leaves, his last image of Dorothy being of her leaning against the railing, as she smokes a cigarette and stares into the night sky.

At dawn Hermie meets Oscy and the two share a moment of reconciliation, with Oscy informing Hermie that Miriam will recover. Oscy, in an uncharacteristic act of sensitivity, lets Hermie be by himself, departing with the words, "Sometimes life is one big pain in the ass."

Trying to sort out what has happened, Hermie goes back to Dorothy's house. Dorothy has fled the island in the night and an envelope is tacked to the front door with Hermie's name on it. Inside is a note from Dorothy, saying she hopes he understands she must go back home as there is much to do. She assures Hermie she will never forget him, and he will find his way of remembering what happened that night. Her note closes with the hope that Hermie may be spared the senseless tragedies of life.

In the final scene, Hermie, suddenly approaching manhood, is seen looking at Dorothy's old house and the ocean from a distance before he turns to join his friends. To bittersweet music, the adult Raucher sadly recounts that he has never seen Dorothy again or learned what became of her.

Cast

- Jennifer O'Neill as Dorothy
- Gary Grimes as Hermie
- Jerry Houser as Oscy
- Oliver Conant as Benjie
- Katherine Allentuck as Aggie
- Christopher Norris as Miriam
- Lou Frizzell as Druggist
- Robert Mulligan (*uncredited voice*) as Narrator/Older Herman Raucher
- Walter Scott (*uncredited*) as Dorothy's husband
- Maureen Stapleton (*uncredited voice*)

Production

Herman Raucher wrote the film script in the 1950s during his tenure as a television writer, but "couldn't give it away."[3] In the 1960s, he met Robert Mulligan, who had just finished directing *To Kill a Mockingbird*. Raucher showed Mulligan the script, and Mulligan took it to Warner Bros., knowing that the studio was looking for a follow up to *Mockingbird*. Mulligan argued the film could be shot for the relatively low price of $1 million, and Warner approved it.[3] They had so little faith in the film becoming a box-office success, though, they shied from paying

Raucher outright for the script, instead promising him ten percent of the gross.[3]

When casting for the role of Dorothy, Warner Bros. declined to audition any actresses younger than the age of 30; Jennifer O'Neill's agent, who had developed a fondness for the script, convinced the studio to audition his client, who was only 22 at the time. O'Neill auditioned for the role, albeit hesitantly, not wanting to perform any nude scenes. O'Neill got the role and Mulligan agreed to find a way to make the film work without blatant nudity.[4]

Though the film took place on Nantucket, by the 1970s the island was too far modernized to be convincingly transformed to resemble a 1940s resort, so production was taken to Mendocino, California, on the West Coast of the US.[3] Shooting took place over eight weeks, during which Jennifer O'Neill was sequestered from the three boys cast as "The Terrible Trio," in order to ensure that they didn't become close and ruin the sense of awkwardness and distance that their characters felt towards Dorothy. Production ran smoothly, finishing on schedule.[3]

After production, Warner Bros., still wary about the film only being a minor success, asked Raucher to adapt his script into a book.[3] Raucher wrote it in three weeks, and Warner Bros. released it prior to the film to build interest in the story.[3] The book quickly became a national bestseller, so that when trailers premiered in theatres, the film was billed as being "based on the national bestseller," despite the film having been completed first.[3][5] Ultimately, the book became one of the best selling novels of the first half of the 1970s, requiring 23 re-prints between 1971 and 1974 to keep up with customer demand.[5]

Factual basis

The film (and subsequent novel) were memoirs written by Herman Raucher; they detailed the events in his life over the course of the summer he spent on Nantucket Island in 1942 when he was fourteen years old.[3] Originally, the film was meant to be a tribute to his friend Oscar "Oscy" Seltzer, an Army medic killed in the Korean War.[3][6] Seltzer was shot dead on a battlefield in Korea whilst attending to a wounded man; this happened on Raucher's birthday, and consequently, Raucher has not celebrated a birthday since. During the course of writing the screenplay, Raucher came to the realization that despite growing up with Oscy and having bonded with him through their formative years, the two had never really had any meaningful conversations or gotten to know one another on a more personal level.[3]

Instead, Raucher decided to focus on the first major adult experience of his life, that of falling in love for the first time. The woman (named Dorothy, like her screen counterpart) was a fellow vacationer on the island whom Raucher had befriended one day when he helped her carry groceries home; he became a friend of her and her husband and helped her with chores after her husband was called to fight in World War II. Raucher went to bed with her one night when he came to visit her, arriving only minutes after she received notification of her husband's death.[3] The next morning, Raucher discovered that she had left the island, leaving behind a note for him (which is read at the end of the film and reproduced in the book). He never saw her again; his last "encounter" with her, recounted on an episode of *The Mike Douglas Show*, came after the film's release in 1971, when she was one of over a dozen women who wrote letters to Raucher claiming to be "his" Dorothy.[7] Raucher recognized the "real" Dorothy's handwriting, and she confirmed her identity by making references to certain events only she could have known about.[7] She told Raucher that she had lived for years with the guilt that she had potentially traumatized him and ruined his life. She told Raucher that she was glad he turned out all right, and that they had best not re-visit the past.[3][7]

In a 2002 Scripps Treasure Coast Publishing interview, Raucher lamented never hearing from her again and expressed his hope that she was still alive.[3] Raucher's novelization of the screenplay, with the dedication, "To those I love, past and present," serves more as the tribute to Seltzer that he had intended the film to be, with the focus of the book being more on the two boys' relationship than Raucher's relationship with Dorothy. Consequently, the book also mentions Seltzer's death, which is absent from the film adaptation.[5]

Reception and awards

The film became a blockbuster upon its release, grossing over $32 million, making it the sixth highest-grossing film of 1971 and one of the most successful films in history, with an expense to profit ratio of 1:32;[8] beyond that, it is estimated video rentals and purchases in the United States since the 1980s have produced an additional $20.5 million.[9] On this point, Raucher says his ten percent of the gross, in addition to royalties from book sales, has "paid bills ever since."[3]

As well as being a commercial success, *Summer of '42* also received rave critical reviews. It went on to be nominated for over a dozen awards, including Golden Globe Awards for "Best Motion Picture – Drama" and "Best Director", and five Academy Award nominations for Best Original Music Score, Best Cinematography, Best Editing, Best Writing-Story and Best Screenplay.[10] Ultimately, the film won two awards: the 1972 44th Academy Awards Oscar for Original Dramatic Score, and the 1971 BAFTA Anthony Asquith Award for Film Music, both to Michel Legrand. Still, it counted among its fans Stanley Kubrick, who had the film play on a television in a scene in *The Shining*.

Sequel

In 1973, the film was followed by *Class of '44*, a slice-of-life film made up of vignettes about Herman Raucher and Oscar Seltzer's experiences in college prior to fighting in the Korean War; because the timeline of Raucher's life was altered for *Summer of '42*, *Class of '44* involves the boys facing army service in the closing days of WWII rather than Korea. The only crew member from *Summer of '42* to return to the project was Raucher himself, who wrote the script; a new director and composer were brought in to replace Mulligan and Legrand. Of the principal four cast members of *Summer of '42*, only Jerry Houser and Gary Grimes returned for prominent roles, with Oliver Conant making two brief appearances totaling less than two minutes of screen time. Jennifer O'Neill did not appear in the film at all, nor was the character of Dorothy mentioned.

The film is noted for featuring a young, slim John Candy briefly appearing in his first film role. The film met with poor critical reviews; the only three reviews available at Rotten Tomatoes are resoundingly negative,[11][12] with Channel 4 calling it "a big disappointment,"[13] and *The New York Times* stating "The only things worth attention in 'Class of 44' are the period details," and "'Class of '44' seems less like a movie than 95 minutes of animated wallpaper."[14]

Soundtrack

Summer of '42: Original Motion Picture Score	
Soundtrack album by Michel Legrand	
Released	April 24, 2001
Label	Warner Bros. Records

The film's soundtrack consists almost entirely of compositions by Michel Legrand, many of which are variants upon "The Summer Knows", the film's theme. Lyrics are by Marilyn and Alan Bergman. In addition to Legrand's scoring, the film also features the song "Hold Tight" by The Andrews Sisters and the theme from *Now, Voyager*.

Summer of '42: Original Motion Picture Score

No.	Title	Length
1.	"Summer of '42 (Main Theme)"	3:51
2.	"Summer Song"	4:21
3.	"The Bacchanal"	1:48
4.	"Lonely Two"	2:04
5.	"The Danger"	2:13
6.	"Montage: But Not Picasso / Full Awakening"	3:32
7.	"High I.Q"	2:11
8.	"The Summer Knows"	1:47
9.	"The Entrance to Reality"	3:04
10.	"La Guerre"	3:15
11.	"Los Manos de Muerto"	3:29
12.	"Awakening Awareness"	2:26
13.	"And All the Time"	1:43
Total length:		**35:44**

Cultural impact

Music

Legrand's theme song for the film, "The Summer Knows," has since become a pop standard, being recorded by such artists as Peter Nero (who had a charting hit with his 1971 version), Biddu, Tony Bennett, Frank Sinatra, Andy Williams, Jonny Fair, Scott Walker, Jackie Evancho and Barbra Streisand.

The 1973 song "Summer (The First Time)" by Bobby Goldsboro has almost exactly the same subject and apparent setting, although there is no direct credited link. Bryan Adams has, however, credited the film as being a partial inspiration for his 1985 hit "Summer of '69."[15]

Film and television

In Stanley Kubrick's 1980 film version of Stephen King's *The Shining*, Wendy (Shelley Duvall) is shown watching *Summer of '42* on television (a brief clip of the scene featuring Hermie helping Dorothy bring her groceries in the house is playing on the television in the background during the scene).

An episode of the 1970s sitcom *Happy Days* was loosely based upon *Summer of '42,* with Richie Cunningham befriending a Korean War widow.

The Simpsons episode "Summer of 4 Ft. 2" (alternately titled 'Summer of 4'2"') was largely a parody of *Summer of '42,* replacing the romantic desire of Hermie for Dorothy with Lisa's desire to befriend a group of beach dwellers. It amalgamated scenes from another early 1970s coming-of-age film, *American Graffiti* (both acknowledged in the DVD commentary for the episode).

In the *Family Guy* episode "Play It Again, Brian", Brian wins an award for an essay, and reads an excerpt that includes the lines: "Nothing from the first day I saw her, and no one that has happened to me since, has ever been as frightening and as confusing, for no person I've ever known has ever done more to make me feel more sure, more insecure, more important and less significant." The excerpt is almost verbatim the conclusion of the narrator's opening monologue in *Summer;* later in that episode, Brian admits that he "ripped off" most of the essay from

Summer of '42.

Remakes

In the years since the film's release, Warner Bros. has attempted to buy back Raucher's ten percent of the film as well as his rights to the story so it could be remade; Raucher has consistently declined.[3] The 1988 film *Stealing Home* has numerous similarities to both *Summer of '42* and *Class of '44*, with several incidents (most notably a subplot dealing with the premature death of the protagonist's father and the protagonist's response to it) appearing to have been directly lifted from Raucher's own life; Jennifer O'Neill stated in 2002 she believes "*Home*" was an attempted remake of "*Summer*."[16]

There are also similarities between *Summer of '42* and 2000's *Malèna,* another coming-of-age film set in the context of World War II, and starring Monica Bellucci and Giuseppe Sulfaro.

Off-Broadway musical

In 2001, Raucher consented to the film being made into an off Broadway musical play.[3] He was on hand opening night, giving the cast a pep-talk which he concluded, "We've now done it every possible way – except go out and piss it in the snow!"[17] The play met with positive critical and fan response, and was endorsed by Raucher himself, but the play was forced to close down in the aftermath of the September 11 attacks.[3] Nevertheless, the play was enough to spark interest in the film and book with a new generation, prompting Warner to re-issue the book (which had since gone out of print, along with all of Raucher's other works) for sale with Barnes & Noble's online bookstore, and to restore the film and release it on DVD.[3] The musical has since been performed across the country, at venues such as Kalliope Stage in Cleveland Heights, Ohio in 2004 (directed by Paul Gurgol) and Mill Mountain Theatre in Roanoke, Virginia, (directed by Jere Hodgin and choreographed by Bernard Monroe), and was subsequently recorded as a concert by the York Theatre Company in 2006.

Alternate sequel

In 2002, O'Neill claimed to have obtained the rights to make a sequel to *Summer of '42*, based on a short story she wrote, which took place in an alternate reality where Herman Raucher had a son and divorced his wife, went back to Nantucket in 1962 with a still-living Oscar Seltzer, and encountered Dorothy again and married her.[4] As of 2006, this project – which O'Neill had hoped to produce with Lifetime television[18] – has not been realized, and it is unknown whether O'Neill is still attempting to get it produced, or if Raucher consented to its production.

References

[1] "*SUMMER OF '42* (X)" (http://www.bbfc.co.uk/releases/summer-42). *British Board of Film Classification.* 1971-04-15. . Retrieved 2013-02-06.
[2] "Summer of '42, Box Office Information" (http://www.the-numbers.com/movies/1971/0SM42.php). The Numbers. . Retrieved January 12, 2012.
[3] Interview with Herman Raucher by TC Palm (http://web.tcpalm.com/specialreports/summerof42/raucher.html). *tcpalm.com.* Retrieved July 5, 2006.
[4] "Jennifer O'Neill Interview (extended)" (http://web.tcpalm.com/specialreports/summerof42/oneill.html). *tcpalm.com.* June 2002. . Retrieved February 8, 2012.
[5] Raucher, Herman. Summer of '42. 23rd Edition. New York: Dell, 1974.
[6] Korean War Memorial – Oscar Seltzer (http://www.koreanwar.org/html/korean_war_project_remembrance.html?KCCF1__KEY=26993) *koreanwar.org.* Retrieved July 5, 2006.
[7] The Mike Douglas Show, Interview with Herman Raucher. Original date of broadcast unknown.
[8] Allmovie: Summer of '42 (http://www.allmovie.com/work/summer-of-42-47639) *allmovie.com.* Retrieved September 3, 2010.
[9] Internet Movie Database: Summer of '42 Business Data (http://imdb.com/title/tt0067803/business) *IMDb.com* Retrieved July 3, 2006.
[10] "Summer of '42 (1971) – Misc Notes" (http://www.tcm.com/tcmdb/title/19262/Summer-of-42/misc-notes.html). TCM.com. . Retrieved February 8, 2012.
[11] Rotten Tomatoes: Class of '44 (http://www.rottentomatoes.com/m/class_of_44/) *rottentomatoes.com* Retrieved August 11, 2006

[12] Timeout Film Review: Class of '44 (http://www.timeout.com/film/69355.html) *timeout.com* Retrieved August 11, 2006,

[13] Channel 4 Film Reviews: Class of '44 (http://www.channel4.com/film/reviews/film.jsp?id=102128) *channel4.com* Retrieved August 11, 2006

[14] New York Times Film Review: Class of '44 (http://movies2.nytimes.com/mem/movies/review.html?_r=1&title1=&title2=Class of '44 (Movie)&reviewer=VINCENT CANBY&v_id=9822&partner=Rotten Tomatoes&oref=slogin) *nytimes.com* Retrieved August 11, 2006

[15] Summer of '69 lyrics explained by co-author (http://www.jimvallance.com/01-music-folder/songs-folder-may-27/pg-song-adams-summer-of-69.html) *jimvallance.com* Retrieved July 6, 2006.

[16] Jennifer O'Neill in 2002 (http://www.tv-now.com/intervus/oneill/index.html) *tv-now.com* Retrieved August 11, 2006 Archived (http://web.archive.org/20060829114811/http://www.tv-now.com/intervus/oneill/index.html) August 29, 2006 at the Wayback Machine

[17] Theatermania.com (http://www.theatermania.com/content/news.cfm/story/1848), Starry, Starry Morning: Charles Nelson's Casts and Forecasts. Retrieved September 3, 2007

[18] Summer of '42 Plus Twenty (http://www.usatoday.com/life/books/2002/2002-04-09-oneill.htm) usatoday.com. Retrieved July 6, 2006.

External links

- *Summer of '42* (http://www.imdb.com/title/tt0067803/) at the Internet Movie Database
- *Summer of '42* (http://www.thewordslinger.com/posts.php?id=82) by Andy Williamson – The Wordslinger dated April 14, 2008

The Dean Martin Show

The Dean Martin Show

Martin with guest Florence Henderson, 1968.

Genre	Variety/Comedy
Written by	Arnie Kogen Ed. Weinberger
Directed by	Greg Garrison
Presented by	Dean Martin
Country of origin	United States
Language(s)	English
No. of seasons	9
No. of episodes	264
Production	
Producer(s)	Greg Garrison
Location(s)	NBC Studios Burbank, California
Running time	60 minutes
Broadcast	
Original channel	NBC
Original run	September 16, 1965 – April 5, 1974
Chronology	
Followed by	*The Dean Martin Celebrity Roast*

The Dean Martin Show also known as The Dean Martin Variety Show is a TV variety-comedy series that ran from 1965 to 1974 for 264 episodes. It was broadcast by NBC and hosted by crooner Dean Martin. The theme song to the series was his 1964 hit "Everybody Loves Somebody."

Nielsen Ratings

- Season 1 (September 16, 1965 - May 5, 1966, 31 episodes): out of the top-30
- Season 2 (September 8, 1966 - April 27, 1967, 33 episodes): #14
- Season 3 (September 14, 1967 - April 4, 1968, 30 episodes): #8
- Season 4 (September 19, 1968 - April 24, 1969, 30 episodes): #8
- Season 5 (September 18, 1969 - June 18, 1970, 31 episodes): #14
- Season 6 (September 17, 1970 - April 8, 1971, 28 episodes): #24
- Season 7 (September 16, 1971 - April 13, 1972, 28 episodes): out of the top-30
- Season 8 (September 14, 1972 - April 12, 1973, 28 episodes): out of the top-30
- Season 9 (September 6, 1973 - April 5, 1974, 25 episodes): out of the top-30

The series was a staple for NBC, airing Thursdays at 10:00 for 8 years, until its move to Fridays at 10:00 for the final season and change in format.

The Dean Martin Celebrity Roast, a series of specials spun off from the final season, generated solid ratings for 10 years on NBC.

Development

Martin was initially reluctant to do the show, partially because he did not want to turn down movie and nightclub performances. His terms were deliberately outrageous: he demanded a high salary and that he need only show up for the actual taping of the show. To his surprise the network agreed. As daughter Deana Martin recalled after meeting the network and making his demands Martin returned home and announced to his family, "They went for it. So now I have to do it."[1]

Martin believed that an important key to his popularity was that he did not put on airs. His act was that of a drunken, work-shy playboy, although the ever-present old-fashioned glass in his hand often only had apple juice in it. The show was heavy on physical comedy rather than just quips (he made his weekly entrance by sliding down a fireman's pole onto the stage.) Martin read his dialogue directly from cue cards. If he flubbed a line or forgot a lyric, Martin would not do a retake, and the mistake — and his recovery from it — went straight to tape and onto the air.

The Dean Martin Show was shot on color videotape beginning in 1965 at Studio 4 Stage 1 inside NBC's massive color complex at 3000 West Alameda Avenue in Burbank, California. The same studio was used for Frank Sinatra's yearly TV specials in the late 1960s, and Elvis Presley's 1968 "Comeback Special". Studio 4 is currently one of two used in the production of the soap opera *Days Of Our Lives*.

Regular segments

- Martin sang two solo numbers per show, one a serious ballad. He would join his weekly guests in song medleys, trading lyrics back and forth. Some of these duets were deliberately played for laughs—Dean and Liberace, for example—with special lyrics by Lee Hale to suit the performers.

- One recurring segment was based on Martin's club act, in which he would begin to sing a popular song and suddenly insert a gag punchline. Martin often tried to make his pianist, Ken Lane, laugh hard enough to break his concentration. The segment usually began with Martin leaping onto Lane's piano; in one episode the real piano was secretly replaced with a phony one. When Martin did his leap the entire faux-piano collapsed under his weight, all to the surprise and delight of the studio audience.

- A knock on the "closet" door occurred each week, with Martin opening the door to reveal an unannounced celebrity guest. Most of the time, Martin did not know who the guest would be, to keep his reactions more spontaneous, according to Hale's book *Backstage at the Dean Martin Show*.

- A regular gag during one season was the "Mystery Voice Contest," wherein Dean invited viewers to write in to guess who was singing a particular song. Invariably, it was the famous Frank Sinatra hit "Strangers in the Night." Finally on one episode, Sinatra himself showed up to announce that he was the mystery singer. Martin dutifully handed over the prize — a trip to Los Angeles, the city where the two of them already lived.

- The finale was typically a production number featuring Dean and the guest stars. Occasionally it would be a musical sketch with Martin appearing as "Dino Vino," a disc jockey who played old records. A vintage record would then be heard, with Dean and his cronies mouthing the words and pantomiming outrageously for comic effect.

- One of the most highly rated of Martin's programs was a Christmas episode featuring only his and Frank Sinatra's family members: Martin's wife Jeanne with children Craig, Claudia, Gail, Deana, Dean Paul, Ricci and Gina along with Sinatra's three children, Tina, Nancy and Frank Jr.

- During the show's 8th season, the finale was a selection of songs from a popular MGM film musical. Clips from the film in question would be shown, with Martin and guests singing a medley from the films. Among those saluted were *Easter Parade*, *Words and Music*, *Till the Clouds Roll By*, and the 1951 film version of *Show Boat*.

- When the show was cancelled in 1974, a series of *Dean Martin Celebrity Roasts* was produced in Las Vegas at the MGM Grand Hotel. This tradition was started during the final season of the variety show, and continued until 1984.

Regulars and recurring guests

In later seasons, many regular performers were added, such as Dom DeLuise and Nipsey Russell in sketches set in a barber shop; Kay Medford and Lou Jacobi in sketches set in a diner, and Medford also pretending to be the mother of Martin's pianist, Ken Lane. Leonard Barr, Guy Marks, Tom Bosley, Marian Mercer, Charles Nelson Reilly, and Rodney Dangerfield were also featured on multiple occasions, while bandleader Les Brown was a regular.

During the inaugural 1965-1966 season, The Krofft Puppets were seen regularly. Their stint, however, only lasted 8 episodes.[2] Sid and Marty Krofft were fired because Martin felt he was being upstaged by their puppets.[3]

Summer replacement series

For Martin's Thursday night time slot, the network and Martin's production crew created original summer programming (without Martin) to hold his usual weekly audience. Rowan and Martin hosted one of Dean Martin's summer series in 1966, which proved so successful that it spawned one of television's most memorable series, *Rowan and Martin's Laugh-In*.

From July to September 1967, the summer show was co-hosted by Martin's daughter Gail Martin, Vic Damone and Carol Lawrence.

In 1968, Martin's staff came up with a new format: a salute to the 1930s, with a variety show performed as if television existed at that time. Producer Greg Garrison recruited a dozen chorus girls, naming the group "The Golddiggers" after the Warner Brothers musicals of the '30s. The series, *Dean Martin Presents the Golddiggers*, starred Frank Sinatra, Jr. and Joey Heatherton as musical hosts, with comedy routines by Paul Lynde, Stanley Myron Handelman, Barbara Heller, comic impressionists Bill Skiles and Pete Henderson, and neo-vaudeville musicians The Times Square Two.

The summer show was a hit, returning the following year with a new cast. Lou Rawls and Gail Martin took over for Sinatra and Heatherton, and six-foot-six dancer Tommy Tune was featured.

The Golddiggers also toured the nation's nightclubs as a live attraction. Some of the members grew tired of traveling and dropped out, to be replaced by other hopefuls. After the summer series ran its course, the Golddiggers were seen on Martin's own program, and four of them were used in another group, the Ding-a-Ling Sisters.

Toward the end of the Thursday-night run, the summer series was devoted to European comedians. Marty Feldman was featured in *Dean Martin's Comedy World*, hosted by Jackie Cooper.

Awards

Emmy Award Nominations

- Outstanding Individual Performance in a Variety or Music Program Foster Brooks (1974)
- Outstanding Individual Performance in a Variety or Music Program Ruth Buzzi (1974)
- Outstanding Variety, Music or Comedy Series (1972)
- Outstanding Music and Lyrics Lee Hale (1971)
- Outstanding Variety, Music or Comedy Series (1970)
- Outstanding Variety, Music or Comedy Series (1969)
- Outstanding Variety, Music or Comedy Series (1968)
- Outstanding Music and Lyrics Lee Hale (1968)
- Outstanding Variety, Music or Comedy Series (1967)
- Outstanding Writing in a Variety, Music or Comedy Program (1967)
- Outstanding Directing for a Variety, Music or Comedy Program Greg Garrison (1967)
- Outstanding Directing for a Variety, Music or Comedy Program Greg Garrison (1966)

Golden Globe Award Wins

- Best Actor in a Television Comedy Series Dean Martin (1967)

Golden Globe Award Nominations

- Best Actor in a Television Comedy Series Dean Martin (1970)
- Best Actor in a Television Comedy Series Dean Martin (1969)
- Best Actor in a Television Comedy Series Dean Martin (1968)

DVD

From 2003 until August 2007, a 29-volume *Best of The Dean Martin Variety Show* collection was sold by direct marketing firm Guthy-Renker via infomercials and a website.

In mid-2007, NBC Universal filed suit in U.S. District Court against several parties, including Guthy-Renker, claiming copyright infringement, forcing G-R to temporarily withdraw the DVDs from sale. The lawsuit was in regard to a dispute over rights to footage used in the DVD series, material to which NBC claimed it still held the copyright. The conflict was discovered when NBC Universal looked into plans to release its own DVD set.

Also named as one of the defendants in the lawsuit was longtime *Dean Martin Show* producer Greg Garrison, who, NBC claims, had rights to use only excerpts from selected episodes of *The Dean Martin Show* for the DVDs—episodes which, according to NBC, Garrison purchased years earlier from the network for a syndicated run of *The Dean Martin Show* that aired worldwide from 1979 to 1981. Garrison died in 2005, before the lawsuit was brought forward.[4]

A settlement among all of the parties to the suit was reached on January 2, 2008. As a consequence, the Guthy-Renker website once again began selling the collection, and infomercials advertising it returned to the small screen.

There remain two other lawsuits pending over rights to material used in the *Best of Dean Martin Variety Show* series, but neither of those suits affected sales of the home video collection.

Unaffected by legal disputes were the *Dean Martin Celebrity Roast* specials, which continue to be marketed on DVD by Guthy-Renker. Total revenues from Dean Martin DVD sales have been rumored to be in the hundreds of millions of dollars. The Martin shows have not been on television since their original telecasts.

On February 3, 2011, it was revealed that a brand new package of DVDs featuring footage from The Dean Martin Show would be released on May 24, 2011 by Time-Life Video. Unlike the earlier Guthy-Renker collection, which was marketed via mail order subscription, these new sets would be aimed largely at the retail sector.[5]

On March 21, 2011, NBC Universal TV Consumer Products Group issued a press release disclosing its participation with Time-Life on the project.[6]

In an online report posted July 9, 2011, Deana Martin, one of Dean's daughters, told columnists Marilyn Beck and Stacy Jenel Smith that the first sets of Dean Martin Show DVDs released by Time-Life in the late Spring had sold so well that a second collection was already being planned, and that she (Deana) would be contributing commentary to it.[7] This information has been independently confirmed by officials at both Time-Life and NBCUniversal.

By the end of the summer of 2011, release dates were disclosed for the second wave of *Dean Martin Show* DVDs produced by Time-Life and featuring footage supplied by the series' originating network, NBC. Entitled *King of Cool: The Best of The Dean Martin Variety Show*, the new collection would be made available in 1- and 6-disc configurations.

Full List of Guest Stars

Note: only the first appearance by the guest star is listed

Season 1 (1965-1966)

- Don Adams
- Eddie Albert
- Van Alexander
- Herb Alpert & the Tijuana Brass
- Allen & Rossi
- Steve Allen
- The Andrews Sisters
- Paul Anka
- Louis Armstrong
- Frankie Avalon
- Pearl Bailey
- Lucille Ball
- Gene Baylos
- Tony Bennett
- Polly Bergen
- Milton Berle
- Shelley Berman
- John W. Bubbles
- Sam Butera & the Witnesses
- Donna Butterworth
- John Byner
- Sid Caesar
- Godfrey Cambridge
- Diahann Carroll
- Jack Carter
- Charo
- Barrie Chase
- Imogene Coca

- Bill Cosby
- Xavier Cugat
- Bill Dana (as José Jiménez)
- Vic Dana
- Dave Clark Five
- Phyllis Diller
- Dino, Desi & Billy
- Dukes of Dixieland
- Nanette Fabray
- Ferrante & Teicher
- Eddie Fisher
- Ella Fitzgerald
- Phil Ford and Mimi Hines
- Pete Fountain
- The Four Step Brothers
- John Gary
- George Gobel
- Robert Goulet
- Buddy Greco
- Joel Grey
- Tammy Grimes
- Jan & Dean
- Joey Heatherton
- Stanley Holloway
- Homer and Jethro
- Bob Hope
- Mahalia Jackson
- George Jessel
- Jack Jones
- Louis Jordan & His Tympany Five
- Lainie Kazan
- Morgana King
- Kirby Stone Four
- Lisa Kirk
- Abbe Lane
- Carol Lawrence
- Peggy Lee
- Hal Le Roy
- The Lettermen
- Shari Lewis and Lamb Chop
- Liberace
- Rich Little
- Julie London
- Dorothy Loudon
- Gisele MacKenzie
- Gordon MacRae
- Sheila MacRae

- Rose Marie
- Jackie Mason
- Johnny Mathis
- The McGuire Sisters
- Barbara McNair
- Ethel Merman
- Roger Miller
- Jane Morgan
- The New Christy Minstrels
- Bob Newhart
- Janis Paige
- Patti Page
- Marguerite Piazza
- Jane Powell
- Louis Prima and Gina Maione
- Juliet Prowse
- Line Renaud
- Frankie Randall
- The Righteous Brothers
- Chita Rivera
- Mickey Rooney
- Rowan & Martin
- Soupy Sales
- Tommy Sands
- The Serendipity Singers
- Allan Sherman
- Frank Sinatra
- Kate Smith
- Keely Smith
- Kay Starr
- The Supremes
- Pat Suzuki
- The Swingle Singers
- Danny Thomas
- The Treniers
- Leslie Uggams
- Shani Wallis
- John Wayne
- Jonathan Winters
- Gretchen Wyler
- The Young Americans

Season 2 (1966-1967)

- Edie Adams
- Eddy Arnold
- Gene Barry
- Shirley Bassey
- Janet Blair
- Ray Bolger
- George Burns
- Red Buttons
- Vikki Carr
- Don Cherry
- Petula Clark
- Tim Conway
- Bing Crosby
- Vic Damone
- Dom DeLuise
- Vince Edwards
- Duke Ellington
- Alice Faye
- Frank Fontaine
- Tennessee Ernie Ford
- Eddie Foy Jr.
- Sergio Franchi
- Connie Francis
- Arthur Godfrey
- Frank Gorshin
- Buddy Hackett
- Phil Harris
- Florence Henderson
- Herman's Hermits
- Sally Ann Howes
- Kessler Twins
- The Kim Sisters
- George Kirby
- Gene Krupa
- Trini Lopez
- Tony Martin
- Patrice Munsel
- Jan Murray
- Dorothy Provine
- Dinah Shore
- Kaye Stevens
- Caterina Valente
- Jackie Vernon
- Adam West
- Paul Winchell

Season 3 (1967-1968)

- Woody Allen
- Nancy Ames
- Carl Ballantine
- John Barbour
- Pat Boone
- Pat Buttram
- Cyd Charisse
- Rosemary Clooney
- Pat Cooper
- Norm Crosby
- Billy De Wolfe
- Buddy Ebsen
- Barbara Eden
- Jack Gilford
- Vic Grecco and Fred Willard
- Lorne Greene
- Shecky Greene
- Barbara Heller
- Pat Henry
- Lena Horne
- Van Johnson
- Julius LaRosa
- Janet Leigh
- Ross Martin
- The Mills Brothers
- Ricardo Montalban
- Byron Nelson
- Donald O'Connor
- Buck Owens
- Minnie Pearl
- Professor Backwards
- Don Rickles
- Roy Rogers and Dale Evans
- Sandler and Young
- Phil Silvers
- Frank Sinatra Jr.
- Nancy Sinatra
- Skiles and Henderson
- David Steinberg
- James Stewart
- Orson Welles
- Flip Wilson
- Henny Youngman

Season 4 (1968-1969)

- Edgar Bergen
- Victor Borge
- Ben Blue
- Pat Crowley
- Dan Dailey
- Bobby Darin
- Angie Dickinson
- David Frye
- Paul Gilbert
- Peter Graves
- Stanley Myron Handelman
- David Janssen
- Fran Jeffries
- Shirley Jones
- Will Jordan
- Michael Landon
- Gina Lollobrigida
- Gloria Loring
- Paul Lynde
- Bobbi Martin
- Zero Mostel
- Sue Raney
- Lou Rawls
- Avery Schreiber
- Sammy Shore
- Elke Sommer
- Ray Stevens
- Milburn Stone
- Dennis Weaver
- Raquel Welch

Season 5 (1969-1970)

- Ann-Margret
- Barbara Anderson
- Patti Austin
- Orson Bean
- Nino Benvenuti
- Shirley Booth
- Walter Brennan
- Albert Brooks
- Sebastian Cabot
- Carol Channing
- Lee J. Cobb
- Susan Cowsill
- Sammy Davis Jr.
- Barbara Feldon

- Margot Fonteyn
- Eva Gabor
- Alice Ghostley
- Gale Gordon
- Rocky Graziano
- Andy Griffith
- Morty Gunty
- Goldie Hawn
- Arte Johnson
- Paula Kelly
- Nancy Kwan
- Virna Lisi
- Danny Lockin
- Greg Morris
- Rudolf Nureyev
- Fess Parker
- Charles Nelson Reilly
- Marty Robbins
- Dale Robertson
- Irene Ryan
- Romy Schneider
- Forrest Tucker
- Tommy Tune
- Jennifer Warren
- Nancy Wilson

Season 6 (1970–1971)

- Lucie Arnaz
- Ronnie Barker and Ronnie Corbett
- Joey Bishop
- Eubie Blake
- Ernest Borgnine
- Jim Brown
- Raymond Burr
- Ruth Buzzi
- Glen Campbell
- Odia Coates
- Britt Ekland
- The Everly Brothers
- Peter Falk
- Marty Feldman
- Glenn Ford
- Joe Frazier
- Kathleen Freeman
- David Frost
- Engelbert Humperdinck
- Milt Kamen

- Meredith MacRae
- Kay Medford
- Joe Namath
- Maureen Reagan
- Debbie Reynolds
- Sugar Ray Robinson
- Kenny Rogers & The First Edition
- Jill St. John
- Alan Sues
- The Temptations
- Dionne Warwick

Season 7 (1971-1972)

- Dan Blocker
- Tom Bosley
- Joyce Brothers
- Art Carney
- Johnny Carson
- Richard S. Castellano
- Mike Connors
- Howard Cosell
- Lou Jacobi
- Jack Kruschen
- Meredith Mercer
- Don Meredith
- Wayne Newton
- Carroll O'Connor
- Jo Ann Pflug
- Ginger Rogers
- Elaine Stritch
- Rip Taylor

Season 8 (1972-1973)

- Lynn Anderson
- Eve Arden
- Jack Benny
- Karen Black
- Lloyd Bridges
- Joseph Campanella
- William Conrad
- Rodney Dangerfield
- Bobby Goldsboro
- Monty Hall
- Dennis Hopper
- Gene Kelly
- Steve Landesberg
- Steve Lawrence

- Martin Milner
- Anna Moffo
- Anne Murray
- Olivia Newton-John
- Hugh O'Brian
- Gilbert O'Sullivan
- Charley Pride
- Richard Roundtree
- Nipsey Russell
- Peter Sellers
- O.C. Smith

Season 9 (1973-1974)

- Dorsey Burnette
- Doug Dillard
- Donna Fargo
- Tom T. Hall
- William Holden
- Ferlin Husky
- Doug Kershaw
- Gladys Knight & the Pips
- Kris Kristofferson and Rita Coolidge
- Loretta Lynn
- Audrey Meadows
- Ray Price
- Charlie Rich
- Jeannie C. Riley
- Johnny Russell
- The Statler Brothers

References

[1] Classic Hollywood: Dean Martin does TV his way (http://www.latimes.com/entertainment/news/
      la-et-classic-hollywood-20110523,0,6902137.story) Los Angeles Times May 24, 2010
[2] Hal Erickson, "E! True Hollywood Story:" The Weird World of Sid & Marty Krofft
[3] (http://www.youtube.com/watch?v=w5pxHq9Qe-w) Sid & Marty Krofft Interview, Part 1 of 5
[4] TV Shows on DVD. (http://www.tvshowsondvd.com/news/Dean-Martin-Subscription-DVDs-Halted-Per-NBC-Lawsuit/8087)
[5] Dean Martin Show DVDs Announced (http://www.tvshowsondvd.com/news/Dean-Martin-DVDs-Announced/14986)
[6] NBCU Press Release re New Dean Martin Show DVDs (http://www.nbcumv.com/mediavillage/distribution/nutvconsprod/
      pressreleases?pr=contents/press-releases/2011/03/21/thebestofthedea1300743481250.xml)
[7] Beck/Smith Hollywood (http://becksmithhollywood.com/?tag=deana-martin)

Further reading

- Hale, Lee. *Backstage at the Dean Martin Show*. Taylor Trade Publishing, 2000. ISBN 0-87833-170-0.

External links

- *The Dean Martin Show* (http://www.imdb.com/title/tt0058797/) at the Internet Movie Database
- *The Dean Martin Show* (http://www.tv.com/shows/the-dean-martin-show/) at TV.com

The House of Blue Lights (song)

"The House of Blue Lights" is a popular song published in 1946, written by Don Raye and Freddie Slack. It was first recorded by Freddie Slack with singer Ella Mae Morse, and was covered the same year by The Andrews Sisters.

Notably for the time, the song featured a "hipster"-style spoken introduction by Slack and Morse:

> *"Well, whatcha say, baby? You look ready as Mr. Freddy this black. How 'bout you and me goin' spinnin' at the track?"*

> *"What's that, homie? If you think I'm goin' dancin' on a dime, your clock is tickin' on the wrong time."*

> *"Well, what's your pleasure, treasure? You call the plays, I'll dig the ways."*

> *"Hey daddy-o, I'm not so crude as to drop my mood on a square from way back......."*

The version by Morse and Slack reached # 8 on the *Billboard* pop chart, and the version by The Andrews Sisters reached # 15.[1]

Little Richard made reference to the "house of blue lights" in his 1958 hit "Good Golly, Miss Molly". The song itself was later recorded by Chuck Miller, Earl Richards, Merrill Moore, Chuck Berry, Jerry Lee Lewis, Freddy Cannon, Canned Heat, Commander Cody & His Lost Planet Airmen, The Flamin' Groovies, Asleep at the Wheel, George Thorogood and others.

References

[1] Jim Dawson and Steve Propes, *What Was The First Rock'n'Roll Record*, 1992, ISBN 0-571-12939-0, pp.14-17

The Lennon Sisters

This article refers to the American singing group. For John Lennon's Aunt Mimi see Mimi Smith.

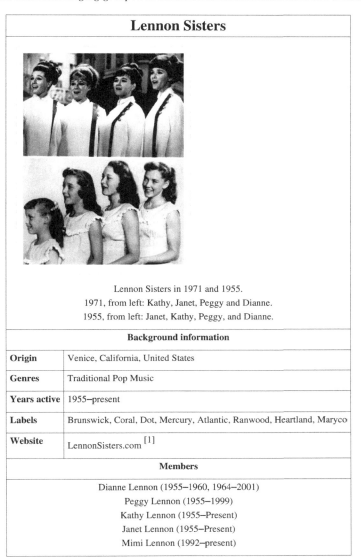

Lennon Sisters

Lennon Sisters in 1971 and 1955.
1971, from left: Kathy, Janet, Peggy and Dianne.
1955, from left: Janet, Kathy, Peggy, and Dianne.

Background information

Origin	Venice, California, United States
Genres	Traditional Pop Music
Years active	1955–present
Labels	Brunswick, Coral, Dot, Mercury, Atlantic, Ranwood, Heartland, Maryco
Website	LennonSisters.com [1]

Members

Dianne Lennon (1955–1960, 1964–2001)
Peggy Lennon (1955–1999)
Kathy Lennon (1955–Present)
Janet Lennon (1955–Present)
Mimi Lennon (1992–present)

The Lennon Sisters are an American singing group initially consisting of four siblings: **Dianne** (born December 1, 1939), **Peggy** (born April 8, 1941), **Kathy** (born August 2, 1943), and **Janet** (born June 15, 1946). They were all born in Los Angeles, California of German/Irish and Mexican ancestry. The group were a regular on the weekly television show, *The Lawrence Welk Show*. The original quartet were the eldest four in a family of twelve siblings. In 1992, younger sister Mimi replaced second sister Peggy who retired. Sister Dianne (DeeDee) has also retired. The current group line-up, appearing mostly at Welk resorts, consists of Mimi, Janet and Kathy.

Career

The quartet debuted on *The Lawrence Welk Show* on Christmas Eve 1955[2] after their school classmate, Larry Welk, son of Lawrence Welk, brought them to the attention of his father. Welk was home, sick in bed, when his son brought the sisters in to sing for him. He was so impressed he picked up the phone and booked them for that week's show. They were a mainstay on the show until they left to start a career of their own in 1968. The quartet was only three members from 1960 to 1964; oldest sister Dianne (also called Dee Dee) married, left the group, and then rejoined them. Peggy sang the high harmony part, Kathy the low harmony, and Janet and Dianne sang the middle harmony and lead parts. Janet also specialized in barbershop or counter-harmony, taught her by her Dad (who performed during the big band era as one of a quartet with his own three brothers), and the girls idolized Patti Page's multi-track vocal sound, feeling they achieved something close to her smooth blend in their Dot recording of "Stars Fell On Alabama." Kathy was especially fond of Connie Francis, evident in her solo Spanish recording of "Malaguena Salerosa," which showcased her impressive vocal range, & the sisters made no secret that they were huge fans of the innovative, intricate musical stylings of both The Andrews Sisters and The Mills Brothers.[3]

Their first hit, "Tonight, You Belong to Me" reached to #15 on the charts in 1956. This was followed by their 1961 single, "Sad Movies (Make Me Cry)", (Dot 16255), which turned out to be their highest-charting record. It provided them with the only number #1 single of their career, reaching the top of the charts in Japan. While much is written of the group's singing on television, they also recorded frequently for Dot Records in the 1950s & 1960s, producing over a dozen stereo albums featuring their own interpretations of tried and true standards like "Among My Souvenirs," "Moon River," "Twilight Time," & many other popular songs, including some that they were best associated with, like "Scarlet Ribbons," "Greensleeves," and Schubert's "Ave Maria." A themed LP entitled "Dominique" featured the singers with their musically talented siblings & cousins performing a variety of 1960s folk songs, including "Where Have All the Flowers Gone," "If I Had My Way (The Sermon of Samson)," as well as the title track. They recorded briefly for Mercury Records after leaving Dot, focusing on more contemporary pop/light-rock fare, such as "Can't Take My Eyes Off of You" and "Never My love." Their three best received, most popular albums were "Lawrence Welk presents The Lennon Sisters: Best-Loved Catholic Hymns (Dot);" "Christmas with The Lennon Sisters (Dot); and "Noel," their Christmas album for Mercury Records. Their full-bodied, homestyle yet choir-like blend added greatly to such yuletide favorites as "Adeste Fideles," "Christmas Island," "Faith of Our Fathers," "The Star Carol," and "Home for the Holidays."[4]

Items such as coloring books, paper dolls and story books were produced with the Lennon sisters.[5]

In 1969, the sisters starred in their own variety show, *Jimmy Durante Presents the Lennon Sisters Hour*. Six weeks before the show premiered on August 12, the sisters were forced to deal with the shooting death of their father, William Lennon, by a stalker named Chet Young, who believed himself married to Peggy and claimed their father stood in the way and had to be eliminated. Young shot William Lennon in the parking lot of the Marina Del Rey golf course; two months later he used the same weapon to commit suicide. The sisters discovered an unopened letter containing a cut out of their father, a picture of a gun pointed at his head, and the words "High Noon" (the time of the murder). (Source, Dr. Doreen Orion, *I Know You Really Love Me*) In the wake of the murder, *Jimmy Durante Presents The Lennon Sisters Hour* lasted one season before it was cancelled by ABC.

In the 1970s, the sisters performed regularly on *The Andy Williams Show*, and toured with Williams across the country including engagements at Caesar's Palace in Las Vegas. They also appeared on several game shows as well, such as *Family Feud*, *Tattletales* and *The Hollywood Squares*. From 1994 to 2004, the quartet performed as headliners at the Welk Champagne Theater in the Ozark community of Branson, Missouri. When Peggy retired from singing in 1999, younger sister Mimi took her place, and when Dianne left for a second time in 2001, the act became a trio again for the rest of its run in Branson.[6]

While continuing to play tour dates, Kathy and Janet Lennon have branched out into the toy market, designing and selling their "Best Pals" dolls. In addition to the dolls, the sisters have recorded CDs of favorite children songs for their "Best Pals" line. In addition, Kathy appeared on a religious TV show called *Search*, produced by Catholic TV

Studios in California.

The four original Lennon Sisters wrote their autobiography *Same Song, Separate Voices*, which was originally published in 1985 and updated a decade later.

Two of their five brothers, Kipp & Pat Lennon make up part of the band Venice along with first cousins Michael and Mark Lennon. [7]

Members

The Lennon Sisters

	Dianne	Peggy	Kathy	Janet
Born:	December 1, 1939	April 8, 1941	August 2, 1943	June 15, 1946
Spouse(s):	Dick Gass m. October 16, 1960–present three children	1) Dick Cathcart (1924–1993) m. May 24, 1964 six children 2) Robert Felt m. July 2, 1995–present	1) Mahlon Clark (1923–2007) m. June 26, 1967 divorced 1979 2) Jim Daris m. April 24, 1982–present	1) Lee Bernhardi m. May 7, 1966 divorced three children 2) John Bahler m. September 25, 1976–present two children

Awards

In 2001 The Lennon Sisters were inducted into the Vocal Group Hall of Fame.[8]

References

[1] http://www.lennonsisters.com
[2] http://www.welkmusicalfamily.com/lennonsisters.html
[3] Sforza, John: "Swing It! The Andrews Sisters Story;" University Press of Kentucky, 2000; 289 pages.
[4] Sforza, John: "Swing It! The Andrews Sisters Story;" University Press of Kentucky, 2000; 289 pages.
[5] http://www.imdb.com/name/nm1293376/bio
[6] vocal group.com (http://www.vocalgroup.org/inductees/the_lennon_sisters.html)
[7] http://www.venicecentral.com/faq.html
[8] http://www.vocalgroup.org/concert.htm

External links

- The Lennon Sisters' Website (http://www.lennonsisters.com/)
- Lennon Sisters page from Welk Musical Family.com (http://www.welkmusicalfamily.com/lennonsisters.html)
- The Lennon Sisters (http://www.imdb.com/name/nm1293376/) at the Internet Movie Database
- The Lennon Sisters (http://www.allmusic.com/artist/p30438) at Allmusic
- 'The Lennon Sisters' Vocal Group Hall of Fame Page (http://www.vocalgroup.org/inductees/the_lennon_sisters.html)
- The Lennon Sisters: Untainted Pop Princesses (http://popcultureaddict.com/music/lennonsisters.htm) Lennon Sisters profile at Confessions of a Pop Culture Addict

The McGuire Sisters

The McGuire Sisters	
Origin	Middletown, Ohio, United States
Genres	Traditional pop
Years active	1952–1968
Past members	
Christine McGuire Dorothy McGuire Phyllis McGuire	

The McGuire Sisters were a singing trio in American popular music. The group was composed of three sisters: **Christine McGuire** (born July 30, 1926); **Dorothy McGuire** (February 13, 1928 – September 7, 2012); and **Phyllis McGuire** (born February 14, 1931). Among their most popular songs are "Sincerely" and "Sugartime".[1]

History

The McGuire sisters were born in Middletown, Ohio[2] and grew up in Miamisburg. Their mother, Lillie, was an ordained minister of the Miamisburg First Church of God (Anderson, Indiana), where, as young girls, they sang in the church at weddings, funerals and church revivals. When they started singing in 1935, the youngest sister, Phyllis, was four years old. Eventually, they sang at occasions outside church and, by 1949, were singing at military bases and veterans' hospitals. They incorporated a more diverse repertoire for those events. Christine has two children, Herold and Asa; Dorothy had two, Rex and David. Phyllis has no children.

Career

They signed with Coral Records in 1952. That same year they appeared on *Arthur Godfrey's Talent Scouts*, and Godfrey hired them for his other shows, where they remained for seven years. *Cosmopolitan*'s November 1953 issue called them "Godfrey's Merry McGuires". The sisters often were compared to The Andrews Sisters. Maxene Andrews once said during an interview with Joe Franklin on WOR (AM) Radio in 1979, "The McGuire Sisters were fine once they stopped imitating The Andrews Sisters" .

In early McGuire recordings Phyllis' voice almost can be mistaken for that of Patty Andrews'. The McGuires and Andrewses met several times throughout their careers. Phyllis credited Patty, Maxene, and LaVerne during a television interview with Maxene in the 1990s, hosted by Sally Jessy Raphael, saying that she and her sisters met the Andrews Sisters in New York in the early 1950s and received important advice. Much like The Andrews Sisters, the McGuires moved when they sang, often executing dance routines during lavish production numbers on countless television specials (something The Andrews Sisters had originated in films during the 1940s, really becoming the first female vocal group to move when they sang, rather than just standing at a microphone). Phyllis and her sisters mimicked the singing style of The Andrews Sisters, as well as The Mills Brothers and The Dinning Sisters. From very young ages when they would perform short shows for family and friends in their parents' living room. While Phyllis is fond of saying in interviews that she and her sisters did not know any popular songs when they became famous (only the church hymns taught them by their minister mother), the trio often imitated other singing groups long before their success. [3]

They performed for five Presidents of the United States (Richard Nixon, Gerald Ford, Jimmy Carter, Ronald Reagan and George H. W. Bush) and for Queen Elizabeth II. In 1958, their mother appeared as a guest challenger on the television game show *To Tell the Truth*. The sisters maintained a busy television schedule, making frequent appearances on popular variety hours hosted by Ed Sullivan, Dean Martin, Danny Kaye, Milton Berle, Andy Williams, Perry Como and Red Skelton. The trio was dressed and coiffed identically and performed their synchronized body movements and hand gestures with military precision. Their recordings of "Sincerely," "Picnic," and 1958's "Sugartime" all sold more than one million copies.[2]

They retired from public appearances in 1968, giving their last performance that year on The Ed Sullivan Show. Phyllis McGuire continued to perform solo for a time. The demise of the group is often attributed to Phyllis' long-standing personal relationship with mobster, Sam Giancana (although she has always claimed that their friendship was strictly platonic), which reportedly blacklisted the group. During one of his 1960s court appearances for which Phyllis was subpoenaed, Giancana told reporters outside the courthouse that "Phyllis knows everything" about the rumored, unethical behaviors of John F. Kennedy and his brother, Robert. Phyllis has resided in a famously showcased mansion in Las Vegas for decades, boasting its own beauty parlor, a swan moat, and a replica of the Eiffel Tower which actually rose through the home's roof. When asked by Barbara Walters during a 1980s ABC-TV "20/20" interview from within the mansion if any of the money to build the lavish home came from Giancana, Phyllis denied the innuendo, claiming that she invested heavily in oil when the sisters were at the height of their popularity.[3]

The sisters reunited in 1986, performing at Toronto's Royal York Hotel for the first time since their retirement.[4] Numerous nightclub engagements followed in Las Vegas, Atlantic City, and New York City's Rainbow & Stars, showcasing the group and Phyllis' impersonations of Peggy Lee, Judy Garland, Pearl Bailey, Ethel Merman and even Louis Armstrong. Singing their greatest hits as part of their act, they were also featured performing specialty numbers like the frantic "I Love a Violin," the a cappella "Danny Boy," and a segment during which Phyllis retired backstage as Christine and Dorothy shared the spotlight playing a concert arrangement of "The Way We Were" on twin pianos. Other highlights in the act were a comical Trinidad-flavored tune, a soft rendering of "Memory" from Broadway's "Cats," and a "Money Medley," which they also performed live on the Jerry Lewis MDA Telethon in 1994. Since then, the sisters have made occasional public appearances together, including in 2004, when they reunited to perform in a PBS special *Magic Moments: Best of '50s Pop*.[5][6] It was plain to see on this 2004 program that at least Phyllis underwent some type of plastic surgery (most notably on her lips, which appeared much larger than ever before, even changing her speech), and the sisters' command of their vocal cords and harmonious blend had significantly diminished.[3]

They were inducted into the National Broadcasting Hall of Fame in 1994, and in 2001 they were inducted into the Vocal Group Hall of Fame. They also have been inducted into the Coca-Cola Hall of Fame and the Headliners' Hall of Fame.[7] They were inducted into the Hit Parade Hall of Fame in 2009.

After their careers wound down, they opened a restaurant in Bradenton, Florida, calling it McGuire's Pub.[8]

On September 7, 2012, Dorothy McGuire died at her son's home in Paradise Valley, Arizona,[9] after suffering from Parkinson's disease and age-related dementia; she was 84.[10]

Discography

Year	Single	Chart positions		
		US	US AC	UK[11]
1954	"Pine Tree, Pine Over Me"	26	-	—
	"Goodnite, Sweetheart, Goodnite"	7	-	—
	"Muskrat Ramble"	10	-	—
	"Lonesome Polecat"	28	-	—
	"Christmas Alphabet"	25	-	—
1955	"Sincerely"	1	-	14
	"No More"	17	-	20
	"It May Sound Silly"	11	-	—
	"Doesn't Anybody Want Me?"	flip	-	—
	"Something's Gotta Give"	5	-	—
	"Rhythm 'n Blues"	flip	-	—
	"He"	10	-	—
	"Give Me Love"	95	-	—
1956	"Missing"	44	-	—
	"Picnic"	13	-	—
	"Delilah Jones"	37	-	24
	"Weary Blues"	32	-	—
	"In the Alps"	63	-	—
	"Ev'ry Day of My Life"	37	-	—
	"Endless"	52	-	—
	"Goodnight, My Love, Pleasant Dreams"	32	-	—
1957	"Sugartime"	1	-	14
	"Ding Dong"	25	-	—
1958	"Volare"	80	-	—
1959	"May You Always"	11	-	15
	"Summer Dreams"	55	-	—
	"Peace"	85	-	—
1960	"Livin' Dangerously"	97	-	—
	"The Last Dance"	99	-	—
1961	"Just For Old Time's Sake"	20	-	—
	"Tears On My Pillow"	59	12	—
	"Just Because"	99	-	—
1962	"Sugartime Twist"	107	-	—
1964	"I Don't Want To Walk Without You" (Phyllis solo)	79	13	—
1966	"Truer Than You Were"	-	30	—

Songs recorded

- "Achoo-Cha-Cha" (flip side of "May You Always") (1958)
- "Are You Looking for a Sweetheart" (flip side of "You Never Know Till Monday") (1953)
- "Around the World" (flip side of "Interlude") (1957)
- "Baby Be Good to Me" (flip side of "My Baby's Got Such Loving Ways") (1956)
- "Banana Split" (flip side of "Sugartime") (1957)
- "Beginning to Miss You" (flip side of "Rock Bottom") (1957)
- "Blue Skies" (flip side of "He's Got Time") (1957)
- "Candy Heart" (flip side of "Dear Heart") (1964)
- "Christmas Alphabet" (flip side of "Give Me Your Heart for Christmas") (1954)
- "Cling to Me" (flip side of "Pine Tree, Pine over Me") (1954)
- "Compromise" (flip side of "Red River Valley") (1959)
- "Cordially Invited" (flip side of "Summertime (Is the Time for Love)") (1963)
- "Dear Heart" (flip side of "Candy Heart") (1964)
- "Delilah Jones" (flip side of "Theme from *Picnic*") (1956)
- "Ding Dong" (flip side of "Since You Went Away to School") (1958)
- "Doesn't Anybody Love Me" (flip side of "It May Sound Silly") (1955)
- "Don't Take Your Love from Me" (date unknown, flip side unknown)
- "Do You Love Me Like You Kiss Me" (flip side of "Volare") (1958)
- "Drowning in Memories" (flip side of "Please Don't Do That To Me") (1957)
- "Endless" (flip side of "Ev'ry Day of My Life") (1956)
- "Ev'ry Day of My Life" (flip side of "Endless") (1956)
- "Forgive Me" (flip side of "Kiss Them for Me") (1957)
- "Give Me Love" (flip side of "Sweet Song Of India") (1955)
- "Give Me Your Heart for Christmas" (flip side of "Christmas Alphabet") (1954)
- "Goodnight My Love" (flip side of "Mommy") (1956)
- "Goodnite, Sweetheart, Goodnite" (flip side of "Heavenly Feeling") (1954)
- "Goody-Goody"
- "Grazia" (flip side of "Truer Than You Were") (1966)
- "Have a Nice Weekend" (flip side of "Some of These Days") (1959)
- "He" (flip side of "If You Believe") (1955)
- "Heart" (flip side of "Young and Foolish") (1955)
- "Hearts of Stone" (flip side of "Naughty Lady of Shady Lane") (1954)
- "Heavenly Feeling" (flip side of "Goodnight Sweetheart Goodnight") (1954)
- "He's Got Time" (flip side of "Blue Skies") (1957)
- "Hey Mr. Cotton Picker" (flip side of "Tell Us Where The Good Times Are") (1953)
- "Honorable Congratulations" (flip side of "Santa Claus Is Coming to Town") (1957)
- "I Can Dream, Can't I?" (flip side of "Time") (1961)
- "I'd Like to Trim a Tree with You" (flip side of "Littlest Angel") (1955)
- "I Do I Do I Do" (flip side of "Just Because") (1961)
- "I Don't Know Why" (flip side of "To Be Loved") (1960)
- "I Don't Want to Walk Without You" (flip side of "That's Life") (1964)
- "If It's a Dream" (flip side of "Kiss Me and Kill Me with Love") (1955)
- "If You Believe" (flip side of "He") (1955)
- "I Give Thanks" (flip side of "The Unforgiven") (1960)
- "I'll Think of You" (flip side of "Sweetie Pie") (1958)
- "I'll Walk Alone" (flip side of "Ticket to Anywhere") (1965)

- "Interlude" (flip side of "Around the World") (1957)
- "In the Alps" (flip side of "Weary Blues") (1956)
- "I Really Don't Want to Know" (flip side of "Mama's Gone Goodbye") (1962)
- "It May Sound Silly" (flip side of "Doesn't Anybody Love Me") (1955)
- "Just Because" (flip side of "I Do I Do I Do") (1961)
- "Just for Old Time's Sake" (flip side of "Really Neat") (1961)
- "Kid Stuff" (flip side of "Without Him") (1957)
- "Kiss Me and Kill Me with Love" (flip side of "If It's a Dream") (1955)
- "Kiss Them for Me" (flip side of "Forgive Me") (1957)
- "The Last Dance" (flip side of "Nine O'Clock") (1960)
- "Littlest Angel" (flip side of "I'd Like To Trim a Tree With You") (1955)
- "Livin' Dangerously" (flip side of "Lovers' Lullaby") (1960)
- "Lonesome Polecat" (released on two different singles, one with "Uno Due Tre" as the flip side, the other with one version of "Muskrat Ramble" as the flip side) (1954)
- "Lovers' Lullaby" (flip side of "Livin' Dangerously") (1960)
- "Mama's Gone Goodbye" (flip side of "I Really Don't Want to Know") (1962)
- "May You Always" (flip side of "Achoo-Cha-Cha") (1958)
- "Melody of Love" (flip side of "Open Up Your Heart") (1954)
- "Missing" (flip side of "Tell Me Now") (1956)
- "Miss You" (flip side of "Tootle-Loo-Siana") (1952)
- "Mommy" (flip side of "Goodnight My Love") (1956)
- "More Hearts are Broken That Way" (flip side of "Sugartime" [remake]) (1962)
- "Muskrat Ramble" (released on two different singles, one with "Not As a Stranger" as the flip side, the other with one version of "Lonesome Polecat" as the flip side) (1954)
- "My Baby's Got Such Loving Ways" (flip side of "Baby Be Good to Me") (1956)
- "My Happiness" (flip side of "Vaya Con Dios") (1966)
- "The Naughty Lady of Shady Lane" (flip side of "Hearts of Stone") (1954)
- "Never" (flip side of "Now and Forever") (1964)
- "Nine O'Clock" (flip side of "The Last Dance") (1960)
- "No More" (flip side of "Sincerely") (1954)
- "Not as a Stranger" (flip side of one version of "Muskrat Ramble") (1954)
- "Now and Forever" (flip side of "Never") (1964)
- "One Two Three Four" (flip side of "Picking Sweethearts") (1952)
- "Open Up Your Heart" (flip side of "Melody of Love") (1954)
- "Peace" (flip side of "Summer Dreams") (1959)
- "Picking Sweethearts" (flip side of "One Two Three Four") (1952)
- "Theme from *Picnic*" (flip side of "Delilah Jones") (1956)
- "Pine Tree, Pine over Me" (flip side of "Cling to Me") (1954)
- "Please Don't Do That To Me" (flip side of "Drowning In Memories") (1957)
- "Really Neat" (flip side of "Just For Old Time's Sake") (1961)
- "Red River Valley" (flip side of "Compromise") (1959)
- "Rhythm and Blues" (flip side of "Something's Gotta Give") (1955)
- "Rock Bottom" (flip side of "Beginning To Miss You") (1957)
- "Run to My Arms" (flip side of "Somebody Else Is Taking My Place") (1965)
- "Santa Claus Is Coming to Town" (flip side of "Honorable Congratulations") (1957)
- "Shuffle Off to Buffalo"
- "Sincerely" (flip side of "No More") (1954)

- "Since You Went Away to School" (flip side of "Ding Dong") (1958)
- "Somebody Else Is Taking My Place" (flip side of "Run to My Arms") (1965)
- "Some of These Days" (flip side of "Have a Nice Weekend") (1959)
- "Something's Gotta Give" (flip side of "Rhythm And Blues") (1955)
- "Space Ship" (flip side of "Tears on My Pillow") (1961)
- "Sugartime" (flip side of "Banana Split") (1957)
- "Sugartime" (remake) (flip side of "More Hearts are Broken That Way") (1962)
- "Summer Dreams" (flip side of "Peace") (1959)
- "Summertime (Is the Time for Love)" (flip side of "Cordially Invited") (1963)
- "Sweetie Pie" (flip side of "I'll Think of You") (1958)
- "Sweet Song of India" (flip side of "Give Me Love]") (1955)
- "Teach Me Tonight"
- "Tears on My Pillow" (flip side of "Space Ship") (1961)
- "Tell Me Now" (flip side of "Missing") (1956)
- "Tell Us Where the Good Times Are" (flip side of "Hey Mr. Cotton Picker") (1953)
- "That's Life" (flip side of "I Don't Want To Walk Without You") (1964)
- "Ticket to Anywhere" (flip side of "I'll Walk Alone") (1965)
- "Time" (flip side of "I Can Dream, Can't I?") (1961)
- "To Be Loved" (flip side of "I Don't Know Why") (1960)
- "Tootle-Loo-Siana" (flip side of "Miss You") (1952)
- "Truer Than You Were" (flip side of "Grazia") (1966)
- "The Unforgiven" (flip side of "I Give Thanks") (1960)
- "Uno Due Tre" (flip side of one version of "Lonesome Polecat") (1954)
- "Vaya Con Dios" (flip side of "My Happiness") (1966)
- "Volare (flip side of "Do You Love Me Like You Kiss Me") (1958)
- "Weary Blues" (flip side of "In the Alps") (1956)
- "Without Him" (flip side of "Kid Stuff") (1957)
- "You Never Know Till Monday" (flip side of "Are You Looking for a Sweetheart?") (1953)
- "Young and Foolish" (flip side of "Heart") (1955)
- "You're Driving Me Crazy"

In popular culture

The McGuire Sisters, and most especially Phyllis McGuire, who lives in Las Vegas, were the subjects of the 1995 HBO movie *Sugartime*, which depicted a romantic relationship between Phyllis and mobster Sam Giancana. Giancana was played by actor John Turturro, and Phyllis was played by actress Mary-Louise Parker.

References

[1] McGuire Sisters official Web site (http://www.mcguiresisters.com)
[2] Murrells, Joseph (1978). *The Book of Golden Discs* (2nd ed.). London: Barrie and Jenkins Ltd. p. 75. ISBN 0-214-20512-6.
[3] Sforza, John: "Swing It! The Andrews Sisters Story;" University Press of Kentucky, 2000; 289 pages.
[4] [*PEOPLE* magazine, "The Mcguire Sisters, Those Sugartime Princesses of Pop, Have Reunited After a 17-Year Split," March 3, 1986]
[5] "Magic Moments: Best of '50s Pop" PBS special (http://www.njn.net/television/highlights/04june/mymusicbestof50spop.html)
[6] Musician Guide, "The McGuire Sisters Biography" (http://www.musicianguide.com/biographies/1608002499/The-McGuire-Sisters.
     html)
[7] AZCentral.com article, "50th anniversary party reunites legendary trio," by Kathy Shayna Shocket, 12/10/2008 (http://www.azcentral.com/
     community/scottsdale/articles/2008/12/10/20081210sr-maguire1211.html)
[8] "The McGuire Sisters" (http://www.answers.com/topic/the-mcguire-sisters). answers.com. . Retrieved 9 September 2012.
[9] Christe, Bob. "Dorothy McGuire of McGuire Sisters dies at 84" (http://my.bresnan.net/news/read.php?rip_id=<DA16D1180@news.ap.
     org>&ps=1016). Associated Press. . Retrieved 9 September 2012.

[10] 5:27PM BST 11 Sep 2012 (2012-09-11). "Dorothy McGuire" (http://www.telegraph.co.uk/news/obituaries/culture-obituaries/ music-obituaries/9536563/Dorothy-McGuire.html). Telegraph. . Retrieved 2012-10-21.

[11] Roberts, David (2006). *British Hit Singles & Albums* (19th ed.). London: Guinness World Records Limited. p. 339. ISBN 1-904994-10-5.

External links

- McGuire Sisters' page on the National Broadcasters Hall of Fame (NBHF) (http://www.infoage.org/exhibits/ national-broadcasters-hall-of-fame/hall-of-fame-articles/267-mcguire-sisters-1994) site
- McGuire Sisters' page on the Primarily A Cappella (http://www.singers.com/group/McGuire-Sisters/) site
- McGuire Sisters on [[Hit Parade Hall of Fame (http://www.hitparadehalloffame.com/Inductees_all/ McGuireSisters.html)] site]
- McGuire Sisters' page on the Vocal Group Hall of Fame (http://www.vocalgroup.org/inductees/ the_mcguire_sisters.html) site
- Cincinnati Enquirer article on the sisters' home (http://www.enquirer.com/editions/2003/07/27/ loc_mcguires27.html)
- The McGuire Sisters (http://www.imdb.com/name/nm1311370/) at the Internet Movie Database
- Christine McGuire (http://www.imdb.com/name/nm0570175/) at the Internet Movie Database
- Dorothy McGuire (http://www.imdb.com/name/nm0570193/) at the Internet Movie Database
- Phyllis McGuire (http://www.imdb.com/name/nm0570279/) at the Internet Movie Database
- The McGuire Sisters (http://www.findagrave.com/cgi-bin/fg.cgi?page=gr&GRid=96787336) at *Find a Grave*

The Puppini Sisters

The Puppini Sisters	

The Puppini Sisters (O'Brien, Puppini and Mullins) at an open-air concert during the City of London Festival in 2008	
Background information	
Origin	London, England
Genres	A cappella, pop, jazz, Close harmony, Swing
Years active	2004–present
Labels	UCJ (UK), Verve (U.S.)
Website	ThePuppiniSisters.com [1]
Members	
Marcella Puppini Kate Mullins Emma Smith	
Past members	
Terrianne Passingham Stephanie O'Brien Rosanna Schura	

The Puppini Sisters are a close harmony vocal trio composed of Italian Marcella Puppini and English Kate Mullins and Emma Smith. Although the three are not related, the name was chosen in tribute to The Andrews Sisters. Puppini first studied fashion design at St. Martins School of Art, and later music at Trinity College of Music in London where she met Mullins and original member Stephanie O'Brien. The trio are backed by a three-piece band featuring Blake Wilner on guitar, Henrik Jensen on double bass and Peter Ibbetson on drums. After eight years with the group, O'Brien decided to leave and she was replaced by Emma Smith. Critic Arion Berger described them as part of "Retro's futuristic vanguard" and characterized their sound as "swing-punk". The group is associated with a burlesque revival.[2]

History

The group was founded in 2004 by Marcella Puppini after she was inspired by the animated film *Les Triplettes de Belleville* (2003). In 2005 they were signed by UCJ (Universal Classics and Jazz). The Puppini Sisters' debut single, "Boogie Woogie Bugle Boy", was a cover of the hit single by The Andrews Sisters. The Puppini Sisters' second album, *The Rise and Fall of Ruby Woo* includes original compositions by Puppini, Stephanie O'Brien and Kate Mullins.

The Puppini Sisters television appearances include *This Morning*, *Loose Women*, *The Alan Titchmarsh Show*, *Big Brother's Little Brother*, *Hell's Kitchen*, CBeebies' *Space Pirates*, *The View* (on ABC), and 2011's *A Michael Bublé Christmas* on NBC. The group also appeared in the 2009 Jonathan Creek New Year's special "The Grinning Man", performing their 2007 single "Spooky". The trio was also featured on the soundtracks for the US TV series *Greys Anatomy* and *Chuck*.

The group performed at Glastonbury Festival 2009 on 27 June.[3] as well as performing at Goodwood Vintage Festival on 15 August.

On 27 June 2012, O'Brien announced via the group's Facebook page that she was leaving The Puppini Sisters.[4] It was later revealed that Terrianne Passingham would replace O'Brien.[5] However, Passingham also left the group and shortly thereafter Emma Smith took her place. The singer made her debut with The Puppini Sisters on *The Graham Norton Show* in November 2012.[6]

Influences

According to their MySpace page, acts that have influenced the Puppini Sisters include The Andrews Sisters, The Boswell Sisters, Marlene Dietrich, Fred Astaire and Ginger Rogers, Kate Bush, Mike Flowers, Joan Crawford, The Smiths, and Tom Waits.

According to Marcella Puppini, the group sings about modern and risqué subjects in a quaintly old-fashioned way. This comes from their interest in 1940s songs such as "Hold Tight (Want Some Seafood Mama)" that have sexual undertones despite their overtly innocent lyrics.[7]

Awards

The Puppini Sisters won a Gold Disc for international sales of their first CD, *Betcha Bottom Dollar*, in 2007.[8]

The Puppini Sisters website won the 2008 Cream of Yorkshire awards "Gold Award" for best website. The digital advertising agency twentysix won the top award the "overall Grand Prix award" for its design of a website for Universal Music showcasing the group.[9]

Discography

Singles

- "Boogie Woogie Bugle Boy (From Company B)" (2006)
- "Jingle Bells/Silent Night (Little Match Seller)" (December 2006) iTunes-only release
- "Spooky" (2007)
- "Crazy in Love" (2007)
- "Jilted" (2008)
- "Apart of Me" with The Real Tuesday Weld (2008)
- "Diamonds Are a Girl's Best Friend" (2011)

Videos

- "Boogie Woogie Bugle Boy" (2006)
- "Spooky" (2007)
- "Apart of Me" with The Real Tuesday Weld directed by Alex de Campi (2007)
- "Jilted" directed by Alex de Campi (2008)
- "(I Can't Believe I'm Not a) Millionaire" directed by Alex de Campi (2008)
- "Diamond's Are a Girl's Best Friend" directed by Alex de Campi (2011)

Albums

- *Betcha Bottom Dollar* (July 31, 2006 U.K., May 1, 2007 U.S., March 2008 France). According to the official website the album reached number two on the U.S. Jazz Charts and number nine on the U.S. new artist chart[10]
- *The Rise and Fall of Ruby Woo* (October 1, 2007 U.K.), (February 2008 U.S., January 2009 France) featuring classic covers, 1940s style reworkings of contemporary music, and a selection of original compositions. According to *Billboard*'s official website, the album peaked at number 5 in the US Jazz Charts in 2008.[10]
- *Christmas with the Puppini Sisters* (October 5, 2010 USA), reworkings of classic Christmas songs on Verve Records
- *Hollywood* (Autumn 2011 France), (December 26, 2011 UK), Hollywood musical themed tracks and one original Universal[11]

Compilations

- Could It Be Magic appears on *Magicians OST Universal* (2007)
- Crazy in Love on *Swing Style - Swing Beats for Dancing Feets* Compiled and mixed by Gulbahar Kultur, *Lola's World* (2008), *100 Hits - Voices DEM* (2009), *Radio Modern - The ABC of Swing, Bop'n'Roll EMI Belgium* (2010)
- In The Mood appears on *Actrices* OST *Milan Music* (2008)
- It Don't Mean A Thing (If It Ain't Got That Swing) appears on *Jazzism 1* from *Jazzism Magazine* (2008)
- I Will Survive appears on *Tom Middleton Presents Crazy Covers 2 UCJ* (2007), *Bolero Fashion Sound compiled by Olivier Rohrbach Universal* (2007), *Jazziz 8: Women compilation by Jazziz Magazine* (2007), *You're Beautiful - 40 Inspiring Songs UCJ* (2007), *Smile Style 2* compilation by DJ Weritos Lounge *Wave Music* (2009), *Intelligent Music Favorites Vol 7* (2009), *Peppermint Candy UMTV* (2011)
- Jilted appears on *Back To Soul - New Soul Queens and Legendary Divas UCJ* (2008)
- Jingle Bells appears on *A Classic Christmas UCJ* (2006), *Now That's What I Call Xmas Virgin* (2006), *Now This Is Christmas 2008 UCJ* (2008), *Wonderland, Spectrum Audio* (2008), *Now That's What I Call Christmas! 3 UCJ* (2009), *Christmas With The Stars Spectrum Audio* (2010), *Merry Christmas Everybody Spectrum Audio* (2010), *Now That's What I Call Xmas EMI UK* (2010)
- Libertango appears on *Lost Vagueness OST Universal* (2007)
- Mele Kalikimaka appears on *Christmas Tales 2010 Raar FM* (2010)
- Mr Sandman appears on *The Jazz Album 2006 UCJ* (2006)
- Panic appears on *Jazz For Dinner UCJ* (2006), *Party Jazz UMGI* (2010)
- Side By Side appears on *Kit Kittredge: An American Girl OST compilation from film of the same name by New Line Records* (2008)
- Spooky appears on *100 Hits - Voices DEM* (2009)
- Sway appears on *The Jazz Album 2006 UCJ* (2006), *100 Hits - Voices DEM* (2009), *TSF Jazz 1999-2009 10 Ans Nova* (2009)
- Tu Vuo Fa L' Americano appears on *The Very Best of Latin Jazz UCJ* (2007), *New York New York Compact Disc Club* (2008)

- We Have All The Time In The World appears on *You Raise Me Up 2008 UCJ* (2008)

Collaboration

Christmas 2011 saw the release of "Jingle Bells" recorded with Michael Bublé for his end of year album.[12] They also recorded "Frosty the Snowman" with Buble on the same album, as a bonus track on the Deluxe Edition.

The group recorded a close harmony version of the song "Apart of Me", by Stephen Coates of The Real Tuesday Weld, and acted in the video for the song, playing "a corpse, murdering waitresses, worms and chickens". Two versions of the song exist, one being that which was used for the video and the other is a track on The Real Tuesday Weld 2008 CD *The London Book of the Dead*.

The group used period costumes designed by Vivienne Westwood in their video for "Jilted", an original song written by Marcella Puppini (not to be confused with the 1954 Theresa Brewer country number). Jesse Quin, bassist of the British band Keane appears in the video as extra.

Further reading

- Heawood, S (2007-09-29). "Meet the sisters of swing" [13]. *Music* (The Times). Retrieved 2007-10-03. (login required)

Live reviews

- Verrico, Lisa (2007-10-05). "The Puppini Sisters" [14]. *Music* (The Times). Retrieved 2007-10-08. (login required)
- Hasted, N (2009-01-06). "The Puppini Sisters, Queen Elizabeth Hall, London" [15]. *Music* (The Independent). Retrieved 2009-01-15.

References

[1] http://www.thepuppinisisters.com/

[2] "Swinging Sister: Marcella Puppini Express Magazine 12 June 2008" (http://www.readexpress.com/read_freeride/2008/06/ sister_act_marcella_puppini.php). Readexpress.com. 2008-06-12. . Retrieved 2011-01-02.

[3] 11:11pm (2009-06-29). "Glastonbury: Best of the Rest BBC 27 June 2009" (http://www.bbc.co.uk/blogs/bbcmusic/2009/06/ with_at_least_23_official.html). Bbc.co.uk. . Retrieved 2011-01-02.

[4] "Official announcement" (https://www.facebook.com/puppinisisters/posts/481344405212803). Facebook.com. 2012-06-27. . Retrieved 2012-06-27.

[5] "The Puppini Sisters" (http://www.neilobrienentertainment.com/portfolio/the-puppini-sisters). Neil O'Brien Entertainment. . Retrieved 26 November 2012.

[6] "What a way to welcome the wonderful Emma Smith into the fold!" (http://www.facebook.com/puppinisisters/posts/382386051846362). Facebook.com. 24 November 2012. . Retrieved 26 November 2012.

[7] "The Puppini Sisters Christmas Metrolife 23 December 2008" (http://www.metro.co.uk/metrolife/article. html?The_Puppini_Sisters_Christmas&in_article_id=456293&in_page_id=9). Metro.co.uk. 2008-12-23. . Retrieved 2011-01-02.

[8] https://www.classicsandjazz.co.uk/plink/The+Puppini+Sisters;jsessionid=539CE63626A4E6ADB341B4C36A3945B9.front2_1

[9] "twentysix wins three top awards in one night creativematch 5 November 2008" (http://www.creativematch.co.uk/viewNews/?96544). Creativematch.co.uk. 2008-11-05. . Retrieved 2011-01-02.

[10] http://www.billboard.com/bbcom/retrieve_chart_history.do?model.chartFormatGroupName=Albums&model.vnuArtistId=773557& model.vnuAlbumId=903738

[11] http://www.concertlive.fr/breves/10186/the-puppini-sisters-nouvel-album-et-serie-de-concerts-en-france-cet-automne

[12] http://www.ctv.ca/CTVNews/Entertainment/20110715/michael-buble-shania-twain-110715/

[13] http://entertainment.timesonline.co.uk/tol/arts_and_entertainment/music/article2529113.ece

[14] http://entertainment.timesonline.co.uk/tol/arts_and_entertainment/music/live_reviews/article2591615.ece

[15] http://www.independent.co.uk/arts-entertainment/music/reviews/the-puppini-sisters-queen-elizabeth-hall-london-1227740.html

External links

- Official website (http://www.thepuppinisisters.com)
- National Public Radio (U.S.) interview (http://www.npr.org/templates/story/story.php?storyId=9937587)
- Audio interview (http://www.bbc.co.uk/wiltshire/content/articles/2007/10/01/ puppini_sisters_interview_feature.shtml) at BBC Wiltshire (http://www.bbc.co.uk/wiltshire)

The Three Belles

The Three Belles	
Genres	close harmony
Occupations	Musicians / Actresses
Years active	2010–present
Associated acts	The Bevin Boys
Website	www.thethreebelles.com [1]

The Three Belles are Anneka Wass, Sally Taylor and Isabelle Moore, a British vintage acting and singing trio specialising in The Andrews Sisters style performances and 1940s Experience nights[2]. They are notable for maintaining throughout their live performances three distinct 1940s personas, 'Betty' (Wass), 'Gail' (Taylor) and 'Dorothy' (Moore).

They are the Heart FM Breakfast House Band [3] and are also the subject of a digital and hard copy novel by Matthew Wingett entitled "The Three Belles Star In We'll Meet Again".[4][5].

The Three Belles are also strongly featured in Richard Grudens' book on vintage style singing groups, "Perfect Harmony"[6][7] with foreword by Patty Andrews of The Andrews Sisters and were featured as an 'emerging band' in 'Nyne Magazine'[8].

They are closely connected with the city of Portsmouth, where the band formed at the University of Portsmouth[9] and have given performances of their own 1940s experience show 'In The Mood' at the major south coast venue Portsmouth Guildhall. The Belles also produce a 1940s theatre show called 'Sing Sing Sing', the production includes music and readings from World War II[10].

Other appearances include The Isle of Wight Festival [11] and the Twinwood Festival [12].

References

[1] http://www.thethreebelles.com/

[2] 'From Students To Stage Stars In A Year', The News, Portsmouth May 15 2012 by Mischa Allen http://www.portsmouth.co.uk/lifestyle/from-students-to-stage-stars-in-a-year-1-3841330

[3] 'Heart Breakfast House Band' http://www.heart.co.uk/cambridgeshire/on-air/breakfast/heart-breakfast-house-band/

[4] 'The Three Belles Star In "We'll Meet Again"' by Matt Wingett, Smashwords (2012), digital edition Amazon.co.uk review (http://www.amazon.co.uk/Three-Belles-Portsmouth-Stories-ebook/dp/B006UFDVH8/).

[5] 'The Three Belles Star In "We'll Meet Again"', Life Is Amazing (2012), paperback edition http://www.amazon.co.uk/gp/offer-listing/0957241305/ref=tmm_pap_new_olp_sr?ie=UTF8&qid=1339514134&sr=1-1&condition=new

[6] 'Perfect Harmony' by Richard Grudens, [Patty Andrews], paperback, 2012, http://www.amazon.com/Perfect-Harmony-Singing-Groups-20th-Century/dp/098478781X

[7] 'Belles Of The Ball' http://www.planetjive.freeuk.com/news5.html

[8] 'Nyne Talks To The 1940s-Style Vocal Trio The Three Belles' in Nyne Magazine Issue 3, April 23rd 2012, pp10-13 http://issuu.com/nyne.magazine/docs/3_final

[9] 'The Three Belles: Graduate Profile' http://www.port.ac.uk/update/2012/05/graduate-profile-the-three-belles/

[10] 'Sing Sing Sing at the Elgiva Theatre' http://www.elgiva.com/index.php/whats-on-details/events/the-three-belles-sing-sing-sing-1321.html

[11] 'The Isle of Wight Festival, Hipshaker Lounge' http://www.isleofwightfestival.com/hipshaker-lounge.aspx

[12] 'Twinwood Festival 2012' http://www.twinwoodevents.com/

External links

- http://thethreebelles.com/ (http://thethreebelles.com/)
- http://www.portsmouth.co.uk/lifestyle/the-guide/stage/a-bit-of-nostalgia-1-3834479 (http://www.portsmouth.co.uk/lifestyle/the-guide/stage/a-bit-of-nostalgia-1-3834479)
- http://issuu.com/thevintageragmag/docs/vintage-rag-mag-march-2012/1 (http://issuu.com/thevintageragmag/docs/vintage-rag-mag-march-2012/1)
- http://3d-car-shows.com/2012/fun-for-all-the-family-at-best-of-british-show/ (http://3d-car-shows.com/2012/fun-for-all-the-family-at-best-of-british-show/)
- http://www.planetjive.freeuk.com/news5.html (http://www.planetjive.freeuk.com/news5.html)
- http://www.port.ac.uk/update/2012/05/graduate-profile-the-three-belles/ (http://www.port.ac.uk/update/2012/05/graduate-profile-the-three-belles/)

The Three Bells

"**The Three Bells**", also known as "**Jimmy Brown**" or "**Little Jimmy Brown**", is a song made popular by The Browns in 1959.[1] The single reached number one on the U.S. country and pop charts,.[2] outperforming a competing version by Dick Flood. The version by The Browns also hit number ten on the Hot R&B Sides chart.[3] It was based on the 1945 French language song "Les trois cloches" by Jean Villard Gilles and Marc Herrand. The English lyrics were written by Bert Reisfeld and first recorded by Melody Maids in 1948. The song was a major 1952-53 hit by Edith Piaf and Les Compagnons de la chanson. The song documents three stages of the life of "Jimmy Brown"—his birth, his marriage, and his death.

Recorded versions

Among the many artists who covered the song are Edith Piaf and Les Compagnons de la chanson (who recorded the original French version), Tina Arena, Brian Poole and The Tremeloes, Ray Charles, Nana Mouskouri, Roy Orbison, Johnny Cash, Floyd Cramer, Daniel O'Donnell, Chet Atkins, Elaine Paige, Sha Na Na and Alison Krauss & Union Station. It was also recorded in Dutch as "De drie klokken" and "Bim bam", in Italian as "Le Tre Campane" by Schola Cantorum, and in Spanish, retaining the title "Jimmy Brown", by the vocal group Mocedades.

"The Three Bells (The Jimmy Brown Song)" was also recorded for Decca Records in 1951 by The Andrews Sisters, the WWII boogie-woogie group of Patty, Maxene & LaVerne. While it did not prove to be the big hit that Billboard predicted it would be for The Andrews Sisters, it was nonetheless a very moving, harmonious rendition, in which the trio was accompanied by Gordon Jenkins' orchestra & chorus. The German title was "Wenn die Glocken hell erklingen".

Jim Ed Brown, one-third of the Browns, released a cover in 1969.

In 1974, Naďa Urbánková recorded Czech version (with her own lyrics) as "Zvony nelžou"[4] ("The bells never lie").

The song was parodied by The Barron Knights as "The Chapel Lead Is Missing" on their 1978 LP *Night Gallery*.

With lyrics in Swedish by Britt Lindeborg, Kikki Danielsson covered the song in 1979 on her debut album, *Rock'n Yodel*, as "Och vi hörde klockor ringa" ("And we heard bells ringing").

Chart position

The Browns

Chart (1959)	Peak position
U.S. *Billboard* Hot Country Singles	1
U.S. *Billboard* Hot 100	1
Australian Singles Chart	1
Norway VG-Lista Charts	6

Jim Ed Brown

Chart (1969)	Peak position
U.S. *Billboard* Hot Country Singles	29
Canadian *RPM* Country Tracks	22

The Tremeloes

Chart (1965)	Peak position
U.K. Singles Charts	17

Brian O'Donnell

Chart (1993)	Peak position
U.K. Singles Charts	71

References

[1] Show 11 - Tennessee Firebird. [Part 3], Big Rock Candy Mountain. [Part 1] : UNT Digital Library (http://digital.library.unt.edu/ark:/67531/metadc19759/m1/)

[2] Whitburn, Joel (2004). *The Billboard Book Of Top 40 Country Hits: 1944-2006, Second edition*. Record Research. p. 59.

[3] Whitburn, Joel (2004). *Top R&B/Hip-Hop Singles: 1942-2004*. Record Research. p. 88.

[4] http://www.nadaurbankova.cz/nada-urbankova-zvony-nelzou/

External links

- "Les trois cloches" (http://www.originals.be/en/originals.php?id=6449) from *The Originals* website

The Woodpecker Song

"**The Woodpecker Song**" (*Reginella Campagnola*) is an originally Italian song. The music was written by Eldo Di Lazzaro in 1939, while the Italian lyrics were written by Bruno Cherubini[1] (pseudonym "C. Bruno"). The English lyrics were written by Harold Adamson. The song became a hit in 1940 recorded by Glenn Miller, The Andrews Sisters and Kate Smith in 1940.

The Glenn Miller recording on RCA Bluebird reached #1 on the *Billboard* charts in 1940.[2]

Recorded versions

- Glenn Miller & His Orchestra. Vocalist: Marion Hutton. Recorded on January 29, 1940. Released on a 78 rpm record by Bluebird Records as catalog number 10598 backed with "Let's All Sing Together".[3]
- The Andrews Sisters. Recorded on February 21, 1940. Released on a 78 rpm record by Decca Records as catalog number 3065A[4]
- Kate Smith with Jack Miller Orchestra. Recorded on February 25, 1940. Released on a 78 rpm record by Columbia Records as catalog number 35398[5]

Other song

The song is not The Woody Woodpecker Song composed later in the 1940s by George Tibbles and Ramey Idriess and used in the Woody Woodpecker cartoon series.

References

[1] The Woodpecker Song Lyrics (http://www.songlyrics.com/glenn-miller-his-orchestra/the-woodpecker-song-lyrics/)
[2] Song arist 6 - Glenn Miller.tsort.info. (http://tsort.info/music/jkgsu0.htm)
[3] Bluebird Records in the 10500 - 10999 series (http://www.78discography.com/BB10500.htm)
[4] Decca Records in the 3000 - 3499 series (http://www.78discography.com/BB10500.htm)
[5] Columbia Records in the 35200 to 35499 series (http://www.78discography.com/BB10500.htm)

There's No Business Like Show Business

"**There's No Business Like Show Business**" is an Irving Berlin song, written for the musical *Annie Get Your Gun* and orchestrated by Ted Royal. The song, a slightly tongue-in-cheek salute to the glamour and excitement of a life in show business, is sung in the musical by members of Buffalo Bill's Wild West Show in an attempt to persuade Annie Oakley to join the production. It is reprised three times in the musical.

The song is also featured in the 1954 movie of the same name, where it is notably sung by Ethel Merman as the main musical number. The movie, directed by Walter Lang, is essentially a catalog of various Berlin's pieces, in the same way that *Singin' in the Rain*—which starred Donald O'Connor as well—was a collection of Arthur Freed songs. There was also a disco version of the song made during the 1970s, with Merman reprising her singing role (see *The Ethel Merman Disco Album*). The song became one of Ethel Merman's standards and was often performed by her at concerts and on television.

Other singers to have recorded the song include Judy Garland, The Andrews Sisters (with Bing Crosby and Dick Haymes), Susannah McCorkle, and Bernadette Peters.

In his liner notes for Susannah McCorkle's version of the song on her *Ballad Essentials* album Scott Yanow writes "usually performed as a corny razzle-dazzle romp, that piece was drastically slowed down by Susannah who performed all of its known lyrics, including stanzas that show Irving Berlin's lyrics were actually quite touching and meaningful".

Tenor saxophonist Sonny Rollins did a rendition of the tune on his 1956 Prestige album, Work Time.

In popular culture

- The Ethel Merman recording is featured in the film *All That Jazz* (1979).
- From 1976 to 2007 the rock band Genesis played the Ethel Merman recording at the end of gigs—it can be heard at the end of their 1977 live album *Seconds Out*.
- During the credits of "Noises Off (film)", Niki Haris sings a form of the song.
- In the 2000 musical film version of *Love's Labour's Lost*, Nathan Lane sings a form of the song.
- In Desperate Housewives, Felicity Huffman's character Lynette Scavo sang a line from this song after telling her sister's boyfriend that she would sing Ethel Merman "at the top of her lungs" in an attempt to make him consider taking her sister back.

Liza Minnelli performed a portion of the song on her 1992 album "Live From Radio City Music Hall."

References

- *America's Songs: The Stories Behind the Songs of Broadway, Hollywood, and Tin Pan Alley*, Philip Furia, Michael L. Lasser. Routledge, 2006, ISBN 978-0-415-97246-8, p. 206

Tico-Tico no Fubá

Tico-Tico no Fubá is the title of a renowned Brazilian choro music piece composed by Zequinha de Abreu in 1917. Its original title was *Tico-Tico no Farelo*, but since Brazilian guitarist Américo Jacomino Canhoto (1889–1928) had a work with the same title,[1] Abreu's work was given its present name in 1931.

Choro (literally translated meaning *lament*) is also popularly known as *chorinho* in the affectionate diminutive form of Brazilian Portuguese. "Fubá" is a type of maize flour, and "tico-tico" is the name of a bird, the rufous-collared sparrow (*Zonotrichia capensis*). Hence, "tico-tico no fubá" means "tico-tico on the cornmeal".

The first recording of the work was made by Orquestra Colbaz (Columbia 22029, 1931).[2]

Tico-Tico no Fubá was recorded and made popular internationally by Carmen Miranda (who performed it onscreen in *Copacabana* (1947)) and Ray Conniff. Another well known recording was made by first lady of the organ, Miss Ethel Smith on the Hammond organ.

A biographical movie by the same title was produced in 1952 by the Brazilian film studio *Companhia Cinematográfica Vera Cruz* with Anselmo Duarte playing the main role.

The song was also featured in the "Aquarela do Brasil" segment of the Walt Disney film *Saludos Amigos* (1942) and in Woody Allen's *Radio Days* (1987). It was also featured in the MGM film *Bathing Beauty* (1943).

The expression also features in the lyrics to the song *O Pato* made famous by João Gilberto.

Lyrics

> *The complete version of Aloysio de Oliveira's original Portuguese lyrics:*
>
> O tico tico tá, tá outra vez aqui,
> o tico tico tá comendo o meu fubá.
> Se o tico tico tem, tem que se alimentar,
> Que vá comer umas minhocas no pomar.
> O tico tico tá, tá outra vez aqui,
> o tico tico tá comendo o meu fubá.
> Eu sei que ele vem viver no meu quintal,
> e vem com ares de canário e de pardal.
>
> Mas por favor tira esse bicho do celeiro,
> porque ele acaba comendo o fubá inteiro.
> Tira esse tico de lá, de cima do meu fubá.
> Tem tanta fruta que ele pode pinicar.
>
> Eu já fiz tudo para ver se conseguia.
> Botei alpiste para ver se ele comia.
> Botei um gato um espantalho e um alçapão,
> mas ele acha que o fubá é que é boa alimentação.
>
> *Loose translation of the original lyrics:*

The tico tico is here, it is here again,
the tico tico is eating my cornmeal.
If that tico tico has to feed itself,
it better eat a few earthworms at the orchard.
The tico tico is here, it is here again,
the tico tico is eating my cornmeal.
I know that it comes to live in my yard,
and that it puts on airs like a sparrow and a canary.

But please take this animal off my granary,
because it will end up eating all the cornmeal
Throw that tico out of here, from the top of the cornmeal (heap),
it has so much fruit to eat from.

I have done everything to see if I could,
Threw it canary feed to see if it ate it.
Let a cat loose, and (even) set up a trap,
but it finds cornmeal to be good nutrition.

English version (not a translation):

Oh tico-tico tick!
Oh tico-tico tock!
This tico-tico - he's the cuckoo in my clock.
And when he says: "Cuckoo!" he means it's time to woo;
It's "tico-time" for all the lovers in the block.
I've got a heavy date -
a tête-à-tête at eight,
so speak, oh tico, tell me is it getting late?
If I'm on time, "Cuckoo!" but if I'm late, "Woo-woo!"
The one my heart has gone to may not want to wait!

For just a birdie, and a birdie who goes no-where,
He knows of ev'ry Lovers' Lane and how to go there;
For in affairs of the heart, my Tico's terribly smart,
He tells me: "Gently, sentiment'ly at the start!"

Oh-oh, I hear my little tico-tico calling,
Because the time is right and shades of night are falling.
I love that not-so-cuckoo cuckoo in my clock:
tico-tico tico-tico-tico tock!

Miscellaneous

This was often performed by the Grateful Dead during their tuning jams which often happened in between songs.

This song was also played as an instrumental by James Booker with the Jerry Garcia Band.

In Quebec the song has been used for several decades in commercials for Sico paint.

The song was recorded by The Andrews Sisters in 1944.

The flamenco guitarist Paco de Lucía also performed this song in 1967.

References

[1] Discography of Américo Jacomino Canhoto (http://www.dicionariompb.com.br/canhoto/discografia), Discography of Américo Jacomino
     Canhoto 2 (http://aochiadobrasileiro.webs.com/GravacoesRaras/GravacoesCanhotoAmericoJacomino.htm)
     CD reissue: Violão Imortal – Canhoto Américo Jacomino (http://www.revivendomusicas.com.br/produto_detalhe.asp?id=4534); Rvpc
     008; Revivendo
[2] CD reissue (http://www.revivendomusicas.com.br/produto_detalhe.asp?id=1028), Orquestra Colbaz (http://www.dicionariompb.com.
     br/orquestra-colbaz/discografia), Gravações Raras (http://www.aochiadobrasileiro.webs.com/GravacoesRaras/
     GravacoesZequinhadeAbreu.htm), 1 (http://teses.musicodobrasil.com.br/pixinguinha-e-a-genese-do-arranjo-musical-brasileiro-.pdf)

External links

- 61 versions of Tico Tico (http://blog.wfmu.org/freeform/2005/11/61_versions_of_.html) at WFMU's blog
- Four hands and one guitar (https://www.youtube.com/watch?v=CcsSPzr7ays) on YouTube Cecilia Siqueira and Fernando Lima
- Paco de Lucia (https://www.youtube.com/watch?v=HIXLC5SRC7w) on YouTube
- http://www.whitegum.com/introjs.htm?/songfile/TICOTICO.HTM
- Tico tico guitar (http://www.youtube.com/watch?v=DZgf9JfjaRs&feature=channel_video_title)

Underneath the Arches (song)

"**Underneath the Arches**" is a 1932 popular song[1] with words and music by Bud Flanagan, and additional lyrics by Reg Connelly.[2] It was one of the most famous songs of the duo Flanagan and Allen.

According to a television programme broadcast in 1957, Bud Flanagan said that he wrote the song in Derby in 1927, and first performed it a week later at the Pier Pavilion, Southport.[3] It refers to the arches of Friar Gate railway bridge and to the homeless men who slept there during the Great Depression.[4]

Covers

The song has also been covered by Primo Scala, The Andrews Sisters, and Andy Russell in the United States. A well-known version in the United Kingdom was made by Max Bygraves. A sequel to the song *Where the Arches Used To Be* was sung by Flanagan and Allen in the film *A Fire Has Been Arranged* in which the arches are knocked down and flats built in their place.

The Primo Scala recording, with The Keynotes, was released by London Records as catalog number 238. The record first reached the *Billboard* charts on August 6, 1948, and lasted 16 weeks on the chart, peaking at #6.[5]

The Andrews Sisters' recording was released by Decca Records as catalog number 24490 (the flip side of their recording of *You Call Everybody Darlin'*). The record first reached the *Billboard* charts on August 27, 1948, and lasted 10 weeks on the chart, peaking at #10.[5]

The Andy Russell recording was released by Capitol Records as catalog number 15183. The record first reached the *Billboard* charts on October 1, 1948 and lasted 5 weeks on the chart, peaking at #21.[5]

In 1970 the artist duo Gilbert & George performed the song in Nigel Greenwood Gallery, which launched their career as "singing and living sculptures".

The song is used in the television mini-series *A Perfect Spy*, based on the John le Carré novel, while father and son (the key figures) are running under arches near a British beach. It was also the signature tune for the Radio London *Underneath the Arches* programme.

Notes

[1] Ray Piper, *Underneath the Arches*, Publisher Lulu.com, 2005, ISBN 1-4116-5440-4, ISBN 978-1-4116-5440-2, 104 pages (page 6 (http://books.google.co.uk/books?id=gK6OQZSNrDIC&lpg=PA6&dq="Underneath the Arches" Flanagan&pg=PA6#v=onepage&q="Underneath the Arches" Flanagan&f=false))

[2] *Catalog of copyright entries: Musical compositions, Part 3*, Publ. Library of Congress. Copyright Office, 1932 (page 727 (http://books.google.co.uk/books?id=-wxhAAAAIAAJ&dq=Underneath the Arches Connelly Flanagan&pg=PA727#v=onepage&q="Underneath the Arches" Connelly Flanagan&f=false))

[3] *Together Again* (http://ftvdb.bfi.org.uk/sift/title/472914?view=synopsis), TV Programme broadcast 19 April 1957

[4] " On Top of Friar Gate Bridge (http://www.bbc.co.uk/derby/content/articles/2008/10/20/friargate_bridge_feature.shtml)", BBC website, Oct 2008, retrieved 26 Nov 2011

[5] Whitburn, Joel (1973). *Top Pop Records 1940-1955*. Record Research.

Vocal Group Hall of Fame

The **Vocal Group Hall of Fame** was organized to honor outstanding vocal groups throughout the world by Tony Butala, also the founder of The Lettermen. It is headquartered in Sharon, Pennsylvania, United States. It includes a theater and a museum.

The VGHF typically inducts sixteen artists annually. Unlike the Rock and Roll Hall of Fame, artists are inducted within categories. Each category has at least one representative. The categories are 40s, 50s, 60s, 70s, 80s, and duos. Only groups are eligible; solo artists may be inducted if they have a legitimate backing band with backing singers (for example, Tom Petty and the Heartbreakers). The Vocal Group Hall of Fame releases a public ballot; allowing everyone to vote for both the nominees and the inductees.

It was originally organized in 1998. The original administration closed it in October 2001 and a new nonprofit organization took over, reopening it in April 2002.

In November 2004, the museum moved out of its rented three-story facility and is currently in the process of relocating to the ca. 1920-built Columbia Theatre, also in Sharon, which it is renovating to serve both as its central office and as the location for its annual induction ceremony and benefit concerts. The museum is being moved to a three-story restaurant building adjacent to the theater (the restaurant portion will become a vocal group-themed bar and grill). Also planned is the opening of two museum annexes, one of which will be located in Las Vegas and the other in Wildwood, New Jersey.

They are currently advertising the Truth In Music Bill, announcing whenever it passes in specific states. The Truth In Music Bill was created to protect the artists from identity theft.[1]

Due to lack of funds, the VGHF announced it would induct its classes of 2008-09 in 2011. Unfortunately, this never came to fruition.

Address

Vocal Group Hall of Fame and Museum, 82 West State Street, Sharon, PA 16146

- Chairman/Founder: Tony Butala
- CEO: Bob Crosby

Vocal Group Hall of Fame Inductees

1998-2002

1998	1999	2000	2001	2002
• The Ames Brothers • The Andrews Sisters • The Beach Boys • The Boswell Sisters • The Five Blind Boys of Mississippi • Crosby, Stills & Nash • The Golden Gate Quartet • The Original Drifters • The Mills Brothers • The Manhattan Transfer • The Platters • The Ravens • Sonny Til & The Orioles • The Supremes	• The Coasters • The Delta Rhythm Boys • The Four Seasons • The Four Tops • Hank Ballard & The Midnighters • Ink Spots • Jackson Five • Little Anthony & The Imperials • The Modernaires • The Moonglows • Peter, Paul & Mary • The Revelers • The Spinners • The Temptations	• The Bangles • Dion & The Belmonts • Dixie Hummingbirds • The Drifters • The Flamingos • Frankie Lymon & The Teenagers • The Kingston Trio • The Mamas & The Papas • The Skylarks • The Soul Stirrers • Three Dog Night	• The Bee Gees • The Chordettes • The Eagles • The Four Aces • The Four Freshmen • Gladys Knight & The Pips • The Lennon Sisters • The Lettermen • The McGuire Sisters • The Oak Ridge Boys • The Pied Pipers • Smokey Robinson & The Miracles • The Vogues • The Weavers	• ABBA • The Chantels • The Clovers • The Fifth Dimension • The Five Keys • The Four Knights • The Harptones • Jay & The Americans • The Marcels • The Shirelles • The Skyliners • The Swan Silvertones

2003-2007

2003	2004	2005	2006	2007
• The Association • The Charioteers • The Commodores • Earth Wind & Fire • The Five Satins • The Four Lads • The Impressions • Isley Brothers • Danny & The Juniors • The Merry Macs • Peerless Quartet • Martha & The Vandellas • The Whispers	• Alabama • American Quartet • The Beatles • The Cadillacs • The Crests • The Dells • The Diamonds • The Doobie Brothers • The Everly Brothers • The Four Tunes • The Jordanaires • The Marvelettes • The O'Jays • The Penguins • The Ronettes • The Stylistics • The Tokens	• The Angels • Brooklyn Bridge • The Chiffons • The Chi-Lites • The Crystals • The Del Vikings • Fleetwood Mac • The Hilltoppers • The Mel-Tones • The Neville Brothers • The Pointer Sisters • The Rascals • The Righteous Brothers • Sons of the Pioneers • The Spaniels • The Tymes	• America • Bread • The Byrds • Deep River Boys • Billy Ward & The Dominoes • The Duprees • The Fleetwoods • Hayden Quartet • The Hi-Lo's • The Hollies • Journey • The Lovin' Spoonful • The Moody Blues • Queen • The Shangri-las • Simon & Garfunkel	• The Five Red Caps • The Chords • The Four Preps • Maurice Williams and the Zodiacs; The Gladiolas • The Capris • The Dixie Cups • The Jive Five • The Monkees • Ruby & The Romantics • Sly & The Family Stone • Tony Orlando and Dawn • Harold Melvin & The Blue Notes • Kool & The Gang • The Traveling Wilburys • Sam & Dave • The Hoboken Four

References

[1] Truth In Music Bill - Vocal Group Hall of Fame Foundation (http://www.vghf.com/truth.htm)

External links

• Vocal Group Hall of Fame (http://www.vocalgroup.org/) home page

Winter Wonderland

"**Winter Wonderland**" is a winter song, popularly treated as a Christmastime pop standard, written in 1934 by Felix Bernard (music) and Richard B. Smith (lyricist). Through the decades it has been recorded by over 150 different artists.

History

Dick Smith, a native of Honesdale, Pennsylvania, was reportedly inspired to write the song after seeing Honesdale's Central Park covered in snow. Smith had written the lyrics while in the West Mountain Sanitarium, being treated for tuberculosis, better known then as consumption.[1] The West Mountain Sanitarium is located off N. Sekol Ave. in Scranton, Pennsylvania.

The original recording was by Richard Himber and his Hotel Ritz-Carlton Orchestra on RCA Bluebird in 1934. At the end of a recording session with time to spare, it was suggested that this new tune be tried with an arrangement provided by the publisher. This excellent "studio" orchestra included many great New York studio musicians including the legendary Artie Shaw. The biggest chart hit at the time of introduction was Guy Lombardo's orchestra, a top ten hit.[2] Singer-songwriter Johnny Mercer took the song to #4 in Billboard's airplay chart in 1946. The same season, Perry Como hit the retail top ten. Como would record a new version for his 1959 Christmas album.

Due to its seasonal theme, "Winter Wonderland" is often regarded as a Christmas song in the Northern Hemisphere, although the holiday itself is never mentioned in the lyrics. There is a mention of "sleigh-bells" several times, implying that this song refers to the Christmas period. In the Swedish language lyrics, *Vår vackra vita vintervärld*, the word tomtar is mentioned.

Parson Brown

The bridge of the song contains the following lyrics:

> "In the meadow we can build a snowman,
> then pretend that he is Parson Brown.
> He'll say 'Are You Married?' We'll say 'No man,
> but you can do the job while you're in town!'"

In the period when this song was written, parsons (now known as Protestant ministers) often traveled among small rural towns to perform wedding ceremonies for denominational followers who did not have a local minister of their own faith.

Children's Lyric

The original bridge, about a couple who make a spur-of-the-moment decision to get married, was supposedly considered inappropriate for children. A 1953 version of the sheet music contains the following replacement bridge[3]

> In the meadow we can build a snowman,
>
> and pretend that he's a circus clown.
>
> We'll have lots of fun with Mister Snowman,
>
> until the other kiddies knock 'im down!
>
> When it snows, ain't it thrillin'?
>
> Tho' your nose, gets a chillin'
>
> We'll frolic and play, the Eskimo way,
>
> Walkin' in a Winter Wonderland.

In addition, the fact that (as noted above) the circuit-traveling country parson trekking from village to village is no longer part of the American cultural scene has also contributed to the circus clown replacing Parson Brown. However, some musicians have performed and even recorded the song with both stanzas - Parson Brown and Circus Clown.

Recorded versions

• A Fine Frenzy from the album *Oh Blue Christmas*	• Donny and Marie Osmond	• Mormon Tabernacle Choir
• Abney Park	• Doris Day (1964) for The Doris Day Christmas Album	• Neil Diamond
• Aimee Mann	• Durant	• Neil Sedaka
• Air Supply	• Eddy Arnold	• Olivia Holt
• Alexis Stone Lopez	• Ednita Nazario	• Ozzy Osbourne & Jessica Simpson
• Al Green	• Ella Fitzgerald	• The Partridge Family
• Aly & AJ	• Elvis Presley	• Pat Boone
• America	• Engelbert Humperdinck	• Pat Green
• Amy Grant	• Enrico Ruggeri	• Paul Anka
• The Andrews Sisters	• Erich Kunzel and the Cincinnati Pops Orchestra	• Paul Carrack
• Andy Williams	• Etta James	• Peggy Lee
• Anne Murray	• Eurythmics from the album *A Very Special Christmas* (1987)	• Percy Faith
• Annie Lennox	• Fleming and John	• Perry Como
• Aretha Franklin	• Frank Sinatra	• Peter Alexander (in German: "Winterwunderland")
• Arthur Fiedler and the Boston Pops	• Faith Hill	• Peter Nero
• Ashanti	• Garth Brooks	• Phantom Planet
• August Burns Red	• Gary Hoey	• The Platters
• Babyface	• George Strait	• Point of Grace
• Banaroo	• The Golddiggers	• Postmarks
• Barbara Mandrell	• Goldfrapp	• Radiohead
• Barry Manilow	• Grandaddy as "Alan Parsons in a Winter Wonderland" (2000)	• Randy Travis
• Bert Kaempfert	• Guy Lombardo	• Rankin Bass
• Bette Midler from the album *Cool Yule* (2006)	• Harry Connick, Jr. (instrumental on the soundtrack of *When Harry Met Sally...*, vocal on *What a Night! A Christmas Album*)	• Ray Charles
• Billy "Crash" Craddock	• Hellogoodbye	• Ray Conniff

- Billy Gilman from the album *Classic Christmas*
- Billy Idol
- Bing Crosby
- Blake Shelton
- Bob Dylan
- Booker T & The MGs from *In the Christmas Spirit* (1966)
- Boston Pops Orchestra
- Brad Paisley
- Brenda Lee
- Brooks & Dunn
- Burl Ives
- Byron Lee & the Dragonaires
- The California Raisins
- The Canadian Brass
- Cap'n Jazz
- Carnie Wilson & Wendy Wilson
- The Carpenters (as part of a medley with "Silver Bells" and "White Christmas")
- Cascada from *It's Christmas Time* (2012)
- Celtic Thunder
- Charlotte Church (*Dream a Dream, 2000*)
- Chet Atkins
- Chicago
- Children's Christmas
- Christina Christian
- Clay Aiken
- The Cocteau Twins
- Colbie Caillat from *Christmas In The Sand* (2012)
- Connie Francis
- Connie Talbot
- Cravin' Melon
- Cyndi Lauper
- The Nashville Brass
- Darlene Love
- Dave Brubeck
- Dave Koz
- Dean Martin from "A Winter Romance" (1959)
- The Del Rubio Triplets
- Demi Lovato
- Diamond Rio
- Diana Krall
- Herb Alpert & The Tijuana Brass
- Inge & Sonja (Winterwunderland)
- Jackie Gleason
- James Taylor
- Jamie Cullum
- Jason Mraz
- Jesse McCartney
- Jewel
- Joey McIntyre on his album *Come Home for Christmas*
- Johnny Mathis
- Johnny Mercer
- Jonas Brothers
- Joy Electric
- The Judds
- Kate Havnevik
- Kathy Troccoli
- Keahiwai
- Kenny G
- Kikki Danielsson (as part of a medley with "Sleigh Ride") [4]
- Kiri Te Kanawa
- Larry Carlton
- Larry Groce on the album *Disney's Christmas Favourites*
- Leon Redbone
- Lionel Richie
- Liz Phair
- Louis Armstrong
- Lou Rawls
- Macy Gray
- Madison Park
- Mandy Moore
- The Manhattan Transfer from the album *An Acapella Christmas*
- Mannheim Steamroller
- Mantovani
- Martina McBride from the album "White Christmas"
- Michael Bolton
- Michael Bublé
- Miley Cyrus
- Mireille Mathieu (in German)
- Mitch Miller
- Rene De Haan (*Kerstfeest In Ons Mooie Nederland*)
- Rene Marie
- Reparata and the Delrons
- Ricky Van Shelton
- Ringo Starr
- Robert Goulet
- Rockapella
- Rod Stewart
- The Ronettes
- Rosemary Clooney
- Royce Campbell
- Sammy Kershaw
- The Saturdays
- Selena Gomez & The Scene
- Scott Weiland
- Shirley Horn
- Sin City Sinners
- Smokey Robinson & The Miracles from *Christmas with The Miracles* (1963)
- Steve Goodman
- Steve Lukather
- Steven Curtis Chapman
- Steve Taylor
- Stryper
- Sugarland
- Take 6
- Tanya Tucker
- Tara MacLean
- Taylor Horn
- Ted Weems
- The Three Tenors
- The Toasters
- Till Brönner (feat. Stevie Woods)
- Tina Robin (*Winter Wonderland Cha Cha*)
- Toby Keith
- Tony Bennett
- Tony Christie
- Travis Tritt
- Tuck Andress
- Vanessa Hudgens
- Vic Damone

• Diana Ross		• Victoria Justice
• Dolly Parton (as part of a medley with "Sleigh Ride")		• Vince Gill
		• Whitney Keyes with Holly Players Orchestra
		• Willie Nelson
		• Wynonna Judd

In addition, the song was incorporated by Michael Kamen as a suspense theme into his score for the 1988 film *Die Hard*.

Fan versions

The song has been parodied by Bob Rivers as "Walkin' 'Round in Women's Underwear", and by Elsa Boreson as "Walkin' in My Winter Underwear". Both songs are frequently played on Dr. Demento's radio show. Jason Lytle of Grandaddy later wrote "Alan Parsons in a Winter Wonderland" as a promotional single that saw an appearance on the compilation album The Windfall Varietal.

In Britain, many football teams sing variations of the song to celebrate a particular player or manager. There is also a version by supporters of British boxer, Ricky Hatton,[5] and another sung by supporters of darts player Phil Taylor.

Awards and achievements

In Nov 2007, ASCAP, a performance rights organization in the United States, listed "Winter Wonderland" as the most-played ASCAP-member-written holiday song of the previous five years, and cited the Eurythmics' version of the song is the one most commonly played.[6]

References

[1] Kunerth, Jeff (December 9, 2010). "The story behind Winter Wonderland" (http://blogs.orlandosentinel.com/features-the-religion-world/ 2010/12/09/the-story-behind-winter-wonderland/). *The Religion World* (*Orlando Sentinel*). .

[2] Guy Lombardo Chart Hits at TsorT.info (http://tsort.info/music/2f3rk3.htm)

[3] Bernard, Felix & Smith, Dick. Winter Wonderland. New York: Bregman, Vocco and Conn, Inc. (1953) Catalog number B.V.C.883-3

[4] Kikki Danielsson, Nu är det advent (http://smdb.kb.se/catalog/id/001548791) Retrieved November 29, 2011

[5] Mayweather-Hatton - Chanting In A Boxing Wonderland (http://www.e-sports.com/articles/2090/1/ Mayweather-Hatton---Chanting-in-a-boxing-wonderland/Page1.html) Retrieved November 29, 2011

[6] ASCAP Announced Top 25 Holiday Songs (http://www.ascap.com/press/2007/111207_holiday.aspx). 12 November 2007

The Andrews Sisters

The Andrews Sisters	
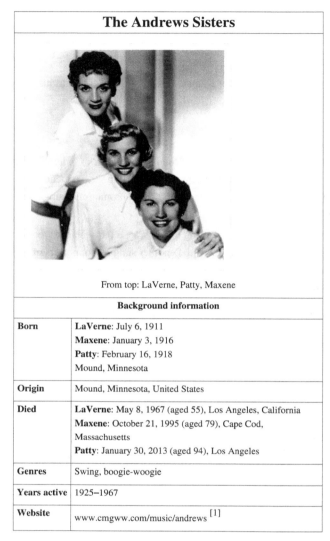 From top: LaVerne, Patty, Maxene	
Background information	
Born	**LaVerne**: July 6, 1911 **Maxene**: January 3, 1916 **Patty**: February 16, 1918 Mound, Minnesota
Origin	Mound, Minnesota, United States
Died	**LaVerne**: May 8, 1967 (aged 55), Los Angeles, California **Maxene**: October 21, 1995 (aged 79), Cape Cod, Massachusetts **Patty**: January 30, 2013 (aged 94), Los Angeles
Genres	Swing, boogie-woogie
Years active	1925–1967
Website	www.cmgww.com/music/andrews [1]

The Andrews Sisters were a American close harmony singing group of the swing and boogie-woogie eras. The group consisted of three sisters: contralto **LaVerne Sophia** (July 6, 1911 – May 8, 1967), soprano **Maxine Angelyn "Maxene"** (January 3, 1916 – October 21, 1995), and mezzo-soprano **Patricia Marie "Patty"** (February 16, 1918 – January 30, 2013).[1] Throughout their long career, the sisters sold well over 75 million records (the last official count released by MCA Records in the mid-1970s). Their 1941 hit "Boogie Woogie Bugle Boy" can be considered an early example of rhythm and blues[2][3] or jump blues.

The Andrews Sisters' harmonies and songs are still influential today, and have been covered by entertainers such as Bette Midler, The Puppini Sisters, Christina Aguilera, and The Three Belles. The group was inducted into the Vocal Group Hall of Fame in 1998.[4] Writing for *Bloomberg*, Mark Schoifet said the sisters became the most popular female vocal group of the first half of the 20th century.

Early life

The Andrews Sisters were born in Mound, Minnesota, to Greek immigrant father, Peter Andreus (1884–1949), and Norwegian American mother, Olga "Ollie" (*née* Sollie) Andrews (1886–1948).[5][6]

Patty, the youngest and the lead singer of the group, was only seven when the group was formed, and just 12 when they won first prize at a talent contest at the local Orpheum Theatre in Minneapolis, where LaVerne played piano accompaniment for the silent film showings in exchange for free dancing lessons for herself and her sisters. Following the collapse of their father's Minneapolis restaurant, the sisters went on the road to support the family.[6] Once the sisters found fame and settled in California, their parents lived with them in a Brentwood estate in Los Angeles until their deaths.

Career

They started their career as imitators of an earlier successful singing group, the Boswell Sisters. After singing with various dance bands and touring in vaudeville with the likes of Ted Mack, Leon Belasco, and comic bandleader Larry Rich, they first came to national attention with their recordings and radio broadcasts in 1937, most notably via their major Decca record hit, *Bei Mir Bist Du Schön* (translation: "To Me, You Are Beautiful"),[7] originally a Yiddish tune, the lyrics of which Sammy Cahn had translated to English and which the girls harmonized to perfection. They followed this success with a string of best-selling records over the next two years and they became a household name by the 1940s.[8]

World War II

During World War II they entertained the Allied forces extensively in America, Africa and Italy, visiting Army, Navy, Marine and Coast Guard bases, war zones, hospitals, and munitions factories.[9] They encouraged U.S. citizens to purchase war bonds with their rendition of Irving Berlin's song Any Bonds Today?. They also helped actress Bette Davis and actor John Garfield found California's famous Hollywood Canteen, a welcome retreat for servicemen where the trio often performed, volunteering their personal time to sing and dance for the soldiers, sailors and marines (they did the same at New York City's Stage Door Canteen during the war). While touring, they often treated three random servicemen to dinner when they were dining out. They recorded a series of Victory Discs (V-Discs) for distribution to Allied fighting forces only, again volunteering their time for studio sessions for the Music Branch, Special Service Division of the Army Service Forces, and they were dubbed the "Sweethearts of the Armed Forces Radio Service" for their many appearances on shows like "Command Performance", "Mail Call", and "G.I. Journal."[10]

Career interruption

The Andrews Sisters broke up in 1951 when Patty joined another group, with her husband acting as her agent. Patty traces the breakup to the deaths of their parents: "We had been together nearly all our lives," Patty explained in 1971. "Then in one year our dream world ended. Our mother died (in 1948) and then our father (in 1949). All three of us were upset, and we were at each other's throats all the time."[1]

When Maxene and LaVerne learned of Patty's decision from newspaper gossip columns rather than from their own sister, it caused a bitter two-year separation, especially when Patty decided to worsen matters by suing LaVerne for a larger share of their parents' estate.[11] Maxene and LaVerne tried to continue the act as a duo and met with good press during a 10-day tour of Australia, but a reported suicide attempt by Maxene in December 1954[12] put a halt to any further tours (Maxene spent a short time in the hospital after swallowing 18 sleeping pills, an occurrence that LaVerne told reporters was an accident). The sisters' private relationship was often troubled and Patty blamed it on Maxene: "Ever since I was born, Maxene has been a problem," she said.[13]

The trio reunited in 1956. They signed a new recording contract with Capitol Records (for whom Patty had become a featured soloist) and released a dozen singles through 1959, some rock-and-roll flavored and not very well received, and three hi-fi albums, including a vibrant LP of songs from the dancing 1920s with Billy May's orchestra. In 1962, they signed with Dot Records and recorded a series of stereo albums until 1964, both re-recordings of earlier hits, as well as new material, including "I Left My Heart In San Francisco", "Still", "The End of the World", "Puff the Magic Dragon", "Sailor", "Satin Doll", the theme from *Come September*, and the theme from *A Man and a Woman*. They toured extensively during the 1960s, favoring top nightclubs in Las Vegas, Nevada, California, and London, England.

Eldest sister LaVerne died of cancer in 1967 after a year-long bout with the illness,[14] during which she was replaced by singer Joyce DeYoung. LaVerne had founded the original group, and often acted as the peacemaker among the three during the sisters' lives, more often siding with her parents, to whom the girls were extremely devoted, than with either of her sisters. Their last appearance together as a trio was on The Dean Martin Show on September 27, 1966.

After LaVerne died, Maxene and Patty continued to perform as a duo until 1968, when Maxene announced she would become the Dean of Women at Tahoe Paradise College,[15] teaching acting, drama and speech at a Lake Tahoe college and worked with troubled teens, and Patty was once again eager to be a soloist.[16]

Comeback

Patty and Maxine's careers experienced a resurgence when Bette Midler recorded her own version of their song "Boogie Woogie Bugle Boy" in 1973. The next year, the pair debuted on Broadway in the Sherman Brothers' nostalgic World War II musical: *Over Here!* which premiered at the Shubert Theatre to rave reviews. This was a follow-up to Patty's success in "Victory Canteen", a 1971 California revue. *Over Here!* starred Maxene and Patty (with Janie Sell filling in for LaVerne and winning a Tony Award for her performance) and was written with both sisters in mind for the leads. It launched the careers of many now notable theater, film, and television icons including John Travolta, Marilu Henner, Treat Williams and Ann Reinking. It was the last major hurrah for the sisters and was cut short due to a lawsuit initiated by Patty's husband against the show's producers, squashing an extensively scheduled road tour.[17]

Patty immediately distanced herself from Maxene, who claimed until her death that she was not aware of Patty's motives regarding the separation. She appealed to Patty for a reunion, personally if not professionally, both in public and in private, but to no avail. Maxene suffered a serious heart attack while performing in Illinois in 1982 and underwent quadruple bypass surgery, from which she successfully recovered. Patty visited her sister while she was hospitalized. Now sometimes appearing as "Patti" (but still signing autographs as "Patty") she re-emerged in the late 1970s as a regular panelist on *The Gong Show*. Maxene had a successful comeback as a cabaret soloist in 1979 and toured worldwide for the next 15 years, recording a solo album in 1985 entitled "Maxene: An Andrews Sister" for Bainbridge Records. Patty started her own solo act in 1981, but did not receive the critical acclaim her sister had for her performances, even though it was Patty who was considered to be the "star" of the group for years. The critics' major complaint was that Patty's show concentrated too much on Andrews Sisters material, which did not allow Patty's own talents as a very expressive and bluesy vocalist to shine through.

The two sisters did reunite, albeit briefly, on October 1, 1987, when they received a star on Hollywood's Walk of Fame, even singing a few bars of "Beer Barrel Polka" for the *Entertainment Tonight* cameras. An earthquake shook the area that very morning and the ceremony was nearly cancelled, which caused Patty to joke, "Some people said that earthquake this morning was LaVerne because she couldn't be here, but really it was just Maxene and me on the telephone." Besides this, and a few brief private encounters, they remained somewhat estranged for the last few years.

Shortly after her Off-Broadway debut in New York City in a show called *Swingtime Canteen*, Maxene suffered another heart attack and died at Cape Cod Hospital on October 21, 1995, making Patty the last surviving Andrews

Sister. Not long before she died, Maxene told music historian William Ruhlmann, "I have nothing to regret. We got on the carousel and we each got the ring and I was satisfied with that. There's nothing I would do to change things if I could...Yes, I would. I wish I had the ability and the power to bridge the gap between my relationship with my sister, Patty."[18] Upon hearing the news of her sister's death, Patty became very distraught. As her husband Wally went to her, he fell on a flight of stairs and broke both wrists. Patty did not attend her sister's memorial services in New York, nor in California. Said Bob Hope of Maxene's passing, "She was more than part of The Andrews Sisters, much more than a singer. She was a warm and wonderful lady who shared her talent and wisdom with others."[18]

Retirement and deaths

Instrumental to the sisters' success over the years were their parents, Olga and Peter; their orchestra leader and musical arranger, Vic Schoen (1916–2000); music publishing giant Lou Levy, who died only days after Maxene, and was their manager from 1937–51 and was also Maxene's husband from 1941–49;[19] and Jack and David Kapp, who founded Decca Records. Maxene was the mother of two adopted children, Peter and Aleda Ann.

LaVerne married Lou Rogers,[14] a trumpet player in Vic Schoen's band, in 1948, and remained with him until her death (he died in 1995, five days after Maxene's death and five days before Levy's).[20] Patty Andrews married agent Marty Melcher in 1947 and left him in 1949, when he pursued a romantic relationship with Doris Day. She then married Walter Weschler, the trio's pianist, in 1951. Patty Andrews died of natural causes at her home in Northridge, California on January 30, 2013, just 17 days before her 95th birthday. Walter Wechsler, her husband of 60 years, died on August 28, 2010, at the age of 88. [6] Patty and Walter were parents to foster daughter Pam Dubois.[13] The sisters were interred in the Forest Lawn Memorial Park Cemetery in Glendale, California, close to their parents.[21]

Legacy

Until the advent of the Supremes, the sisters were the most imitated of all female singing groups and influenced many artists, including Mel Tormé, Les Paul and Mary Ford, The Four Freshmen, The McGuire Sisters, The Manhattan Dolls, The Lennon Sisters, The Pointer Sisters, The Manhattan Transfer, The Puppini Sisters, Barry Manilow, and Bette Midler. Even Elvis Presley was a fan. Most of the Andrews Sisters' music has been restored and released in compact disc form, yet over 300 of their original Decca recordings, a good portion of which was hit material, has yet to be released by MCA/Decca in over 50 years. Many of these Decca recordings have been used in such television shows and Hollywood movies as *Homefront, ER, The Brink's Job, National Lampoon's Christmas Vacation, Swing Shift, Raggedy Man, Summer of '42, Slaughterhouse-Five, Maria's Lovers, Harlem Nights, In Dreams, Murder in the First, L.A. Confidential*, American Horror Story, *Just Shoot Me*, Gilmore Girls, *Mama's Family, War and Remembrance, Jakob the Liar, Lolita, The Polar Express, The Chronicles of Narnia, Molly: An American Girl on the Home Front, Memoirs of a Geisha*, and *Bon Voyage, Charlie Brown (and Don't Come Back!!)*. Comical references to the trio in television sitcoms can be found as early as *I Love Lucy* and as recently as *Everybody Loves Raymond*. In 2007, their version of "Bei Mir Bist Du Schön" was included in the game *BioShock*, a first-person shooter that takes place in an alternate history 1960, and later in 2008, their song "Civilization" (with Danny Kaye) was included in the Atomic Age-inspired video game *Fallout 3*. The 2010 video game *Mafia II* features numerous Andrews Sisters songs, with 'Boogie Woogie Bugle Boy', 'Strip Polka' and 'Rum And Coca-Cola'. The 2011 video game *L.A. Noire* features the song Pistol Packin' Mama, where the sisters perform a duet with Bing Crosby.

Christina Aguilera used the Andrews Sisters' "Boogie Woogie Bugle Boy" to inspire her song "Candyman" (released as a single in 2007) from her hit album *Back to Basics*. The song was co-written by Linda Perry. The London based trio the Puppini Sisters uses their style harmonies on several Andrews Sisters and other hits of the 1940s and 1950s as well as later rock and disco hits. The trio has said their name is a tribute to The Andrews Sisters. The Manhattan Dolls, a New York City-based touring group, performs both the popular tunes sung by the Andrews Sisters and some of the more obscure tunes such as "Well Alright" and "South American Way" as well.

In 2008 and 2009, the BBC produced *The Andrews Sisters: Queens of the Music Machines*, a one-hour documentary on the history of the Andrews Sisters from their upbringing to the present. The American premier of the show was June 21, 2009, in their birthplace of Mound, Minnesota. In 2008, Mound dedicated "The Andrews Sisters Trail". The sisters spent summers in Mound[1] with their uncles Pete and Ed Solie, who had a grocery store there. Maxene Andrews always said that the summers in Mound created a major sense of "normalcy" and "a wonderful childhood" in a life that otherwise centered on the sisters' careers. The Westonka Historical Society has a large collection of Andrews Sisters memorabilia.[22]

Musical innovators

When the sisters burst upon the music scene in the late 1930s, they shook a very solid musical foundation: producing a slick harmonic blend by singing at the top of their lungs while trying - successfully - to emulate the blare of three harmonizing trumpets,[23] with a full big band racing behind them. Some bandleaders of the day, such as Artie Shaw and his musicians, resented them for taking the focus away from the band and emphasizing the vocals instead. They were in as high demand as the big bandleaders themselves, many of whom did not want to share the spotlight and play back-up to a girl trio.

Nevertheless, they found instant appeal with teenagers and young adults who were engrossed in the swing and jazz idioms, especially when they performed with nearly all of the major big bands, including those led by Glenn Miller, Benny Goodman, Buddy Rich, Tommy Dorsey, Jimmy Dorsey, Gene Krupa, Joe Venuti, Freddie Slack, Eddie Heywood, Bob Crosby (Bing's brother), Desi Arnaz, Guy Lombardo, Les Brown, Bunny Berigan, Xavier Cugat, Paul Whiteman, Ted Lewis, Nelson Riddle and mood-master Gordon Jenkins, whose orchestra and chorus accompanied them on such successful soft and melancholy renditions as "I Can Dream, Can't I?" (which shot to number one on *Billboard* and remained in the Top 10 for 25 weeks), "I Wanna Be Loved", "There Will Never Be Another You", and the inspirational "The Three Bells" (the first recorded English version of the French composition), along with several solo recordings with Patty, including a cover version of Nat King Cole's "Too Young", "It Never Entered My Mind", "If You Go", and "That's How A Love Song Is Born".

"Boogie Woogie Bugle Boy" can be considered an early recording of rhythm and blues or jump blues.

Many styles

While the sisters specialized in swing, boogie-woogie, and novelty hits with their trademark lightning-quick vocal syncopations, they also produced major hits in jazz, ballads, folk, country-western, seasonal, and religious titles, being the first Decca artists to record an album of gospel standards in 1950. Their versatility allowed them to pair with many different artists in the recording studios, producing Top 10 hits with the likes of Bing Crosby (the only recording artist of the 1940s to sell more records than The Andrews Sisters), Danny Kaye, Dick Haymes, Carmen Miranda, Al Jolson, Ray McKinley, Burl Ives, Ernest Tubb, Red Foley, Dan Dailey, Alfred Apaka, and Les Paul. In personal appearances, on radio and on television, they sang with everyone from Rudy Vallee, Judy Garland and Nat "King" Cole to Jimmie Rodgers, Andy Williams, and The Supremes. Some obvious 1930's song styles can be heard with early contemporary harmonizers of their day with the Boswell Sisters, and the Three X Sisters.

Films

Maxene, Patty, and LaVerne appeared in 17 Hollywood films. Their first picture, *Argentine Nights*, paired them with another enthusiastic trio, the Ritz Brothers.[24] Universal Pictures, always budget-conscious, refused to hire a choreographer, so the Ritzes taught the sisters some eccentric steps. Thus, in *Argentine Nights* and the sisters' next film, *Buck Privates*, the Andrews Sisters dance like the Ritz Brothers.

Buck Privates, with Abbott and Costello, featured the Andrews Sisters' best-known song, "Boogie Woogie Bugle Boy". This Don Raye-Hughie Prince composition was nominated for Best Song at the 1941 Academy Awards ceremony.

Universal hired the sisters for two more Abbott and Costello comedies, and then promoted them to full-fledged stardom in B musicals. *What's Cookin', Private Buckaroo,* and *Give Out, Sisters* (the latter portraying the sisters as old women) were among the team's popular full-length films.

The Andrews Sisters have a specialty number in the all-star revue *Hollywood Canteen* (1944). They can be seen singing "You Don't Have to Know the Language" with Bing Crosby in Paramount's *Road to Rio* with Bob Hope, that year's highest-grossing movie. Their singing voices are heard in two full-length Walt Disney features ("Make Mine Music"[25] which featured Johnny Fedora and Alice Blue Bonnet, and "Melody Time", which introduced *Little Toot,* both of which are available on DVD today).

Stage and radio shows

The Andrews Sisters were the most sought-after entertainment property in theater shows worldwide during the 1940s and early 1950s, always topping previous house averages. The trio headlined at the London Palladium in 1948 and 1951 to sold-out crowds. They hosted their own radio shows for ABC and CBS from 1944–1951, singing specially-written commercial jingles for such products as Wrigley's chewing gum, Dole pineapples, Nash motor cars, Kelvinator home appliances, Campbell's soups, and Franco-American food products.

Setting records

They recorded 47 songs with crooner Bing Crosby, 23 of which charted on *Billboard*, thus making the team one of the most successful pairings of acts in a recording studio in show business history. Their million-sellers with Crosby included "Pistol Packin' Mama", "Don't Fence Me In", "South America, Take It Away", and "Jingle Bells", among other yuletide favorites.

The sisters' popularity was such that after the war they discovered some of their records had actually been smuggled into Germany after the labels had been changed to read "Hitler's Marching Songs". Their recording of *Bei Mir Bist Du Schön* became a favorite of the Nazis, until it was discovered that the song's composers were of Jewish descent. Still, it did not stop concentration camp inmates from secretly singing it, this is most likely since the song was originally a Yiddish song "Bei Mir Bistu Shein", and had been popularized within the Jewish community before it was recorded as a more successful "cover" version by the Andrews sisters.

Along with Bing Crosby, separately and jointly, The Andrews Sisters were among the performers who incorporated ethnic music styles into America's Hit Parade, popularizing or enhancing the popularity of songs with melodies originating in Brazil, Czechoslovakia, France, Ireland, Israel, Italy, Mexico, Russia, Spain, Sweden and Trinidad, many of which their manager chose for them.

The Andrews Sisters became the most popular female vocal group of the first half of the 20th century.[26]

- between 75-100 million records sold from a little over 600 recorded tunes
- 113 charted Billboard hits, 46 reaching Top 10 status (more than Elvis Presley or The Beatles)
- 17 Hollywood films (more than any other singing group in motion picture history)[27]
- record-breaking theater and cabaret runs all across America and Europe;

- countless appearances on radio shows from 1935 to 1960 (including their own)
- guest spots on every major television show of the 1950s and 1960s, including those hosted by Ed Sullivan, Milton Berle, Perry Como, Frank Sinatra, Dean Martin, Sammy Davis, Jr., Johnny Carson, Joey Bishop, Art Linkletter and Jimmy Dean.

Early comparative female close harmony trios were the Boswell Sisters, the Pickens Sisters, and the Three X Sisters.

Repertoire

Hit records

Year	Single	Chart positions		
		US	US R&B	US Country
1938	"Bei Mir Bist Du Schön"	1	-	-
	"Nice Work If You Can Get It"	12	-	-
	"Joseph, Joseph"	18	-	-
	"Ti-Pi-Tin"	12	-	-
	"Shortenin' Bread"	16	-	-
	"Says My Heart"	10	-	-
	"Tu-li-Tulip Time"	9	-	-
	"Sha-Sha"	17	-	-
	"Lullaby To a Jitterbug"	10	-	-
1939	"Pross-Tchai (Goodbye)"	15	-	-
	"Hold Tight, Hold Tight"	2	-	-
	"You Don't Know How Much You Can Suffer"	14	-	-
	"Beer Barrel Polka (Roll Out the Barrel)"	4	-	-
	"Well All Right (Tonight's the Night)"	5	-	-
	"Ciribiribin (They're So In Love)"(with Bing Crosby)	13	-	-
	"Yodelin' Jive"(with Bing Crosby)	4	-	-
	"Chico's Love Song"	11	-	-
1940	"Say Si Si (Para Vigo Me Voy)"	4	-	-
	"The Woodpecker Song"	6	-	-
	"Down By the O-Hi-O"	21	-	-
	"Rhumboogie"	11	-	-
	"Ferryboat Serenade"	1	-	-
	"Hit the Road"	27	-	-
	"Beat Me Daddy, Eight to the Bar"	2	-	-

1941	"Scrub Me, Mama, With a Boogie Beat"	10	-	-
	"Boogie Woogie Bugle Boy"	6	-	-
	"I Yi, Yi, Yi, Yi (I Like You Very Much)"	11	-	-
	"(I'll Be With You) In Apple Blossom Time"	5	-	-
	"Aurora"	10	-	-
	"Sonny Boy"	22	-	-
	"The Nickel Serenade"	22	-	-
	"Sleepy Serenade"	22	-	-
	"I Wish I Had a Dime (For Every Time I Missed You)"	20	-	-
	"Jealous"	12	-	-
1942	"The Shrine of St. Cecilia"	3	-	-
	"I'll Pray For You"	22	-	-
	"Three Little Sisters"	8	-	-
	"Don't Sit Under the Apple Tree"	16	-	-
	"Pennsylvania Polka"	17	-	-
	"That's the Moon, My Son"	18	-	-
	"Mister Five By Five"	14	-	-
	"Strip Polka"	6	-	-
	"Here Comes the Navy"	17	-	-
1943	"East of the Rockies"	18	-	-
	"Pistol Packin' Mama"(with Bing Crosby)	2	3	1
	"Victory Polka"(with Bing Crosby)	5	-	-
	"Jingle Bells"(with Bing Crosby)	19	-	-
	"Shoo-Shoo Baby"	1	-	-
1944	"Down In the Valley"	20	-	-
	"Straighten Up and Fly Right"	8	-	-
	"Tico Tico"	24	-	-
	"Sing a Tropical Song"	24	-	-
	"Is You Is Or Is You Ain't My Baby"(with Bing Crosby)	2	-	-
	"A Hot Time In the Town of Berlin"(with Bing Crosby)	1	-	-
	"Don't Fence Me In"(with Bing Crosby)	1	9	-
1945	"Rum and Coca Cola"	1	3	-
	"Accentuate the Positive"(with Bing Crosby)	2	-	-
	"The Three Caballeros"(with Bing Crosby)	8	-	-
	"One Meat Ball"	15	-	-
	"Corns For My Country"	21	-	-
	"Along the Navajo Trail"(with Bing Crosby)	2	-	-
	"The Blond Sailor"	8	-	-

Year	Title			
1946	"Money Is the Root of All Evil"	9	-	-
	"Patience and Fortitude"	12	-	-
	"Coax Me a Little Bit"	24	-	-
	"South America, Take It Away"(with Bing Crosby)	2	-	-
	"Get Your Kicks On Route 66"(with Bing Crosby)	14	-	-
	"I Don't Know Why"	17	-	-
	"House of Blue Lights"	15	-	-
	"Rumors Are Flying"(with Les Paul)	4	-	-
	"Winter Wonderland"(with Guy Lombardo)	22	-	-
	"Christmas Island"(with Guy Lombardo)	7	-	-
1947	"Tallahassee"(with Bing Crosby)	10	-	-
	"There's No Business Like Show Business"(with Bing Crosby and Dick Haymes)	25	-	-
	"On the Avenue"	21	-	-
	"Near You"	2	-	-
	"The Lady From 29 Palms"	7	-	-
	"The Freedom Train"(with Bing Crosby)	21	-	-
	"Civilization (Bongo, Bongo, Bongo)"(with Danny Kaye)	3	-	-
	"Jingle Bells"(with Bing Crosby)(re-entry)	21	-	-
	"Santa Claus Is Comin' To Town"(with Bing Crosby)	22	-	-
	"Christmas Island"(with Guy Lombardo)(re-entry)	20	-	-
	"Your Red Wagon"	24	-	-
	"How Lucky You Are"	22	-	-
1948	"You Don't Have To Know the Language"(with Bing Crosby)	21	-	-
	"Teresa"(with Dick Haymes)	21	-	-
	"Toolie Oolie Doolie (The Yodel Polka)"	3	-	-
	"I Hate To Lose You"	14	-	-
	"Heartbreaker"	21	-	-
	"Sabre Dance"	20	-	-
	"Woody Woodpecker"(with Danny Kaye)	18	-	-
	"Blue Tail Fly"(with Burl Ives)	24	-	-
	"Underneath the Arches"	5	-	-
	"You Call Everybody Darling"	8	-	-
	"Cuanto La Gusta"(with Carmen Miranda)	12	-	-
	"160 Acres"(with Bing Crosby)	23	-	-
	"Bella Bella Marie"	23	-	-

1949	"Christmas Island"(with Guy Lombardo)(re-entry)	26	-	-
	"The Pussy Cat Song (Nyow! Nyot! Nyow!)"(Patty Andrews w/Bob Crosby)	12	-	-
	"More Beer!"	30	-	-
	"I'm Bitin' My Fingernails and Thinking of You"(with Ernest Tubb)	30	-	2
	"Don't Rob Another Man's Castle"(with Ernest Tubb)	-	-	6
	"I Can Dream, Can't I?"	1	-	-
	"The Wedding of Lili Marlene"	20	-	-
	"She Wore a Yellow Ribbon"(with Russ Morgan)	22	-	-
	"Charley, My Boy"(with Russ Morgan)	15	-	-
1950	"Merry Christmas Polka"(with Guy Lombardo)	18	-	-
	"Have I Told You Lately That I Love You"(with Bing Crosby)	24	-	-
	"Quicksilver"(with Bing Crosby)	6	-	-
	"The Wedding Samba"(with Carmen Miranda)	23	-	-
	"I Wanna Be Loved"	1	-	-
	"Can't We Talk It Over"	22	-	-
	"A Bushel and a Peck"	22	-	-
1951	"A Penny a Kiss, a Penny a Hug"	17	-	-
	"Sparrow in the Tree Top"(with Bing Crosby)	8	-	-
	"Too Young"(Patty Andrews)	19	-	-
1955	"Suddenly There's a Valley"(Patty Andrews)	69	-	-

Other songs

Highest chart positions on Billboard; with Vic Schoen and his orchestra, unless otherwise noted:

- "Joseph! Joseph!" (1938) (#18)
- "Ti-Pi-Tin" (1938) (#12)
- "Shortenin' Bread" (1938) (#16)
- "Says My Heart" (1938) (#10)
- "Tu-Li-Tulip Time" (with Jimmy Dorsey and his orchestra) (1938) (#9)
- "Sha-Sha" (with Jimmy Dorsey and his orchestra)(1938) (#17)
- "Lullaby to a Jitterbug" (1938) (#10)
- "Pross Tchai (Goodbye-Goodbye)" (1939) (#15)
- "You Don't Know How Much You Can Suffer" (1939) (#14)
- "Ciribiribin (They're So in Love)" (with Bing Crosby & Joe Venuti and his orchestra) (1939) (#13)
- "Chico's Love Song" (1939) (#11)
- "The Woodpecker Song" (1940) (#6)
- "Down By the O-HI-O" (1940) (#21)
- "Rhumboogie" (1940) (#11)
- "Hit the Road" (1940) (#27)
- "Scrub Me Mama with a Boogie Beat" (1940) (#10)
- "I Yi, Yi, Yi, Yi (I Like You Very Much)" (1941) (#11)
- "Aurora" (1941) (#10)
- "Sonny Boy" (1941) (#22)

- "The Nickel Serenade" (1941) (#22)
- "Sleepy Serenade" (1941) (#22)
- "I Wish I Had a Dime (For Ev'rytime I Missed You)" (1941) (#20)
- "Jealous" (1941) (#12)
- "I'll Pray For You" (1942) (#22)
- "Three Little Sisters" (1942) (#8)
- "Pennsylvania Polka" (1942) (#17)
- "That's the Moon, My Son" (1942) (#18)
- "Mister Five By Five" (1942) (#14)
- "Strip Polka" (1942) (#6)
- "Here Comes the Navy" (1942) (#17)
- "East of the Rockies" (1943) (#18)
- "Down in the Valley (Hear that Train Blow)" (1944) (#20)
- "Straighten Up and Fly Right" (1944) (#8)
- "Sing a Tropical Song" (1944) (#24)
- "Tico-Tico no Fubá" (1944) (#24)
- "Corns for My Country" (1945) (#21)
- "The Three Caballeros" (with Bing Crosby) (1945) (#8)
- "One Meat Ball" (1945) (#15)
- "The Blond Sailor" (1945) (#8)
- "Money Is the Root of All Evil (Take it Away, Take it Away, Take it Away)" (with Guy Lombardo and his Royal Canadians) (1946) (#9)
- "Patience and Fortitude" (1946) (#12)
- "Coax Me a Little Bit" (1946) (#24)
- "Get Your Kicks on Route 66" (with Bing Crosby) (1946) (#14)
- "I Don't Know Why (I Just Do)" (1946) (#17)
- "The House of Blue Lights" (with Eddie Heywood and his orchestra) (1946) (#15)
- "Winter Wonderland" (with Guy Lombardo and his Royal Canadians) (1946) (#22)
- "Christmas Island" (with Guy Lombardo and his Royal Canadians) (1946: #7; 1947: #20; 1949: #26)
- "Tallahassee" (with Bing Crosby) (1947) (#10)
- "There's No Business Like Show Business" (with Bing Crosby and Dick Haymes) (1947) (#25)
- "On the Avenue" (with Carmen Cavallaro at the piano) (1947) (#21)
- "The Lady from 29 Palms" (1947) (#7)
- "The Freedom Train" (1947) (#21)
- "Your Red Wagon" (1947) (#24)
- "How Lucky You Are" (1947) (#22)
- "You Don't Have to Know the Language" (with Bing Crosby) (1948) (#21)
- "Teresa" (with Dick Haymes) (1948) (#21)
- "Heartbreaker" (with The Harmonica Gentlemen) (1948) (#21)
- "(Everytime They Play the) Sabre Dance" (with The Harmonica Gentlemen) (1948) (#20)
- "I Hate to Lose You" (1948) (#14)
- "The Woody Woodpecker Song" (with Danny Kaye and The Harmonica Gentlemen) (1948) (#18)
- "The Blue Tail Fly (Jimmy Crack Corn)" (with Burl Ives, vocal and guitar accompaniment) (1948) (#24)
- "You Call Everybody Darling" (recorded in London with Billy Ternant and his orchestra) (1948) (#8)
- "Cuanto La Gusta" (with Carmen Miranda) (1948) (#12)
- "A Hundred and Sixty Acres" (with Bing Crosby) (1948) (#23)
- "Bella Bella Marie" (1948) (#23)

- "More Beer!" (1949) (#30)
- "I'm Biting My Fingernails and Thinking of You" (with Ernest Tubb and The Texas Troubadors directed by Vic Schoen) (1949) (#30)
- "The Wedding of Lili Marlene" (with Gordon Jenkins and his orchestra and chorus) (1949) (#20)
- "The Pussy Cat Song (Nyow! Nyot Nyow!)" (Patty Andrews and Bob Crosby) (1949) (#12)
- "She Wore a Yellow Ribbon" (with Russ Morgan and his orchestra) (1949) (#22)
- "Charley, My Boy" (with Russ Morgan and his orchestra) (1949) (#15)
- "Merry Christmas Polka" (with Guy Lombardo and his Royal Canadians) (1950) (#18)
- "Have I Told You Lately that I Love You?" (with Bing Crosby) (1950) (#24)
- "Quicksilver" (with Bing Crosby) (1950) (#6)
- "The Wedding Samba" (with Carmen Miranda) (1950) (#23)
- "Can't We Talk it Over?" (with Gordon Jenkins and his orchestra and chorus) (1950) (#22)
- "A Bushel and a Peck" (1950) (#22)
- "A Penny a Kiss-A Penny a Hug" (1950) (#17)
- "Sparrow in the Treetop" (with Bing Crosby) (1951) (#8)
- "Too Young" (Patty Andrews with Victor Young and his orchestra) (1951) (#19)
- "Torero" Capitol F 3965 (recorded on March 31, 1958)

Film and theatre

(partial list)

Filmography

- *Argentine Nights* (Universal Pictures, 1940)[28]
- *Buck Privates* (Universal Pictures, 1941)
- *In the Navy* (Universal Pictures, 1941)[28]
- *Hold That Ghost* (Universal Pictures, 1941)
- *Private Buckaroo* (Universal Pictures, 1942)[28]
- *Give Out, Sisters* (Universal Pictures, 1942)
- *How's About It* (Universal Pictures, 1943)
- *Always a Bridesmaid* (Universal Pictures, 1943)
- *Swingtime Johnny* (Universal Pictures, 1943)
- *Moonlight and Cactus* (Universal Pictures, 1944)
- *Follow the Boys* (Universal Pictures, 1944)
- *Hollywood Canteen* (Warner Brothers, 1944)
- *Her Lucky Night* (Universal Pictures, 1945)
- *Make Mine Music* (Walt Disney Studios, 1946)
- *Road to Rio* (Paramount Pictures, 1947)[28]
- *Melody Time* (Walt Disney Studios, 1948)[28]
- *Brother, Can You Spare a Dime?* (1975)

Soundtracks

- *What's Cookin'?* (Universal Pictures, 1942)[28]
- *Breach* (background music) (2007)
- *Land of the Lost* (2009)

Broadway

- *Over Here!* (1974; Shubert Theater, New York City, 9 months)

Dance

- *Company B* (1991; Choreographed by Paul Taylor, Performed by Paul Taylor Dance Company, American Ballet Theatre, and Miami City Ballet)

As Muppets

They were parodied on "Sesame Street" as the Androoze Sisters, named Mayeeme (Audrey Smith), Pattiz (Maeretha Stewart), and Lavoorrnee (Kevin Clash).

References

[1] http://www.foxnews.com/entertainment/2013/01/30/last-surviving-andrews-sisters-member-patty-andrews-dies-at-4/?test=latestnews

[2] boogie-woogie (http://www.collinsdictionary.com/dictionary/english/boogie-woogie). CollinsDictionary.com. Collins English Dictionary - Complete & Unabridged 11th Edition. Retrieved November 26, 2012.

[3] The American Heritage Dictionary of the English Language, Fourth Edition copyright ©2000 by Houghton Mifflin Company, Updated in 2009 CITED IN "Boogie-Woogie" (http://www.thefreedictionary.com/boogie-woogie), *FreeDictionary.com.*

[4] "Vocal Group Hall of Fame - The Andrews Sisters" (http://www.vocalgroup.org/inductees/andrews_sisters.htm). . Retrieved January 31, 2013.

[5] (http://uk.real.com/music/artist/The_Andrews_Sisters/). UK Real.com article on The Andrews Sisters.

[6] http://www.startribune.com/entertainment/189120371.html

[7] SHOLOM SECUNDA The Story of Bei Mir Bist du Schön (http://www.dvrbs.com/swing/SholomSecunda-BeiMirBistDuSchoen.htm)

[8] Jill Serjeant (January 30, 2013). "Last of 1940s hitmakers Andrews Sisters dies in California" (http://www.reuters.com/article/2013/01/30/us-pattyandrews-idUSBRE90T1HW20130130). "Reuters". . Retrieved February 3, 2013.

[9] Andrews, Maxene and Bill Gilbert. *Over Here, Over There: The Andrews Sisters and the USO Stars in World War II.* New York: Kensington Publishing Corp, 1993.

[10] Adam Bernstein (January 30, 2013). "Patty Andrews, the last surviving member of the Andrews Sisters, dies at 94" (http://articles.washingtonpost.com/2013-01-30/local/36647222_1_boswell-sisters-sister-act-andrews-sisters). "Washington Post". . Retrieved February 3, 2013.

[11] Bob Beverage, Ron Peluso. "Christmas of Swing" (http://www.historytheatre.com/files/play-guide_christmas-of-swing_2012.pdf). "HistoryTheater.com". p. 4. . Retrieved February 3, 2013.

[12] Los Angeles Times article (http://proquest.umi.com/pqdweb?did=435022642&sid=5&Fmt=10&clientId=48776&RQT=309&VName=HNP) (PDF) December 22, 1954.

[13] Natalie Finn (January 30, 2013). "Patty Andrews Dies, Singer Was Last Surviving Member of the Andrews Sisters" (http://www.eonline.com/news/383541/patty-andrews-dies-singer-was-last-surviving-member-of-the-andrews-sisters). "E Online.com". . Retrieved February 3, 2013.

[14] Los Angeles Times article (http://proquest.umi.com/pqdweb?did=521603392&sid=6&Fmt=10&clientId=48776&RQT=309&VName=HNP) (PDF) May 9, 1967.

[15] St Petersburg Times August 10, 1968 (http://news.google.com/newspapers?id=cqJQAAAAIBAJ&sjid=u1wDAAAAIBAJ&pg=5642,6029172&dq=andrews+sisters&hl=en)

[16] St. Petersburg Times (http://news.google.com/newspapers?id=hR0MAAAAIBAJ&sjid=u1wDAAAAIBAJ&dq=andrews sisters&pg=5682,6029193) August 10, 1968.

[17] http://news.google.com/newspapers?id=cD9SAAAAIBAJ&sjid=hHkDAAAAIBAJ&pg=4875,1202172&dq=andrews+sisters&hl=en St. Petersburg Times - December 27, 1974.

[18] Sforza, John (2004). *Swing It!: The Andrews Sisters Story* (http://books.google.com/books?id=IPoMEFUgOwUC&pg=PA171). United States of America: University Press of Kentucky. p. 171. ISBN 9780813190990. .

[19] Los Angeles Times article (http://proquest.umi.com/pqdweb?did=408941231&sid=1&Fmt=10&clientId=48776&RQT=309&VName=HNP) PDF February 4, 1940.

[20] http://books.google.com/books?id=9mE2-RxDyZsC&pg=PA409

[21] "The Andrews Sisiters - Bio" (http://www.imdb.com/name/nm1679536/bio). "IMDb". . Retrieved Fevruary 3, 2013.

[22] Westonka Historical Society (http://www.westonkahistoricalsociety.org/movestory.html)

[23] "Patty Andrews, last surviving member of Andrews sisters, remembered for rallying troops" (http://www.washingtonpost.com/ entertainment/music/patty-andrews-last-surviving-member-of-singing-andrews-sisters-dead-at-94/2013/01/30/ 2da038ec-6b45-11e2-9a0b-db931670f35d_story.html). The Associated Press. The Washington Post. January 31, 2013. . Retrieved February 1, 2013.

[24] Los Angeles Times article (http://proquest.umi.com/pqdweb?did=409280301&sid=1&Fmt=10&clientId=48776&RQT=309& VName=HNP) PDF May 15, 1940.

[25] Los Angeles Times article (http://proquest.umi.com/pqdweb?did=415221731&sid=3&Fmt=10&clientId=48776&RQT=309& VName=HNP) (PDF) Hedda Hopper. June 30, 1946.

[26] Schoifet, Mark (January 30, 2013). "Patty Andrews, Last Survivor of Wartime Sister Trio, Dies at 94" (http://www.businessweek.com/ news/2013-01-30/patty-andrews-last-survivor-of-wartime-sister-trio-dies-at-94). *Bloomberg* (BusinessWeek). . Retrieved January 31, 2013.

[27] "Biography for The Andrews Sisters" (http://www.imdb.com/name/nm1679536/bio). IMDb.com. . Retrieved January 31, 2013.

[28] "The Andres Sisters" (http://www.imdb.com/name/nm1679536/). IMDb. . Retrieved February 3, 2013.

- Nimmo, H. Arlo. *The Andrews Sisters.* Jefferson: McFarland & Co, Inc., 2004.
- Sforza, John. *Swing It! The Andrews Sisters Story.* Lexington: The University Press of Kentucky, 2000.

External links

- Andrews Sisters Official website (http://www.cmgww.com/music/andrews/)
- Andrews Sisters on BigBands.net (http://www.bigbands.net/andrewsbio.htm)
- Vocal Group Hall of Fame page on the Andrews Sisters (http://www.vocalgroup.org/inductees/ andrews_sisters.htm)
- Maxene Andrews (http://www.findagrave.com/cgi-bin/fg.cgi?page=gr&GRid=3052) at *Find a Grave*
- Laverne Andrews (http://www.findagrave.com/cgi-bin/fg.cgi?page=gr&GRid=2092) at *Find a Grave*
- Patty Andrews (http://www.findagrave.com/cgi-bin/fg.cgi?page=gr&GRid=104311861) at *Find a Grave*

Article Sources and Contributors

The Andrews Sisters *Source*: http://en.wikipedia.org/w/index.php?oldid=538687232 *Contributors*: 13westrn, 17Drew, 2001:558:6011:11:50F3:7123:CE1E:EB5D, 23skidoo, 28bytes, Addshore, Ajuk, Alan Canon, Alexdan loghin, All Hallow's Wraith, Alphacatmarnie, Alphalurion, AmericanLeMans, And we drown, Arpad13, Ashley Pomeroy, Aspects, Avicennasis, BRG, Bellczar, Bensin, Bigroger27509, Blakegripling ph, Bloodholds, Boing! said Zebedee, Brian the Editor, Bro rick, Burbridge92, C777, CAWylie, CSWarren, Cabe6403, Calmer Waters, Cameronc, CapitalR, CatherineMunro, Catperson12, Ccgrimm, Cellofury, Chanlyn, Chowbok, Chris the speller, Ckruschke, Cluth, Coinmanj, Colonies Chris, Common Man, Crooner62, D6, DBigXray, Dagonet, Danny, Dave Andrew, DavidRF, Davidecross, Dcoetzee, Discographer, Docu, Dogru144, Donaldd23, Download, DrakeLuvenstein, Dumelow, Dutchmonkey9000, ERcheck, Eco84, EdGl, Edgar181, Edkollin, Effajay, Egghead06, Entheta, Erianna, Eric Schutte, Esprit15d, Evil Monkey, Fayenatic london, Filmsaboutstuff, Freakofnurture, Fuddle, Furrycat66, GBrady, Ganymead, Ghmyrtle, GiantSnowman, Gilliam, Gingerandfred, Giovannii84, Gl873, GoingBatty, Grafen, Graham87, Gregoing, Grstain, Gujuguy, Guroadrunner, Gyrobo, Hailey C. Shannon, Ham1000, HandsomeFella, Harry Nimmo, Hattrem, Herr von underpants, Hifihitman, Hirolovesswords, Homerrocks, Hoof Hearted, Howard352, Htfiddler, Indopug, Infrogmation, Inscription, Iridescent, IsarSteve, It Is Me Here, Italo9, JCaesar, JGKlein, Jack1956, Jbarta, Jimknut, Jmgonzalez, Joefromrandb, Joel Mc, Jogers, JohnRogers, JoleneKat, Jonpetteroie, Josh Rumage, Jusdafax, JustAGal, Jwy, Kak500, Karlos the Jackal, Kcoutu, Kellyprice, Ken Gallager, Keraunoscopia, Kevinmon, KhryssoHeart, Kintetsubuffalo, Kmweber, Leoni2, Lightmouse, LilHelpa, Lincher, Lisko33, Lkop56, Lolliapaulina51, Lpmiller, LucilleBall, LukeSurl, Lwellsnyc, MBlume, MER-C, Mago266, Mandarax, Markhurd, MarnetteD, Mattbr, Mattgirling, MatthewTStone, Mauitunes, May Cause Dizziness, Mike Dillon, Mike Halterman, Minnesota cold, Miopportunity, Mlisko, Moncrief, MoreMetal, MrDolomite, Mrceleb2007, Mrestko, Mulad, Mutley1989, Mykleavens, NawlinWiki, Nedrutland, Nepal2030, Niceguyedc, NickyBeth, Nihiltres, Niteowlneils, No1lakersfan, Nonstandard, Notheruser, Nwbeeson, Oanabay04, Od Mishehu, Oobopshark, Open2universe, Operagal52, Otto4711, PDH, Pascal.Tesson, Paul A, Paul Erik, Pcpcpc, Perohanych, Philip Trueman, PieBoysMama, PigFlu Oink, Pigmonkeyandsuzi, Piledhigheranddeeper, Ponyo, PrettyMuchBryce, PsychoNiff, Qballbuster2, Quentin X, R'n'B, Ragtimeacres97, Raulsebrook, Rees11, Replysixty, Rich Farmbrough, Rich257, Richardcavell, Richhoncho, Richwales, Rjd0060, Rossrs, Roygbiv666, Rusty201, Salliesatt, Sasake662, SchreiberBike, SchuminWeb, SebastianHelm, Serlin, Shadow1, ShelfSkewed, Shir-El too, Shlomke, Sicamous, Sjc, Sluzzelin, Slysplace, Snezzy, Snowmanradio, Son of Somebody, Spellcast, Starcheerspeaksnewslostwars, Studerby, SusanLesch, Syrthiss, Tabledhote, Tacllews, Tal1962, Tassedethe, Ted Wilkes, Tednor, TenPoundHammer, Tesscass, Thanatos666, Themidwestprincess, Threeafterthree, Tim!, Timrollpickering, Tjmayerinsf, Tkynerd, Tombarrister, TooCleverDuck, Tribal44, Triplestop, Trystan, TutterMouse, Tvoz, Twinchester, TypoBoy, USRoute66, Ulric1313, VIGNERON, Vague Rant, Valentinejoesmith, Vegan4Life, Vertigo Man-iac, Vgirly, Virginboi6969, Voltaire137, Vorash, Vulturell, Vyruss, W guice, WBardwin, Wahkeenah, Waldir, Walter Görlitz, Wareismike, Wasell, Wasted Time R, Wdchk, We hope, Welsh, WesleyDodds, WikHead, Wikianon, Wildhartlivie, Wolfluver2013, Wool Mintons, Wrnchhead76, Xmanager, YUL89YYZ, Zazaotm, Zmjezhd, Zytsef, 466 anonymous edits

(I'll Be With You) In Apple Blossom Time *Source*: http://en.wikipedia.org/w/index.php?oldid=535603179 *Contributors*: Bonnie13J, Ghmyrtle, JustAGal, Richhoncho, 2 anonymous edits

A Bushel and a Peck *Source*: http://en.wikipedia.org/w/index.php?oldid=499012033 *Contributors*: BRG, Danmuse, Delvingup, Edward, Eric444, Flami72, Gareth E Kegg, Grstain, Harvick3829, Hmains, Jogers, Jpgordon, Kkerr63, Labalius, Levineps, Merillupin, Nickellmusic, Pinirico65, Pmsyyz, Runt, Smmurphy, 13 anonymous edits

Beat Me Daddy, Eight to the Bar *Source*: http://en.wikipedia.org/w/index.php?oldid=527191706 *Contributors*: Alton.arts, Auspicion, Brian the Editor, ChrisQvNguyen, Cit helper, Florescent, GoingBatty, Gsupittman, Guiltyfeet, Jker81278poe, Jlloyd81278, JustAGal, Lawlar, Morgan Wright, Ojorojo, Richhoncho, Ssbohio, Technopat, Woohookitty, YUL89YYZ, Zbxgscqf, Ὁ οἶστρος, 13 anonymous edits

Beer Barrel Polka *Source*: http://en.wikipedia.org/w/index.php?oldid=535914655 *Contributors*: Accordion Noir, AlanUS, Algabal, Amchow78, AnonMoos, Ary29, BigT2006, Btilm, Cetange23, Chalkieperfect, Chancemichaels, Ckatz, DJ Clayworth, DWaterson, Dcelano, Dyfsunctional, Erianna, Fang Aili, Flightsoffancy, Fritzpoll, Gumruch, Ianmacm, Iaroslavvs, Ikescs, Javierme, Kevlar67, Levineps, Mbakkel2, Miraceti, Moonriddengirl, Nickellmusic, Oanabay04, Oashi, Oldiesmann, Olessi, Pmj, Postcard Cathy, Pustelnik, Qertis, Ratgris, Ross.Hedvicek, Sluzzelin, Stev0, Tjmayerinsf, Tulkolahten, Wereon, William Avery, 73 anonymous edits

Bei Mir Bistu Shein *Source*: http://en.wikipedia.org/w/index.php?oldid=539387614 *Contributors*: Akristol, AlbertSM, Aleksandr Grigoryev, Amcbride, Angr, Anomalocaris, Argyriou, Avoran, B00P, BRG, Balihb, Boyajian, Brewcrewer, CharlesMartel, Cst17, Cyberevil, Dancter, Danny-w, Darena mipt, Deus Homoni, DirtyMohair, Download, Durova, Ecoleetage, Edward Hyde, Espoo, Fundamentisto, Fvasconcellos, Gement, Ghirlandajo, HG, Haeinous, Harxor, Htfiddler, IZAK, Ilari.scheinin, Imeriki al-Shimoni, Imz, It Is Me Here, JackofOz, Jmabel, JohnRogers, Johnsmusicbox, Jonpetteroie, Jpgordon, Kbdank71, KeyboardWarriorOfZion, Koavf, Kosboot, KremBrule, Lamaybe, Laurencebeck, Loew Galitz, Lumos3, Lynchkenney, Macrakis, Maikel, Malikbek, Marchfishka, Miguel Andrade, MiguelMunoz, Mild Bill Hiccup, Nareek, NawlinWiki, Notreallydavid, Parishan, Pasna, Paul Miil, Pegship, Pemilligan, Piccone, PositiveBeta, Remi505, Retroman, Rlendog, Rosenbluh, Salamurai, SchreiberBike, ShelfSkewed, Smmurphy, Soundroll, SpaceFlight89, Tguignar, The Anome, The Gnome, Toddsschneider, Tsca, Uglinessman, Wikianon, Wje600, Wonder al, Yms, Ynhockey, 128 ,חובבשירה anonymous edits

Bette Midler *Source*: http://en.wikipedia.org/w/index.php?oldid=539306148 *Contributors*: 14Adrian, 19204, 5 albert square, AMK1211, Abrech, Absalom89, Acalamari, Ace Class Shadow, Adammichael, Aervanath, Ageekgal, Aguilac, Ajd, Ajleung, Akendall, Akira625, Alakazam, Alecsdaniel, Alison, All Hallow's Wraith, Allusernamestaken, Amy3grant, AndrewAllen15, Andycjp, Anirvan, Antandrus, Antares33712, Anthropocentrism, Appsmountaineer, Argos'Dad, Arjayay, ArkansasTraveler, Arniep, Arrataz, Ash, Aspects, Astorknlam, Austinfidel, BDrischBDemented, BRG, BalticPat22, Barrympls, Bcharles, Bearcat, Beijingcoffeecake, Benjiboi, Bergamini, Bette08, Betteisdivine, Betteontheboards, Bigjimr, Bigweeboy, Binrochus, Bjones, Bogdangiusca, Bohed, Bovineboy2008, Bryan Seecrets, Buffy1994, Bus stop, Butter Bandit, Cadr, CanOfWorms, Candy156sweet, CanisRufus, Canyouhearmenow, Cburnett, Charleenmerced, Charlie White, Charshi, Chowbok, ChrisB, ChrisGualtieri, Christie2012?, Cimon Avaro, Cinemaniac86, Cliff1911, Clinicalupset, Coder Dan, Colonies Chris, ConoscoTutto, Coppertop Guy, Courcelles, CrazyLegsKC, Cretanforever, Crystallina, D6, DAJF, Dabegra, Dadofsam, Dajuna, DanMS, Danny oldsen, Darcherj, Dark jedi requiem, Darth Panda, DauntBooks, Davemackey, DavidFarmbrough, Deflective, Den81164, DepressedPer, Derek R Bullamore, Deville, DickClarkMises, Dimadick, Discographer, Dismas, Djay70k, Djbj16, Dobie80, Doc glasgow, Drakehottie, Dreamer.se, DropDeadGorgias, Dtowng, Duckie7, E Wing, E-Kartoffel, E2eamon, EarthlyAlien, East718, EdGl, Edwy, Eeyen, Egmontaz, Ejfetters, Elipongo, Embryomystic, Emerson7, Empoor, EoGuy, Erfan24, Ericorbit, Erikb88, Ernio48, Escape Orbit, Este83, EurekaLott, Eurleif, Evan1200, Everard Proudfoot, Exploding Boy, Extraordinary Machine, Falkreon, Fallout boy, Fat&Happy, Faustlin, FeralDruid, Filll, Flami72, FocalPoint, Frank, Frecklefoot, Fridakahlo, Frschoonover, Furrykef, Futurebird, Fuzzy510, Fæ, G-Long42, GCord52, Gadfium, Garing, Gaudio, GcSwRhIc, Gemini86 618, Getreddy78, Gfad1, Gidonb, Gilliam, Gilmore1316, Glennwells, Gmosaki, Gobonobo, GoingBatty, Golbez, Goldnpuppy, Gongshow, Graham87, Greenspun Interactive, GregorB, Grenavitar, Grstain, GusF, Guy M, Hakushu8, Hall Monitor, Harout72, Hasbro, Haynesy, Heatherbuff, Heatherbuff22, Heegoop, Hiphats, Hit bull, win steak, Hoary, Hologram900, Hooperbloob, Hotholly95, Hucz, HuggaBounce, Hut 8.5, Hydrogen Iodide, IAmTheCoinMan, IBO, Igoldste, Iheartu213, Ilovemeganmullally, IndyLawSteve, Isaiah lowe, J-B, J.R. Hercules, JGKlein, Jack O'Lantern, JackO'Lantern, JamesB3, JamesMLane, Jamesontai, Japanese Searobin, Jauers, JayKeaton, Jedi94, Jerry, Jerzy, Jerzymare, Jesyjond, Jet0425, Jhsounds, Jidanni, Jimbobjoe456, Jmc29, JohnI, Johnnya2k6, Johnpacklambert, Jon Kay, Joncaire, Jonluvsmaddy, Joseph Solis in Australia, Josh Rumage, Jpgordon, JustAGal, Justme89, Jwarhol, Jweiss11, Jzummak, KaiAdin, Kaisersanders, Katieh5584, Kaykay123, Kbdank71, KeithH, Kevin Gorman, Kevinbrogers, Koavf, Krylonblue83, Kurt Shaped Box, Kwamikagami, Kyra4325, Kyriosity, L Kensington, L1975p, Lappado, Lauren, Levineps, Lhademmor, Lightmouse, LilHelpa, Lilshortstack, Ling.Nut, LiteraryMaven, Little Savage, Los besos, Luckyz, MJEH, Macaire, Mandarax, MarcK, Marchije, Mareino, Mark Arsten, MarnetteD, Martynjsimpson, Masirahos, Materialscientist, Mattbr, MaxPride, McSly, MegX, Mel Etitis, Melissa Dilo, Mentifisto, Michael Hardy, MichaelCaricofe, Mickey gfss2007, Microwave ov, Midway, Mike Halterman, MikeyChalupa, Missdiatribe, Mj161, Monni95, Movieguru2006, Mr. Nacho de la Libre, Muntzorama, NGPriest, Nancy, Nashvilledon, Nationalparks, Nick Levinson, Nneonneo, Noboyo, Nofoolz, Northofdc, Notmicro, Nrswanson, Ocaasi, Ohconfucius, Oneiros, Openmy, Orange Suede Sofa, Orphan Wiki, Ottre, P0lit0o, Padillah, Pascal666, Paul-L, Pcpcpc, Pearle, Peloneous, Peruvianllama, Phaeton23, Pigman, Pinethicket, Pinkadelica, Pogoman, Pointillist, Polly, Potatoswatter, Professor Von Pie, Proxmire2000, Pwillson, Q8-falcon, Qaqaq, Qiq, Quadell, QuasyBoy, QuickMotion, Quixoticattimes, R. fiend, RAFAELANGEL12, RED DAVE, RHaworth, RHodnett, RSekulovich, RadioKirk, RainbowOfLight, Random contributor, RattleandHum, Redeagle688, Reidca, Ricardogomes1983, Richdiesal, Rje, Robert Moore, Robertissimo, Rogerd, Rollsroyce88, Roodngis, Rossrs, RoyBoy, Rsugden, Ryan032, RyanGerbil10, Ryanb006, S Marshall, SFTVLGUY2, SP-KP, Sabbut, Sandcherry, Sannse, Scarian, SchfiftyThree, Schmiteye, Semorrison, Ser Amantio di Nicolao, SexyColin, Shaniafan, ShelfSkewed, Shicrbs, Shortride, SidP, Silverchair3, SimonP, SkyWalker, Somebody9973, SpikeJones, Ssilvers, Suffusion of Yellow, Suprarider1, Synchronism, T8520, TSOP, Tabledhote, Tabletop, Taker2008, Tassedethe, Ted87, Tfts, Thatguy820, The Devil's Advocate, The Honorable, The Librarian at Terminus, TheCustomOfLife, Thebadboys, Thecheetah, Threeafterthree, Thumbelina, Tide rolls, Tiggertrouble, Tinton5, Tjmayerinsf, Tlesher, TonyTheTiger, Toon05, Toyan1019, TrafficBenBoy, Trancer78, Tregoweth, Tribal44, Turnstep, Ulric1313, Uncle Dick, Unclemikejb, Unused000701, Uytingco, Vanderbilt8, Vegaswikian, Vincelord, Viriditas, Vulturell, Vuruless, WBardwin, Wasted Time R, WayKurat, Wayne Slam, WereSpielChequers, WikEd, WikHead, Wikieditor06, Wildhartlivie, Wmahan, Woohookitty, Yobmod, Zalgo, Zero Diggity, ZimZalaBim, Zoe, Zzyzx11, 876 anonymous edits

Bing Crosby *Source*: http://en.wikipedia.org/w/index.php?oldid=539187711 *Contributors*: -Lemmy-, 09aidepikiw, 0x6D667061, 777sms, A Stop at Willoughby, ACSE, Aardvarkzz, Abenzev, Abrazame, Abrech, Abtinb, Academic Challenger, Accubam, Acroterion, Adam McMaster, After Midnight, Ahunt, Ajraddatz, Alan W, Aleal, Alex2706, Alexander336, Alexbonaro, Alexvincent2, AliveFreeHappy, All Hallow's Wraith, Allthewhile, Altenmann, AmiSue, Andland, AndrewHowse, Andrewa, Andyvanhout, Angelique, Anger22, Angr, Animum, AnonMoos, Anthony Winward, Anthropocentrism, Aphid360, Apteva, Arakunem, Aranel, Arbor to SJ, ArglebargleIV, Ary29, Aryonoco, Ashtin16, Askedoffer, Astral, Auror, AussieLegend, Austinmurphy, Ayapota, BD2412, BRG, Baa, Babygrand1, Badgernet, Bantosh, Barek, Barrympls, Bbb23, Bbsrock, Bcp67, Bede735, Before My Ken, Bemoeial, Bender235, BertSen, Best name, Bevo, Bgruber, BigDunc, Billy Hathorn, Bingcrosby Enterprises, Binksternet, Bioprof, Bioprofessor, Biruitorul, Black Kat, BobJones77, Bobblewik, Bobo192, Bohouse, Bojars, Bokan, Bongwarrior, Boris Crépeau, Bporopat, BrianHansen, BrigidHarry, Bryan Derksen, Brycem, Btphelps, Bumhole123, C.Fred, CIreland, Calabe1992, CambridgeBayWeather, Can't sleep, clown will eat me, Carl savich, Carr, Cassandre H., Causa sui, Cavepiggy, Cburnett, Cgilbert76, Changalangadingdong, Chanheigeorge, Chanlyn, CharlesRFord, Cheesemaster, ChittyChittyBangBang49, Choster, Chowbok, Cindamuse, Clarityfiend, Clockster, Commander Keane, Conversion script, Cooksi, Couillaud, Courcelles, Cresix, Crosbylilis, Crox in the Box, Cst17, Cvieg, Cygnature, D6, D7240, DONOVAN, Da Main Event, Dale Arnett, Dalinian, Damirgraffiti, DangTungDuong, Database, David Martland, Dbzsamuele120, Ddlfan, DeadEyeArrow, DeadlyAssassin, Deanos, Deb, Deejaytalk, Demiurge, Dennette, Deyyaz, Dferg47, DiamondDave, Dicklyon, Digby scallops, Dirkbb, Discographer, Discospinster, Diskpocket, Dk1965, Dlobo74, Doh286, Domingo Portales, Doniago, Donreed, DougHill, Dougie monty, Download, Dpbsmith, Dr. Blofeld, Dranster, Dreftymac, Dudesleeper, Dunks58, EJBanks, EagleOne, Ed Poor, Edetic, Edgar181, Edgars2007, Eep²,

Eliz81, Ellekit, Elsquared, Emerson7, Emricha, Enviroboy, Ericorbit, Ericpelland, Ericynot, Esrever, Evan1200, Everyking, Eyesnore, F1list, FMAFan1990, Fabiform, Facts, Famous Goof Bally, Farosdaughter, Fat&Happy, FeanorStar7, Ffirehorse, Flami72, FloK, Francs2000, FrankBlissett, Freightgod, Froid, Fryede, Fuhghettaboutit, Fyyer, GTubio, Gaius Cornelius, Gamaliel, Ganymead, Gareth Aus, Gareth E Kegg, Garrett p, Garzo, Gaudio, Gelingvistoj, Ghaly, Ghirlandajo, Ghmyrtle, Gigliotti, Gil Gamesh, Gilliam, Giraffedata, Godfrey Daniel, Gogo Dodo, Goldnpuppy, Gongshow, Good Olfactory, Gracenotes, Granttrial1, Grapester, Grenavitar, Griffinofwales, Grika, Grimhim, Grstain, Guat6, Gujuguy, Gurch, Haham hanuka, Hall Monitor, Handicapper, Harout72, HarveyCarter, Havershaw, Hayythere, Headius, Hedwig in Washington, Heegoop, Hekerui, Helga76, Hendren, Hifihitman, Hmains, Horizens, Horsemen4life, Hotwine8, Hoverfish, Howard352, Howard85, Hullaballoo Wolfowitz, Hydrafoil, Hydrargyrum, IP4240207xx, Ianblair23, Ilikelotsofnumbers, IllaZilla, ImpossiblyLost, In Defense of the Artist, Informationfountain, Infrogmation, Insanity Incarnate, IsarSteve, Istuart0, Ithink72wp, ItsElectric7, J.J. Popplewick, J.delanoy, JASpencer, JCSantos, JFreeman, JGKlein, JHP, Jab843, Jack Cox, JackHearne, Jackelfive, JackofOz, Jackson008, Jafeluv, Jaraalbe, Jarbie01, Jasminegetfresh, Jauerback, Jax 0677, Jayhare, JerH, Jerzy, Jessiejames, Jfrlkb, Jhlynes, Jim1138, JimVC3, Jjacobsmeyer, Jjwaltrip, Jm307, Jmabel, Jmw1959, JoBrLa, Joao Xavier, JoetheMoe25, Joey80, John, John of Reading, JohnRogers, Johnpacklambert, Jokestress, Jolomo, Jolsonmhd, JordoCo, Joseph Solis in Australia, Josh Rumage, Journalist, Jpgordon, Jpo51, Jrpowell, Judyschmid, Julia Gordon, June w, Justme89, Jwarmbrodt, K-ray913, KXL, Kammat, KaneTW, Karanacs, Karlos the Jackal, Katsuya, Kbdank71, Kedar63, Kelly Martin, Keraunoscopia, Ketil3, Ketiltrout, KillerChihuahua, Killiondude, Kimchi.sg, KingDaevid, Kingboyk, KingdomHearts25, Kingpre, Kingturtle, Kintetsubuffalo, Kitty Davis, Kleinzach, Kneberle, Koavf, Koro Neil, Koyaanis Qatsi, Kumioko (renamed), Kungfuadam, Kuralyov, Kyhiking, Ladydayelle, Laureapuella, Leon7, Levent, Levineps, Lhb1239, Lilac Soul, Lilredrooster, Lin Anderson, Ling.Nut, Locke Cole, Lockeownzj00, Logain, Loganperm, LorenzoB, Lucky 6.9, Lugnuts, Luna Imper, Luna Santin, MACWILMSLO, MATHTEACHER4, MJEH, Maarten1963, Magioladitis, Manto1261, Manuel Trujillo Berges, Marcus Brute, Marcus2, Mark K. Jensen, Markhh, Marxo22, Matthew Fennell, Mauri96, MaxPride, Maximus Rex, Maxviwe, Mayumashu, Mboverload, Mddake, Meco, Mediaace, MegX, Mehrunes Dagon, Mercury, MichaelSH, Michaelt54, Mike Dillon, MikeWazowski, Missy1234, Mkoyle, Mnewhous, Monkeymanman, Moreschi, MovieBuff74, Moviefan, Mr Hall of England, Mr. Nacho de la Libre, Mr.Baker, MrChupon, Mslevy, Mtstroud, Muboshgu, Murph24, Music&Medicine, My toof itz bwoke, NETTKNUT, NHRHS2010, Nabokov, Nandesuka, NatureLover106, New Living Wiki Editor, NewEnglandYankee, Niceguyedc, Njerseyguy, No Guru, Noirish, Northamerica1000, Nues20, Number87, Oanabay04, Obli, OctoberRamonOctober, OettingerCroat, Ohconfucius, OrthodoxCelt, Osomec, Ow i hurt my toof, Owen, POTA, PTJoshua, Panhandleman, Parable1991, Parklandspanaway, Pascoevale, Paul A, Paul Del Delaney, Paul MacDermott, Paul210, Pcpcpc, Pdcook, Peachey88, Pegship, Penguinonice4, Pepso2, Peter Fleet, PhantomS, PhilKnight, Philg88, Philip Stevens, Philip Trueman, Pinethicket, Polyhymnia, Porterhse, Prime-daedalus, Prodego, Professor Von Pie, ProhibitOnions, PuppyOnTheRadio, Purplebackpack89, Pwotter, Quadell, Qwyrxian, RGorman, RHodnett, RSP196607, Radar01, Radio gaga, RadioChuck, RadioFan, Railroad Runners, Rainwarrior, RandomP, Raudys, Raymondwinn, Rdgambola, Reginmund, RenamedUser01302013, Retired and loving it, Rhoffman2, Rich Farmbrough, Rich257, Richard David Ramsey, Richardw, Rick Block, RickK, Rickbolger, Rillian, Ringhorne, RjLesch, Rjwilmsi, Rmhermen, Rms125a@hotmail.com, Rodney Ruff, Rogerd, Rojomoke, Ronbo76, Roo72, Room429, Rossrs, Rothorpe, Rower131, Rschmidt12, Ryssby, S19991002, SILUFND, SMP0328., SNIyer12, Saforrest, Sal Massaro, Salamurai, Sallieparker, Sam, Sam Korn, Sametype23, SarahStierch, SarekOfVulcan, Savantas83, Savolya, Scewing, Schatman, SchuminWeb, ScottSteiner, Seaaron, SeanO, Seaoneil, Searscard, Severa, Shadow1, Shadowjams, Shaun J. Kirkpatrick, Shell Kinney, Shimmera, Shiuheng, Sicamous, SigPig, SilkTork, Simplybarbaric, Simxp, Sintonak.X, Sir Isaac Lime, Sky Captain, Skymasterson, Smashville, Snowolf, Somsack, Somsack101, Spangineer, Sparky222b, Spshu, StAnselm, Steel, Steffaustri, Stephen Bain, Stephenb, Stevecov, StevenInLv, Still Gnash, Strikehold, Studerby, Stwalkerster, Sumahoy, Superbu, Surachit, Surtsicna, Suupa Koopa, Swarto112, T. Anthony, TUF-KAT, Tabercil, Tamfang, Tarohi, Tassedethe, Taykel, Teelie, Teepeetea, TenPoundHammer, Terence, Tesscass, The Man in Question, The Red, The wub, TheGrappler, TheMadBaron, Thingg, Thomas Aquinas, Thortondundee, Tide rolls, TigerShark, Tikiwont, Tills, Timc, Time Dilation Theory, Timothybb, Timrollpickering, Tinton5, Tjmayerinsf, Tomcat7, Tony1, TonyTheTiger, Toof en chocolate, Toofy mcjack, Tregoweth, Tresiden, Trident13, Tuneman42, TyA, UberCryxic, Upsmiler, Vague Rant, ValueForYourPay, Vaquero100, Vchimpanzee, Vcmartin, Versageek, VeryVerily, Vikki1965, Vilartatim, Vintage Music, Violetriga, Vulturell, WFinch, Walloon, Wasted Time R, Wastetimer, Wavelength, We hope, Webclient101, Wedg, Weldc1jr, Wiki libs, WikiBob47, Wikiklrsc, Wild 'n' Flicky, WildCowboy, Wildhartlivie, WimTexas, Wittkowsky, Wknight94, Wmadavis, Wmahan, Woogee, Woohookitty, Wool Mintons, WooteleF, Worthong, X96lee15, Xiahou, Xymmax, YUL89YYZ, Yinzland, Ylee, Zafonic, ZapThunderstrike, Zimmy08210, Zoe, Zytsef, Zzyzx11, ^demon, 1160 anonymous edits

Bob Crosby *Source*: http://en.wikipedia.org/w/index.php?oldid=537940117 *Contributors*: ASK, Aeromedia, Analog Kid, Arjayay, Asnav, BRG, Baseball Bugs, Bblegacy, Betacommand, Billy Hathorn, BurmaShaver, BurtTurgler, Calliopejen1, Chubbles, Crystallina, D6, Dellhpapple, Dionysusacropolis, Dnyhagen, Ebyabe, Eurodog, Fifties, Fiveless, Foofbun, Fuddle, GiantSnowman, Gregbrown, Grutness, Guat6, Igoulet, Ilyanep, JJansen, JazzWard, Jeffrey Mall, John of Reading, Kam Solusar, Ksnow, Kumioko (renamed), Kwiki, Lockley, Lucobrat, Mattbr, Max.inglis, Michael Snow, Mind meal, MrX, Nethgirb, Nickellmusic, Nono64, Number87, Parablooper, Paraparanormal, Pepso, Philip Cross, Piano non troppo, RMHED, Radiohist, Rossrs, SemoArchives, Shadow1, Shimarenda, Sicamous, Steveiz, Strephon, Sweetalkinguy, T. Anthony, Technopat, TenOfAllTrades, TestsPoint, The Prince of Darkness, The Thing That Should Not Be, TheBearPaw, TheParanoidOne, Urhixidur, Ustye, V v p, Vometia, Wayne Slam, We hope, Welsh, Whouk, Wikievil666, Woohookitty, Δ, 110 anonymous edits

Boogie-woogie *Source*: http://en.wikipedia.org/w/index.php?oldid=537110338 *Contributors*: 100keystone, AMCKen, Ahoerstemeier, Alansohn, Altenmann, Andux, AndyBoyd, Andycjp, Anomalocaris, BD2412, Bearian, Bemoeial, BenCrookston, Bibliorock, Bobo192, Brendan Moody, Brunetton, CN3777, Camembert, CanadianLinuxUser, ChristTrekker, Darkcrobat, Dave Bass, Dave314159, Derek R Bullamore, DocterJ1595, Durova, Dvorsky, E2eamon, Everyking, Ewlyahoocom, Fraggle81, Furrykef, Gandydancer, Geekybroad, Gene Nygaard, Gentgeen, Ghmyrtle, Giannioneill, Gilliam, Gwib, Habj, Hmains, Holroy, Hyacinth, Infrogmation, Ish ishwar, J.delanoy, Jacob walker, Jafeluv, Jamespoke, Jerryleelewis1, Jevansen, Jlitton12, Jmg99, Jo.Salmoretti, Joey-das-WBF, Johnpseudo, Jpers36, Jpfagerback, Kaleeyed, Kyng, Lateg, Liftarn, LittleWink, Looneytunas, Lumos3, MXER, Macaronlover, Maddy Mud, Mago266, Marchendoe, Mark91, Matthew Fennell, Mckeanm, Mets501, Mogism, Mooquackwooftweetmeow, Morgan Wright, Mutant Despot, Nadflah, NatureA16, Nickboogie, Nickellmusic, Nickyus, Oldhamlet, OnBeyondZebrax, Ortolan88, Parnas, PedanticallySpeaking, Pedro, Piano58, PigFlu Oink, Pilotguy, Pleasantville, RadioBroadcast, Ragesoss, Red Gown, Redheylin, Rich Farmbrough, Righteous65, Rjwilmsi, RobertG, Rodhullandemu, SJP, Sabrebd, Seraphimblade, Shanes, Shlishke, ShotokanTuning, Sluzzelin, Slysplace, Ssbohio, Steve Pastor, Syp, TUF-KAT, Tarquin, Tekmatic38, That Guy, From That Show!, Topbanana, Vendettax, Verne Equinox, Vidkun, Wikipelli, Woohookitty, Xron, Yossarian, 222 anonymous edits

Boogie Woogie Bugle Boy *Source*: http://en.wikipedia.org/w/index.php?oldid=535785804 *Contributors*: 23skidoo, Absath, Akira625, Alan Liefting, AlanUS, Albaum, Banality, Bevo, Beyond My Ken, Bibliotrope, BigT2006, BokuAlec, Brian the Editor, Buzzz, C colorado, Carlossfsu, Cgingold, Chrisa0001, David Rush, Derek R Bullamore, Design, Durova, Dutchmonkey9000, Exploding Boy, Extraordinary Machine, Feydey, Freakyfoe, GVnayR, Gbleem, George Ho, GoingBatty, GyozaMan, Hhelibeb, InnocuousPseudonym, Internet Czar, Iridescent, J-B, Jack1956, JamesBWatson, Jorgebarrios, Jwrosenzweig, Koavf, Krysee, Lairor, Laoshi888, Leadegroot, Levdr1, MOK120, Mago266, Markt3, Mboverload, Mo ainm, Morgan Wright, Muchness, Omokabish, Plummer, Poohze, Qballbuster2, R'n'B, Rev40e, Rich Farmbrough, Richhoncho, Serein (renamed because of SUL), ShelfSkewed, Snowball1988, Starcheerspeaksnewslostwars, Steelbeard1, Steve Pastor, Tamarkot, Tearlach, TheOldJacobite, Tonyloyals, Trivialist, Ustye, Verne Equinox, WAS, Wasted Time R, Wikid77, Winchelsea, Wolfer68, Woohookitty, Wouh, Ὁ οἶστρος, 100 anonymous edits

Buck Privates *Source*: http://en.wikipedia.org/w/index.php?oldid=532102629 *Contributors*: Altenmann, Altzinn, AttoRenato, Beyond My Ken, Binksternet, Cinemaniac, Coltenstokes, David Gerard, Dhodges, Dmacw6, Donaldd23, Dutchy85, Foofbun, Ghmyrtle, Ian Rose, Jafeluv, Jauerback, Johnsp1, Kelisi, Lugnuts, Mallanox, Mark5677, MarnetteD, Mild Bill Hiccup, Mteson, MysteryDog, Plummer, Polisher of Cobwebs, Queenmomcat, Rettetast, Rev40e, Skier Dude, Sledgeh101, Supernumerary, TheMovieBuff, Tim!, Tjmayerinsf, Waukegan, Wool Mintons, Xufanc, 16 anonymous edits

Burl Ives *Source*: http://en.wikipedia.org/w/index.php?oldid=539206230 *Contributors*: 47SweetBirdofYouth85, Achromatic, AdamBMorgan, After Midnight, Agrophobe, Aldengirl, All Hallow's Wraith, Ameliorate!, Anastrophe, Anonymous from the 21st century, Anthony Winward, Arthemius x, Aruffo, Asmaybe, Aspects, Azumanga1, Bearcat, Bernie Sokolov, Betacommand, Bevo, Big Bird, Billdescoteaux, Billy Hathorn, Biruitorul, Bkalafut, Blkmagwom, BlueMoonlet, Blueboar, Bluebusy, Brholden, Brianhe, BuffaloBob, BuzzWoof, COLA1956, Cburnett, Charles Matthews, ChemMater, Chicheley, Chironomia, Chowbok, Chris66, Chuck72908, Ckim, Coldlullaby, Courcelles, Cresix, Cryptic, Cstaffa, D6, DCEdwards1966, DIDouglass, DL77, Dancing is Forbidden, Darguz Parsilvan, David spector, DavidOaks, Deadguy71, Deb, Deliboo24, Deltabeignet, Denimadept, Dgabbard, Diosprometheus, Download, Dusti, Ebobnar, Emb021, Enviroboy, Eric444, Everyking, Excelsior51, Ferky123, Finwailin, Firsfron, FlashSheridan, Flyingw, Foofbun, Fratrep, Gaius Cornelius, Gamaliel, Garion96, Garr1984, GcSwRhIc, GoingBatty, Good Olfactory, Gr8lyknow, Graham87, Grye, Gwernol, HJKeats, Hamamelis, HarryHenryGebel, Hayford Peirce, Hedgey42, Herostratus, Hifihitman, Hiphats, Hmains, Hmcnally, Hotwine8, Howcheng, Htfiddler, Hydrargyrum, Iconoclast.horizon, Iful, IndulgentReader, Informationfountain, InthePast, IsaacAA, J.delanoy, JFreeman, JGKlein, JMyrleFuller, JSweit8573, JackofOz, Jason Recliner, Esq., Jbarnett49, Jbill007, Joey80, John Price, Johnpacklambert, JustAGal, Justme89, Jzummak, Karaboom, Kchishol1970, Keane4, Ken Burch, Ketiltrout, KevinOKeeffe, Koavf, Konczewski, Kranar drogin, Kriple3, Kumioko (renamed), Lazugod, LenBudney, Leon7, Lhb1239, LilHelpa, Lilmul123, LordHuffNPuff, LtNOWIS, Magda, Manuel Trujillo Berges, Marchi1856, MarnetteD, MartinUK, Masked Mutant, Mattbrundage, Mauitunes, Mayumashu, Mcsteven, Mdumas43073, MegX, Mike 7, MontanaMax, MrDolomite, Msw1002, Muhandes, Music2611, Nevermore27, NitekMobilian, Noviracer, Numskll, OGO50, Oanabay04, Od Mishehu, OnBeyondZebrax, PCSammons, PacificBoy, Patchyreynolds, Paul MacDermott, Peregrine Fisher, Peterkehoe2468, Phaedra1970, Phaeton23, Philip Cross, Pigman, Pinkadelica, Quebec99, RGS31, RadioBroadcast, Raymondwinn, Recognizance, Red Slash, Redlentil, Ricky81682, Rjwilmsi, Rlevse, RobDe68, RobH103, Robearsn, Rossrs, Sam, Sandstein, SavageHenry77, Scarpy, SchuminWeb, Shadow6677, Shadowfax521, Shuttrbug53, Sillyfolkboy, SlubGlub, Spartaz, Sq178pv, Stoopsklan, Studerby, Sumahoy, TJRC, TPIRFanSteve, TRBP, Tassedethe, Ted Wilkes, Teeb, TenPoundHammer, Terrence Fraser, The Wookieepecian, Thefourdotelipsis, Thismightbezach, Thofts, Tinton5, Tjmayerinsf, TopScumOne, Tregoweth, Truthanado, Tyros1972, Unschool, UnvoicedConsonant, Valentinejoesmith, Varlaam, VeryVerily, Vjamesv, W guice, Waacstats, Wachholder0, Wbwn, Wildhartlivie, Woohookitty, Zav, Zephyrnthesky, Zoe, Zzyzx11, Ὁ οἶστρος, 314 anonymous edits

Candyman (Christina Aguilera song) *Source*: http://en.wikipedia.org/w/index.php?oldid=537610362 *Contributors*: -Majestic-, 17Drew, 1zackman, 23sk, Aaktt, Acalamari, Addie555, AdrianoMoura, Aguilerlittle, Ahmetyal, AlbertSM, Alecsdaniel, Alexianna1988, Ali, Amylee-britney, Angel310, Angmering, Another Believer, Anotherwikipedian, Artisticguy99, Aspects, BGTopDon, Baby16, Babyjazspanail, Barbas5, Basinger19, Beagle5589, Bellatrix Kerrigan, Bgwhite, Bhaggers, Bhiinoe, Biagio2103, Bigjimr, Binksternet, BoneStorm, Bouncehoper, Bull Borgnine, Buzzz, C777, CND, Calabe1992, Candyo32, CarbonRod85, Cardcapturs, Catsmartie, Chad427, Chrisdogz, Christopher Higgins 93, Chronisgr, Cocoaguy, Coko1284, Correctordj, Crazy in Love with Beyonce, Crocodileman, Crumbsucker, DKfan1, DanV, Dancebert, Davidwr, Dbunkley6, DepressedPer, Derek R Bullamore, Dirrtykidd, Dobie80, Dragunova, Dutchmonkey9000, Easy4me, Efe, Electric Storm89, Emanspinners, Enanoj1111, Ericorbit, Esprit15d, Everyking, Flojo2008, Frazzle, Froxen11, Froxxen, GSNFFJTR, GassyGuy, Genieofmusic, Geokaii, Gimmetoo, Glane23, Goldddfish, Gonzalet, Goodforlife, Hahc21, Hayleymarilyn, HereIam11, Hiltonhampton, Hotwiki, I teh yuh, Iokerapid, J 1982, JGabbard, JYi, Jameboy, Jaydec, Jeffq, Jellyfish99, Jesscharmed7, Jllb21, Joeyjackpot, Jonpro, JustAGal, Justincovington, Karin127, Karleysuen, Kmc stripped, Kminato5, Koavf, Kraft., Kransky, Kumioko (renamed), Kww, Lallybrooky, Latka, Lazy610, Libra15, LilHelpa, Lillygirl, LindsayH, Ljósgeisli, Los besos, MZMcBride, Magioladitis, Magnius, Manofradio, Mariglee2012, Marmac87, Martin19, Mas 18 dl,

Olfactory, GorillaWarfare, Gossipbangbang, GotMilk3, GothGrrrl, Gpratts06, GraemeL, Graham87, Great Scott, GreekStar12, GreenKid, Greg 2me, Gregstoll, Grenno, Grey Shadow, Grinv, Gritironskillet, Grubber, Grumpyy, Guanaco, Guat6, Gubel, Gurch, Gurubrahma, Gwernol, H, H Bruthzoo, HJKeats, HTurtle, Hadal, Hadima, HaeB, Hagerman, Haham hanuka, Hailey C. Shannon, Hall Monitor, Hallucinations, Hamletg, Hammersoft, Hapsiainen, Harman18, Harrisju, Harry**, Harry-potter-mania, Harvey100, Hatefest, Hatto0467, Hbent, Hdt83, Headbomb, HelenMB, Hellowgow20, Henry Flower, Hephaestos, Heraldro, HereIam11, Heroin-owns-my-life, HeyNow10029, Heycherry, Hiltonhampton, Hippi ippi, Hmains, Hml13, Hmwith, Hobo joe 3rd, Hog2, Honbicot, Hot acid, Hotwiki, Hotwine8, HowardRob, Hu, Hunny 90, Huntster, Hydrogen Iodide, Hyenaste, Hynca-Hooley, I have puppets made from SOCKS (wink wink), I'll bring the food, I-Podfreak123, IJALB, INXS-Girl, Iam, Iamthecheese44, Ian Pitchford, Ianblair23, Ibanez RYM, Icemanofbarcelona101, Iconoclast09, Idealintellect, Iggy Ax, Ik.pas.aan, Ikkomuitnederland, Illegitimate Barrister, Ilyan, ImNotRichImStillLyin, Imcsister, In Defense of the Artist, IndulgentReader, Informationadvocate, Insaneace1, Inter, Interestedscholar, Irishguy, Irk, Isinbill, Isittruebabyyy, Istabo, ItsZae, Itsbydesign, Ivan Bajlo, Ixfd64, J Di, J Milburn, J-love-lee, J.MENSAH, J.delanoy, JHMM13, JHunterJ, JJKL7, JJonathan, JLaTondre, JRHorse, JT312, JYi, JYolkowski, Jack O'Lantern, JackO'Lantern, Jackal09, Jackol, Jaga185, Jaganath, Jamalar, James26, JamesAM, JamesBWatson, JamesHeil, Jamieli, Janejellyroll, Janilson1995, Jaqura, Jarajet89, Jarble, JarlaxleArtemis, Jarryl, Jarvis03, Jason voorhees, JasonRR, Jasonguy13, Jaxl, Jay2009m, Jayojay, Jayy008, Jaz-Low, Jazdanziger, Jazz2210, Jd027, Jeanenawhitney, Jedi Striker, Jeff Muscato, JeffHCross, Jeffklein, Jeffykan, Jem5218, Jemiller226, Jennica, Jenniferpress, Jeremy0506, Jesus bronze85, Jesus878, Jfabulash, Jgera5, Jh51681, Jigsaw9, Jim Douglas, Jim Michael, Jimarey, Jimmjet89, Jkelly, Jllb21, Jmusc85, Jmyx, Jnorton7558, Jodeh, JoelHorton 1, Joey Penguine, John, John Broughton, John FitzGerald, John Lake, John Vandenberg, John254, JohnKG, Johnciacci, Johnleemk, Johnny Sumner, Johnnya2k6, Johnpacklambert, Joliefille, JonathanNoyola, Jonathannew7, Jonel, Jonhmayer-fã, Jorgex16, Joseph Solis in Australia, Josephishere, Josh Rumage, Journalist, Jpagan09, Jpbowen, Jpete, Jphil126, Js2Jo, Jsc83, Jtkiefer, Julius1990, Jump01, JuneGloom07, Juruco, Justincovington, Jvbishop, Jw21, JzG, K4ng, KJS77, Kageorge, Kaiwhakahaere, KanditaChampion, Kane5187, Kanjiiroo, Kanonkas, Kanyam, Karaveks voice, Karleysuen, Kate, Katwmn6, Kbdank71, Ke$ha-fa, KeithH, KellyRoche, Kellyclarkson22, Kellycya, Kencokamo, Kennan1, Keraunoscopia, Kernow, Kevin, KevinC2125, Kevindl1985, Khalif, Khoiifiish, KickoMan69, Kidlittle, Kigono, Kikkokalabud, Kilka, Kimchi.sg, Kimiko20, Kimon, King Bee, Kingspice, Kinnitch, Kintetsubuffalo, Kiran Gopi, KittenKlub, Kj8744, Kjmt, Kjoonlee, Kleinzach, Klutzulmaniack, Kmayhew, Kmc stripped, KnowledgeOfSelf, Knucmo2, Koavf, Kobe1444, Kokokaykay, Kraft., KrakatoaKatie, Kristina2477, Krystina10, Ksood91, Kubigula, Kukini, Kungfuadam, Kuru, Kusunose, Kww, Kyla, Kyorosuke, L.a.m.b, LAUGH90, LAX, LSmith, LaTraviata1453, Labird, Lakers, Laps87, Larry Yuma, Larry laptop, Lawrence Cohen, Lay Muthaphukkin T, Ldog00, Leafyplant, Leftus, LegatoXxXxXxXx, Legolas2186, Legomyeggo252, Lehla, Lemonade51, Lenin1991, Leonaistheoneforever, Leroyinc, Les Invisibles, Leszek Jańczuk, Levineps, Lewiscarrol, Lhademmor, LiDaobing, LibLord, LifeloverElena, Lightdarkness, Lightmouse, LightningHD, Lights, Lil Flip246, Lil bratz gurl00, Lil devil20002, Lil-luke93, Lil-unique1, LilHelpa, Lilac Soul, Lilplayboii, Lilteen17, Lilypada94, LinaMishima, Liquid6908, Lisasmall, Little Mountain 5, LittleOldMe, LittleWink, Livelikemusic, Lizzy Green, Ljhenshall, Llbegines, Llola11, Lloydhackl, Lmz00, Loca pixie, LonerXL, Loop202, Lopeztonight, Lordelliott, Lordmontu, Los besos, Louievanstone, Louisdf, Love me 33, LoveXtina-x, Lovelette81, LovelieHeart, Lucas RdS, Lucas233, Luckyslimester, Lugnuts, Luigi-ish, Luigiboy18, Luis m luque, LukeDG, LukeM212, Luna Santin, Lupo, Lxhizy, Lynzie2000jt, Lyricposter, Lyricremover, M.O.X, MC MasterChef, MC-Balazs, MCRGIRL, MER-C, MK, MK8, MONGO, MPA40, MZMcBride, Ma xyz, MacGyverMagic, Mad Hatter, Mad akhil 96, MadGuy7023, MadJack, Madchester, Maddyfan, Madeleine1728, Magic-Bunny, Magiciandude, Magister Mathematicae, Mahalkitta, Mahanga, Mahdiislam, Mailer diablo, Maine12329, Majinsnake, Majorly, Malcolmo, Malkinann, Malli19, Malo, Mappychris, Marc-André Aßbrock, Marc-Olivier Pagé, Mareino, Marek69, MariAna Mimi, Marioh13, Mark.deane, MarkSutton, MarkWegener, Marketdiamond, MarkusBJoke, Marshall, Marsvin123, Martianmen, Martin H., Martin villafuerte85, Martin19, Martyy1, Mashcash13, Mason.Jones, Master Jay, MasterPiece99, Masónico, Matheus!, Mathiassandell, Mattgirling, MatthewMain, Mav, Max Liron, Maxim04, Maxwell Derwinee, Mayumashu, Mayur, McMare's, Mcbridelr, Mcelite, Meanubeanu, Meelar, MegX, Megaasdfjk, Megastrike14, Mel Etitis, Melander, Melonkelon, Memo952, Merchbow, Merlito, Meryl-H, Messy Thinking, Metropolitan90, MgCupcake, Mhiji, Michael Devore, MichaelSkinsFan, Michaelas10, Michaelpremsrirat, Michbich, Michiganb2323, MickWithoutGlasses, Midas touch, MightyWarrior, Migospia, Mikaey, Mike 7, Mike F, Mikmoonie, MilCivHR, MilaSveta13, Minesweeper, Mini-Geek, Miss Rara, Missy1234, MissyMusic13, Mistermagoo90, Mlaffs, Mlowin, Mmckee350, Mnpeter, Modulatum, Mogism, Mohammed Alrubay, Mommaloveuk, Moondyne, Morenooso, Morhange, Mormegil, Morning Sunshine, Morwen, Moxy, Mpo90, Mr Ar-Br, MrBCochrane, MrBubulino, MrFacts2xx, MrFish, MrFizyx, Mrmagoo2006, Mrschimpf, Mrwhatchacallit, Mrxerox, MsJessicaDevlin, Msteal2342, Mstreysongz1, Mszvicious, Muffynbear, Mushroom, MusicGeek101, Musicpvm, Muéro, Mwanner, MyNoseSmellsLikePork, Myke209, Mynewall22, Myownworst, Myrockstar, Mysid, Mystic chick, Mysticmartin, N1mr0d, NBJames, NHRHS2010, NJZombie, NRGKutKlose, Nakon, Narayan89, Nathan Johnson, Nathan jones244, Nathan86, Natx, Naur, NawlinWiki, Nburden, Ndgp, Ndugu, Necromanticism, Need some hypnotherapy, Neilc, Nellua, Nelson m, Nelstar, Neptunekh2, Nerrawllehctim, Neurolysis, Nevermore27, NewWaveRomantic, Newone, NiallHatchell1996, Nicastar, Nicblais, Nick, Nicolas Love, Nicole401, Nightquest, Nigosh, Nihiltres, Nikai, Nikki, Nikki wiggins, Nikki311, NinjaChucks, Nishkid64, Niteowlneils, Njoku06, Nlu, No Guru, NoOne898, Nodoubt9203, Nofoolz, Nohansen, Nomaam57, Nonstopdrivel, Noolmusic, Norahjones-cover, Not69usickobut96, Notepadzone, Notheruser, Nowhy, NrDg, Nrswanson, Nummer29, Nuttycoconut, Nymf, Nzseries1, OVERM1ND, Oatmeal batman, Obacoomb, Oda Mari, Ohconfucius, OhitstragikX, Oidia, OjeB, Okmjuhb, Okoku, Olbap, Old Right, Oldelpaso, Olijven, Oliver Pereira, Oliver202, Olivewildes, Olivia Bush, Olliyeah, OmegaXmutantX, Omernos, Omicronpersei8, OnBeyondZebrax, OnFire, Oneononetvseries, Only, Oogity boogity, Opinoso, Oppman, OregonD00d, Orginalinfo, Orphanannie, Ortolan88, Ottawa4ever, Otto ter Haar, OutOfControl2, OutbackKidd, OwenX, Oxcarlima, Oxymoron83, Ozkithar Salas, P toolan, PJ05, PMS1234, PTSE, PXE-M0F, PacifistPrime, Pandyzee, Panfakes, Paperdoll51, Pardy, Parisfan0000, Part of me 2, Parys, Patesta, Pathoschild, PatrikR, Patstuart, Paul A, Paul August, Paul Erik, Paulobr, PaultjeKwik, Pcpcpc, Pcsbr, PeaceNT, Pedia6, Pepepe2009, Perfect77, Perfectblue97, Perkyville, Persian Poet Gal, PersianiMalibran, Peruvianllama, Petee, Peter2012, PeterS32, Petergriffin9901, Peterkostos, Pgan002, Pgk, Phan1991, Phatcat68, Philippe, Phoenix Hacker, Phoenix V, PhoenixPrince, Piano non troppo, Pil56, Pilotguy, PinkKnight, Piranga, Plavalagunanbanshee, Ploghbill, Plumadesabiduría, Plumphumps, Poikpoik, Poisonparadise98, Pojojo, Pompertown, Portillo, Poshb, Powelldinho, Powerofrussia2, Ppinette, Ppoi307, Prayer for the wild at heart, Premeditated Chaos, Prepelos, Preshpopa2910, Presidentluis, Prof. MagneStormix, Prolog, Prophet101, Prunejuicemontes, Pseudo-Richard, Psy guy, Puertorico1, Punishinglemur, Punk ryder88, Purgatory Fubar, Pwqn, Qforq, Qhalilipa, Qtboy120, Quanto2010, Quark7, Quasipalm, QuasyBoy, Queerbubbles, QuiteUnusual, Qxz, R&Blover1996, R7604, RB972, RBBrittain, RC1995, RHaworth, RKMiner5, Rada526, Radan92, RadicalBender, Radmatt1021, Raine r pierre, Rama, Ramanujanredux, Randee15, RandomEnigmaReborn, RandomXYZb, Ranggaeuy224, Ranveig, RaqiwasSushi, Rararanging, Rasgfsadgas, RattleandHum, Raul654, Raventime, Ray-zin, Rayato, Rdsmith4, Realist2, Realityme, Recliner Man, Red Director, RedRose333, RedWolf, Reidlos, RememberTheTime, Renné, Reptileeater, Reqluce, Requiem&Dream, Retiono Virginian, Rettetast, Revived, Revth, RexNL, Rg3, Rhrad, Ric168, Rich Farmbrough, Richard Arthur Norton (1958-), Riker5589, Risteard B, Ritchie333, Rito Revolto, Rjanag, Rjwilmsi, Rklawton, Rlest, Rmurkowsk, Robert Moore, Robert.newham, Robinepowell, Robinhio84, Robmicklethwaite, Rocastelo, RockStar50, Rocksteadyman2, RodrigoCC, Rodrigogomespaixao, Rojamariposa5285, Roleplayer, Ronhjones, Roscelese, Rossrs, Roux, RoySmith, RoyalBlueStuey, Royalbroil, Rrhyno, Rs09985, Rsolermo, Rtg1980, Ruddager, RudolfRed, Rudwolf, Rusted AutoParts, RuurdWoltring, Rwolf040, RxS, Ryan Postlethwaite, Ryan3074, Ryannnn2, Ryn2me, Ryoga Godai, Ryulong, SD6-Agent, SE7, SMC89, SMasters, SNIyer12, SQB, ST47, SU Linguist, Sadistik, Saguamundi, Salamurai, Sally Drizzleschlitz, Salsb, Salviiboii617, Sam Blacketer, Sam Hocevar, Samfim, Samspam3, Samuel.hinch@hotmail.com, Sandstein, Santiagokdasilva1, Sapient one, Saranghae honey, Sashak90, Sasquatch, Save-Me-Oprah, Sawoe, Sbrools, Sc135, Scarian, Sceptre, Schroeder74, SchuminWeb, ScorpionSeven, Sct72, Sdma89, Seanfs2010, Seanmathis, Seanmathis26, Sebascoaster, Secfan, Securiger, Sef aguilera, SemiramideSutherland, Ser Amantio di Nicolao, Sesmith, Seth Ilys, Seán Travers, ShadowRanger, Shadowjams, Shakesomeaction, Shanel, Shanes, Shawis, Sherool, Shikaidou, Shimmera, Shirulashem, ShoShoGirl, Shoessss, Shotcaller8, Shultze, SidP, Siemens2, Sietse Snel, SillyHoe, Silvergoat, Silvermen, SimonP, Simpsoboy, Simpsonian, Sintonak.X, Sir Louis, Sixtyplace9472, Sjakkalle, Sjorford, Sk8erock, SkyWalker, Skye 0913, Sl84, Slgrandson, Smash, Smegans, Smilemean, Smilingsuzy, Smokefan2007, Snail2, Snail456, SnapSnap, Snoyes, SoWeirdBoy, Soetermans, Sofffie7, Solomon7968, Solotwilight, Somemoron, Sometimesdee, Soonpush, Sophie52, Soulsiren244, SpLoT, Spanglej, Spellcast, Spencerlaf2009, Spiceitup08, Spitts88, SpuriousQ, Squeak90, SqueakBox, SrSeniorCitizen, Srushe, StAnselm, Staecker, Stakelum, Stan weller, StarbucksFreak, Starswept, Status, Steel, Stephenchou0722, Stevertigo, Stevey7788, Sticksandstonesxy1, Stifle, Stinkyturd andrew, Stizz, Storched, Stpatty91, Stranded Pirate, Strippedx, Strokeofluck, Stupid Corn, Stwalkerster, Suduser85, Sugarcubez, Suicidalhamster, Summer Song, SummerPhD, Sunbeam22, Supermatique, SupremoJunior, Surfeited, Suyw, Svick, Sweetloulou, Sylent, Syncere, SyntaxError55, T. Anthony, TAnthony, TBM10, TCR11, TFOWR, TGZ, THF, TKD, TPIRFanSteve, TR122, TUF-KAT, TV1981HS, Tabercil, Tabletop, Takenages, Talkwithme, Tamagotchirules, Tamara4006, Tanaats, Tarheelz123, Tasie, Tassedethe, Tayduh, Tbhotch, Teachereddie, Techi2ee, Tekks, Tellmex3baby, Teman13, Tenebrae, Terneris, Terrence235, ThaddeusB, Thankyoubaby, Thatnewguy, Thatsthewaytodoit, The Candyboy, The Man in Question, The Rambling Man, The Rogue Leader, The dude 2, The undertow, The wub, The-G-Unit-Boss, ThePointblank, TheRee BritneySpears, TheRevolution7, TheRingess, TheSeez, TheVerificator, Thebatman312, Theda, Thehalfside, Thehelpfulone, Theroadislong, Therockishot, Thesadisticcheeseburgerpickle1, Thevampireashlee, Thingg, Thinker12, ThisIsMyName, Thomas Aquinas, Thomas G Graf, ThomasK, Thorpe, Thunderbunny, Tide rolls, Tigermichal, Tikkuy, Tim riley, Timclare, Timmansfield, Timmystix, Timrollpickering, Tinton5, Tiptoety, Titoxd, Tjvalerio, Tkynerd, Tlatito, Tmorin, Todaealas, Tom Reedy, Tomdobb, Tommyindahouseuk@hotmail.com, Tonsofpcs, Tony1, Tony221268, Torrmallin, Tra, Tracibaby10, Tranquility2007, TravisTX, Tregoweth, TrentJones, Treybien, Triggy, Trivialist, Triwbe, Trnhgduoc2222, Trontonian, Trunks ishida, Trusilver, Truth005, TruthGal, Trödel, Tsadaqbmein, Tuba mirum, Tubby, Tubesurfer, Tubeyoumania, TucsonDavid, Tugaygs1905, Turkishbob, Turzh, Twopenguins, Txtcircus, Tzipi, U.S.A.U.S.A.U.S.A., UNDISCOVERED, Uglinessman, Ulrikke1994, Ultatri, Ultimate Star Wars Freak, UltraEdit, Ultralord910, Unbreakable kat, Underneath-it-All, Unisycho56, UnknownDude, Unreal7, Unyoyega, Uolll, Urb1972, Urmomsbuttsmells, Utcursch, UtherSRG, Vanessahudgens22, Vanilla ninja, Vanished user alaij23jrkef8hj4fiu34t34, Vanished188, Vanyca, Varlaam, VegaDark, Veggiegirl, Velten, VictoriousUser, Victorshang, Vikramsidhu, Violetriga, Vipetthegreat, Vis-a-visconti, Vj rom, Vorash, Vulturell, WJetChao, WLU, Wackley, Walklikealegend, Wallstowalls90, Wandering Ghost, Ward3001, Warriorboy85, Wasell, Wasted Time R, WatchAndObserve, Watquaza, Wavelength, WazzerAlvin, Webelongtogether2005, Weex121, Wei Farg, Welsh, WereWolf, Wereon, Werldwayd, Wesley1995, Wester, Weyes, Whitty4u, Whollabilla, Wi-king, Widr, Wifione, WikHead, Wiki Raja, Wiki alf, Wiki edit Jonny, WikiLeon, WikiRedactor, Wikid77, Wikilebrity, Wikiscribe, Wildhartlivie, Will Beback Auto, Willallen93, Willi173, Williamborg, Wimt, Winnermario, Witan, Wknight94, Wmahan, Wneedham02, Wo78, Wolfkeeper, Woodstock in Bangock, Woohookitty, Wwfanz, X LadySweetness x, X-Tina Eddie's Mamacita, XHugoTheNerd, Xcali, Xeno, Xezbeth, Xionel, Xiong Chiamiov, Xkillinourownx, Xmen4ever8290, Xtin21bass, Xtina knowles, Xtina4eva07, Xtremejet, XuxiRawe22, Xx kidschoice xx, YOPMISMO, Yamla, Yancyfry jr, Yanksox, Yboris, Yeldarb68, Yestyle, Yodler, Your gamerican, Yourseeisme, Yrymar, Yuckfoo, Yummygjd, Yvesnimmo, Z.E.R.O., Zacharee, Zaxby, Zengarden17, Zethraith, ZhaoHong, Zimbardo Cookie Experiment, Zippanova, Zoe, Zondor, Zouavman Le Zouave, Zuracech lordum, Zvar, Zzuuzz, Zzzzzzus, ^demon, Δ, 5360 anonymous edits

Ciribiribin *Source*: http://en.wikipedia.org/w/index.php?oldid=525979393 *Contributors*: Baseball Bugs, Graham87, Lantana11, Nickellmusic, RMc, Richhoncho, Robert Worthing, Starzynka, Wlexxx, 10 anonymous edits

Civilization (song) *Source*: http://en.wikipedia.org/w/index.php?oldid=525015788 *Contributors*: Ary29, BRG, Bernium, DarthBinky, Durova, FallingOut, GamerPro64, Guoguo12, JoeShmoe64, Jpbowen, Koavf, Larrybob, Markoff Chaney, Mbakkel2, Pi zero, PotentialDanger, Richhoncho, SidP, Soetermans, 22 anonymous edits

Dan Dailey *Source*: http://en.wikipedia.org/w/index.php?oldid=539379170 *Contributors*: 1962monroe, After Midnight, All Hallow's Wraith, Amcaja, Anthony Winward, Bbahler, Bearcat, Bender21435, Billy Hathorn, Blaxthos, Bobo192, Broadweighbabe, CanisRufus, Cburnett, Charles A. Brown, Clarityfiend, Cliff1911, D-Rock, D6, Darkwind, Debresser, Delirium, Embram,

Foofbun, Gary4362, Grimmnj, Guanaco, Gymclasshero90, IndulgentReader, Infrogmation, J. Van Meter, JGG59, JGKlein, JackofOz, Jaimelare, JillandJack, Johnpacklambert, Kbdank71, Kumioko (renamed), LaVidaLoca, LiteraryMaven, Lockley, Love Crusader, Manuel Trujillo Berges, MisfitToys, Monkeyzpop, Oobopshark, Otto4711, PamD, Papa November, Pearle, Qdiderot, REVUpminster, Rjwilmsi, Rock4arolla, Ron whisky, Rossrs, Sallyrob, Savolya, Ser Amantio di Nicolao, ShelfSkewed, Sjkoblentz, Sumahoy, TheCustomOfLife, Tjmayerinsf, TonyW, UtherSRG, Vary, Welsh, Wrightaway, Wytzox1, Zoe, 33 anonymous edits

Danny Kaye *Source*: http://en.wikipedia.org/w/index.php?oldid=539353640 *Contributors*: 1exec1, ANTONIOROCKS, Absalom89, Academic Challenger, Adam Bishop, Afterwriting, Agather, AgentPeppermint, Aka, AlbertSM, All Hallow's Wraith, Allan warren, Amazinrick, Ameliorate!, Amicon, And we drown, Anthony Winward, Anthony22, Archer3, Aruffo, AvatarMN, BalthCat, Bart, Baseball Bugs, Bbsrock, Bergfalke2, Beta m, Bettyc, BigHaz, Biglez, Billy Hathorn, Bisbis, Blaxthos, Blueporch, Bobblewik, Bobdaman123123, Bunnyhop11, BurmaShaver, Buzzlightyear, Bwmodular, CONFIQ, CanisRufus, Carlj7, Carlton30458AZ, Cburnett, Chicheley, Chirop, Chowbok, Christian List, Clarityfiend, Cleduc, Cliff1911, Closedmouth, Cocoinfolol, CommonsDelinker, Connormah, Conscious, Contaldo80, ContiAWB, Conversion script, Coren, Crouchend, Cst17, D6, David spector, Davolson, Ddkkll, Deb, Denovoid, Design, Dhodges, Discospinster, Dizmaster, Dougie monty, Dpbsmith, Drmargi, Dungodung, E-Kartoffel, Efilipek, Emerson7, Exocet1, FT2, Fetchcomms, Fg2, Figaro, Filpaul, Firsfron, Flami72, Flyguy33, Foofbun, Franck Holland, Gareth E Kegg, Gcstackmoney, Gilliam, Gogue2, Goomoo, Gotrexman, Graham87, GrahamColm, Green Cardamom, Hendren, Hesca419, Heslopian, Hydroxonium, Hymanbrown, IP4240207xx, Ianblair23, Ilikeflylady, InManusTuas, Informationfountain, Infrogmation, JMiall, Jack O'Lantern, JackFloridian, JackofOz, Janke, Japanese Searobin, Jarro 2783, JasonAQuest, Jcb10, Jeanenawhitney, Jeff G., Jeff Muscato, Jengod, Jimknut, Jleigh.nolan, Joefromrandb, John Craig Sharpe, Johnpdeever, Jtdirl, Julia Rossi, JustAGal, Justme89, Jwgrayson51, Jzummak, Kaiwhakahaere, Kak500, Karen Johnson, Kbdank71, Keane4, Keith D, Kennvido, Kevlar67, Kingturtle, Kintetsubuffalo, Kiwegapa, KoaWood, Koyaanis Qatsi, Krkey, Ktr101, Kukla22, Kumioko (renamed), Kurykh, Levineps, LilHelpa, Lord Opeth, Lucobrat, Lufiend, Lugnuts, Lwc, M.A.Dicker, MachoCarioca, Majorly, Malcolmxl5, Mangwanani, MarnetteD, Matchups, Mattbr, Mayumashu, MegX, Mercurywoodrose, Michael David, Michael Devore, Mrblondnyc, Mrodowicz, Msignor, Muboshgu, Mwprods, N5iln, Nandt1, Neddyseagoon, NielsenGW, Nono64, Notmicro, Oanabay04, OlEnglish, Omizzle77, Orbicle, PDH, PJM, Paul A, Paul MacDermott, Pauli133, Paxsimius, Penale52, Pensativa, Piceainfo, Piperdown, Pissant, Plasticspork, Politepunk, Ponyo, Professor Von Pie, Prolog, Purplebackpack89, R sirahata, RHodnett, RSido, Radiojane, Railwayfan2005, Reywas92, Rhapsodyrock, Rich Farmbrough, Richard K. Carson, Rjstern, Rjwilmsi, Rodhullandemu, Rogerd, Ron Davis, Rossrs, Rynasaurus, SE7, Salamurai, Sam, Sam Blacketer, SatyrTN, Savolya, ScarlettW, Ser Amantio di Nicolao, Shir-El too, Shsilver, SidP, Siryendor, Skylap, Skysmith, Smartie2thaMaxXx, Someone else, Somerwind, Spamer123, Srich32977, Ssbohio, StAnselm, Straw Cat, Stroppolo, Sumahoy, Surtsicna, TMC1982, Tassedethe, Tborsari, Tham153, The News Hound, TheCustomOfLife, Theonemacduff, Thismightbezach, Thor Dockweiler, Tim Thomason (usurped), Tinton5, Tjmayerinsf, Tobias Hoevekamp, Toddsschneider, Tony Sidaway, Tony1, TonyTheTiger, Topbanana, Trevor MacInnis, Trovatore, Unimaginable666, Upsmiler, Utcursch, Vancouveriensis, Vanished user 5zariu3jisj0j4irj, Vis-a-visconti, Vobor, Vocaro, W guice, WBardwin, WHPratt, Wahkeenah, We hope, Werdnawerdna, Who, Wikievil666, Wikiwatcher1, Wildhartlivie, WilliamSommerwerck, Wjvanb, Wlmg, Woohookitty, Wool Mintons, Zaslav, Zeiden, Zenomax, Zhicks, Ziko, Ὁ οἶστρος, 283 anonymous edits

Dick Haymes *Source*: http://en.wikipedia.org/w/index.php?oldid=538404146 *Contributors*: AdamantAzoth, Aldengirl, AmyNelson, Attilios, BRG, Barry Moreno, Bobby H. Heffley, CelticJobber, Colonies Chris, Coppertop Guy, D6, Destry, Elonka, Emory20, Ericorbit, Findline, Frank0102, Fredrik, Gaius Cornelius, Ghmyrtle, Gimmetoo, Good Olfactory, Hb2019, Hffan1, Hifihitman, JackofOz, Joefromrandb, John of Reading, JohnRogers, Kariteh, Kellogg257, Korny O'Near, Kumioko (renamed), Lugnuts, Marcus2, Mattbr, Nickellmusic, NuclearWarfare, Otrfan, Paul MacDermott, Pepso2, Pfw, Pinkadelica, Professor Von Pie, Reality Maker, RexNL, Richigi, Rjwilmsi, Rms125a@hotmail.com, Rossrs, Saugekaktus, Seaaron, SimonP, SmartyBoots, Srich32977, Symphony Girl, TGC55, TV Tony, Tassedethe, Tcrimans, Tiniuk, Tjmayerinsf, Trident13, Wildhartlivie, Wolfer68, 49 anonymous edits

Don't Fence Me In (song) *Source*: http://en.wikipedia.org/w/index.php?oldid=533310331 *Contributors*: 3pny, Abderitestatos, Airproofing, Alandeus, Algabal, AndrewHowse, Derdingle, Desert2mtngirl, Durova, Freakofnurture, Giovannii84, GoingBatty, Hmains, Hydrargyrum, InnocuousPseudonym, JohnRogers, Kindii, Kiyoweap, Korky Day, Martarius, Mbakkel2, Owenc@hubris.net, Ozzieboy, Perey, Rlcantwell, Russell corbyn, Somsack, Sparsefarce, Starcheerspeaksnewslostwars, Tassedethe, TenPoundHammer, TestsPoint, Theda, Trivialist, WandaRMinstrel, Warpozio, WikHead, Wikid77, Wm. H. Young, Wolfer68, Woohookitty, Ὁ οἶστρος, 38 anonymous edits

Don't Rob Another Man's Castle *Source*: http://en.wikipedia.org/w/index.php?oldid=535784509 *Contributors*: AjaxSmack, Carlossfsu, Housewatcher, LongLiveMusic, Richhoncho

Dot Records *Source*: http://en.wikipedia.org/w/index.php?oldid=538081677 *Contributors*: 78.26, AlbertSM, Avs5221, BRG, Barrympls, Bearcat, Chubbles, Circozoppe, Craggiehope, DYNAMIC D, Derek R Bullamore, DougHill, EddieHugh, Eric444, FMAFan1990, Fratrep, Gaius Cornelius, Garr1984, Give2ThumbsUp, Gyrofrog, H.W. Tiedtke, Infrogmation, Itsfullofstars, Izzy007, Jimgiz, Jnocook, JohnRogers, JustAGal, Ketiltrout, Klemen Kocjancic, Kody-the-Fox, Ks45, Lindagaph, Lugnuts, Mdoc7, Middayexpress, Oatmeal batman, OlEnglish, Oldiesplayer, Parkwells, PhilKnight, Pjs012915, Plasticup, Plrk, Rothorpe, Rschroeder000, Steelbeard1, Stormyhawn, Svick, TTillman7, TenPoundHammer, Theseekerhp, Tregoweth, Varlaam, Verne Equinox, Viajero, Warpozio, Waterthedog, Wbwn, Wellsjc, Wknight94, Xenhark, Zephyrad, 87 anonymous edits

Down in the Valley (folk song) *Source*: http://en.wikipedia.org/w/index.php?oldid=538988486 *Contributors*: Athaenara, Gil Gamesh, GoingBatty, IMagainstYOU, Jamestowne, Jbvoinet, Kourkoumelis, LightningMan, Marcus Brute, Mathonius, Muhandes, PorchPostPapa, Waacstats, Winter Maiden, 27 anonymous edits

Ernest Tubb *Source*: http://en.wikipedia.org/w/index.php?oldid=537567557 *Contributors*: Aboutmovies, Airproofing, Angela, Anger22, Antediluvian67, BD2412, Badbilltucker, Bluerasberry, Brianyoumans, Briguy52748, Brycechandlertubb, BuffaloBob, Camembert, Cartman0128, Cfreese1977, Chuckiesdad, Cmdrjameson, Crystallina, D6, DabMachine, DavidWBrooks, Derek R Bullamore, Doover, Empirecontact, Eric444, Everyking, Goodshoped35110s, Hifihitman, Infrogmation, JNW, Jimerb, John Abbe, Johnnymackmusic, JustAGal, Kaldari, Kennethhari, Ketiltrout, KittenKlub, Leodmacleod, Mattbr, Mdebets, MegX, Michael David, Miller17CU94, Mukadderat, Nv8200p, Popiloll, R'n'B, RadioBroadcast, Rees11, Scott Frans, Scwlong, Ted Wilkes, Teeb, TenPoundHammer, Tijuana Brass, Vipinhari, Waacstats, WereSpielChequers, Wiki libs, William G Edgar, Wisekwai, 46 anonymous edits

Fallout 3 *Source*: http://en.wikipedia.org/w/index.php?oldid=538971507 *Contributors*: (jarbarf), -Majestic-, 057SAsh, 11ccupp, 2600:1003:B015:1717:0:47:87D8:E701, 2D, 2m2m1984, 388383838h, 4twenty42o, 9Chunk20, A British Nerd, A.Roaf, A3RO, A520, A8UDI, AGGoH, AP Shinobi, AWEInCA, Aar, AarnKrry, Abce2, Abi79, Abu-Dun, Aceya, Achawgo164, Acroterion, Adamc7, AeonicOmega, Aergoth, Aficonado, Agnus, Ajutla, Aktsu, Alai, Alansohn, Ale jrb, Alex360, Alex3600, Alex5670, AlexJFox, Allmightyduck, Alpha Monkey357, Alsotop, Amog, Anarchangel, And4e, Andpet47, Angel riu, Angelus1753, AnimalMother617, Anionis, Anna Lincoln, Anna.McFaith, Annabelee, Annonnimus, Annoyedbeef, Anonymous Dissident, Ant field, Ant man24, Anunimportantperson, Apoxalex, Appropriate Username, Aquatech, Archer23, Archon888, ArtemusB, Asatruer, Asm2750, Asnav, Assassin1234567890, Astatine211, Auntof6, Aurongurdian, Ausir, Autonova, Avoided, Avono, Azarkiowa, B-RadShock3, B34stm0d3upinhere, BI Str, BLACKLightt, BURNyA, Baardhimself, Baby jokill, Bachihii, Bahahs, Baiken, Banej, Bantinsay, Batista98, Batobatobato, Bean23, Beem2, Belanidia, Bellinger2112, Bellyzbad, BenjaminFerrari, Benparfitt, Beyond silence, Bfcdan, Bignole, Bilbo571, Billy Liakopoulos, Bistro7, Bkonrad, Black Falcon, Blakvswite, Blingonmywrist, Blockman7771234, Bloodholds, BloodyFox, BlueMario1016, Blueshade, BobTheMad, Bobbyb373, Bobfordsgun, Bonadea, Bongwarrior, Boomshadow, Bozzi90, Brad101, Bradjohns10, Bradley652, Brigandsmc, Brinlong, Brozozo, Bsadowski1, Btilm, Budbuddingding299, Buddha iz str8, Bunnyhop11, Butcake, C.Fred, CTZMSC3, Cabe6403, Calabreseboy, Calamity-Ace, Calendar, Caltas, Cameronsacount, CampbellSinnett, Camw, Capc, Capricorn42, Carboneclectic, CardinalNZ, Cartch123, CaveatLector, Cbh, Celystia, Centrx, Cerejota, Cglassey, Chadnewman, Chainmail, Chamal N, Changster308, Cheese7272, Cheeseman Muncher, Cheezy duzit, Chensiyuan, Chiefegg, ChildrenEdit, ChilliSauce59, ChimpanzeeUK, Chris L. Reynolds, Chriso1290, Chromatikoma, Church of emacs, Cjottawa, Closedmouth, Cody14.howell, Cometstyles, Commdor, CommonsDelinker, Compactsoul2, Coolman1081, Corvoe, Courcelles, CranialNerves, Crash Underride, Crazy5dolphin, CrazyChemGuy, Crossmr, Csaetre, Cselm, Cuchullain, Cwass85, CyberRaptor, CyberSkull, Cyberalien18, Cyclonius, DARTH SIDIOUS 2, DGaw, DLong0331, DMacks, DVdm, Da thunda, Daa89563, Dac04, Daduzi, DamageW, Damicatz, Damien Russell, Danbrab, Danial27b, Daniel J. Leivick, Dark verdant, Darkness2005, Darkpower, Darkskyz, Darkwarriorblake, Darth Mike, Darth Panda, Dashiel, Daveydweeb, Davideogamer, Dawormie, Dca5347, Dead Echo DX, Deathtrap3000, Debresser, Deerrr, Deftera, Dell9300, Deltwalrus, DerHexer, Deus257, Dewritech, Dgies, Dherb, Dibol, Diewelt, Diogo Pinto, DiscipleOfKnowledge, Discospinster, Dispenser, Diw321, Doberman Pharaoh, Dodman123, Doniago, Dou Gweler, Doubledose 2, Dougofborg, Doulos Christos, Download, Dr v, Dr. XIII, Dr. Yingst, Dr.x38, Draglikepull, Dragon239, Dragonmazula, Drgyen, Duki47, Dumnass100, Dvavasour, Dylan is cool, Dynaflow, E662, EEMIV, EastTN, EdBever, Edgerunner76, Edthefreak, Eeekster, Eekerz, Eik Corell, ElKevbo, ElSturge, ElTchanggo, Elisa Woods, Ellusion, Elmindreda, ElseJon, Emssme, Emstidor, Enviroboy, EoGuy, Epbr123, Erebus Morgaine, Erjhguieruigyeruigw, Eseb, Eva2pare, Everchanging02, Evilgohan2, Eviltrance, Excirial, Exeunt, Exhipigeonist, Experts4games, Explicit, Eyesnore, F3nNec, FPS Mc Duck, Falcon9x5, Fallout0101, Fallout3bh1, Falloutnewdlc, Faramir1138, Fastily, Fat kid with no life, Favonian, Feinoha, Ferr3t, Ferret, Fieldday-sunday, FiercedeitylinkX, Figureskatingfan, Fildon, Fireato, Fish and karate, Fishguy234, FlashHawk4, Flatneck, Flibolimay, Fortresseurope, Freaky Dug, Frecklefoot, FreddyKrueger69, Friginator, FrozenPurpleCube, Funnysheep, Fyyer, Fæ, G-J, GDallimore, GODhack, GVnayR, Gaaramax1235, Gabenewellthefattroll, Gail, Galaviz413, Gamer007, GamerPro64, GargoyleMT, Ged UK, GeneralAtrocity, Geniac, Genralmills44, Gerrardperrett, Gfoley4, Ghepeu, Gibbons91, Ginsengbomb, GlassCobra, Gman3zm, Gman451, GoShow, Godheval, Goffrie, Gogo Dodo, GoodLunaLove, Grayshi, GreatSnake666, Greatrobo76, GreenFallout3, Grinevitski, GroundZ3R0 002, Gtdp, Guam00, GucciManeLaFlare, Gumbie777, Gunman47, Gunmetal Angel, Guyhunger, Gwaser, H1nkles, HDCase, Haigh21, Hairy Dude, Halo77mac, Halohunter, Hammersoft, HappyInGeneral, HarryHenryGebel, Haunt9, Headbomb, Hefner1, Hellfire29, Hikari, Hikui87, Hinotori, Hmains, Hoddyman666, HolmesSPH, Honette, Hqb, Hujjiy, Hujjiy 2, Hujjiy 3, Huntster, Hurracane, Hydrogen Iodide, I dream of horses, ICEBreaker, IGeMiNix, II MusLiM HyBRiD II, IQpierce, IRP, IWantToSayNo, IceCream66, Icealien33, Icearmy2000, Icseaturtles, IdahoEv, Iliev, Illegitimate Barrister, Imamathwiz, ImperatorExercitus, InTeGeR13, Ingolfson, Inkheart667, Inmate42392, Innonexess, Intelati, InternetMeme, Irishsourcer, Ironcito, Island Monkey, Itanius, Izno, J.delanoy, J0nas3, JAF1970, JForget, JGXenite, JHunterJ, JRD3, Ja 62, JaGa, JabbaXErnie, Jack Cox, Jacoplane, Jagged 85, Jamestheferrit, Jamiee24, Jared555, Jarlaxlecq, JasonS2101, Jchap, Jecowa, Jeff G., Jeff790, Jeffrey Mall, Jerry teps, Jerry220, Jim1138, Jim15936, JimBrownish, JimmyBlackwing, Jizo7, Jochickenlikepie, Joffeloff, Jofishtrick, John of Reading, JohnnyPolo24, Jojhutton, JokeySmurf, Jonalton92, Jonashart, Josette, JrChurchXtrM, Jspoel, Jtg12, Jules.lt, Juliancolton, JuneGloom07, Justicepie, Jweiss11, K1Bond007, KOZ92, KPalicz, Kaini, Kandres4, KarKnowsItForTrue, Karoken, Kasun Gunasekara, Kbdank71, Kehrbykid, Keilana, Kermitron, Kflester, KhalienBB, Khing, Kida1011, Kilibear, Kimon, King Newby 1995, King of Hearts, King of the Wontons, Kingmundi, Kingofkong288, Kirachinmoku, KishKiai, Kittoo, Klilidiplomus, Kliu1, Klon-immortal, Kman618, Knobsheller, Knoxfett, Knulclunk, Kokoas12345, KokoroTechnix, Komitet, Kooperfan, KronicTOOL, Ks0stm, Kukule, Kungfujoe, Kurtis, Kyle1278, L337 kybldmstr, LN2, LaBelle24, Labranewf, Landon1980, Law, Lax15o, LeaveSleaves, LepricahnsGold, Leujohn, Lewiscb, Lightmouse, LilHelpa, Liljak, Limulus, Linny56, Liquid Silencer, Liverpool37, Lmorton575, Lololx, Lord Bone de Ham, Lorddragon, Lordvaldor2, Loren.wilton, Lthornsb, LucaviX, Luminite2, LxRv, M-le-mot-dit, M00npirate, MASLEGOMan, MASQUERAID, MASTER GNOME JH, MScire, MUSE1795, MZMcBride, Magicmat, Majoramask, Makarius, Makswel, Malleus Fatuorum, Mallimaster, ManOfSummer, Mandarax, Maquis196, Marco.pietersen, Marek69, Marginoferror, Mark Arsten, Markypoo20, MarnetteD, Martarius, Martoine,

Marxisabadasssssssss, MasahiroHayamoto, Master Deusoma, Masterchief22134, Masterchief411, Mat wang, Mato, Matt7895, MattParker 119, Mattgirling, MattieTK, Mattyboy89, MaulYoda, MaxWilder, Maxinuk, Mazza453, McGeddon, McSly, Meelar, Megaman en m, Megamattman, Mentifisto, Metalmulisha333, Metathink, Metricopolus, Metroid014, Mfpvehicles, Michformer, Michigan31, Mika1h, Mikael GRizzly, Mikaey, Mild Bill Hiccup, Millahnna, Milton Stanley, Minimac, Mipadi, Miquonranger03, Mirelurk, Misstemperance, Mist17, MisterVodka, Mk03s1, Modernist, MoffAvinoff, Mojoworker, Moochocoogle, Mookie89, Moonraker0, Morgankevinj huggle, Moshe Constantine Hassan Al-Silverburg, Moskevap, Mps, Mr. ?, Mr. ghujkj, Mr.Z-man, Mr.cliickz, MrRadioGuy, Mrbrefast, Mrtraver, Mrzaius, Mshe, Mtpt, Mttcmbs, MushroomCloud, Muspar, Myscrnnm, N. Harmonik, N419BH, NHRHS2010, Nanzilla, Nathan Johnson, Nathan13954, NawlinWiki, Nczempin, Ndboy, Ndrost, Necroptic, NellieBly, Neo139, NerdyScienceDude, Nergaal, Netito777, Neurolysis, New Age Retro Hippie, Next-Genn-Gamer, Nick Ottery, Nick Swanson, NickW557, Nickin, Niemti, Nikkimaria, Nimbusania, Nneonneo, Nonagonal Spider, Nono64, Nour josen, Nrbnerd17, Nufy8, Nukeman8000, Nukleon, Num43, Nv8200p, Nymf, O VERTiGO O, Oaktowndrummer, Oarias, Odessaukrain, Odie5533, Ominae, OnWithTheShow, Onesimos, Oren0, Oriol003, Orracle107, Oscar86, Ost316, OutOfTimer, Oxymoron83, P924 CarreraGTS, PL290, PV1Viokni, Papa emo, Papercutbiology, Parsecboy, Pasi, Patato, Pathoschild, Patrikas2, Patrikor, Pauli133, Paxsimius, Pele Merengue, Persian Poet Gal, PeterSymonds, Petrarch, Philip Trueman, Piano non troppo, Pinethicket, Pinkadelica, Pistolpete852, Pitel, Pkaulf, Planet-man828, Playclever, Playstation1105, Pockack, Polemos, Poohunter, Popisfizzy, Portillo, Poseidon1224, Possum, Potaterfilms, Pparazorback, Professor Ninja, Proofreader77, Ps1on1c99, Pts925, Puffin, Purpleturple, Puskar487, QSquared, QuasiAbstract, Quindie, Quirk, R3tr0, RAKSTHESAVIOUR, RG2, RJFJR, RJHall, RKN1987, RainbowOfLight, RamirBorja, RandomLittleHelper, Ranix, Rapturous, Ratwar, Razor2988, Razorflame, ReCover, Readmore, Reason turns rancid, Rebochan, Reconman43, Regalvanman, Rehevkor, Reliableforever, Rhettfight, Richard Arthur Norton (1958-), Richbunk, Richiekim, Rjwilmsi, Rmosler2100, Rmp1978, Robertlyon, Rockfang, Ronhjones, Rotzo, Royxomonuchi, Rror, Rusanton99, Ruthlessraccoon, Ry Fryy, SCB '92, SSJ3Brian, SYSS Mouse, Sabbalabba, SaderBiscut, Sakkath, Sallystang, Sammayel, Saturn star, Scalesjordan, Sceptre, SchfiftyThree, Schmidty226, Scott is great, Scoutmatt2, Sdaffer, Sdornan, Secleinteer, Second hand toilet paper 7, Sector001, Seriema, Sesu Prime, SethAJS, Sgtrico2, ShadowFusion, ShadowMan1od, Shadowjams, Shak 10, ShaleZero, Shane dawson for real, SharkD, Shawn in Montreal, Shayne is awesome, Sherzo, Shirik, Shlomke, Shorty35P, Shriram, Shyam, Sidasta, Sillygostly, Silver Edge, Simon KHFC, Sixtimes, Skinnytie, Skomorokh, SkyWalker, Skydayer1, Slamnose2345678910, Slicing, Smalljim, Smett, Smurfy, Snigbrook, Snoopdawg45, SnowmanC, Snowolf, Sobolewski, Soetermans, Solberg, Soliloquial, Solvebreaky, Somersxxx, Something12356789101, Somethingofpie, Somthinofpie, Soundwaveonacid, SpK, SpaceFlight89, Spacemarine2552, Specs112, Sportzguy1006, Stabby Joe, StarScream1007, StarryWorld, StaticGull, Steakbuns, Steel, Stephenb, Steve71694, Steveprutz, Stickee, StrAtgeir, Subash.chandran007, SuckaFreeM3, Superbowlbound, Supertegwyn, Susfele, SwissIrishAmerican, Symplectic Map, SynergyBlades, Syremusic, TCR6V, TDC, TDogg310, THEN WHO WAS PHONE?, THeGaJmAn, TJ Spyke, TOMNORTHWALES, TPIRman, Tabicoleman, Tadman, TaerkastUA, TallNapoleon, TangSC, Taotriad, Tbhotch, Teancum, Techman224, TehPhil, Tempodivalse, Tenraixtreme, TerraHikaru, Tgeairn, Th1rt3en, The Apokalips, The Clawed One, The Illusive Man, The Moose, The Rogue Penguin, The Simonator, The Stick Man, The Thing That Should Not Be, The Watchtower, The wub, The-carrot, The1337gamer, TheEarlyStrike, TheSilencedScream, TheVaultDweller, Thedoodonline, Thegamingninja, Thekittycat97, Theseven7, Thesis4Eva, Thingg, Think4aSec!, Thisisborin9, Thomas Connor, ThommoX12, ThreadbareSock, Threedots dead, Thu, Thumperward, Tidablishan, Tide rolls, TigerK 69, Tim1357, Timstuff, Timur9008, Tiptoety, Tlesher, Tnewe, Tom Lennox, Tommy2010, Tommy758, Tony1, Tonyjk78, Tozir, Tpbradbury, TrafficHaze, Traxs7, Tree Biting Conspiracy, Trinexx, Trisklow, Tronno, Troubling, Trusilver, Tsmith2345, TunnelSnakesRule, Turtlekid118, Twas Now, Typhoon966, Tyrantus, Tyrone0308, Ubergeekguy, UltraIPman, UncannyGarlic, Uncle Dick, Unclejedd, Unibod, Upcomplaygame, Uucp, Uzumakiwalid, VAINDAL, VD6661, VI, Valdusaurus, Valentine82, VanisherX, Vantine84, Vault dweller 26, Vercingeterix, Vermaden, Vermaletta, Versus22, Vianello, Vicenarian, Victory93, Vifee, Vincetti, Vipinhari, Voidvector, Voracious reader, Vrenator, Vrinan, WORLDWAR4ACE, WOSlinker, Wardrift, Warreed, Wayne Slam, Weirdsqurl2, Werthead, Wes Richards, Wesker73, White 720, WhosAsking, Whsc6, WikiBob42, Wikih101, Wikipelli, Wildfire9909, Wildhartlivie, Wilester, Willking1979, Winterheart, Winterus, Wjfox2005, Wknight94, Wookie501, Word2that, Wwegreenandchris, Wysprgr2005, X!, X201, Xaldoth, Xanzzibar, Xavexgoem, Xblackfirex1, Xeno, Xenowiki, Xeon25, Xhaoz, Xinoph, Xombi p, Xover, Xpsychedelico, XxRunescapexOwnsxx, XxdbzxX, Yakiv Gluck, Yamamoto Ichiro, Yuefairchild, Z-man123465, Zad68, Zeekyman, Zewis28, Zidonuke, Ziggy in Oz, Zigmar, Zimjimmy, Zpops, Zyvo1, Éclusette, Артур Коровкин, 2842 ,קליפורניה anonymous edits

Follow the Boys *Source*: http://en.wikipedia.org/w/index.php?oldid=538834356 *Contributors*: After Midnight, Brumski, Debonairchap, Hydraton31, JGKlein, Lockley, Lugnuts, MPoint, Milowent, NoahVail, Orbicle, Polisher of Cobwebs, Skymasterson, Storyliner, Tassedethe, TheMovieBuff, Tjmayerinsf, WFinch, Wool Mintons, 2 anonymous edits

Frank Sinatra *Source*: http://en.wikipedia.org/w/index.php?oldid=539300326 *Contributors*: 007steve3, 152.163.197.xxx, 1jrb, 23skidoo, 2812, 3finger, 440william, 5 albert square, 7, 75pickup, ABF, Aaron Bowen, Aaronjhill, Ablebakerus, Absalom89, Abtract, Acalamari, Ace2541, Acegikmo1, Acevan, Acrazy007, Acroterion, AdamB, Adambro, Adashiel, Adishesha, Aff123a, Afghana, Ahoerstemeier, Ahsirakh, Ajax-and-Achilles, Alakey2010, Alanfeld, Alansohn, AlbertSM, Aldaron, Alessgrimal, AlexP525, AlexWilkes, Alexbonaro, Alikah23, All Hallow's Wraith, Allens, Allthewhile, Ally OBE, Alpha Quadrant, Altris77, Amazzing5, Ameliorate!, AmericanLeMans, Amiodarone, Anakronik, Anaraug, Anaxial, Andonic, Andreasegde, Andreasmperu, Andrew Gray, Andrew Levine, AndrewAllen, Andrewxxl, Andy M. Wang, Andy Marchbanks, AndySimpson, Anetode, Anger22, Ani td, AnnaFrance, Anonymouseman101, Another Believer, Antandrus, Anthony, Anthony Winward, Antonio.napoli, Aphid360, Apple1013, Aranel, Arbero, Arbor to SJ, Arcade McAleney, ArielGold, Artaxiad, Ary29, Asalrifai, Asarelah, Asm english, Asn, AspenShrines, Ataro21, Atomician, AtticusX, Aucociscokid, Auric, Auréola, Austindeadhead, Avoided, Axem Titanium, Azumanga1, Azuris, B2u6951, BD2412, BRG, BTzombie, Backslash Forwardslash, Badagnani, Badsy, Baiji, Baird, Baldghoti, Banana04131, Bapples81, Barnabat, Barrympls, Bart133, Barticus88, Baseball Bugs, Bassclarinet99, BastianOfArt, Bbatsell, Beardo, Bearian, Before My Ken, Bellerophon5685, Ben eggers, Bender235, Benducharme, BeniNgimarsonfc, Benny215, Berean Hunter, Best O Fortuna, Betempte, Bhny, Big Brother 1984, Big Jock Knew, Bigmac31, Bignole, Biker Biker, BillyH, Billyfutile, Binksternet, BizarreLoveTriangle, Bjarki S, Bkell, Black Falcon, Blackjays1, Blood sliver, Bloomington882005, Blueeyes711, Bmearns, Bobdaman123123, Bobo192, Bobosthecatlover, Bodnotbod, Bonadea, Bongwarrior, Bono24, Bookkeeperoftheoccult, BorgQueen, BozMo, Bped1985, Brandmeister (old), Brandon97, Bratsche, Brianga, Brianhenke, Briansokoloff, Brilliance, Britanica54, Brittanyy93, BrokenSegue, Brooksthomas99, Brusegadi, Bryanimal, Bryates999, Btmeacham, Bucephalus, Bucketsofg, Bueller 007, Bunnyhop11, BurmaShaver, Burnberrytree, Bvo66, C colorado, C777, CJAllbee, CRKingston, CWY2190, Cacique, Cacophony, Calliopejen1, Callmarcus, Calmer Waters, Caltas, CalumH93, CambridgeBayWeather, CamperStrike, Can't sleep, clown will eat me, CanOfWorms, CanadianLinuxUser, CanisRufus, Canute, Capricorn42, Casper2k3, Cassivs, Catbar, Catgut, Causa sui, Cburnett, Ccockkkk, Cdyson37, Cgersten, Cgilbert76, Chad44, Chairman S., Changalangadingdong, Chanlyn, CharlotteWebb, Chaser, Chasingsol, Chasnip, Chefgclef, ChiMaster XIX, Chicheley, Chicken Collar Guy, Chochopk, Choiboi00, Cholmes75, Chris Halpin (2nd), Chris5369, ChrisHamburg, ChrisRed, Chrism, Chrisphase, Christian List, Christofurio, ChristopherJamesGill, Chrysaor, Cinemaretro, Ckatz, Clarificationgiven, Clausule, Closeapple, Cntras, Collio33, Colonies Chris, Common Sense7, Con67mac, Connormah, Conteuse, ContribWiki82, Contributor777, Conversion script, Cooksi, Cookster6, CopperSquare, Corpx, Cosprings, Courcelles, Cp111, Crackshoe, Creatednewaccount, Creativeoutsourceoptions, Cremepuff222, Crimson Cherry Blossom, Croat Canuck, Crox in the Box, Crystallina, Cschroll, Csigabi, Cst17, CuteHappyBrute, Cwiki, CyeZ, Cyril1984, Cyrius, D. Recorder, D6, DARTH SIDIOUS 2, DBigXray, DCEdwards1966, DVD R W, DWaterson, Da Joe, Daisykc, Dale Arnett, Damirgraffiti, Dancon7, Dandv, Dano999, Dark Lord of the Sith, Darklilac, Dasani, Dave2, Daveman 84, DaveyJones1968, David Couch, David in DC, David.Monniaux, Davidovich60, Davidwr, Dawn Bard, Dawnseeker2000, Dctoedt, Deb, Debresser, Deflective, Delldot, Dellwebb, Den fjättrade ankan, Denisarona, Deor, Derek R Bullamore, Desmay, Dgmoran, Diegovh, Dionysius525, Discographer, Discospinster, Diskpocket, Dissolve, Djdynasty, Dobie80, DocWatson42, Doczilla, Domingo Portales, Dominic, Dominic Hardstaff, Dominik92, Don4of4, Donreed, Dooyar, DougHill, Dougie monty, Dr. Blofeld, Drake Redcrest, DrunkenSmurf, Drutt, Dtjensen, Dudesleeper, Dwayne, Dxco, Dysepsion, E Wing, E-Kartoffel, EBCurtis, EEMIV, EWikist, EdoDodo, Edwy, Eevans23, Ego White Tray, El Greco, Elassint, Elephantitis12345, ElfMage, ElinorD, Elipongo, Elpablo123, Elsker, Elvis1935, Emerson7, Emersoni, Emijrp, Ems57fcva, Endlessdan, Enigmabooks, Enigmaman, Enki Nabu, Enter Movie, EoGuy, Epbr123, Erebus Morgaine, Erebus555, Eric-Wester, EricEnfermero, Ernest747, Eroteme, Esfr, Esrever, Ethan Shay, Ethan c.00, Eugrus, Eurodog, Evan1200, Evanreyes, Evercat, Everyking, Everyme, Evil1987, Excirial, Exert, FF2010, FactCheck150, Falcon8765, Faradayplank, Farmokopole, FastFred, Fat&Happy, Father McKenzie, Favonian, Fayenatic london, FeanorStar7, Felipegaspars, Fg2, Filipmk01, Filmflavor, Finishlosmith, Firsfron, FisherQueen, Fjarlq, Flami72, Flewis, Flooch, Flowerparty, Fluffernutter, Flyguy33, Folks at 137, Footwarrior, Fordmadoxfraud, Foriamunusal, Fourthords, FrankEldonDixon, FrankySin, Fratrep, FredR, Fredrik, Free2kill14, FriscoKnight, Fru1tbat, FruitFlies32794, Frymaster, Fschoenm, Fvw, G.S.K.Lee, GAYNIGGER ON WHEELS, GCord52, GDonato, GDuwen, GTBacchus, GWP, Gadfium, Gaius Cornelius, Gamaliel, Gamer112, Garbage101, Gareth E Kegg, Garion96, Garret500, GcSwRhIc, Ged UK, Geniac, Gennaro Prota, Georg Kolling, GeorgannP, George Ho, George805, GeorgeLouis, Gerarding, Getcrunk, Gggh, Gigliotti, Gilliam, Gillwill, Gioto, Giraffedata, Girlylicious, GlassCobra, GoPurpleNGold24, Gobonobo, Godjirra, GoingBatty, Good Olfactory, Goofy Freaks, Gr8lyknow, Gragox, Graham87, Grahams, Grapeindie, GreatWhiteNortherner, Gregums, Greogory, Griffin4prez, Griffinofwales, GrimGrinningGuest, Groeneveldp, Ground Zero, Grstain, Gulfstorm75, Gurch, Guy M, Guðsþegn, Gventi, Gwernol, HOT L Baltimore, Hadal, Hafmark, Hagerman, Hal Raglan, HalJor, Halmstad, Hammer1980, Hammon27, Hamsaladpants, Happy-melon, Happyme22, Head, Hede2000, Heegoop, Heidi.kapesy, Hello32020, Henry Flower, Henry the heron, Herbythyme, Heslopian, Hidudes1000, Hifihitman, Hjasud, Hjorten, Hmains, Hoangkid, Homie524, Hongooi, Hoo man, HorsePunchKid, Hraefen, Htasch, Husker Jay, Husond, Hydrargyrum, Hydrogen Iodide, IGG8998, ITAPEVI, Iambret, Iamtall47, Ian Pitchford, Ian Stapleford, Ian13, Ianblair23, Ibeb1, Ibtuten, Icey, Iggiv44, Ihuxley, Ijayasin, Ikmarchini, Iliank, Illegitimate Barrister, Illyria05, Imasleepviking, In Defense of the Artist, Indexme, IndulgentReader, Infamous30, Infocidal, Infrogmation, Iohannes Animosus, Irish4life91, IrishPete, Irishguy, IronGargoyle, Irregulargalaxies, Issac500, ItsZippy, Ivessays, Izagig0506, J Milburn, J.R. Hercules, J.delanoy, JDG, JDezGnomes4Life, JDoorjam, JEA13, JForget, JFreeman, JGKlein, JKevin01, JWPowell, Jaan, Jacek Kendysz, Jack Cox, Jack O'Lantern, Jackelfive, JackofOz, Jailerdaemon, Jakew, Jamesgibbon, Jamie213jkd, Jamiereidit, Jan1nad, January, Japanese Searobin, Jason S. Klepp, Jasonanaggie, Jauerback, Jay-W, Jayhare, Jazz N Media, Jazzeur, Jb413, Jclemens, Jebba, Jeffman52001, Jehfes, Jengod, Jeppi, Jeremy Visser, Jeromemoreno, Jerry Ritcey, Jessemcgregor, Jessiejames, Jesster79, Jesusthemessiah, Jhsounds, JimmB, Jimmorrisonpapa, Jimthing, Jmlk17, JoWal, JoanneB, Joao Xavier, Joecashfire, Joefilm, Joey80, John, John O'C, John Paul Parks, JohnInDC, JohnRobertBrown, JohnRogers, Johnjoe2345, Johnleemk, Johnny Sumner, Johnny Weissmuller, Johnny locks sudbury, Jojhutton, Jolsonmhd, Jorian-Kell, Joseph Solis in Australia, Josh Rumage, Joshk, Jossi, Journalist, Jpete, Jprg1966, Jpvandijk, Jriver44, Jschnur, Jsondow, Jtclarkjr, Juankevindani, Juicifer, Jumbo Snails, Jusdafax, Jusses2, JustAGal, Jvcdude, Jzummak, K. Annoyomous, KHLehmann, KJS77, KUBILM, Kablammo, Kaisershatner, Kanogul, Kap42, Katalaveno, Katydidit, Kbdank71, Kellogg257, Kelly Martin, Kerotan, Kevin B12, Kevin j, Khazar2, Kibiusa, Kierzek, Kilgoretrout89, Killiondude, Kimchi.sg, King of Hearts, KingStrato, Kingsfold, Kkm010, Kleinzach, Klow, Kmg90, KnowledgeOfSelf, Koavf, Koeberlein, Korg, Kornfan71, Kosmotheoria, Kpwla, Ktr101, Kubigjay, KudzuVine, Kuru, Kustard100, Ky1958, L Kensington, L'Especial, L33th4x0rguy, LAX, LaVidaLoca, Lady Lotus, Ladyofsongandverse, LarryGilbert, Lauriepk, Laveol, LeaveSleaves, Leevclarke, Legomyeggo252, Leiser18, Lesonyrra, Lestrade, Leszek Jańczuk, Levineps, Liberatus, Light current, Lightdarkness, Lightmouse, LilHelpa, Limxzero, Lindsaywinn, Linlasj, LinoPop, Linuxbeak, Liquidmetalrob, Listentotiesto, Little Mountain 5, LittleWink, Livefastdieold, LizardJr8, Llort, Lmharnisch, Logan, Longhair, Lord Cestern, Lordoddie, Loren.wilton, Love Krittaya, Love8, Lowzeewee, LuK3, Lucas1111, LucasVB, Lucky 6.9, Lugia2453, Lugnad, Lugnuts, Luigilos, Luk, Luna Santin, Lunchscale, Lupo, LéonTheCleaner, M4, MELOVEMUSIC, MER-C, MK2, MONGO, Maarten1963, MackSalmon, Macktheknifeau, Madcap Mary, Madman, Magioladitis, Magister Mathematicae, Maher-shalal-hashbaz, Majsnsjid, Mako shshsh ki, Mandsford, Mani1, Marcus Brute, Marcus2, Mark.deane, MarkGallagher, MarkSweep, Markonen, MarnetteD, Martarius, Masterofzen, Math Champion, Matt Traywick, Mattbr, Mattbrundage, Matthew Fennell, MatthewTStone, Mausmalone, Mav, Mawbid, MaxBassanetti, Mayumashu, Mboverload, McGeddon, McLennonSon, Meaghan, Mean as custard, Meco, MegX, Megakibbles, Megas888, MegastarLV, Meisam, Melgibstone, Mentifisto, Merchbow, Mercury McKinnon, Merienda, Metasailor, Metropolitan90, MetsJetsFan4Life, Mhiji, Michael Bednarek, Michael Snow, Michaelas10, Michæl, Mike Rosoft, Mikeblas, Mikeoconnelljr, Mind meal, Minimac,

MinnesotanConfederacy, Miopportunity, Miranda, Miroglio69, MisfitToys, MissionInn.Jim, Misterrick, Misto, Mlaffs, Mmyers1976, Mnealon, Modus Vivendi, Moe Epsilon, Moeron, Moncrief, Monkeyinredresponse, MonoAV, Monty845, MoogleEXE, Moomoomoocow, Morenooso, Mormegil, Morten, Mr. DogmA, Mr. Nacho de la Libre, Mr.Baker, Mr.S, Mr.Vibrato, MrDolomite, MrKing84, MrX, Mrmaroon25, Ms. Fashion, Mschel, Mshecket, Msignor, Mushroom, MusicaBaroque, MuzikJunky, Mwh6288, NE Ent, NamibiaCoastGuard, NapoleonX, Naraht, Nasnema, Nat Miller, Nathanael Bar-Aur L., Nathann sc, Natl1, Nehrams2020, Neko-chan, Neon white, Nepenthes, Neutrality, Nevadaresident, NewEnglandYankee, Niceguyedc, Nick C, Nickderiso, NickelShoe, Nickhorder, Nightfox2020, Nightscream, Nihiltres, NikitaO113, Nknight, No1lakersfan, Nodios, Noirish, Nolancatingub, Nono64, Noodle123, Norm mit, Norwikian, NotACow, Nposs, Nunh-huh, Nv8200p, Nwbeeson, O.Koslowski, Ocaasi, Ocatecir, OettingerCroat, Offenbach, OfficialRollingStone, Ohconfucius, Ol32, Ol33, Oldlaptop321, Oliphaunt, Ollieollieollie, Omg1995, Omizzle77, Onebravemonkey, Optimist on the run, OrangeDog, Orbicle, Oreos, Oroso, Ortolan88, Ottawa4ever, Otto4711, Oxymoron83, P. Rollin, PCHS-NJROTC, PDH, PETEYTHEREF, PJtP, PL290, Palzoo, ParaDoxus, Parkjunwung, Paroxysm, Pascal.Tesson, Paterakis, Patkickass, PatrickFisher, Paul A, Paul August, Paul Barlow, Paul Benjamin Austin, Paul MacDermott, Paul20070, Paul210, Pdcook, Pegship, Pekaje, Pepso, Pepso2, Per Ardua, PetersPiper, Petrb, Pezzonovante, Pgk, PhantomS, Phantomsteve, Phatcat68, Philip Trueman, Philip.t.day, Phoenix2, Phototakinluver, Phyco man, Piano non troppo, Pichpich, Pinclip, Pinethicket, Pink!Teen, Pithecanthropus, Plateofshrimp, Plazak, Plrk, Poiuytrewq69, Politepunk, Pompton15041, Portillo, Postmarc, Powelldinho, Poxto, Prattlement, PrestonH, Prestonmag, PrinceRegentLuitpold, Princegetsitin, Prodego, Professor Von Pie, Professorpickles, Prolog, Protonk, Pseudomonas, Puceron, Pudsey UK, Puertogerm, Purgatory Fubar, Pyrotec, Que-Can, R'n'B, RA0808, RHodnett, RICHARD GRUDENS, RP88, RThompson82, Rabidpiano, Racingstripes, RadioKirk, RafikiSykes, Rainwarrior, Rasmus Faber, RattleandHum, Rawgreenbean, Rawracat222, Rbbloom, Rdsmith4, Reaper Eternal, RedWolf, Redfarmer, Redxx, Refusecollection, Regancy42, Rekiwi, Retired username, RexNL, Reywas92, Rhavers, Rhebus, RicDod, Rich Farmbrough, Richard Arthur Norton (1958-), Richhoncho, Riddley, Rikstar, Riotrocket8676, Rizan, Rjwilmsi, Rlquall, Rms125a@hotmail.com, RobbieNomi, Rocketrod1960, RodC, Rodgerd, Rodhullandemu, Rogerd, Ronbo76, Ronhjones, Root Beers, Rosestiles, Rossrs, Rothorpe, RoyBoy, Rror, Rrostrom, Runnerupnj, Runt, Ruy Lopez, RyanGerbil10, S.Curls, SCJohnson77, SD5, SDC, SEWilco, SJFriedl, SJP, SK8erT, SMC, SQGibbon, Saalstin, Saga City, Salamurai, Salvio giuliano, Sam'sTheJazzMan, Sammy8912, SandyGeorgia, SarekOfVulcan, Satellizer, Saulisagenius, Scewing, SchfiftyThree, Schmiteye, SchnitzelMannGreek, SchuminWeb, Scientist3993, Scohoust, Scooteristi, ScottSteiner, Seaaron, Seadog365, SeanO, Seaphoto, Searscard, Seneca91, Serendipia, Sevenplusone, Sfniall, Sgeureka, Sgt. R.K. Blue, Shadowjams, Shamrox, Shanes, Sharkentile, ShelfSkewed, Shifty86, Shisock, Shyam, Shymian, Sicamous, Signaleer, Signinstranger, Silence, SimonLyall, Sinatra1969, SinatraDJ, SinatraElvis, Sinn, Siobob1, Sjakkalle, Skamecrazy123, Skizzik, Skysmith, SlapAyoda, Sljaxon, Sluzzelin, Smalljim, Smdudle, Smiffy99, Smileblame, Smilesfozwood, Smileyface11945, Smitty, Smokizzy, Snigbrook, Snowolf, Soerfm, Soetermans, Someguy1221, SonicAD, Spangineer, Sparsefarce, Spartan, Spartaz, Spellcast, Spiderverse, Spitfire, Splash, Squirepants101, Srich32977, Sssoul, Star3709, Stargaze, Stefanomione, Stellarag, Stellmach, Stepanovas, Stephenb, SteveO, Stevenmeven, Steviestare, StovePicture, Struway, SubSeven, Suddenly There Is a Valley, Sue Rangell, Sugar-Baby-Love, SummerPhD, SunKing, SuperHamster, Superastig, Suruena, Swarm, Swishfish, Switcher, Swoonatra, Synchronism, TFOWR, THEN WHO WAS PHONE?, TOMBOCHI, TUF-KAT, TURNUPSANDZEBRAS, Tablesaw, Tariqabjotu, Tassedethe, Tbhotch, TearJohnDown, Ted87, Teepeetea, Teklund, Tempshill, The Almighty King, The Anome, The Devil's Advocate, The JPS, The Thing That Should Not Be, The stuart, The undertow, The wub, The-verver, TheGoofyGolfer, TheKMan, ThePrairieDawg, TheProf07, Thebogusman, Theda, Thedjatclubrock, Thegreatmonkey, Thehelpfulone, Theopolisme, Thesilverbail, Thingg, Thinkcover, Thiseye, Thismightbezach, Thomas Aquinas, ThomasK, Thorsen, Thumperward, Thussaiththewalrus, Tide rolls, TigerShark, Tim Thomason (usurped), Tim1357, Tim2567, Timothybb, Timrollpickering, Tinmoran, Tinton5, Tjmayerinsf, Tnayin, Tobby72, Tom-, Tomer T, Tony1, TonyTheTiger, Townmouse, Trampikey, Tregoweth, Trevor MacInnis, Treybien, Treyt021, Tripnoted, TroisiemeLigne, Tropicalisle23, Trusilver, Trypsin, Tsemii, Tslocum, Tstew11, Ttonyb1, Twas Now, TylerDregerKelowna, USAIR, UberCryxic, Ulric1313, Uncle Dick, Underdawg, UnicornTapestry, Unimaginative Username, Unreal7, Upsmiler, Uranuskid228, Useight, User2563, Ustye, Utcursch, Uzzo2, VakKarapetian, Vampiregabe, Van Heusen Music, Vanischenu, Vanished User 3388458, Vanished user 39948282, Vegaswikian, Veghead221, Ventur, Versus22, VeryVerily, Viajero, Villwock, Violetriga, Vobor, Volatile, Vorash, Vrenator, Vudujava, W guice, WAJWAJ, WWGB, Wafulz, Wallie, Wasted Time R, WayKurat, We hope, Wegngis, Wertuose, WesleyDodds, WhatAGal, WhatamIdoing, Where, WhisperToMe, Whkoh, WikHead, Wiki alf, Wiki libs, Wiki13, WikiBob47, WikiLaurent, Wikijazz, Wikiwatcher1, Wiktacular, Wildhartlivie, Willerror, Williamnilly, Willy99, WillyK999, Wimt, Winona laura, Wintonian, Wis2fan, Wjfox2005, Wknight94, Woohookitty, Wtmitchell, X-factor, X96lee15, Xanderer, Xioyux, Xyzzyva, YUL89YYZ, Yachtsman1, Yeepsi, Yellar, Yinzland, Ylee, Yoda of Borg, YodaRULZ, YoungRonJeremy, YourPTR!, Youre dreaming eh?, Yourmom1234567, Yoursvivek, Zabadinho, Zanimum, Zarniwoot, Zeledi, Zenexp, Zenohockey, Zephyrnthesky, Zimbabweed, Zippanova, Zoe, Zzyzx11, Žiedas, Žiga, Саша Стефановић, 2912 anonymous edits

Freddie Slack *Source*: http://en.wikipedia.org/w/index.php?oldid=535768479 *Contributors*: All Hallow's Wraith, D6, DutchDevil, Fifties, Ghmyrtle, GregorB, JGKlein, Morgan Wright, Ojorojo, RFD, Stevage, Technopat, Trontonian, Waacstats, Wis2fan, 24 anonymous edits

George Martin Lane *Source*: http://en.wikipedia.org/w/index.php?oldid=536005964 *Contributors*: CanisRufus, D6, Dassiebtekreuz, Delirium, FeanorStar7, Gzuckier, Hmains, Hohenloh, J. Van Meter, Jonathan Groß, Sam, Scewing, Ser Amantio di Nicolao, 5 anonymous edits

Hollywood Canteen *Source*: http://en.wikipedia.org/w/index.php?oldid=520683892 *Contributors*: After Midnight, Amatulic, AmiDaniel, AndrewHowse, BrownHairedGirl, Btorrence1, ChuckG92, Colonies Chris, Dave Andrew, David Gerard, Dawkeye, EoGuy, Ermanon, Firsfron, Fratrep, Gareth E Kegg, Graham87, Hmains, Jevansen, Khatru2, LiviaFrye, Loren.wilton, Lugnuts, Mandarax, Matthew Auger, Mild Bill Hiccup, Ninly, Orbicle, Ospalh, Quentin X, R, R'n'B, SarahStierch, SchreiberBike, Selbymayfair, Shanes, Tassedethe, Ted Wilkes, Truthanado, Ulric1313, Valfontis, WereSpielChequers, Wildhartlivie, Woohookitty, ZouBEini, 70 anonymous edits

Hollywood Canteen (film) *Source*: http://en.wikipedia.org/w/index.php?oldid=529106275 *Contributors*: A. Carty, Bencherlite, Black Falcon, Bovineboy2008, Comar4, CowboySpartan, Dutchy85, Foofbun, Funandtrvl, Girolamo Savonarola, Hmains, IndianCaverns, LiviaFrye, Lugnuts, MovieBuff74, Polisher of Cobwebs, Stetsonharry, Tassedethe, TheMovieBuff, Tjmayerinsf, Truthanado, Ulric1313, Victorcoutin, Wool Mintons, 27 anonymous edits

I, Yi, Yi, Yi, Yi (I Like You Very Much) *Source*: http://en.wikipedia.org/w/index.php?oldid=533700778 *Contributors*: 78.26, Hyju, Paul MacDermott, SwisterTwister, Wolfer68, 10 anonymous edits

I Don't Know Why (I Just Do) *Source*: http://en.wikipedia.org/w/index.php?oldid=490897722 *Contributors*: Alansohn, BRG, DISEman, Dsreyn, Eric444, J04n, Jafeluv, Kak500, Korny O'Near, Lightmouse, ShelfSkewed, Warofdreams, 6 anonymous edits

I Wanna Be Loved *Source*: http://en.wikipedia.org/w/index.php?oldid=537487639 *Contributors*: BRG, Bonnie13J, Discographer, Giovannii84, Jacowium, Magioladitis, Richhoncho, 5 anonymous edits

Is You Is or Is You Ain't My Baby *Source*: http://en.wikipedia.org/w/index.php?oldid=531944875 *Contributors*: AEMoreira042281, Bicycle legs, Bokan, Carlossfsu, Crystallina, DaHuzyBru, Darth Panda, Dawynn, Durova, Emurphy42, Furnituregirl, Ghirlandajo, Ghmyrtle, HkCaGu, Hmains, ISTB351, InnocuousPseudonym, J04n, Jayunderscorezero, Kintetsubuffalo, LenGoforth, Levin, Marcus Brute, MartinP1983, Morrisp, Nikkimaria, OliverTwisted, QuiteUnusual, Richhoncho, Shuvayev, Skier Dude, Stevecudmore, Tide rolls, Tony2Times, Wysinger, Zeldabalooney2006, 42 anonymous edits

Leon Belasco *Source*: http://en.wikipedia.org/w/index.php?oldid=523756832 *Contributors*: JGKlein, Jack1956, Johnpacklambert, Leszek Jańczuk, NuclearWarfare, SandyGeorgia, Ser Amantio di Nicolao, Timrollpickering, Walor, Yoninah

Les Paul *Source*: http://en.wikipedia.org/w/index.php?oldid=538236077 *Contributors*: 1ForTheMoney, 2D, 2T, 37uie7548347, 4twenty42o, 75pickup, 78.26, A-research, A. Parrot, A58pacer, AV3000, Abdullais4u, Acalora, Adverb, Agateller, Ahoerstemeier, Airproofing, Ajraddatz, Akersmc, Alakey2010, Alansohn, AldRC, Alhutch, Alison, All Hallow's Wraith, Altenmann, Andrewa, Angel Alice, Anger22, Animum, Annunciation, Anovikov2345, Antandrus, Arbor to SJ, Arejayess, Arisa, Art LaPella, Arwel Parry, Ary29, Astonmartini, AtheWeatherman, AuburnPilot, Auréola, Aussie Ausborn, Avm815, Avoided, BRG, BSTemple, Bacchus87, BanyanTree, BaronLarf, BaseballDetective, Bbb2007, Bear475, Bearian, BennyQuixote, Beponoj, Beyondthislife, Bhaanchod, Bigbearsarecool, Bigdumbdinosaur, Bigjimr, Binksternet, BizarreLoveTriangle, Blanchardb, BlindEagle, Bluechakka, Bluerasberry, Bobblewik, Bobo192, Boing! said Zebedee, Bongwarrior, Brandon3378, Bratsche, BravesFan2006, Brian McNeil, BritishWatcher, BrokenSegue, Brossow, Bsssalm, Bubba hotep, Bubba73, C1911a, COMPFUNK2, Cacycle, Caeruleancentaur, Camtoonz, Canadaolympic989, CanadianLinuxUser, Capricorn42, Captain Kirk, CardinalDan, Carel.jonkhout, Catpoop1234, Cbing01, Cboard2, Ccarlini, Centism, Chafinsky, Chasingsol, Chench, Chevyboy666, Chickendinner1506, Chitoboy, Chitt66, Ciphers, Cirt, Ckatz, Clarityfiend, Cleric2145, Clicknclip, Cntras, Cobain, Collegebookworm, Cometstyles, Cool3, Coolmax06, Coralmizu, Cosprings, Courcelles, Creativewright, Crisis, Crohnie, Crombiedood09, Cyanidethistles, D6, DARTH SIDIOUS 2, DC, DMacks, DVdm, DaltreyEntwistleMoonTownshend, Dancter, Danger, Daniel Musto, DanielLevitin, Darguz Parsilvan, DarkDynasty, Dashnick, Davemackey, Davewho2, David Levy, David Regimbal, David Unit, Deb, Deineka, Deltabeignet, Deon Steyn, DerHexer, Derek R Bullamore, Desmay, Dfrankow, Dhartung, Dhp1080, DiScOrD tHe LuNaTiC, Dina, Dirac66, Discospinster, Dismas, Djdaedalus, Dktrfz, Dljone9, Dmarquard, Donald gadwall, DoxTxob, Dr. Blofeld, DragonflySixtyseven, Dream out loud, Duedilly, Dunks58, Dwmr, Dwpaul, EALacey, Eclecticology, Ed Poor, Edaudio, Eddy1174, Editingisbad, Editit, Edward321, Effectkid, Eleggiero, Elsapucai, Emmaaslan, Epbr123, Epeefleche, Eric444, Ericoides, Esprit15d, Exert, Eyesnore, Fair Deal, Famspear, Fastily, Fauxhawk13, Federalist51, FisherQueen, FlirmLi, Floaterfluss, Flowanda, Flowerpotman, Floydmaniax, Fod210, Fozforus, Frank, Frankt, Fred Yowazup:D, Freddiem, Freddy S., Freekee, Freshfighter9, Funeral, Furrykef, GFHandel, Gamesccr7, Garr1984, Gatemansgc, GcSwRhIc, Gegege13, Gerkinstock, Gfoley4, Ghuj, Gigidon, Glane23, Glowleaf, Gmchambless1, Gogo Dodo, GoingBatty, Goodnightmush, Gow343, GraemeL, Gramadeb, Ground Zero, Guitarman.tyrel, Gunmetal Angel, Gurch, Gwen Gale, H.E. Hall, Halcionne, Harro, Hawaiian717, Hifihitman, Hobartimus, Hobedits, Holdenbuckley, Holtben0, Hooperbloob, Hosbar1019, Hu, Huntingj38, Husond, Hyacinth, ILike2BeAnonymous, Iain, Impy4ever, Information yes, Infrogmation, Iridescent, Iriekl777, IronChris, Ithildraug, Ixfd64, Izzy007, J P M7791, J.WILL777, J.delanoy, JGKlein, JJARichardson, JMikeD, JNW, Jack Cox, Jack nickols, Jack8597, JackLumber, Jackfork, Jafeluv, Jakeopm, Jameboy, Jaranda, Jaydec, Jazz77, Jefah, Jeffrey Mall, Jennaalyssa, Jeremiad, Jessiejames, Jflorin, Jhessian Zombie, Jim62sch, Jimregan, Jivecat, Jjohnson1120, JmacBrown, Jmrowland, Jnc, Jnivekk, John, John Price, John of Reading, John254, JordoCo, Jovianeye, Jparenti, Jpers36, Jrcla2, Jstyninger, Jte.daman, Jusdafax, Justinfr, Kablammo, Kalathalan, Kaleeyed, Kartano, Katalaveno, Katharineamy, Keegan, Khukri, Killing Vector, Kinaro, Kingpin13, Kinkyturnip, Kintetsubuffalo, Koavf, Kooo, Kriselle009, Kritikos99, Ksgant, Kubrickrules, Kudret abi, Kumioko (renamed), Kuru, Kwamikagami, L Kensington, Lahiru k, Lampman, Laxgirl15, Lcarscad, Lccccm9080, Leahtwosaints, Leandrod, LedgendGamer, Lekindem, Les boys, Lightmouse, Lilac Soul, Littlebum2002, Livitup, Lockley, Loneagle, LoneliedSphere, Lotje, Lriley47, Luk, Luminifer, Lumos3, Lwellsnyc, MER-C, Madguitar5, Maikel, Maj. Brain, Mallocks, Manway, MarB4, Markhelmy1, MarnetteD, Marshall Stax, Martian, Mashford, Master of Puppets, Materialscientist, Mattbr, Mattgirling, Maurice Lelaix, Maxim,

Mechanical digger, MegX, Melos Antropon, Metallicpunk, Mhking, Michael David, Michael Hardy, Michael Snow, Midway, MightyWarrior, MikeP996, Mikeo, Mind meal, Minimac's Clone, Miss-Meeeee, Mm40, Mogism, Mona, Moproducer, Morahman7vn, Mothmolevna, Motorider57, Mr. Brain, Mr.Z-man, Mrm092890, Mrschimpf, Msr69er, Muboshgu, Mungo Kitsch, Mutleybird, Mwanner, My76Strat, NJA, Naraht, NawlinWiki, Nburden, Nick carson, Nicolaiplum, Nigelj, Night Gyr, Nightscream, Nk, Noctibus, Nsaa Nscheffey, Nukeage, Nurg, Obituarist, Oblivy, Obscurans, Offenbach, Officerveets, Ojorojo, Olessi, Omar35880, Only Child, Ophitke38, Ortolan88, OverlordQ, P-fuzz, PJM, Paganin, Paradiso, Parmesan, Patrick lovell, Paul August, Penmachine, Pepso2, Petchboo, Peter Fleet, Petiatil, Pharaoh of the Wizards, Philco49, Philip Cross, Philip Trueman, Phs72, Phyllis1753, Pi zero, Piano non troppo, Piccadilly, Pigx, Ponyo, Postdlf, Potentialwell, Primarycontrol, Proxy User, Psage, Pshent, QYV, Quebec99, Quicke007, R'n'B, RFD, Radiovoice2, Randomdude411, Randompickle, RavingRocker98, Razorflame, Rebell813, Red Rooster 69, RefrencesOnly, RegenerateThis, Remz, RenamedUser01302013, René Vincent Jansen, Ret8, Rettetast, Rich941, Richard Arthur Norton (1958-), Rjwilmsi, Robert K S, Robert.Harker, RobertG, Rodparkes, Rogerd, Ronark, Roregan, RottweilerCS, Royalbroil, Rtetzloff, Runt, SGGH, SINFJ, Sabbah67, Saint-Paddy, Sala427, Salamander135, Sam Blacketer, Savidan, Sc0ttkclark, Schmorgluck, SchreyP, SchuminWeb, Sclotdebro, Scorpion0422, Scriptwriter, Sdcrocks, SeanO, Seaphoto, Seeker alpha806, Sensei48, Seqsea, Seth Ilys, Shadow2700, Shadowjams, Sheepdontswim, Shoeofdeath, Simmiecity, Sintaku, Slashburst, SlayerXT, Slon02, Slornish, Snow1215, Snowolf, SoCalDonF, Sochwa, Soldat44, Soliloquial, Some guy, Some jerk on the Internet, SpaceFlight89, Spacerules1, Spartaz, Special Cases, Spellcast, Spencer, Spike Wilbury, Spursn17, Star cobra, Starmanforte, Steve.russ, Steve69uc, Steveprutz, Subash.chandran007, Subitopiano, Suduser85, Sunny256, TFBCT1, TUF-KAT, Tbhotch, Tbone762, Television fan, Tgbauer77, Tgeairn, The Thing That Should Not Be, The smilodon, TheGrappler, TheHYPO, TheMadBaron, Thedce, Theking17825, Theopolisme, Theturtleguy, ThewilliNilli, Thgoiter, Thingg, Thumperward, Tiddly Tom, Tide rolls, Tiggerchen, Tim Messer, Timrollpickering, Tinton5, Titodutta, Tjmayerinsf, Tnxman307, Toddsschneider, Tomalak geretkal, Tomasjpn, Tommy2010, Totallybananas, Tpbradbury, Treybien, TronTonian, TuneyLoon, TutterMouse, Twsx, Ucanlookitup, Ulric1313, Ultimateedit, Unibond, Unused0022, User03, Userpd, Valerius Tygart, Verne Equinox, Versus22, Vince lombardi, Vincelord, VonFrenchie, Vytal, WWGB, Wavelength, Wawzenek, Wayne Slam, We hope, Welsh, WereSpielChequers, WereWolf, Wether B, Whouk, Wik, Wiki libs, WikiDon, WikiMazter, WikiZorro, William Avery, Willking1979, Willzeee, Woohookitty, Wspock50, Wtmitchell, Wuffyz, XXleashXx, Xtramental, XxSKULSKIxx, Y2kcrazyjoker4, Yachtsman1, Ymp11, ZX81, Zigger, ZooFari, 1475 anonymous edits

Lou Levy (publisher) *Source*: http://en.wikipedia.org/w/index.php?oldid=529191135 *Contributors*: MegX, Nick Number, Rich Farmbrough, Richhoncho, Tassedethe, Ubiquity, Zoicon5, 1 anonymous edits

Mafia II *Source*: http://en.wikipedia.org/w/index.php?oldid=538897392 *Contributors*: 1exec1, 1wolfblake, 24DeathRow173, AGToth, AS, Acasperw, Ace Oliveira, Acowsik, Afiq1998, Airplaneman, Alansohn, Aled607, Alexius08, Alpheta, Andruś ŠŁ, Anthony77fx, Arbero, Arjayay, AusMooney, Avoided, BD2412, Bilbo571, BlackDragon2026, Blakegripling ph, BluWik, Boddahboy, Bongwarrior, Boobeckett, Bovineboy2008, Brebear15, Bruce1ee, Buffgorilla, Bunnyhop11, Bücherwürmlein, CPO Pieman, Calabe1992, Catgut, Chevrolet01, ChicagoHistory1950, ChimpanzeeUK, Chris TC01, Claviere, Comatmebro, Count druckula, Crankerman, Crimsoninja, Cryuffpl, Cyko149, DanDud88, Dancter, Davie247, DeeYay, Deerstop, Diannaa, Dizzzer, Don Vendetti, Dongareth, Douglasrs, Dougweller, Drobec85, Dudemandude440, Dugahole, DulE3, E2eamon, Elguima, Elk Salmon, Emerald94, EoGuy, Evalowyn, Falcon8765, Falcon9x5, Favonian, Fazm1bico, Fiftyquid, Flask, FlieGerFaUstMe262, Foosyer, Fyyer, GDuwen, GODFATHER, GRKiller, Gargaj, Geoff B, Ghmyrtle, Grandia01, GregorB, Gtrwizrd, Guinea pig warrior, Gunmetal Angel, Guy Harris, Gwenavirre, Happynoodleboycey, Hazard-SJ, Heimdall58, Henry Merrivale, Heterozygous4442, Hgfshgshgh, Hippo99, Hmrox, Honette, Hotlikefrosty, HuntingBear, Hydrogen Iodide, IBoy2G, IGeMiNix, Illegitimate Barrister, Insanity Incarnate, Ints13, Ionutzmovie, IronGargoyle, J.delanoy, JForget, Joel7687, JonBroxton, Jordheck, Joshuarembrandt, Judake2010, Juliofranco, Jvs.cz, Kakinend, Kariteh, Kerim90, Khazar, Klippdass, Koveras, Kozuch, Krillfish, Kubigula, Kumkwat, L Kensington, Labranewf, Layonard, Legend6, Legija, Levangvilava, LilHelpa, Little Mountain 5, Lumidek, MAINEiac4434, MGD11, MOOOOOPS, MaartenJan Roeleveld, Man It's So Loud In Here, Mandarax, Marek69, Mark Arsten, Martarius, Master Deusoma, Math Champion, MattyDienhoff, McGeddon, McSly, Mcris6, Megata Sanshiro, Mercy, Mika1h, Mike Rosoft, MikeWazowski, Mikeo, Minna Sora no Shita, Mobster 1930, Moeinfriends, Motorheadx, MrMarmite, MrMoonshine, N5iln, NYCSlover, Ndboy, NellieBly, Nerdinthebasement, Netalarm, New Age Retro Hippie, Nicholas0, Nickin, Nicko22, Nitr0uk, NoobToober45, Nymf, Ocaasi, Off2riorob, Ost316, Parker1919, Pharaoh of the Wizards, Pikramenos, Plastikspork, Pongley, Poppingcherry, Portillo, Postwar, Pseudomonas, Psykocyber, PyroOnFire, QuantumWake, Qwfp, Qwyrxian, Rabatin, Raptor Messiah, Raul13, Reach Out to the Truth, Rex Blaze, Rider28031, Rjwilmsi, S@bre, SPIRIdk, Saint Ryan, Salamurai, Samanas, SarzzeR, SeanMooney, Sekol, Septuater, Sercan0053, Shadowhawk27, Shangas, Sharplesats, Shopingjs, Simon Beavis, SingularX12, SkyWalker, Slushbunny, Smalljim, Smartcom5, Smurfy, SoWhy, Soetermans, Some guy, Sosaited, Spippy, Spunking, Stabby Joe, StaticGull, Steven Zhang, Sun Creator, Svetovid, Swatjester, TaerkastUA, Tbhotch, Team.terminal, TeleComNasSprVen, Telfordbuck, TenPoundHammer, The PC Gamer, TheOldJacobite, TheQuestofVegeance, TheTruthiness, TheWarPope, Theburn77, Thejadefalcon, Timppis, TobyDZ, TomUSA, Tommy2010, TommykCZ, Topher hkr, Trap The Drum Wonder, Tsuchiya Hikaru, Twas Now, Twentysixpurple, UltimateSin01, Umairanwer, Userpd, V2Blast, Veneration, Victory93, Vighipedia, Vinnie1337, Vipinhari, Vishal1082, Wajalama, Wangry, Widr, WikiDao, WikiPediaAid, Wikipelli, Wisecracker555, Wiz-Pro3, Wknight94, Woohookitty, Wrathsputin, Wtmitchell, Wuxley, X06, X201, XX55XX, Yerolo, Youcandoitlars, Zlatko, Zntrip, Zombie111, 1200 anonymous edits

Make Mine Music *Source*: http://en.wikipedia.org/w/index.php?oldid=539151377 *Contributors*: 16@r, 78.26, AdamDeanHall, Agustinaldo, AlbertSM, Aldo samulo, Alro, Andrzejbanas, André Koehne, AnmaFinotera, B Touch, BRG, Badbats, Blitz Lutte, Bovineboy2008, Calabe1992, Cartoon Boy, Cattus, Chicgeek, Chris1219, Clarityfiend, Clerks, CommonsDelinker, Dante Alighieri, Darkness2005, Deggert, Delcity, Discospinster, Disneyfolly2, DoctorHver, EdJogg, Esn, Estrose, FaceMoss4077, Fanatix, Finebelikethat, Flair Girls, Floydgeo, Fpastor, FriscoKnight, FuriousFreddy, Gabrielkat, Garion96, Hailey C. Shannon, Hellboy10, Hydrargyrum, Igolder, Ihategirls349, Jevansen, Junkfly, Jvsett, Jwelch5742, Kevin j, Klow, Lalli, Leapman, Lilac Soul, Lugnuts, MHarrington, Malakith, Markhh, MarnetteD, McDoobAU93, Mepolypse, Merqurial, Michael Harrington, Minotaurgirl, Mona, MonkeeJuice, NeilEvans, Nemeses9, Noirish, Ost316, PM Poon, PacificBoy, Pathoschild, Paul 012, Paul A, Phantomsteve, R'n'B, Rjwilmsi, Robsinden, Rosalbissima, ST47, Scarecroe, SchreiberBike, SchuminWeb, Silentaria, Sjones23, Skulblaka shur'tugal, Smartie2thaMaxXx, Smjwalsh, SonyWonderFan, Soulessnake, SpikeJones, TheMovieBuff, Thefourdotelipsis, ThomasAnime, Thow1615, ToddSweeney, Tregoweth, Trivialist, Trovatore, Varlaam, Visokor, Wafulz, Wetman, 179 anonymous edits

Mel Tormé *Source*: http://en.wikipedia.org/w/index.php?oldid=535872444 *Contributors*: 23skidoo, 2T, Alan W, All Hallow's Wraith, AllyD, Anthropocentrism, Ar-wiki, Astynax, AttoRenato, BRG, Bacteria, Bellagio99, Benreynolds4, Betacommand, Billy Hathorn, Bokan, Breffni Whelan, Buckboard, BurmaShaver, Cavalcabo, Chowbok, Closeapple, Coppertop Guy, Coreman, Courcelles, Crystallina, D6, David Regimbal, Deb, Dennman, Derek R Bullamore, Design, Dixjaw, DonPevsner, Donaldd23, Download, Downwards, DrDaveHPP, Duritzgirl, Edwy, Elisson1, Emerson7, Emmaaslan, Engineer Bob, Fc21, FentonGlass, Firsfron, First Word Sounds Like, Fox2k11, Fpastor, Fraggle81, Frdeb, Gareth E Kegg, Garion96, Gene Nygaard, GiantSnowman, Good Olfactory, Graham87, Grstain, Hifihitman, HutchinsonKS, ItsAlwaysLupus, JGKlein, Jack O'Lantern, Jackhynes, Jaldridge86, Jburlinson, Jessiejames, Jimstahl333, Jpgordon, Kaihoku, Kbdank71, Kelainoss, Khaosworks, Khatru2, Kinkyturnip, Klooka, LAlawMedMBA, Lentisco, Levineps, LilHelpa, Lockley, Luckypuppy, Lugnuts, Marchfishka, Markkawika, Marylandstater, Mateo SA, Mattbr, Mav, Maywither Dragon, Meribona, Mhiseley, Michellewillendrof, Mind meal, MrDolomite, MrX, Nietzsche 2, Nsk92, Oanabay04, Obiwan57, Orpheus, Ortolan88, PDD, Panfish123, Pascal666, Paul Arnott, Paul MacDermott, Paul Richter, Paul20070, Paulo cavalcanti, Pete3194, Piano non troppo, Pudgenet, Q0, Qzm, RachelBrown, Radioguy91, Ramisses, Raul654, RickK, Rjwilmsi, Rms125a@hotmail.com, Rocks and rolls, Rossmer, Rubioblanca, Sanguinity, Satori Son, SeanO, Shatner1, Shiai, Shoeofdeath, Shsilver, Sirmrmatt, Siryendor, Sk'py Skwrrrl, Skymasterson, Slysplace, Snelson66, Soetermans, Softcoverage, Spalding, Special-T, Sray, Ssilvers, Stackja1945, Steve71575, Supergee, TJ Spyke, TUF-KAT, Tabletop, TheDarkOneLives, Tommix, Twh66, UCBCalBear, Unbreakable10000, VMS Mosaic, Verne Equinox, Viajero, Waacstats, WandaRMinstrel, We hope, WereSpielChequers, Wikiwakiwoo, Will Wilberson, Woof, Woohookitty, Wvkevin, Zone46, Борат Сагдиев, 196 anonymous edits

Melody Time *Source*: http://en.wikipedia.org/w/index.php?oldid=539159969 *Contributors*: AlbertSM, AnmaFinotera, B Touch, Badbats, Benzband, Biblomaniac15, Bovineboy2008, Catamorphism, Catpedantic, Cattus, Chris1219, Coin945, Cyberfreeworld, Darkness2005, Deggert, Disneyfolly2, DoctorHver, Dsreyn, Esn, Estrose, Fanatix, FigmentJedi, Flair Girls, Flowerpotman, Floydgeo, Formula 86, FriscoKnight, FuriousFreddy, Garion96, Geonarva, GünniX, Heartmac, Hrdinský, Hyenaste, Ieditwiki, Ihategirls349, Iridescent, JamesBurns, Jedi94, Junkfly, Jvsett, Leapman, Luxoman237, MHarrington, Markhh, MarnetteD, Mboverload, McDoobAU93, Mepolypse, Michael Harrington, MonkeeJuice, Morel, Nintendo Maximus, Ost316, PMDrive1061, PacificBoy, Paul A, PeruAlonso, Pigby, PrawnRR, Rhindle The Red, Robsinden, Rosalbissima, SchuminWeb, Scottbadman, Sjones23, Smartie2thaMaxXx, Soulessnake, SpikeJones, TAnthony, TMC1982, TheMovieBuff, Thefourdotelipsis, Tregoweth, Trivialist, Ulric1313, Zhanzhao, Žiedas, 127 anonymous edits

Mound, Minnesota *Source*: http://en.wikipedia.org/w/index.php?oldid=531136863 *Contributors*: Altenmann, Antandrus, Appraiser, Blackice123, Bobak, CR85747, Catbar, Cbl62, Coasttrip, Conman2k, Damon207, Dyre, Eco84, Eric Wester, Firsfron, Freakofnurture, Fusionmix, Ginobusinaro, Glitterspray, Gogo Dodo, Hebig07, Hobbitguy, Irregulargalaxies, Jamo2008, Jllm06, Justinfr, Kerms316, Kubigula, Mal7798, Mallardfan, Mboverload, MisfitToys, Mithridates, Mnlakegal, Monegasque, Mwmnp, Nacho2001, Nanabozho, Nickedward23, Nik-renshaw, Nyttend, Ohnoitsjamie, Pearle, Pooblatt, Rahk EX, Ram-Man, Rawskifartknocker, Rawskipoop, RedSpruce, Rich Farmbrough, Seugster, SpuriousQ, Stewie814, Streater2005, TEDIUM07, Tomshuman, Trafton, Vhyntsze, Waggers, WeijiBaikeBianji, Zachlipton, 102 anonymous edits

Near You *Source*: http://en.wikipedia.org/w/index.php?oldid=537191096 *Contributors*: BRG, Brianyoumans, Briguy52748, Carlossfsu, David829, Dipper3, Durova, Eric444, Iss246, Koavf, MarcoLittel, Pianoman2, Richhoncho, Runt, Starcheerspeaksnewslostwars, TenPoundHammer, TonyTheTiger, 10 anonymous edits

Nice Work If You Can Get It (song) *Source*: http://en.wikipedia.org/w/index.php?oldid=535529703 *Contributors*: Alexiusnovius, BRG, Bib, Colonies Chris, D7240, David Kernow, Durova, Engelbaet, Freewa, Giovannii84, Ilphin, Inscription, J04n, JRy2, Kbdank71, Pharaoh of the Wizards, Sjorford, Thumper2, Usgnus, Whyaduck, Xsmasher, 24 anonymous edits

Over Here! *Source*: http://en.wikipedia.org/w/index.php?oldid=532086614 *Contributors*: Angelic-alyssa, Dugwiki, Flami72, Harmil, Howard352, Iohannes Animosus, JGKlein, Kbdank71, LiteraryMaven, MusicMaker5376, Omtay38, PrestonH, SFTVLGUY2, Tassedethe, Trivialist, Varlaam, WereSpielChequers, Ztrawhcs, 37 anonymous edits

Private Buckaroo *Source*: http://en.wikipedia.org/w/index.php?oldid=519148363 *Contributors*: Bensin, Colonies Chris, Courcelles, Foofbun, Johnsp1, Khazar, Kubigula, Lockley, Lugnuts, Macy, Michael Veenswyk, S2grand, Skier Dude, Tassedethe, Tjmayerinsf, TubularWorld, WereSpielChequers, Wool Mintons, Ymmv99

Road to Rio *Source*: http://en.wikipedia.org/w/index.php?oldid=529108723 *Contributors*: Alan Smithee, B3t, BBCD, BRG, Baseball Bugs, Bede735, Clarityfiend, Colonies Chris, David Kernow, Dlobo74, Donaldd23, Dutchy85, Elesi, Estrose, Eugenebiscardi, FMAFan1990, Filll, FreplySpang, Hiphats, Jaxl, Jevansen, Jg325, JosephMurillo, Kidlittle, Louklou, Lugnuts, Marine

69-71, MarnetteD, Mikomaid, Nehrams2020, Pagingmrherman, Paul MacDermott, Rl, Sreejithk2000, Steven Andrew Miller, Storyliner, Tassedethe, TheMovieBuff, Tjmayerinsf, Tobb, Wool Mintons, Xezbeth, Ὁ οἶστρος, 15 anonymous edits

Route 66 (song) *Source:* http://en.wikipedia.org/w/index.php?oldid=537262578 *Contributors:* 0dd1, 23skidoo, Aiko, Alex Ray. Ramirez, Amchow78, Anja, Another Believer, Apple1013, Ary29, Bedient, Bellczar, Bigjimr, Bluemargay, Bobby H. Heffley, Braceout, Brickie, Burro, Captain Kirk, Catquach2341, Chzz, Crash Underride, Csc2.71, Cwarheit, Dch888, Dennissell, Depeche mode freak, Derek R Bullamore, Discospinster, Dmurawski, Doulos Christos, DutchmanInDisguise, E-Kartoffel, Epbr123, Erianna, Eric444. Esprit15d, EvilEntity, Extraordinary Machine, Flowerparty, Fratrep, Froid, GoingBatty, Graham87, Grstain, Hyju, Imzadi1979, Jcb, Jenolen, Jim1138, Jogers, Jonnymela, Jtervin, KConWiki, Ken from Dublin, King of Hearts, KingDaevid, Koavf, Kstarsinic, Kukini, Kww, Ladyofsongandverse, Mardruck, Markcant, Marmelmm, MaxBrowne, Mdumas43073, MegX, Merovingian, Mike Selinker, Mlpearc, Mlpearc Public, Mo0, Moabdave, Morefun, Mwalimu59, Njbob, Nono64, Ortolan88, Pat Holscher, Pecos2, Pepepitos, Phantom in ca, Pxcasey, R sirahata, Rajah, Richhoncho, RickBusciglio, Rm w a vu, Rt66lt, Schmegal, Scooter, ShelfSkewed, Signalhead, Suriel1981, Tcatron565, Tekmatic38, Thom84, Tom.k, Tombrend, Tomcat7, TonyTheTiger, Trivialist, Vchimpanzee, Wahkeenah, Webzu, Yorkshiresky, Yuriybrisk, 158 anonymous edits

Rumors Are Flying *Source:* http://en.wikipedia.org/w/index.php?oldid=471271359 *Contributors:* Abderitestatos, BRG, Deeplogic, Durova, Giovannii84, Robina Fox, 1 anonymous edits

Sabre Dance *Source:* http://en.wikipedia.org/w/index.php?oldid=537079506 *Contributors:* 23skidoo, AHMartin, Alpha Ursae Minoris, Amire80, Araxhiel, Beyond My Ken, BilabialBoxing, Brighat, Caitlin.barton, Centaur81, CesarFelipe, Chaojoker, Chevellefan11, Chris Roy, CommonsDelinker, Crisis, DO'Neil, DavidRF, Dcelano, DeNoel, Debresser, Dick Laurent, Diloretojazz, Edmunter, Electroguv, Emurphy42, Esn, Evercat, Francis Schonken, Frencheigh, Gevorg89, Gidonb, GoingBatty, Graham87, GregorB, Grey ghost, Guroadrunner, Guru Larry, Gus Polly, Hearfourmewesique, Iluvcapra, Jdcooper, Jnelson09, KplFlUSA, Kville105125, Lonelymiesarchie, M czerniewski, Mapsax, Matt McIrvin, Maury Markowitz, Mbakkel2, Mbecker, Mdd4696, MegA, Melah Hashamaim, Michael Bednarek, Mkuehn10, Mrzuko, Nabokov, Nedrutland, Nonagonal Spider, Oos, Pantonal, Paquis, Paul Richter, PaulGarner, Pbrady917, PhilKnight, Pianoplonkers, RoyBoy, Rsduhamel, STBR, Saeed Jahed, Seb Patrick, Shalom Yechiel, ShelfSkewed, Shocking Blue, SidP, Slowking Man, Son of Somebody, Spylab, StAnselm, The Diamond Apex, Theo10011, Thinking of England, Toddcs, Trivialist, Tyciol, Woohookitty, WoundedWolfgirl, Yerevanci, Zscout370, 107 anonymous edits

Sailor (song) *Source:* http://en.wikipedia.org/w/index.php?oldid=539090068 *Contributors:* CharlotteWebb, Cherrylimerickey, Dannys-777, Ddermott, E-Kartoffel, Lithorien, Mbakkel2, Michaelelizarraraz, PamD, Pjedicke, Retro junkie, Rich Farmbrough, RobinCarmody, Ulric1313, WikHead, 12 anonymous edits

Say "Si Si" *Source:* http://en.wikipedia.org/w/index.php?oldid=538634227 *Contributors:* BRG, Bgwhite, Mattisse, Picus viridis, Tombarrister, 4 anonymous edits

Shoo Shoo Baby (song) *Source:* http://en.wikipedia.org/w/index.php?oldid=494220034 *Contributors:* CDBPDX1, Carlossfsu, Goroslair, GregorB, Hippie Metalhead, JustAGal, NoahVail, Patyo1994, Smalljim, Suddenly There Is a Valley, 10 anonymous edits

Sonny Boy (song) *Source:* http://en.wikipedia.org/w/index.php?oldid=533196213 *Contributors:* JGKlein, Mbakkel2, Pinkadelica, Stephencdickson, Terrka, Woohookitty, 6 anonymous edits

Sparrow in the Treetop *Source:* http://en.wikipedia.org/w/index.php?oldid=453643704 *Contributors:* BRG, Durova, Eric444, Housewatcher, InnocuousPseudonym, LongLiveMusic, Nickellmusic, Qirex

Summer of '42 *Source:* http://en.wikipedia.org/w/index.php?oldid=536929754 *Contributors:* Aardvarkzz, Abrahamjoseph, Ajmilner, AlbertSM, Americanfreedom, Andrzejbanas, Arbero, Arwcheek, BD2412, Barefeetdude, Before My Ken, Bmathew, Bookgrrl, Bovineboy2008, Brighterorange, Bubba73, Canterbury Tail, Cvene64, Danielhoward, Dark Kubrick, David Gerard, Dobie80, DrKiernan, DrSamba, Dutchmonkey9000, Dyl, Everyking, Fratrep, FrickFrack, Fritz Saalfeld, Gimmetoo, GoingBatty, Goustien, Graham87, Hegria66, Hifrommike65, Hrdinský, Hushpuckena, IllaZilla, Ineuw, Iridescent, Itxia, J Milburn, Jagged 85, Janggeom, Jaranda, JimmyBlackwing, JoanneB, Joelr31, Josh Parris, Judesba, KSmrq, Kbdank71, Kelly Martin, KevCureton, Kozuch, Ldavid1985, Lightmouse, Lotje, LtNOWIS, Lugnuts, Marcd30319, Markt3, MarnetteD, Mattbr, Mdumas43073, MegX, Merope, Mike65535, MisfitToys, Mistergrind, Muzicalb, MwNNrules, Nabokov, Ndboy, Nehrams2020, Noirish, NuncAutNunquam, Ommnomnomgulp, Outriggr, Owhanee, PhillipgreyIII, PseudoAnoNym, Rich Farmbrough, SGGH, Sadads, Sbrasel, Schmiteye, Seans Potato Business, Sgeureka, Shirt58, Ssilvers, Stevouk, Sugar Bear, TMC1982, Taninao0126, Ted Wilkes, ThatFilmGuy92, The JPS, TheMovieBuff, Thefixing, Thismightbezach, Tony1, Tpbradbury, Trapped in a parallel dimension, Trekphiler, Treybien, Trezjr, Varlaam, Violetriga, Wikid77, Wildhartlivie, Wmahan, Worldedixor, Zad68, Ὁ οἶστρος, 124 anonymous edits

The Dean Martin Show *Source:* http://en.wikipedia.org/w/index.php?oldid=538582520 *Contributors:* 19Josh03, 23skidoo, AarHan3, Aaron Booth, AlbertSM, Altenmann, Alvestrand, Amjaabc, Ancientflounder, AnonMoos, Azumanga1, Bearcat, Ben76266, Bovineboy2008, Choster, Chris the speller, Ckatz, Clarityfiend, Cliff1911, Crovney76, Crystallina, Dgabbard, Dwanyewest, Gareth E Kegg, Gekritzl, Hamburglerosis, Informationfountain, Interbang, JMyrleFuller, Jafeluv, JeffJonez, JustAGal, Kharkless, Krash, LarryJeff, LittleWink, Mark Arsten, Marstalsson, MegastarLV, Michael Bednarek, Mike Halterman, NameIsRon, Oanabay04, Pinkadelica, Professor2789, RainbowCrane, Rjwilmsi, SimonP, Squamate, Stevietheman, Stundra, TMC1982, Ustye, VinnieRattolle, We hope, Wildhartlivie, Yyop, Zanimum, Zoicon5, 91 anonymous edits

The House of Blue Lights (song) *Source:* http://en.wikipedia.org/w/index.php?oldid=530119854 *Contributors:* DynamoDegsy, Eric444, Ghmyrtle, Richhoncho, Ὁ οἶστρος, 4 anonymous edits

The Lennon Sisters *Source:* http://en.wikipedia.org/w/index.php?oldid=528444557 *Contributors:* 1archie99, Arjayay, Bcorr, Brianhenke, Britmax, Bro rick, Burnwelk, C.Kent87, CCRoxtar, Cali567, Carel.jonkhout, Cgingold, Chuq, Dansham, Davidovic, Dhartung, Discospinster, Dlsnider, Dugwiki, Foofbun, Fractalchez, Garion96, Hu12, Icaims, Jaldridge86, JavierMC, Jclemens, Jeffrey O. Gustafson, Jevansen, Johnpacklambert, June w, Ken Gallager, Kralizec!, Kyiaj, Michaelcarraher, Mike Garcia, Mike Halterman, Minos P. Dautrieve, MrNeutronSF, NickelShoe, Nsaa, Pinkadelica, Pnerger, Pufnstuf, QuiteUnusual, RadioBroadcast, Rjwilmsi, Rms125a@hotmail.com, SchuminWeb, Shenme, Shirleygrrl, Starcheerspeaksnewslostwars, Tabletop, Tclpups, TheCustomOfLife, Tomrom, Tony1, TooCleverDuck, We hope, Zephyrnthesky, 81 anonymous edits

The McGuire Sisters *Source:* http://en.wikipedia.org/w/index.php?oldid=535937974 *Contributors:* 78.26, Amazinrick, Aristophanes68, Aspects, AuthorAuthor, Avicennasis, BD2412, BRG, Bobet, Boojum, Burbridge92, BuzzDog, CRKingston, Carel.jonkhout, Cattus, Cavrdg, Cliff1911, Crystallina, Cvbear, Derek R Bullamore, Dobie80, Doremimi, Dwtpa97, E-Kartoffel, EJM22, Elyaqim, Enochlau, Fryede, Gilliam, Giraffedata, Goat0809, Grepman, Herostratus, Hoof Hearted, Huntster, Hushpuckena, Hydrargyrum, Indexme, Jbrownconsulting, Jim1138, Jogers, Katydidit, Kennvido, Koavf, LongLiveMusic, Mandarax, Manxwoman, MarkDonna, MegX, MutterErde, Naniwako, Natrajdr, NorthernThunder, Nouse4aname, Onkelringelhuth, Ontheveldt, Otto4711, Owen, Pattonre, Paul MacDermott, Paul20070, Phileasson, Pinkadelica, Producerguy101, Professor Von Pie, PrometheusX303, Proteus, Regan1973, Richard David Ramsey, Rjwilmsi, Rms125a@hotmail.com, Rogerd, SchuminWeb, ShelfSkewed, Spidermedicine, Sunray, TFBCT1, Tabletop, Tassedethe, TiMike, Tikiwont, TooCleverDuck, Usmale83814, Ustye, Vegaswikian, Vegaswikian1, Zolland, Zundark, 71 anonymous edits

The Puppini Sisters *Source:* http://en.wikipedia.org/w/index.php?oldid=524881473 *Contributors:* Alitheblond, Alpha Quadrant, Aspects, Auntieflo, BD2412, Binderskagnaes, Blakegripling ph, BokuAlec, Bonetm, CapitalLetterBeginning, Cooldude292, Cricket02, Danio, Bibliophylax, DazB, Derek R Bullamore, Dmitry iljinih, Edkollin, Efe, Exploding Boy, Fjolsfdr, Garik, Gimmetoo, GoingBatty, GuanoLad, Gurch, Hajatvrc, Indie leo sayer, Iridescent, Jmbranum, John, JohnRogers, JoseMartinez443, JuneGloom07, Keith D, Kew, Legofreck, LilHelpa, Longhair, Majorclanger, Malcolmxl5, Mauitunes, Nareek, Nouse4aname, Nutfortuna, Percy Snoodle, Peterwill, Pole 2 pole, Polly, Quentin X, R'n'B, RadioBroadcast, Rjwilmsi, Roscelese, Schipli, SchuminWeb, Seeadam, Serein (renamed because of SUL), ShelfSkewed, SigPig, Sin-man, Siormarse1, StAnselm, Starcheerspeaksnewslostwars, Tamfang, Tassedethe, TheRedPenOfDoom, Thir, Tim riley, Timclare, Tjmayerinsf, Tpacw, Upkdm, Vanished user 194difuh2ruhqwdoinxojakdjncno234r, Verne Equinox, Versus22, Vianello, Wikievil666, Woohookitty, Wool Mintons, YUL89YYZ, Yourfrienddave, 166 anonymous edits

The Three Belles *Source:* http://en.wikipedia.org/w/index.php?oldid=526377751 *Contributors:* Mark Arsten, Mattwingett, Sionk, Thethreebelles, WOSlinker, 14 anonymous edits

The Three Bells *Source:* http://en.wikipedia.org/w/index.php?oldid=534346264 *Contributors:* AlbertSM, BRG, BravesFan2006, CanadianLinuxUser, CapnHawk, Carlossfsu, Carptrash, Derek R Bullamore, DougHill, ElvisFan1967, Eric Lipmann, Eric444, Ericorbit, Falcorian, Fried Gold, GassyGuy, Hattrem, J 1982, Jposey3, Manbemel, Mike Selinker, Nickellmusic, OldakQuill, Omar35880, Pastor Theo, Pinus pinea, Renata, Richhoncho, RobertCMWV1974, Rreagan007, Shalom Yechiel, Sijtze Reurich, Sjorford, Spblat, Starcheerspeaksnewslostwars, Staxringold, THEN WHO WAS PHONE?, TenPoundHammer, Triona, Ward3001, 34 anonymous edits

The Woodpecker Song *Source:* http://en.wikipedia.org/w/index.php?oldid=532230372 *Contributors:* Carl savich, Cethegus, Durova, Graham87, NawlinWiki, Richhoncho, Rusty201, Scapler, Very trivial, 19 anonymous edits

There's No Business Like Show Business *Source:* http://en.wikipedia.org/w/index.php?oldid=531818109 *Contributors:* AmbigDexter, BD2412, BRG, BostonRed, DocWatson42, Edward, GBS2, Gelingvistoj, Gilliam, Giovannii84, Graham87, Hardy1956, Invertzoo, Juliancolton, Kbdank71, Leftfoot69, MarkRae, Noirish, PJtP, PercyWM, Richhoncho, Talking image, TheJazzDalek, TonyTheTiger, 21 anonymous edits

Tico-Tico no Fubá *Source:* http://en.wikipedia.org/w/index.php?oldid=505462288 *Contributors:* Benkarm, Bepp, Bubba73, CalJW, Cosprings, David Moerike, Deborahjay, Dr. Blofeld, Flowerysong, Hmains, Hugo999, Hyju, Jahami14, Joaosac, Kaikhosru, Ktotam, Languagehat, Looney1023, Lugnuts, Luiscarlosrubino, Marek69, Ovens for sale, Pasquale, Paul Richter, PaulTanenbaum, Pengo, PlatypeanArchcow, Rnestle, Simener, Vejvančický, Walter Görlitz, YUL89YYZ, Yaroslav Blanter, 36 anonymous edits

Underneath the Arches (song) *Source*: http://en.wikipedia.org/w/index.php?oldid=507598536 *Contributors*: Andrewa, BRG, Bezapt, Binglee, DragonflySixtyseven, Durova, Engineer Bob, Flyingw, Hugo999, Iantresman, Jogers, Jonpetteroie, Kbthompson, Kleon3, Labalius, LilHelpa, Lord Cornwallis, NawlinWiki, RMHED, Rich Farmbrough, RobinCarmody, Rothorpe, Salamurai, Shantavira, ShelfSkewed, Slowtalk, Timeineurope, Welsh, Wolfer68, Xensyria, Y control, 8 anonymous edits

Vocal Group Hall of Fame *Source*: http://en.wikipedia.org/w/index.php?oldid=531423293 *Contributors*: 5060apwj, Aec is away, AmericanLeMans, Antæus Feldspar, B Touch, BRG, Bearcat, Cab88, Chuck the writer, Commander Keane, Comprendo, DavidBailey, Derek R Bullamore, Discographer, DutchDevil, Eagle4000, GDibyendu, Gadfium, Godlord2, Grstain, Haemo, Hajor, Haleyga, Jake Nelson, JamesBurns, Jax 0677, Jllm06, Lquilter, Peterbasix, RadicalBender, Retromaniac, Rick Block, Ricky, Rodii, Stevenspiegel, Taestell, Tim!, Topbanana, Tregoweth, Twice25, Willgee, Wknight94, Zoicon5, 122 anonymous edits

Winter Wonderland *Source*: http://en.wikipedia.org/w/index.php?oldid=535314459 *Contributors*: 2602:304:AB8B:FAD9:88DD:1258:7CB4:F987, 5 albert square, Achangeisasgoodasa, Alansohn, Androl, Andycjp, Anomieman, Another Believer, Apolomchak, ApprenticeFan, Auntof6, BRG, Baseball Bugs, Belovedfreak, Bennewsome, Bib, Brendan4hsm, Brettalan, Bugmenot2006, Bwilkins, CTF83!, CambridgeBayWeather, Cascada0121, Cgray4, Chironomia, ChristalPalace, Closeapple, Daeyeol lee, Dah31, DanCole42, Danemaricich13, Darwinek, Das Baz, Davandron, Davidbix, Delanotolhuisen, Derek R Bullamore, Dffb23, Dhanuri Ariyananda, Dobie80, Dravecky, Elrox, Eric444, Fishnet37222, FordPrefect42, Freddyprospect, Fuhghettaboutit, GeeFour, Gekritzl, Generation talk123, Georgia guy, Giovannii84, Giuliopp, Gnowxilef, Goethi, Gongshow, Good Olfactory, Grapefruit8, Graphicbryan, Grushenka, Harryboyles, HonorTheKing, Housewatcher, Ianthegecko, ImperatorExercitus, Iowamutt, It'sOnlyU, Izzy007, J 1982, JoeSmack, Joefromrandb, JohnInDC, Issfrk, JustAGal, Koavf, Korossyl, Kwekubo, Lee0405, Leonardo.radoiu, Lightmouse, Little green rosetta, LizardJr8, LongLiveMusic, Mamahopper, Matti-92, Mauitunes, Mcbill88, Mild Bill Hiccup, Monckmann, Myname808, NeonMerlin, Nespresso, Nickellmusic, Njmike, Nomenclator, Paulhemmer, Pearle, Philip Trueman, Piast93, Pjoef, Producercunningham, Quentin X, Reaper Eternal, Rednikki, Redxx, Richhoncho, Richmeister, RickH86, Rje, Rpeh, Rsolermo, Sarcha 45, Scwlong, Seandaichi95, Seduisant, Setsuna29, ShelfSkewed, Sine Nomine, Slagathor, Sliv812, Spjuvern17, Streamside, Stux, SuperHamster, T-Dub, Talkingbirds, TashkentFox, TboltUSA, TheAllSeeingEye, TheRatedRKOLegendKiller, Thief12, Tide rolls, Tinton5, Torqtorqtorq, Tsbuzash, Tsnash, Ttc817, Twsheely, USN1977, Uncle Dick, Uncle G, Uzerakount, Wesley M. Curtus, Wiikipedian, WikkanWitch, Willirennen, Willlenzie, Wis2fan, Wmcewenjr, Wolf530, Woodshed, Woohookitty, Xxmatt2010xx, Yip1982, Younghsim, Zzyzx11, 316 anonymous edits

The Andrews Sisters *Source*: http://en.wikipedia.org/w/index.php?oldid=539391203 *Contributors*: 13westrn, 17Drew, 2001:558:6011:11:50F3:7123:CE1E:EB5D, 23skidoo, 28bytes, Addshore, Ajuk, Alan Canon, Alexdan loghin, All Hallow's Wraith, Alphacatmarnie, Alphalurion, AmericanLeMans, And we drown, Arpad13, Ashley Pomeroy, Aspects, Avicennasis, BRG, Bellczar, Bensin, Bigroger27509, Blakegripling ph, Bloodholds, Boing! said Zebedee, Brian the Editor, Bro rick, Burbridge92, C777, CAWylie, CSWarren, Cabe6403, Calmer Waters, Cameronc, CapitalR, CatherineMunro, Catperson12, Ccgrimm, Cellofury, Chanlyn, Chowbok, Chris the speller, Ckruschke, Cluth, Coinmanj, Colonies Chris, Common Man, Crooner62, D6, DBigXray, Dagonet, Danny, Dave Andrew, DavidRF, Davidecross, Dcoetzee, Discographer, Docu, Dogru144, Donaldd23, Download, DrakeLuvenstein, Dumelow, Dutchmonkey9000, ERcheck, Eco84, EdGl, Edgar181, Edkollin, Effajay, Egghead06, Entheta, Erianna, Eric Schutte, Esprit15d, Evil Monkey, Fayenatic london, Filmsaboutstuff, Freakofnurture, Fuddle, Furrycat66, GBrady, Ganymead, Ghmyrtle, GiantSnowman, Gilliam, Gingerandfred, Giovannii84, Gl873, GoingBatty, Grafen, Graham87, Gregoing, Grstain, Gujuguy, Guroadrunner, Gyrobo, Hailey C. Shannon, Ham1000, HandsomeFella, Harry Nimmo, Hattrem, Herr von underpants, Hifihitman, Hirolovesswords, Homerrocks, Hoof Hearted, Howard352, Htfiddler, Indopug, Infrogmation, Inscription, Iridescent, IsarSteve, It Is Me Here, Italo9, JCaesar, JGKlein, Jack1956, Jbarta, Jimknut, Jmgonzalez, Joefromrandb, Joel Mc, Jogers, JohnRogers, JoleneKat, Jonpetteroie, Josh Rumage, Jusdafax, JustAGal, Jwy, Kak500, Karlos the Jackal, Kcoutu, Kellyprice, Ken Gallager, Keraunoscopia, Kevinmon, KhryssoHeart, Kintetsubuffalo, Kmweber, Leoni2, Lightmouse, LilHelpa, Lincher, Lisko33, Lkop56, Lolliapaulina51, Lpmiller, LucilleBall, LukeSurl, Lwellsnyc, MBlume, MER-C, Mago266, Mandarax, Markhurd, MarnetteD, Maitbr, Mattgirling, MatthewTStone, Mauitunes, May Cause Dizziness, Mike Dillon, Mike Halterman, Minnesota cold, Miopportunity, Mlisko, Moncrief, MoreMetal, MrDolomite, Mrceleb2007, Mrestko, Mulad, Mutley1989, Mykleavens, NawlinWiki, Nedrutland, Nepal2030, Niceguyedc, NickyBeth, Nihiltres, Niteowlneils, No11akersfan, Nonstandard, Notheruser, Nwbeeson, Oanabay04, Od Mishehu, Oobopshark, Open2universe, Operagal52, Otto4711, PDH, Pascal.Tesson, Paul A, Paul Erik, Pcpcpc, Perohanych, Philip Trueman, PieBoysMama, PigFlu Oink, Pigmonkeyandsuzi, Piledhigheranddeeper, Ponyo, PrettyMuchBryce, PsychoNiff, Qballbuster2, Quentin X, R'n'B, Ragtimeacres97, Raulsebrook, Rees11, Replysixty, Rich Farmbrough, Rich257, Richardcavell, Richhoncho, Richwales, Rjd0060, Rossrs, Roygbiv666, Rusty201, Salliesatt, Sasake662, SchreiberBike, SchuminWeb, SebastianHelm, Serlin, Shadow1, ShelfSkewed, Shir-El too, Shlomke, Sicamous, Sjc, Sluzzelin, Slysplace, Snezzy, Snowmanradio, Son of Somebody, Spellcast, Starcheerspeaksnewslostwars, Studerby, SusanLesch, Syrthiss, Tabledhote, Tacllews, Tal1962, Tassedethe, Ted Wilkes, Tednor, TenPoundHammer, Tesscass, Thanatos666, Themidwestprincess, Threeafterthree, Tim!, Timrollpickering, Tjmayerinsf, Tkynerd, Tombarrister, TooCleverDuck, Tribal44, Triplestop, Trystan, TutterMouse, Tvoz, Twinchester, TypoBoy, USRoute66, Ulric1313, VIGNERON, Vague Rant, Valentinejoesmith, Vegan4Life, Vertigo Man-iac, Vgirly, Virginboi6969, Voltaire137, Vorash, Vulturell, Vyruss, W guice, WBardwin, Wahkeenah, Waldir, Walter Görlitz, Wareismike, Wasell, Wasted Time R, Wdchk, We hope, Welsh, WesleyDodds, WikHead, Wikianon, Wildhartlivie, Wolfluver2013, Wool Mintons, Wrnchhead76, Xmanager, YUL89YYZ, Zazaotm, Zmjezhd, Zytsef, 466 anonymous edits

Image Sources, Licenses and Contributors

License

CPSIA information can be obtained at www.ICGtesting.com
Printed in the USA
LVOW02s1118240215

428132LV00013B/144/P